AGRICULTURAL DEVELOPMENT

THE JOHNS HOPKINS STUDIES IN DEVELOPMENT
Vernon W. Ruttan and T. Paul Schultz, Consulting Editors

REVISED AND EXPANDED EDITION

AGRICULTURAL DEVELOPMENT

An International Perspective

Yujiro Hayami and Vernon W. Ruttan

The Johns Hopkins University Press • Baltimore and London

The Johns Hopkins University Press,
701 West 40th Street,
Baltimore, Maryland 21211
The Johns Hopkins Press Ltd., London

The paper in this book is acid-free and meets the guidelines for permanence and durability of the Committee on Production Guidelines for Book Longevity of the Council on Library Resources.

Library of Congress Cataloging in Publication Data

Hayami, Yūjirō.
  Agricultural development.
  (The Johns Hopkins studies in development)
  Includes index.
  1. Agriculture—Economic aspects. I. Ruttan,
Vernon W. II. Title. III. Series.
HD1415.H318   1985   338.1   84-23386
ISBN 0-8018-2348-X (alk. paper)
ISBN 0-8018-2376-5 (pbk. : alk. paper)

To Kazushi Ohkawa and Theodore W. Schultz

Contents

vii

Illustrations

Tables

1

Introduction

In the first three decades following World War II the agricultural productivity gap between the developed and developing countries widened sharply.

During the late 1960s a series of technical breakthroughs created a new potential for rapid increases in grain production in the less developed countries of the tropics and subtropics. A major issue facing policymakers and planners in many developing nations today is whether the potential agricultural surpluses can be converted into a viable basis for sustained economic growth.

Economic doctrine with respect to the relative contribution of agricultural and industrial development to national economic growth has experienced a sharp transition during the last several decades. In the 1950s development economists were emphasizing the critical contribution of urban industrial growth to agricultural development. By the 1960s they were equally impressed with the importance of an agricultural surplus for economic development. Analysts who were skeptical of the willingness of peasant producers in poor countries to adopt new technology became disturbed by the price and income distribution effects of the new technology. And by the 1970s scholars who had earlier been skeptical of the willingness of peasant producers to respond to economic incentives became aware that the price distortions resulting from government interventions in factor and product markets had become a burden on agricultural development.

In part this change in emphasis is a product of the new range of development problems with which economists have begun to concern themselves. Western economies are characterized by rapid technical progress in agriculture, relatively modest rates of population growth, and a declining response in the demand for farm products to income growth. Rapid urban-industrial development has been perceived as clearly essential if rural labor, made redundant by the rapid gains in labor productivity in agriculture, is to escape from low-productivity employment in the rural sector and make an important contribution to national economic growth. This has been particu-

1

larly true in the less industrialized regions of major national economies, such as the southeastern United States, and the less industrialized nations of multinational economic systems, such as the southern European members or associate members of the European Economic Community (EEC).

After World War II the attention of economists shifted increasingly to a concern with the problem of economic development in low-income national economies that had not yet solved the problem of how to transform traditional agriculture into a viable source of sustained growth in food production.

This shift in orientation reflected an increasing concern for the agricultural development problems of nations characterized by static agricultural technology, rapid increases in the demand for farm products in response to population and income growth, and the "pathological" growth of urban centers. It also represents a pragmatic response to the lack of success of much of the development effort and development assistance that has been attempted by both national and international agencies in areas outside of the Western economic system—in Asia, Africa, and Latin America.

No clear-cut system of "new development economics" has yet emerged to dominate the fields of economic development theory and policy as completely as Keynesian macroeconomics once dominated income and employment theory. But a new consensus seems to have emerged that an effective economic development strategy, particularly during the early stages of economic growth, depends critically on the achievement of rapid technical change.

This consensus has not yet been accompanied by comparable agreement regarding the processes by which rapid productivity and output growth can be achieved in the agricultural sector. In his iconoclastic book *Transforming Traditional Agriculture* (1964), Theodore W. Schultz has suggested that significant growth in productivity cannot be brought about by the reallocation of resources in traditional agricultural systems. Significant opportunities for growth will become available only through changes in technology—new husbandry techniques, better seed varieties, more efficient sources of power, and cheaper plant nutrients. Investment in such activities as agricultural research, leading to the supply of new inputs, and in the education of the farm people who are to use the new inputs will provide the basis for technical change and productivity growth in agriculture. The Schultz theory of agricultural development is consistent with the more general perspective advanced by Simon Kuznets in his book *Modern Economic Growth* (1966) (and elsewhere), which identified the development of economic and social institutions for the systematic application of scientific knowledge to economic activity as the primary source of sustained growth in productivity and in per capita income during the epoch of modern economic growth.

We attempt, in this book, to develop the Kuznets-Schultz perspective further to incorporate resource allocation to, and within, the sector that produces and supplies the new inputs. This sector consists of the suppliers of the new inputs, such as innovative farmers, public research institutions, and agricultural supply firms. It competes with other sectors of the economy in the use of scarce resources. The issue of how a society allocates resources to the technology supply sector and how the resources are allocated among different activities within the sector is fundamental to the agricultural development process. Some of the products of this sector (for example, new husbandry techniques) are not traded through the market, which raises the question of how information concerning product demand and factor endowments can be effectively conveyed to the suppliers of new inputs.

There is also the more difficult question of the relationship between technological and institutional changes. By what processes are economic institutions transformed to enable society to capture the gains implicit in new technical potentials? The interplay between technical change and institutional change is a theme that has been explored since the last century by Karl Marx and his followers and more recently by the "new institutional economics" school.

Our approach to an operationally meaningful theory of agricultural development involves the incorporation of the economic behavior of public and private sector suppliers of knowledge and new inputs and the economic response of institutions to new economic opportunities as components of the economic system rather than treating technical institutional change as exogenous to the system.

The years since World War II have been characterized by uneven rates of growth in food production among countries and over time. Modest fluctuations in production about favorable long-run trends have given rise to much sharper price fluctuations in world commodity markets. And these fluctuations have induced exaggerated waves of optimism and pessimism about the capacity of developing countries to meet their food needs. We anticipate that short-run fluctuations in economic activity will continue to generate waves of optimism and pessimism. But the fundamental forces that guide economic development are not to be discerned in the momentary behavior of commodity markets. We would like our readers to keep in mind, as they are confronted with the systemic noise of future waves of optimism and pessimism, that the progress of history is characterized by rolling contours rather than sharp curves.

In this book we attempt to show how a model, in which technical and institutional changes are treated as endogenous factors, responding to economic forces, can aid in the historical analysis of agricultural growth, particularly in Japan and the United States. We believe this model represents a significant advance in the foundations upon which a more complete theory of economic development can be built.

Our main concern, then, is to identify the necessary conditions for agricultural growth. We accept as fundamental that in most societies, growth in agricultural output is essential to the development process and that the contribution of agricultural growth to the development process is positively related to the rate of productivity growth in the agricultural sector. Furthermore, we regard the new methods, materials, and opportunities associated with technical advance as a fundamental source of institutional change in modernizing societies.

It is not a major purpose of this book to investigate the conditions under which productivity growth in agriculture will be translated into national economic growth. The resources made available to society by productivity growth in the agricultural sector create an opportunity for the growth of material welfare in the total society. We look to others to provide a more complete analysis of the conditions under which these opportunities for overall economic growth are fully realized. Such study will require careful analysis of the conditions under which the potential dividends of agricultural productivity growth remain unrealized because of failures in social, political, and economic organization, and of the forces that lead to the dissipation of the potential for growth in a pursuit of the symbols rather than the reality of national development.

HYPOTHESIS

Our basic hypothesis is that a common basis for success in achieving rapid growth in agricultural productivity is the capacity to generate an ecologically adapted and economically viable agricultural technology in each country or development region. Successful achievement of continued productivity growth over time involves a dynamic process of adjustment to original resource endowments and to resource accumulation during the process of historical development. It also involves an adaptive response on the part of cultural, political, and economic institutions in order to realize the growth potential opened up by new technical alternatives. We have outlined this hypothesis more formally in an induced innovation model. The model attempts to make more explicit the process by which technical and institutional changes are induced through the responses of farmers, agribusiness entrepreneurs, scientists, and public administrators to resource endowments and to changes in the supply and demand of factors and products.

The state of relative endowments and accumulation of the two primary resources, land and labor, is a critical element in determining a viable pattern of technical change in agriculture. Agriculture is characterized by much stronger constraints of land on production than most other sectors of the economy. Agricultural growth may be viewed as a process of easing the constraints on production imposed by inelastic supplies of land and labor. Depending on the relative scarcity of land and labor, technical change embodied in new and more productive inputs may be induced primarily either (a) to save labor or (b) to save land.

The nonagriculture sector plays an important role in this process. It absorbs labor from agriculture. And it supplies to agriculture the modern technical inputs that can be substituted for land and labor in agricultural production. We hypothesize that the high agricultural productivity of the developed countries is based on (a) the development of a nonagriculture sector capable of transmitting increased productivity to agriculture in the form of cheaper sources of power and plant nutrients (for example, tractors and chemical fertilizers) and (b) the capacity of society to generate a continuous sequence of technical innovations in agriculture which increases the demand for the inputs supplied by the industrial sector. A continuous stream of new technical knowledge and a flow of industrial inputs in which the new knowledge is embodied are necessary for modern agricultural development. This stream of new technical inputs must be complemented by investments in general education and in production education for farmers and by efforts to transform institutions to be consistent with the new growth potentials if the full productive potential of the new knowledge and the new inputs is to be realized. We hypothesize that the expected returns to political entrepreneurs or leaders from institutional changes that facilitate the exploitation of new technical opportunities are one of the major inducements to institutional innovation.

The critical element in this process is an effective system of market and nonmarket information linkages among farmers, public research institutions, private agricultural supply firms, and political and bureaucratic entrepreneurs. It is hypothesized that the proper functioning of such interactions is a key to success in the generation of the unique pattern of technical change necessary for agricultural development in any developing economy.

APPROACH

The tests of the induced innovation hypothesis presented in this book are based on international time-series and cross-sectional comparisons of the levels of production, productivity, and inputs in agriculture. The patterns of technical change and growth in agriculture evidenced in the experiences of various countries can be generalized only through such comparisons. The international comparisons also offer an opportunity to test the induced innovation hypothesis over a much broader range of variation in variables, especially factor proportions, than would be possible within any single economy.

The first test of the hypothesis regarding the interaction among resource endowments and technical change is obtained from an intercountry cross-section comparison of agricultural production. The hypothesis is subjected to a further test based on time-series data for the United States and Japan. Both the United States and Japan have been successful in achieving growth in agricultural output and productivity for at least a century, despite enormous differences in resource endowments, through the development of unique institutions to generate and diffuse appropriate technologies. The analysis is extended further to include the processes by which the scientific and technical capacity to generate an ecologically adapted and economically viable agricultural technology is transferred to the less developed countries. The historical experiences of Japan, Taiwan, and Korea are compared with those of the tropical countries, which are currently experiencing major technical advances in grain production.

We are also able to test the interrelationships among resource endowments, technical change, and institutional change at a microeconomic level by drawing on a number of village studies in the Philippines and Indonesia. These village-level studies also enable us to test whether the new biologically based "green revolution" technology has become a source of greater equality or inequality in the distribution of income in rural communities.

PLAN OF THE BOOK

This book consists of five major parts. In Part I (Chapters 2, 3, and 4) we develop the theoretical framework in some detail. In Chapter 2 we review the received theories of economic development to see what insight they provide on the critical role played by agriculture in the overall development process. In Chapter 3 we extract, from the diverse literature in the field of agricultural development, the main themes that should enter into a more comprehensive theory of agricultural development. In Chapter 4 we develop the theory of induced technical and institutional change that serves as our basic theoretical framework for the analysis in later chapters.

In Part II (Chapters 5 and 6) we examine the nature and sources of the gap in agricultural productivity among countries. In Chapter 5 we show that the productivity gap between developed and developing countries has continued to widen during the postwar period. In Chapter 6 we analyze the sources of this gap. We then explore how countries with different resource endowments should direct their investments to overcome the constraints imposed by unfavorable resource endowments, agricultural technology, and human capital.

In Part III (Chapters 7 and 8) we draw on the agricultural development experience of Japan and the United States to explore the sources and impact of technical change in the process of economic development. In Chapter 7 we explore how the different resource constraints in the two countries have induced different paths of technical change. In Chapter 8 we examine the institutional basis for the generation of technical change, and we explore the adjustment problems faced by the agricultural sector in Japan and the United States in response to technical change.

In Part IV (Chapters 9 and 10) we explore the conditions for successful transfer of agricultural technology among countries. In Chapter 9 we show that the transfer of scientific knowledge through the development of agricultural research institutions is far more essential in the international transfer of technology than the transfer of specific designs, materials, or techniques. As an illustration, the experience of the transfer of rice production technology from Japan to Korea and Taiwan is examined. In Chapter 10 we show how the successful transfer of agricultural technology, under conditions of the severe land constraints that characterize many developing countries, is dependent on complementary investments in land and water development.

In Part V (Chapters 11, 12, and 13) we attempt to give a strategic perspective on the causes of success and failure in agricultural development among countries. In Chapter 11 we address the widely debated issue of the relationship between growth and equity in the process of agricultural development. In Chapter 12 we examine the institutional and policy problems underlying the widening gap in productivity and income between the developed and the developing countries. And in Chapter 13 we explore, from the induced technical and institutional innovation perspective, some of the guidelines that must inform agricultural policy if the developing countries are to take advantage of the opportunities for economic growth now available to them.

I

PROBLEMS AND THEORY

2

Agriculture in Economic
Development Theories

There has been a sharp transition in economic doctrine with respect to the relative contribution of agricultural and industrial development to national economic growth. There has been a shift away from an earlier "industrial fundamentalism" to an emphasis on the significance of growth in agricultural production and productivity for the total development process. As economists have become involved in the analysis of development problems in nations characterized by static agricultural technology and rapid growth in demand for agricultural products, attention has shifted increasingly to a concern with the conditions under which an agricultural surplus can occur and be sustained.

In this chapter the literature on the role of agriculture in economic development is reviewed in order to show the significance of the problem to be treated in this book for development theory and policy.[1]

As already noted, no clear-cut system of "new development economics" has emerged to dominate the field of economic development theory as completely as Keynesian economics once dominated income, employment, and growth theory.[2] Three approaches have been used frequently in attempts to

1. The reader may want to supplement the material presented in this chapter with the comprehensive review of literature relating to agriculture's role in economic development by John W. Mellor, *The Economics of Agricultural Development* (Ithaca: Cornell University Press, 1966); Bruce F. Johnston and Peter Kilby, *Agriculture and Structural Transformation: Economic Strategies in Late Developing Countries* (New York: Oxford University Press, 1975); Louis Malassis, *Agriculture and the Development Process* (Paris: Unesco Press, 1975); and Carl K. Eicher and John M. Staatz, *Agricultural Development in the Third World* (Baltimore: Johns Hopkins University Press, 1984).

2. Albert Hirschman has argued that the emergence of development economics as a separate subdiscipline after World War II was facilitated by the discredit into which orthodox neoclassical economics had fallen as a result of the depression of the 1930s and the emergence of Keynesian macroeconomics. The case for a separate subdiscipline was reinforced by a perception that the developing economies were distinguished from the developed primarily by (a) rural underemployment and (b) late industrialization. This view in turn led to a policy paradigm consisting of three strategic themes: (a) rapid capital accumulation, (b) mobilization of underemployed manpower, and (c) industrial development guided by the state. During the 1960s and 1970s the consensus with respect to both the structural characteristics of underdevelopment and to develop-

stake out the boundaries of a new development economics. One of these is the growth-stage or leading sector approach, which, in post–World War II literature, is identified with W. W. Rostow.[3] A second is the dual-economy approach along lines originally set forth by W. Arthur Lewis and developed by Dale W. Jorgenson and by John C. H. Fei and Gustav Ranis.[4] A third is the structuralist and dependency perspectives that have emerged from the work of Raúl Prebisch and Paul Baran to become a dominant theme for a broad spectrum of Third World economists, political scientists, and sociologists.[5]

It seems useful, therefore, to review the evolution of thought on the relative contribution of industrial and agricultural development to the process of economic growth within the framework of these three approaches. First we present a brief introduction to the classical model of economic development, which has served as a point of departure for more recent development thought.

THE CLASSICAL BACKGROUND

Current thought on the role of agriculture in economic development remains strongly influenced by the "magnificent dynamics" of the classical school, principally that of Adam Smith, Thomas A. Malthus, and David Ricardo.[6]

ment policy gradually eroded. See Albert O. Hirschman, "The Rise and Decline of Development Economics," in *The Theory and Experience of Economic Development: Essays in Honor of Sir W. Arthur Lewis,* ed. Mark Gersovitz, Carlos F. Diaz-Alejandro, Gustav Ranis, and Mark Rosenzweig (London: George Allen & Unwin, 1982), pp. 372–90; and, Amartya Sen, "Development: Which Way Now?" *Economic Journal* 93 (December 1983): 745–62.

3. W. W. Rostow, "The Take-off into Self-sustained Growth," *Economic Journal* 66 (March 1956):25–48; *The Stages of Economic Growth: A Non-Communist Manifesto* (Cambridge: Cambridge University Press, 1960).

4. W. Arthur Lewis, "Economic Development with Unlimited Supplies of Labor," *Manchester School of Economic and Social Studies* 22 (May 1954):139–91; Dale W. Jorgenson, "The Development of a Dual Economy," *Economic Journal* 71 (June 1961):309–34; Jorgenson, "Testing Alternative Theories of the Development of a Dual Economy," *The Theory and Design of Economic Development,* ed. Irma Adelman and Erik Thorbecke (Baltimore: Johns Hopkins Press, 1966), pp. 45–60; "Surplus Agricultural Labour and the Development of a Dual Economy," *Oxford Economic Papers* 19 (November 1967):288–312; "The Role of Agriculture in Economic Development: Classical versus Neoclassical Models of Growth," *Subsistence Agriculture and Economic Development,* ed. Clifton R. Wharton, Jr. (Chicago: Aldine, 1969), pp. 320–48; Gustav Ranis and J. C. H. Fei, "A Theory of Economic Development," *American Economic Review* 51 (September 1961):533–65; John C. H. Fei and Gustav Ranis, *Development of the Labor Surplus Economy: Theory and Policy* (Homewood, Ill.: Irwin, 1964); Fei and Ranis, "Agrarianism, Dualism, and Economic Development," *Theory and Design of Economic Development,* ed. Adelman and Thorbecke, pp. 3–41.

5. Raúl Prebisch, *The Economic Development of Latin America and Its Principal Problems* (Lake Success, N.Y.: United Nations Department of Economic Affairs, 1950); Paul A. Baran, "On the Political Economy of Backwardness," *Manchester School of Economic and Social Studies* 20 (January 1952):66–84.

6. Useful discussions of the classical model are presented in Erskine McKinley, "The

The classicals agreed that the accumulation of capital was a fundamental source of growth. They also agreed that the possibilities for productivity growth in agriculture opened up by division of labor and by invention were sharply different from those in manufacturing. In manufacturing, the progress of invention might more than offset the tendency for diminishing returns. But in agriculture, and in the natural resource sectors generally, it was held that the progress of invention would be incapable of offsetting the effects of diminishing returns.[7] Finally, they agreed that at the institutionally determined "natural" wage rate the long-run supply of labor is perfectly elastic.

The dynamics of the Ricardian model, the most rigorously developed classical model, can be illustrated by tracing the effect of an increase in production resulting from a new invention. A similar sequence could be developed as the result of the discovery of new land or new raw materials.

- The increase in production creates a surplus over and above the amount necessary to cover the subsistence wage. This disposable surplus represents a "wages fund" that capitalists can use to hire more labor.

- The increase in the wages fund results in competition among capitalists for the inelastic (in the short run) supply of labor. The effect is a rise in the wage rate and a decline in the rate of return to capital.

- The higher wage rate results in an increase in the rate of population growth. The rise in wage rates and the increase in population generate a rise in the demand for food.

- The rise in the demand for food is met by bringing progressively lower-quality land into production—land on which the marginal product of an incremental dose of capital and labor is lower than on the land already in use.

- The price of food rises to cover the cost of production on the marginal land. The effect of rising food prices is to reduce the real wage rate. As the

---

Theory of Economic Growth in the English Classical School," *Theories of Economic Growth,* ed. Bert F. Hoselitz et al. (Glencoe, Ill.: Free Press, 1960), pp. 89–112; Irma Adelman, *Theories of Economic Growth and Development* (Stanford: Stanford University Press, 1961); Luigi L. Pasinetti, *Lectures on the Theory of Production* (New York: Columbia University Press, 1977), pp. 8–18. See also Keith Tribe, *Land, Labor and Economic Discourse* (London: Routledge and Kegan Paul, 1978), pp. 110–46, for development of the classical synthesis between the publication in 1771 of Adam Smith's *Wealth of Nations* (ed. Edwin Cannan [New York: Random House, 1937]), and the publication in 1817 by David Ricardo of *The Principles of Political Economy and Taxation* (London: J. M. Dent & Sons, Ltd., 1911).

7. The principle of decreasing returns to incremental doses of capital and labor applied to land was based on what Ricardo's followers referred to as (a) the case of the Extensive Margin— as population increases, poorer and poorer soils have to be taken into cultivation and equal increments of capital and labor produce progressively smaller increments of production, and (b) the case of the Intensive Margin—equal increments of capital and labor successively applied to a given piece of land will also, after a point, produce progressively smaller increments of production. The principle of diminishing returns did not originate with the classicals. It was formulated in something approaching its modern form by Turgot in 1767. See Joseph A. Schumpeter, *History of Economic Analysis* (New York: Oxford University Press, 1954), pp. 257–62.

FIGURE 2-1. The Ricardian model.

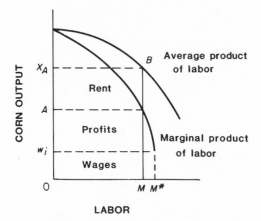

LABOR

Source: Lance Taylor, *Macro Models for Developing Countries* (New York: McGraw-Hill, 1979), p. 143.

Note. Given the average product of labor schedule, employment M results in a total corn output of $OMBX_A$. Landlords receive as rent the difference between the average and the marginal product of labor times the number of people employed. On the last bit of marginal land brought into production by capitalist farmers renting from landlords, rent will be driven to zero. Profits and wages are determined by the size of the wages fund relative to the number of workers. When the number of workers increases from M to M^*, profits will fall to zero and wages will be equal to the institutionally determined subsistence wage.

wage rate approaches the subsistence level the rate of population growth declines.

- The production surplus that gave rise to the higher profits and the higher wage rates initially realized by capitalists and workers is absorbed by a combination of higher land rents and the subsistence wages of a larger labor force. When the surplus has been fully absorbed, a new stationary equilibrium is reached at which all the surplus above the laborers' minimum subsistence is captured by landlords. A new round of growth is dependent on new inventions or new discovery.

In the classical model, diminishing returns to increments of labor and capital applied to an inelastic supply of land represented a fundamental constraint on economic growth. Ricardo's policy prescription was to repeal the Corn Laws on the theory that liberalization of food imports would prevent the domestic terms of trade from turning against the industrial sector.[8] Thus the

8. Donald Grove Barnes, *A History of the English Corn Laws from 1660-1846* (rpr. New York: Augustus M. Kelley, 1961), notes that the shift of comparative advantage from agriculture to manufacturing associated with the Industrial Revolution was reinforced by the lower food prices resulting from repeal of the Corn Laws. He states that "only for a brief period in Great Britain were the interests of the manufacturers and consumers identical. Both wanted cheap food,

Ricardian model provided ideological support for the economic interests of the emerging industrial capitalists in their efforts to achieve political ascendancy over the landed aristocracy.

In retrospect, it is clear that Ricardo was overly pessimistic about the potential of technological progress in agriculture. Empirical studies for developed countries today indicate that total factor productivity in agriculture has risen in the process of economic development. The real cost of agricultural production has declined in spite of the land resource constraint.[9] In contrast to the prediction of the Ricardian model, the share of land in national income has declined in the process of economic development.[10] Technical change in agriculture has released the constraints on growth implied by inelastic resource supplies.

GROWTH STAGE THEORIES

Efforts to systematize the process of economic growth within a framework of sequential stages, with general application across national and cultural boundaries, represent a persistent tendency in economic thought. The earlier growth-stage literature was primarily a product of the nineteenth-century German economic historians. It was not a coincidence that the growth-stage approach emerged originally in Germany in the nineteenth century, because Germany was then a latecomer to industrialization (relative to Britain), and the promotion of industrialization and economic growth were regarded as major goals of German nationalism. With the rebirth of interest in economic

---

although for different reasons, and hence they united against their common enemy, the agriculturalists, and brought in free trade'' (p. 293).

9. For the United States see the total and partial productivity indexes for the agricultural sector published annually by the U.S. Department of Agriculture, *Economic Indicators of the Farm Sector* (Washington, D.C.: U.S. Department of Agriculture, Economic Research Service, Statistical Bulletin No. 679, January 1982). An incomplete list of total productivity studies for other developed countries includes the following: I. F. Furniss, "Agricultural Productivity in Canada: Two Decades of Gains," *Canadian Farm Economics* 5 (1970):16–27; Robert A. Young, "Productivity Growth in Australian Rural Industries," *Quarterly Review of Agricultural Economics* 24 (1971):185–205; J. C. Toutain, *Le Produit de l'agriculture française, 1700 à 1958* (Paris: L'Institut de Science Economique Appliquée, 1961); Saburo Yamada, "Changes in Conventional and Nonconventional Inputs in Japanese Agriculture since 1880," *Food Research Institute Studies* 7 (1967):372–413; Yujiro Hayami (in association with Masahatsu Akino, Masahiko Shintani, and Saburo Yamada), *A Century of Agricultural Growth in Japan* (Tokyo: University of Tokyo Press, and Minneapolis: University of Minnesota Press, 1975).

There are also several total productivity studies for less developed countries. See, for example, the studies of Taiwan (by Lee and Chen), Korea (by Ban), and the Philippines (by David and Barker) in Yujiro Hayami, Vernon W. Ruttan, and Herman Southworth, eds., *Agricultural Growth in Japan, Taiwan, Korea, and the Philippines* (Honolulu: University Press of Hawaii, 1979); for India see Robert E. Evenson and Dayanatha Jha, "The Contribution of the Agricultural Research System to Agricultural Production in India," *Indian Journal of Agricultural Economics* 27 (October–December 1973):212–30.

10. Theodore W. Schultz, *The Economic Organization of Agriculture* (New York: McGraw-Hill, 1953), pp. 125–45.

growth during the last several decades, economists and historians have joined in the effort to satisfy the demand for a general development theory by dividing economic history into discrete linear segments.[11]

The German Tradition

There are two major traditions in the nineteenth-century German literature of growth-stage theories: (a) Friedrich List and the German Historical School and (b) Karl Marx and the Marxists. Both List and Marx emphasized five stages in the development process, but their stages were based on entirely different principles.

List based his stage classifications on shifts in occupational distribution. His five stages include savage, pastoral, agricultural, agricultural-manufacturing, and agricultural-manufacturing-commercial.[12] Both the List stages and the numerous other stage schema developed by the German Historical School (Bruno Hildebrand, Karl Bücher, Gustav Schmoller) are little more than "a simple expository device for impressing upon beginners (or the public) the lesson that economic policy has to do with changing economic structures."[13]

Yet the work of List is of contemporary interest because of his emphasis on nationalist industrial and commercial policies in achieving a transition from an agricultural to an industrial economy. In List's view, progress in agriculture could occur only under the stimulus of export demand or the impact of domestic industrial development. Of these two sources, domestic industrial development was considered the more important generator of agricultural progress, because of the double impact of the increased demand for farm products from an expanding nonfarm sector and the development of more efficient production methods resulting from the application of science and technology. List's policy prescription for the developing economies of the nineteenth century was to encourage industrialization through the protection of "infant industries" so as to promote the growth of both import substitutes and industrial exports.[14] These prescriptions continue to have great intuitive

---

11. Bert F. Hoselitz, "Theories of Stages of Economic Growth," *Theories of Economic Growth,* ed. Hoselitz et al., pp. 193–238. Political scientists have not been immune to the penchant for development "staging." See Robert T. Holt and John E. Turner, *The Political Basis of Economic Development: An Exploration in Comparative Political Analysis* (Princeton: D. Van Nostrand, 1966), pp. 39–50.

12. Friedrich List, *The National System of Political Economy* (London: Longmans, Green and Co., 1885; repr. Augustus M. Kelley, New York, 1966). For a review of the significance of List's work see K. William Kapp, "Friedrich List's Contribution to the Theory of Economic Development," *Hindu Culture, Economic Development and Economic Planning in India,* ed. D. William Kapp (New York: Asia Publishing House, 1963), pp. 165–70; and Hoselitz, "Theories of Stages of Economic Growth."

13. Joseph A. Schumpeter, *History of Economic Analysis* (New York: Oxford University Press, 1954), p. 442.

14. List did not regard protectionism as an end in itself, but rather as a means to achieve the greatest development of national productive power. In the introductory essay to the 1904 English edition, J. S. Nicholson pointed out that List held that "nations must modify their systems

appeal to the industrial entrepreneurs and political leaders of developing countries.

Marx based his stage classification on changes in production technology and associated changes in the system of property rights and ideology. His stages include primitive communism, ancient slavery, medieval feudalism, industrial capitalism, and socialism. In the Marxian system, economies evolve through these stages, driven by the forces generated by struggles between two classes, one controlling the means of production to combine with labor and the other possessing no means of production but labor. The class struggle reflects the continuing contradiction between the evolution of economic institutions and progress in production technology.[15]

In spite of the unrealistic assumption that society is organized in two socioeconomic classes with mutually inconsistent interests engaged in a continuous struggle over the division of income, the "Marxist analysis is the only genuinely evolutionary economic theory that the period produced."[16] Apart from ideological considerations, the work of Marx is of contemporary significance because of the major importance which he gave to the role of technical change in shaping economic institutions. In the Marxian system, changes in technology represent the dynamic source of changes in social organization. Marx considered growth of agricultural productivity as a "precondition" to the emergence of industrial capitalism.[17] In contrast to the classical economists, he viewed increasing returns to scale as an important source of growth in the agricultural as well as in the industrial sector. Marx was impressed by the efficiency of large-scale farming in England and regarded structural

---

according to the measure of their own progress. In the first stage they must adopt free trade with the more advanced nations as a means of raising themselves from a state of barbarism and of making advances in agriculture. In the second stage they must resort to commercial restrictions to promote the growth of manufactures, fisheries, navigation, and foreign trade. In the last stage, 'after reaching the highest degree of wealth and power,' they must gradually revert to the principle of free trade and of unrestricted competition in the home as well as in foreign markets, so that their agriculturists, manufacturers, and merchants may be preserved from indolence and stimulated to retain the supremacy which they have acquired." List, *National System of Political Economy* (reprinted without page numbers following p. 444).

15. This perspective is expressed in a number of Marx's works, typically Karl Marx, *A Contribution to the Critique of Political Economy*, trans. N. I. Stone (Chicago: Charles H. Kerr, 1918). For a review of the Marxian historical perspective see Mandell Morton Bober, *Karl Marx's Interpretation of History* (Cambridge, Mass., Harvard University Press, 2d ed. rev., 1948).

16. Schumpeter, *History of Economic Analysis*, p. 441.

17. Karl Marx, *Capital, A Critique of Political Economy*, ed. Friedrich Engels (New York: Modern Library, copyright, 1906, by Charles H. Kerr and Co.). According to Marx, "Technology discloses man's mode of dealing with Nature, the process of production by which he sustains his life, and thereby also lays bare the mode of formation of his social relations, and of the mental conceptions that flow from them," p. 406n. For a review of the Marxian perspective on the role of technical change see Bober, *Interpretation of History*. Karl Marx, "The So-Called Primitive Accumulation," Part VIII in *Capital: A Critical Analysis of Capitalist Production*, Vol. 1, ed. Friederich Engels (Moscow: Progress Publishers, 1965), pp. 713–74. See also Bober, *Interpretation of History*, pp. 56–63.

changes leading to the elimination of peasant farming as an essential step in agricultural development.

Structural Transformation

The "resemblance between List's three last stages and the concept of primary, secondary and tertiary production, developed in the 1930s by Allan G. B. Fisher and propagated further by Colin Clark," has been emphasized by Bert F. Hoselitz. Fisher emphasized the "steady shift of employment and investment from the essential 'primary' activities . . . to secondary activities of all kinds, and to a still greater extent into tertiary production" which accompanies economic progress. In Clark's formulation the economic growth which accompanies this transformation is achieved, first, by increases in output per worker in any sector and, second, by the transfer of labor from sectors with low output per worker to sectors with higher output per worker.[18]

Fisher, as did List, held that such a transition was closely associated with the advance of science and technology. But an intense empiricism inhibited Clark from attempting an adequate theoretical foundation for his transition generalization. Nor did he provide any significant policy guidance for the problem of how a predominantly agricultural society might proceed to achieve a successful transition to a modern industrial society.

The important impact of the Fisher-Clark generalizations on economic thought and on economic policy during the decade immediately following World War II must be attributed to three factors: (a) the weight of empirical evidence generated by Clark's massive scholarship; (b) a felicitous choice of a value-loaded terminology; and (c) the equating of economic progress with industrialization by the planners and policymakers of countries which were attempting to emerge from economic and/or political colonization.

By the mid-1950s the analytical validity and statistical evidence, as well as the policy implications of the Fisher-Clark generalizations, were being questioned.[19] Analytical criticisms were directed toward the arbitrariness of the distinctions and lack of uniformity of income elasticity of demand among products classed within each of the three categories. A number of critics pointed to the tendency of official statistics to conceal the high proportion of

18. Hoselitz, "Theories of Stages of Economic Growth," pp. 202–3; Allan G. B. Fisher, *Economic Progress and Social Security* (London: Macmillan, 1945), p. 6. For Fisher's earlier works, see *The Clash of Progress and Security* (London: Macmillan, 1935), pp. 25–43; and "Production, Primary, Secondary, and Tertiary," *Economic Record* 15 (March 1939):24–38. The best exposition of Clark's approach is found in Colin Clark, "The Morphology of Economic Growth," Chapter X, *The Conditions of Economic Progress,* ed. Colin Clark (London: Macmillan, 1940), pp. 337–73. This chapter has been omitted in later editions.

19. P. T. Bauer and B. S. Yamey, "Economic Progress and Occupational Distribution," *Economic Journal* 61 (December 1951):741–55; and "Further Notes on Economic Progress and Occupational Distribution," ibid. 64 (March 1954):98–106; Simon Rottenberg, "Notes on 'Economic Progress in Occupational Distribution,'" *Review of Economics and Statistics* 35 (May 1953):168–70; S. G. Triantis, "Economic Progress, Occupational Redistribution and International Terms of Trade," *Economic Journal* 63 (September 1953): 627–37.

time spent by the rural population in secondary (handicraft, etc.) and tertiary (transport, trading, personal service, etc.) activities in economies in which occupational specialization is limited.

Other analysts have focused on the constraints that impinge on rapid structural transformation. Folke Dovring demonstrated that the size of the agricultural sector relative to the rest of the economy limits the rate at which workers can be shifted to nonagricultural employment. In an economy that is primarily agricultural, the share of the labor force in agriculture will decline slowly even when the growth of employment in the industrial and service sectors is very rapid. Bruce Johnston and Peter Kilby have emphasized two additional constraints. The domestic demand for the commodities produced by the agricultural sector is limited by the small size of the urban-industrial sector and the low income of workers in the industrial and service sectors. And these demand side constraints in turn limit "the farm sector's demand for manufactured consumer goods and purchased inputs such as fertilizer and farm equipment."[20] Johnston and Kilby also emphasize the importance of farm size distribution for the development of efficient intersectoral factor and commodity markets. They argue that a rural economy characterized by a highly unequal (bimodal) farm size distribution imposes severe constraints on the development of strong rural markets for the products of domestic industries.

The structural transformation theme remains an important organizing principle for both development thought and development policy. But the easy gains from interindustry resource transfers implied by the structural transformation thesis have been difficult to realize. As a result, the attention of development economists and planners has shifted to give greater attention to the constraints on rapid structural transformation in primarily agrarian economies.

Leading Sectors

The decline of professional interest in the Fisher-Clark stages during the 1960s was due, at least in part, to the emergence of Rostow's "leading sector" growth-stage approach.[21] Rostow identifies five stages in the transition from a primitive to a modern economy: the traditional society, the preconditions for take-off, the take-off, the drive to maturity, and the age of high mass consumption. These stages are, except for the first and last, transition stages rather than a succession of equilibrium positions.

Rostow was primarily concerned with the process by which a society

---

20. Folke Dovring, "The Share of Agriculture in a Growing Population," *FAO Monthly Bulletin of Agricultural Economics and Statistics* 8 (August–September 1959):1–11, reprinted in Food and Agriculture Organization, *FAO Studies in Agricultural Economics and Statistics, 1952–1977* (Rome: Food and Agriculture Organization of the United Nations, 1978), pp. 186–96; Johnston and Kilby, *Agriculture and Structural Transformation*, p. xvii.

21. Rostow, "The Take-off into Self-sustained Growth," and *Stages of Economic Growth*.

moves from one stage to another, and his historical analysis was conducted with the objective of providing policy guidance to the leaders of the developing countries, since "it is useful, as well as roughly accurate, to regard the process of development now going forward in Asia, the Middle East, Africa, and Latin America as analogous to the stages of preconditions and take-off of other societies, in the late eighteenth, nineteenth, and twentieth centuries."[22]

Rostow's approach starts from the empirical premise that "deceleration is the normal optimum path of a sector, due to a variety of factors operating on it, from the side of both supply and demand."[23] The problem of transition and hence of growth, therefore, becomes how to offset the tendency for deceleration in individual sectors to achieve growth in the total economy.

On the supply side, Rostow introduces the concept of a sequence of leading sectors which succeed each other as the basic generators of growth. On the demand side, declining price and income elasticities of demand are introduced as technical factors dampening the growth rate of leading sectors and transforming them to sustaining or declining sectors. Technology plays an important role in both the emergence of new leading sectors and the elimination of older sectors.

All three growth-stage theories reviewed here treat the transition from an agricultural to an industrial society as the major problem of development policy. Rostow's system, like that of Marx, clearly specifies a dynamic role for the agricultural sector in the transition process. In an open economy, primary sector industries may act as leading sectors and, at a particular time, carry the burden of accelerating growth. In addition, agriculture must provide food for a rapidly increasing population, provide a mass market for the products of the emerging industrial sectors, and generate the capital investment and labor force for new leading sectors outside of agriculture.[24]

Rostow, as well as the other growth-stage proponents, has not escaped criticism. Most of the papers presented at the 1960 conference of the International Economic Association on "The Economics of the Take-Off into Sustained Growth" rejected either Rostow's dating of the take-off for presently advanced countries or the concept of the take-off itself. A. K. Cairncross and Simon Kuznets have vigorously attacked the analytical criteria employed to identify successive stages, the leading sector hypothesis, and the historical validity of Rostow's empirical generalizations concerning the take-off stage for the presently developed countries.[25]

22. Ibid. (1960), p. 3.
23. Ibid., p. 13.
24. This is roughly equivalent to the role which Marx assigned to agriculture. What he termed "primitive accumulation" was a precondition for the emergence of industrial capitalism.
25. W. W. Rostow, ed., *The Economics of Take-off into Sustained Growth* (London: Macmillan, 1964); see also the review of the volume by W. Paul Strassmann, *American Economic Review* 54 (September 1964): 785–90; A. K. Cairncross, "Essays in Bibliography and Criticism XLV: The Stages of Economic Growth," *Economic History Review,* 2d ser., 13 (April 1961): 450–58; Simon Kuznets, "Notes on the Take-off," *The Economics of Take-off,* ed. Rostow, pp. 22–43. In his more recent work Rostow tends to view his stage schema more as an expository

Rostow himself has had some difficulty in dating the take-off. He identifies the Turkish take-off as 1937 but noted that there was still some doubt in the late 1950s whether Turkey had made a successful transition to self-sustaining growth. Students from less developed countries have found even greater difficulty in identifying their experience with any particular stage. One article reached the startling conclusion that "after entering into the 'take-off' stage in 1957, the [Philippine] economy immediately slipped back into the 'preconditions' . . . stage."[26] Furthermore, the approach contains no mechanism to explain why countries such as Argentina, Chile, Ceylon, and Burma, all of which experienced very rapid growth during the latter years of the nineteenth century, failed to achieve a successful take-off.

Rostow's recognition of the critical importance of rapid growth in agricultural output during the early stages of economic development led to a rapid "diffusion" of the leading sector model among students of agricultural development. A sequence of three agricultural development stages, which roughly parallel the precondition, take-off, and drive-to-maturity stages in the Rostow model, has been presented by Maurice Perkins and Lawrence Witt, Bruce F. Johnston and John W. Mellor, and Forrest F. Hill and Arthur T. Mosher.[27]

Perkins and Witt have followed Rostow in emphasizing the importance of leading commercial sectors within agriculture, in contrast to the more static subsistence sectors, in the adoption of technological innovations and as a source of much of the increase in the output of food and export commodities. Johnston and Mellor, using Japan and Taiwan as models, emphasize the possibilities of transforming the subsistence sector into a small-scale commercial sector. The difficulty of resolving this issue, within the framework of growth-stage analysis, is symptomatic of the difficulty faced by stage approaches in generating useful guides to agricultural development policies at any particular time in economic history. W. David Hopper has made a similar point in his comment that "every developing country . . . fits each of the stages."[28]

device than as a theory of development. Walter W. Rostow, *The World Economy: History and Prospect* (Austin: University of Texas Press, 1978), pp. 365–72.

26. Gabriel Y. Itchon, "Philippines: Necessary Condition for 'Take-off,' " *Philippine Economic Journal* 1 (First Semester, 1962): 30.

27. Maurice Perkins and Lawrence Witt, "Capital Formation: Past and Present," *Journal of Farm Economics* 43 (May 1961):333–43; Bruce F. Johnston and John W. Mellor, "The Role of Agriculture in Economic Development," *American Economic Review* 51 (September 1961):566–93. The Johnston-Mellor approach has been elaborated in a series of articles by J. W. Mellor, "Increasing Agricultural Production in Early Stages of Economic Development: Relationships, Problems and Prospects," *Indian Journal of Agricultural Economics* 17 (April-June 1962):29–46; and "The Process of Agricultural Development in Low-income Countries," *Journal of Farm Economics* 44 (August 1962):700–16. Forrest F. Hill and Arthur T. Mosher, "Organizing for Agricultural Development," in *Science, Technology and Development*, vol. 3, *Agriculture*, United States papers prepared for the United Nations Conference on the Application of Science and Technology for the Benefit of the Less Developed Areas (Washington, D.C.: U.S. Government Printing Office, 1962), pp. 1–11.

28. W. David Hopper, "Discussion: The Role of Agriculture in the World Economy," ibid. 43 (May 1961):347.

DUAL ECONOMY MODELS

The dual-economy approach emerged out of an attempt to understand the relationship (or lack of relationship) between a lagging traditional sector and a growing modern sector within non-Western societies affected by the economic, political, and military intrusions of Western colonialism. The static dual-economy models emphasized the limited interaction between the traditional and modern sectors. The newer dynamic dual-economy models identify agriculture as the traditional sector and industry as the modern sector and attempt to trace the increasing interaction between the two sectors in the process of development.

Static Dualism

Two distinct variations of static dualism can be identified in the literature: (a) a "sociological dualism," which stresses cultural differences leading to distinct "Western" and "non-Western" concepts of economic organization and rationality, and (b) an "enclave dualism," which emphasizes the perverse behavior of labor, capital, and product markets through which the modern industrial nations of the West interact with traditional societies in other parts of the world.[29] Both variants are important to an understanding of the assumptions about the structure and economic behavior of developing economies that have been incorporated into modern dual-economy models.

Sociological dualism was primarily the product of inquiry by the Dutch economist J. H. Boeke into the reasons for the failure of Dutch colonial policy in Indonesia.[30] The failure of the liberal economic policies adopted in 1870 to reverse the "diminishing welfare" of the Indonesian masses, particularly in Java, led to an intensive reevaluation of colonial policy. Beginning with his doctoral thesis in 1910, Boeke argued that Western economic thought was not applicable to tropical-colonial conditions and posited the need for a separate theoretical approach to the problems of such economies. "Where . . . there is a sharp, deep, broad cleavage dividing the society into two segments, many social and economic issues take on a quite different appearance and western economic theories lose their relation to reality—and hence their value."[31] Boeke thus assumes, as a precondition for his dualism, the coexistence of two social systems, which interact only marginally through very limited contact in the product and labor markets.

29. We are indebted to Richard Hooley, "The Concept of Dualism in the Theory of Development" (National Planning Association Center for Development Planning, M-9285, March 1968, mimeo.) for clarification of this distinction.

30. J. H. Boeke, *Economics and Economic Policy of Dual Societies as Exemplified by Indonesia* (New York: Institute of Pacific Relations, 1953). For an excellent summary of Boeke's work see *Indonesian Economics: The Concept of Dualism in Theory and Policy*, vol. 6 of *Selected Studies of Indonesia* by Dutch Scholars (The Hague: W. Van Hoeve Publishers, 1961). In addition to Boeke's classic article, "Dualistic Economics," the book contains several of his other articles, as well as a critical review of his work by other Dutch scholars.

31. Dutch Scholars, ibid., p. 170.

The central tenet of Boeke's thesis is a fundamental distinction between the objectives of economic activity in Western and Eastern society. He argued that while economic activity in the West, and in the Western enclaves in the East, is based on the stimulus of economic need, the Indonesian is guided primarily by social needs. He is particularly critical of attempts to explain the allocation of resources or the distribution of income in terms of neoclassical marginal productivity theory, mainly because of the great immobility of resources in Eastern society.

The major policy implication of the Boeke analysis is the futility of attempting to introduce Western technology and Western institutions into Indonesian, and, by inference, other Asian economic systems. The only effect of efforts to bring about technological change in traditional agriculture through the introduction of new inputs from outside the agricultural sector is an acceleration in the rate of population growth.

Boeke's static dualism has been strongly criticized by a number of Dutch economists, almost from its first appearance. Benjamin Higgins has questioned the accuracy of Boeke's empirical observations and has suggested specific examples of the usefulness of Western economic analysis to counter the examples he presented. Indeed, he suggests that Boeke's criticisms of Western thought stem in part from his unfamiliarity with Western thought since Alfred Marshall and Joseph Schumpeter.[32]

Academic criticism of the Boeke thesis has not prevented it from exerting a substantial impact on economic policy. In spite of its "colonialist" origin it has been widely accepted, either explicitly or implicitly, among members of the intellectual elite and the bureaucracy in the economic policy and planning agencies in many new nations. It provides an intellectual rationalization for an industrialization policy that avoids investment in fertilizer, agricultural chemicals, and farm equipment industries in favor of other heavy industry and import substitutes. And Boeke's "backward bending supply curve" provides a rationalization for failure to achieve productivity gains in agriculture, in spite of (a) failure to invest in agricultural research, education, irrigation, and manufactured inputs and (b) the adoption of price policies that provide only minimal incentives to use available technology.

Enclave dualism, as a variant of static dualism, reflects very heavily the efforts of a number of trade theorists to explain "the spectacle of . . . : a high productivity sector producing for export coexisting with a low productivity sector producing for the domestic market."[33] Higgins, explicitly rejecting the sociological dualism of Boeke, traces the origin of dualism to differences in

32. Ibid.; Benjamin Higgins, "The 'Dualistic Theory' of Underdeveloped Areas," *Economic Development and Cultural Change* 4 (1955-56):99–115. The sociological dualism model has also been used to interpret differences in economic behavior between the indigenous and expatriate sectors in African agriculture. For a review and criticism see Montague Yudelman, *Africans on the Land* (Cambridge, Mass.: Harvard University Press, 1964), pp. 90–103.

33. H. W. Singer, "The Distribution of Gains between Investing and Borrowing Countries," *American Economic Review* (Proceedings) 40 (May 1950):475.

technology between the modern and subsistence sectors.[34] In his view, the modern sector concentrates heavily on the production of primary commodities in mining and on plantations. It imports its technology from abroad. The imported technology employed in the modern sector is basically labor-saving, with relatively high and fixed capital coefficients. This is in contrast to the technology employed in the traditional sector, which is characterized by wide substitution possibilities between capital and labor and the use of labor-intensive production methods. Expansion of the modern sector is primarily in response to demand in foreign markets, and its growth has relatively little impact on the local economy. Expansion of the traditional sector is limited by shortages of savings.

Hla Myint goes beyond Higgins in emphasizing the significance of the capital market as a basis for enclave dualism.[35] In his system the access of the modern commercial, industrial, and agricultural sectors to modern financial markets makes capital available to them at a fraction of the cost of capital to the traditional sectors, thus leading to the adoption of more capital-intensive technology and higher levels of labor productivity. He also suggests that the enclave financial sector tends to produce a net inflow of capital from the subsistence sector and a net outflow to international financial centers. The impact of the modern enclave on local economic development is thus limited by both its low demand for labor and its failure to channel investment into the local economy.

Dynamic Dualism

Although recent interest in dynamic dualism focuses very heavily on the work of Jorgenson and of Fei and Ranis, the now classical article by W. Arthur Lewis, "Economic Development with Unlimited Supplies of Labor," represents the intellectual "take-off" for the Jorgenson, Fei and Ranis, and most other recent dual-economy literature. Indeed, Lewis's work can be regarded as the bridge between dynamic dualism and both the classical and static dualism traditions.[36]

34. Higgins, "The 'Dualistic Theory' of Underdeveloped Areas,"; Benjamin Higgins, *Economic Development: Principles, Problems, and Policies* (New York: Norton, 1959), pp. 325–33, 424–31.

35. Hla Myint, *The Economics of the Developing Countries* (London: Hutchinson University Library, 1964), pp. 69–84.

36. Jorgenson, "The Development of a Dual Economy,""Testing Alternative Theories," "Surplus Agricultural Labour," and "The Role of Agriculture in Economic Development"; Ranis and Fei, "A Theory of Economic Development"; Fei and Ranis, *Development of the Labor Surplus Economy,* and "Agrarianism, Dualism, and Economic Development"; W. Arthur Lewis, "Economic Development with Unlimited Supplies of Labour," *Manchester School of Economics and Social Studies* 22 (May 1954):139–91, and "Unlimited Labour: Further Notes," ibid. 26 (January 1958):1–32. Three major contributions to the dual economy literature which appear to owe little intellectual debt to Lewis's earlier work are Anne O. Krueger, "Interrelationships between Industry and Agriculture in a Dual Economy," *Indian Economic Journal* 10 (July 1962):2–13; William H. Nicholls, "An 'Agricultural Surplus' as a Factor in Economic Development," *Journal of Political Economy* 71 (February 1963):1–29; and G. S. Tolley and S.

The dynamic dual-economy models accept the static typology of "sociological" and "enclave" dualism as essentially valid for a broad class of underdeveloped economies, particularly the postcolonial economies of South and Southeast Asia and Africa and the Latin American economies with large indigenous populations. According to Fei and Ranis, these economies "are characterized by the coexistence of two sectors: a relatively large and overwhelmingly stagnant subsistence agricultural sector in which institutional forces determine the wage rate, and a relatively small but growing commercialized industrial sector in which competitive conditions obtain in the input markets."[37]

The main thrust of the dynamic dual-economy models has been to explore the formal relationships that would permit an escape (a) from the Malthusian trap, which Boeke regards as the inevitable consequence of attempting to introduce new technology into the native agriculture, and (b) from the lack of effective labor and capital market relationships between the modern enclave and the traditional economy. Indeed, productivity increases in agriculture become, in the dynamic models, the mechanism that permits a continuous reallocation of labor from the agricultural to the industrial sector.

In the Fei-Ranis model (Figure 2.2) the subsistence sector is characterized by (a) disguised unemployment and underemployment; (b) a positive "institutionally determined" wage rate for agricultural labor, which approximates the average productivity of labor in the subsistence sector; (c) a marginal productivity of labor lower than the wage rate; and (d) fixed land inputs. Fei and Ranis argue that under these conditions it is possible to transfer labor from the subsistence sector to the commercial-industrial sector without reducing agricultural output and without increasing the supply price of labor to the industrial sector during the early stages of development. Indeed, the transfer of one worker from the subsistence to the nonsubsistence sector results in an agricultural surplus which then becomes available as an investment fund for

Smidt, "Agriculture and the Secular Position of the U.S. Economy," *Econometrica* 32 (October 1964):554–75. Krueger refers to previous work by Sayre P. Schatz, "A Dual-Economy Model of an Underdeveloped Country," *Social Research* 23 (Winter 1956):419–32, which discusses some of the features of an economy characterized by enclave dualism. Gustav Ranis and John C. H. Fei, "Lewis and the Classicists," *Theory and Experience of Economic Development*, ed. Gersovitz, Diaz-Alejandro, Ranis, and Rosenzweig, pp. 31–42. We do not, in this section, review a second class of dynamic dual-economy models that owes its intellectual origins to neoclassical growth theory. In these models it is typically assumed that one sector produces capital goods and the other consumption goods. See, for example, Hirofumi Uzawa, "On a Two-Sector Model of Economic Growth, I," *Review of Economic Studies* 29 (October 1961):40–47, and "On a Two-Sector Model of Economic Growth, II," *Review of Economic Studies* 30 (June 1963):105–18. The Uzawa and other two sector models based on capital goods—consumption goods dualism— do not provide a useful framework for examining issues related to agricultural development. In retrospect, it is apparent that the growth-theory tradition, which has typically confined itself to the formal analysis of the dynamic and equilibrium properties of growth models, has not been a fruitful inspiration either for analysis of the historical experience of developing economies or as a guide to development policy.

37. Fei and Ranis, *Development of the Labor Surplus Economy*, p. 3.

FIGURE 2-2. A simplified representation of the Fei-Ranis dual-economy model.

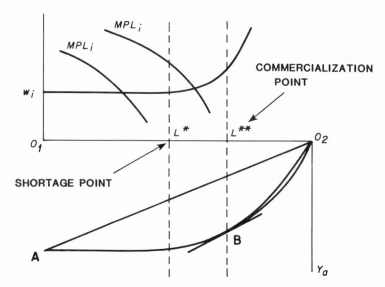

Source: Adapted from John C. H. Fei and Gustav Ranis, *Development of the Labor Surplus Economy: Theory and Policy* (Homewood, Ill.: Irwin, 1964), p. 25, and from Avinash Dixit, "Models of Dual Economies," *Models of Economic Growth,* ed. J. A. Mirrlees and N. H. Stern (New York: Wiley, 1973), p. 340.

Note. O_1O_2 represents the total labor force with industrial labor measured from O_1 to the right and agricultural labor from O_2 to the left. Curve O_2BA is the total product curve for food. Line w_i is the supply curve for labor to the industrial sector. If the agricultural labor force is greater than O_2L^* (the shortage point) the marginal product of labor is zero. If the agricultural labor force is less than O_2L^{**} (the commercialization point) the marginal product of labor exceeds the constant institutional wage rate ($\bar{y} = Y/L^*$). As long as the demand for labor in the industrial sector (MPL_i) is less than O_1L the transfer of labor from the agricultural sector does not reduce agricultural output and labor is available to the industrial sector at the constant institutional wage rate. When the demand for labor in the industrial sector exceeds O_1L^* (MPL_i), transfer of labor from agriculture leads to a decline in food output, a relative increase in the price of food, and a rise in wage rates in the industrial sector. If the demand for labor in the industrial sector exceeds L^{**} (the commercialization point), the wage rate in the agricultural sector rises along with the wage rate in the industrial sector. The agricultural surplus available to the industrial sector then declines further both because of the effect of the decline in the agricultural labor force on production and the rise in food consumption resulting from the higher wages received by agricultural workers.

the development of the industrial sector. Fei and Ranis also envisage additional agricultural surpluses as a result of productivity increases from labor-intensive capital improvements. Agriculture, in this system, contributes both workers and surplus production in the form of a wage fund for the expansion of the industrial sector. In such a system the major functions of public policy are (a) to design institutions that transfer the ownership of such surpluses from the agricultural sector to the government or to the entrepreneurs in the commercial-industrial sector and (b) to avoid dissipation of the potential surplus through higher consumption in the rural sector.

One of the critical points in the development of the dual economy, within the context of the Fei-Ranis model, occurs at the time when the marginal value product of agricultural labor begins to rise above zero. At this point, which is called the "shortage point," the transfer of one worker from the subsistence to the commercial-industrial sector does not release a sufficiently large wage fund to support his consumption in the commercial-industrial sector. The result is a "worsening of the terms of trade" against the industrial sector, which can be offset only by productivity growth in agriculture or by deceleration in the growth of the commercial-industrial sector.

Another critical point, called the "commercialization point," occurs when the marginal value product of labor exceeds the "institutionally determined" wage rate in the agricultural sector. At this point, a rise in the industrial wage is required if the commercial-industrial sector is to compete effectively with the subsistence sector for labor. If, at this stage, rapid productivity growth in the agricultural sector is achieved, the "dualistic" features of the economy atrophy and agriculture increasingly takes on the role of an appendage of the one-sector economy taken as a whole.

In the Jorgenson dual-economy model, the assumptions of (a) zero marginal productivity of labor and (b) an institutionally determined wage rate in the subsistence sector are dropped. Wage rates are determined in an intersector labor market even during the initial stages of development. As a result labor is never available to the industrial sector without sacrificing agricultural output, and the terms of trade move against the industrial sector continuously throughout the development process rather than after substantial development in the commercial-industrial sector.[38]

In Jorgenson's system, an economy's ability to generate an agricultural surplus depends on only three parameters: (a) the rate of technical progress in agriculture; (b) the rate of population growth; and (c) the elasticity of output in the agricultural sector with respect to changes in the agricultural labor force. For an economy caught in a low-level equilibrium trap, an escape is possible through (a) changes in the rate of introduction of new technology in agricultural production and (b) changes in medical knowledge and practices that lower the birth rate more rapidly than the death rate. Note that in the Jorgenson model, technological change must be introduced into the agricultural sector from the very beginning of the growth process.

The Jorgenson model has moved somewhat closer to operational relevance than the Fei-Ranis model. The Fei-Ranis assumption that the marginal productivity of labor in the subsistence sector is lower than an institutionally

38. It has become conventional to label the Fei-Ranis model "classical" and the Jorgenson approach "neoclassical" on the basis of their different assumptions about the elasticity of supply of labor to the industrial sector. Avinash Dixit notes that "the neoclassical approach emphasizes the rate at which agricultural labor can be released for industrial work, while the classical approach concentrates on the scarcity of industrial capital available for the potentially usable labour," "Growth Patterns in a Dual Economy," *Oxford Economic Papers* 22 (July 1970):233.

determined wage rate is not consistent with the findings of a number of empirical studies of labor productivity in subsistence agriculture.[39]

This weakness in their formal model does not imply that Ranis and Fei are unaware of the critical importance of agricultural productivity growth in the early economic development process. On the contrary, they insist that "any underdeveloped economy which attempts to force the pace of industrialization while disregarding the need for a priori—or at least simultaneous—revolution in its agricultural sector will . . . find the going most difficult. We are thus keenly aware of the fact that any success criterion which concentrates only on the industrial sector's ability to absorb labor is merely an index which implicitly summarizes the simultaneous capacity of the agricultural sector to release labor."[40] The zero marginal labor productivity assumption of Ranis and Fei represents a convenient but misleading pedagogical device. This assumption should be relaxed or replaced by more realistic assumptions with respect to intersector labor market behavior in drawing policy implications from their model.

The major weakness of the Jorgenson model relative to the Fei-Ranis model involves the Malthusian population response mechanism and a zero income elasticity of demand for food.[41] Population growth is constrained by food supply up to the point that per capita food consumption is no longer

39. Charles H. C. Kao, Kurt R. Anschel, and Carl K. Eicher, "Disguised Unemployment in Agriculture: A Survey," *Agriculture in Economic Development,* ed. Carl Eicher and Lawrence Witt (New York: McGraw-Hill, 1964), pp. 129–44; Theodore W. Schultz, *Transforming Traditional Agriculture* (New Haven: Yale University Press, 1964); W. David Hopper, "Allocative Efficiency in a Traditional Indian Agriculture," *Journal of Farm Economics* 47 (August 1965):611–24; Morton Paglin, "Surplus Agricultural Labor and Development: Facts and Theories," *American Economic Review* 55 (September 1965):815–34. More recent theoretical work has demonstrated that the assumption of zero marginal productivity of labor is less critical than originally assumed. If production can be described by a neoclassical production function and leisure is an inferior good, the transfer of labor to the modern sector may change the work-leisure equilibrium of the workers remaining in agriculture and compensate for those who have left in such a way that there is no loss of output. See Amartya K. Sen, "Peasants and Dualism with or without Surplus Labor," *Journal of Political Economy* 74 (October 1966):425–50; and Paul Zarembka, *Toward a Theory of Economic Development* (San Francisco: Holden Day, 1972), pp. 9–25. Empirical estimates by Howard N. Barnum and Lyn Squire, "An Econometric Application of the Theory of the Farm-Household," *Journal of Development Economics* 6 (March 1979):79–102, and by Mark Rosenzweig, "Determinants of Wage Rates and Labor Supply Behavior in the Rural Sector of a Developing Country," *Contractual Arrangements, Employment, and Wages in Rural Labor Markets in Asia,* ed. Hans P. Binswanger and Mark Rosenzweig (New Haven: Yale University Press, 1984), indicate less than full compensation at the farm level.

40. Fei and Ranis, *Development of the Labor Surplus Economy,* pp. 121, 151–99.

41. The most thorough comparison and criticism of the dynamic economy models has been presented in a series of papers by Avinash Dixit, "Growth Patterns in a Dual Economy"; "Short-Run Equilibrium and Shadow Prices in the Dual Economy," *Oxford Economic Papers* 23 (November 1971):384–400; "Models of Dual Economies," *Models of Economic Growth,* ed. J. A. Mirrlees and N. H. Stern (New York: John Wiley & Sons for International Economic Association, 1973), pp. 325–52. For other reviews and criticisms see Alvin H. Marty, "Professor Jorgenson's Model of the Dual Economy," *Indian Economic Journal* (April–June 1965):437–41; and R. Ramanathan, "Jorgenson's Model of a Dual Economy—An Extension," *Economic Journal* 77 (June 1967):322–27.

responsive to income growth. At this point, in the Jorgenson model, the rate of population growth declines and there is a sudden drop in the income elasticity of demand for food from one to zero. All increases in consumption are devoted to goods produced in the industrial sector. These assumptions clearly are not consistent with either demographic or food consumption behavior. The rate of population growth typically begins to decline while the income elasticity of demand for food is well above zero. And the income elasticity of demand for food does not decline to zero in even the highest-income countries.

Perhaps the most serious limitation in both models stems from the treatment of productivity gains in agriculture as results of neutral and exogenous shifts in the production function without imposing any demand on resource inputs other than labor-intensive capital improvements such as land reclamation and development.[42] The production of technical change in agriculture is itself, however, a relatively capital-intensive activity, particularly when one considers the human investment involved. Furthermore, it frequently requires a relatively long gestation period and has highly uncertain returns. The short-run supply of new technical knowledge appears to be relatively inelastic with respect to increases in expenditure on research personnel in both developed and less developed countries. Technical change is difficult for a country in the early stages of economic development to produce. And when it does become available, it is typically channeled into the agricultural sector embodied in the form of inputs, such as fertilizer and insecticides, which are purchased from the nonagricultural sector. Failure to incorporate resource flows into the agricultural sector unnecessarily restricts the use of technical changes embodied in inputs that must be purchased from the modern sector. It is entirely possible, in an open dual-economy model, that it would appear appropriate in some situations to have a net flow of savings into the agricultural sector.[43]

A second major limitation is that both models ignore the problem of resource use in the intersector commodity markets. Markets are treated as disembodied communications systems through which resources and commodities are transferred between the modern and traditional sectors without absorbing either capital or labor in the process. The transfer of labor from the farm to the nonfarm sector is viewed as the source of a wages fund which then becomes available to support development in the nonagricultural sector. In most underdeveloped countries, substantial labor and capital resources are

42. This point has also been made by Dixit, "Growth Patterns in a Dual Economy." According to Dixit the assumption of exogenous and neutral technical change and no capital accumulation in the agricultural sector means that there must be "an absolute decline in agricultural labour, before the surplus-labour phase can end. But if there is surplus labour, a very important role of technical progress is that of rendering this labour productive. Technical progress in a real labour-surplus economy will clearly be induced by this necessity" (p. 232). We develop an induced innovation model of agricultural development in Chapter 4.

43. Shigeru Ishikawa, *Economic Development in Asian Perspective* (Tokyo: Kinokuniya Bookstore, 1967), pp. 290–356.

absorbed in the storage, transportation, and trading activities involved in making the marketable surpluses produced by the agricultural sector available to urban consumers. Thus a shift of workers from a rural or village location to an urban location associated with growth in employment in the nonsubsistence sector typically requires a substantial increase in labor and capital inputs allocated to the marketing sector.[44] As development occurs, a higher and higher portion of food flows through wholesale and retail channels. For countries starting out with a relatively low ratio of food passing through wholesale and retail channels, the rate of increase in resources devoted to marketing can be explosive, as the share of the population residing in urban centers rises and even modest gains in per capita income levels are achieved. These very substantial "leakages" of agricultural surpluses into the marketing process imply more severe constraints on the potential for growth resulting from the simple transfer of labor resources from the subsistence to the modern sector than implied by the modern dual-economy models.

In spite of these qualifications both the Jorgenson and Fei-Ranis dual-economy models have made important contributions to our understanding of the role of the agricultural sector in the process of economic development. The sectoral division, whether modern-traditional or industrial-agricultural, captures economic and social distinctions that are important in developing economies. There are important differences in the elasticity of supply of land and in the forms of capital used in the industrial sector. The intersector labor markets are characterized by substantial disequilibrium in the earnings of agricultural and industrial workers. Both models confirm, in formal terms, the intuitive judgment (a) that a shift in the domestic terms of trade toward agriculture signals a breakdown in the transformation to sustained economic growth and (b) that this shift can be offset only by some combination of a more rapid rate of technological change in agriculture and/or a dampening of the rate of population growth. The very simplicity of the models, a major source of their insight into the fundamental process of development, however, has led to substantial underestimation of the difficulties that face poor countries in achieving such a transformation.

Toward Contemporary Relevance

The early 1970s witnessed a third stage in the evolution of dual-economy models. Efforts were made to extend these models to incorporate more realistic assumptions about the behavior of intersectoral factor markets, commodity demand and supply relationships, and the rate and bias of technical

44. Robert D. Stevens, *Elasticity of Food Consumption Associated with Changes in Income in Developing Countries* (Washington, D.C.: U.S. Department of Agriculture, Economic Research Service, FAER No. 23, March 1965); Vernon W. Ruttan, "Agricultural Product and Factor Markets in Southeast Asia," *Economic Development and Cultural Change* 17 (July 1969):501–19. Dixit, "Models of Dual Economies," notes that "a major drawback of dualistic theories . . . is the total neglect of the service sector" (p. 326).

change. Efforts were also made to "open up" the closed dual-economy models to explore the possibility of exporting labor-intensive industrial products and importing capital goods and land-extensive agricultural commodities to offset the domestic constraints on growth.

Perhaps the most ambitious attempt to extend the dual-economy model to incorporate factor and product market behavior and technical change and to test the implications against historical experience has been made by Allen C. Kelley, Jeffrey G. Williamson, and Russell J. Cheetham.[45]

Kelley, Williamson, and Cheetham (KWC) proceed in two steps. They first develop an equilibrium model that incorporates dualism between the agricultural and industrial sectors. They then introduce more realistic disequilibrium assumptions into the behavior of factor and product markets and compare the results of simulations based on the equilibrium and disequilibrium models. Initial conditions and parameter values were selected to be consistent with historical experience in Japan and contemporary experience in Southeast Asia.

A major contribution of the KWC work for development policy is the addition to our understanding of the interactions between technical change and wage rates in the two sectors. In the disequilibrium model, rapid capital formation and rapid technical change result in a widening of the gap between wages in the agricultural and nonagricultural sectors.

The "closed economy" tradition of the early Fei-Ranis and Jorgenson dual-economy models, continued in the KWC model, has been another factor that has limited their usefulness in interpreting contemporary development experience.[46] Since the mid-1970s there have been a number of efforts to

45. See Allen C. Kelley, Jeffrey G. Williamson, and Russell J. Cheetham, "Biased Technological Progress and Labor Force Growth in a Dualistic Economy," *Quarterly Journal of Economics* 86 (August 1972):426–47; and, *Dualistic Development: Theory and History* (Chicago: University of Chicago Press, 1972). Another contribution of somewhat similar nature by Mitoshi Yamaguchi and Hans P. Binswanger, "The Role of Sectoral Technical Change in Development: Japan, 1880-1965," *American Journal of Agricultural Economics* 57 (May 1975):269–78, represents an extension of a model developed for the U.S. economy by G. S. Tolley and S. Smidt, "Agriculture and the Secular Position of the U.S. Economy." For a further application to the Japanese economy see Mitoshi Yamaguchi, *Nihon Keizai no Seicho Kaikei Bunseki* (Growth accounting for the Japanese economy: Population, agriculture, and economic development) (Tokyo: Yuhikaku, 1982). We do not, in this section, attempt to review a number of planning models which have their intellectual roots in the dual-economy literature. Dixit, in "Models of Dual Economies," classifies dual-economy models into historical-descriptive (or mechanistic) and planning (or teleological) types. The first analyze the effects of specific behavioral and technical assumptions; the second assume a greater degree of freedom in behavioral and technical relationships. Although an understanding of behavior would seem to be a prerequisite for planning, the two bodies of literature have evolved with only limited reference to each other. For an extreme example, see Lance Taylor, *Macro Models for Developing Countries* (New York: McGraw-Hill, 1979). Taylor manages to deal with most of the issues discussed in the dynamic dual-economy literature without mentioning either the Jorgenson or the Fei-Ranis contributions.

46. See, for example, the criticisms by J. M. Hornby, "Investment and Trade Policy in the Dual Economy," *Economic Journal* 78 (March 1968):96–107; Dixit, "Short-Run Equilibrium and Shadow Prices in the Dual Economy."

repair this deficiency.[47] The Fei-Ranis interpretation of the experience of Taiwan and Korea, within the framework of an open dualistic model, makes a particularly valuable contribution to our understanding of agricultural development processes.

In the open dualistic models they identify, in addition to the shortage and commercialization points on which attention was focused in the closed model, there are three other transition points in the development of the open dualistic economies:

- *the reversal point,* when the agricultural labor force begins to decline absolutely;

- *the export-substitution point,* when labor-intensive industrial exports replace (or substitute for) the traditional agricultural exports; and

- *the switching point,* when a natural-resource-poor region switches from being a net exporter to being a net importer of agricultural commodities.

The open dual-economy model facilitates the analysis of a wider range of policy choices than the closed dual-economy model during the transition from a labor-surplus to a fully commercialized economy. These options can be illustrated by the contrasts between Taiwan and Korea. In Taiwan, technical change in agriculture was sufficiently rapid to meet domestic food requirements and provide the foreign exchange earnings needed to support the importation of capital goods and raw materials for the industrial sector. Taiwan began to import substantial amounts of feed grains to sustain rapid growth in livestock production in the mid-1960s but did not become a net importer of agricultural commodities until the early 1970s. Korea, on the other hand, was a net importer of agricultural commodities even in the mid-1950s. Agricultural imports continued to grow rapidly to compensate for the slow growth in productivity in the agricultural sector. Fei and Ranis note that from the early 1950s the agricultural sector in Taiwan played a much more positive role in supporting expansion of the industrial sector than in Korea. In the case of Korea, the agricultural sector was "pulled along" by a dynamic industrial sector. In Taiwan, a dynamic agricultural sector "pushed" the development of the industrial sector. Thus in Korea the "switching point" preceded the "reversal point" by a substantial margin, whereas in Taiwan they occurred almost simultaneously.

Another important extension of the dual-economy model has involved the

---

47. Douglas S. Paauw and John C. H. Fei, *The Transition in Open Dualistic Economies: Theory and Southeast Asia Experience* (New Haven: Yale University Press, 1973); John C. H. Fei and Gustav Ranis, "Agriculture in the Open Economy," *The Role of Agriculture in Economic Development,* ed. Erik Thorbecke (New York: Columbia University Press for National Bureau of Economic Research, 1969), pp. 129–59; "A Model of Growth and Employment in the Open Dualistic Economy: The Cases of Korea and Taiwan," *Journal of Development Studies* 11 (January 1975):32–63; "Agriculture in Two Types of Open Economies," *Agriculture in Development Theory,* ed. Lloyd G. Reynolds (New Haven: Yale University Press, 1975), pp. 355–72.

incorporation of duality into modern sector labor markets.[48] In the model introduced by John R. Harris and Michael P. Todaro the sources of dualism in the modern sector are institutional, such as minimum wage legislation or trade union power that maintain modern sector wages above the supply price of labor from the traditional sector. Harris and Todaro argue that in spite of substantial urban unemployment and underemployment, rural to urban migration is individually rational as long as the expected urban wage exceeds average labor income in rural areas. The economic effect of an institutionally determined wage rate in excess of the equilibrium wage rate is, however, to induce premature rural to urban migration, excessive unemployment and underemployment in the urban sector, and loss of potential production of both agricultural commodities and manufactured goods. The policy recommendations that emerge from the Harris-Todaro analysis are either a limited wage subsidy to reduce urban unemployment or a migration restriction policy to reduce the rate of rural to urban migration. But neither policy is capable of moving the economy to the optimal level of intersectoral distribution of employment that could be achieved with competitive wage determination.

DEPENDENCY PERSPECTIVES

The growth-stage approach looks largely within the national economy for the timing of the transition to more advanced stages. The dual-economy models also look within the national economy for the transformation of industrial structure. The dependency perspective insists that the key to differential development between the developed countries of the "center" and the underdeveloped countries of the "periphery" is to be found in the growth of the international economic system—in the world system.

Dependency theory as it has emerged in the last several decades has joined several intellectual and ideological traditions. It has absorbed and incorporated the unequal exchange concepts that were central to the Latin American structuralist school. It has drawn on Marxian economics for a view of the state as an instrument of the ruling class. But the distinguishing feature of the dependency perspective is an insistence on the dominance of the economic forces operating in the international system over those operating within national systems.

48. Interest in modern sector dualism stems largely from the seminal article by Michael P. Todaro, "A Model of Labor Migration and Urban Unemployment in Less Developed Countries," *American Economic Review* 59 (March 1969):138–48. See also John R. Harris and Michael P. Todaro, "Migration, Unemployment and Development: A Two-Sector Analysis," *American Economic Review* 60 (March 1970):125–42; Joseph E. Stiglitz, "Wage Determination and Unemployment in LDC's," *Quarterly Journal of Economics* 88 (May 1974):194–227. For a useful review and criticism of modern sector dualism see Trent Bertrand and Lyn Squire, "The Relevance of the Dual Economy Model: A Case Study of Thailand," *Oxford Economic Papers* 32 (November 1980):480–511. Bertrand and Squire fail to find evidence to support either the traditional sector dualism or the modern sector dualism in Thailand.

The Structuralist Model

The central argument of the structuralist school is that the countries of the periphery have experienced, and will continue to experience, long-run deterioration in their terms of trade with the center.[49] Deterioration in the terms of trade is generated by the combined effect of (a) low price and income elasticity of demand in the center for the products of the periphery and (b) high demand elasticities for imports from the center by the periphery. The tendency is reinforced in the structuralist model by a belief that productivity growth, measured in output per worker, is inherently slower in primary production, the source of exports by the periphery, than in the industrial sectors on which the center relies for its major exports. The structuralists also argue that the periphery sells its products in competitive markets and the center sells its products in monopolistic markets. The basis for this argument is an assertion that because the periphery's products, such as agricultural commodities and minerals, are homogeneous and undifferentiated they must be sold in competitive markets. In contrast, the products of the center, such as consumer durables and industrial equipment, are differentiable and their producers can therefore extract monopolistic prices from purchasers in the peripheral economies.

In the structuralist view, "the great industrial centers not only keep for themselves the benefit of the use of new techniques in their own economy, but are in a favorable position to obtain a share of that deriving from the technical progress of the periphery."[50] As a consequence of differential demand elasticities and differential rates of productivity growth, the countries of the periphery are forced into the unattractive alternative of growing more slowly or of restraining imports by tariff protection or subsidies to import-substituting industries.

The Underdevelopment Perspective

A major presumption in orthodox Marxian theory, as well as other growth-stage theories of development, was that the force of technological change (the forces of production) interacting with changes in institutions (the relations of production) and with culture and ideology (the superstructure) would cause

---

49. The structuralist model is developed most fully in the work of Raúl Prebisch and his associates in the Economic Commission for Latin America. Raúl Prebisch, *The Economic Development of Latin America: Toward a Dynamic Development Policy for Latin America* (New York: United Nations, 1963); "Commercial Policy in the Underdeveloped Countries," *American Economic Review* 49 (May 1959):251–73. See also H. W. Singer, "The Distribution of Gains between Investing and Borrowing Countries," *American Economic Review* 40 (May 1950):473–85. For a history of the emergence of the structuralist model in Latin American economic thought see Albert O. Hirschman, "Ideologies of Economic Development in Latin America," in *A Bias for Hope: Essays on Development and Latin America* (New Haven: Yale University Press, 1971), pp. 270–311. For a critical review see M. June Flanders, "Prebisch on Protectionism: An Evaluation," *Economic Journal* 74 (June 1964):305–26.

50. Prebisch, *Economic Development of Latin America,* p. 14.

economic growth in the advanced and backward countries to converge along a common path. In the words of Marx, "The country that is more developed industrially only shows, to the less developed, the image of its own future."[51]

The divergent paths followed by the developed industrial and the underdeveloped agrarian economies led a number of scholars, working within the Marxian tradition, to challenge the convergent growth hypothesis. The perspective that has emerged out of this challenge insists that the underdevelopment of Africa, Asia, and Latin America has been a product of the same forces that have led to development in Europe and North America. The integration of backward areas into the world capitalist system is viewed as a major source of underdevelopment.[52] Integration of formerly isolated sectors of the underdeveloped world has been accompanied by the extraction of surpluses by the capitalist center from the colonial and postcolonial economies of the periphery. This perspective has led to a relatively easy joining of the structuralist and underdevelopment perspectives. The appeal of the underdevelopment perspective to the structuralist school is that it adds a richer explanation, in the working out of class interests in a dependent economic system, to the economic considerations involved in the structuralist model. The dependency model has also had a strong appeal to nationalist sentiment because it focuses reform effort on inequities in the international system rather than on domestic policy.

The underdevelopment school has built on the orthodox Marxian view of the capitalist state as an administrative body of the ruling class. But in their hands the model has been opened up, and economic relationships between the center and the periphery have been used to account for the differential com-

51. Karl Marx, "Author's Preface I," *Capital,* Vol. 1, 1st American edition, ed. Ernest Unterman (Chicago: C. H. Kerr & Co., 1912), p. 13.

52. For a classical treatment of the underdevelopment perspective see Paul A. Baran, "On the Political Economy of Backwardness." See also Baran, *The Political Economy of Growth* (New York: Monthly Review Press, 1957). For an important extension of the dependency perspective see Andre Gunder Frank, "The Development of Underdevelopment," *Monthly Review* 18 (September 1966):17–31; and Theotonio Dos Santos, "The Structure of Dependence," *American Economic Review* 60 (May 1970):231–36.

For an interpretation of the historical development within the dependent perspective see Immanuel Wallerstein, *The Modern World System: Capitalist Agriculture and the Origins of the European World-Economy in the Sixteenth Century* (New York: Academic Press, 1974). For a sympathetic review see Frederick C. Lane, "Economic Growth in Wallerstein's Social Systems: A Review Article," *Comparative Studies in Society and History* 18 (1976):517–32. The implications of the dependency perspective for contemporary economic development have been elaborated fully in Samir Amin, *Accumulation on a World Scale: A Critique of the Theory of Underdevelopment,* Vols. 1 and 2 (New York: Monthly Review Press, 1974).

The underdevelopment perspective has generated more interest among political scientists and sociologists than among economists. Economists have tended to be put off by the colorful rhetoric that often seems to substitute for analysis in dependency literature. For two useful reviews see Ronald H. Chilcote, "Dependency: A Critical Synthesis of the Literature," *Latin American Perspectives* 1 (1974):4–29; Raymond D. Duvall, "Dependence and Dependencia Theory: Notes toward Precision of Concept and Argument," *International Organization* 32 (Winter 1978):51–78.

position of the ruling class in the center and the periphery.[53] Baran argues, for example, that in the center, capitalist enterprise sets in motion a momentous expansion of productivity and material welfare in which the lower classes participate. But in the underdeveloped countries of the periphery, capitalism was not achieved, he argues, through the growth of indigenous enterprise but was introduced by the transfer of advanced monopoly capitalism from the center.

In the periphery, in this view, capitalist development was not accompanied by the rise of an economically and politically powerful middle class. Instead, the economic and political system was dominated by an alliance between a new national elite based on the monopolization of trade and industrial relations with the center and the older, socially and politically powerful agrarian elite. Where the process of indigenous industrial development had been initiated, it was "decapitalized" and "denationalized" by the penetration of the more technically advanced and more capital-intensive industry of the center. Pressures for political and economic reform by a radicalized industrial labor force led not to accommodation of workers' demands for wage increases and social programs, as in the case of the progressive capitalism of the center, but to repression and the emergence of the authoritarian state in the periphery.

Agrarian Development in the Periphery

The implications of the dependency perspective for agrarian development, particularly in the Latin American context, have been elaborated by Alain de Janvry.[54]

In de Janvry's view, rural poverty in Latin America is largely explained by a three-level chain of exploitive relations:

- At the international level between the dominant countries of the center and the dependent countries of the periphery—as a result of the unequal exchange between raw materials and industrial capital goods.

- At the sectoral level between capital-intensive industry, which produces commodities for the upper classes in the periphery and for the world market, and the labor-intensive industrial and agricultural sectors, which produce mass-consumption items with cheap labor. The subsistence sector produces cheap food for the laborers in the commercial sectors of agriculture, which in turn produce cheap food for the urban-industrial sector.

53. Lack of rigor in the analysis of the role of internal class structure has represented a major criticism of the dependency perspective by orthodox Marxist scholars. See Chilcote, "Dependency," pp. 9, 14.

54. Alain de Janvry, *The Agrarian Question and Reformism in Latin America* (Baltimore: Johns Hopkins University Press, 1981); also, de Janvry, "The Political Economy of Rural Development in Latin America: An Interpretation," *American Journal of Agricultural Economics* 57 (August 1975):490–99; Alain de Janvry and Carlos Garramón, "The Dynamics of Rural Poverty in Latin America," *Journal of Peasant Studies* 4 (April 1977):206–16; Carmen Diana Deere and Alain de Janvry, "A Conceptual Framework for the Empirical Analysis of Peasants," *American Journal of Agricultural Economics* 61 (November 1979):601–11.

• At the social level between landlords and agricultural laborers, including the minifundia, driven by the need for cheap food and cheap labor in the urban sector.

Thus in the de Janvry view the marginalization of peasants in the periphery is a consequence of the peculiar pattern of dependent industrial development—wages and incomes remain low in rural areas because capital-intensive industrial development creates little demand for labor, and labor-intensive industrial development can expand only as long as wage rates remain low.

In the center, labor is incorporated into development but remains marginal to the development process in the periphery. In the center the distribution of income between capital and labor determines growth—the center is the primary consumer of its own output, and wages are an important source of demand as well as a cost of production. But in the peripheral economy labor is only a cost. Low wages are an important determinant of the ability to export labor-intensive primary and industrial products and to import capital equipment and luxury consumer products.

De Janvry rejects the Schultz "poor-but-efficient" characterization of traditional agriculture (see the discussion of the high-payoff model in Chapter 3). Underdevelopment of agriculture in backward areas can be understood only in terms of the market relations between backward and advanced areas. "Because agriculture serves as a natural refuge for marginal populations enabling them to satisfy part of their subsistence needs, rural poverty should be analyzed in the framework of marginality rather than traditional culture." Marginalism is a consequence of modernization: "They are the farmers who lose control of the means of production because they cannot withstand the competitive pressure of the modern sector or . . . who see their economic condition deteriorate as they retain traditional production techniques, but in both cases they cannot sufficiently proletarianize themselves to compensate for the income loss because they cannot be absorbed or fully sustained by the modern sector. Inevitably they join the ranks of marginals as *minifundistas* and subsistence farmers who cannot find employment in the modern sector."[55]

The implications of dependency theory for agricultural development stand in sharp contrast to the growth-stage and dual-economy theories. The growth-stage theories attempt to explain the process of transformation from a primarily agrarian to an industrial economy. In the dynamic dual-economy models incorporation of peasants into the market results in the disappearance of dualism. The dependency perspective attempts to explain why the periphery remains trapped in a backward agrarian state. In the dependency view incorporation of rural areas into the market is the source of marginalization—it perpetuates rather than erodes dualism.

---

55. De Janvry, "Political Economy of Rural Development," p. 491.

Dependency Theory and Development Policy

What are the policy implications of dependency theory? Acceptance of the dependency thesis that the peripheral countries can only lose by trade with the center leads to a strategy of "self-reliant development," which requires an extended period of autarky and a reallocation of productive capacity toward the production of mass-consumption goods. During this stage the domestic elites are forced to redirect their investments toward the domestic rather than the international economy.

Empirical evidence in support of the thesis of dependency theorists is slim. The terms of trade have not turned consistently against the raw materials produced by the periphery.[56] And growth rates appear to be positively rather than negatively related to both the stock and flow of foreign investment. The earlier evidence that has sometimes been used to support the argument of declining terms of trade could more appropriately be interpreted as a result of declining real costs of transportation between the center and the periphery. In retrospect, the failure of many countries of the periphery to make the investments in physical and institutional infrastructure needed to expand the volume of agricultural and raw material exports is a more significant source of lag in development than overdependence on exports.

It is more difficult to confront the intuitive analyses of the underdevelopment variants of the dependency perspective than the logic of the structuralist school.[57] In spite of insistence on the importance of history, the perspectives are overly static. They provide no mechanism to explain the process by which peripheral countries have become incorporated into the center. During the first half of the nineteenth century the center was occupied only by Great Britain. By the beginning of the twentieth century the center included most of western Europe and North America. Today the market economies of East Asia must also be counted as part of the center. And Brazil and Mexico appear to be in the process of transition from periphery to center. None of these countries has followed an autarkic "self-reliant" growth strategy.[58]

56. See the careful analysis by John Spraos, "The Statistical Debate on the Net Barter Terms of Trade between Primary Commodities and Manufacturers," *Economic Journal* 90 (March 1980):107–28. Spraos concludes that the evidence points to a deteriorating trend in the relative prices of primary products from 1870 to the late 1930s. The trend was, however, much less pronounced than suggested by Prebisch. When the analysis is conducted for the 1900–1970 period, however, it does not provide clear support for either decline or improvement in the relative terms of trade for primary products.

57. The argument has been made that the term *dependence* is intended to connote a general "frame" rather than a precise "data container" and hence cannot be subject to the normal empirical tests. Duvall, "Dependence and Dependencia Theory," p. 57. For a contrary view see Vincent A. Mahler, *Dependency Approaches to International Political Economy: A Cross-National Study* (New York: Columbia University Press, 1980). Duvall and his colleagues have attempted to specify core concepts formulated as a set of dynamic distributed lag relationships. But he holds out little hope that the model test can actively be empirically implemented.

58. Argentina, Mexico, the Republic of Korea, Singapore, Portugal, Brazil, Hong Kong, the Philippines, and Spain are identified as semiperiphery by James A. Caporaso, "Industrialization in the Periphery: The Evolving Global Division of Labor," *International Studies Quarterly* 25 (September 1981):347–84.

Nor does the dependency perspective provide any clear guide for the development of the dependent rural areas of the peripheral economies. The dominant theme in the dependency literature is that the reversal of the forces leading to underdevelopment in rural areas depends on the communal organization of agricultural production within the framework of a socialist economy. Alain de Janvry has argued, however, that a combination of (a) land reform that breaks the alliance between the national industrial capitalists and the traditional landed elite and (b) technical change resulting in the generation of new income streams in rural areas could result in the incorporation of marginal classes as more active participants in the national economic and political system. With the decentralization of economic and political resources implied by these changes it then becomes possible to design other rural development programs that further facilitate economic and social incorporation.

Many dependency theorists would argue, however, that the changes suggested by de Janvry are feasible only as part of a set of structural economic and political changes leading to a more self-reliant development strategy. And the critics of the dependency theory would insist that only economies that have achieved successful development—that are making the transition from periphery to center status—have followed a pattern of open export-oriented growth. Korea and Taiwan, two recent success stories, have effectively combined an export-oriented growth strategy in the industrial sector with land reform and rural development programs.

A MICROECONOMIC PERSPECTIVE

In this chapter, we have identified a number of significant insights into the process of economic development that have been contributed by economists working within the classical, growth-stage, dual-economy, and dependency traditions. We have also outlined several of the specific limitations of the historical generalizations, development theories, growth models, and perspectives that have emerged from these traditions.

The classical analysis continues to represent an important foundation for development thought. It continuously sets before society the consequences of the failure to make effective use of the available knowledge of the technical and institutional sources of development. The growth-stage models represent useful pedagogical devices for enlarging our understanding of the structural changes that take place in a growing economy. But they provide few guides to development policy or planning.

The dual-economy models have contributed more powerful insights into the development process. They represented a significant advance over the

---

The process by which countries of the center become reduced to semiperiphery or periphery is also neglected. Italy, Spain, and Portugal, which, according to Wallerstein, formed part of the core in the sixteenth century, had by the middle of the seventeenth century been reduced to the status of the semiperiphery and by the beginning of the nineteenth century to the periphery.

post-Keynesian one-sector, one-input models of the Harrod-Domar-Mahalanobis type. As the dual-economy models have evolved, they have become more sophisticated. They have contributed to the interpretation of economic history and to the evolution of growth-stage concepts that are more firmly grounded analytically than the earlier generalizations. As a result, it is increasingly recognized that "the functions which the agricultural and industrial sectors must perform in order for growth to occur are totally interdependent."[59] This is clearly an important contribution to economic doctrine when contrasted with the naive industrialization-first doctrines of the 1950s.

The dependency perspective has attempted to provide an integrated view of the interrelationships between political and economic forces in international economic relationships. It has directed attention to the limits of national autonomy in an interrelated world economy. And it has helped to focus concern on the poorest and weakest groups in the developing countries— those on the periphery. But it has also served as an excuse for failure. It has provided intellectuals in developing countries with an ideology that excuses lack of rigorous analysis of national economic performance and policy. And it has provided national political leadership with a rationale for policies that are a burden on rather than a source of development.

In our 1971 book we noted that during the 1950s and 1960s development theory, research, and policy had been excessively focused at the macro level.[60] During the 1970s a refocus at the micro level has resulted in significant advances in our understanding of agricultural and rural development processes. Among these advances have been (a) a more adequate understanding of the source and process of technical and institutional innovations and (b) the economics of consumption, demographic, and production behavior of rural households. We draw on the advances in both areas in subsequent chapters.

The 1970s were also characterized by the emergence of several new development program thrusts. The community development movement of the 1950s was resurrected under the label of integrated rural development. The living standards movement of the 1930s has been reformulated as the basic needs approach to development. Rising concern about the distributional implications of rapid development has led to better empirical measures of income distribution in poor countries. These issues of development policy are also addressed in later sections of this book.

This book, like our earlier book, represents an attempt to employ the theory and method of microeconomics to advance the understanding of the process of agricultural development.

59. Erik Thorbecke, Introduction, *The Role of Agriculture in Economic Development,* ed. Erik Thorbecke (New York: Columbia University Press, 1969), p. 4.
60. Yujiro Hayami and Vernon W. Ruttan, *Agricultural Development: An International Perspective* (Baltimore: Johns Hopkins Press, 1971).

3

Theories of Agricultural Development

The review of development economics literature in the previous chapter indicates that a new consensus has emerged to the effect that agricultural growth is critical (if not a precondition) for industrialization and general economic growth. Nevertheless, the process of agricultural growth itself has remained outside the concern of most development economists. Both technical change and institutional evolution have been treated as exogenous to their systems.

The central focus of this book is the agricultural development process itself. A first step in any attempt to evolve a meaningful perspective on agricultural development is to abandon the view of agriculture in pre-modern or traditional societies as essentially static.[1] Sustained rates of growth in agricultural output in the range of 1.0 percent per year were feasible in many preindustrial societies. With the advent of industrialization, potentials for the growth of agricultural output shifted upward to the range of 1.5–2.5 percent per year. Following the Industrial Revolution, rates of growth in this range occurred over relatively long periods in western Europe, North America, and Japan. Since the middle of the twentieth century, the growth potential of agricultural production has apparently again shifted upward to annual growth rates of over 4.0 percent. Sustained growth rates in this range have been

1. Even in premodern times, agriculture was characterized by the continuous, though relatively slow, development of agricultural tools, machines, plants, animals, and husbandry practices. The rate of development was influenced by long-run patterns of population growth and price fluctuations. For a review of the state of knowledge of change in agricultural technology in prehistory and ancient civilization see Ester Boserup, *Population and Technological Change* (Chicago: University of Chicago Press, 1981). For western Europe see S. H. Slicher van Bath, *The Agrarian History of Western Europe, A.D. 500-1850* (London: Edward Arnold, 1963). Comparable historical detail is not available for Asia. However, the view expressed here is consistent with the material presented by Shigeru Ishikawa, *Economic Development in Asian Perspective* (Tokyo: Kinokuniya Bookstore Co., 1967). See also Ester Boserup, *The Conditions of Agricultural Growth: The Economics of Agrarian Change under Population Pressure* (Chicago: Aldine, 1965); Clifford Geertz, *Agricultural Involution: The Process of Ecological Change in Indonesia* (Berkeley: University of California Press, 1966).

observed primarily in newly developing economies such as Mexico, Brazil, Taiwan, and Israel, rather than in the older industrial economies.[2]

Viewed in a historical context, the problem of agricultural development is not that of transforming a static agricultural sector into a modern dynamic sector, but of accelerating the rate of growth of agricultural output and productivity, consistent with the growth of other sectors of a modernizing economy. Similarly, a theory of agricultural development should provide insight into the dynamics of agricultural growth—into the changing sources of growth—in economies ranging from those in which output is growing at a rate of 1.0 percent or less to those in which agricultural output is growing at an annual rate of 4.0 percent or more.

In this chapter we review the theories of agricultural development that are reflected, either explicitly or implicitly, in the literature on agricultural and economic development. We have characterized the literature on agricultural development under six general approaches: (a) the resource exploitation; (b) the conservation; (c) the location; (d) the diffusion; (e) the high-payoff; and (f) the induced innovation models. In this chapter we review the contribution of the first five models. The next chapter is devoted to a more complete exposition of the induced innovation model. It should be emphasized that we do not regard these models as stages in the agricultural growth process. Rather, they are designed to capture the changing sources of growth during the process of agricultural development. In most countries agricultural growth draws on all of the sources identified in each of the several models.[3]

THE RESOURCE EXPLOITATION MODEL

Throughout most of history, expansion in the areas cultivated or grazed has been the main means of increasing agricultural production.[4] The most dramatic example in Western history was the opening up of new continents—North

2. Between 1960 and 1980 agricultural production increased at an annual rate of 1.9 percent in the developed market economies; 3.4 percent in the more advanced (middle stage) developing economies; and 2.9 percent in the least developed countries (Table 13-1). A number of developing countries achieved annual rates of increase of over 4.0 percent for the entire twenty-year period. Because of more rapid population growth rates in the developing countries, however, per capita food production in the least developed countries increased at only 0.4 percent per year as compared to 1.3 percent in the more advanced developing countries and 1.1 percent in the developed countries. In a number of developing countries, particularly in Africa, per capita food production actually declined. See Terry N. Barr, "The World Food Situation and Global Grain Prospects," *Science* 214 (December 4, 1981):1087–95; Glenn Fox and Vernon W. Ruttan, "A Guide to LDC Food Balance Projections," *European Review of Agricultural Economics* 10 (1983):325–56; World Bank, *World Development Report, 1982* (New York: Oxford University Press, 1982).

3. For alternative typologies see Hans Ruthenberg, *Farming Systems in the Tropics* (Oxford: Clarendon Press, 1971); David B. Grigg, *The Agricultural Systems of the World: An Evolutionary Approach* (London: Cambridge University Press, 1974).

4. We do not, in this section, attempt to explore the role of the frontier in the formation of national character or social and political institutions. These were the major concerns in the

and South America and Australia—to European settlement during the eighteenth and nineteenth centuries.[5] With the advent of cheap transport during the latter half of the nineteenth century, the countries of the new continents became increasingly important sources of food and agricultural raw materials for the metropolitan countries of western Europe.

In earlier times, similar processes had proceeded, though at a less dramatic pace, in the peasant and village economies of Europe, Asia, and Africa. The first millennium A.D. saw the agricultural colonization of Europe north of the Alps, the Chinese settlement of the lands south of the Yangtze, and the Bantu occupation of Africa south of the tropical forest belts. Population pressure resulting in intensification of land use in existing villages was followed by pioneer settlement, the establishment of new villages, and the opening up of forest or jungle land to cultivation. In western Europe there was a series of changes from neolithic forest fallow to systems of shifting cultivation on bush and grassland followed by short fallow systems and later by annual cropping.

A substantial literature in economic history and in development economics has attempted to interpret the implications of agricultural development in newly settled regions. It includes the "staple" model developed by the Canadian economic historian Harold A. Innis to explain the rapid growth of commodity production and exports in the newly settled areas of North America.[6] Innis's research convinced him of the crucial importance of export staples, furs, and fish in early Canadian history and timber and grain at a later stage in shaping the economic development of Canada. Innis's perspective has been widely adopted by other historians and economists whose work has focused on the national and regional development of more recently settled areas.

A second body of literature, termed the "vent-for-surplus" model, has emerged out of the efforts of the Burmese economist Hla Myint to explain the rapid growth of production and trade in a number of tropical countries during the nineteenth century.[7] Myint was particularly interested in explaining the

---

"frontier thesis" as initially formulated by Frederick Jackson Turner, *The Frontier in American History* (New York: Henry Holt & Co., 1920). The Turner thesis has stimulated a large literature on the role of the frontier in the formation of other national societies such as Australia, Brazil, Canada, Russia, and South Africa. See, for example, Marvin W. Mikesell, "Comparative Studies in Frontier History," *Annals of the Association of American Geographers* 50 (March 1960):62–74.

5. Grigg, *Agricultural Systems of the World,* pp. 24–43; Alfred W. Crosby, Jr., *The Columbian Exchange: Biological and Cultural Consequences of 1492* (Westport, Conn.: Greenwood Publishing Co., 1972).

6. Harold A. Innis, *The Fur-Trade of Canada* (Toronto: University of Toronto Library, 1927); *The Cod Fisheries: The History of an International Economy* (New Haven: Yale University Press; Toronto: Ryerson Press, 1940); *Problems of Staple Production in Canada* (Toronto: Ryerson Press, 1933). For a review and exposition of the staple theory see Melville H. Watkins, "A Staple Theory of Economic Growth," *Canadian Journal of Economics and Political Science* 29 (May 1963):141–58. For an interpretation of regional development in terms of the staple theory see Douglass C. North, "Location Theory and Regional Economic Growth," *Journal of Political Economy* 63 (June 1955):243–58.

7. Hla Myint, "The 'Classical Theory' of International Trade and the Underdeveloped Countries," *Economic Journal* 68 (June 1958):317–37. For a review of the vent-for-surplus

rapid growth of production and exports by peasant producers of, for example, rice in Burma and Thailand during the latter half of the nineteenth century. He noted that peasant export production usually expanded as rapidly as that of the plantation sectors while remaining self-sufficient in production of food crops. His explanation is that surplus land and labor capacity enabled peasant producers, even though confronting relatively fixed technical coefficients, to expand production rapidly under the stimulus of new markets opened up by the reduction of transport costs. An example was the dramatic increase in rice production for export in the great river deltas of continental Southeast Asia (the Mekong Delta in Vietnam, the Chao Phraya Delta in Thailand, and the Irrawaddy Delta in Burma) that occurred in the late nineteenth century in response to the lower transport costs between Southeast Asia and Europe associated with the opening of the Suez Canal and the development of the steamship.

In the past, in some areas, exploitation of natural resources along the lines suggested by the staple and vent-for-surplus models has been a major source of agricultural and economic development. But there are relatively few remaining areas of the world where development along the lines of the resource exploitation model will continue to represent an efficient source of growth. The 1970s saw the closing of the frontier in most areas of Southeast Asia. In Latin America and Africa the opening up of new lands awaits the development of technologies for control of pests and diseases in the tsetse fly–infested plains of Africa; for the release and maintenance of the productivity of problem soils of the Brazilian campos cerado and the Venezuelan and Colombian llaños; and for the development of conservation systems of farming that are capable of maintaining fertility on the upland soils in the humid tropics of Africa.[8]

This century is experiencing a transition from an era when most of the increases in world agricultural production occurred as a result of the expansion in area cultivated to a period when most of the growth in crop and animal production must come from increases in the frequency and intensity of cultivation—from changes in land use which make it possible to crop a given

---

model and a comparison with the staple theories see Richard E. Caves, " 'Vent for Surplus' Models of Trade and Growth," *Economics of Trade and Development,* ed. James D. Theberge (New York: John Wiley & Sons, 1968), pp. 211–30. For an interpretation of Nigerian agricultural development within the framework of the vent-for-surplus model see Gerald K. Helleiner, "Typology in Development Theory: The Land Surplus Economy (Nigeria)," *Food Research Institute Studies* 6 (1966):181–94.

8. Michael Nelson, *The Development of Tropical Lands: Policy Issues in Latin America* (Baltimore: Johns Hopkins University Press, 1973); Martin T. Katzman, "The Brazilian Frontier in Comparative Perspective," *Comparative Studies in Society and History* 17 (July 1975):266–85. For a more optimistic perspective on the potential of sustained agricultural production under tropical conditions see Pedro A. Sanchez, Dale E. Bandy, J. Hugo Villachica, and John J. Nicholaides, "Amazon Basin Soils: Management for Continuous Crop Production," *Science* 216 (May 21, 1982):821–27.

area of land more frequently and more intensively and hence to increase the output per unit area per unit of time.

The primary concerns of the scholars who articulated the staple and vent-for-surplus theories were to explore the conditions by which underutilized natural resources could be exploited to generate growth in agricultural output and to identify the processes by which the agricultural surpluses could be mobilized to generate growth in the total economy. The resource exploitation model provides little insight into the problem of how to generate growth in land and labor productivity when the slack resulting from underutilized natural resources has been exhausted. In those few areas where new lands are still available for pioneer settlement or plantation development the resource exploitation model remains relevant. But attempts to achieve continued growth along the path outlined by the staple or vent-for-surplus theorists will be increasingly confronted by the limits to growth inherent in the classical model of economic development—to diminishing marginal productivity from additional increments of land, labor, and capital.

Agricultural growth based on the resource exploitation model is not sustainable over the long run. In order to sustain agricultural growth it is necessary to make a transition from resource exploitation to (a) development of resource-conserving or enhancing technologies such as crop rotation and manuring, (b) substitution of modern industrial inputs such as fertilizer for natural soil fertility, and (c) development of modern fertilizer-responsive crop varieties. To gain access to these new sources of growth, discussed in the next several sections of this chapter, a society must invest in the development of land and water infrastructure, the industrial capacity needed to produce modern inputs, and the human capital and scientific research needed to develop new technology and use it effectively.

THE CONSERVATION MODEL

The conservation model of agricultural development evolved from the advances in crop and livestock husbandry associated with the English agricultural revolution and the concepts of soil exhaustion suggested by the early German soil scientists. This theory was reinforced by the concept of diminishing returns to labor and capital applied to land in the English classical school of economics and the traditions of ethical, aesthetic, and philosophical naturalism of the American conservation movement.

The English agricultural revolution consisted of the evolution of an intensive, integrated, crop-livestock husbandry system.[9] In the process, the Nor-

---

9. In recent years agricultural historians have stressed the "evolutionary" in contrast to the "revolutionary" aspects of these changes. "The increase in agricultural output does not appear to have been due primarily to the discovery of new ways of doing things. The improved methods were the result of the accumulation of a very large number of small adaptations, and while a few

folk-crop-rotation system replaced the open-three-field system in which arable land was allocated between permanent cropland and permanent pasture. This involved the introduction and more intensive use of new forage and green manure crops and an increase in the availability and use of animal manures. This "new husbandry" permitted the intensification of crop-livestock production through the recycling of plant nutrients, in the form of animal manures, to maintain soil fertility. The advances in technology were accompanied by the consolidation and enclosure of farms and by investments in land development. The net effect was a substantial growth in both total agricultural output and output per acre. The inputs used in this conservation system of farming were largely supplied by the agricultural sector itself. This system, which had evolved over several centuries, was popularized in the late eighteenth and early nineteenth centuries by Arthur Young and other exponents of agricultural science. Its diffusion provided the technical basis for English "high farming" as it evolved in 1850–70, following the repeal of the Corn Laws.[10]

The British doctrine of "new husbandry" was transplanted to Germany by its ardent advocates, Albrecht Thaer and his followers. Their investigations of the nature and principles of soil and plant nutrition led to a doctrine of soil exhaustion. This doctrine held that the danger of soil exhaustion was so great that any permanent system of agriculture must provide for the complete restoration to the soil of all the elements removed by a crop. According to Abbott P. Usher, "The doctrine of soil exhaustion first took shape in the latter part of the eighteenth century, when the humus theory of plant-nutrition was dominant. It was then supposed that plants derived their food from the organic matter in the soil, collectively designated as humus."[11] This led to a presumption that good farming practice should maintain the organic content of the soil at a definite level, usually the level natural to the particular soil.

---

of them do sum up to methods which can legitimately be regarded as new (the advances in cattle breeding, for example), the substitution of turnips and grass crops for fallow, the technique responsible for the most revolutionary changes, was already known. That is to say, the increase in output, where it was not merely the result of the employment of more men and land, arose from the spread of the best existing techniques rather than from the invention of new ones." H. J. Habakkuk, "Economic Functions of English Landowners in the Seventeenth and Eighteenth Centuries," *Essays in Agrarian History*, vol. I, ed. W. E. Minchinton (New York: Augustus M. Kelley, 1968), p. 190 (first published in *Exploration in Entrepreneurial History*, vol. 6, 1953). For a survey of the more recent perspectives on the English agricultural revolution see David B. Grigg, *The Dynamics of Agricultural Change* (New York: St. Martin's Press, 1982), pp. 177–92.

10. For further discussion see Lord Ernle, *English Farming, Past and Present*, 6th ed. (London: Heinemann, 1961); G. E. Mingay, "The Agricultural Revolution in English History: A Reconsideration," in Minchinton, ed., *Essays in Agrarian History*, vol. II, pp. 11–27 (reprinted from *Agricultural History* 37 [July 1963]); C. Peter Timmer, "The Turnip, the New Husbandry, and the English Agricultural Revolution," *Quarterly Journal of Economics* 83 (August 1969):375–95.

11. See Abbott Payson Usher, "Soil Fertility, Soil Exhaustion, and Their Historical Significance," *Quarterly Journal of Economics* 37 (May 1923):385–411.

With the demonstration of the relation of soil minerals to plant growth by Justus von Liebig and others during the second quarter of the nineteenth century, the soil exhaustion doctrine was extended to include the maintenance of the mineral content of the soil.[12] The investigations of German soil scientists thus appeared to provide a scientific basis for the hypothetical calculations by the English classical economists, from Malthus and Ricardo to Mill, of diminishing returns to labor and capital applied to agricultural production.

The tradition of naturalism, which represented in many respects a reaction to the mechanistic conception of nature associated with the scientific revolution, was compatible with the experience of the English agricultural revolution, the classical theory of diminishing returns (see Chapter 2), and the growing body of natural resource literature.[13] The synthesis led to the formulation of a more sophisticated doctrine of natural resource scarcity.[14] Sum-

12. "Liebig's explanation of plant growth rested upon four propositions: (1) that the nitrogen needed by plants was derived from the air; (2) that the plants utilized the mineral elements in inorganic forms; (3) that the amounts of minerals required by plants could be ascertained by analysis of the ash; (4) that plant growth would be directly proportioned to the supply of the mineral least abundantly furnished by the soil. . . . The new theory seemed not only to make the fertility of soils minutely calculable, but also to indicate a relatively brief period of productivity for most soils. Soil exhaustion thus became a corollary of the mineral theory as well as of the humus theory, and Liebig judged all agricultural practices in terms of their relation to the maintenance of the mineral content of the soil." Ibid., p. 389.

13. Liebig attributed the decline of classical civilization to soil exhaustion. This view of the relationship between soil exhaustion and the decline of civilization has remained a persistent threat in the "underworld" of conservation literature. For several more recent restatements see Fairfield Osborn, *Our Plundered Planet* (Boston: Little, Brown, and Co., 1948); William Vogt, *Road to Survival* (New York: William Sloane and Associates, Inc., 1948); Tom Dale and Vernon Gill Carter, *Topsoil and Civilization* (Norman: Oklahoma University Press, 1955). For a discussion of some of the doctrines about soils, see Charles E. Kellogg, "Conflicting Doctrines about Soils," *Scientific Monthly* 66 (June 1948):475–87.

14. The two major contributions to the evolution of doctrine during the last half of the nineteenth century were Darwin and Marsh. According to Barnett and Morse, "Darwin, with a social impact perhaps even larger than Malthus' original impact, generalized as a law of nature the concept of the 'struggle for food.' And, although Malthus, no less than Darwin, claimed to be stating natural law, there was the added force of Darwin's greater prominence and the fact that his contribution emanated from a practicing scientist and many of the leaders of the Conservation Movement were natural scientists themselves. Second, and more important perhaps, the Darwinian contribution played a central role in the development and propagation of the popularized version of naturalistic philosophy that was so strong in the Conservation philosophy." Harold J. Barnett and Chandler Morse, *Scarcity and Growth, the Economics of Natural Resource Availability* (Baltimore: Johns Hopkins Press, 1963), p. 88. In reviewing the work of George P. Marsh, *Man and Nature: Physical Geography as Modified by Human Action* (New York: Charles Scribner, 1864, [rev. ed., 1874]; and Cambridge: Harvard University Press, 1965) Barnett and Morse comment that "there are, in Marsh's view, such extensive possibilities of modification of the balance of man and nature—favorable and unfavorable—that the scarcity doctrines of Malthus and Ricardo presumably could not for him be natural laws. Since scarcity is no longer an ineluctable force, its effects are no longer inescapable. Before Marsh, and in the eyes of the classical economists, there was no question that scarcity was always operative. . . . After Marsh, if his lessons are believed, the question became empirical since man and his environment are so susceptible to change," Barnett and Morse, *Scarcity and Growth*, p. 93.

marized in economic terms, the doctrine asserts that natural resources are scarce, that the scarcity increases with economic growth, and that resource scarcity threatens to impair levels of living and economic growth.[15]

In recent years the scarcity doctrine has been subject to substantial reexamination and revision. The reexamination has proceeded at three levels. First, there has been a reexamination of the possibilities of agricultural growth under the conditions of the preindustrial technology assumed by the classical economists. Second, there has been an attempt at the hands of land and resource economists to "rationalize" the theory of conservation. Finally, there is the attempt, of which this book is an example, to examine the implications of industrialization for advances in mechanical, chemical, and biological technology for the long-term growth of agricultural output.

The classical view is now regarded as based on an inadequate understanding of the history of agricultural development, even in England and western Europe.[16] Its major deficiency, even for a preindustrial society, stemmed from an oversimplified view of the role of land in agricultural development. The history of land use, both in temperate and tropical regions, indicates that the supply of land services has been much more elastic than implied by the static view of land either as the "original and indestructible powers of the soil" or as a "natural" agent of production.[17]

The most extreme challenge to the classical position has been suggested by Ester Boserup.[18] In a survey of historical patterns of land use under prein-

15. Barnett and Morse, *Scarcity and Growth*, p. 49. For a formal statement and analysis of the scarcity model see pp. 101–47.

16. The classical view did not go without challenge even in its initial statement, "The American economist, H. C. Carey, . . . asserted that the real law of agricultural expansion is the very reverse of that stated by Ricardo and affirmed by Mill. He argued that agricultural land was not used in the order of best quality first. Rather cultivation begins with poorer lands, and later extends to more fertile ones. The result is that expansion of agricultural output is carried on under conditions of increasing returns. The reason that settlers in a new country do not use the lands of greatest quality first is that river lowlands are unhealthy, or require considerable prior investment in clearance and drainage. Settlement, therefore, commences on lands that are high and less fertile. Only as population increases and wealth accumulates are the more fertile lands eventually brought into use." Ibid., p. 67. For a recent clarification of the Ricardo-Carey controversy see Ralph Turvey, "A Finnish Contribution to Rent Theory," *Economic Journal* 65 (June 1955):346–48.

17. "The use of soils in agricultural production commonly means a change in the environment from that in which the soils were formed. Man clears the forest and plows the prairie. He drains extra water out of some soils and adds extra water to others through irrigation. In extreme cases, he may rearrange soils entirely, as has been done in rice paddies of Japan and with peats and dune sands in Holland. More changes are usually made in chemical than in physical properties. Furthermore, the changes tend to reduce differences among soils as they are used for agricultural purposes." Roy W. Simonson, "Changing Place of Soils in Agricultural Production," *Scientific Monthly* 81 (October 1955):173–82. "A particular parcel of land suitable for farming is a complex physical structure in which there is embedded, as one approaches the surface, an intricate biological mechanism. How much or how little of it is natural or original or indestructible has little or no meaningful relation to its productivity." Theodore W. Schultz, *The Economic Organization of Agriculture* (New York: McGraw-Hill, 1953), p. 140.

18. Boserup, *Conditions of Agricultural Growth*.

dustrial conditions in both temperate and tropical regions, Boserup suggests a pattern of continuous development from more extensive to intensive systems. The sharp distinction between cultivated and uncultivated land, implied by the concepts of the intensive and extensive margin, is replaced by a concept of increasing frequency of cropping and by changes ranging from forest and bush fallow to multicropping systems in which the same plot bears two or more crops each year. In this view, soil fertility is a dependent variable, responding to the intensity of land use, rather than a determinant of the intensity of land use.

Both the classicals and their critics do, however, share the perspective of agriculture as a relatively self-contained system. The inputs used in agricultural production were, by and large, supplied by the agricultural sector itself. Industrial inputs were not viewed as playing a significant role at either the extensive or intensive margin. Increased land productivity was achieved, as during the English agricultural revolution, primarily through labor-intensive methods of fertility enhancement (such as green manuring and forage livestock systems), land development (such as drainage and irrigation), and capital formation in the form of livestock and fruit- and nut-bearing trees.

The movement by economic historians and land and resource economists to "rationalize" the theory of conservation began in the mid-1920s with an attempt to explore the economic importance of conservation principles, particularly in the field of fertility maintenance, as a guide to agricultural practice.[19] By the early 1950s a new body literature embracing both technical (soils, plant nutrition, agronomic, engineering) and economic considerations was leading to a more rational view of both the farm management and public policy aspects of soil fertility and of the role of land in agricultural development.[20]

In the United States this attempt at rationalization was under continuous pressure, however, as a result of the stagnation in the national economy

19. Abbott Payson Usher, "Soil Fertility, Soil Exhaustion, and Their Historical Significance," *Quarterly Journal of Economics* 37 (May 1923):385–411. According to Usher, "It is steadily becoming clearer that science affords no basis for the static concept of the fertility program. The calculation of the minerals removed by the crop does not furnish a certain or adequate guide to fertilization. For high farming it may be necessary to add much more of some elements than is removed: low farming may be justified in limiting its fertility program to the maintenance of nitrogen and organic matter. The modern farmer, too, is not primarily concerned with maintenance of the 'original' powers of the soil; his problem is to modify the natural soil in accordance with his needs" (pp. 410–11). See also John Ise, "The Theory of Value as Applied to Natural Resources," *American Economic Review* 15 (June 1925):284–91; Siegfried von Ciriacy-Wantrup, "Soil Conservation in European Farm Management," *Journal of Farm Economics* 20 (February 1938):86–101.

20. Much of the work is summarized in Arthur C. Bunce, *The Economics of Soil Conservation* (Ames: Iowa State College Press, 1942); Siegfried von Ciriacy-Wantrup, *Resource Conservation: Economics and Policies* (Berkeley: University of California Press, 1952); and R. Burnell Held and Marion Clawson, *Soil Conservation in Perspective* (Baltimore: Johns Hopkins Press, 1965).

during the 1930s,[21] the resource drains resulting from World War II,[22] a neo-Malthusian perspective generated by the postwar population explosion,[23] the concern with the resource constraints on economic growth associated with the environmental movement in the late 1960s, and the energy crisis of the early and mid-1970s.[24]

In retrospect, a fundamental limitation of both the "conservation fundamentalists" and the early attempts to "rationalize" the conservation princi-

21. It was claimed that the solution to the depressed conditions in agriculture was to be found in an agrarian philosophy of subsistence and conservation. "How many of our farm families, in difficult financial circumstances today, would be better off tomorrow under an altered agriculture that placed subsistence above market cash, and substituted scientific methods for habit in the use of land?" H. H. Bennett, *The Land We Defend*, U.S. Department of Agriculture, Soil Conservation Service (Washington, D.C.: U.S. Government Printing Office, July 1940), pp. 13–14. This romantic view of agricultural development has again emerged as an important theme in the 1970s. See Wendell Berry, *The Unsettling of America: Culture and Agriculture* (New York: Avon Books, 1978).

For a more serious consideration of the technical and economic considerations involved in the development of modern farming systems more consistent with the conservation model see USDA Study Team on Organic Farming, *Report and Recommendations on Organic Farming* (Washington, D.C.: U.S. Department of Agriculture, July 1980).

Robert C. Oelhaf, *Organic Agriculture: Economic and Ecological Comparisons with Conventional Methods* (Montclair, N.J.: Allanheld, Osmun, & Co., 1978); *Organic and Conventional Farming Compared* (Ames, Iowa: Council for Agricultural Science and Technology, Report No. 84, October 1980).

22. The concern led to a series of postwar appraisals of the resource needs of the American economy. These include (a) U.S. Department of Agriculture, Bureau of Agricultural Economics, *Agriculture's Capacity to Produce, Possibilities under Specified Conditions* (Washington, D.C.: U.S. Department of Agriculture, Agriculture Information Bulletin No. 88, June 1952); (b) President's Materials Policy (Paley) Commission, *Resources for Freedom* (Washington, D.C.: U.S. Government Printing Office, June 1952); (c) President's Water Resources (Cooke) Policy Commission, *A Water Policy for the American People* (Washington, D.C.: U.S. Government Printing Office, 1950).

23. For an excellent historical perspective see M. K. Bennett, "Population and Food Supply: The Current Scare," *Scientific Monthly* 68 (January 1949):17–26. According to Bennett, the English-speaking world has experienced three waves of pessimism about food supply since the first one touched off by Malthus. The second came in the 1890s, the third a few years after World War I, and the fourth after World War II. If Bennett were writing in 1980 instead of 1949 he would have identified a fifth wave in the mid-1960s and a sixth wave in the early and mid-1970s.

24. In this second post–World War II wave of concern with natural resource scarcity the traditional concern with the adequacy of the natural resource base to sustain economic growth was supplemented by an intense concern with the stress on the environment associated with economic growth. This new wave of concern was dramatized by the publication, under the sponsorship of the Club of Rome, of Donella H. Meadows et al., *The Limits to Growth* (New York: Universe Books, 1972). For a perspective on these concerns see Vernon W. Ruttan, "Technology and the Environment," *American Journal of Agricultural Economics* 53 (December 1971):707–17; William D. Nordhaus, "World Dynamics: Measurement without Data," *Economic Journal* 83 (December 1973):1156–83; Robert M. Solow, "The Economics of Resources or the Resources of Economics," *American Economic Review* 64 (May 1974):1–14. For a more thorough analytical treatment see the papers in V. Kerry Smith, ed., *Scarcity and Growth Reconsidered* (Baltimore: Johns Hopkins University Press, 1979), and P. S. Dasgupta and G. M. Heal, *Economic Theory and Exhaustible Resources* (Welwyn, Eng.: J. Nisbet,, 1979). For a major attempt to assess the empirical significance of resource scarcity see the Council on Environmental Quality (U.S.) and the Department of State, *The Global 2000 Report to the President: Entering the Twenty-First Century*, vol. 2 of 3 vols. (Washington, D.C.: U.S. Government Printing Office, 1980–81).

ples was the failure to recognize the full impact of technical change on resource use and productivity in agriculture. In the United States the period between 1900 and 1925 was one of relative stagnation in agricultural productivity. The impact of the stagnation was reflected in higher food prices during the first two decades of this century. Even after 1925 the growth in productivity was obscured by the depression and by World War II. As a result, it was not unreasonable for postwar resource assessment studies to reflect a scarcity perspective.[25] It was not until the mid-1950s that the new perspective on the relationship between technical change and resource availability and output growth became widely accepted, even in economics literature.[26]

With this new perspective it has been possible to analyze and test the resource-scarcity doctrine more rigorously than in the past. In their definitive study *Scarcity and Growth,* Harold J. Barnett and Chandler Morse first analyze the implications of the scarcity doctrine under the classical assumption of a parametrically invariant world and then in a world characterized by technical progress.[27] In their empirical analysis Barnett and Morse test what they refer to as "strong" and "weak" versions of the scarcity hypothesis.

The *strong scarcity test* is based on changes in the "unit cost of extractive output." Unit costs are defined as the labor and capital required to produce a unit of extractive output—a ton of steel or rice, for example. The strong scarcity definition is based directly on the classical notion that as the quality of "land" that is brought into production declines, larger and larger doses of labor and capital are required to produce a unit of extractive output (Chapter 2). The *weak scarcity test* is based on changes in the relative price of extractive products. A rise (decline) in the price of the extractive product relative to the general price level is taken to indicate an increase (decrease) in scarcity. The weak scarcity test is generally regarded as a more relevant measure because the prices of extractive products reflect, at least to some

25. The President's Water Resources Policy Commission concluded that "present food surpluses are transitory. The real agricultural problem is how to assure sufficient production to meet the requirements of an expanding population," Report of President's Water Resource Policy Commission, p. 159. The report of the President's Material Policy Commission projected a 1975 index of land inputs of 111 (1950 = 100). As a result of increased land productivity, the cropland index actually declined, standing at ninety (1950 = 100) in 1968; *Changes in Farm Production and Efficiency; A Summary Report, 1970* (Washington, D.C.: U.S. Department of Agriculture Statistical Bulletin No. 233, June 1970).

26. Schultz had pointed out, as early as 1932, that agriculture in Iowa seemed to be characterized by increasing returns stemming from technological advance. Theodore W. Schultz, "Diminishing Returns in View of Progress in Agricultural Production," *Journal of Farm Economics* 14 (October 1932):640–49. For references to more recent literature see Theodore W. Schultz, "A Framework for Land Economics—The Long View," ibid. 33 (May 1951):204–15; Schultz, *Economic Organization of Agriculture,* pp. 146–51; Vernon W. Ruttan, "The Contribution of Technological Progress to Farm Output: 1950-75, *Review of Economics and Statistics* 38 (February 1956):61–69: Theodore W. Schultz, "Connections between Natural Resources and Economic Growth," *Natural Resources and Economic Growth,* ed. J. J. Spengler (Washington, D.C.: Resources for the Future, 1961), pp. 1–9.

27. Barnett and Morse, *Scarcity and Growth.*

degree, the effect of expectations regarding the future costs of exploration, discovery, and extraction and of productivity growth in the extractive industries.

The empirical tests, based on data for 1870–1957, result in rejection of both scarcity hypotheses for the total extractive sector and for the agricultural sector alone. In an update of the earlier analysis, using data for 1870–1970, Barnett was again unable to find support for either the strong or the weak scarcity hypothesis.[28]

This review of the evolution of the conservation model of agricultural development, the criticism of it, and its refinements should not be taken as a rejection of it as an approach to agricultural development. Agricultural development within the framework of the conservation model has been capable, in many parts of the world, of sustaining rates of growth in agricultural production in the range of 1.0 percent per year over long periods of time. The most serious effort in recent history to develop agriculture within the conservation model framework was made by the People's Republic of China in the 1950s and 1960s. It became readily apparent, however, that the growth rates that could be achieved, even with a rigorous emphasis on the recycling of plant, animal, and human manures, were not compatible with modern rates of growth in the demand for agricultural output—which typically fall in the 3–5 percent range in the less developed countries.

A more modest role for development within the framework of the conservation model is appropriate in both developed and developing economies. The rise in energy prices in the early 1970s redirected the attention of plant and soil scientists and agricultural planners toward greater reliance on biological sources of plant nutrition, energy-saving methods of cultivation, and more efficient farming systems.

Agricultural development efforts carried out within the framework of the conservation model can continue to make an important contribution to productivity growth. And in the developed countries it will remain an important source of inspiration to the organic farming movement and agrarian fundamentalists.

THE LOCATION MODEL

In the conservation model, locational divergences in agricultural development were related primarily to differences in environmental factors. Developments in the nonagricultural sectors were not brought, explicitly, into the

---

28. Harold J. Barnett, "Scarcity and Growth Revisited," *Scarcity and Growth Reconsidered*, ed. Smith, pp. 163–217. Several of the essays in *Scarcity and Growth Reconsidered* are critical of the Barnett-Morse methodology. See also V. Kerry Smith, "Measuring Natural Resource Scarcity: Theory and Practice," *Journal of Environmental Economics and Management* 5 (May 1978):150–71.

agricultural development process. The location model was initially formulated to explain geographic variations in the location and intensity of agricultural production in an industrializing economy. Efforts in this direction draw their primary intellectual inspiration from the early efforts of Johann Heinrich von Thünen (1783–1850) to determine both the optimal intensity of cultivation and the optimal farm organization or combination of crop and animal "enterprises."[29] Von Thünen generalized the Ricardian theory of rent to show how urbanization determines the location of production of agricultural commodities and influences the techniques and intensity of cultivation.[30]

In the United States the implications of the von Thünen thesis have attracted the attention of both historians and economists. Agricultural historians have drawn on the von Thünen model to explore the dynamics of agricultural expansion. They have been particularly interested in the changing distribution of commodity production in response to changes in transport cost and variations in the national environment as commercial farming moved into the American interior in the nineteenth century.[31] Agricultural economists have been more interested in the impact of differential rates of growth of urban-industrial development on productivity and income differences among areas.

The implications of the location model for modern agricultural development were formulated by Theodore W. Schultz in 1953: "(1) Economic development occurs in a specific locational matrix. . . . (2) These locational matrices are primarily industrial-urban in composition. . . . (3) The existing economic organization works best at or near the center of a particular matrix of economic development and it also works best in those parts of agriculture which are situated favorably in relation to such a center."[32]

29. J. H. von Thünen, *Von Thünen's Isolated State*, trans. Carla M. Wartenberg and edited with an introduction by Peter Hall (Oxford: Pergamon Press, 1966). Von Thünen was the inspiration for Marshall's treatment of marginal productivity, his analysis of rent, his distinction between partial and total equilibrium, and his distinction between the short and the long term. For useful expositions of the von Thünen thesis see Edgar S. Dunn, Jr., *The Location of Agricultural Production* (Gainesville, Fla.: University of Florida Press, 1954); Grigg, *Dynamics of Agricultural Change*, pp. 135–50. For a history of the impact of von Thünen's work on economic thought see Joosep Nõu, *Studies in the Development of Agricultural Economics in Europe* (Uppsala: Almqvist and Wiksells, 1967), pp. 184–230. Von Thünen, like Arthur Young and other founders of agricultural sciences, viewed agricultural economics as part of an integrated science of agriculture.

30. H. D. Dickinson, "Von Thünen's Economics," *Economic Journal* 79 (December 1969):894–902.

31. John T. Schlebecker, "The World Metropolis and the History of American Agriculture," *Journal of Economic History* 20 (June 1960):187–208; Richard Peet, "Von Thünen Theory and the Dynamics of Agricultural Expansion," *Explorations in Economic History* 8 (Winter 1970–71):181–201.

32. Schultz, *Economic Organization of Agriculture*, p. 147. The Schultz "urban-industrial impact hypothesis" bears a striking similarity, in its conception of the process of urban-industrial development, to the "growth pole" hypothesis that was also advanced during the early 1950s by François Perroux, "Economic Space: Theory and Applications," *Quarterly Journal of Economics* 64 (1950):89–104. The "growth pole" perspective has had a substantial impact on thought in the area of regional economics and planning. There has been relatively little attention in the growth

In formulating the "urban-industrial impact hypothesis" Schultz draws on the Fisher-Clark structural transformation model of general economic development (Chapter 2) as well as on the von Thünen traditions of location and land economics.

He was particularly concerned with the development of a hypothesis that would explain the failure of agricultural production and price policy to remove the substantial regional disparities in the rate and level of development in American agriculture. Schultz presented a rationale for the urban-industrial impact hypothesis in terms of more efficient functioning of factor and product markets in areas of rapid urban-industrial development than in areas where the urban economy had not made a transition to the industrial stage. Major attention was placed on structural imperfections in labor and capital markets. The role of the urban-industrial sector as a source of new and more productive inputs was also stressed.

Formulation of the urban-industrial impact hypothesis generated a series of studies designed to test both the validity of (a) the empirical generalizations and (b) the factor and product market rationale.[33] Results of these studies have generally sustained the validity of Schultz's empirical generalizations with respect to the impact of urban-industrial growth in geographic differentials in per capita or per worker farm income. The tests of the factor and product market rationale, however, have been much less conclusive.

The impact of urban-industrial growth, transmitted through the intersector product and factor markets, on agricultural development has been widely recognized. Some development economists have viewed this contact as an essential requirement for modernization. Others have viewed it as a source of exploitation. But the only significant tests of the urban-industrial impact hypothesis in a less developed country with which we are familiar are the studies by William H. Nicholls and by Martin T. Katzman for the states of São Paulo and Goias in Brazil.[34] Before 1940, economic development in

pole literature to the implications for agricultural development. For a useful review see John B. Parr, "Growth Poles, Regional Development, and Central Place Theory," *Papers of the Regional Science Association* 31 (1973):173–212.

33. Vernon W. Ruttan, "The Impact of Urban-Industrial Development on Agriculture in the Tennessee Valley and the Southeast," *Journal of Farm Economics* 37 (February 1955):38–56; Daniel G. Sisler, "Regional Differences in the Impact of Urban-Industrial Development on Farm and Nonfarm Income," ibid. 41 (December 1959):1100–1112; Anthony M. Tang, *Economic Development in the Southern Piedmont, 1860-1950: Its Impact on Agriculture* (Chapel Hill: University of North Carolina Press, 1958); William H. Nicholls, "Industrialization, Factor Markets, and Agricultural Development," *Journal of Political Economy* 69 (August 1961):319–40; Dale E. Hathaway, "Urban-Industrial Development and Income Differentials between Occupations," *Journal of Farm Economics* 46 (February 1964):56–66; Dale E. Hathaway, J. Allen Beegle, and W. Keith Bryant, *People of Rural America* (A 1960 Census Monograph) (Washington, D.C.: U.S. Government Printing Office, 1968).

34. Douglas S. Paauw and John C. H. Fei, *The Transition in Open Dualistic Economies: Theory and Southeast Asian Experience* (New Haven: Yale University Press, 1973), pp. 112–15; Alain de Janvry, *The Agrarian Question and Reformism in Latin America* (Baltimore: Johns Hopkins University Press, 1981), pp. 141–81; William H. Nicholls, "The Transformation of Agriculture in a Semi-Industrialized Country: The Case of Brazil," *The Role of Agriculture in*

Brazil had occurred primarily in response to a series of export-based commodity booms along lines suggested by the staple or vent-for-surplus models of trade and development. The series of commodity booms served as a stimulus for São Paulo's rapidly growing industrial sector. The coffee boom was particularly important in generating a demand for industrial inputs and commercial services. Nicholls indicates that after 1940 there were clear indications that urban-industrial development in São Paulo was sufficiently large and dynamic to begin exerting an independent differential impact on labor productivity in São Paulo agriculture by facilitating the flow of capital into and the flow of labor out of agriculture. The urban-industrial impact was limited, however, because of the locational impact of resource-based opportunities for development and the failure of the Brazilian government to invest in the research capacity and the agricultural services necessary to permit the agricultural sector to respond to growth in the urban-industrial sector.

The Goias Test by Katzman, which covers the period 1940–70, is particularly interesting because it focuses on a frontier region that has experienced rapid urbanization as a result of the relocation of the national capital to Brasilia (in southeastern Goias), the relocation of the state capital to Goiana, and the construction of the Belem-Brasilia highway. In his study Katzman tests an integrated model, which incorporates the implications of the von Thünen model for farming intensity and enterprise selection and the implication of the Schultz model for income disparity among regions. His results indicate that the agricultural counties located closer to the market were characterized by higher product prices, land values, and rates of land use. Access to urban-industrial centers was also associated with machinery investment per hectare and per man but had little effect on other inputs. Katzman concludes by noting that the integrated model opens up powerful insights into the relationship between urban and rural development.

Development policies based on the urban-industrial impact model of agricultural development appear to have limited scope in the poorest of the less developed countries, where (a) a major problem is to initiate and accelerate economic growth at a sufficient rate to absorb the growing labor force rather than the geographic distribution of economic activity; (b) the technology necessary for rapid agricultural growth is not available; and (c) the "pathological" growth of urban centers resulting from population inflow from rural areas is running ahead of growth in the demand for nonfarm workers.[35] For

Economic Development, ed. Erik Thorbecke (New York: Columbia University Press, 1969), pp. 311–78; also G. Edward Schuh, "Comment," ibid., pp. 379–85; Martin T. Katzman, "The von Thünen Paradigm, the Industrial-Urban Hypothesis, and the Spatial Structure of Agriculture," *American Journal of Agricultural Economics* 56 (November 1974):683–96; Martin T. Katzman, "Regional Development Policy in Brazil: The Role of Growth Poles and Development Highways in Goias," *Economic Development and Cultural Change* 24 (October 1975):75–107.

35. For a model of the rural-urban labor migration process in economics characterized by chronic unemployment and underemployment of a high proportion of the urban labor force, see Michael P. Todaro, "A Model of Labor Migration and Urban Unemployment in Less Developed Countries," *American Economic Review* 59 (March 1969):138–48.

the newly industrializing countries, however, where there is some scope for discretion in industrial location, the model has much more significant implications for agricultural development. Industrial development policies that encourage decentralization can contribute to more effective intersector factor and product market linkages.

THE DIFFUSION MODEL

The diffusion of better husbandry practices and of crop and livestock varieties has been a major source of productivity growth in agriculture. The classical studies by Carl O. Sauer and N. I. Vavilov and the more recent cytogenetic studies of plant origins have forced a recognition of the extensive diffusion of cultivated plants and domestic animals in prehistory and in the classical civilizations.[36] Such diffusion must have been an important element in the evolution of preindustrial labor- and land-intensive conservation systems.

By the last half of the nineteenth century the process of plant exploration and discovery had become highly institutionalized. In the British Empire the effort was organized through a system of botanic gardens that were developed to facilitate the transfer, testing, and introduction of plant materials.[37] In the United States crop exploration and introduction became a major activity of the U.S. Department of Agriculture.[38] Similar programs became an integral part of all of the leading national agricultural research programs.[39]

A second source of the diffusion approach to agricultural development draws on the empirical observation of substantial differences in land or labor productivity among farmers in any agricultural region, from the most advanced to the most backward. The route to agricultural development is, in this

36. Carl O. Sauer, *Agricultural Origins and Dispersals; The Domestication of Animals and Foodstuffs*, 2d ed. (Cambridge: Massachusetts Institute of Technology Press, 1969), pp. 113–34. N. I. Vavilov, *The Origin, Variation, Immunity and Breeding of Cultivated Plants*, trans. K. Starr Chester, vol. 13, nos. 1-6, of *Chronica Botanica*, 1949-50. For an engaging nontechnical account of advances in the study of plant origins and diffusion see Edgar Anderson, *Plants, Man and Life* (Berkeley: University of California Press, 1967). For useful references to livestock adaptation and diffusion see Ralph W. Phillips, *Breeding Livestock Adapted to Unfavorable Environments* (Washington, D.C.: FAO Agricultural Studies No. 1, January 1948).

37. For an interesting account, written from a dependency theory perspective, of the role of the Royal Botanic Gardens in the international transfer of agricultural technology see Lucile H. Brockway, *Science and Colonial Expansion: The Role of the British Royal Botanic Gardens* (New York: Academic Press, 1979).

38. Nelson Klose, *America's Crop Heritage: The History of Foreign Plant Introduction by the Federal Government* (Ames: Iowa State College Press, 1950).

39. In the USSR, Vavilov's commitment to a major program of plant introduction provided a focus for the attack, by T. D. Lysenko, on the plant breeding program that Vavilov headed at the All-Union Institute of Plant Breeding. Lysenko held that the inheritance of acquired characteristics, cold tolerance for example, eliminated the need to collect and introduce exotic genetic material as a basis for crop improvement. Zhores A. Medvedev, *The Rise and Fall of T. D. Lysenko* (New York: Columbia University Press, 1969).

view, through more effective dissemination of technical knowledge and a narrowing of dispersion in productivity among individual farmers and among regions.

The men whose researches contributed to the evolution of the agricultural sciences were impressed with the innovations in methods of cultivation made by farmers themselves. Young, the ideologue of the English agricultural revolution in the eighteenth century, regarded such knowledge as the only foundation on which scientific farming could be based. Liberty Hyde Bailey, writing a century later, insisted, "At the present time, every intelligent farmer is an experimenter . . . this cumulative body of experience of the best farmers is capable of yielding better results than similar work which might be undertaken at an experiment station. . . . An experiment station, which is necessarily constituted for scientific research, cannot touch many of the most vital problems of farming."[40]

Even in nations with well-developed agricultural experiment station systems, a significant portion of the total effort, until as late as the 1930s or 1940s, was devoted to the testing and refinement of farmer innovations and to the testing and adaptation of exotic crop varieties and animal species. It seems likely that even in the most advanced agricultural nations this activity contributed more to the growth of agricultural productivity than the more scientific work carried on by the experiment stations until at least the middle of this century.[41]

The diffusion model of agricultural development has provided the major intellectual foundation for much of the research and extension effort in farm management and production economics since the emergence, in the last half of the nineteenth century, of agricultural economics as a separate sub-discipline linking the agricultural sciences and economics. The developments that led to the establishment of active programs of farm management research and extension occurred at a time when experiment station research was making only a modest contribution to agricultural productivity growth. This led to a heavy emphasis on the economic analysis of farmer innovations. A stimulus for refinement in survey methods, accounting techniques, and statistical methods developed by farm management economists was the desire to determine with greater precision the sources of productivity and income differentials among farmers.[42]

The theoretical and empirical basis for farm management research was subject to intensive review following the advances in the theory of the firm in

40. Nōu, *Development of Agricultural Economics,* pp. 85–107; L. H. Bailey, "Extension Work in Horticulture" (Ithaca: Cornell University Agricultural Experiment Station, January 1896), Bulletin 110, pp. 130–31.

41. For a specific example see Martin L. Mosher, *Early Iowa Corn Yield Tests and Related Later Programs* (Ames: Iowa State University Press, 1962).

42. For a review of these developments in the United States see Henry C. Taylor and Anne Dewees Taylor, *The Story of Agricultural Economics in the United States, 1840-1932* (Ames: Iowa State University Press, 1952), pp. 326–446.

the late 1930s. These conceptual advances were complemented by simultaneous advances in quantitative methods and data-processing techniques. A synthesis of the theoretical implications of the neoclassical theory of the firm and the utilization of modern quantitative techniques in the analysis of farm management and production economics was achieved by the modern production economists by the early 1950s.[43] With this new synthesis, the interest of agricultural economists centered even less around the problem of choice of technology than that of the farm management economists, whose methodology the production economists rejected. The problem of economic growth, both of the individual firm and of the agricultural sector, was cast firmly within the context of reorganizing production inputs to achieve increases in output per unit of input by improving the efficiency with which the existing inputs are allocated.

A further contribution to the effective diffusion of known technology was provided by the research of rural sociologists on the diffusion process. Models were developed emphasizing the relationship between diffusion rates and the personality characteristics and educational accomplishments of farm operators.[44] The insights into the dynamics of the diffusion process contributed to the effectiveness of the agricultural extension service and strengthened the confidence of agricultural administrators and policymakers in the validity of the diffusion model. The pervasive acceptance of its validity, when coupled with the observation of wide agricultural productivity gaps among developed and less developed countries and with the firm presumption of inefficient resource allocation among "irrational tradition-bound" peasants, produced an extension bias in the choice of agricultural development strategy during the 1950s.[45] These programs were expected to transform tradition-bound peasants into "economic men" who would respond more rationally to the tech-

43. The landmark in this initial synthesis was the publication by Earl O. Heady, *Economics of Agricultural Production and Resource Use* (Englewood Cliffs, N.J.: Prentice-Hall, 1952). See also Earl O. Heady and John I. Dillon, *Agricultural Production Functions* (Ames: Iowa State University Press, 1961). For a critical review of these developments see Glenn L. Johnson, "Stress on Production Economics," *Australian Journal of Agricultural Economics* 7 (June 1963):12–26; Harald R. Jensen, "Farm Management and Production Economics, 1946–70," *A Survey of Agricultural Economics Literature I*, ed. Lee R. Martin (Minneapolis: University of Minnesota Press, 1977), pp. 3–89.

44. For a review of diffusion research by rural sociologists see Everett M. Rogers, *Diffusion of Innovations*, 3d ed. (New York: Free Press, 1983); Everett M. Rogers, "Motivations, Values, and Attitudes of Subsistence Farmers: Toward a Subculture of Peasantry," *Subsistence Agriculture and Economic Development*, ed. Clifton R. Wharton, Jr. (Chicago: Aldine, 1969), pp. 111–35. For a more complete discussion of the international transmission of technology see Chapter 9.

45. According to Moseman this extension bias was partially based on the successful experience of transfer of hybrid corn technology from the United States to Western Europe under the Marshall Plan. This transfer was successful because the climate in Western Europe is reasonably close to that in corn-producing areas in the United States, and there was indigenous human capital, in the form of agricultural scientists and technicians in Europe, to conduct adaptive research. Albert H. Moseman, *Building Agricultural Research Systems in the Developing Nations* (New York: Agricultural Development Council, Inc., 1970), pp. 66–67.

nical opportunities that were available to them and who would reallocate resources more efficiently in response to economic incentives.

The limitations of the diffusion model as a foundation for the design of agricultural development policies became increasingly apparent as technical assistance and community development programs, based explicitly or implicitly on the diffusion model, failed to generate either rapid modernization of traditional farms or rapid growth in agricultural output.

THE HIGH-PAYOFF INPUT MODEL

The inadequacy of policies based on the diffusion model led, in the 1960s, to a reexamination of the assumptions regarding the availability of a body of agricultural technology that could be readily diffused from the high-productivity to the low-productivity countries and the existence of significant disequilibrium in the allocation of resources among progressive and lagging farmers in the developing economies.

The result was the emergence of a new perspective that agricultural technology is highly "location specific" and that techniques developed in advanced countries are not, in most cases, directly transferable to less developed countries with different climates and different resource endowments. Evidence was also accumulated to the effect that only limited productivity gains are to be had by the reallocation of resources in traditional peasant agriculture.[46] This iconoclastic perspective was developed most vigorously by Schultz in his book *Transforming Traditional Agriculture*. In much of the social science literature the economic behavior of peasants had been dominated by an assumption of subsistence orientation. Economic relationships in peasant society had been viewed as organized by considerations of dependence and reciprocity rather than by market relationships.[47] Schultz insisted

46. W. David Hopper, "Allocation Efficiency in a Traditional Indian Agriculture," *Journal of Farm Economics* 47 (August 1965):611–24; Benton F. Massell, "Farm Management in Peasant Agriculture: An Empirical Study," *Food Research Institute Studies* 7, no. 2 (1967):205–15; Pan A. Yotopoulos, *Allocative Efficiency in Economic Development: A Cross Section Analysis of Epirus Farming* (Athens: Center of Planning and Economics Research, 1968); Pan A. Yotopoulos, "On the Efficiency of Resource Utilization in Subsistence Agriculture," *Food Research Institute Studies* 8, no. 2 (1968):125–35. See also the review of studies of supply response in traditional agriculture by Raj Krishna, "Agricultural Price Policy and Economic Development," *Agricultural Development and Economic Growth*, ed. Herman M. Southworth and Bruce F. Johnston (Ithaca: Cornell University Press, 1967), pp. 497–540. Many of the early tests of the hypothesis of allocative efficiency in peasant agriculture drew on Asian experience. For a more recent study drawing on African experience see David W. Norman, "Economic Rationality of Traditional Hausa Dryland Farmers in the North of Nigeria," *Tradition and Dynamics in Small-Farm Agriculture: Economic Studies in Asia, Africa, and Latin America*, ed. Robert D. Stevens (Ames: Iowa State University Press, 1977), pp. 63–91.

47. For a review of the literature on peasantry see Everett M. Rogers, "Motivations, Values, and Attitudes of Subsistence Farmers," pp. 111–35. Rogers identifies ten central elements in a subculture of peasantry: mutual distrust, lack of innovativeness, fatalism, low aspiration levels, lack of deferred gratification, limited time perspective, familism, dependence on government authority, locality orientation, and lack of empathy.

that peasants in traditional agriculture are rational, efficient resource allocators and that they remain poor because in most poor countries there were only limited technical and economic opportunities to which they could respond.

In Schultz's opinion, the key to transforming a traditional agricultural sector into a productive source of economic growth is investment to make modern high-payoff inputs available to farmers in poor countries. We may call this view the high-payoff input model, and according to Schultz:

> Economic growth from the agricultural sector of a poor country depends predominantly upon the availability and price of modern (nontraditional) agricultural factors. . . . The principal sources of high productivity in modern agriculture are reproducible sources. They consist of particular material inputs and of skills and other capabilities required to use such inputs successfully. . . . But these modern material inputs are seldom ready-made. They can rarely be taken over and introduced into farming in a typically poor community in their present form. . . . There are very few reproducible agricultural factors in technically advanced countries that are ready-made for most poor communities. In general, what is available is a body of useful knowledge which has made it possible for the advanced countries to produce for their own use factors that are technically superior to those employed elsewhere. This body of knowledge can be used to develop similar, and as a rule superior, new factors appropriate to the biological and other conditions that are specific to the agriculture of poor communities.[48]

This implies three types of relatively high-productivity investments for agricultural development: (a) in the capacity of agricultural experiment stations to produce new technical knowledge; (b) in the capacity of the industrial sector to develop, produce, and market new technical inputs; and (c) in the capacity of farmers to use modern agricultural factors effectively. High private and social returns to investment in education and research have been demonstrated by a series of studies. (Tables 3.A1, 3.A2, and 3.A3).

The enthusiasm with which the high-payoff input model has been accepted and translated into an economic doctrine has been substantially the result of the success of efforts to develop high-yielding modern grain varieties suitable for the tropics.[49] The high-yielding wheat and corn varieties were developed in Mexico, beginning in the 1950s, and high-yielding rice varieties in the Philippines in the 1960s. These varieties were highly responsive to industrial inputs, such as fertilizer and other chemicals, and to more effective soil and water management. The high returns associated with the adoption of the new varieties and the associated technical inputs and management practices led to rapid diffusion of the new varieties among farmers in several countries in Asia, Africa, and Latin America. The impact of farm production and income

48. Theodore W. Schultz, *Transforming Traditional Agriculture* (New Haven: Yale University Press, 1964), pp. 145–47.

49. E. C. Stakman, Richard Bradfield, and Paul C. Mangelsdorf, *Campaigns against Hunger* (Cambridge: Harvard University Press, 1967); Lester R. Brown, *Seeds of Change* (New York: Praeger, 1970); Moseman, *Building Agricultural Research Systems.*

has been sufficiently dramatic to be heralded as a "green revolution."[50] The significance of the high-payoff input model is that policies based on the model appear capable of generating a sufficiently high rate of agricultural growth to provide a basis for overall economic development consistent with modern population and income growth requirements.

As interpreted generally, the model is sufficiently inclusive to embrace the central concepts of the conservation, location, and diffusion models of agricultural development. Advances in conservation systems of agriculture, as, for example, the Norfolk crop rotation as propagated in England in the eighteenth century, represented a new high-payoff input in that period. The rate of diffusion of agricultural technology can be viewed as a function of the profitability of the new inputs or techniques. The impact of urban-industrial development changes the relative profitability of alternative techniques through the growth of demand and the capacity to supply the new technical inputs. The unique implications of the model for agricultural development policy are the emphasis placed on accelerating the process of development and propagation of new inputs or techniques through public investment in scientific research and education.

Evidence with respect to the impact of the new high-payoff investments on rural equity and level of living has been less clear than that on improvements in land and labor productivity and on growth of agricultural output. There have been a variety of reformist and radical criticisms of the impact of the modernization of agricultural production on rural income distribution and on the viability of rural institutions. These equity issues will be discussed in Chapter 11 and the implications for rural institutions in Chapter 12.

Our major concern at this point, however, is that the high-payoff input model remains incomplete as a theory of agricultural development. Typically, education and research are public goods, not traded through the marketplace. The mechanism by which resources are allocated among education, research, and other alternative public and private sector economic activities is not fully incorporated into the model.[51] The model does treat investment in research as

---

50. Although the term "green revolution" is used at a number of points in this study to refer to the impact of the new cereals technology, our view is essentially similar to that of Dovring: "Evidently there is no general consensus on the meaning of the term 'revolution.' This term has been over used to the point of losing any distinctive meaning." Folke Dovring, "Eighteenth Century Changes in European Agriculture: A Comment," *Agricultural History* 63 (January 1969):181–86. The use of the term "green revolution" to describe the new high-yielding cereals technology represents an interesting footnote in the history of the international diffusion of terminology. The term was first suggested by the administrator of US AID, William Gaud, in 1968. William S. Gaud, "The Green Revolution: Accomplishments and Apprehensions," address before the Society for International Development, Washington, 1968. Later the term became widely used in popular press accounts and in the professional literature. In the interwar period the term "green revolution" was used to refer to the radical peasant political movements in Eastern Europe. See David Mitrany, *Marx against the Peasant* (Chapel Hill: University of North Carolina Press, 1951), pp. 118–45.

51. Schultz has stressed the need to direct research toward the analysis of this process. Theodore W. Schultz, "The Allocation of Resources to Research," *Resource Allocation in*

the source of new high-payoff techniques. But it does not explain how economic conditions induce the development and adaptation of an efficient set of technologies for a particular society. Nor does it attempt to specify the process by which factor and product price relationships induce investment in research in a particular direction.

Moreover, the high-payoff input model does not explain how economic conditions induce the development of new institutions such as publicly supported agricultural experiment stations to enable both individuals and society to take fuller advantage of new technical opportunities. Nor does it attempt to specify the process by which farmers organize collective action for the creation of public infrastructure such as irrigation and drainage systems. That peasants in traditional agriculture can be viewed as rational and efficient in the allocation of the resources available to them does not guarantee efficient resource allocation at the level of the rural community. In fact, it is common to observe in rural villages that communal irrigation canals are choked by silt because of villagers' inability to organize themselves for maintenance work and that communal pasture land is overgrazed resulting in serious soil depletion because of their inability jointly to agree on and enforce efficient stocking rates.

The model of agricultural and economic development remains incomplete unless the process is specified by which collective action, from the local community to the central government level, is organized for the supply of public goods, including new technical knowledge and institutional arrangements, in response to changes in economic conditions. In the next chapter, we try to incorporate the high-payoff input model, along with the resource exploitation, conservation, location, and diffusion models, into a more general model in which both technical and institutional changes are treated as endogenous to the economic system.

Agricultural Research, ed. Walter L. Fishel (Minneapolis: University of Minnesota Press, 1971), pp. 90–120.

TABLE 3-A1.　Summary of studies of agricultural research productivity

Study	Country	Commodity	Time period	Annual internal rate of return (%)
Index Number:				
Griliches, 1958	USA	Hybrid corn	1940–55	35–40
Griliches, 1958	USA	Hybrid sorghum	1940–57	20
Peterson, 1967	USA	Poultry	1915–60	21–25
Evenson, 1969	South Africa	Sugarcane	1945–62	40
Barletta, 1970	Mexico	Wheat	1943–63	90
Barletta, 1970	Mexico	Maize	1943–63	35
Ayer, 1970	Brazil	Cotton	1924–67	77+
Schmitz and Seckler, 1970	USA	Tomato harvester, with no compensation to displaced workers	1958–69	37–46
		Tomato harvester, with compensation of displaced workers for 50% of earnings loss		16–28
Ayer and Schuh, 1972	Brazil	Cotton	1924–67	77–110
Hines, 1972	Peru	Maize	1954–67	35–40[a] 50–55[b]
Hayami and Akino, 1977	Japan	Rice	1915–50	25–27
Hayami and Akino, 1977	Japan	Rice	1930–61	73–75
Hertford, Ardila, Rocha, and Trujillo, 1977	Colombia	Rice	1957–72	60–82
		Soybeans	1960–71	79–96
		Wheat	1953–73	11–12
		Cotton	1953–72	none
Pee, 1977	Malaysia	Rubber	1932–73	24
Peterson and Fitzharris, 1977	USA	Aggregate	1937–42	50
			1947–52	51
			1957–62	49
			1967–72	34
Wennergren and Whitaker, 1977	Bolivia	Sheep	1966–75	44
		Wheat	1966–75	−48
Pray, 1978	Punjab (British India)	Agricultural research and extension	1906–56	34–44
	Punjab (Pakistan)	Agricultural research and extension	1948–63	23–37
Scobie and Posada, 1978	Bolivia	Rice	1957–64	79–96
Pray, 1980	Bangladesh	Wheat and rice	1961–77	30–35
Regression Analysis:				
Tang, 1963	Japan	Aggregate	1880–38	35
Griliches, 1964	USA	Aggregate	1949–59	35–40
Latimer, 1964	USA	Aggregate	1949–59	not significant

TABLE 3-A1. (Continued)

Study	Country	Commodity	Time period	Annual internal rate of return (%)
Peterson, 1967	USA	Poultry	1915–60	21
Evenson, 1968	USA	Aggregate	1949–59	47
Evenson, 1969	South Africa	Sugarcane	1945–58	40
Barletta, 1970	Mexico	Crops	1943–63	45–93
Duncan, 1972	Australia	Pasture Improvement	1948–69	58–68
Evenson and Jha, 1973	India	Aggregate	1953–71	40
Cline, 1975 (revised by Knutson and Tweeten, 1979)	USA	Aggregate	1939–48	41–50c
		Research and	1949–58	39–47c
		extension	1959–68	32–39c
			1969–72	28–35c
Bredahl and Peterson, 1976	USA	Cash grains	1969	36d
		Poultry	1969	37d
		Dairy	1969	43d
		Livestock	1969	47d
Kahlon, Bal, Saxena, and Jha, 1977	India	Aggregate	1960–61	63
Evenson and Flores, 1978	Asia—national	Rice	1950–65	32–39
			1966–75	73–78
	Asia— International	Rice	1966–75	74–102
Flores, Evenson, and Hayami, 1978	Tropics	Rice	1966–75	46–71
	Philippines	Rice	1966–75	75
Nagy and Furtan, 1978	Canada	Rapeseed	1960–75	95–110
Davis, 1979	USA	Aggregate	1949–59	66–100
			1964–74	37
Evenson, 1979	USA	Aggregate	1868–1926	65
	USA	Technology oriented	1927–50	95
	USA	Science oriented	1927–50	110
	USA	Science oriented	1948–71	45
	Southern USA	Technology oriented	1948–71	130
	Northern USA	Technology oriented	1948–71	93
	Western USA	Technology oriented	1948–71	95
	USA	Farm management research and agricultural extension	1948–71	110

Source: Robert E. Evenson, Paul E. Waggoner, and Vernon W. Ruttan, ''Economic Benefits from Research: An Example from Agriculture,'' *Science* 205 (September 14, 1979):1101–7. Copyright 1979 by the American Association for the Advancement of Science.

aReturns to maize research only.

bReturns to maize research plus cultivation ''package.''

cLower estimate for 13-, and higher for 16-year time lag between beginning and end of output impact.

dLagged marginal product of 1969 research on output discounted for an estimated mean lag of 5 years for cash grains, 6 years for poultry and dairy, and 7 years for livestock.

The results of many of the studies reported in this table have previously been summarized in the following works:

Thomas M. Arndt, Dana G. Dalrymple, and Vernon W. Ruttan, eds., *Resource Allocation and Productivity in National and International Agricultural Research* (Minneapolis: University of Minnesota Press, 1977), pp. 6,7.

James K. Boyce and Robert E. Evenson, *Agricultural Research and Extension Systems* (New York: Agricultural Development Council, 1975), p. 104.

Robert Evenson, Paul E. Waggoner, and Vernon W. Ruttan, "Economic Benefits from Research: An Example from Agriculture," *Science* 205 (September 14, 1979):1101–7.

Robert J. R. Sim and Richard Gardner, *A Review of Research and Extension Evaluation in Agriculture* (Moscow, Idaho: University of Idaho, Department of Agricultural Economics Research Series 214, May 1978), pp. 41, 42.

Sources for individual studies:

H. Ayer, "The Costs, Returns and Effects of Agricultural Research in São Paulo, Brazil" (Ph.D. dissertation, Purdue University, 1970).

H. W. Ayer and G. E. Schuh, "Social Rates of Return and Other Aspects of Agricultural Research: The Case of Cotton Research in São Paulo, Brazil," *American Journal of Agricultural Economics* 54 (November 1972):557–69.

N. Ardito Barletta, "Costs and Social Benefits of Agricultural Research in Mexico" (Ph.D. dissertation, University of Chicago, 1970).

M. Bredahl and W. Peterson, "The Productivity and Allocation of Research: U.S. Agricultural Experiment Stations," *American Journal of Agricultural Economics* 58 (November 1976): 684–92.

Philip L. Cline, "Sources of Productivity Change in United States Agriculture" (Ph.D. dissertation, Oklahoma State University, 1975).

Jeffrey S. Davis, "Stability of the Research Production Coefficient for U.S. Agriculture" (Ph.D. dissertation, University of Minnesota, 1979).

R. C. Duncan, "Evaluating Returns to Research in Pasture Improvement," *Australian Journal of Agricultural Economics* 16 (December 1972):153–68.

R. Evenson, "The Contribution of Agricultural Research and Extension to Agricultural Production" (Ph.D. dissertation, University of Chicago, 1968).

———, "International Transmission of Technology in Sugarcane Production" (New Haven, Conn.: Yale University, mimeographed paper, 1969).

R. E. Evenson and P. Flores, *Economic Consequences of New Rice Technology in Asia* (Los Baños, Laguna, Philippines: International Rice Research Institute, 1978).

R. E. Evenson and D. Jha, "The Contribution of Agricultural Research Systems to Agricultural Production in India," *Indian Journal of Agricultural Economics* 28 (1973):212–30.

P. Flores, R. E. Evenson, Y. Hayami, "Social Returns to Rice Research in the Philippines: Domestic Benefits and Foreign Spillover," *Economic Development and Cultural Change* 26 (April 1978):591–607.

Z. Griliches, "Research Costs and Social Returns: Hybrid Corn and Related Innovations," *Journal of Political Economy* 66 (1958):419–31.

———, "Research Expenditures, Education and the Aggregate Agricultural Production Function," *American Economic Review* 54 (December 1964):961–74.

Y. Hayami and M. Akino, "Organization and Productivity of Agricultural Research Systems in Japan," *Resource Allocation and Productivity in National and International Agricultural Research*, ed. Thomas M. Arndt, Dana G. Dalrymple, and Vernon W. Ruttan (Minneapolis: University of Minnesota Press, 1977), pp. 29–59.

R. Hertford, J. Ardila, A. Rocha, and G. Trujillo, "Productivity of Agricultural Research in Colombia," *Resource Allocation and Productivity in National and International Agricultural Research*, ed. Thomas M. Arndt, Dana G. Dalrymple, and Vernon W. Ruttan (Minneapolis: University of Minnesota Press, 1977), pp. 86–123.

J. Hines, "The Utilization of Research for Development: Two Case Studies in Rural Modernization and Agriculture in Peru" (Ph.D. dissertation, Princeton University, 1972).

A. S. Kahlon, H. K. Bal, P. N. Saxena, and D. Jha, "Returns to Investment in Research in India," *Resource Allocation and Productivity in National and International Agricultural Research,* ed. Thomas M. Arndt, Dana G. Dalrymple, and Vernon W. Ruttan (Minneapolis: University of Minnesota Press, 1977), pp. 124–47.

M. Knutson and Luther G. Tweeten, "Toward an Optimal Rate of Growth in Agricultural Production Research and Extension," *American Journal of Agricultural Economics* 61 (February 1979):70–76.

R. Latimer, "Some Economic Aspects of Agricultural Research and Extension in the U.S." (Ph.D. dissertation, Purdue University, 1964).

J. G. Nagy and W. H. Furtan, "Economic Costs and Returns from Crop Development Research: The Case of Rapeseed Breeding in Canada," *Canadian Journal of Agricultural Economics* 26 (February 1978):1–14.

T. Y. Pee, "Social Returns from Rubber Research on Peninsular Malaysia" (Ph.D. dissertation, Michigan State University, 1977).

W. L. Peterson, "Return to Poultry Research in the United States," *Journal of Farm Economics* 49 (August 1967):656–69.

W. L. Peterson and J. C. Fitzharris, "The Organization and Productivity of the Federal State Research System in the United States," *Research Allocation and Productivity in National and International Agricultural Research,* ed. Thomas M. Arndt, Dana G. Dalrymple, and Vernon W. Ruttan (Minneapolis: University of Minnesota Press, 1977), pp. 60–85.

C. E. Pray, "The Economics of Agricultural Research in British Punjab and Pakistani Punjab, 1905–1975" (Ph.D. dissertation, University of Pennsylvania, 1978).

———, "The Economics of Agricultural Research in Bangladesh," *Bangladesh Journal of Agricultural Economics* 2 (December 1979):1–36.

A. Schmitz and D. Seckler, "Mechanized Agriculture and Social Welfare: The Case of the Tomato Harvester," *American Journal of Agricultural Economics* 52 (November 1970): 569–77.

G. M. Scobie and R. Posada T., "The Impact of Technical Change on Income Distribution: The Case of Rice in Colombia," *American Journal of Agricultural Economics* 60 (February 1978):85–92.

A. Tang, "Research and Education in Japanese Agricultural Development," *Economic Studies Quarterly* 13 (February–May 1963):27–41 and 91–99.

E. B. Wennergren and M. D. Whitaker, "Social Return to U.S. Technical Assistance in Bolivian Agriculture: The Case of Sheep and Wheat," *American Journal of Agricultural Economics* 59 (August 1977):565–69.

In addition to the studies listed in the table, there have been several other important research impact studies in which results are reported in a cost-benefit rather than an internal rate of return format:

L. L. Bauer and C. R. Hancock, "The Productivity of Agricultural Research and Extension Expenditures in the Southeast," *Southern Journal of Agricultural Economics* 7 (December 1975):117–22.

J. S. Marsden, G. E. Martin, D. J. Parham, T. J. Risdill, and B. G. Johnston, *Returns on Australian Agricultural Research: The Joint Industries Assistance Commission—CSIRO Benefit-Cost Study of the CSIRO Division of Entomology* (Canberra: Commonwealth Scientific and Industrial Research Organization, 1980).

H. Graham Purchase, "The Etiology and Control of Marek's Disease of Chickens and the Economic Impact of a Successful Research Program," *Virology in Agriculture: Beltsville Symposium in Agricultural Research–1,* ed. John A. Romberger (Montclair, N.J.: Allanheld, USMUN, 1977), pp. 63–81.

TABLE 3-A2. Summary of studies of education's effects and environmental variables

Author, region, and sample	N	Formal Education			Nonformal Education			Environmental Variables				
		Functional form*	Gain in output per 1 yr education (%)	SE of estimate of % gain†	Variable	Regression coefficient on output	t-statistic	Modernizing environment‡	Extension present or not§	GNP per capita	Crop	Adult literacy rate (%)
Halim, Philippines:												
1963	274	2	2.2	1.3	Nonlog—of weighted contacts	.0063	3.435	0	1	285.16	Rice	72.0
1968	273	2	1.92	1.5		.0036	2.4	0	1	343.83	Rice	—
1973	220	2	2.74	1.2		-.00017	-.772	0	1	314.38	Rice	—
Haller:												
Chinchiná	77	1	-.29	2.2	—	—	—	1	0	—	Coffee	74.0
Espinal	74	1	6.10	3.5	—	—	—	1	0	—	Mixed	—
Málaga	74	1	3.09	3.3	—	—	—	-1	0	452.66	Tobacco	—
Moniquirá	75	1	-3.12	3.0	—	—	—	-1	0	—	Mixed	—
Jamison and Lau:												
Korea												
Mechanical	1,363	2	2.22	.4	—	—	—	1	0	525.23	Mixed	91.0
Nonmechanical	541	2	2.33	.8	—	—	—	1	0	—	Mixed	—
Malaysia	403	3	5.11	2.2	Adult education participation	.2369	1.732	1	1	764.20	Rice	89.0
Thailand:												
Chemical	91	2	3.15	1.5	Nonlog—whether extension was available in village	-.09182	-1.098	1	1	317.42	Rice	82.0
Nonchemical	184	2	2.43	1.1		.08538	2.225	1	1	—	Rice	—
Moock, Kenya	152	3	1.73	1.1	Factored variables	.0027	0.77	1	1	216.00	Maize	30.0
Pachico and Ashby:												
Candelaria	117	3	2.69	3.3	N of contacts	-.010	-2.5	-1	1	—	Mixed	68.0
Garibaldi	101	3	4.60	2.7		—	—	-1	1	—	Mixed	—
Guarani	63	3	1.49	2.9		—	—	-1	1	1,225.87	Mixed	—
Taquari	101	3	5.53	3.8		—	—	1	1	—	Mixed	—

TABLE 3-A2. (Continued)

Author, region, and sample	N	Formal Education			Nonformal Education			Environmental Variables				
		Functional form*	Gain in output per 1 yr education (%)	SE of estimate of % gain†	Variable	Regression coefficient on output	t-statistic	Modernizing environment‡	Extension present or not§	GNP per capita	Crop	Adult literacy rate (%)
Patrick and Kehrberg:												
Alto Saõ Francisco	82	2	-1.29	2.0	Nonlog—of	.00432	.977	0	1	–	Mixed	68.0
Conceicao de Castelo	54	2	-.90	1.2	visits	.00901	2.650	-1	1	–	Coffee	–
Paracatu	86	2	-1.79	1.2		.00056	.203	-1	1	955.04	Mixed	–
Resende	62	2	1.01	.9		.00099	.124	-1	1	–	Dairy	–
Viscosa	337	2	2.33	.8		.00268	1.026	1	1	–	Mixed	–
Pudasaini, Nepal	102	2	1.3	.8	–	–	–	0	-1	97.21	Rice	14.0
Sharma, Nepal:												
Wheat	87	3	5.09	3.1	–	–	–	1	-1	108.62	Wheat	14.0
Rice	138	3	2.85	1.7	–	–	–	0	-1	–	Rice	–
Sidhu, India:												
Traditional and												
Mexican wheat	236	1	1.49	.8	–	–	–	0	0	125.02	Wheat	36.0
Mexican wheat	369	1	1.41	.6	–	–	–	0	0	–	Wheat	36.0
Wu, Taiwan:												
1971, rice	333	2	.70	1.3	–	–	–	1	0	583.69	Rice	73.0
1971, banana and pineapple	316	2	3.87	1.4	–	–	–	1	0	–	Mixed	–
1977	310	2	.9	1.0	–	–	–	1	0	997.35	Mixed	73.0
Yotopoulos, Greece	430	1	6.47	3.2	–	–	–	-1	0	1,356.68	Mixed	82.0

*Numbers correspond to the Cobb-Douglas production function specifications given in eqq. (1)–(3).

†In order to calculate SE in the estimate of the percentage gain in output for 1 yr of education, one needs the value of the coefficient on education in the original regression (β), the estimated SE in the estimate of β (σβ), and the functional form of the original regression. For all studies reported in this table the functional form was that of equation (1), (2), or (3) of Sec. I, and the corresponding formulas for SE are:

$$(1')\quad SE = \left[\!\left[\exp\!\left[2\beta \ln\!\left(\frac{\bar{E}+0.5}{\bar{E}-0.5}\right)\right]\exp\!\left[\ln\!\left(\frac{\bar{E}+0.5}{\bar{E}-0.5}\right)^{2}\sigma\beta^{2}\right]\left\{\exp\!\left[\ln\!\left(\frac{\bar{E}+0.5}{\bar{E}-0.5}\right)^{2}\sigma\beta^{2}\right]-1\right\}\right]\!\right]^{1/2}$$

where $\bar{E}$ is the mean number of years of education in the sample;

$$(2')\quad SE = (e^{2\beta}e^{\sigma\beta^{2}}(e^{\sigma\beta^{2}}-1))^{1/2};\ \text{and}$$

$$(3') \quad SE = \left\{ \frac{1}{N^2} [e^2 \beta e^{\alpha\beta^2} (e^{\alpha\beta^2} - 1)] \right\}^{1/2}$$

where N is the number of years of completed education signified by the indicator variable D.

‡ − 1 = nonmodernizing environment; 1 = modernizing environment; and 0 = no information or a transitional environment.

§ − 1 = no extension service available; 1 = availability of extension service in region; and 0 = no information on availability of extension.

Source for Table: Marlaine E. Lockhead, Dean T. Jamison, and Lawrence J. Lau, "Farmer Education and Farm Efficiency: A Survey," *Economic Development and Cultural Change* 29 (October 1980):73–74.

Sources for the individual studies:

Abdul Halim, "Schooling and Extension and Income Producing Philippine Household [*sic*]," mimeographed (Bangladesh: Department of Agriculture Extension and Teachers Training, Bangladesh Agricultural University, 1976).

Thomas E. Haller, "Education and Rural Development in Colombia" (Ph.D. dissertation, Purdue University, 1972. *Dissertation Abstracts International* 33A, no. 6 (1972):898. University Microfilms no. 72-30898.

Dean T. Jamison and Lawrence J. Lau, *Farmer Education and Farm Efficiency* (Baltimore: Johns Hopkins University Press, 1982).

Peter R. Moock, "Education and Technical Efficiency in Small Farm Production" (Paper presented at the Comparative and International Education Society Annual Meeting, Mexico City, March 1978).

Douglas H. Pachico and Jacquiline A. Ashby, "Investments in Human Capital and Farm Productivity: Some Evidence from Brazil" (Unpublished paper, Cornell University, Ithaca, N.Y., 1976).

George F. Patrick and Earl W. Kehrberg, "Costs and Returns of Education in Five Agricultural Areas of Eastern Brazil," *American Journal of Agricultural Economics* 55 (1973):145–54.

Som P. Pudasaini, "Resource Productivity Income and Employment in Traditional and Mechanized Farming of Bara District, Nepal" (Master's thesis, University of the Philippines at Los Baños, 1976).

Shalik R. Sharma, "Technical Efficiency in Traditional Agriculture: An Econometric Analysis of the Rupandehi District of Nepal" (Master's thesis, Australian National University, 1974).

Surjit S. Sidhu, "The Productive Value of Education in Agricultural Development," Staff Paper P76-17, Department of Agricultural and Applied Economics, University of Minnesota, 1976.

Surjit S. Sidhu and Carlos A. Baanante, "Farm-level Fertilizer Demand for Mexican Wheat Varieties in the Indian Punjab," *American Journal of Agricultural Economics*. 61(1979):455–62.

Craig C. Wu, "The Contribution of Education to Farm Production in a Transitional Farm Economy" (Ph.D. dissertation, Vanderbilt University, 1971. *Dissertation Abstracts International* 32A, no. 5 (1971):338. University Microfilms no. 71-29338).

———, "Education in Farm Production: The Case of Taiwan," *American Journal of Agricultural Economics* 59 (November 1977):699–709.

Pan A. Yotopoulos, "The Greek Farmer and the Use of His Resources," *Balkan Studies* 8 (1967):365–86.

In addition to the studies listed in the table, there have been a number of other important education impact studies which do not lend themselves to summarization in the form used in Table 3-A2:

P. Calkins, "Shiva's Trident: The Effect of Improving Horticulture on Income, Employment and Nutrition" (Ph.D. dissertation, Cornell University, 1976).

D. P. Chaudhri, "Effect of Farmer's Education on Agricultural Productivity and Employment: A Case Study of Punjab and Haryana States of India (1960–1972)," mimeographed (Armidale: University of New England, 1974).

———, *Education, Innovation and Agricultural Development: A Study of North India (1961–72)* (London: Croom Helm, Ltd., 1979).

Bruce R. Harker, "The Contribution of Schooling to Agricultural Modernization: An Empirical Analysis," *Education and Rural Development*, ed. P. Foster and J. R. Sheffield (London: Evans Bros., 1973).

K. Y. Hong, "An Estimated Economic Contribution of Schooling and Extension in Korean Agriculture" (Ph.D. dissertation, University of the Philippines at Los Baños, 1975).

Peter N. Hopcraft, "Human Resources and Technical Skills in Agricultural Development: An Economic Evaluation of Educative Investments in Kenya's Small-Farm Sector" (Ph.D. dissertation, Stanford University, 1974).

Peter R. Moock, "Managerial Ability in Small Farm Production: An Analysis of Maize Yields in the Vihiga Division of Kenya" (Ph.D. dissertation, Columbia University, 1973).

Ezra Sadan, Chava Nachmias, and Gideon Bar-Lev, "Education and Economic Performance of Occidental and Oriental Family Farm Operators," *World Development* 4 (1976):445–55.

TABLE 3-A3. Summary of returns to extension studies

Study	Country (Data set year)	Type of study	Conclusion
1. Patrick and Kehrberg (1973)	Brazil–Eastern (1968)	Production function	Extension, number of direct contacts of farmers with extension agents during the study year, had positive but generally not statistically significant effects on value added in farm production.
2. Evenson and Jha (1973)	India (1953–54 to 1970–71)	Productivity change	Extension, index of maturity of extension program, contributes significantly to agricultural productivity change only through interaction with research programs. Investment in extension programs yields a 15%–20% social rate of return.
3. Huffman (1974)	United States–Corn Belt (1959–64)	Allocative efficiency-production	Extension (days, average for 1958 and 1960, allocated to crops by agents doing primarily agricultural work) and education are substitutes in inducing optimal nitrogen fertilizer usage on hybrid corn. The marginal value of extension time on this one decision is estimated at $4.48 per hour of extension agent time allocated to crops or a social rate of return of 1.3%. Total social return from enhanced decision-making suggested to be in excess of 16%.
4. Mohan and Evenson (1975)	India (1959–60 to 1970–71)	Productivity change	The Intensive Agricultural Districts Program (presence vs. absence) contributed to more rapid agricultural productivity change. The social rate of return realized on the investment was 15%–20%.
5. Huffman (1976a)	United States, Iowa, North Carolina, Oklahoma (1964)	Production function	Extension, agent days allocated three years earlier to crops and livestock activities by agents doing primarily agricultural work, contributes significantly to level of agricultural production. The marginal product of extension is $1,000–3,000 per day.
6. Mooch (1976, 1978)	Kenya-Vihiga, (a western division) (1971)	Production function	An index of crop related extension contact with male and female farm operators during the last year contributes significantly to corn (maize) yields. Extension and education are substitutes in corn production; extension interacts positively with the rate of nitrogen fertilizer application on male operated farms (1978).
7. Huffman (1976b)	United States, Iowa, North Carolina, Oklahoma (1964)	Production function	Same as for Huffman (1976a) except marginal product of extension $1,000–2,500 per day.

8. Halim (1977)	Philippines-Laguna Province (1963–68–73)	Production function	An index of extension contact with farms, derived by weighting frequency of contact over previous five years, contributes positively and significantly to agricultural production. Marginal products imply a "relatively high return of extension contact."
9. Huffman (1977)	United States-Corn Belt (1959–64)	Allocative efficiency	Same as Huffman (1974) except marginal value of extension time on this one decision is estimated at $600 per day of extension agent time allocated to crops or a social rate of return of 110%.
10. Evenson (1978)	United States (1949–71)	Productivity change	Extension, expenditures on applied farm management research and on applied agricultural engineering research are combined with expenditures on extension activity and deflated by number of commodity-subregions, interacts negatively with education and positively with applied research. The internal rate of return on extension expenditures is 110%.
11. Huffman (1978)	United States, Iowa, North Carolina, Oklahoma (1964)	Production function	Extension is measured as days allocated to crops, livestock, and planning and managing farm businesses and as days allocated to the separate components. Emphasis is placed on holding factors constant that may be correlated with the extension variables. Marginal product of extension is sensitive to output mix (livestock vs. crop), ranging from very large to negative values. Crop extension performs better than other components.
12. Pudasaini (1981)	Nepal, Bara, and Gorkha Districts (1979–80)	Production and profit functions	Extension, contacts with farmers during the study year (in rice, wheat, sugarcane, or total farm in modernizing Bara; or in rice, wheat, maize, or total farm in more traditional Gorkha district), had positive or negative but generally not statistically significant effects on the individual crop output, value added, gross revenue, or profits of the farms of both districts. The above findings remained valid even when extension was included as three separate variables (x_1: 1–5 contacts, x_2, 6–9 contacts and x_3; more than 9 contacts) rather than a single variable, or even when it was included as a zero-one variable rather than a continuous variable. Education and extension were weak substitutes in the farm decision-making process.

Source: Adapted from Wallace E. Huffman, "Assessing Returns to Agricultural Extension," *American Journal of Agricultural Economics* 60 (December 1978):973.
Note: Huffman identifies four potential sources of bias in the measurement of returns to extension: (a) production function estimates, which focus on the effect of extension on production, do not capture the effect on factor choice (downward bias); (b) extension is typically treated as a current input rather than a capital input (upward bias); (c) most studies, except Evenson and Jha neglect the interaction between research and extension (upward bias); (d) none of the studies include the effect of private sector information activities (upward bias). Huffman concludes that after taking into account the potential sources of bias the rate of return to extension is modest or better in the United States, modest in India, and difficult to assess in the other countries. In our judgment failure to include private sector information may result in very little bias since the cost of the information activity is included in the cost of inputs purchased from the private sector.

TABLE 3-A3. (Continued)

Sources of the individual studies:

Robert E. Evenson, "Research, Invention, Extension and Productivity Change in U.S. Agriculture: An Historical Decomposition Analysis" (Paper presented at Symposium on Research and Extension Evaluation, Moscow, Idaho, May 21–23, 1978).

Robert E. Evenson and D. Jha, "The Contribution of Agricultural Research System to Agricultural Production in India," *Indian Journal of Agricultural Economics* 28, (1973):212–30.

Abdul Halim, "The Economic Contribution of Schooling and Extension to Rice Production in Laguna, Philippines," *Journal of Agricultural Economics and Development* 7 (1977):33–46.

Wallace E. Huffman, "Allocative Efficiency: The Role of Human Capital," *Quarterly Journal of Economics* 91 (1977):59–79.

———, "Decision Making: The Role of Education," *American Journal of Agricultural Economics* 56 (1974):85–97.

———, "The Productive Value of Human Time in U.S. Agriculture," *American Journal of Agricultural Economics* 58 (1976a):672–83.

———, "Returns to Extension: An Assessment" (Paper presented at Symposium on Research and Extension Evaluation, Moscow, Idaho, May 21–23, 1978).

———, "The Value of the Productive Time of Farm Wives: Iowa, North Carolina, and Oklahoma," *American Journal of Agricultural Economics* 58 (1976b):836–41.

R. Mohan and R. E. Evenson, "The Intensive Agricultural Districts Program in India: A New Evaluation," *Journal of Developmental Studies* 11 (1975):135–54.

P. R. Mooch, "Education and Technical Efficiency in Small Farm Production" (Unpublished paper, Columbia University, January 1978).

G. F. Patrick and E. W. Kehrberg, "Cost and Returns of Education in Five Agricultural Areas in Eastern Brazil," *American Journal of Agricultural Economics* 55 (1973):145–53.

Som P. Pudasaini, "The Effects of Education in Agriculture: Evidence from Nepal," *American Journal of Agricultural Economics* 65 (August 1983):509–15.

———, "The Contribution of Education to Agricultural Productivity, Efficiency and Development" (Ph.D. dissertation, University of Minnesota, 1981).

72

4

Toward a Theory of Technical and Institutional Change

In this chapter we attempt to build an integrated theory of agricultural development, drawing on the agricultural and economic development theories outlined in the two previous chapters. A major step forward from the existing theories is the attempt to incorporate changes in technology and institutions as endogenous to the economic system—as directed by the conditions of factor supply and product demand. We also incorporate recursive interactions between technical and institutional change, and we attempt to show how both are critically influenced by the cultural endowment specific to each society.[1]

ALTERNATIVE PATHS OF TECHNOLOGICAL DEVELOPMENT

The attempt to develop a model of agricultural development in which technical change is treated as endogenous to the development process, rather than as an exogenous factor that operates independently of other development processes, must start with the recognition that there are multiple paths of technological development. Technology can be developed so as to facilitate the substitution of relatively abundant (hence cheap) factors for relatively scarce (hence expensive) factors in the economy. For example, high-yielding crop varieties are essentially an input designed to facilitate the substitution of fertilizer (or other inputs) for land. For purposes of illustration we compare, in Table 4-1, the yield response to nitrogen of indigenous rice varieties in Bangladesh and of some older improved varieties in Japan. The comparison

1. In the first edition of *Agricultural Development* (1971) we outlined the elements of an induced innovation model of agricultural development. Since then our thinking has been strongly influenced by our own research and by research undertaken in collaboration with colleagues. See particularly, *Induced Innovation: Technology, Institutions and Development*, ed. Hans P. Binswanger and Vernon W. Ruttan et al. (Baltimore: Johns Hopkins University Press, 1978); Yujiro Hayami and Masao Kikuchi, *Asian Village Economy at the Crossroads: An Economic Approach to Institutional Change* (Tokyo: University of Tokyo Press, 1981, and Baltimore: Johns Hopkins University Press, 1982).

TABLE 4-1.   Yield response to nitrogen input by rice varieties

	Yield (lb./acre) at the levels of N				Marginal product of N	
	(1) 95 lb./acre		(2) 150 lb./acre		$\frac{(2)-(1)}{55}$	
Variety	Paddy	Straw	Paddy	Straw	Paddy	Straw
Habiganj[a]	4,785	7,948	4,372	10,478	−7.5	46.0
Batak[a]	5,445	9,488	5,875	11,743	7.8	41.0
Kamenoo[b]	5,417	5,500	6,077	7,617	12.0	38.5
Norin 1[c]	6,352	7,205	7,700	8,225	24.5	18.5
Norin 87[c]	5,118	6,352	6,517	7,892	25.4	28.0
Rikuu 232[c]	5,802	6,902	7,425	8,553	29.5	30.0

Source: Institute of Asian Economic Affairs, *Ajia no Inasaku* (Rice Farming in Asia) (Tokyo, 1961), p. 14.

[a]Indigenous varieties in Bangladesh.

[b]A variety selected by a veteran farmer, the use of which became prevalent in Japan from 1905 to 1925.

[c]Varieties selected through hybridization by agricultural experiment stations in Japan after the nationwide co-ordinated experiment system called "Assigned Experiment System" was established in 1926–27.

shows that the yields of the indigenous varieties were as high as those of the improved varieties at a low level of fertilization, but that they respond negatively or only modestly to higher levels of fertilizer. With the indigenous varieties a larger dose of fertilizer results in a larger output of straw but not of grain. The lack of response of the indigenous varieties to higher levels of fertilization represents a particularly serious constraint on growth of agricultural output in economies characterized by high population densities and an inelastic supply of land. Increases in output depend on the development of an agricultural technology, including fertilizer-responsive crop varieties, that can release the constraints on growth imposed by the inelastic supply of land.

Likewise, in an economy characterized by a relative scarcity of labor, substitution of land and capital for labor would be made possible primarily by improving agricultural implements and machinery. In the United States, for example, when horses were used for plowing, the substitution of additional land and power (horses) for labor was constrained by the technical limits of "horse mechanization." Introduction of tractors facilitated substitution by making it easier for a worker to command more power and to cultivate a larger land area.

An important consideration is that new techniques, such as new husbandry practices or new seeds, are not substitutes for labor or land by themselves; but they are the inputs which behave as catalysts to facilitate the substitution of the relatively scarce factors for the less scarce factors. It seems reasonable, according to the definition of John R. Hicks, to call techniques designed to facilitate the substitution of other inputs for labor "labor-saving" and ones designed to facilitate the substitution of other inputs for land "land-saving."[2]

In agriculture, two kinds of technology generally correspond to this taxonomy: mechanical technology to "labor-saving" and biological and chemical technology to "land-saving."[3] The former is designed to facilitate the substitution of power and machinery for labor. Typically land is substituted for labor because higher output per worker through mechanization usually requires that the worker cultivate a larger land area. The latter, which we will hereafter identify as biological technology, is designed to facilitate the substitution of labor and/or industrial inputs for land. This substitution may be accomplished through increased recycling of soil fertility by more labor-intensive conservation systems; through use of chemical fertilizers; and through husbandry practices, management systems, and inputs (insecticides) that permit an optimal yield response.

We recognize, of course, that the distinction between mechanical and biological technology employed in this study may be overdrawn for expositional purposes. All mechanical innovations are not necessarily motivated by incentives to save labor, nor are all biological innovations necessarily motivated by incentives to save land. For example, in Japan, horse plowing was developed as a device to cultivate more deeply, so as to increase yield per hectare, and the use of herbicides may save labor as well as prevent yield losses.

In the United States in recent years attempts have been made to develop crop varieties more suitable for mechanical harvesting. For example, tomatoes have been developed which have a sturdier skin and ripen at the same time, in order to facilitate mechanical harvesting. This research illustrates that the development of mechanical technology may be land-saving, and the development of biological technology may be labor-saving. Yet, historically, the dominant factor for saving labor has been the progress of mechanization; and the dominant factor for saving land has been biological innovations.

2. According to Hicks's original definition, considering two production factors, labor (L) and capital (K), technical change is L-saving and K-using or L-using and K-saving depending on whether it increases or decreases L's marginal product relative to K's for a given (L/K) ratio. It follows that the (L/K) ratio increases for a given wage-rental ratio if technological change is L-saving and K-using, and vice versa if technological change is L-using and K-saving. See John R. Hicks, *The Theory of Wages* (London: Macmillan & Co., 1932). In extending the concept to include more than two factors, technical change that is ith factor-saving reduces the ith factor input relative to other factor inputs for a given set of relative factor prices.

3. The distinction made here between "mechanical" and "biological" technology has also been employed by Earl O. Heady, "Basic Economic and Welfare Aspects of Farm Technological Advance," *Journal of Farm Economics* 31 (May 1949):293–316. It is similar to the distinction between "laboresque" and "landesque" capital employed by Sen. See A. K. Sen, "The Choice of Agricultural Techniques in Underdeveloped Countries," *Economic Development and Cultural Change* 7 (April 1959):279–85. Hiromitsu Kaneda employs the terms mechanical-engineering and biological-chemical. See Hiromitsu Kaneda, "Economic Implications of the 'Green Revolution' and the Strategy of Agricultural Development in West Pakistan," *Pakistan Development Review* 9 (Summer 1969):111–43.

At the most sophisticated level, technological progress depends on a series of simultaneous advances in both biological and mechanical sciences and techniques. In the case of the mechanization of tomato harvesting, the plant-breeding research and the engineering research were conducted cooperatively in order to invent new machines capable of harvesting the tomatoes specifically bred for mechanical handling.[4]

Mechanical Processes

The mechanization of farming in Great Britain, and to an even greater degree in the United States, has been intimately associated with the Industrial Revolution. The precise interrelationship between the industrial and agricultural revolutions of the eighteenth century is still a matter of debate among economic historians. It is generally agreed, however, that the relative scarcity of labor represented an inducement to adopt more capital-intensive methods in both the industrial and agricultural sectors in the United States than in Britain.[5]

Although progress of agricultural and industrial mechanization represents a response to the same set of fundamental economic forces, the mechanization of agriculture cannot be treated as simply the adaptation of industrial methods of production to agriculture. The spatial nature of agricultural production results in significant differences between agriculture and industry in the pattern of machinery use. It imposes severe constraints on the efficiency of large-scale production in agriculture.[6]

4. Wayne D. Rasmussen, "Advances in American Agriculture: The Mechanical Tomato Harvester as a Case Study," *Technology and Culture* 9 (October 1968):531–43; and Andrew Schmitz and David Seckler, "Mechanized Agriculture and Social Welfare: The Case of the Tomato Harvester," *American Journal of Agricultural Economics* 52 (November 1970):569–77. More recently this development has become the focus for considerable controversy because of its impact on labor displacement. See Alain de Janvry, Phillip Le Veen, and David Runsten, "Mechanization of California Agriculture: The Case of Canning Tomatoes," mimeographed (Berkeley: University of California, Department of Agricultural and Resource Economics, September 1980). Also Vernon W. Ruttan, *Agricultural Research Policy* (Minneapolis: University of Minnesota Press, 1982), pp. 186–92, 336–38.

5. H. J. Habakkuk, *American and British Technology in the Nineteenth Century: The Search for Labour Saving Inventions* (Cambridge: Cambridge University Press, 1962), p. 14. Habakkuk argues that "the course of agricultural technology in the early decades of the nineteenth century may well have accentuated the disparity between the terms on which labour was available to industry in the U.S.A. and England. In America improvements in agriculture took the form primarily of increasing output per head and the increase initially was probably more rapid than in industry; in England on the other hand, agricultural improvement was devoted primarily to increasing yields per acre and, even where there was an increase in output per head, the abundance of labour made it difficult for the labourer to enjoy the increase. In America agricultural improvements raised, and in England prevented, a rise in the terms on which labour was available to industry."

6. John M. Brewster, "The Machine Process in Agriculture and Industry," *Journal of Farm Economics* 32 (February 1950):69–81: "In pre-machine times, farming and manufacturing were alike in that operations in both cases were normally done sequentially, one after another; usually by the same individual or family. The rise of the machine process has forced agriculture and industry to become progressively different in respect to the sequence in which men once per-

In the industrial sector, the replacement of handcraft methods of production with machine methods forced a factory system of organization in which the individual worker becomes specialized in one particular operation or function. In farming, the sequence of operations from preplanting to postharvesting remains as widely separated by time intervals after mechanization as before. The spatial dimension of crop production requires that the machines suitable for agricultural mechanization must be mobile—they must move across or through materials that are immobile, in contrast to moving materials through stationary machines, as in most industrial processes. The seasonal or time characteristic of agricultural production requires a series of specialized machines—for land preparation, planting, weed control, and harvesting—specifically designed for sequential operations, each of which is carried out only a few days or weeks in each season. This also means that it is no more feasible for workers to specialize in one operation in mechanized agriculture than in premechanized agriculture. In addition, it means that in a "fully mechanized" agricultural system, because of the mobility and specialization characteristics, investment per worker is frequently higher than in industry.[7] The mobility characteristic means that the machine must not only have the power to perform the specific operation but must be able to move itself across frequently unfavorable terrain while performing the operation. The specialization characteristic means that machines employed in agriculture must be adapted to perform operations that require their use for only a short time each year.

It is clear, regardless of the impact of the economic organization of agriculture, that the major economic force leading to the greater use of mechanical equipment in agriculture is the drive to reduce labor costs. The major consequence is a rise in labor productivity—output per worker or per man-hour. In economies where the price of labor is low and where the price of

formed both farm and industrial operations. For in substituting machine for hand power and manipulations in agriculture, individuals in no wise disturb their pre-machine habit of doing their production steps one after another whereas in making the same substitution in industry men thereby force themselves to acquire increasingly the new habit of performing simultaneously the many operations in a production process. As a consequence, the 'Industrial Revolution' in agriculture is merely a spectacular change in the implements of production whereas in industry it is a further revolution in the sequence (order) in which men use their implements" (pp. 69–70). See also Nicholas Georgescu-Roegen, "Process in Farming versus Process in Manufacturing: A Problem of Balanced Development," *Economic Problems of Agriculture in Industrial Societies,* ed. Ugo Papi and Charles Nunn (London: Macmillan, and New York: St. Martin's Press, 1969), pp. 497–528.

7. Paul Zarembka, "Manufacturing and Agricultural Production Functions and International Trade: United States and Northern Europe," *Journal of Farm Economics* 48 (November 1966):952–66; Allen G. Smith, "Comparative Investment per Worker in Agriculture and Manufacturing Sectors of the Economy," *American Journal of Agricultural Economics* 53 (February 1971):101–2. In 1979 the five hundred largest industrial corporations in the United States had $49,500 of assets per employee, while production assets per farm worker were about $150,000. Reported in D. Gale Johnson, "International Capital Markets, Exchange Rates and Agricultural Trade," University of Chicago, Agricultural Economics Research Paper 82-17, August 25, 1982.

material goods—of machinery—is high, there is little economic incentive to mechanize field operations. As the value of labor rises, either as a result of rising demand for labor in the urban-industrial sector or as a result of greater domestic or international demand for agricultural commodities, mechanization is typically adopted first for those activities in which stationary power sources can be used—for pumping water and threshing grain, for example. Mechanization of motive power for machines that must move across the landscape typically represents a later stage in farm mechanization.[8]

The implications of progress in mechanical technology on labor productivity are illustrated by many examples from the historical experiences of the United States, Canada, England, and other Western economies. The impact of the evolution of harvesting machinery in the United States during the nineteenth century, as calculated from documentation by Leo Rogin, is illustrated in Figure 4-1.[9]

The usual method of harvesting wheat, before the adoption of horse-drawn machinery, was to reap it with a hand sickle. With the sickle, a worker could harvest between one-third and one-half acre per day. The cradle, a scythe with a frame composed of tapering wooden fingers attached alongside the blade to permit simultaneous cutting and "bunching" of the grain, was introduced toward the end of the colonial period, and its use permitted an approximate doubling of the acres harvested per day per worker. The cradle represented an answer to the relative labor scarcity in North America when settlement was still concentrated east of the Appalachian Mountains. The first horse-drawn reapers, which permitted a second doubling of acreage harvested per worker per day, were patented in the 1830s and were in widespread use by 1850. This innovation corresponded to the dramatic expansion in cultivable land area relative to labor after the opening up of the Midwest. A series of improvements followed, permitting a further doubling of labor productivity during the 1860s. The next major advance came with the invention of wire and twine binders, which replaced the self-rake reaper and the hand-binding harvester. The incorporation of automatic binding equipment, together with other improvements in size and efficiency of operation, permitted a doubling or tripling of labor productivity in grain harvesting. The ultimate step in the evolu-

8. Historically this has been the general sequence of mechanization. The stationary and mobile power sources may, however, be adopted by some developing countries concurrently, rather than in sequence, because the progress of farm mechanization has made a more complete set of farm mechanization devices available. In other countries, the adoption sequence may be considerably shortened. Even where tractor power is introduced fairly early in the development process, however, it tends to be used first in those areas, such as land preparation, where its advantage relative to animal power or hand methods is greatest. See W. J. Chancellor, "Mechanization of Small Farms in Thailand and Malaysia by Tractor Hire Services," *Transactions of the American Society of Agricultural Engineers* 14 (1971):847–59.

9. Leo Rogin, *The Introduction of Farm Machinery in Its Relation to the Productivity of Labor in the Agriculture of the United States during the Nineteenth Century* (Berkeley: University of California Press, 1931); Paul A. David, *Technical Choice Innovation and Economic Growth* (London: Cambridge University Press, 1975):195–232.

tion of harvesting methods began with the introduction of the combine—a combined harvester and thresher. Except for limited adoption in the extensive wheat-growing areas of California and the Red River Valley of the north, the advantage of using a combine was not great, relative to the twine binder, until after the development of machinery having more efficient motive power than the large steam tractors available at the turn of the century.

The entire significance of this sequence of innovations in grain harvesting was to increase labor productivity. To the extent that any impact on land productivity was involved, it was a factor contributing to the extension of grain production into the drier areas of the Great Plains, where grain yields were lower than in the eastern grain-producing regions.

From this discussion, it seems reasonable to hypothesize an agricultural production function in which mechanical equipment is viewed primarily as a substitute for labor; and evolution of the mechanical equipment is designed to bring about larger output per worker by increasing the land area that can be operated per worker. Furthermore, it seems apparent that the production functions which described the individual grain-harvesting technologies, from the sickle to the combine, were induced by changes in relative factor costs, reflecting the rising resource scarcity of labor relative to other inputs.

Biological and Chemical Processes

In agriculture, biological and chemical technology and processes are more fundamental than mechanization or machine processes. The implications of biological and chemical processes for the economic development and organization of agriculture are generally not well understood by social scientists, planners, and political leaders. Until the development and diffusion of modern high-yielding varieties of rice and wheat in the tropics since the late 1960s, commonly referred to as the green revolution, the treatment of biological and chemical innovations in a typical treatise on economic development was passed over with a quick reference to the need for new seeds and improved methods of cultivation, with apparently little insight into the significance of this terminology. The technical changes associated with mechanization seemed to imply a sharp break with the past and the prospect of instant modernization. Advances in biological and chemical technology typically pose neither the threat nor the promise of a radical reorganization of the agricultural production systems that have characterized the mechanization of motive power in agriculture.

Advances in biological and chemical technology have been induced primarily by a desire to increase crop output per unit of land area or to improve the yield of animal products per unit of feed or per unit of breeding stock. In crop production, these advances have typically involved one or more of the following three elements: (a) land and water resource development to provide a more satisfactory environment for plant growth; (b) modification of the environment by the addition of organic and inorganic sources of plant nu-

FIGURE 4-1. Evolution of harvesting machinery in the United States during the nineteenth century.

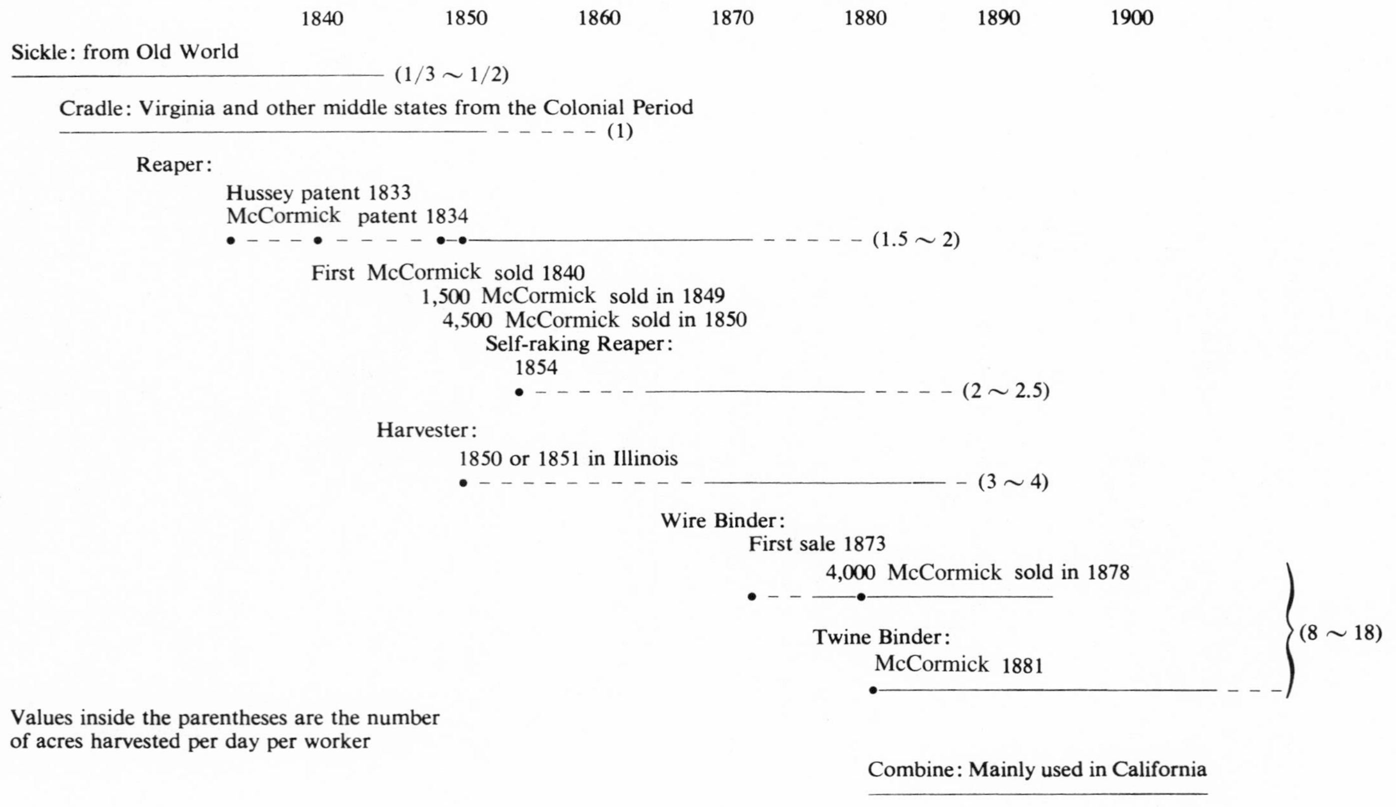

1840   1850   1860   1870   1880   1890   1900

Sickle: from Old World
(1/3 ~ 1/2)

Cradle: Virginia and other middle states from the Colonial Period
- - - - (1)

Reaper:
Hussey patent 1833
McCormick patent 1834
First McCormick sold 1840
1,500 McCormick sold in 1849
4,500 McCormick sold in 1850
(1.5 ~ 2)

Self-raking Reaper:
1854

Harvester:
1850 or 1851 in Illinois
(2 ~ 2.5)

(3 ~ 4)

Wire Binder:
First sale 1873
4,000 McCormick sold in 1878

Twine Binder:
McCormick 1881

(8 ~ 18)

Combine: Mainly used in California

Values inside the parentheses are the number
of acres harvested per day per worker

Source: Leo Rogin, *The Introduction of Farm Machinery in Its Relation to the Productivity of Labor in the Agriculture of the United States during the Nineteenth Century* [Berkeley: University of California Press, 1931].

Note: Man-labor requirements for harvesting small grains (reaping, binding, and shocking):

		Acres/day/worker
Sickle	1/3 ~ 1/2 acres/day/worker	1/3 ~ 1/2
Cradle	2 acres/day/2 workers (one cutter plus one binder)	1
Reaper	10 ~ 12 acres/day/6 ~ 7 workers (1 driver plus 1 raker plus 4 ~ 5 binders)	1.5 ~ 2
Self-raking Reaper	10 ~ 12 acres/day/5 ~ 6 workers (1 driver plus 4 ~ 5 binders)	2 ~ 2.5
Harvester	10 ~ 12 acres/day/3 workers (1 driver plus 2 binders)	3 ~ 4
Self-binder		
2 horse case	8 acres/day/worker	8
3 horse case	10 ~ 12 acres/day/worker	10 ~ 12
4 horse case	18 acres/day/worker	18

trients to the soil to stimulate plant growth and the use of biological and chemical means to protect plants from pests and disease; and (c) selection and design of new biologically efficient crop varieties specifically adapted to respond to those elements in the environment that are subject to man's control. Similar processes can be observed in advances in livestock agriculture.

The implications of biological and chemical innovations can be illustrated from English, United States, Japanese, Taiwanese, and other historical experiences. Two examples, one from the English and one from the Taiwanese experience, are particularly instructive.

The English agricultural revolution of the eighteenth century is regarded by economic historians as a critical complement of the Industrial Revolution. As explained in the previous section, the agricultural revolution consisted of the development of an integrated crop-livestock system of husbandry. Intensive rotation of arable land between food grains and feed crops replaced the traditional open-field system in which one-third of the arable land was left fallow. In many areas, the use of the turnip, for both green forage and winter fodder, was a key innovation in the new system, although in some areas new grasses and legumes played a critical role.

This new system increased the livestock-carrying capacity of the land. The increase in livestock population produced the dung necessary to improve soil fertility and raise the yield of grain crops. The marketed value of both crops and livestock per unit of land area was substantially increased. On the better-managed operations, increases in the marketable value of crops and livestock in the neighborhood of 50 percent were feasible.

The increase of net returns to labor was considerably less dramatic. The new system was much more labor-intensive than the traditional system. Turnips were a labor-intensive crop, and labor requirements increased almost as much as output. Labor requirements, however, were distributed more evenly throughout the year, thus contributing to a rise in the number of days worked, that is, in labor input per agricultural laborer.

The primary impact of the English agricultural revolution of the eighteenth century was to increase land, not labor, productivity. According to C. Peter Timmer, "The agrarian revolution apparently did not supply surplus labor for an industrial army of workers. It did provide food for the rapidly rising population from which both an increased agricultural and industrial labor force were recruited."[10]

Taiwan represents a partcularly useful case in which to examine the utilization of the several technological and institutional elements associated with rapid agricultural development.[11] All of the three elements which we have

10. C. Peter Timmer, "The Turnip, the New Husbandry, and the English Agricultural Revolution," *Quarterly Journal of Economics* 83 (August 1969):384.

11. For a more detailed discussion of the material on Taiwan summarized in this section, see S. C. Hsieh and T. H. Lee, *Agricultural Development and Its Contribution to Economic Growth in Taiwan: Input-Output and Productivity Analysis of Taiwan Agricultural Development* (Taipei:

identified with biological technology have been involved in the transformation of Taiwanese agriculture. By the mid-1920s, under Japanese administration, Taiwan had acquired a number of the essential elements needed for rapid growth of its rice economy: (a) the development of improved rice varieties, initially through selection of the best local varieties and later through a program of crossbreeding designed to adapt fertilizer-responsive Japanese varieties to local conditions; (b) the availability of irrigation systems capable of delivering water to much of the rice land throughout the year; and (c) the availability of technical inputs, such as chemical fertilizers, through an economic integration with the Japanese economy. In addition, economic integration also resulted in rapid development of the local transportation and marketing systems, opening up the Japanese market and creating incentives to increase the marketable surplus of rice in Taiwan.

The Japonica varieties developed by Japanese breeders in Taiwan are referred to as Ponlai varieties. The first Ponlai variety was introduced commercially in 1922 on four hundred hectares of land. By 1940 Ponlai varieties were planted on half of the total rice area. The development of the new Ponlai varieties and the development of irrigation systems were intimately related to rapid growth in the use of commercial fertilizer in rice production after the mid-1920s. The introduction of the Ponlai varieties, with a complementary improvement in cultural practices and investment in irrigation, resulted in rapid increases in yield per hectare, over 2 percent per year until 1938, when the Japanese military efforts began to direct resources away from development objectives. (For details, see Chapters 9 and 10.)

In contrast to the English agricultural revolution, labor productivity in Taiwan, and the labor earnings of individual cultivators, rose concurrently with the rise in land productivity associated with the introduction of modern biological technology. A factor in the rise in output per worker was the rise in the multiple cropping rates, facilitated by irrigation development, that permitted an increase in labor inputs per worker per year by more than 50 percent. A remarkable aspect was that the significant gains in labor productivity were realized despite the decline in the land-labor ratio (see Figure 10-2, Chapter 10).

From this discussion, it seems reasonable to consider that the new husbandry techniques or the new seeds in which new biological and chemical technologies are embodied can be viewed primarily as the inputs which facilitate

Chinese-American Joint Commission on Rural Reconstruction, Economic Digest Series no. 17, April 1966); S. C. Hsieh and V. W. Ruttan, "Environmental, Technological and Institutional Factors in the Growth of Rice Production: Philippines, Thailand, and Taiwan," *Food Research Institute Studies*, vol. 7, no. 3 (1967):307–41; Raymond P. Christensen, *Taiwan's Agricultural Development: Its Relevance for Developing Countries Today* (Washington, D.C.: U.S. Department of Agriculture, Foreign Agriculture Economic Report 39, April 1968); and T. H. Lee, "Intersectoral Capital Flows in the Economic Development of Taiwan, 1895–1960," *Journal of Agricultural Economics* (Taiwan) 7 (June 1969):69–97.

the substitution for land of artificial sources of plant nutrients, either purchased or produced by more labor-intensive conservation systems.

INDUCED TECHNOLOGICAL INNOVATION

It seems clear from the previous discussion that multiple paths of technical change in agriculture are available to a society. The constraints imposed on agricultural development by an inelastic supply of land may be offset by advances in biological technology. The constraints imposed by an inelastic supply of labor may be offset by advances in mechanical technology. The ability of a country to achieve rapid growth in agricultural productivity and output seems to hinge on its ability to make an efficient choice among the alternative paths. Failure to choose a path that effectively loosens the constraints on growth imposed by resource endowments can depress the entire process of agricultural and economic development. An effective theory of agricultural development should incorporate the mechanism by which a society chooses an optimal path of technological change in agriculture.

The process by which technical change is generated has traditionally been treated as exogenous to the economic system—as a product of autonomous advances in scientific and technical knowledge. The theory of induced innovation represents an effort to interpret the process of technical change as endogenous to the economic system. In this view technical change represents a dynamic response to changes in resource endowments and to growth in demand.

Induced Innovation in the Theory of the Firm

The theories of induced innovation have been developed mainly within the framework of the theory of the firm. There have been two traditions in the attempt to incorporate into economic theory the innovative behavior of profit-maximizing firms. One is the Hicks tradition that focused on the factor-saving bias induced by changes in relative factor prices resulting from changes in relative resource scarcities.[12] Another is the Schmookler-Griliches tradition

12. Hicks, *Theory of Wages*, pp. 124–25. Interest by economists in the issue opened up by Hicks lagged until the 1960s. Two papers by William Fellner were particularly important in directing attention to the issue of induced technical change: "Two Propositions in the Theory of Induced Innovations," *Economic Journal* 71 (June 1961):305–8, and "Does the Market Direct the Relative Factor-Saving Effects of Technological Progress?" *The Rate and Direction of Inventive Activity,* a report of the National Bureau of Economic Research, ed. Richard R. Nelson (Princeton: Princeton University Press, 1962), pp. 171–93. An extended dialogue followed over the theoretical foundations and the macroeconomic implications of induced technical change beginning with the article by Charles Kennedy, "Induced Bias in Innovation and the Theory of Distribution," *Economic Journal* 74 (September 1964):541–47; Paul A. Samuelson, "A Theory of Induced Innovation Along Kennedy-Weisäcker Lines," *Review of Economics and Statistics* 47 (November 1965):343–56; Charles Kennedy, "Samuelson on Induced Innovation," *Review of Economics and Statistics* 48 (November 1966):442–44; Paul A. Samuelson, "Rejoinder: Agreements, Disagreements, Doubts, and the Case of Induced Harrod-Neutral Technical Change,"

that focused on the influence of the growth of product demand on the rate of technical change.[13]

In the dynamic process of economic development, changes in product demand and relative factor prices are inseparably related. For example, when food demand rises because of growth in population and/or per capita income, the demand for factor inputs in food production increases more or less proportionally. When increases in factor demands are confronted with different factor supply elasticities, the result is changes in relative factor prices. The different rates of change in factor prices result, in turn, in changes in the level of income and income distribution among factor owners, thereby affecting the aggregate product demand. A fully developed general equilibrium theory of induced innovation that is capable of explaining the dynamic process of agricultural development should incorporate the mechanisms by which changes in both product demand and factor endowments interact with each other to influence the rate and direction of technological change.

The Hicks theory of induced innovation implies that a rise in the price of one factor relative to that of other factors induces a sequence of technical changes that reduces the use of that factor relative to the use of other factor inputs. As a result, the constraints on economic growth imposed by resource scarcity are released by technical advances that facilitate the substitution of relatively abundant factors for relatively scarce factors. The Hicks theory has

---

Review of Economics and Statistics 48 (November 1966):444–48; Syed Ahmad, "On the Theory of Induced Invention," *Economic Journal* 76 (June 1966):344–57; William Fellner, "Comment on the Induced Bias," *Economic Journal* 77 (September 1967):662–64; Syed Ahmad, "Reply to Professor Fellner," *Economic Journal* 77 (September 1967):664–65; Charles Kennedy, "On the Theory of Induced Invention—A Reply," *Economic Journal* 77 (December 1967):958–60; Syed Ahmad, "A Rejoinder to Professor Kennedy," *Economic Journal* 77 (December 1967):960–63. For other contributions see E. M. Drandakis and E. S. Phelps, "A Model of Induced Invention, Growth and Distribution," *Economic Journal* 76 (December 1966):823–40; John Conlisk, "A Neoclassical Growth Model with Endogenously Positioned Technical Change Frontier," *Economic Journal* 79 (June 1969):348–62; Th. van de Klundert and R. J. de Groof, "Economic Growth and Induced Technical Progress," *De Economist* (The Netherlands) 125 (1977):505–24. For reviews of this and related literature see Henry Y. Wan, Jr., *Economic Growth* (New York: Harcourt Brace Jovanovich, 1971), pp. 215–26; William D. Nordhaus, "Some Skeptical Thoughts on the Theory of Induced Innovation," *Quarterly Journal of Economics* 87 (May 1973):208–19; Hans P. Binswanger, "Induced Technical Change: Evolution of Thought," *Induced Innovation*, pp. 13–43.

13. Zvi Griliches, "Hybrid Corn: An Exploration in the Economics of Technical Change," *Econometrica* 25 (1957):501–22; Jacob Schmookler, "Changes in Industry and in the State of Knowledge as Determinants of Industrial Invention," *Rate and Direction of Inventive Activity,* ed. Nelson, pp. 195–232; Jacob Schmookler, *Invention and Economic Growth* (Cambridge: Harvard University Press, 1966). David Mowery and Nathan Rosenberg, "The Influence of Market Demand upon Innovation: A Critical Review of Some Recent Empirical Studies," *Research Policy* 8 (April 1979):102–53, have argued that in a number of recent studies "the notion that market demand forces 'govern' the innovation process is simply not demonstrated by the empirical analyses which have claimed to support that conclusion" (p. 104). In a recent study, using a more complete data base, F. M. Scherer, "Demand Pull and Technological Invention: Schmookler Revisited," *Journal of Industrial Economics* 30 (March 1982):225–38, concludes that "the relationship between demand pull and the flow of innovations was much weaker, though still significant."

been criticized by W. E. G. Salter and others for its lack of a microeconomic foundation based on the optimizing behavior of the innovating firm.[14]

Salter's criticism runs somewhat as follows: Firms are motivated to save total cost for a given output; at competitive equilibrium, each factor is being paid its marginal value product; therefore, all factors are equally expensive to firms; hence there is no incentive for competitive firms to search for techniques to save a particular factor.

The difference between our perspective and Salter's results partly from a difference in the definition of the production function. Salter defined the production function to embrace all possible designs conceivable by existing scientific knowledge and called the choice among these designs "factor substitution" instead of "technical change." Salter admits, however, that "relative factor prices are in the nature of signposts representing broad influences that determine the way technological knowledge is applied to production."[15] If we accept Salter's definition, the allocation of resources to the development of high-yielding and fertilizer-responsive varieties adaptable to the ecology of Bangladesh, which are comparable to the improved varieties in Japan (Table 4-1), for example, cannot be considered as a technical change. Rather, it is viewed as an application of existing technological knowledge (breeding techniques, plant-type concepts, and the like) to production.

Although we do not deny the case for Salter's definition, it is clearly not very useful in attempting to understand the process by which new technical alternatives become available. We regard technical change as any change in production coefficients resulting from the purposeful resource-using activity directed to the development of new knowledge embodied in designs, materials, or organizations.[16] In terms of this definition, it is entirely rational for competitive firms to allocate funds to develop a technology that facilitates the substitution of increasingly more expensive factors for less expensive factors. Syed Ahmad clearly shows, assuming entrepreneurs conceive alternative new technical possibilities that can be developed by the same amount of research costs, that, if one factor becomes more expensive relative to another over time, the innovative efforts of entrepreneurs will be directed toward saving the factor that becomes more expensive.[17] Similarly, in a country in which a factor is more expensive relative to another factor than it is in a second country, innovative efforts will be directed toward saving the relatively more expensive factors.

14. W. E. G. Salter, *Productivity and Technical Change* (Cambridge: Cambridge University Press, 1960), pp. 43–44. See also the literature cited in note 13.

15. Ibid., p. 16.

16. Paul M. Hohenberg, *Chemicals in Western Europe, 1850–1914* (Chicago: Rand McNally and Co., 1967), p. 57.

17. Ahmad, "On the Theory of Induced Invention." See also discussion by Fellner and Ahmad in Fellner, "Comment on the Induced Bias," pp. 662–64; Ahmad, "Reply to Professor Fellner," pp. 664–65; discussions by Kennedy, "On the Theory of Induced Invention—A Reply," pp. 958–60; and Ahmad, "A Rejoinder to Professor Kennedy," pp. 960–63.

More recently, Hans P. Binswanger has developed an induced innovation model incorporating a research production function. By assuming decreasing marginal productivity of research resources in applied research and development he was able to construct a model of induced factor-saving bias in technical change based on the profit-maximizing behavior of the firm without resorting to the restrictive assumption of a fixed research budget.[18] Binswanger also incorporates into the model the effect of product demand on research resource allocation. In his model, the growth in product demand increases the marginal value product of resources devoted to research, thereby increasing the optimal level of research expenditure for the profit-maximizing firm. The larger research budget implies a shift of the innovation possibility curve (IPC), defined as an envelope of unit isoquants corresponding to the alternative technologies that can potentially be developed for a given research budget at a given state of art, toward the origin. In the Binswanger model, technical change is guided along the IPC by changes in relative factor prices, while the IPC itself is induced to shift inward toward the origin by the growth in product demand. Thus he was able to incorporate both the Hicks approach, which focused on the effect of relative factor prices on factor-saving bias, and the Schmookler-Griliches approach, which focused on the effect of product demand on the rate of technological change, into a single model of induced technical change.

Induced Innovation in Public Research Institutions

Innovative behavior in the public sector has largely been ignored in the literature on induced innovation.[19] This is a particularly critical limitation in attempting to understand the process of scientific and technical innovation in agricultural development. In most countries that have been successful in achieving rapid rates of technical progress in agriculture, "socialization" of agricultural research has been deliberately employed as an instrument of modernization in agriculture.

Our view of the mechanism of induced innovation in public sector agricultural research is similar to the Hicksian theory of induced innovation in the private sector. A major extension of the traditional argument is that we base the innovation inducement mechanism not only on the response to changes in

18. Hans P. Binswanger, "A Microeconomic Approach to Induced Innovation," *Economic Journal* 84 (December 1974):940–58; and "The Microeconomics of Induced Technical Change," *Induced Innovation*, ed. Binswanger and Ruttan, pp. 91–127. Two particularly bothersome assumptions in the Kennedy growth-theory tradition of induced innovation were those of (a) an exogenously given budget for research and development and (b) a stable "fundamental" trade-off or transformation function (the IPF) between the rate of labor augmentation (or reduction in labor requirements) and the rate of capital augmentation (or reduction in capital requirements).

19. For an attempt to assess the role of the public sector as a source of technical change see Richard R. Nelson, "Government Stimulus of Technological Progress: Lessons from American History," *Government and Technical Progress: A Cross-Industry Analysis*, ed. Richard R. Nelson (New York: Pergamon Press, 1982), pp. 451–82.

the market prices of profit-maximizing firms but also on the response by research scientists and administrators in public institutions to resource endowments and economic change.

We hypothesize that technical change is guided along an efficient path by price signals in the market, provided that the prices efficiently reflect changes in the demand and supply of products and factors and that there exists effective interaction among farmers, public research institutions, and private agricultural supply firms. Farmers are induced, by shifts in relative prices, to search for technical alternatives that save the increasingly scarce factors of production. They press the public research institutions to develop the new technology and also demand that agricultural supply firms supply modern technical inputs that substitute for the more scarce factors. Perceptive scientists and science administrators respond by making available new technical possibilities and new inputs that enable farmers profitably to substitute the increasingly abundant factors for increasingly scarce factors, thereby guiding the demand of farmers for unit cost reduction in a socially optimal direction.

The dialectic interaction among farmers and research scientists and administrators is likely to be most effective when farmers are organized into politically effective local and regional farm "bureaus" or farmers' associations. The response of the public sector research and extension programs to farmers' demand is likely to be greatest when the agricultural research system is highly decentralized, as in the United States. In the United States, for example, each of the state agricultural experiment stations has tended to view its function, at least in part, as to maintain the competitive position of agriculture in its state relative to agriculture in other states. Similarly, national policymakers may regard investment in agricultural research as an investment designed to maintain the country's competitive position in world markets or to improve the economic viability of the agricultural sector producing import substitutes. Given effective farmer organizations and a mission- or client-oriented experiment station system, the competitive model of firm behavior can be usefully extended to explain the response of experiment station administrators and research scientists to economic opportunities.

In this public sector–induced innovation model, the response of research scientists and administrators represents the critical link in the inducement mechanism. The model does not imply that it is necessary for individual scientists or research administrators in public institutions to respond consciously to market prices, or directly to farmers' demands for research results in the selection of research objectives. They may, in fact, be motivated primarily by a drive for professional achievement and recognition.[20] It is

---

20. For a useful analysis of the problem of resource allocation and productivity within bureaucratic organizations and the response of bureaucratic organizations to market and nonmarket incentives, see Stephen A. Hoenack, *Economic Behavior within Organizations* (Cambridge: Cambridge University Press, 1983). See also William A. Niskanen, "The Peculiar

necessary only if there exists an effective incentive mechanism to reward the scientists or administrators, materially or by prestige, for their contributions to the solution of significant problems in the society.[21] Under these conditions, it seems reasonable to hypothesize that the scientists and administrators of public sector research programs do respond to the needs of society in an attempt to direct the results of their activity to public purposes. Furthermore, we hypothesize that secular changes in relative factor and product prices convey much of the information regarding the relative priorities which society places on the goals of research.

The response in the public research sector is not limited to the field of applied science. Scientists trying to solve practical problems consult with or ask cooperation of those working in more basic fields. If the basic scientists respond to the requests of the applied researchers, they are in effect responding to the needs of society. It is not uncommon that major breakthroughs in basic science are created through the process of solving the problems raised by research workers in the more applied fields.[22] It appears reasonable, therefore, to hypothesize, as a result of the interactions among the basic and applied sciences and the process by which public funds are allocated to research, that basic research tends to be directed also toward easing the limitations on production imposed by relatively scarce factors.

We do not argue, however, that technical change is wholly of an induced character. There is a supply (an exogenous) dimension to the process as well as a demand (an endogenous) dimension. In addition to the effects of resource endowments and growth in demand, technical change reflects the progress of general science and technology. Progress in general science (or scientific innovation) which lowers the cost of technical and entrepreneurial innovations may have influences on technical change unrelated to changes in factor pro-

---

Economics of Bureaucracy," *American Economic Review* 58 (May 1968):293–305; Maury E. Bredahl, W. Keith Bryant, and Vernon W. Ruttan, "Behavior and Productivity Implications of Institutional and Project Funding of Research," *American Journal of Agricultural Economics* 62 (August 1980):371–83.

21. Incentive is a major issue in many developing economies. In spite of limited scientific and technical manpower many countries have not succeeded in developing a system of economic and professional rewards that permits them to have access to, or make effective use of, the resources of scientific and technical manpower that are potentially available.

22. The symbiotic relationship between basic and applied research can be illustrated by the relation between work at the International Rice Research Institute in (a) genetics and plant physiology and (b) plant breeding. The geneticist and the physiologist are involved in research designed to advance understanding of the physiological processes by which plant nutrients are transformed into grain yield and of the genetic mechanisms or processes involved in the transmission from parents to progenies of the physiological characteristics of the rice plant which affect grain yield. The rice breeders use this knowledge from genetics and plant physiology in the design of crosses and the selection of plants with the desired growth characteristics, agronomic traits, and nutritional value. The work in plant physiology and genetics is responsive to the need of the plant breeder for advances in knowledge related to the mission of breeding more productive varieties of rice. For a model of the relationships between basic and applied science see Ruttan, *Agricultural Research Policy,* pp. 56–60.

portions and product demand.[23] Even in these cases, the rate of adoption and the impact on productivity of autonomous or exogenous changes in technology will be strongly influenced by the conditions of resource supply and product demand, as these forces are reflected through factor and product markets.

Thus the classical problem of resource allocation, which was rejected as an adequate basis for agricultural productivity and output growth in the high-payoff input model, is, in this context, treated as central to the agricultural development process. Under conditions of static technology, improvements in resource allocation represent a weak source of economic growth. The efficient allocation of resources to open up new sources of growth is, however, essential to the agricultural development process.

A Model of Induced Technical Change in Agriculture

A model of induced technical innovation, consistent with the research resource allocation process at both private firms and public institutions, is illustrated in Figure 4-2. The model incorporates the characteristics of both factor substitution and complementarity associated with advances of biological and mechanical technologies.

The process of advance in mechanical technology is shown in the left-hand panel of Figure 4-2. I_0^* represents the innovation possibility curve (IPC) at time zero; it is the envelope of less elastic unit isoquants that correspond, for example, to different types of harvesting machinery. A certain technology—a reaper, for example—represented by I_0 is invented when the price ratio XX prevails for some time. Correspondingly, the minimum-cost equilibrium point is determined at P with a certain optimal combination of land, labor, and nonhuman power to operate the reaper. In general, the technology that enables cultivation of a larger area per worker requires a higher animal or mechanical power per worker. This implies the complementary relationship between land and power, which may be drawn as a line representing a certain combination of land and power $[A, M]$. In this simplified presentation, land-cum-power is assumed to be substituted for labor in response to a change in wage relative to an index of land and power prices, though, of course, in actual practice land and power are substitutable to some extent.

I_1^* represents the IPC of period 1. Let us assume that from period 0 to 1 labor becomes more scarce relative to land, for example, because of the transfer of labor to industry in the course of economic development, resulting in the decline in land rent relative to wage rates. Also assume that the price of power declines relative to the wage rate for labor because of the supply of a cheaper power source from industry. The change in the price ratio from XX to ZZ induces the invention of another technology—such as the combine—

23. Richard R. Nelson, "The Economics of Invention: A Survey of the Literature," *Journal of Business* 32 (April 1959):101–27; Jacob Schmookler, *Invention and Economic Growth* (Cambridge, Mass.: Harvard University Press, 1966).

FIGURE 4-2. A model of induced technical change in agriculture.

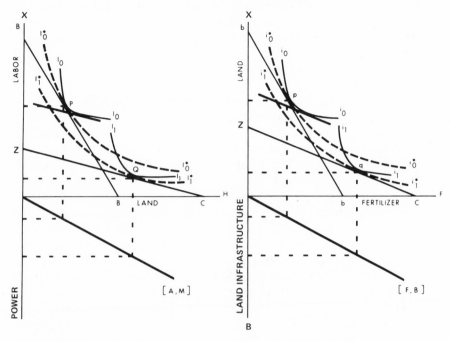

represented by I_1, which enables a farm worker to cultivate a larger land area using a larger amount of power.

The process of advance in biological technology is illustrated in the right-hand panel of Figure 4-2. Here, i_0^* represents an IPC embracing less elastic land-fertilizer isoquants, such as i_0, corresponding to different crop varieties and cultural practices. When the fertilizer-land price ratio declines from xx to zz from time period 0 to 1, a new technology—a more fertilizer-responsive variety, for example—represented by i_1 is developed along i_1^*, the IPC of time 1. In general, the technology that facilitates substitution of fertilizer for land, such as fertilizer-responsive, high-yielding crop varieties, requires better control of water and better land management. This suggests a complementary relationship between fertilizer and land infrastructure in the form of irrigation and drainage systems, as implied by the linear relationship $[F, B]$.[24]

24. In the model of induced innovation in Figure 4.2 we have treated, for pedagogical purposes, the impact of advances in mechanical and biological technology on factor ratios as if they were completely separable, even though they are interrelated. Furthermore, some biological innovations are labor-saving and some mechanical innovations are land-saving. Also, we do not deny the possibility of autonomous or innate bias in technical change unrelated to changes in factor prices. If, for example, the rate of advance in mechanical technology exceeds the rate of advance in biological technology, because of autonomous bias in technological potential, it may force a rise in the land-labor ratio even if there is no change in the land-labor price ratio. See, for example, the discussion by Colin G. Thirtle, ''Induced Innovation in United States Agriculture''

In later chapters the model presented in this section is used to interpret the process of agricultural development in the United States and Japan (Chapter 7) and in Taiwan, Korea, and the Philippines (Chapters 9 and 10). The model provides powerful insight into the development process in both developed and developing countries.[25]

Dynamic Sequences

It would be misleading if the model illustrated in Figure 4-1 were to leave the impression that induced innovation proceeds as a smooth adjustment along the IPC in response to change in relative factor prices. In the dynamic process of development, the emergence of imbalance or disequilibrium is a critical element in inducing technical change and economic growth. Disequilibrium among the several elements in the system creates the bottlenecks that focus the attention of scientists, inventors, entrepreneurs, and public administrators on the solution of problems for attaining more efficient resource allocation.[26]

The introduction of reapers in U.S. agriculture in the mid-nineteenth century, for example, was induced as a result of an imbalance in the labor requirements between the planting and harvesting operations. In U.S. agriculture, as the frontier pushed rapidly to the west, land became progressively abundant relative to labor. In order to prevent crop spoilage the reaper was invented, in response to a compelling need to harvest wheat crops within a

---

(Ph. D. dissertation, Columbia University, 1982), p. 183; also, Thirtle, "The Microeconomic Approach to Induced Innovation: A Reformulation of the Hayami and Ruttan Model," *Manchester School of Economic and Social Studies* (forthcoming, 1984), and "Induced Innovation in United States Field Crops, 1939–78," *Journal of Agricultural Economics* (January 1985).

25. The induced innovation model has also been tested successfully against the agricultural development experience of Denmark, France, Germany, and Great Britain. See Vernon W. Ruttan, Hans P. Binswanger, Yujiro Hayami, William W. Wade, and Adolf Weber, "Factor Productivity and Growth: A Historical Interpretation," *Induced Innovation*, ed. Binswanger and Ruttan, pp. 44–80; William W. Wade, *Institutional Determinants of Technical Change and Agricultural Productivity Growth: Denmark, France, and Great Britain, 1870–1965* (New York: Arno Press, 1981). Several recent studies have demonstrated the power of the induced innovation model in interpreting the process of technical change in the industrial sector. See, for example, William H. Phillips, "Induced Innovation and Economic Performance in Late Victorian British Industry," *Journal of Economic History* 42 (March 1982):97–103.

26. Rosenberg has suggested a theory of induced technical change based on "obvious and compelling need" to overcome the constraints on growth instead of relative factor scarcity and factor relative prices. See Nathan Rosenberg, "The Direction of Technological Change: Inducement Mechanisms and Focusing Devices," *Economic Development and Cultural Change* 18 (October 1969):1–24. The Rosenberg model is consistent with the model suggested here, since his "obvious and compelling need" is reflected in the market through relative factor prices. C. Peter Timmer has pointed out (in an October 9, 1970, letter) that in a linear programming sense the constraints that give rise to the "obvious and compelling need" for technical innovation in the Rosenberg model represent the "dual" of the factor prices used in our model. For further discussion of the relationships between Rosenberg's approach and that outlined in this section see Yujiro Hayami and Vernon W. Ruttan, "Professor Rosenberg and the Direction of Technological Change: A Comment," *Economic Development and Cultural Change* 21 (January 1973):352–55.

limited number of days. It was designed to solve the harvesting bottleneck in an economic environment in which the supply of land was expanding more rapidly than the supply of labor.[27] Inventive efforts were focused on solving this obvious need of farmers resulting from the relative labor scarcity in the economy.

A solution to the problems that result from one bottleneck generally creates another bottleneck. This acts as a device for transmitting technical change from one process of production to another. A classical example may be seen in the English cotton industry in the early period of the Industrial Revolution: "Key's flying shuttle led to the need for speeding up spinning operations; the eventual innovations in spinning in turn created the shortage of weaving capacity which finally culminated in Cartwright's introduction of the power loom."[28]

Progress in farm mechanization is no exception to this general pattern. Original models of reapers saved cutting labor but made raking and binding operations the bottleneck. The successive introduction of self-raking reapers and binders clearly illustrates the process of cumulative sequences in technical change (see Figure 4-1).[29] Mechanization of harvesting also created a bottleneck in threshing, calling for the introduction of power threshers. Through these cumulative sequences, the United States succeeded in developing a mechanical technology in agricultural production which facilitated the substitution of the relatively more abundant land and capital for the relatively more scarce labor.

The linkages between innovations in the nonagricultural sector with advances in agricultural technology are also critical. The secular decline in fertilizer prices, resulting from cost-reducing innovations in the fertilizer industry, served to focus attention on the limited capacity of traditional grain varieties to respond to higher levels of fertilizer. The decline in the price of fertilizer, relative to the prices of output and land, has induced efforts by experiment station researchers to overcome this bottleneck by developing more fertilizer-responsive grain varieties.

27. This bottleneck would not have emerged had not land become more abundant relative to labor. Technically it would have been possible to prevent crop spoilage at reduced acreage while maintaining the same level of output by developing a labor-intensive technology based on scientific crop rotation and commercial fertilizers; in fact, such technology was developed in Germany and other countries in Europe in the mid-nineteenth century. U.S. farmers did not adopt such labor-intensive technology because it was less profitable for their relative factor prices.

28. Rosenberg's historical reconnaissance gives an excellent perspective on this process. The quotation is in Nathan Rosenberg, "The Direction of Technological Change: Inducement Mechanisms and Focusing Devices," *Economic Development and Cultural Change* 18 (October 1969):1–24.

29. The process of cumulative synthesis of individual innovations in the evolution of major or strategic innovations or sequences of inventions is described in the classical study by Abbott Payson Usher, *A History of Mechanical Inventions* (Cambridge, Mass: Harvard University Press, 1954), pp. 56–83.

INDUCED INSTITUTIONAL INNOVATION

The disequilibria in economic relationships resulting from technical change represent a major source of institutional change. For example, technical change in fertilizer production resulted in a decline in the price of fertilizer, both in real terms and relative to the price of land, that has persisted in most industrialized countries for over a century. But traditional grain varieties were characterized by only limited yield response to higher levels of fertilization. These disequilibria induced the growth, in Germany, the United States, Japan, and the other industrial countries, of a system of national and regional agricultural research institutions that had as a major objective the development of crop varieties capable of responding to higher levels of fertilization. More recently similar changes have led to the strengthening of national agricultural research systems and to the establishment of a network of international agricultural research institutes in the tropics (Chapter 9).

The public research institutions that have been a major source of growth in agricultural output obtain their resources in the political marketplace and allocate their resources through bureaucratic mechanisms. The success of the theory of induced technical change gives rise, therefore, to the need for understanding the sources of institutional innovation—including the entrepreneurial behavior of politicians and bureaucrats.

In this section we elaborate a theory of institutional innovation in which shifts in the demand for institutional innovation are induced by changes in relative resource endowments and by technical change. We also consider the impact of advances in social science knowledge and of cultural endowments on the supply of institutional change. After examining the forces that act to shift the demand and supply of institutional innovation we then present the elements of a more general model of institutional change.

What Is Institutional Innovation?

Institutions are the rules of a society or of organizations that facilitate coordination among people by helping them form expectations which each person can reasonably hold in dealing with others. They reflect the conventions that have evolved in different societies regarding the behavior of individuals and groups relative to their own behavior and the behavior of others.[30]

---

30. There is considerable disagreement regarding the meaning of the term *institution*. A distinction is often made between the concepts of institution and organization. The broad view which includes both concepts is most useful for our purpose and is consistent with the view expressed by both John R. Commons, *The Economics of Collective Action* (New York: Macmillan, 1950), p. 24, and Frank H. Knight, "Institutionalism and Empiricism in Economics," *American Economic Reveiw* 42 (May 1952):51. Our definition also encompasses the classification employed by Lance E. Davis and Douglass C. North, *Institutional Change and American Economic Growth* (Cambridge: Cambridge University Press, 1971), pp. 8 and 9. We employ the more inclusive definition so as to be able to consider changes in the rules or conventions that govern behavior (a) within economic units such as families, firms, and bureaucracies, (b) among economic units as in the cases of the rules that govern market relationships, and (c) between

In the area of economic relations they have a crucial role in establishing expectations about the rights to use resources in economic activities and about the partitioning of the income streams resulting from economic activity. Carlisle Ford Runge has noted that "institutions provide *assurance* respecting the actions of others, and give order and stability to expectations in the complex and uncertain world of economic relations."[31]

In order to perform the essential role of forming reasonable expectations in dealings among people, institutions must be stable for an extended time period. But institutions, like technology, must also change if development is to occur. Anticipation of the latent gains to be realized by overcoming the disequilibria resulting from changes in factor endowments, product demand, and technical change is a powerful inducement to institutional innovation.[32] Institutions that have been efficient in generating growth in the past may, over time, come to direct their efforts primarily to protecting the vested interests of some of their members by maintaining the status quo and thus become obstacles to further economic development.[33] The growing disequilibria in resource allocation resulting from institutional constraints generated by economic growth create opportunities for political entrepreneurs or leaders to organize collective action to bring about institutional changes.

Our perspective on the sources of demand for institutional change is similar to the traditional Marxian view.[34] Marx considered technological change as

---

economic units and their environment, as in the case of the relationship between a firm and a regulatory agency.

31. Carlisle Ford Runge, "Institutions and Common Property Externalities: The Assurance Problem in Economic Development" (Ph.D. dissertation, University of Wisconsin–Madison, 1981), p. xvi. Formal analysis of the role of institutions in providing assurance of stability in economic relationships emerged from dissatisfaction with the implications of the assumption of strict dominance of individual strategy in modern welfare economics. See Amartya K. Sen, "Isolation, Assurance and the Social Rate of Discount," *Quarterly Journal of Economics* 81 (February 1967):112–24; Carlisle Ford Runge, "Common Property Externalities: Isolation, Assurance, and Resource Depletion in a Traditional Grazing Context," *American Journal of Agricultural Economics* 63 (November 1981):595–606. In a less formal treatment, North argues, in a chapter titled "Ideology and the Free Rider Problem," that shared ideological and ethical perspectives provide assurance that is lacking in models built on the dominance of individual strategies. Douglass C. North, *Structure and Change in Economic History* (New York: W. W. Norton, 1981), pp. 45–58.

32. See Douglass C. North and Robert Paul Thomas, "An Economic Theory of the Growth of the Western World," *Economic History Review* 23 (April 1970):1–17, and *The Rise of the Western World* (London: Cambridge University Press, 1973). Also Theodore W. Schultz, "The Value of the Ability to Deal with Disequilibria," *Journal of Economic Literature* 13 (September 1975):827–46.

33. The role of special interest "distributional coalitions" in slowing society's capacity to adopt new technology and reallocate resources in response to changing conditions is the central theme in Mancur Olson, *The Rise and Decline of Nations* (New Haven: Yale University Press, 1982), p. 74.

34. "At a certain stage of their development, the material forces of production in society come in conflict with the existing relations of production, or—what is but a legal expression for the same thing—with the property relations within which they had been at work before. From forms of development of the forces of production these relations turn into their fetters. Then comes the period of social revolution. With the change of the economic foundation the entire

the primary source of institutional change. Our view is somewhat more complex in that we consider that changes in factor endowments and product demand are equally important sources of institutional change. Nor is our definition of institutional change limited to the dramatic or revolutionary changes of the type anticipated by Marx. Rather, we share with Lance Davis and Douglass North the view that basic institutions such as property rights and markets are more typically altered through the cumulation of "secondary" or incremental institutional changes such as modifications in contractual relations or shifts in the boundaries between market and nonmarket activities.[35]

There is a supply dimension as well as a demand dimension in institutional change. Collective action leading to changes in the supply of institutional innovations involves struggles among various vested interest groups. Clearly, the process is much more complex than the clear-cut, two-class conflict between the property owners and the propertyless as assumed by Marx. In our view, the supply of institutional innovations is strongly influenced by the cost of achieving social consensus (or of suppressing opposition). How costly a form of institutional change is to be accepted in a society depends on the power structure among vested interest groups. It also depends critically on cultural tradition and ideology, such as nationalism, that make certain institutional arrangements more easily accepted than others.

Advances in knowledge in the social sciences (and in related professions such as law, adminstration, planning, and social service) can reduce the cost of institutional change in a somewhat similar manner as advances in the natural sciences reduce the cost of technical change. Education, both general and technical, that facilitates a better understanding among people of their common interests can also reduce the cost of institutional innovation.

Our insistence that important advances in the understanding of the processes of institutional innovation and diffusion can be achieved by treating institutional change as endogenous to the economic system represents a clear departure from the tradition of modern analytical economics.[36] This does not

---

immense superstructure is more or less rapidly transformed." Karl Marx, *A Contribution to the Critique of Political Economy* (Chicago: Charles H. Kerr & Co., 1913), pp. 11–12. For a discussion of the role of technology in Marxian thought see Nathan Rosenberg, *Inside the Black Box: Technology and Economics* (New York: Cambridge University Press, 1982), pp. 34–51.

35. Davis and North, *Institutional Change and American Economic Growth*, p. 9.

36. The orthodox view of a generation ago was expressed by Paul A. Samuelson, *Foundations of Economic Analysis*, Harvard Economic Studies, vol. 80 (Cambridge, Mass.: Harvard University Press, 1948): "The auxiliary [institutional] constraints imposed upon the variables are not themselves the proper subject of welfare conomics but must be taken as given" (pp. 221–22). Contrast this with the more recent statement by Andrew Schotter, *The Economic Theory of Social Institutions* (Cambridge: Cambridge University Press, 1981): "We view welfare economics as a study . . . that ranks the system of rules which dictate social behavior" (p. 6). There are now five fairly well-defined "political economy" traditions that have attempted to break out of the constraints imposed by traditional welfare economics and treat institutional change as endogenous. These include (a) the theory of property rights, (b) the theory of economic regulation, (c) the theory of interest group rent-seeking, (d) the liberal-pluralist theories of government, and (e) the neo-Marxian theories of the state. In the property rights theories the government plays a

mean that we abandon analytical economics. On the contrary, we try to expand the scope of modern analytical economics by treating institutional change as endogenous.

Demand for Institutional Innovation—Property Rights and Market Institutions

In some cases the demand for institutional innovation can be satisfied by the development of new forms of property rights, more efficient market institutions, or evolutionary changes arising out of direct contracting by individuals at the level of the community or the firm. In other cases, in which externalities are involved, substantial political resources may have to be brought to bear to organize nonmarket institutions to provide for the supply of public goods.

In this section we illustrate, from the agricultural history of a number of countries, how changes in factor endowments, technical change, and growth in product demand have induced change in property rights and contractual arrangements in order to promote more efficient resource allocation through the market.

The agricultural revolution that occurred in England between the fifteenth and the nineteenth centuries involved a substantial increase in the productivity of land and labor. It was accompanied by the enclosure of open fields and the replacement of small peasant cultivators, who held their land from manorial lords, by a system in which large farmers used hired labor to farm the land they leased from the landlords. The First Enclosure Movement, in the fifteenth and sixteenth centuries, resulted in the conversion of open arable fields and commons to private pasture in areas suitable for grazing. It was induced by expansion in the export demand for wool. The Second Enclosure Movement in the eighteenth century involved conversion of communally managed arable land into privately operated units. It is now agreed that it was largely induced by the growing disequilibrium between the fixed institutional rent that landlords received under copyhold tenures (with lifetime contracts) and the higher economic rents expected from adoption of new technology which became more profitable as a consequence of higher grain prices and lower wages. When the land was enclosed there was a redistribution of income from farmers to landowners, and the disequilibrium was reduced or eliminated.[37]

---

relatively passive role; the economic theory of regulation focuses on the electoral process; the rent-seeking and liberal-pluralist theories concentrate on both electoral and bureaucratic choice processes; and the theory of the state attempts to incorporate electoral, legislative choice, and bureaucratic choice processes. For a review and criticism see Gordon C. Rausser, Erik Lichtenberg, and Ralph Lattimore, "Developments in Theory and Empirical Applications of Endogenous Governmental Behavior," *New Directions in Econometric Modeling and Forecasting in U.S. Agriculture,* ed. Gordon C. Rausser (New York: Elsevier, 1982), pp. 547–614.

37. There has been a continuing debate among students of English agricultural history about whether the higher rents that landowners received after enclosure was because (a) enclosed farming was more efficient than open-field farming, or (b) enclosures redistributed income from

In nineteenth-century Thailand, the opening up of the nation for international trade and the reduction in shipping rates to Europe resulted in a sharp increase in the demand for rice. The land available for rice production, which had been abundant, became more scarce. Investment in land development for rice production became profitable. The response was a major transformation of property rights. Traditional rights in human property (corvée and slavery) were replaced by more precise private property rights in land (fee-simple titles).[38]

In Japan, at the beginning of the feudal Tokugawa period (1603–1867), peasants' rights to cropland had been limited to the right to till the soil with the obligation to pay a feudal land tax in kind. As the population grew, commercialization progressed and irrigation and technology were developed to make intensive farming more profitable. Some peasants divided their holdings into smaller units and leased them out to former servants or extended family members. Some accumulated land through mortgaging arrangements that made other peasants de facto tenants. As a result of the accumulation of illegal leasing and mortgaging practices, peasants' property rights in land approximated those of a fee-simple title by the end of the Tokugawa period. These rights were readily converted to the modern private property system in the succeeding Meiji period.[39]

Research conducted by Yujiro Hayami and Masao Kikuchi in the Philippines during the late 1970s has enabled us to examine a contemporary example of the interrelated effects of changes in resource endowments and technical change on the demand for institutional change in land tenure and labor relations.[40] The case is particularly interesting because the institutional innovations occurred as a result of private contracting among individuals. The study is unique in that it is based on a rigorous analysis of microeconomic data in a village over a period of about twenty years.

Changes in technology and resource endowments.   Between 1956 and 1976, rice production per hectare in the study village rose dramatically, from 2.5 to 6.7 metric tons per hectare per year. This increase resulted from two technical innovations. In 1958, the national irrigation system was extended to the village, which permitted double-cropping to replace single-cropping,

---

farmers to landowners. See Jonathan D. Chambers and G. E. Mingay, *The Agricultural Revolution, 1750–1880* (London: B. T. Batsford, and New York: Schocken Books, 1966); Carl J. Dahlman, *The Open Field System and Beyond: A Property Rights Analysis of an Economic Institution* (Cambridge: Cambridge University Press, 1980); Robert C. Allen, "The Efficiency and Distributional Consequences of Eighteenth Century Enclosures," *Economic Journal* 92 (December 1982):937–53.

38. David Feeny, *The Political Economy of Productivity: Thai Agricultural Development, 1880–1975* (Vancouver: University of British Columbia Press, 1982).

39. Hayami and Kikuchi, *Asian Village Economy at the Crossroads*, p. 28.

40. Masao Kikuchi and Yujiro Hayami, "Inducements to Institutional Innovations in an Agrarian Community," *Economic Development and Cultural Change* 29 (October 1980):21–36; Hayami and Kikuchi, *Asian Village Economy at the Crossroads*, pp. 99–123.

thereby doubling the annual production per hectare. The second major technical change was the introduction in the late 1960s of the modern high-yielding rice varieties. The diffusion of modern varieties was accompanied by increased use of fertilizer and pesticides and by the adoption of improved cultural practices such as straight-row planting and intensive weeding.

Population growth in the village was rapid. Between 1966 and 1976 the number of households rose from 66 to 109 and the population rose from 383 to 464, while cultivated area remained virtually constant. The number of landless laborer households increased from 20 to 54. In 1976 half of the households in the village had no land to cultivate, not even land for rent. The average farm size declined from 2.3 to 2.0 hectares.

The land is farmed primarily by tenants. In 1976 only 1.7 of the 108 hectares of cropland in the village were owned by village residents. Traditionally, share tenancy was the most common form of tenure. In both 1956 and 1966, 70 percent of the land was farmed under share tenure arrangements. In 1963, a new agricultural land reform code was passed which was designed to break the political power of the traditional landed elite and to provide greater incentives to peasant producers of basic food crops.[41] A major feature of the new legislation was an arrangement that permitted tenants to initiate a shift from share tenure to leasehold, with rent under the leasehold set at 25 percent of the average yield for the previous three years. Implementation of the code between the mid-1960s and the mid-1970s resulted in a decline in the percentage of land farmed under share tenure to 30 percent.

Institutional innovation. The shift from share tenure to lease tenure was not, however, the only change in tenure relationships that occurred between 1966 and 1976. There was a sharp increase in the number of plots farmed under subtenancy arrangements. The number increased from one in 1956, to five in 1966, and to sixteen in 1976. Subtenancy is illegal under the land reform code. The subtenancy arrangements are usually made without the formal consent of the landowner. All cases of subtenancy were on land farmed under a leasehold arrangement. The most common subtenancy arrangement was fifty-fifty sharing of costs and output.

It was hypothesized that an incentive for the emergence of the subtenancy institution was that the rent paid to landlords under the leasehold arrangement

41. Although the passage and implementation of the Land Reform Code of 1963 was exogenous to the economy of the village, the land reform of the 1960s has been interpreted as the result of efforts by an emerging industrial elite simultaneously to break the political power of the more conservative landowning elite and to provide incentives to peasant producers to respond to the rapid growth in demand for marketable surpluses of wage goods, primarily rice and maize, needed to sustain urban-industrial development. Thus the Land Reform Code can be viewed as an institutional innovation designed to facilitate realization of the opportunities for economic growth that could be realized through rapid urban-industrial development. See Vernon W. Ruttan, "Equity and Producivity Issues in Modern Agrarian Reform Legislation," *Economic Problems of Agriculture in Industrialized Societies,* ed. Ugo Papi and Charles Nunn (London: Macmillan; New York: St. Martin's Press, 1969), pp. 581–600.

TABLE 4-2. Factor shares of rice output per hectare, 1976 wet season

	Number of plots	Area (ha)	Rice output	Current inputs	Factor shares[a]			Labor	Capital[b]	Operators' surplus
					Land					
					Landowner	Sublessor	Total			
				‑‑‑‑‑‑‑‑kg/ha‑‑‑‑‑‑‑‑						
Leasehold land	44	67.7	2,889 (100.0)	657 (22.7)	567 (19.6)	0 (0)	567 (19.6)	918 (31.8)	337 (11.7)	410 (14.2)
Share tenancy land	30	29.7	2,749 (100.0)	697 (25.3)	698 (25.4)	0 (0)	698 (25.4)	850 (30.9)	288 (10.5)	216 (7.9)
Subtenancy land	16	9.1	3,447 (100.0)	801 (23.2)	504 (14.6)	801[c] (23.2)	1,305 (37.8)	1,008 (29.3)	346 (10.1)	−13 (−0.4)

Source: Yujiro Hayami and Masao Kikuchi, Asian Village Economy at the Crossroads, An Economic Approach to Institutional Change (Tokyo: University of Tokyo Press, 1981, and Baltimore: Johns Hopkins University Press, 1982), pp. 111–13.
[a]Percentage shares are shown in parentheses.
[b]Sum of irrigation fee and paid and/or imputed rentals of carabao, tractor, and other machines.
[c]Rents to subleasors in the case of pledged plots are imputed by applying the interest rate of 40 percent crop season (a mode in the interest rate distribution in the village).

was below the equilibirum rent—the level that would reflect both the higher yields of rice obtained with the new technology and the lower wage rates implied by the increase in population pressure against the land.

To test this hypothesis, market prices were used to compute the value of the unpaid factor inputs (family labor and capital) for different tenure arrangements during the 1976 wet season. The results indicate that the share-to-land was lowest and the operators' surplus was highest for the land under leasehold tenancy. In contrast, the share-to-land was highest and no surplus was left for the operator who cultivated the land under the subtenancy arrangement (Table 4-2). Indeed, the share-to-land when the land was farmed under subtenancy was very close to the sum of the share-to-land plus the operators' surplus under the other tenure arrangement.

The results are consistent with the hypothesis. A substantial portion of the economic rent was captured by the leasehold tenants in the form of operators' surplus. On the land farmed under a subtenancy arrangement, the rent was shared between the leaseholder and the landlord.

A second institutional change, induced by higher yields and the increase in population pressure, has been the emergence of a new pattern of employer-labor relationship between farm operators and landless workers. According to the traditional system called *hunusan,* laborers who participated in the harvesting and threshing activity received a one-sixth share of the paddy (rough rice) harvest. By 1976, most of the farmers (83 percent) adopted a system called *gamma,* in which participation in the harvesting operation was limited to workers who had performed the weeding operation without receiving wages.

The emergence of the *gamma* system can be interpreted as an institutional innovation designed to reduce the wage rate for harvesting to a level equal to the marginal productivity of labor. In the 1950s, when the rice yield per hectare was low and labor was less abundant, the one-sixth share may have approximated an equilibrium wage level. With the higher yields and more abundant supply of labor, the one-sixth share became larger than the marginal product of labor in the harvesting operation.[42]

To test the hypothesis that the *gamma* system was adopted rapidly primarily because it represented an institutional innovation that permitted farm operators to equate the harvesters' share of output to the marginal productivity of labor, imputed wage costs were compared with the actual harvesters' shares (Table 4-3). The results indicate that a substantial gap existed between the imputed wage for the harvesters' labor alone and the actual harvesters'

42. Real wages for agricultural labor declined significantly between the mid-1950s and the mid-1960s in the Philippines. See Azizur Rahman Khan, "Growth and Inequality in the Rural Philippines," *Poverty and Landlessness in Rural Asia* (Geneva: International Labour Office, 1977), pp. 233–49. Thus, although we cannot be certain that the labor market was in equilibrium in the 1950s, it is clear that the degree of disequilibrium widened, as a result of both higher yields and lower wage rates, before the introduction and diffusion of the *gamma* system.

TABLE 4-3.   Comparison between the imputed value of harvesters' share and the imputed cost of *gamma* labor

	Based on employers' data	Based on employees' data
Number of working days of *gamma* labor (days/ha)[a]		
Weeding	20.9	18.3
Harvesting/threshing	33.6	33.6
Imputed cost of *gamma* labor (P/ha)[b]		
Weeding	167.2	146.4
Harvesting/threshing	369.6	369.6
(1) Total	536.8	516.0
Actual share of harvesters:		
In kind (kg/ha)[c]	504.0	549.0
(2) Imputed value (P/ha)[d]	504.0	549.0
(2) − (1)	−32.8	33.0

Source: Yujiro Hayami and Masao Kikuchi, *Asian Village Economy at the Crossroads: An Economic Approach to Institutional Change* (Tokyo: University of Tokyo Press, 1981, and Baltimore: Johns Hopkins University Press, 1982), p. 121.
[a]Includes labor of family members who worked as *gamma* laborers.
[b]Imputation using market wage rates (daily wage = P8.0 for weeding, P11.0 for harvesting).
[c]One-sixth of output per hectare.
[d]Imputation using market prices (1 kg = P1).

shares. This gap was eliminated if the imputed wages for harvesting and weeding labor were added.

Those results are consistent with the hypothesis that the changes in institutional arrangements governing the use of production factors were induced when disequilibria between the marginal returns and the marginal costs of factor inputs occurred as a result of changes in factor endowments and technical change. Institutional change, therefore, was directed toward the establishment of a new equilibrium in factor markets.

Efficiency and equity implications.   It is important to recognize that subtenancy and *gamma* contracts were the institutional innovations to facilitate more efficient resource allocations through voluntary agreements by assigning more complete private property rights. The land reform laws gave tenants strong protection of their tenancy rights with the result that a part of land property rights, which is the right to continue tilling the soil at a rent lower than the marginal product of land, was assigned to tenant operators. But the laws prohibited tenants from renting their land to someone else who might use it more efficiently, when they became elderly or found more profitable off-farm employment, for example. Subtenancy was developed to reduce such inefficiency resulting from the institutional rigidity in the land rental market based on the land reform programs. Likewise, the *gamma* system was developed to counteract the institutional rigidity in the labor market based on the traditional custom in the rural community of a fixed harvester's share.

It might appear that these institutional innovations increased efficiency at the expense of equity. But if the subtenancy system had not been developed, the route would have been closed for some of the landless laborers to become farm operators and use their entrepreneurial abilities more profitably. If the implicit wage rate for harvesting work had been raised in the absence of the *gamma* contract, it might have encouraged mechanization in threshing and thereby reduced employment and labor earnings. It must be recognized that the institutional innovations to develop more efficient markets by assigning more complete private property rights do not necessarily impair equity, as is often argued by Marxist and populist critiques against private market institutions.

In the case reviewed here the induced innovation process leading toward the establishment of equilibrium in factor markets occurred very rapidly even though many of the transactions—between landlords, tenants, and laborers—were less than fully monetized. Informal contractual arrangements or agreements were used. The subleasing and the *gamma* labor contract evolved without the mobilization of substantial political activity or bureaucratic effort. Indeed, the subleasing arrangement evolved in spite of legal prohibition. When substantial political and bureaucratic resources must be mobilized to bring about technical or institutional change, the changes occur much more slowly, as in the cases of the English enclosure movements and the Thai and Japanese property rights cases referred to at the beginning of this section.

The Demand for Institutional Innovation—Nonmarket Institutions for the Supply of Public Goods

The examples of institutional change advanced in the previous section, such as the enclosure in England and the evolution of private property rights in land in Japan and Thailand, have contributed to the development of a more efficient market system. Institutional changes of this type are profitable for society only if the costs involved in the assignment and protection of rights are smaller than the gains from better resource allocation. If those costs are very high, it may be necessary to design nonmarket institutions in order to achieve more efficient resource allocation.[43]

In Japan, for example, although the system of private property rights was

43. Harold Demsetz has pointed out that the relative costs of using market and political institutions is rarely given explicit consideration in the literature on market failure. An appropriate way of interpreting the "public goods" versus "private goods" issue is to ask whether the costs of providing a market are too high relative to the cost of nonmarket alternatives. Harold Demsetz, "The Exchange and Enforcement of Property Rights," *Journal of Law and Economics* 7 (October 1964):11–26. A similar point is made by Leonid Hurwicz, "Organized Structures for Joint Decision Making: A Designer's Point of View," *Interorganizational Decision Making,* ed. Matthew Tiute, Roger Chisholm, and Michael Radnor (Chicago: Aldine, 1972):37–44.

developed on cropland during the premodern period, communal ownership at the village level permitted open access to large areas of wild and forest land which were used for the collection of firewood, leaves, and wild grasses to fertilize rice fields. Over time, detailed common property rules were stipulated for the use of communal land so as to prevent resource exhaustion.[44]

Detailed stipulations of the time and place of use of communal land as well as rules for mobilizing village labor to maintain communal property (such as applying fire to regenerate pasture) were often enforced with religious taboos and rituals. Those communal village institutions remained viable because it was much more costly to demarcate and partition wild and forest land than crop land among individuals and to enforce exclusive use. Any villager's use of communal land involves externality. For example, his collection of firewood reduces the availability of firewood for other villagers. If property rights are not assigned, there may be only limited incentive for resource conservation. This is not a serious problem if the resource that is subject to open access is abundant relative to population. As population pressure begins to rise, however, a common understanding regarding appropriate use, reinforced by social sanctions, may act to limit excessive exploitation. But as population growth continues to press against limited land resources and the market value of the resource product rises, it becomes necessary to impose more formal regulations regarding the access of individual villagers to communal land.

Group action to supply public goods, such as the maintenance of communal land, may work effectively if the size of the group involved is small, as in the case of a village community. If a large number of people are involved in the use of a public good, however, as in the case of marine fisheries, it is more difficult to regulate their resource use or to prevent free riders by means of voluntary agreements.[45] Action by a higher authority with coercive power, such as government, may be required to limit free riding.

The "socialization" of agricultural research, as discussed earlier in this

44. For the distinction between open access and common property, see S. V. Ciriacy-Wantrup and R. C. Bishop, " 'Common Property' as a Concept in Natural Resource Policy," *Natural Resources Journal* 15 (October 1975):713–27. In the case of open access, use rights have not been fully established. In the case of common property, rules have been established that govern joint use. Common property is therefore a form of land use that lies between the extremes of open access and fully exclusive private rights. The problem of resource exhaustion in open-access properties was elaborated in Harold Demsetz, "Toward a Theory of Property Rights," *American Economic Review* 57 (May 1967):347–59; and Armen A. Alchian and Harold Demsetz, "The Property Right Paradigm," *Journal of Economic History* 33 (March 1973):16–27.

45. Mancur Olson, Jr., *The Logic of Collective Action: Public Goods and the Theory of Groups* (New York: Schocken Books, 1968). Several students of institutional change have emphasized that coordinated or common expectations, resulting from the assurance provided by traditional institutions or common assumptions about equity or ideology, have permitted much larger groups to engage in either implicit or explicit voluntary cooperation than is implied by Olson's model. See Runge, "Institutions and Common Property," pp. 189–99; North, *Structure and Change*. North notes that "the premium necessary to induce people to become free riders is positively correlated with the perceived legitimacy of the existing institution" (p. 54).

chapter, is common not only in socialist economies but also in market economies. This can be explained by the failure of the market to allocate resources efficiently for the supply of public goods for a large, unidentifiable clientele group. New information or knowledge resulting from research is typically endowed with the attributes of a public good characterized by *nonrivalness* or jointness in supply and use and *nonexcludability* or external economies.[46] The first attribute implies that the good is equally available to all. The second implies that it is impossible for private producers to appropriate through market pricing the full social benefits arising directly from the production (and consumption) of the good—it is difficult to exclude from the use of the good those who do not pay for it. A socially optimal level of supply of such a good cannot be expected if its supply is left to private firms. Because present institutional arrangements are such that much information resulting from basic research is nonexcludable, it has been necessary to establish nonprofit institutions to advance basic scientific knowledge.[47]

A unique aspect of agricultural research, particularly that directed to advancing biological technology, is that many of the products of research—even in the applied area—are characterized by nonexcludability. Protection by patent laws is either unavailable or inadequate. The nature of agricultural production would make it difficult to restrict information about new technology or practices. Furthermore, even the largest farms are relatively small units and would not be able to capture more than a small share of the gains from inventive activity. Private research activities in agriculture have been directed primarily toward developing mechanical technology for which patent protection is established.[48]

46. Yujiro Hayami and Saburo Yamada, "Agricultural Research Organization in Economic Development: A Review of the Japanese Experience," *Agriculture in Development Theory*, ed. Lloyd G. Reynolds (New Haven: Yale University Press, 1975), pp. 224–49. For a characterization of the nonrivalness and nonexcludability attributes of public goods see Paul A. Samuelson, "The Pure Theory of Public Expenditure," *Review of Economics and Statistics* 36 (1954):387–89; "Diagrammatic Exposition of a Theory of Public Expenditure," *Review of Economics and Statistics* 37 (1955):350–56; "Aspects of Public Expenditure Theories," *Review of Economics and Statistics* 40 (1958):332–38; and Richard A. Musgrave, *The Theory of Public Finance* (New York: McGraw-Hill, 1959).

47. Nonrivalness is an essential attribute of information. The use of information about a new farming practice (contour plowing, for example) by a farmer is not hindered by the adoption of the same practice by other farmers. There is no capacity limit for its use.

Nonexcludability, in contrast, is not a natural attribute of information but rather is determined by institutional arrangements. In fact, patent laws are an institutional arrangement that makes a certain form of information (called an "invention") excludable, thereby creating profit incentives for private creative activities. Retention of trade secrets is another legally sanctioned method of retaining control over inventions or other forms of new technical knowledge. These arrangements are designed to promote more efficient resource allocation through market arrangements, as discussed in the previous section.

48. In a number of countries "breeders' rights" and "petty patent" legislation have induced rapid growth in private sector research and development agriculture. Vernon W. Ruttan, "Changing Role of Public and Private Sectors in Agricultural Research," *Science* 216 (April, 2, 1982):23–29. Donald D. Evenson and Robert E. Evenson, "Legal Systems and Private Sector Incentives for the Invention of Agricultural Technology in Latin America," *Technical Change*

Another important attribute of the research production function is that it has a stochastic form. Research, by nature, is characterized by risk and uncertainty. Success in a research project is like hitting a successful oil well. Any number of dry holes may be bored before the successful one is found. Richard Nelson has pointed out that this stochastic nature of the research production function, which is especially strong in the case of basic research, contributes to the failure of the market in attaining optimal resource allocation over time: "The very large variance of the profit probability distribution from a basic research project will tend to cause a risk-avoiding firm, without the economic resources to spread the risk by running a number of basic-research projects at once, to value a basic-research project at significantly less than its expected profitability and hence . . . at less than its social value."[49]

The public-good attributes of the agricultural research product together with the stochastic nature of the research production function make public support of agricultural research socially desirable. It does not necessarily follow, however, that agricultural research should be conducted in government institutions financed by tax revenue. The social benefit produced by agricultural research can be measured as the sum of increases in consumers' and producers' surpluses resulting from the downward shift in the supply function of an agricultural product. If the benefit consists primarily of producers' surplus, agricultural research may be left to the cooperative activities of agricultural producers (that is, such institutions as agricultural commodity organizations and cooperatives). Research on a number of tropical export crops grown under plantation conditions, such as sugar, bananas, and rubber, is often organized in this manner.

Most agricultural commodities, however, are produced by a very large number of relatively small farmers. Under these conditions voluntary cooperation to support research would be very costly to organize. Furthermore, most agricultural commodities, except those intended for export, are characterized by low price elasticity of demand. As a result, a major share of the social benefit produced by research tends to be transmitted to consumers through lower market prices. In such a situation the cost of agricultural research should be borne by the general public.

If agricultural research were left entirely to the private sector the result would be serious bias in the allocation of research resources. Resources would flow primarily to areas of mechanical technology that are adequately protected by patents and to areas of biological technology in which the results can be protected by trade secrets (such as the inbred lines used in the production of hybrid corn seed). Other areas, such as research on open-pollinated seed varieties, biological control of insects and pathogens, and improvements in

and Social Conflict in Agriculture: Latin American Perspectives, ed. Martin E. Piñeiro and Eduardo J. Trigo (Boulder, Colo.: Westview Press, 1983), pp. 189–216.

49. Richard R. Nelson, "The Simple Economics of Basic Scientific Research," *Journal of Political Economy* 67 (1959):304.

farming practices and management, would be neglected. The socialization of agricultural research or the predominance of public institutions in agricultural research, especially in the biological sciences, can be considered a major institutional innovation designed to offset what would otherwise represent a serious distortion in the allocation of research resources.

The Supply of Institutional Innovation

We have identified the disequilibria in economic relationships associated with economic growth, such as technical change leading to the generation of new income streams and changes in relative factor endowments, as important sources of demand for institutional change. But the sources of supply of institutional innovation are less well understood. The factors that reduce the cost of institutional innovation have not been widely studied by economists or other social scientists.

In the Philippines village case discussed earlier, changes in tenure and labor market institutions were supplied, in response to the changes in demand generated by changing factor endowments and new income streams, through the individual and joint decisions of owner-cultivators, tenants, and laborers. But even at this level it was necessary for gains to the innovators to be large enough to offset the risk of ignoring the land reform code prohibitions against subleasing and the social costs involved in changing traditional harvest-sharing arrangements. Although mobilization of substantial political resources was not required to introduce and extend the new land and labor market institutions, the distribution of political resources within the village did influence the initiation and diffusion of the institutional innovations.

The supply of major institutional innovations necessarily involves the mobilization of substantial political resources by political entrepreneurs and innovators. It is useful to think of a supply schedule of institutional innovation that is determined by the marginal cost schedule facing political entrepreneurs as they attempt to design new institutions and resolve the conflicts among various vested interest groups (or suppression of opposition when necessary). We hypothesize that institutional innovations will be supplied if the expected return from the innovation that accrues to the political entrepreneurs exceeds the marginal cost of mobilizing the resources necessary to introduce the innovation. To the extent that the private return to the political entrepreneurs is different from the social return, the institutional innovation will not be supplied at a socially optimal level.[50]

Thus the supply of institutional innovation depends critically on the power structure or balance among vested-interest groups in a society. If the power

50. See, for example, Norman Frohlich, Joe A. Oppenheimer, and Oran R. Young, *Political Leadership and Collective Goods* (Princeton: Princeton University Press, 1971). For a review and extension of concepts of political entrepreneurship see Joel M. Guttman, ''Can Political Entrepreneurs Solve the Free Rider Problem?'' *Journal of Economic Behavior and Organization* 3 (1982):1–10.

balance is such that the political entrepreneurs' efforts to introduce an institutional innovation with a high rate of social return are adequately rewarded by greater prestige and stronger political support, a socially desirable institutional innovation may occur. But if the institutional innovation is expected to result in a loss to a dominant political block, the innovation may not be forthcoming even if it is expected to produce a large net gain to society as a whole.

It is also possible that socially undesirable institutional innovations may occur if the returns to the entrepreneur or the interest group exceed the gains to society. For example, it is common to observe that government market interventions such as licenses, quotas, rationing, and price controls are promoted by interest groups seeking "institutional rents" or monopoly profits. Rent seeking by interest groups does not contribute to the creation of new income streams in society, but it does entail social costs. These costs result in losses in market efficiency that government interventions produce and the waste of resources used to obtain them, such as lobbying and bribery.[51]

The failure of many developing countries to institutionalize the agricultural research capacity needed to take advantage of the large gains from relatively modest investments in technical change may be caused, in part, by the divergence between social returns and the private returns to political entrepreneurs. In the mid-1920s, for example, agricultural development in Argentina appeared to be proceeding along a path roughly comparable to that of the United States. Mechanization of crop production lagged slightly behind that in the United States. Grain yields per hectare averaged slightly higher. In contrast to the United States, however, output and yields in Argentina remained relatively stagnant between the mid-1920s and the mid-1970s. It was not until the late 1970s that Argentina began to realize significant gains in agricultural productivity. One reason for this lag in Argentine agricultural development was the disruption of export markets in the 1930s and 1940s. Students of Argentine development have suggested that other reasons were the political dominance of the landed aristocracy, the rising tensions between urban and rural interests, and inappropriate domestic policies toward agriculture.[52] In

51. For a seminal work on rent seeking, see Gordon Tullock, "The Welfare Costs of Tariffs, Monopolies and Theft," *Western Economic Journal* 5 (June 1967):224–32. Other major works include George J. Stigler, "The Theory of Economic Regulation," *Bell Journal of Economics and Management Science* 2 (Spring 1971):3–21, and Anne O. Krueger, "The Political Economy of the Rent-Seeking Society," *American Economic Review* 64 (June 1974):291–303. For a useful collection of the emerging literature on rent-seeking see James M. Buchanan, Robert D. Tollison, and Gordon Tullock, *Toward a Theory of the Rent-Seeking Society* (College Station: Texas A&M University Press, 1980). For a literature review see Robert Tollison, "Rent Seeking: A Survey," *Kyklos* 35 (Fasc. 4, 1982):575–602.

52. Alain de Janvry, "A Socioeconomic Model of Induced Innovations for Argentine Agricultural Development," *Quarterly Journal of Economics* 87 (August 1973):410–35; Peter H. Smith, *Politics and Beef in Argentina: Patterns of Conflict and Change* (New York: Columbia University Press, 1969); *Argentina and the Failure of Democracy: Conflict among Political Elites, 1904–1955* (Madison: University of Wisconsin Press, 1974); Domingo Cavallo and Yair Mundlak, *Agriculture and Economic Growth in an Open Economy: The Case of Argentina*

the Argentine case the bias in the distribution of political and economic resources apparently imposed exceptionally costly delays in the institutional innovations needed to take advantage of the relatively inexpensive sources of growth that technical change in agriculture could have made available.

Cultural endowments, including religion and ideology, exert a strong influence on the supply of institutional innovation. They make some forms of institutional change less costly to establish and impose severe costs on others. For example, the traditional moral obligation in the Japanese village community to cooperate in communal infrastructure maintenance has made it less costly to implement rural development programs than in societies lacking such traditions. These activities had their origin in the feudal organization of rural communities in the pre-Meiji period. But practices such as maintenance of village and agricultural roads and of irrigation and drainage ditches through joint activities in which all families contribute labor were still practiced in well over half of the hamlets in Japan as recently as 1970.[53] The traditional patterns of cooperation have represented an important cultural resource on which to erect modern forms of cooperative marketing and joint farming activities. Similar cultural resources are not available in South Asian villages, where, for example, the caste structure inhibits cooperation and encourages specialization.

Likewise, ideology may reduce the cost to political entrepreneurs of mobilizing collective action for institutional change. For example, the Jeffersonian concept of agrarian democracy provided ideological support for the series of land ordinances culminating in the Homestead Act of 1862, which established the legal framework that encouraged an owner-operator system of agriculture in the American West. Strong nationalist sentiment in Meiji Japan, reflected in slogans such as ''A Wealthy Nation and Strong Army'' (Fukoku Kyohei), helped mobilize the resources needed for the establishment of vocational schools and agricultural and industrial experiment stations. In China, communist ideology, reinforced by the lessons learned during the guerrilla period in Yenan, inspired the mobilization of communal resources to build irrigation systems and other forms of social overhead capital.[54] Thus ideology can be a critical resource for political entrepreneurs and an important factor affecting the supply of institutional innovations.

Advances in social sciences that improve knowledge relevant to the design

(Washington, D.C.: International Food Policy Research Institute, Research Report 36, December 1982).

53. Shigeru Ishikawa, *Essays on Technology, Employment and Institutions in Economic Development: Comparative Asian Experience* (Tokyo: Kinokuniya, 1981), pp. 325–47.

54. Willard W. Cochrane, *The Development of American Agriculture: A Historical Analysis* (Minneapolis: University of Minnesota Press, 1979), pp. 41–47, 179–88; Yujiro Hayami, in association with Masakatsu Akino, Masahiko Shintani, and Saburo Yamada, *A Century of Agricultural Growth in Japan* (Minneapolis: University of Minnesota Press, 1975); Peter Schran, ''On the Yenan Origins of Current Economic Policies,'' *China's Modern Economy in Historical Perspective*, ed. Dwight H. Perkins (Stanford: Stanford University Press, 1975), pp. 279–302.

of institutional innovations that are capable of generating new income streams or that reduce the cost of conflict resolution act to shift the supply of institutional change to the right. Throughout history, improvements in institutional performance have occurred primarily through the slow accumulation of successful precedent or as by-products of expertise and experience. Institutional change was generated through the process of trial and error much in the same manner that technical change was generated before the invention of the research university, the agricultural experiment station, or the industrial research laboratory. With the institutionalization of research in the social sciences and related professions the process of institutional innovation has begun to proceed much more efficiently; it is becoming increasingly possible to substitute social science knowledge and analytical skill for the more expensive process of learning by trial and error.

The research that led to advances in our understanding of the production and consumption of rural households in less developed countries is an important example of the contribution of advances in social science knowledge to the design of more efficient institutions.[55] In a number of countries this research has led to the abandonment of policies that viewed peasant households as unresponsive to economic incentives. And it has led to the design of policies and institutions to make more productive technologies available to peasant producers and to the design of more efficient price policies for factors and products.

Similarly, the diffusion of education designed to raise the intellectual level of the general public and to facilitate better understanding of the private and social costs of institutional change may reduce the cost to political entrepreneurs of introducing socially desirable institutions and raise the cost of biasing institutional change in a manner that is costly to society.

TOWARD A MORE COMPLETE MODEL
OF INDUCED INNOVATION

We illustrate, in Figure 4-3, the elements of a model that maps the general equilibrium relationships among resource endowments, cultural endowments, technologies, and institutions.[56] The model goes beyond the conventional

55. Theodore W. Schultz, *Transforming Traditional Agriculture* (New Haven: Yale University Press, 1964); Mark Nerlove, "Household and Economy: Toward a New Theory of Population and Economic Growth," *Journal of Political Economy* 82 (March–April 1974, pt. 2):S200–S218; Hans P. Binswanger, Robert E. Evenson, Cecilia A. Florencio, and Benjamin N. W. White, eds., *Rural Household Studies in Asia* (Singapore: Singapore University Press, 1980).

56. Daniel R. Fusfeld, "The Conceptual Framework of Modern Economics," *Journal of Economic Issues* 14 (March 1980):1–52. Fusfeld uses the terms *pattern* or *Gestalt* model to describe a form of analysis that links the elements of a general pattern together by logical connections. The recursive multicausal relationships of the pattern model imply that the model is always "open"—"it can never include all of the relevant variables and relationships necessary for a full understanding of the phenomena under investigation" (p. 33).

FIGURE 4-3. Interrelationships between changes in resource endowments, cultural endowments, technology, and institutions.

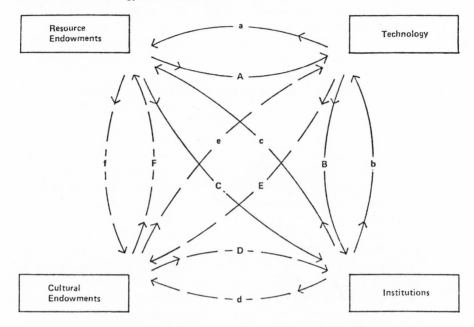

general equilibrium model in which resource endowments, technologies, institutions, and culture (conventionally designated as tastes) are given.[57] In the study of long-term social and economic change the relationships among the several variables must be treated as recursive. The formal microeconomic models that are employed to analyze the supply and demand for technical and institutional change can be thought of as "nested" within the general equilibrium framework of Figure 4-3.

One advantage of the "pattern model" outlined in Figure 4-3 is that it helps to identify areas of ignorance. Our capacity to model and test the relationships between resource endowments and technical change is relatively strong. Our capacity to model and test the relationships between cultural endowments and either technical or institutional change is relatively weak. A second advantage of the model is that it is useful in identifying the compo-

57. In economics the concept of cultural endowments is usually subsumed under the concept of tastes, which are regarded as given, that is, not subject to economic analysis. Our use of the term *culture* is consistent with the definition suggested by Leslie A. White; "When things and events are considered in the context of their relation to the human organism, they constitute behavior; when they are considered . . . in their relationship to one another, they become culture," Leslie A. White, "Human Culture," *Encyclopedia Britannica,* vol. 8, 15th ed. (Chicago: Benton, 1974), p. 1152. We use the term *cultural endowments* to capture those dimensions of culture that have been transmitted from the past. Contemporary changes in resource endowments, technology, and institutions can be expected to result in changes in cultural endowments.

nents that enter into other attempts to account for secular economic and social change. Failure to analyze historical change in a general equilibrium context tends to result in a unidimensional perspective on the relationships bearing on technical and institutional change.

For example, historians working within the Marxist tradition often tend to view technical change as dominating both institutional and cultural change. In his book *Oriental Despotism,* Karl Wittfogel views the irrigation technology used in wet rice cultivation in East Asia as determining political organization.[58] As it applies to Figure 4-3 his primary emphasis was on the impact of resources and technology on institutions (B) and (C).

A serious misunderstanding can be observed in contemporary neo-Marxian critiques of the green revolution. These criticisms have focused attention almost entirely on the impact of technical change on labor and land tenure relations. Both the radical and populist critics have emphasized relation (B). But they have tended to ignore relationships (A) and (C).[59] This bias has led to repeated failure to identify effectively the separate effects of population growth and technical change on the growth and distribution of income. The analytical power of the more complete induced innovation model was illustrated in the work by Yujiro Hayami and Masao Kikuchi, discussed earlier in this chapter, on the impact of both technical change and population growth on changes in land tenure and labor market relationships in the Philippines.

Armen Alchian and Harold Demsetz identify a primary function of property rights as guiding incentives to achieve greater internalization of externalities. They consider that the clear specification of property rights reduces transaction costs in the face of growing competition for the use of scarce resources as a result of population growth and/or growth in product demand. Douglass North and Robert P. Thomas, building on the Alchian-Demsetz paradigm, attempted to explain the economic growth of western Europe between 900 and 1700 primarily in terms of changes in property institutions.[60] During the eleventh and thirteenth centuries the pressure of population against

58. Karl A. Wittfogel, *Oriental Despotism: A Comparative Study of Total Power* (New Haven: Yale University Press, 1957).

59. A major limitation of the Marxian model is the emphatic rejection of a causal link between demographic change and technical and institutional change. North, *Structure and Change,* pp. 60, 61. This blindness to the role of demographic factors, and to the impact of relative resource endowments, originated in the debates between Marx and Malthus. An attempt to correct this deficiency represents the major innovation of the "cultural materialism" school of anthropology. See Marvin Harris, *Cultural Materialism: The Struggle for a Science of Culture* (New York: Random House, 1979).

60. Demsetz, "Toward a Theory of Property Rights"; Alchian and Demsetz, "The Property Right Paradigm"; North and Thomas, "An Economic Theory of the Growth of the Western World," *Economic History Review* 23 (1970):1–17, also in *The Rise of the Western World* (London: Cambridge University Press, 1973). For a critical perspective on the North-Thomas model see Alexander J. Field, "The Problem with Neoclassical Institutional Economics: A Critique with Special Reference to the North/Thomas Model of Pre-1500 Europe," *Explorations in Economic History* 18 (1981):174–98. Field is critical of the attempt by North and Thomas to treat institutional change as endogenous.

increasingly scarce land resources induced innovations in property rights that in turn created profitable opportunities for the generation and adoption of labor-intensive technical changes in agriculture. The population decline in the fourteenth and fifteenth centuries was viewed as a primary factor leading to the demise of feudalism and the rise of the national state (line C). These institutional changes in turn opened up new possibilities for economies of scale in nonagricultural production and in trade (line b).

In a more recent work Mancur Olson has emphasized the proliferation of institutions as a source of economic decline.[61] He also regards broad-based encompassing organizations as having incentives to generate growth and redistribute incomes to their members with little excess burden. For example, a broadly based coalition that encompasses the majority of agricultural producers is more likely to exert political pressure for growth-oriented policies that will enable its members to obtain a larger share of a larger national product than a smaller organization that represents the interests of the producers of a single commodity. Small organizations representing narrow interest groups are more likely to pursue the interests of their members at the expense of the welfare of other producers and the general public. In contrast, an even more broadly based farmer-labor coalition would be more concerned with promoting economic growth than would an organization representing a single sector. But large groups, in Olson's view, are inherently unstable because rational individuals will not incur the costs of contributing to the realization of the large group program—they have strong incentives to act as free riders. As a result, organizational "space" in a stable society will be increasingly occupied by special interest "distributional coalitions." These distributional coalitions make political life divisive. They slow down the adoption of new technologies (line b) and limit the capacity to reallocate resources (line c). The effect is to slow down economic growth or in some cases initiate a period of economic decline.

What are the implications of the theory of institutional innovation outlined in this chapter for the research agenda on the economics of institutional change? In our research on the direction and rate of technical change we were able to advance significantly our knowledge by treating technical change as endogenous—as induced primarily by changes in relative resource endowments and the growth of demand. We have also attempted to develop a theory of induced institutional innovation in which we treat institutional innovation as endogenous. There is now a significant body of evidence that suggests that substantial new insights on institutional innovation and diffusion can be obtained by treating institutional change as an economic response to changes in resource endowments and technical change.

61. Mancur Olson, *The Rise and Decline of Nations: Economic Growth, Stagflation, and Social Rigidities* (New Haven: Yale University Press, 1982). For a review of the Olson work see Douglass C. North, "A Theory of Economic Change," *Science* 219 (January 14, 1983):163, 164.

We also insist on the potential significance of cultural endowments, including the factors that economists typically conceal under the rubric of tastes and that political scientists include under ideology. But our capacity to develop rigorous empirical tests capable of identifying the relative significance of the relationships between cultural endowments and the other elements of the model outlined in Figure 4-3 is unsatisfactory. Until our colleagues in the other social sciences provide us with more helpful analytical tools, we are forced to adhere to a strategy that focuses primarily on the interactions between resource endowments, technical change, and institutional change. The strategy suggested here does have the clear advantage of allowing us to explore how far a strategy based on the straightforward extension of standard microeconomic theory will take us in the analysis of both technical and institutional change.

II

INTERNATIONAL COMPARISONS

5

International Comparisons of Agricultural Productivity

A s a first step in identifying the broad pattern of agricultural development, we attempt in this chapter to compare agricultural
productivity among countries according to output per worker and output per
hectare. The comparisons for 1960 and 1980 reveal not only that intercountry
differences in the partial productivity ratios were very large but also that they
increased during the past two decades. Further, the observed differences in
the partial productivity ratios were associated with differences in the use of
modern industrial inputs as substitutes for land and labor.

From those observations we attempt to construct a more operational model,
suitable for empirical testing, of the induced technical innovation process
outlined in the previous chapter. The model is specifically designed to incorporate the processes by which advances in industrial technology, which reduce the costs of biological and mechanical inputs to the agricultural sector,
induce unique paths of technological change and productivity growth in the
agricultural sector. Our model will be used to generate a series of hypotheses
that are tested in subsequent chapters.

The data used in constructing the intercountry productivity comparisons
are clearly of uneven quality. There are serious conceptual and technical
problems in the collection, organization, and processing of agricultural data,
even for the most advanced countries. The aggregation and index number
problems are nearly insuperable. In spite of these limitations, the intercountry
cross-section analysis provides useful insights. It permits us to draw on the
experiences of nations with an extremely wide range of variation in the
relative endowments of land and labor and land and labor productivity. This
wide range is particularly valuable in helping to clarify relationships that tend
to be obscured by observations based on the experiences of an individual
country or a small number of relatively homogeneous countries.

PRODUCTIVITY AND RESOURCE USE IN AGRICULTURE

In this section the two partial productivity measures, output per unit of labor and output per unit of land, are used to illustrate the wide variations in the relationship between factor endowments and agricultural output among countries and over time.[1] The close association between variations in land productivity and the use of biological technology and variations in the land-labor ratio and the use of mechanical technology is also illustrated.

Comparisons in Partial Productivity Ratios

The intercountry cross-section comparisons of agricultural production and productivity pioneered by Colin Clark were advanced by Yujiro Hayami and associates, who attempted a comprehensive analysis of a cross-section comparison of labor and land productivities among countries for 1960.[2] For the analysis in this chapter, the 1960 data were revised and extended to 1980. The detailed explanations of data sources and methods of organization are presented in Appendix A.

The labor and land productivities of forty-four countries for 1960 and 1980 are shown in Table 5-1. Intercountry differences in these partial productivity

1. This section draws heavily on Toshihiko Kawagoe and Yujiro Hayami, "The Production Structure of World Agriculture: An Intercountry Cross Section Analysis," *Developing Economies* 21 (September 1983):189–206.
2. Colin Clark's pioneering study was *The Conditions of Economic Progress* (London: Macmillan, 1940). A number of intercountry comparative studies that appeared before the mid-1950s were reviewed in Colin Clark, "World Supply and Requirement of Farm Products," *Journal of the Royal Statistical Society,* vol. 117, ser. A, pt. III (1954):263–91; and *The Conditions of Economic Progress,* 3d ed., rev. (London: Macmillan, and New York: St. Martin's Press, 1957). In the late 1960s intercountry comparisons along the lines pioneered by Clark were revived by Hayami and associates: Yujiro Hayami, "Industrialization and Agricultural Productivity: An International Comparative Study," *Developing Economies* 7 (March 1969):3–21; Yujiro Hayami and Kinuyo Inagi, "International Comparison of Agricultural Productivities," *Farm Economist* 11 (1969):407–19; and Yujiro Hayami in association with Barbara B. Miller, William W. Wade, and Sachiko Yamashita, *An International Comparison of Agricultural Production and Productivities,* University of Minnesota Agricultural Experiment Station Technical Bulletin 277, St. Paul, 1971. For a thorough discussion of the methodology of international comparisons of national product and income the reader is referred to the series of reports of the United Nations International Comparison Project directed by Irving B. Kravis and associates: Irving B. Kravis, Zoltan Kenessey, Alan Heston, and Robert Summers, *A System of International Comparisons of Gross Product and Purchasing Power* (Baltimore: Johns Hopkins University Press, 1975); Irving B. Kravis, Alan Heston, and Robert Summers, *International Comparisons of Real Product and Purchasing Power* (Baltimore: Johns Hopkins University Press, 1978); and Irving B. Kravis, Alan Heston, and Robert Summers, *World Product and Income: International Comparisons of Real Gross Product* (Baltimore: Johns Hopkins University Press, 1982).
Several other traditions of international comparative analysis of economic growth focus on the changing sectoral composition of national output associated with economic growth. In a series of ten articles published in *Economic Development and Cultural Change* (1956–67), Kuznets analyzed time-series variations in the sectoral composition of gross national product for a number of developed and developing countries. The results of these studies are consolidated in Simon Kuznets, *Modern Economic Growth: Rate, Structure and Spread* (New Haven: Yale University Press, 1966), and extended in Simon Kuznets, *Economic Growth of Nations: Total Output and Production Structure* (Cambridge, Mass.: Harvard University Press, 1971). Chenery and his associates have employed more formal statistical analyses of patterns of growth among countries.

ratios are indeed great. In 1960, agricultural output per male worker measured in wheat units (WU)—one WU is equivalent to one metric ton of wheat—ranged from 2.0 (Bangladesh) to 140.5 (New Zealand), and output per hectare ranged from .05 (Libya) to 10.34 (Taiwan). By 1980, the ranges had widened further—1.8 (Bangladesh) to 285.1 (United States) for output per worker, and .14 (Libya) to 18.65 (Taiwan) for output per hectare.

The labor and land productivity ratios given in Table 5-1 are plotted in Figure 5-1 with labor productivity (Y/L) on the horizontal axis and land productivity (Y/A) on the vertical axis, both measured in logarithmic scale (Y, L, and A represent, respectively, total output, labor, and land in agriculture). For each country, the 1960 position is connected to the 1980 position by an arrow representing a path of output growth for given changes in labor and land in agriculture. Viewed from the northeast corner of Figure 5-1 (marked $0'$), each country's position represents a combination of labor and land for producing one unit of agricultural output. Thus a contour connecting the United States, New Zealand, Belgium, the Netherlands, and Taiwan may be considered an efficiency frontier, or an efficient unit isoquant of world agriculture, with respect to the use of labor and land.

Since both axes of Figure 5-1 are expressed in logarithmic scale, each of the 45-degree lines represents a uni-land/labor ratio line (uni-A/L line) corresponding to a certain land area per male worker. By identity, labor productivity (Y/L) can be partitioned into land-labor ratio (A/L) and land productivity (Y/A) components:

$$(Y/L) \equiv (A/L) \times (Y/A)$$

or

$$\log(Y/L) \equiv \log(A/L) + \log(Y/A).$$

Therefore, arrows parallel to the uni-A/L lines (such as Taiwan and the Philippines) represent countries following a growth path in which an increase in land productivity was a sole contributor to an increase in labor productivity. Arrows with slopes steeper than the uni-A/L lines (such as Egypt and Peru) represent a path in which the increase in labor productivity was smaller than that in land productivity by the amount of decrease in the land-labor ratio, whereas those with less steep slopes (such as the United States and Canada)

These include several articles and the book by Hollis B. Chenery and Moises Syrquin, *Patterns of Development, 1950–70* (London: Oxford University Press, 1975). A third body of work consists of intercountry and individual country studies designed to test or illustrate the growth-stage typology of Walter W. Rostow, *The World Economy: History and Prospect* (Austin: University of Texas Press, 1978). These studies have reinforced the broad perception outlined in the structural transformation view of economic development. Growth of per capita income is associated with (a) a decline in the share of output and employment accounted for by the primary sectors relative to other sectors and (b) a change in factor proportions involving more rapid growth in physical and human capital relative to land and population. Our approach differs from that of Chenery in that we are concerned with identifying the sources of growth. Thus we draw more directly on the microeconomic theory of production and exchange.

TABLE 5-1. Estimates of land and labor productivities in agriculture, 1960 and 1980

	Output per male worker in WU (Y/L)		Output per hectare in WU (Y/A)		Hectare per male worker (A/L)	
	1960	1980	1960	1980	1960	1980
Argentina	34.9	63.8	0.30	0.44	116.0	146.1
Australia	103.8	256.2	0.09	0.15	1153.1	1764.5
Austria	30.5	90.8	2.32	3.49	13.1	26.0
Bangladesh	2.0	1.8	2.51	3.51	0.8	0.5
Belgium (and Luxemburg)	47.5	174.7	6.12	10.08	7.8	17.3
Brazil	9.3	13.2	0.56	0.72	16.7	18.3
Canada	66.1	193.6	0.58	0.85	113.4	228.5
Chile	11.4	19.8	0.47	0.48	24.1	40.9
Colombia	8.3	17.2	0.79	1.37	10.5	12.5
Denmark	46.4	131.2	4.60	5.58	10.1	23.5
Egypt	4.4	4.6	6.90	9.18	0.6	0.5
Finland	30.5	104.2	2.02	3.34	15.1	31.2
France	32.4	101.8	2.49	4.09	13.0	24.9
Germany, F.R.	37.1	113.7	4.00	5.99	9.3	19.0
Greece	9.1	25.8	1.22	2.21	7.4	11.7
India	2.2	3.1	1.06	1.58	2.0	2.0
Ireland	20.1	58.7	1.52	2.38	13.2	24.6
Israel	25.9	101.8	1.84	4.96	14.1	20.5
Italy	14.5	48.0	3.40	4.97	4.3	9.6
Japan	10.3	27.8	8.64	12.23	1.2	2.3
Libya	3.6	12.9	0.05	0.14	73.8	94.5
Mauritius	10.1	10.6	6.68	7.18	1.5	1.5
Mexico	5.1	7.5	0.27	0.52	19.4	14.3
Netherlands	43.1	109.1	7.21	14.11	6.0	7.7
New Zealand	140.5	235.0	1.21	1.71	116.2	137.6
Norway	31.0	94.0	3.09	4.18	10.0	22.5
Pakistan	3.1	4.2	0.90	1.62	3.5	2.6
Paraguay	4.9	6.5	0.08	0.14	60.9	48.1
Peru	9.6	10.1	0.26	0.37	36.9	27.5
Philippines	3.3	5.9	2.11	3.47	1.6	1.7
Portugal	7.1	18.7	1.70	1.98	4.2	9.5
South Africa	11.2	16.7	0.16	0.30	69.1	55.8
Spain	9.2	44.8	1.12	2.15	8.3	20.9
Sri Lanka	3.6	4.8	2.19	2.98	1.7	1.6
Surinam	13.7	47.3	4.46	9.63	3.1	4.9
Sweden	43.0	122.7	2.33	3.20	18.5	38.4
Switzerland	29.2	77.6	3.38	4.53	8.6	17.1
Syria	7.2	10.0	0.31	0.65	23.4	15.5
Taiwan	7.1	12.4	10.34	18.65	0.7	0.7
Turkey	6.1	12.7	0.59	1.09	10.3	11.7
United Kingdom	47.0	116.3	1.94	3.09	24.2	37.6
United States	93.8	285.1	0.80	1.16	117.0	246.6
Venezuela	7.8	22.7	0.28	0.55	27.6	41.4
Yugoslavia	6.6	14.3	1.14	2.00	5.8	7.2

Source: Data sources are described in detail in Appendix A.

FIGURE 5-1. International comparison of labor and land productivities in agriculture, the 1960 data points connected to the 1980 points by arrows (data from Table 5-1).

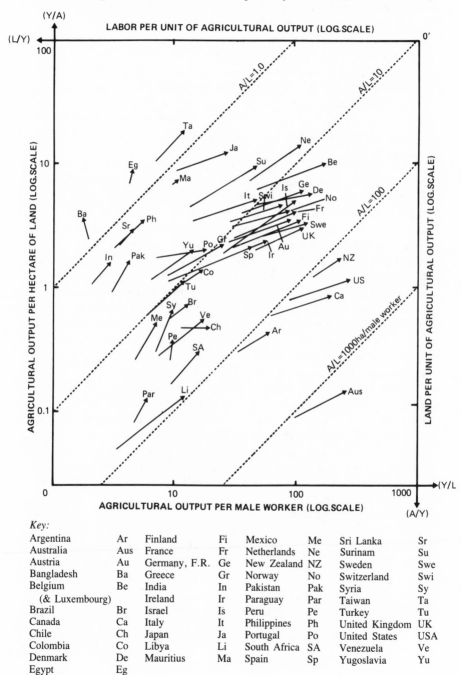

Key:

Argentina	Ar	Finland	Fi	Mexico	Me	Sri Lanka	Sr
Australia	Aus	France	Fr	Netherlands	Ne	Surinam	Su
Austria	Au	Germany, F.R.	Ge	New Zealand	NZ	Sweden	Swe
Bangladesh	Ba	Greece	Gr	Norway	No	Switzerland	Swi
Belgium	Be	India	In	Pakistan	Pak	Syria	Sy
(& Luxembourg)		Ireland	Ir	Paraguay	Par	Taiwan	Ta
Brazil	Br	Israel	Is	Peru	Pe	Turkey	Tu
Canada	Ca	Italy	It	Philippines	Ph	United Kingdom	UK
Chile	Ch	Japan	Ja	Portugal	Po	United States	USA
Colombia	Co	Libya	Li	South Africa	SA	Venezuela	Ve
Denmark	De	Mauritius	Ma	Spain	Sp	Yugoslavia	Yu
Egypt	Eg						

represent a path in which the increase in labor productivity was enhanced by both the increased land productivity and the increased land/labor ratio.

In every country, both government policies and individual farmers' efforts should have been directed to increasing output and income per worker engaged in agricultural production—that is, to moving the country's position in Figure 5-1 to the right. In general, in advanced industrial economies the rates of growth in total population and labor force were low and those of labor absorption by the nonagricultural sectors were high. As a result, the labor force in agriculture decreased rapidly from 1960 to 1980, resulting in marked improvements in the land-labor ratio. Thus the high-income countries were able to increase their labor productivities by moving up along higher A/L lines to the right.

Partly because of the high population growth rates and partly because of insufficient labor absorption by nonagriculture, however, most low-income countries experienced an absolute increase in the agricultural labor force, resulting in deterioration of the land-labor ratio in agriculture between 1960 and 1980. This trend applied not only to the low-income countries in Asia characterized by high population densities but also to those in the new continents (North and South America and Australia), such as Mexico and Peru, which traditionally were endowed with a relatively favorable land-labor ratio. It appears that by the 1960s the strong population pressure in developing countries, even those located in the new continents, had already reached a point at which the marginal cost of opening new land for cultivation began to rise sharply. To counteract the population pressure, serious efforts were made to increase output per unit of land area by investing in the development of land infrastructure, such as irrigation, and in land-saving technologies. Those efforts resulted in increased output per worker along the paths parallel to or steeper than the uni-A/L lines. Yet to the extent that the land-labor ratio was fixed or declined, the rates of growth in labor productivity of the low-income countries were lower than those of the high-income countries.

Such contrasts in agricultural growth patterns between the high-income and the low-income countries are confirmed by a comparison among three groups of countries—seventeen high-income developed countries (DC) with per capita GNP in 1980 higher than U.S.$6,000 (of which four countries are located in the new continents), fifteen middle-stage countries (MC) between $1,500 and $6,000, and twelve low-income less-developed countries (LDC) below $1,500, classified according to the World Bank's *World Development Report 1982*.[3] Results of the comparison, shown in Table 5-2, indicate that the wide gap in labor productivity in agriculture between DCs and LDCs widened further. Agricultural output per male worker in the LDCs increased from 4.7 WU in 1960 to 6.4 WU in 1980, at a growth rate of 1.7 percent per year, and

---

3. World Bank, *World Development Report, 1982* (New York: Oxford University Press, 1982). An exception to this classification rule is Libya, which is classified as an MC despite a per capita GNP higher than $8,000 from a large oil revenue.

TABLE 5-2. Comparison among country groups of agricultural output per male worker (*Y/L*), agricultural output per hectare (*Y/A*), and labor-land ratio (*A/L*), 1960 (1957–62 averages) and 1980 (1975–80 averages)

	Developed countries (DC)			Middle-stage countries (MC)	Less developed countries (LDC)
	Average	New continent	Other		
Labor productivity (*Y/L:* WU/worker)					
1960	41.0	97.5	31.4	9.9	4.7
	(100)	(238)	(77)	(24)	(12)
1980	116.1	240.1	92.8	23.9	6.4
	(100)	(207)	(80)	(21)	(6)
Land productivity (*Y/A:* WU/ha)					
1960	2.20	.48	3.53	.76	1.04
	(100)	(22)	(160)	(35)	(47)
1980	3.29	.70	5.30	1.33	1.61
	(100)	(21)	(161)	(40)	(49)
Land-labor ratio (*A/L:* ha/worker)					
1960	18.6	205.4	8.9	13.1	4.6
	(100)	(1,103)	(48)	(70)	(24)
1980	35.3	342.0	17.5	18.0	4.0
	(100)	(970)	(49)	(51)	(11)
Growth rate, 1960 to 80 (%/year)					
Y/L	5.9	5.1	6.0	5.0	1.7
Y/A	2.3	2.1	2.3	3.2	2.5
A/L	3.6	2.9	3.8	1.8	−.8

Source: Data sources are described in detail in Appendix A.

Note: Data for each country group are shown in parentheses and are computed with the average for developed countries set equal to 100.

DC: New continent countries—Australia, Canada, New Zealand, United States. Other—Austria, Belgium, Denmark, Finland, France, Germany, Italy, Japan, Netherlands, Norway, Sweden, Switzerland, United Kingdom.

MC: Argentina, Brazil, Chile, Mexico, Greece, Israel, Ireland, Libya, Portugal, South Africa, Spain, Surinam, Taiwan, Venezuela, Yugoslavia.

LDC: Bangladesh, Colombia, Egypt, India, Mauritius, Pakistan, Paraguay, Peru, Philippines, Sri Lanka, Syria, Turkey.

that of DCs increased from 41.0 to 116.1 WU, at a rate of 5.9 percent. Thus the labor productivity in the LDCs as a percentage of that in the DCs declined by one-half, from 12 percent in 1960 to only 6 percent in 1980. Meanwhile, the rate of increase in land productivity in the LDCs kept up with that of the DCs. Therefore, the widening gap in labor productivity was explained solely by a decline in the land-labor ratio in the LDCs, both absolutely and relatively. The growth performance of the LDCs was also slower compared with the MCs, where the rates of increases in both land productivity and the land-labor ratio were as fast as in the DCs.

FIGURE 5-2. Stylized patterns of growth in labor and land productivity in agriculture (for key, see Figure 5-1).

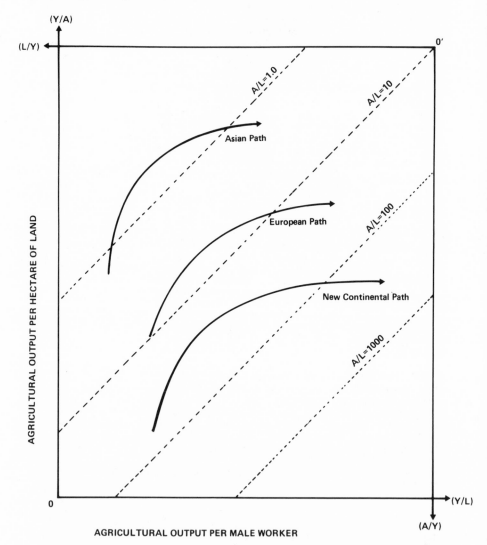

AGRICULTURAL OUTPUT PER MALE WORKER

Although the directions of agricultural productivity growth represented by the arrows in Figure 5-1 are similar among countries at the same stage of economic development, their positions differ depending on initial factor endowments. Three distinct scatters of the arrows can be observed, each representing a long-term growth path: (a) the path indicated by the group of countries in the new continents, including Libya and South Africa, that are scattered around the $A/L = 100$ line; (b) the path indicated by countries in Europe, including Israel, Syria, and Turkey, scattered around the $A/L = 10$ line; and (c) the path indicated by countries in Asia, including Egypt and Mauritius, scattered around the $A/L = 1.0$ line. Stylized patterns of these three growth paths are shown in Figure 5-2. Lack of adequate historical data has prevented us from attempting to identify a distinctly African path, although it is possible to identify some African countries, Egypt for example, with resource endowments that would locate them on the Asian path. Other countries, the Sudan for example, have resource endowments that would locate them on the new continental path.

Each path seems to reflect a long-term process of agricultural growth under alternative man-land ratios. In Asia, land has traditionally been the major factor limiting the increase in output. In countries such as Japan and Taiwan, major efforts have been made throughout history to economize on the use of the limiting factor by substituting man-made inputs, such as fertilizer, for land. This growth process has been accentuated during the past two decades by further deterioration in the man-land ratio resulting from the explosive population growth in the LDCs that began in the 1920s and 1930s and has accelerated since World War II. The dramatic development of modern semi-dwarf varieties of rice and wheat with high-yielding and high fertilizer-absorbing capacities in the tropics since the late 1960s may be considered an innovation induced by a compelling need to sustain agricultural growth under declining man-land ratios. An exception among the Asian countries was Japan, which in the 1950s reached the DC stage of economic development, characterized by an absolute decrease in agricultural labor force.

In the new continents, the most significant constraint on growth of output has traditionally been a relatively inelastic supply of labor. To ease this constraint, farmers have tried to substitute power and machines for labor so as to expand area cultivated per worker. Those efforts have enabled new continent DCs to achieve superiority in labor productivity in agriculture. Rapid population growth during the past several decades, however, has induced many new continent LDCs to seek agricultural growth along a direction similar to the traditional Asian model. This trend will continue until those countries reach the stage at which the agricultural labor force begins to decline absolutely.

Process of Substitution for Labor and Land

In the previous section agricultural growth was viewed as a process involving the substitution of man-made inputs for labor and land. This process may be visualized in Figure 5-3, which shows changes in the land-labor ratio (A/L) associated with tractor horsepower per male worker (M/L), and in Figure 5-4, which shows changes in land productivity (Y/A) associated with fertilizer input per hectare (F/A). Fertilizer is used here as a proxy or index for the factors that substitute for land. Tractor horsepower is used as a proxy for the

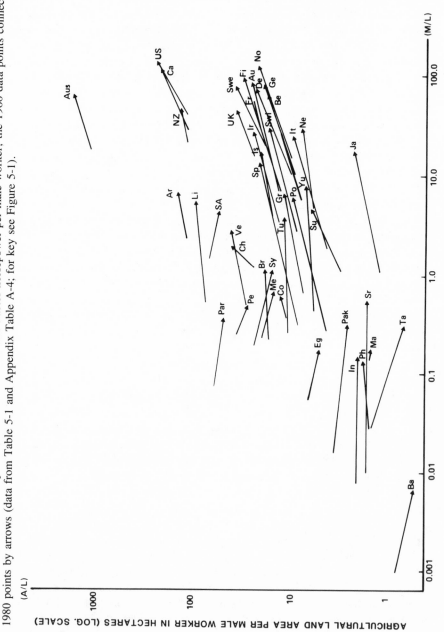

FIGURE 5-3. International comparison of land-labor ratio and tractor horsepower per male worker, the 1960 data points connected to the 1980 points by arrows (data from Table 5-1 and Appendix Table A-4; for key see Figure 5-1).

points by arrows (data from Appendix Table A-4; for key see Figure 5-1).

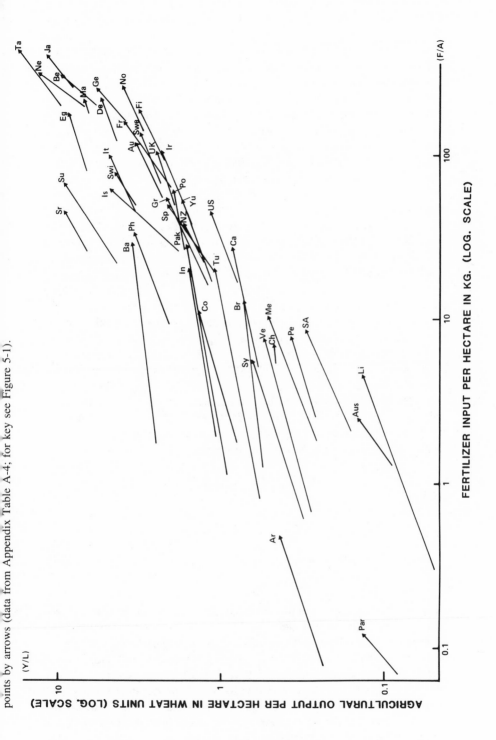

factors that substitute for labor. The positive association between (A/L) and M/L) in Figure 5-3 seems to indicate a process by which the constraints on agricultural production imposed by limited endowments of labor were mitigated through increased investments in power and machinery per worker so that the average land area cultivated by one worker was enlarged. Similarly, the correlation between (Y/A) and (F/A) indicates that the constraints resulting from limited land resource endowments were released by increasing the application of fertilizer (and other yield-increasing inputs) per unit of land.

Even though the land-labor ratio, on the whole, is positively associated with tractor horsepower per worker in Figure 5-3, the relationship varies among regions. Countries in the new continents tend to be located above a common regression line whereas those in Asia tend to be located below that line. An opposite relation holds in Figure 5-4, which shows new continent countries tending to lie below and Asian countries above a common regression line. These relationships seem to reflect differences in land use among the country groups. The new continent countries characterized by sparse population have traditionally used a large percentage of their land as permanent pasture for grazing animals. In contrast, the percentage of arable land has been larger in the countries of older settlement. In general, the requirement for power and machinery is smaller per hectare of land, and average output per hectare is also smaller where a larger percentage of the land is used for permanent pasture.

To test our hypothesis on the relation between the land-labor ratio (A/L) and tractor horsepower per worker (M/L), and between land productivity (Y/A) and fertilizer input per hectare (F/A), the following regressions are estimated by applying the ordinary least squares to the cross-country data:

$$\log\left(\frac{A}{L}\right) = 1.421 + \underset{(.036)}{.350} \ \log\left(\frac{M}{L}\right) - \underset{(.110)}{1.209} \log\left(\frac{C}{A}\right) - \underset{(.188)}{.321D}, \ \bar{R}^2 = .747$$

and

$$\log\left(\frac{Y}{A}\right) = -.598 + \underset{(.037)}{.473} \log\left(\frac{F}{A}\right) + \underset{(.092)}{.389} \ \log\left(\frac{C}{A}\right) - \underset{(.127)}{.111D}, \ \bar{R}^2 = .814$$

where (C/A) represents the ratio of arable land area to total agricultural land area including permanent pasture land; D represents a time dummy (0 for 1960 and 1 for 1980); $\bar{R}^2$ is the coefficient of determination adjusted for the degree of freedom; and standard errors of estimated coefficients are shown in parentheses. The coefficients of (M/L) and (F/A) are, as expected, positive and highly significant; the coefficients of (C/A) are negative for the $(A/L$ equation and positive for the (Y/A) equation. This result is consistent with our hypothesis that land area per worker (A/L) is inversely related to the index of land-use intensity (C/A) and that output per unit of land area (Y/A) is directly related to the index of land-use intensity. The coefficients of determination indicate reasonable fit of the regressions to the data.

These results indicate that a major portion of the intercountry variation in the land-labor ratio and land productivity is explained by variations in the inputs of labor substitutes, represented by tractors, and of land substitutes, represented by fertilizer, respectively, after adjusting for differences in the use of land as represented by differences in the arable land ratio. These relations seem to have remained essentially the same during the past two decades. (The coefficients of the time dummy variable are not different from zero at conventional levels of significance.)

INDUSTRIALIZATION AND AGRICULTURAL PRODUCTIVITY GROWTH

Despite great differences in climate, technology, and output mix, it seems apparent that the major variations in land and labor productivity among countries are associated with differences in the levels of industrial inputs which ease the constraints imposed by the inelastic supply of the primary factors. The relations observed above are consistent with the hypothesis that growth in agricultural productivity is essentially a process of adaptation by the agricultural sector to new opportunities created by the advances in knowledge and by the progress of interindustry division of labor which has accompanied industrialization. The term *industrialization* is used here in a broader sense than simply the expansion of the manufacturing sector. It includes the coordinated growth of manufacturing, service, and related industries, including international trade and transport, that characterizes an industrial economy.

If industrialization is measured by the ratio of the number of male workers in the nonagricultural sector to the total number of male workers, the countries located close to the efficiency frontier implicit in Figure 5-1 are all highly industrialized. The industrialization ratios, based on 1980 data, are 0.93 in Australia, 0.97 in the United States, 0.88 in New Zealand, 0.91 in Denmark, 0.97 in Belgium, 0.93 in the Netherlands, 0.91 in Japan, and 0.72 in Taiwan. In contrast, this ratio is low in countries located near the origin: 0.40 in Paraguay, 0.57 in Peru, 0.55 in Turkey, 0.51 in Syria, 0.44 in India, and 0.13 in Bangladesh. The fact that countries such as Australia and New Zealand, which are major exporters of agricultural products and importers of industrial commodities, also rank high on the industrialization ratio seems to suggest that industrialization interacts with growth in agricultural productivity in a complex manner. The technical inputs supplied by the industrial sector represent a major source of productivity growth in agriculture. Similarly, growth in agricultural productivity results in a rise in the demand for the products of the industrial sector and releases the labor necessary for industrial growth.

The growth implication of the intercountry cross-section observations may be further tested by drawing on the historical experiences of five countries.

Each country was selected for a specific purpose: (a) the United States to illustrate the growth pattern for the group of countries in the new continents, where man-land ratios are particularly favorable; (b) Japan to illustrate the growth pattern for the group of countries in Asia, where unfavorable man-land ratios prevail; and (c) Denmark, France, and the United Kingdom to illustrate the growth pattern in the countries of Europe, where the man-land ratios are intermediate to the two groups above. In terms of the availability of data, as well as the important implications of their historical experiences on development economics, there seems to be little problem in selecting the United States and Japan as the representatives of the first two groups. It was difficult to choose a single country to illustrate the intermediate growth path. Among countries characterized by an intermediate growth path, Denmark, France, and the United Kingdom were selected to represent, respectively, the agricultural product exporting countries, the agriculturally self-sufficient countries, and the agricultural product importing countries.

The time-series paths of agricultural productivity growth in the selected countries are plotted in Figure 5-5. The numbers in parentheses indicate the percentage of male workers in nonagricultural occupations in the total number of male workers. The time-series path of the United States passes through the scatter of new continental countries, and the path of Japan passes through the scatter of Afro-Asian countries. The historical relationships between the level of industrialization and the level of agricultural productivity both in the United States and Japan are similar to the intercountry relationships.

The productivity positions of European countries in 1980 are either within or on the fringe of the envelope formed by the growth paths of Denmark and the United Kingdom. Denmark, which has remained relatively specialized in agricultural production among European countries, has attained a high labor productivity in agriculture by increasing output per unit of land. In contrast, the United Kingdom, which initiated the Industrial Revolution, has attained a relatively high level of agricultural efficiency mainly by enlarging agricultural land area per worker in response to the absorption of labor in nonagricultural occupations. France, which traditionally followed an agrarian policy designed to protect the peasant family farm (*la petite exploitation familiale*) from external competition and internal social change, achieved higher output per hectare than the United Kingdom but slower growth in output per worker than either the United Kingdom or Denmark until the formation of the European Economic Community (EEC). Since 1960, stimulated by increased demand for the protected EEC market, output and productivity of French agriculture have expanded at a very rapid rate. The high productivity of Danish agriculture, in spite of a relatively larger percentage of workers engaged in agriculture, has reflected its specialized role as a supplier of livestock products to the more industrialized British economy.

Although the historical paths of agricultural productivity growth in the selected DCs appear similar to the intercountry cross-section relationships, it

FIGURE 5-5. Historical growth paths of agricultural productivity of Denmark, France, Japan, the United Kingdom, and the United States for 1880–1980, compared with intercountry cross-section observations of selected countries in 1980. Values in parentheses are percent of male workers employed in nonagriculture. (Data from Appendixes A and B; for key see Figure 5-1).

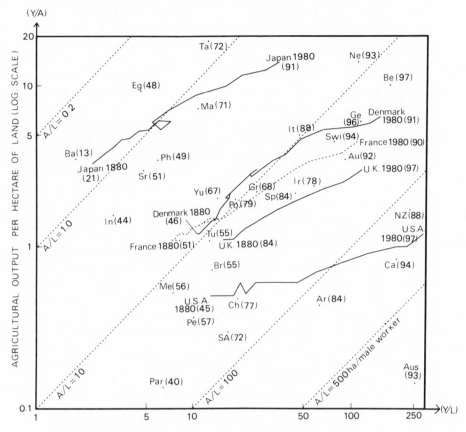

AGRICULTURAL OUTPUT PER MALE WORKER (LOG. SCALE)

is important to recognize that there is also a critical difference. As observed in Figure 5-1, and stylized in Figure 5-2, the man-land ratio in agriculture in the LDCs has deteriorated as a result of explosive population growth. The result is a growth path that is steeper than the uni-A/L line. In their early stages of modern economic growth, the present DCs experienced much lower rates of population growth. Absorption of labor by nonagricultural sectors was sufficient to reduce the absolute size of the labor force in agriculture. As a result, the historical paths of agricultural productivity growth of the DCs were less steep than the uni-A/L line from the early stages of industrialization. Denmark, which specialized in agricultural production in the international division of labor within western Europe, was the major exception. This difference in direction of the productivity growth paths between the DCs and the LDCs indicates greater need for the LDCs to develop land-saving technologies to facilitate substitution of fertilizer for land in order to sustain growth in agricultural output per worker. At the same time, national efforts will be required to modify industrial technology in the labor-using direction in order to increase labor absorption by nonagriculture.

Industrialization can affect agriculture in many ways. Growth of the nonagricultural sector increases the demand for farm products. More favorable factor-product price ratios increase the demand for both mechanical and biological inputs by agricultural producers. The impact of industrialization on factor markets is perhaps even more significant than the product market impact. Industrial development increases the demand for labor in the nonagricultural sector. The effect of increasing returns resulting from the progressive specialization of industry and division of labor and from the application of new knowledge is to reduce the cost of modern agricultural inputs, such as fertilizer, chemicals, and machinery, produced by the industrial sector.[4] A progressive industrial economy also contributes to growth of agricultural productivity through its greater capacity to support agricultural research; through its capacity to support both general education and production education in rural areas; through its capacity to support the development of more effective transportation and communication systems; and through the pervasive strengthening of other elements in the physical and institutional infrastructure serving rural areas.[5]

The capacity of the agricultural sector to respond to the lower prices of

4. Allyn A. Young, "Increasing Returns and Economic Progress," *Economic Journal* 38 (December 1928): 527–42. In his classic discussion of the sources of economic progress, Young regarded increasing returns resulting from the "enlargement of markets" and the associated "progressive division and specialization of industries" and "division of labor" as the principal source of economic progress. The "discovery of new natural resources" and "the growth of scientific knowledge" are treated as "factors which reinforce the influences which make for increasing returns." The role of market expansion, specialization, and division of function in the broad sense outlined by Young has frequently been lost sight of in recent discussions of the contribution of technical change to economic growth. Young's view that the "casual connections between the growth of industry and the progress of science run in both directions, but on which side the preponderant influence lies no one can say" (p. 535) remains valid. Current perspectives would probably place greater emphasis on advances in scientific and technical knowledge than appeared reasonable to Young writing in 1928. For an attempt to allocate the sources of change in efficiency in fertilizer production among sources internal and external to the fertilizer industry see Gian S. Sahota, *Fertilizer in Economic Development: An Econometric Analysis* (New York: Praeger, 1968).

5. The high correlation between the share of nonagricultural population and the literacy rate is indicated by the United Nations Educational, Social and Cultural Organization (UNESCO), *World Illiteracy at Mid-Century* (Paris, 1957). Peterson's analysis clearly shows that in the United States nonagricultural income is a critical variable in explaining the interstate variations in public support for agricultural education, research, and extension. See Willis L. Peterson, "The Allocation of Research, Teaching, and Extension Personnel in U.S. Colleges of Agriculture," *American Journal of Agricultural Economics* 51 (February 1969): 41–56.

modern biological, chemical, and mechanical inputs relative to the prices of land and labor and relative to the prices of agricultural products is critical to the agricultural development process. The positive relationship between industrial development observed in the time-series and cross-sectional observations and elaborated above is not, however, automatic. Industrialization policies which have ignored the potential intersector factor and product market linkages, such as those followed by a number of socialist countries and a number of developing countries, have frequently failed to produce the industrial inputs necessary to release the constraints on agricultural growth imposed by inelastic supplies of land and labor. And failure to invest in agricultural research and in education and other elements of the physical and social infrastructure in rural areas has frequently limited the capacity of the agricultural sector to respond to the potential for growth associated with industrialization.

TECHNICAL CHANGE AND THE METAPRODUCTION FUNCTION: A HYPOTHESIS

At this point it would seem useful to elaborate on the induced development model by formalizing, in operational terms, the process by which changes in the prices of industrial inputs are hypothesized to induce alternative paths of technical change and productivity growth in the agricultural sector of economies such as those observed in the previous section.

It seems clear that opportunities arising from industrialization do not bring about productivity growth unless they are exploited properly. A requisite for agricultural productivity growth is the capacity of the agricultural sector to adapt to a new set of factor and product prices. This adaptation involves not only the movement along a fixed production surface but also the creation of a new production surface which is optimal for the new set of prices. For example, even if fertilizer prices decline relative to the prices of land and farm products, increases in the use of fertilizer may be limited unless new crop varieties are developed which are more responsive to high levels of biological and chemical inputs than are traditional varieties.

Table 4-1 in the previous chapter, which compares the yield response of several rice varieties to fertilizer application, indicated that the yields of the indigenous varieties in Bangladesh were as high as those of the improved varieties in Japan at the low level of fertilization, but that they were less responsive to increases in the level of nitrogen application. For illustrative purposes, the relationship between fertilizer use and yield may be drawn, as in Figure 5-6, letting u_0 and u_1 represent the fertilizer-response curves of indigenous and improved varieties, respectively. For farmers facing u_0, a decline in the fertilizer price relative to the product price from p_0 to p_1 would not be expected to result in much increase in fertilizer application or in yield. The full impact of a decline in the fertilizer price on fertilizer use and output can be

FIGURE 5-6. Shift in fertilizer response curve along the metaresponse curve.

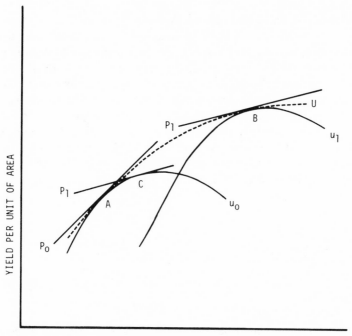

FERTILIZER INPUT PER UNIT OF AREA

fully realized only if u_1 is made available to farmers through the development of more responsive varieties.

Conceptually, it is possible to draw a curve such as U in Figure 5-6, which is the envelope of many individual response curves, each representing a rice variety characterized by a different degree of fertilizer responsiveness. We will identify this curve as a "metaproduction function" or a "potential production function." The metaproduction function can be regarded as the envelope of commonly conceived neoclassical production functions. In the *short run*, in which substitution among inputs is circumscribed by the rigidity of existing capital and equipment, production relationships can best be described by an activity with relatively fixed factor-factor and factor-product ratios. In the *long run*, in which the constraints exercised by existing capital disappear and are replaced by the fund of available technical knowledge, including all alternative feasible factor-factor and factor-product combinations, production relationships can be adequately described by the neoclassical production function. In the *secular period* of production, in which the constraints given by the available fund of technical knowledge are further relaxed to admit all potentially discoverable possibilities, production relationships can be described by a metaproduction function which describes all conceivable technical alternatives that might be discovered.[6]

Thus defined, the metaproduction function may appear to be the same as the innovation possibility curve advanced in Figure 4-2 in the previous chapter. In fact, we consider the metaproduction function an operational definition of the innovation possibility curve—operational in the sense that it can be measured empirically from observable production data. The metaproduction surface drawn in Figure 5-6 is the envelope of the most efficient production points available in the world. It is our basic assumption that such an envelope approximates the innovation possibility curve for the LDCs.

For example, the indigenous varieties in Bangladesh represented by u_0 in Figure 5-6 are considered to be an efficient technology developed over a very long period of time through a process of trial and error by farmers in an environment of high fertilizer prices relative to product and other input prices. Therefore it is difficult, or involves a very high cost, to develop a variety that will yield higher than the available indigenous varieties at a low level of fertilizer input or to make a parallel upward shift of u_0 above U. On the other hand, the technological potential available for Bangladesh agriculture at a high level of fertilizer application has not been fully exploited because it was only recently that research efforts began to be directed to the development of fertilizer-responsive, high-yielding varieties in response to a relative decline in fertilizer prices (from p_0 to p_1).

The germ plasm, plant type concepts, and other ideas and materials needed to develop varieties capable of producing high yields at high levels of fertilizer application are already available in DCs. Only modest adaptive research is required for the LDCs to develop the fertilizer-responsive, high-yielding varieties adaptable to their environments, as represented by u_1, relative to the research required to make a parallel upward shift of U_0. Thus it seems reasonable to assume that the innovation possibility curve for an LDC like Bangladesh can be approximated operationally by the envelope of the most efficient production points presently available in the world (U in Figure 5-6)—the metaproduction function according to our definition.

Following this hypothesis, the low efficiency in agricultural production in the LDCs is represented by point C in Figure 5-6. This suboptimal equi-

6. See Murray Brown, *On the Theory and Measurement of Technological Change* (Cambridge: Cambridge University Press, 1966), pp. 63–76, for a discussion of short-run, long-run, and secular production processes. The relationship between U and the u_i's in Fig. 5.6 is somewhat analogous to the interfirm envelope of a series of intrafirm production functions. See M. Bronfenbrenner, "Production Functions: Cobb-Douglas, Interfirm, Intrafirm," *Econometrica* 12 (January 1944):35–44. For an alternative perspective that views technical change as a process of widening the elasticity of substitution possibilities among factors rather than as a sequence of response functions, see Rolf Färe and Leif Jansson, "Technological Change and Disposability of Inputs," *Zeitschrift für Nationalökonomie* 34 (1974):283–90. For an empirical application see Richard Grabowski and David Sivan, "The Direction of Technological Change in Japanese Agriculture, 1874–1971," *Developing Economies* 21 (September 1983):234–43.

librium is the result of the lag in developing and adopting the fertilizer-responsive variety (u_1) in response to a decline in the relative price of fertilizer from p_0 to p_1. In this example we have used the development of fertilizer-responsive rice varieties as a pedagogical device to illustrate how changes in factor prices induce the development of new short-run production functions along the long-run metaproduction function. Our more general hypothesis is that the relatively low production efficiency of LDC agriculture is explained mainly by the limited capacity of LDC agricultural research systems to develop a new technology in response to changes in relative factor prices and of farmers' capacity to adopt it. This hypothesis will be tested empirically in the next chapter.

We do not consider that the metaproduction function is inherent in nature or that it remains completely stable over time. The metaproduction function will shift in response to the accumulation of general scientific knowledge. We do consider, however, that it is operationally feasible to assume a reasonable degree of stability for a technical "epoch," the time range relevant for many empirical analyses. Shifts in the metaproduction function are much slower than adjustments along the surface, or to the surface from below, of the metaproduction function, especially in LDCs.

It is hypothesized that the adaptation of agriculture to new opportunities in the form of lower relative prices of modern inputs involves an adjustment to a more efficient point on the metaproduction function. According to this hypothesis it may be equally rational for farmers in Japan, where prices of fertilizer are relatively low and prices of rice relatively high, to plant varieties that are more responsive to high levels of fertilization and to fertilize more heavily than farmers in Southeast Asia, where fertilizer prices are relatively high and prices of rice are typically relatively low (see Chapter 9). In extreme cases the relative prices of land and labor may induce completely opposite paths of productivity growth. For example, in the United States, where wage rates are high relative to the price of land, it has been profitable to sacrifice yield per unit area by designing tomato plants that ripen uniformly, in order to permit mechanical harvesting. In Mexico, where wage rates are low and land is expensive, it may be more profitable to develop tomato varieties that have a more extended harvest period and are more responsive to more labor-intensive production practices in order to obtain higher yields per hectare.

From the intercountry cross-section and time-series observations, the relative endowments of land and labor at the time a nation enters into the development process apparently have a significant influence upon the optimal path to be followed in moving along the metaproduction function. Where labor is the limiting factor, the optimum for new opportunities in the form of lower prices of modern inputs is likely to be along a path characterized by a higher land-labor ratio. Movement toward an optimal position on the metaproduction function would involve development and adoption of new mechanical inputs. On the other hand, where land is the limiting factor, the new optimum is likely to be the point at which the yield per hectare is higher for the higher level of fertilizer input. Movement to this point would involve development and adoption of new biological and chemical inputs.

The partial productivity and factor input ratios presented earlier in this chapter suggest that those nations which have achieved relatively high levels of either land or labor productivity have been relatively successful in substituting industrial inputs for the constraints imposed by a relatively scarce factor, either land or labor. It seems possible to explain many of the vast differences in productivity levels and factor input ratios in agriculture among countries by hypothesizing that technical advance in agriculture occurs primarily as a result of new economic opportunities created by developments in the nonagricultural sector. The advances in mechanical and biological technology do not, however, occur without cost. Development of a more fertilizer-responsive crop variety, in response to declining prices of fertilizer, typically requires substantial expenditures on research, development, and dissemination, before it actually becomes available to farmers. Public investment in improvements in water control, land development, and other environmental modifications may also be required before it becomes profitable for farmers to adopt the newly developed varieties.

Farmers seek the new inputs and new techniques in order to move to a more efficient point on the metaproduction function in response to new factor-factor and factor-product price ratios. Only when public research institutions and private farm supply firms accurately anticipate the demands by farmers for profitable opportunities and make the new inputs or methods available to farmers is it possible to move to the optimal point on the metaproduction function. Even then, the capacity of the new variety or breed to respond to higher levels of inputs may not be fully realized until the producer fully masters the modifications in soil and water management and in other cultural practices necessary to achieve the higher yield potential of a new crop variety. Production education programs by public extension services and the private sector suppliers of new inputs are frequently required to convey this information to farmers. Unless this mechanism of dialectic interaction among farmers, suppliers of new inputs, and research scientists and administrators functions properly, productivity growth in agriculture is not assured.

Improvements in human capital in the form of educated, innovative farmers, competent scientists and technicians, and perceptive public administrators and business entrepreneurs are essential if this process is to generate continuous growth in agricultural productivity. We hypothesize that the agricultural productivity gap among countries is based on differences in the prices of modern technical inputs in agriculture and differences in the stock of human capital capable of generating a sequence of innovations which enables agriculture to move along the metaproduction function in response to changes in factor and product price relationships. The precise manner in which investment in resource accumulation, technical inputs, and human capital accounts for differences in labor productivity among countries is examined in the next chapter.

6

Sources of Agricultural Productivity Differences among Countries

Growth in output per worker in agriculture is generally recognized as a necessary condition for economic development (Chapter 2). The great differences in the productivity of agricultural labor among countries, discussed in the previous chapter, have raised serious doubts among national policymakers and planners and among officials in the international aid agencies about the possibility of substantially narrowing the gaps. In this chapter we attempt to identify the sources of the differences in productivity of agricultural labor among countries. We first estimate an aggregate production function based on intercountry cross-section data for 1960, 1970, and 1980. We then use this production function to account for intercountry differences in labor productivity.[1]

During two decades covered by the analysis in this chapter major changes occurred in world agriculture. In the less developed countries, the so-called green revolution—the development and diffusion of modern semidwarf varieties of rice, wheat, and other cereal crops with high fertilizer-absorbing and high-yielding capacity—exerted an appreciable impact on aggregate output and productivity. In developed countries, especially in the United States, the increase in labor productivity in agriculture was extremely rapid, mainly because of (a) the dramatic progress of mechanical technology associated with large decreases in the agricultural labor force during the two decades of economic boom preceding the first oil crisis and (b) the high rates of investment in agriculture during the world food crisis of the mid-1970s.

Despite such remarkable developments, the disequilibrium in world agriculture—underproduction of food and chronic malnutrition in the LDCs and overproduction and depressed farm prices or the accumulation of surpluses in the DCs—has remained serious (Chapter 12). Among the important issues to be confronted in designing national and international agricultural production and market policies is whether the production structure of world agriculture

1. This chapter draws heavily on Toshihiko Kawagoe, Yujiro Hayami, and Vernon W. Ruttan, "The Intercountry Agricultural Production Function and Productivity Differences among Countries," *Journal of Development Economics* (forthcoming).

has changed during the past two decades and what factors underlay the differential changes in agricultural productivity between the DCs and the LDCs.

Our analysis indicates that, despite the dramatic technological developments in both the DCs and the LDCs during the past two decades, the production structure of world agriculture as measured by the production elasticities of conventional and nonconventional inputs remained largely unchanged. The gap in labor productivity in agriculture between the DCs and the LDCs, which widened further between 1960 and 1980, continued to be accounted for in roughly equal importance by the three sources—differences in internal resources (land and livestock), modern technical inputs (fertilizer and machinery), and human capital (general and technical education). When the intercountry agricultural production function was estimated separately for the DCs and the LDCs by pooling the observations for 1960, 1970, and 1980, a major difference in production structure was found. The LDC production function was neutral with respect to farm scale whereas the DC production function was characterized by significant scale economies. This scale-economy effect accounts for about one-fourth of the agricultural productivity gap between the developed and less developed countries.

We do not, in this chapter, attempt to explore the economic and institutional factors that have led some economies to make the investments necessary to supply modern technical inputs to their farmers and to provide them with the knowledge and skill to make productive use of the new inputs. In subsequent chapters, however, we explore how Japan and the United States, two economies with extreme differences in resource endowments, have been able to follow different factor productivity growth paths as they have moved along the metaproduction function.

THE METHOD AND THE DATA

Our approach involves the estimation of an aggregate production function of the Cobb-Douglas type, employing the same set of intercountry cross-section data used in the analysis in Chapter 5. (For details on data sources and processing, see Appendix A.) The production function estimates, together with the data on conventional and nonconventional inputs, are used in accounting for intercountry differences in output per worker. Forty-three countries are classified into subsamples of twenty-one DCs with 1980 per capita GNP above U.S.$4,000 and twenty-two LDCs with 1980 per capita GNP below $4,000: DCs—Australia,* Austria,* Belgium,* Canada,* Denmark,* Finland,* France,* Germany (Federal Republic),* Greece, Ireland, Israel, Italy,* Japan,* Netherlands,* New Zealand,* Norway,* Spain, Sweden,* Switzerland,* United Kingdom,* United States*; and LDCs—Argentina, Bangladesh,* Brazil, Chile, Colombia,* Egypt,* India,* Libya, Mauritius,* Mexico, Pakistan,* Paraguay,* Peru,* Philippines,* Portugal, South Africa,

Sri Lanka,* Syria,* Taiwan, Turkey,* Venezuela, Yugoslavia.[2] The seventeen DCs with asterisks are high-income developed countries (HDC) with a per capita GNP above $6,000; the twelve LDCs with asterisks are low-income, less developed countries (LLDC) with a per capita GNP of less than $1,500. These groupings are used for the later analysis of sources of productivity differences (Table 6-5). (The HDC and LLDC classification used in this chapter is the same as the DC and LDC classification used in Table 5-2 in the previous chapter.)

The specific variables used in the study included labor (L), land (A), livestock (S), fertilizer (F), machinery (M), and general and technical education $(E$ and $T)$. In summing up the effects of resource endowments, technology, and human capital on productivity per worker, land and livestock serve as proxy variables for resource endowments, machinery and fertilizer for technical inputs, and general and technical education in agriculture for human capital.

The land actually being used for agricultural production cannot be regarded as a mere gift of nature. It represents the result of previous investments in land clearing, reclamation, drainage, fencing, and other development measures. Similarly, livestock represents a form of internal capital accumulation. Thus, in our perspective, land and livestock represent a form of long-term capital formation embodying inputs supplied primarily from within the agricultural sector.[3] In the conservation model of agricultural development, internal capital formation of this type was almost the only source of growth in labor productivity. High inputs of both land and livestock per worker tend to be associated with high levels of labor and low levels of land per unit of output.

In contrast, as discussed in Chapter 5, fertilizer, as measured by the N + P_2O_5 + K_2O in commercial fertilizers, and machinery, as measured by tractor horsepower, represent inputs supplied by the industrial sector. Technical advances stemming from both public and private sector research and development are embodied in, or complementary to, these modern industrial inputs. Advances in mechanical technology are usually associated with larger inputs of power and machinery. Biological improvements, such as the development of new high-yielding varieties, are typically associated with higher levels of fertilizer use. In this analysis, these two industrial inputs represent proxies for the whole range of inputs in which modern mechanical and biological technologies are embodied.

All the conventional inputs, as well as outputs, were deflated by the

2. World Bank, *World Development Report 1982* (New York: Oxford University Press, 1982). Surinam, which was included in the analysis of the previous chapter, is excluded from the sample for the analysis in this chapter because of the unavailability of data on the number of farms. Libya is classified as an LDC even though its per capita GNP was higher than $8,000 because of large oil revenues.

3. Perennial plants belong to the same category of inputs as livestock, but they are not included because of lack of data.

number of farms so that the production function is expressed in per-farm terms in order to make inferences about scale economies.

The proxies for human capital include measures of both the general educational level of the rural population and specialized education in the agricultural sciences and technology. Two alternative measures of the level of general education were attempted: (a) the literacy ratio and (b) the school enrollment ratio for the primary and secondary levels.[4] Both sets of data are deficient, in that they apply to the entire population and are not sensitive to differences in the quality of rural and urban education. Education in the agricultural sciences and technology was measured by the number of graduates per ten thousand farm workers from agricultural faculties at above the secondary level. These graduates represent the major source of technological and scientific personnel for agricultural research and extension.

Attempts were also made to incorporate other variables. The ratio of irrigated land to total land area and the ratio of cropland to pastureland were tried to adjust for differences in the quality of land input. But the coefficients of such variables were either negative or nonsignificant, probably because those data are too crude to capture the effect of differences in land quality.

The production function employed in this analysis is of the unrestricted Cobb-Douglas (linear in the logarithms) form.[5] It was used mainly because of its ease of manipulation and interpretation. The coefficients of the Cobb-Douglas production function can be interpreted as indicating the elasticities of production with respect to inputs. Assuming that the factors are specified correctly, the coefficients can also be interpreted as indicating the relative importance of each factor as a source of differences in output among countries.

Multicollinearity is a major statistical problem in estimating a production function that includes as many as seven independent variables. Intercorrelation was especially serious between land and livestock and resulted in nonsignificant or negative coefficients for the land variable when estimated by ordinary least squares (OLS) in previous studies. We have attempted to avoid the multicollinearity problem by using the principal components regressions (PCR) devised by Maurice J. Kendall in addition to OLS.[6] Two alternative

4. The school enrollment ratio is regarded as a somewhat more sensitive educational index than the literacy ratio. See Mary Jean Bowman and C. Arnold Anderson, "Concerning the Role of Education in Development," *Old Societies and New States,* ed. Clifford Geertz (New York: Free Press of Glencoe, 1963), pp. 247–79; the authors emphasize the multidimensional nature of the relationships between education and development.

5. A more general production function of the transcendental logarithmic (translog) form was also tried, but the results of estimation, involving as many as seven variables, were too complicated and unreliable to make a reasonable judgment and interpretation. For the translog function, see Laurits R. Christensen, Dale W. Jorgenson, and Lawrence J. Lau, "Transcendental Logarithmic Production Frontiers," *Review of Economics and Statisitics* 55 (February 1973):28–45.

6. Maurice G. Kendall, *A Course in Multivariate Analysis* (New York: Hafner Publishing Co., 1957).

procedures of deleting principal components were tried, one based on the relative magnitudes of characteristic roots and another based on the Student *t*-ratios of principal components regression coefficients.[7] The results were similar, but those based on the characteristic root criteria were generally more consistent and plausible and are, therefore, the only results reported here.[8] Under these criteria, the principal components having the smallest characteristic roots are deleted. The deletion proceeds to the point at which 95 percent of the total system variations are explained by the remaining components.

A critical assumption in this approach is that the technical possibilities available to agricultural producers in the different countries can be described by the same production function. Richard R. Nelson has argued that the assumptions of a common production function ''get in the way of understanding international differences in productivity—particularly differences between advanced and underdeveloped economies.'' Nelson's objections appear directed primarily to the empirical results obtained from the use of relatively primitive two-factor production functions, as in K. J. Arrow, H. B. Chenery, B. S. Minhas, and R. M. Solow, which relate intercountry differences in value added per worker to the capital-labor ratio. He insists, as a result of differential diffusion of new technology, that ''at any given time one would expect to find considerable variation among firms with respect to the vintage of their technology, certainly between countries, but even within a country.''[9]

We share the Nelson perspective. Agricultural producers in different countries, in different regions of the same country, and on different farms in the same region are not all on the same microproduction function. This reflects differences among producers in their ability to adopt new technology. More important, it is also the result of differential diffusion of agricultural technology, and, to an even greater degree, of differential diffusion of the scientific and technical capacity to invent and develop new mechanical, biological, and chemical technology specifically adapted to the factor endowments and prices in a particular country or region. Furthermore, we view the generation of new technical knowledge in agriculture as endogenous. It is generated in response to changes in relative factor and product prices.

7. See Ron C. Mittelhammer and John L. Baritelle, "On Two Strategies for Choosing Principal Components in Regression Analysis," *American Journal of Agricultural Economics* 59 (May 1977):336–43.

8. The ridge regression (RR) approach developed by Hoerl and Kennard was also tried in order to cope with the multicollinearity problem. The results of RR were largely similar to those of PCR for a relevant range of the *k*-parameter but are not reported here because of the difficulty of selecting a single value for the *k*-parameter. See Arthur E. Hoerl and Robert W. Kennard, "Ridge Regression: Biased Estimation for Nonorthogonal Problems," *Technometrics* 12 (February 1970):55–68.

9. Richard R. Nelson, "A 'Diffusion Model' of International Productivity Differences in Manufacturing Industry," *American Economic Review* 58 (December 1968):1229–30; K. J. Arrow, H. B. Chenery, B. S. Minhas, and R. M. Solow, "Capital-Labor Substitution and Economic Efficiency," *Review of Economics and Statistics* 43 (August 1961):225–50.

According to the hypothesis proposed in Chapter 5, technical change occurs in response to changes in relative prices along the surface of a "metaproduction function." The full range of technological alternatives described by the metaproduction function, which represents the envelope of all known and potentially available production "activities," is only partially available to individual producers in a particular country or agricultural region during any particular historical "epoch." It is, however, potentially available to agricultural scientists.

We consider the common intercountry production function which we have estimated as a metaproduction function. It is assumed that the invention and diffusion of a new location-specific agricultural technology through the application of the concepts of physical, biological, and chemical science and of engineering, craft, and husbandry skill, are capable of making the factor productivities implicit in the metaproduction function available to producers in less developed countries. It is also assumed that the capacity of a country to engage in the necessary research, development, and extension is measured by the two proxy variables for human capital, general education and technical education in agriculture. This effort is not inconsistent with the perspective presented by Nelson in his criticism of the empirical results obtained from two-factor intercountry production functions.

ESTIMATION OF THE PRODUCTION FUNCTION[10]

The results of the estimation of the unrestricted Cobb-Douglas production function based on the cross-country data are summarized in Tables 6-1 and 6-2. Each column reports the results of a regression including estimates of production elasticities and their standard errors (in parentheses), the standard error of estimates, and the coefficient of determination adjusted for the degree of freedom. Table 6-1 presents estimates for 1960, 1970, and 1980 separately based on the data for all forty-three countries. Table 6-2 presents estimates from pooled observations for 1960, 1970, and 1980 for all countries, and for twenty-one DCs and twenty-two LDCs separately.

Considering the crudeness of the data, the levels of statistical significance of the regression coefficients appear satisfactory in most cases. The major exceptions are the OLS estimates of the coefficients for land. The application of PCR improves the estimates of the land coefficient. It increases the magnitudes of the coefficient for land primarily at the expense of the coefficient for livestock because of the high intercorrelation between land and livestock. The PCR estimates are surprisingly good in terms of both our a priori knowledge of the relative magnitudes of production elasticities among factors and the magnitudes of the estimated coefficients relative to their standard errors, even

---

10. Readers who are not interested in the technical details may wish to skip this section and turn directly to the next section.

TABLE 6-1. Estimates of the intercountry agricultural production function based on the sample of 43 countries, for 1960 (1957–62 averages), 1970 (1967–72 averages), and 1980 (1975–80 averages) separately

Period	1960				1970				1980			
Estimation method	OLS		PCR		OLS		PCR		OLS		PCR	
Regression number	(Q1)	(Q2)	(Q3)	(Q4)	(Q5)	(Q6)	(Q7)	(Q8)	(Q9)	(Q10)	(Q11)	(Q12)
Labor (L)	.537	.535	.505	.496	.550	.537	.519	.514	.525	.527	.420	.409
	(.131)	(.128)	(.086)	(.085)	(.125)	(.124)	(.075)	(.075)	(.104)	(.106)	(.060)	(.060)
Land (A)	.045	.040	.099	.100	.048	.040	.062	.057	.014	.009	.080	.080
	(.067)	(.065)	(.018)	(.018)	(.060)	(.060)	(.022)	(.023)	(.058)	(.059)	(.021)	(.022)
Livestock (S)	.303	.309	.157	.164	.235	.249	.177	.194	.318	.326	.184	.195
	(.085)	(.083)	(.020)	(.019)	(.078)	(.079)	(.018)	(.021)	(.082)	(.085)	(.018)	(.018)
Fertilizer (F)	.148	.134	.154	.147	.204	.194	.223	.218	.163	.143	.246	.245
	(.060)	(.061)	(.021)	(.020)	(.086)	(.086)	(.020)	(.020)	(.069)	(.069)	(.022)	(.022)
Machinery (M)	.036	.043	.101	.100	.058	.070	.100	.097	.071	.090	.118	.117
	(.062)	(.060)	(.007)	(.009)	(.070)	(.068)	(.009)	(.011)	(.063)	(.063)	(.008)	(.009)
General education (E):												
Literacy ratio	.129		.141		.226		.163		.390		.316	
	(.146)		(.141)		(.170)		(.161)		(.186)		(.174)	
School enrollment ratio		.271		.288		.320		.214		.506		.346
		(.190)		(.187)		(.255)		(.235)		(.291)		(.274)
Technical education (T)	.194	.173	.156	.135	.172	.160	.166	.163	.151	.153	.119	.126
	(.054)	(.055)	(.045)	(.047)	(.057)	(.060)	(.048)	(.051)	(.053)	(.055)	(.047)	(.050)
LDC dummy	−.299	−.290	−.290	−.139	−.393	−.392	−.236	−.261	−.597	−.606	−.284	−.296
	(.192)	(.188)	(.188)	(.102)	(.201)	(.201)	(.091)	(.084)	(.184)	(.187)	(.075)	(.075)
Coef. of det. (R̄²)	.928	.930	.918	.920	.943	.943	.940	.941	.956	.954	.944	.943
S.E. of estimates	.301	.296	.322	.316	.285	.286	.292	.291	.274	.279	.307	.311
Sum of conventional coefficients	1.070	1.061	1.017	1.006	1.095	1.090	1.081	1.081	1.091	1.095	1.048	1.046
	(.098)	(.097)	(.089)	(.087)	(.082)	(.083)	(.077)	(.077)	(.071)	(.062)	(.072)	(.063)

Note: Equations linear in logarithms are estimated by the ordinary least squares (OLS) and the principal components regression (PCR). The standard errors of coefficients are in parentheses.

144

TABLE 6-2. Estimates of the intercountry agricultural production function, based on the whole sample of 43 countries, and the subsamples of 22 LDCs and 21 DCs, pooling 1960, 1970, and 1980 observations

Country coverage	All countries				LDC				DC			
Estimation method	OLS		PCR		OLS		PCR		OLS		PCR	
Regression number	(Q13)	(Q14)	(Q15)	(Q16)	(Q17)	(Q18)	(Q19)	(Q20)	(Q21)	(Q22)	(Q23)	(Q24)
Labor (L)	.509 (.068)	.503 (.068)	.473 (.043)	.436 (.042)	.608 (.107)	.562 (.103)	.534 (.050)	.551 (.052)	.658 (.083)	.707 (.082)	.667 (.063)	.651 (.068)
Land (A)	.036 (0.35)	.033 (.068)	.090 (.012)	.091 (.012)	-.052 (.063)	-.065 (.063)	.088 (.012)	.094 (.012)	.068 (.033)	.099 (.031)	.101 (.016)	.080 (.016)
Livestock (S)	.302 (.047)	.309 (.048)	.190 (.010)	.195 (.010)	.274 (.089)	.318 (.085)	.140 (.014)	.161 (.017)	.189 (.065)	.150 (.068)	.175 (.007)	.189 (.009)
Fertilizer (F)	.158 (.039)	.154 (.040)	.194 (.012)	.195 (.012)	.084 (.058)	.089 (.057)	.162 (.018)	.142 (.021)	.189 (.077)	.189 (.083)	.219 (.010)	.232 (.011)
Machinery (M)	.061 (.036)	.067 (.035)	.095 (.005)	.109 (.004)	.133 (.053)	.136 (.053)	.072 (.009)	.060 (.014)	.216 (.056)	.175 (.054)	.130 (.011)	.142 (.009)
General education (E): Literacy ratio	.139 (.091)		.091 (.089)		.287 (.111)		.276 (.101)		-1.607 (.767)		-.708 (.485)	
School enrollment ratio		.165 (.128)		.252 (.115)		.405 (.155)		.450 (.146)		-.173 (.267)		-.112 (.252)
Technical education (T)	.180 (.031)	.174 (.032)	.167 (.028)	.064 (.006)	.178 (.040)	.166 (.041)	.158 (.038)	.156 (.035)	.134 (.034)	.142 (.038)	.139 (.033)	.113 (.028)
LDC dummy	-.444 (.111)	-.446 (.111)	-.295 (.053)	-.392 (.043)								
Time dummy: 1970	-.004 (.069)	-.021 (.070)	-.066 (.062)	-.004 (.060)	-.156 (.104)	-.220 (.105)	-.191 (.086)	-.209 (.083)	.045 (.070)	.090 (.068)	.119 (.050)	.089 (.056)
1980	-.044 (.081)	-.070 (.081)	-.121 (.067)	-.001 (.058)	-.330 (.122)	-.428 (.123)	-.330 (.094)	-.367 (.093)	.095 (.087)	.172 (.081)	.203 (.055)	.180 (.067)
Coef. of det. ($\bar{R}^2$)	.943	.943	.938	.932	.913	.913	.902	.902	.965	.963	.963	.962
S.E. of estimates	.292	.293	.304	.319	.314	.314	.334	.333	.178	.185	.184	.188
Sum of conventional coefficients	1.066 (.047)	1.066 (.048)	1.042 (.043)	1.026 (.044)	1.047 (.058)	1.040 (.059)	.996 (.053)	1.007 (.052)	1.320 (.070)	1.320 (.073)	1.293 (.060)	1.294 (.061)

Note: Equations linear in logarithms are estimated by the ordinary least squares (OLS) and the principal components regression (PCR). The standard errors of coefficients are in parentheses.

145

TABLE 6-3.   Covariance-analysis tests of stability in production elasticities over
time and among countries

Stability over 1960, 1970, and 1980	
F-statistics calculated from:	
Q1, Q5, Q9, and Q13	1.25
Q2, Q6, Q10, and Q14	1.29
Q3, Q7, Q11, and Q15	.87
Q4, Q8, Q12, and Q16	1.61
Theoretical F-values with 16 and 102 degrees of freedom:	
5% level of significance	1.75
1% level of significance	2.19
Stability between DC and LDC:	
F-statistics calculated from:	
Q13, Q17, and Q21	4.76
Q14, Q18, and Q22	4.58
Q15, Q19, and Q23	4.35
Q16, Q20, and Q24	5.73
Theoretical F-values with 9 and 109 degrees of freedom:	
5% level of significance	1.97
1% level of significance	2.58

though the PCR estimates involve some bias and, hence, the standard t-tests
are not strictly applicable.

The results shown in Table 6-1 give some indication that the production
elasticities for fertilizer and machinery increased from 1960 to 1980 at the
expense of the elasticity for labor. The F-statistics presented in Table 6-3,
however, support the conclusion that there has been no significant change in
production elasticities over time, although the statistical tests do indicate that
there are significant differences in the production functions between the DCs
and the LDCs. The production elasticities of conventional factors are uniformly larger for the DCs than for the LDCs. As a result, the sum of the
conventional input coefficients for the DCs is significantly larger than one,
whereas for the LDCs the sum is not significantly different from one.[11] Thus
the results indicate that LDC agriculture was characterized by constant returns
to scale, and DC agriculture was subject to increasing returns.

These results are consistent with our knowledge of the basic difference in
agricultural technology between the DCs and the LDCs. For the past two
decades the agricultural labor force in the DCs declined at very rapid rates—
by as much as one-half to two-thirds in most countries. The decreases in the
labor force were associated with dramatic progress in mechanical technology
and acceleration of fixed capital investment in machinery and equipment. The
scale economies usually stem from the lumpiness or indivisibility of fixed
capital. It is reasonable to expect that agricultural technology in the DCs,

11. The sum of conventional coefficients for DCs was not significantly different from one
when the production function was estimated on national aggregate data without being deflated by
the number of farms.

which facilitated substitution of increasingly larger machines for labor, would be characterized by scale economies. Our estimates of the DC production function are consistent with the results of Zvi Griliches's earlier study of the aggregate agricultural production function for the United States.[12] The sum of the coefficients of conventional inputs that he estimated was about 1.3, which is the same as ours. His estimates of the individual factor coefficients were also similar to ours.[13]

In contrast to the DCs, the LDCs experienced absolute increases in their agricultural labor force because of explosive population growth and insufficient labor absorption by the nonagricultural sector. Rapid population growth has resulted in continued decline in the land-labor ratio. In this situation, the major effort of technological development was directed to saving land by applying more labor- and land-substituting inputs, such as fertilizer, per hectare of farmland. This substitution was facilitated by the development of modern fertilizer-responsive high-yielding varieties of rice and wheat in the tropics. It is reasonable to expect that this new land-saving technology in the LDCs was scale-neutral since seeds, fertilizer, and chemicals are highly divisible. Some LDCs did experience significant progress in farm mechanization, such as the installation of power pumps for irrigation and substitution of tractors for draft animals, but the production function estimates seem to indicate that in the LDCs the development of scale-neutral land-saving technology predominated over that of labor-saving mechanical technology.

It is interesting to note that the DC production elasticities for conventional factors are larger than those of the LDCs by approximately equal proportions. For example, if we divide the conventional coefficients in regressions (Q23) and (Q24), by their sums, we obtain:

	Labor (L)	Land (A)	Livestock (S)	Fertilizer (F)	Machinery (M)
(Q23)	.516	.078	.135	.169	.100
(Q24)	.503	.062	.146	.179	.110

12. Zvi Griliches, "Research Expenditures, Education, and the Aggregate Agricultural Production Function," *American Economic Review* 54 (December 1964):961–74.

13. The existence of scale economies in U.S. agriculture has been questioned in an important article by Yoav Kislev and Willis Peterson, "Prices, Technology and Farm Size," *Journal of Political Economy* 90 (June 1982):578–95. They argue that increases in the size of farm in U.S. agriculture have occurred in response to rising wage rates. Wage increases in the nonagricultural sector have resulted in the transfer of labor from the agricultural to the nonagricultural sector and have increased the opportunity cost of labor to agriculture. The loss of labor to the agricultural sector has also created opportunities for the remaining farm operators to enlarge the size of their farms. We agree that the intersector labor market effects emphasized by Kislev and Peterson represent a very important part of the explanation for the increase in farm size in U.S. agriculture. But our analysis (see Chapter 7) also suggests that the higher wage rates have induced advances in mechanical technology, such as an increase in the size of tractors and of grain and forage harvesting and storage equipment, that could be employed economically only on increasingly larger farms. As these new machines have become available, the opportunity to eliminate the disequilibria between existing and optimal farm size generated returns to scale. Thus we view our

which are almost the same as the coefficients of regressions (Q19) and (Q20). These results suggest that the intercountry agricultural production function may be expressed in the following form:

(1) $\log Y = k(\alpha_L \log L + \alpha_A \log A + \alpha_S \log S + \alpha_F \log F + \alpha_M \log M)$
$+ (\beta_E \log E + \beta_T \log T) + \log \gamma$

where $\alpha_L + \alpha_A + \alpha_S + \alpha_F + \alpha_M = 1$ and $k > 1$ for DC and $k = 1$ for LDC, and γ represents an intercept including random disturbances. All the conventional inputs (L, A, S, F, and M) are expressed in per-farm averages for the respective countries. Thus the DC production function differs from the LDC function only by the scale factor k, and the other parameters are approximately the same.

It is apparent from the results in Table 6-2 that there is a major difference in the production elasticities of general education (β_E) between the DCs and LDCs. The general education coefficients were estimated to be negative for the DCs. In the LDCs the coefficients were positive and had magnitudes similar to the estimates based on the entire sample. The negative estimates of the general education coefficients for the DCs should be interpreted with considerable caution. The data ranges of both the literacy and school enrollment ratios were very narrow among the DCs because they were all close to 100 percent. Furthermore, they are very poor proxies of the educational level of the rural labor force. It seems reasonable to assume that if more complete data, such as average schooling years of agricultural workers as used by Griliches for the United States, were available for intercountry cross-section comparisons, a significant coefficient for education would have been obtained for the DCs.[14]

A check on the plausibility of our results can be obtained by comparing them with the results of previous attempts to estimate intercountry agricultural production functions. The results from earlier studies are summarized in Table 6-4. The estimates shown in Table 6-4 represent a modal set in each study (with estimates rounded). On the whole, the results of these previous studies were similar to ours. The major exceptions are those of Jyoti P. Bhattacharjee, which seem subject to serious bias because of incomplete specification. Except for that of John M. Antle, the earlier studies did not attempt to estimate the production functions separately for different country groups. He obtained very poor results with negative or nonsignificant estimates for most production elasticities.

One reason that it has been difficult to obtain reasonable estimates of the

---

hypothesis and the Kislev-Peterson hypothesis as complementary, rather than competing, explanations for changes in farm size. In any case, the empirical evidence for scale neutrality in U.S. agriculture, as advanced by Kislev and Peterson, is more conjectural then conclusive. It must be recognized, however, that the major thrust of their theory is valid even if increasing returns to scale prevail.

14. Kislev and Peterson, "Prices, Technology and Farm Size."

TABLE 6-4. Some previous estimates of the intercountry agricultural production function

Source	Bhattacharjee (1953)	Hayami (1969)	Hayami-Ruttan (1970)	Evenson-Kislev (1975, p. 81)	Nguyen (1979)	Yamada-Ruttan (1980)	Antle (1980)	Mundlak-Hellinghausen (1982)
Number of countries included	22	38	38	36	40	41	66	58
Period for estimation	1949	1960	1955, 60, 65	1955, 60, 65, 68	1970, 75	1970	1965	1960–63
Estimation method[a]	OLS	OLS	OLS & IV	OLS	OLS	OLS	OLS & PC	OLS & PC
Data specification[b]	S:NG	M:NG	M:NG PF & PW	M:NG	M; NG & PH	M:NG	S:NG	S:NG
Coefficients estimated								
Labor	.30	.45	.40	.20	.35	.35	.40	.40
Land	.40	.20	.10	.10	0	0	.15	.20
Livestock	0		.25	.35	.30	.25	.20	.20
Fertilizer	.30	.20	.15	.10	.15	.25	.10	.10
Machinery		.15	.10	.10	.20	.15		.10
General education (School enrollment ratio)		.45	.40		.25	.25	.25	
Technical education		.10	.15	.10	.20	.15	.20	
Research				.10			.20[c]	
Infrastructure								0[d]

Sources: John M. Antle, "Infrastructure and Aggregate Agricultural Productivity: International Evidence," *Economic Development and Cultural Change* 31 (April 1983):609–19.

Jyoti P. Bhattacharjee, "Resource Use and Productivity in World Agriculture," *Journal of Farm Economics* 37 (February 1955):57–71.

Robert E. Evenson and Yoav Kislev, *Agricultural Research and Productivity* (New Haven: Yale University Press, 1975).

Yujiro Hayami, "Sources of Agricultural Productivity Gap among Selected Countries," *American Journal of Agricultural Economics* 51 (August 1969):564–75.

Yujiro Hayami and Vernon W. Ruttan, "Agricultural Productivity Differences among Countries," *American Economic Review* 60 (December 1970):895–911.

Yair Mundlak and Rene Hellinghausen, "The Intercountry Agricultural Production Function: Another View," *American Journal of Agricultural Economics* 64 (November 1982):664–72.

Dûng Nguyen, "On Agricultural Productivity Differences among Countries," *American Journal of Agricultural Economics* 61 (August 1979):565–70.

Saburo Yamada and Vernon W. Ruttan, "International Comparisons of Productivity in Agriculture," *New Developments in Productivity Measurement and Analysis*, ed. John W. Kendrick and Beatrice N. Vaccara (Chicago: University of Chicago Press, 1980), pp. 509–94.

[a] OLS, IV, and PC represent, respectively, ordinary least squares, instrumental variable, and principal components regressions.

[b] S and M represent, respectively, single-year observations and multiple-year averages. NG, PF, PW, and PH represent, respectively, national aggregates, per-farm, per-worker, and per-hectare averages.

[c] Communication and transportation.

[d] Irrigation.

production function separately for DCs and LDCs using a cross-country sample for a single time point is that the data range within each country group is so narrow that large observational errors inherent in the cross-country data tend to overshadow the real effects of explanatory variables. This study was successful in producing reasonable estimates for each country group because by pooling data for three time periods encompassing more than two decades, the data range was sufficiently wide relative to observational errors.

ACCOUNTING FOR PRODUCTIVITY DIFFERENCES

The results obtained from estimation of the agricultural production function in the previous section may be used to account for intercountry differences in labor productivity (output per male worker) in agriculture.

Since the intercountry production function is now specified as equation (1), the labor productivity function can be expressed as:

$$(2) \quad \log (Y/L) = \alpha_A \log (A/L) + \alpha_S \log (S/L) + \alpha_F \log (F/L)$$
$$+ \alpha_M \log (M/L) + \beta_E \log E + \beta_T \log T + (k - 1)\log Z + \log \gamma$$

where $\log Z = \alpha_L \log L + \alpha_A \log A + \alpha_S \log S + \alpha_F \log F + \alpha_M \log M$. By taking the difference in labor productivity between a base country (subscript 0) and a country to be compared (subscript 1) and taking its Taylor expansion to the first-order term, the following approximation formula can be obtained:

$$(3) \quad \frac{\Delta(Y/L)}{(Y/L)_0} \cong \left[\alpha_A \frac{\Delta(A/L)}{(A/L)_0} + \alpha_S \frac{\Delta(S/L)}{(S/L)_0} + \alpha_F \frac{\Delta(F/L)}{(F/L)_0} + \alpha_M \frac{\Delta(M/L)}{(M/L)_0} \right]$$
$$+ (\beta_E \frac{\Delta E}{E_0} + \beta_T \frac{\Delta T}{T_0}) + (k_0 - 1) \frac{\Delta Z}{Z_0} + U$$

where Δ's are absolute differences in respective factors between the base country and the country compared, and their denominators are the base-country values of respective inputs. The first term on the right-hand side of equation (3) represents the contribution of conventional inputs per worker to the percentage difference in output per worker; the second term represents the contribution of human capital variables; the third term represents the effect of scale economies; and the fourth term (U) represents the residual.[15]

15. This residual term is expressed as

$$U = (k_0 - k_1)\log Z_1 + \frac{\Delta_\gamma}{\gamma_0}$$

where the second term is the effect of error in the equation and the first term represents the effect of a shift from the LDC production function to the DC function specific to the comparison between DCs and LDCs (this effect is zero for the comparison within each group). This effect is included in the residual in this analysis because Z_1 is dependent on the scale of input measurement and, hence, there is no way to treat it meaningfully in separation from the residual.

In accounting for productivity differences among countries using equation (3), the following parameters were specified based on the results shown in Tables 6-1 and 6-2: $\alpha_L = .45$, $\alpha_A = .1$, $\alpha_S = .2$, $\alpha_F = .15$, $\alpha_M = .1$, $\beta_E = .2$, $\beta_T = .15$, and $k = 1.3$. Only the school enrollment ratio was used as the general education variable in this accounting, but the results were essentially the same when the literacy ratio was used.

Group Comparisons

A measurement of the sources of differences in labor productivity among country groups is presented in Table 6-5. Case 1 compares twenty-one DCs with twenty-two LDCs demarcated by per capita GNP of U.S.$4,000 in 1980 with the DC as the base of comparison. The difference in labor productivity between the DCs and the LDCs was not only very large originally, but it widened further during the past two decades. In 1960, average agricultural output per worker of the twenty-one DCs was 33.6 WU (wheat units or metric tons of wheat equivalents), whereas that of the twenty-two LDCs was only 6.1 WU, a difference of 81.8 percent.[16] From 1960 to 1980, the LDCs experienced a significant gain in labor productivity, but the rate of increase was faster in the DCs with the result that the difference increased to 90.1 percent in 1980.

The sources of the differences in labor productivity were measured by weighting the percentage differences in input variables by the specified parameters. Internal resource accumulation (land and livestock), modern technical inputs from the industrial sector (fertilizer and machinery), and human capital (general and technical education) each accounts for approximately one-fourth of the difference in labor productivity. The scale-economy effect accounts for about 15 percent, leaving about 10 percent unexplained. When the results for 1980 are compared with those for 1960, the percentage difference explained by human capital variables decreased while that explained by internal resources increased. It is remarkable that the percentage difference accounted for by technical inputs did not increase despite dramatic increases in those inputs in the DCs.

These results reflect major changes in world agriculture during the past two decades. The LDCs were able to increase labor productivity by counteracting a rapid decline in the land-labor ratio with significant technological progress associated with a larger application of fertilizers and other industrial inputs and with improved human resources. But the productivity gap between the DCs and the LDCs widened because the DCs increased their labor productivity at an even faster rate.

Case 2 compares seventeen high-income DCs (HDC) with twelve low-income LDCs (LLDC). In this case the scale-economy effect becomes even

16. In the following analysis, geometric means are taken for averages of outputs and inputs for each country group.

TABLE 6-5. Accounting for differences in labor productivity among country groups

	Case 1 21 DC vs. 22 LDC		Case 2 17 HDC vs. 12 LLDC		Case 3 13 HDC vs. 12 LLDC		Case 4 4 HDC vs. 13 HDC	
	1960	1980	1960	1980	1960	1980	1960	1980
Average output per worker (WU):								
Base countries	33.6	99.3	41.0	116.1	31.4	92.8	97.5	240.1
Countries compared	6.1	9.8	4.7	6.4	4.7	6.4	31.4	92.8
Difference in output per worker (%)	81.8 (100)*	90.1 (100)	88.5 (100)	94.5 (100)	85.0 (100)	93.1 (100)	67.8 (100)	61.3 (100)
Percent of difference explained:								
Internal resources	17.5 (21)	23.3 (26)	23.2 (26)	26.9 (28)	18.4 (22)	24.8 (27)	25.8 (38)	24.7 (40)
Land	5.1 (6)	7.3 (8)	7.6 (8)	8.9 (9)	4.9 (6)	7.7 (8)	9.6 (14)	9.5 (15)
Livestock	12.4 (15)	16.0 (18)	15.6 (18)	18.0 (19)	13.5 (16)	17.1 (19)	16.2 (24)	15.2 (25)
Technical inputs	24.3 (30)	24.2 (27)	24.7 (28)	24.6 (26)	24.6 (29)	24.6 (26)	13.4 (20)	11.3 (18)
Fertilizer	14.5 (18)	14.4 (16)	14.8 (17)	14.7 (16)	14.7 (17)	14.7 (16)	5.9 (9)	7.3 (12)
Machinery	9.8 (12)	9.8 (11)	9.9 (11)	9.9 (10)	9.9 (12)	9.9 (10)	7.5 (11)	4.0 (6)
Human capital	21.5 (26)	17.2 (19)	23.3 (26)	19.7 (21)	22.8 (27)	19.2 (21)	9.2 (14)	10.8 (18)
General education	8.5 (10)	4.4 (5)	9.7 (11)	5.8 (6)	9.4 (11)	5.6 (6)	2.3 (4)	1.2 (2)
Technical education	13.0 (16)	12.8 (14)	13.6 (15)	13.9 (15)	13.4 (16)	13.6 (15)	6.9 (10)	9.6 (16)
Scale economies	14.2 (17)	13.3 (15)	21.3 (24)	20.6 (22)	18.8 (22)	17.9 (19)	19.9 (29)	20.0 (33)
Unexplained residual	4.3 (5)	12.1 (13)	−4.0 (−5)	2.7 (3)	0.4 (0)	6.6 (7)	−.5 (−1)	−5.5 (−9)

*Inside of parentheses are percentages with output per worker set equal to 100.
Case 1: 21 DC (base) with per capita GNP above $4,000 compared with 22 LDC below $4,000.
Case 2: 17 HDC (base) with per capita GNP above $6,000 compared with 12 LLDC below $1,500.
Case 3: 13 HDC (base) excluding Australia, Canada, New Zealand, and the United States compared with 12 LLDC.
Case 4: Australia, Canada, New Zealand, and the United States (base) compared with other 13 HDC.

more important, accounting for about one-fourth of the difference in labor productivity in agriculture, leaving only a negligible percentage unexplained.

Case 3 compares the twelve LLDCs with the thirteen old settlement HDCs. The old settlement HDCs are endowed with meager internal resources relative to the other four new continental HDCs (Australia, Canada, New Zealand, and the United States). The difference in labor productivity between the HDCs and the LLDCs was much smaller in Case 3 than in Case 2. This smaller difference in labor productivity was a result of smaller differences in internal resource endowments and smaller scale-economy effects. The productivity difference between the older HDCs and the LLDCs also increased significantly over time, reflecting increases in the land-labor ratio in the older HDCs corresponding to rapid transfer of the agricultural labor force to industrial and service sectors.

Case 4 presents a comparison within HDCs between four new continental countries and thirteen old settled countries. The labor productivity in agriculture of the old HDCs was lower by 67.8 percent than that of the new HDCs in 1960, when the average national income per capita was lower in the old HDCs by about 40 percent. In 1980, when there was no significant difference in per capita national income between the old and new HDCs, a difference of 61.3 percent in agricultural labor productivity still remained. About 70 percent of the difference in agricultural productivity was explained by differences in internal resource endowments and scale-economy effects. Such results suggest that the comparative advantage in agriculture of the new continental HDCs endowed with favorable land-labor ratios was further strengthened during the past two decades. Significant differences in labor productivity between the new and old HDCs were also explained by differences in the levels of application of technical inputs and/or human capital. It is especially interesting to find that the percentage explained by technical education increased significantly from 1960 to 1980. This finding seems to suggest a hypothesis that the comparative advantage in agriculture of the new continental HDCs was not based solely on their favorable land-labor ratio but also on the greater intensity of agricultural research and extension that facilitated rapid developments in land-saving technology in order to take full advantage of favorable resource endowments.

Individual Comparisons

To provide more concrete insight into the sources of differences in labor productivity, selected countries representing various levels of economic development are compared with the United States. The United States ranked the highest in labor productivity in agriculture in 1980 (285.1 WU) and third in 1960 (93.8 WU). Each row in Table 6-6 compares the percentage differences in agricultural output per workers between each country and the United States with the linear combinations of percentage differences in input variables weighted by the specified production elasticities.

TABLE 6-6. Accounting for differences in labor productivity in agriculture of selected countries from the United States as percent of U.S. labor productivity

Country (per capita GNP in U.S.$ in 1980)		Output per worker (WU)	Difference in output per worker from U.S. as percent of U.S.	Percentage of difference explained by				
				Internal resources	Technical inputs	Human capital	Scale economies	Residual
Low-income countries								
India (240)	1960	2.2	97.7 (100)*	28.0 (29)	25.0 (25)	29.0 (30)	26.4 (27)	−10.8 (−11)
	1980	3.1	98.9 (100)	29.2 (30)	24.9 (25)	24.7 (25)	27.3 (28)	−7.2 (−7)
Philippines (690)	1960	3.3	96.5 (100)	28.8 (30)	24.9 (26)	20.4 (21)	24.8 (26)	−2.4 (−3)
	1980	5.9	97.9 (100)	29.5 (30)	24.9 (25)	16.4 (17)	25.2 (26)	1.9 (2)
Peru (930)	1960	9.6	89.8 (100)	20.7 (23)	24.2 (27)	23.7 (26)	22.6 (25)	−1.5 (−2)
	1980	10.1	96.5 (100)	27.1 (28)	24.8 (26)	18.1 (19)	25.0 (26)	1.5 (2)
Middle-income countries								
Argentina (2390)	1960	34.9	62.8 (100)	−3.1 (−5)	24.3 (39)	19.0 (30)	2.4 (4)	20.2 (32)
	1980	63.8	77.6 (100)	11.3 (15)	24.4 (31)	16.8 (22)	3.1 (4)	22.0 (28)
Greece (4380)	1960	9.1	90.3 (100)	27.2 (30)	23.9 (26)	20.3 (23)	23.4 (26)	−4.5 (−5)
	1980	25.8	91.0 (100)	28.4 (31)	23.6 (26)	16.5 (18)	23.5 (26)	−1.0 (−1)
Israel (4500)	1960	25.9	72.4 (100)	26.5 (37)	21.5 (30)	14.3 (20)	18.7 (26)	−8.6 (−12)
	1980	101.8	64.3 (100)	26.1 (41)	22.0 (34)	13.8 (21)	14.9 (23)	−12.5 (−19)
High-income countries								
Japan (9890)	1960	10.3	89.0 (100)	29.2 (33)	22.4 (25)	8.3 (9)	25.8 (29)	3.3 (4)
	1980	27.8	90.2 (100)	28.9 (32)	22.6 (25)	9.8 (11)	26.2 (29)	2.7 (3)
France (11730)	1960	32.4	65.5 (100)	23.0 (35)	16.9 (26)	17.3 (26)	11.7 (18)	−3.4 (−5)
	1980	101.8	64.3 (100)	23.2 (36)	15.5 (24)	15.7 (25)	11.1 (17)	−1.2 (−2)
Denmark (12950)	1960	46.4	50.6 (100)	17.7 (35)	12.8 (25)	13.9 (28)	3.0 (6)	3.2 (6)
	1980	131.3	54.0 (100)	18.4 (34)	12.7 (24)	14.5 (27)	6.8 (12)	1.6 (3)

*Inside of parentheses are percentages with output per worker set equal to 100.
Note: Per capita GNP in 1980 and agricultural outputs per worker in 1960 and 1980 in the United States are $11,360 and 93.8 and 285.1 WU, respectively.

154

In the three low-income countries—India, Philippines, and Peru—differences in internal resources, technical inputs, human capital, and farm scale each accounted for roughly one-fourth of the difference in labor productivity. Both India and the Philippines experienced substantial gains in labor productivity from 1960 to 1980 largely because of the higher yields associated with the green revolution, although they were handicapped by the decreasing land-labor ratios resulting from rapid population growth. Therefore, the difference in output per worker between those countries and the United States increased mainly because of increased differences in internal resource accumulation per worker and scale-economy effects, even though the difference explained by human capital was reduced. Agricultural labor productivity in the Philippines was nearly twice as high as in India despite very similar resource endowments. The difference between the Philippines and India, compared with the United States, was explained almost solely by different levels of general and technical education.

Compared with the Asian LDCs, Peru was endowed with a more favorable land-labor ratio. In 1960, its labor productivity was almost three times as high as that of the Philippines and four times that of India. But Peru's advantage in internal resource accumulation was seriously undermined during the past decades by explosive population growth that pressed hard on limited land resources. Furthermore, there was no technological breakthrough for Peru's major crops—corn and potatoes—as there was for rice and wheat in Asia. As a result, the comparative position of agricultural labor productivity in Peru vis-à-vis the United States deteriorated from 1960 to 1980 more rapidly than in India and the Philippines.

The deterioration in comparative position, caused by an erosion of an initial advantage in natural resource endowments, was even more pronounced in Argentina. In 1960, in spite of low levels of technical inputs and human capital, labor productivity in Argentine agriculture was roughly equal to that in western Europe, almost entirely because of a favorable land-labor ratio that was comparable to that of the United States. But the initial advantage in land resource endowments has been dissipated, and agricultural output per worker in Argentina has declined to only about one-half the level achieved by western Europe in 1980.

A sharp contrast to Argentina was found in the case of Israel, which is one of the rare cases in which labor productivity in agriculture increased faster than in the United States during the past two decades. The rapid productivity increase in Israeli agriculture was supported both by high rates of investment in modern technical inputs and human capital and by improvements in the land-labor ratio as a result of high rates of labor absorption into the non-agricultural sectors.

Greece was able to maintain a productivity growth rate comparable to that of the United States by investing heavily in technical inputs and human capital. Although the agricultural labor force in Greece declined rapidly, Greek agriculture continued to be handicapped by its unfavorable land-labor ratio and small farm size.

The effect of an unfavorable man-land ratio and small farm size on growth of labor productivity was most pronounced in the case of Japan. In 1960, Japan was still a low-income country. Its per capita GNP was less than one-sixth that of the United States. By 1980 there was almost no difference between Japan and the United States in both average national income per capita and labor wage rates. Yet Japan's agricultural labor productivity remained only one-tenth the U.S. level despite its high level of human capital endowments.[17] Japan's experience illustrates how quickly and completely the comparative advantage in agriculture can be lost when a resource-poor country makes a rapid transition to a major industrial power.

In the countries of western Europe, rapid transfer of agricultural labor to the industrial and service sectors resulted in major improvements in the man-land ratio and in farm size from 1960 to 1980. Technological developments supported by high-quality human capital facilitated the substitution of technical inputs for labor, resulting in major gains in agricultural output per worker at a pace comparable to that of the United States. This process was particularly dramatic in France, where the transfer of labor from agriculture was especially rapid during recent decades because a disproportionately large population had been held in agriculture until the early 1960s by the traditional French policy of protecting its peasant sector. This experience is in sharp contrast to that of Denmark, which had realized substantial agricultural adjustments earlier under a liberal trading system. As a result, the transfer of labor out of agriculture was slower and productivity gains were somewhat lower even though the absolute level of labor productivity in Danish agriculture was among the highest in Europe.

In spite of rapid productivity increases during the past two decades, agricultural output per worker in western Europe remained only about one-third to one-half the U.S. level. It seems likely that labor absorption by the non-agricultural sector will continue to decelerate for some years in the advanced industrial economies as a result of the slow economic growth that began in the mid-1970s. In this event, improvements in the land-labor ratio and farm size will not likely proceed as fast in the 1980s as during the 1960s and 1970s. The comparative disadvantage in agriculture in western Europe relative to the new continental countries such as the United States is likely to persist well into the next century.

---

17. This difference in labor productivity measured in agricultural output per worker may be somewhat exaggerated. Since the proportion of labor man-hours of agricultural workers allocated to nonfarm employment was larger in Japan than in the United States, the labor productivity difference would be narrowed if measured by agricultural output per man-hour.

IMPLICATIONS FOR AGRICULTURAL DEVELOPMENT

The perspective implied by the results of this analysis for agricultural development in the less developed countries is essentially encouraging. It is clear that agricultural output per worker in the LDCs, especially the poorest ones, can be increased by several multiples by adequate investments in education, research, and the supply of modern technical inputs, even if land area per worker continues to decline because of growing population pressure in the rural sector. Support for this conclusion was provided by the experience of low-income Asian LDCs, such as India and the Philippines, that experienced both strong population pressure and rapid growth based on the new seed-fertilizer technology during the 1970–80 period. It is especially encouraging to find that the agricultural production function of the LDCs is neutral with respect to scale. This implies that the low-income LDCs will not be too severely handicapped by the declines in the land-man ratio and farm size, relative to the older developed countries, at least over the next decade or two.

Of course, any slackening of efforts to offset the effects of rising population pressure against land resources in LDCs by technological development will result in a retrogression of agricultural productivity. But if a modest slackening in population growth is accompanied by rapid advances in yield-increasing technology, the low-income LDCs may be able to achieve levels of labor productivity in agriculture roughly comparable to the levels achieved in the older developed countries.

At that stage, a new problem will emerge. As the agricultural labor force begins to stabilize, the agricultural production function is likely to begin to exhibit increasing returns to scale. But the transfer of labor to the non-agricultural sector and the expansion in farm size have, even in Western economies, typically proceeded slowly, often over several generations. During this period the comparative advantage may shift rapidly away from agriculture, as illustrated by the Japanese experience. The lag between the loss of comparative advantage in agriculture and the reallocation of resources (especially labor) between agriculture and the rest of the economy can be expected to give rise to protectionist agricultural policies. This was the experience of western Europe and Japan and will likely be repeated by the newly industrializing countries, especially those located in areas of high population density in Asia. Major efforts to achieve international cooperation for agricultural adjustment will be required to prevent the rise of agricultural protectionism from disrupting the international economic order.

SUPPLEMENT: A TEST OF UNITARY
ELASTICITY OF SUBSTITUTION

In the preceding analysis in this chapter, the production function was specified as being of the Cobb-Douglas type, thus assuming unitary elasticity of substitution. Here we attempt to test this assumption by estimating the parameters of the constant elasticity of substitution (CES) production function by use of an equilibrium condition initially developed by Arrow, Chenery, Minhas, and Solow and modified by Zvi Griliches and V. Ringstad for the case of increasing returns.[18] This test is limited to the elasticity of substitution between labor and the aggregate of other inputs. A more general test by estimating the translog production function was not attempted because of the complexity involved in the estimation of a translog function including as many as seven input variables.

The CES production function is specified as:

$$Y = \gamma[\delta X^{-\rho} + (1 - \delta)L^{-\rho}]^{-k/\rho} Z^{\lambda}$$

where Y is gross output in agriculture; L is labor; X is the aggregate of nonlabor conventional inputs including current inputs; Z is the shorthand notation for nonconventional variables (general and technical education in this study), which is assumed to shift the production neutrally; γ, δ, and ρ are, respectively, parameters representing efficiency, distribution, and substitution; and k is a scale-economy factor.

The equilibrium condition produces:

$$\frac{\partial Y}{\partial L} = \gamma X(1 - \delta) [\delta X^{-\rho} + (1 - \delta)L^{-\rho}]^{-[(k+\rho)/\rho]} L^{-(1+\rho)} Z^{\lambda} = W$$

where W is the agricultural wage rate. From the above two equations we have the elasticity of substitution function as follows:

$$\log (Y/L) = a + b \log W + c \log L = d \log Z$$

where

$$a = \frac{k\sigma}{1 + (k - 1) \sigma} [\log \frac{1}{k(1 - \delta)} + \frac{1 - \sigma}{k\sigma} \log \gamma],$$

$$b = \frac{k\sigma}{1 + (k - 1) \sigma},$$

$$c = \frac{(k - 1) (1 - \sigma)}{1 + (k - 1) \sigma}, \text{ and}$$

$$d = \frac{k\lambda\sigma}{1 + (k - 1)\sigma}.$$

where $\sigma = 1/(1 + \rho)$ is the elasticity of substitution.

Since $b = 1$ and $c = d = 0$ if $\sigma = 1$, the hypothesis of the unitary elasticity of substitution will be accepted if the coefficient of wage rate in the regression

18. Arrow, Chenery, Minhas, and Solow, "Capital-Labor Substitution and Economic Efficiency"; and Zvi Griliches and V. Ringstad, *Economies of Scale and the Form of the Production Function: An Economic Study of Norwegian Manufacturing Establishment Data* (Amsterdam: North-Holland Publishing Co., 1971).

TABLE 6-7. Estimates of the elasticity of substitution function on intercountry cross-section data for 1960, 1970, and 1980

Period	1960 (22 countries)			1970 (23 countries)			1980 (25 countries)		
Regression number	(A1)	(A2)	(A3)	(A4)	(A5)	(A6)	(A7)	(A8)	(A9)
Wage rate (W)	1.157	.906	.953	.915	.783	.787	.813	.631	.638
	(.112)	(.213)	(.212)	(.183)	(.246)	(.226)	(.170)	(.219)	(.220)
Labor (L)	.102	.140	.126	.108	.149	.186	.398	.333	.342
	(.237)	(.242)	(.247)	(.167)	(.177)	(.175)	(.203)	(.211)	(.209)
General education (E):									
Literacy ratio		.306			.450			.167	
		(.447)			(.548)			(.436)	
School enrollment ratio			.169			1.161			.174
			(.545)			(.834)			(.652)
Technical education (T)		.135	.130		.065	.030		.157	.154
		(.110)	(.112)		(.122)	(.118)		(.127)	(.131)
LDC dummy	-.297	-.148	-.148	-.974	-.835	-.776	-.861	-.772	-.790
	(.214)	(.250)	(.255)	(.352)	(.397)	(.384)	(.450)	(.457)	(.456)
Coef. of det. ($\bar{R}^2$)	.861	.862	.858	.899	.893	.900	.870	.869	.868
S.E. of estimates	.433	.433	.438	.387	.399	.386	.499	.501	.502

Note: Equations linear in logarithms are estimated by the ordinary least squares. The standard errors of coefficients are in parentheses.

159

estimate of the elasticity of substitution function is not significantly different from one and those of labor (per farm) and general and technical education are not significantly different from zero.

The availability of wage data limits countries included in the sample for estimation to Argentina (1980), Austria, Belgium, Canada, Denmark, Finland, France, Germany, India, Ireland, Israel (1970, 1980), Japan, Mauritius, Mexico (1960, 1970), Netherlands (1970, 1980), New Zealand, Norway, Pakistan (1980), Peru (1960), Philippines (1960, 1980), Portugal, Spain (1980), Sri Lanka, Sweden (1960, 1970), Syria (1980), Turkey, United Kingdom, United States, and Yugoslavia (1970), including the countries with the years specified in parentheses only for those years. Thus the sample size was twenty-two for 1960, twenty-three for 1970, and twenty-five for 1980. The wage data were averaged for 1952–56, 1962–66, and 1972–74 for the regressions of 1960 (1957–62 averages), 1970 (1967–72 averages), and 1980 (1975–80 averages), respectively, to allow for time lag in production adjustments. Estimates were made for 1960, 1970, and 1980 separately, and estimates based on the pooled data for the three periods were not attempted because of the unavailability of an adequate deflator to make the wage rates comparable among periods.

The results of the estimation of the elasticity of substitution function are summarized in Table 6-7; each column reports the results of a regression including the estimates of coefficients and their standard errors (in parentheses), the standard error of estimates, and the coefficient of determination adjusted for the degree of freedom. Those results are largely consistent with the unitary elasticity of substitution hypothesis: (a) the coefficients of wage rate are not significantly different from one, and (b) the coefficients of labor and two human capital variables are not significantly different from zero at conventional significance levels. Thus there is no strong prima facie evidence against the use of the Cobb-Douglas production function.

III

AGRICULTURAL GROWTH IN
THE UNITED STATES AND JAPAN

7

Resource Constraints
and Technical Change

In the previous chapter we investigated the sources of differences in agricultural productivity among countries. The results of the analysis implied that even in situations characterized by severe constraints on the supply of land or labor a potential for dramatic growth of agricultural output still exists. Realization of this potential depends on growth of technical inputs and human capital. The intercountry cross-section data, however, did not enable us to analyze the dynamic process through which specific economies have overcome resource constraints by generating a sequence of innovations leading to the substitution of technical inputs, such as fertilizer and machinery, for land and labor.

In this chapter and the next we explore this process by analyzing the historical experiences of agricultural development in the United States and Japan for the period 1880 to 1980.[1] As we have seen in Chapter 5 (Figures 5-2 and 5-5), the experiences of the United States and Japan seem to have important implications for two groups of countries: (a) those in the new continents that have a favorable man-land ratio and (b) those in Asia that have an unfavorable man-land ratio. In Chapter 5 we hypothesized that agricultural

1. The first three sections of this chapter draw heavily on Yujiro Hayami and V. W. Ruttan, "Factor Prices and Technical Change in Agricultural Development: The United States and Japan, 1880–1960," *Journal of Political Economy* 78 (September–October 1970):1115–41. The data have been revised and updated. The section "A Test of the Induced Technical Change Hypothesis" draws on Toshihiko Kawagoe, Keijiro Otsuka, and Yujiro Hayami, "Induced Biases of Technical Change in Agriculture: The United States and Japan, 1880–1980," mimeographed (Tokyo Metropolitan University, July 1983). Our earlier results for 1880–1960 have been compared with the experience of Denmark, France, Germany, and the United Kingdom by Adolf Weber and William Wade. See Adolf Weber, "Productivity in German Agriculture, 1850–1970, with Comparisons to the Development of Japan and the United States," *Rural and Development Economics,* ed. Paris Andreou (Nairobi: East African Literature Bureau, 1977); William W. Wade, *Institutional Determinants of Technical Change and Agricultural Productivity Growth: Denmark, France and Great Britain, 1870–1965* (New York: Arno Press, 1981); Vernon W. Ruttan, Hans P. Binswanger, Yujiro Hayami, William Wade, and Adolf Weber, "Factor Productivity and Growth," *Induced Innovation: Technology, Institutions, and Development,* ed. Hans P. Binswanger and Vernon W. Ruttan (Baltimore: Johns Hopkins University Press, 1978), pp. 44–87.

growth in these two countries has been achieved through movement along a common metaproduction function under conditions of extreme difference in resource constraints. The influence of resource endowments on technical changes in agriculture can be usefully illustrated by analyzing these two extreme cases.

The data on which it has been necessary to draw in conducting this study are subject to substantial limitations (see Appendix C).[2] Since much of the data are admittedly crude and comparability of the data for the two countries is less adequate than we would prefer, analysis must of necessity deal with only the broadest trends in the comparative growth experiences of the two countries.

First, let us describe the trends in factor prices and in several significant factor-product and factor-factor ratios in the course of agricultural development in the United States and Japan. After presenting this background material, we will specify more precisely our hypothesis concerning the relationship between factor prices and technical change. We will then subject the hypothesis to a statistical test using time-series data from the United States and Japan.

RESOURCE ENDOWMENTS, PRODUCTION, AND PRODUCTIVITY

In this section we attempt to characterize the differences and similarities in agricultural growth patterns in the United States and Japan for the period 1880–1980. We first point to the extreme differences in factor endowments and factor prices and then compare changes in agricultural output and productivity in the two countries.

2. See the comparison of various time series of agricultural production and productivities in the United States by Charles O. Meiburg and Karl Brandt, "Agricultural Productivity in the United States: 1870–1960," *Food Research Institute Studies* 3 (May 1962):63–85. For a discussion of the conceptual basis of the USDA productivity estimates see American Agricultural Economics Association Task Force on Measuring Agricultural Productivity, *Measurement of U.S. Agricultural Productivity: A Review of Current Statistics and Proposals for Change* (Washington, D.C.: U.S. Department of Agriculture, Economics, Statistics and Cooperatives Service, Technical Bulletin 1614, February 1980). We adopted the USDA agricultural output series because it is consistent with the definition of agricultural output in our intercountry data. The reliability of agricultural production statistics in Meiji Japan has been strongly questioned by Nakamura. See James I. Nakamura, *Agricultural Production and the Economic Development of Japan: 1873–1922* (Princeton: Princeton University Press, 1966). The questions regarding the official statistics of Japan raised by Nakamura have been widely discussed by Japanese and other scholars: Yujiro Hayami, "On the Japanese Experience of Agricultural Growth," *Rural Economic Problems* 4 (May 1968):79–88; Yujiro Hayami and Saburo Yamada, "Agricultural Productivity at the Beginning of Industrialization," *Agriculture and Economic Development: Japan's Experience,* ed. Kazushi Ohkawa, Bruce F. Johnston, and Hiromitsu Kaneda (Tokyo: University of Tokyo Press, 1969), pp. 105–35; J. I. Nakamura, "The Nakamura Versus the LTES Estimates of Growth Rate of Agricultural Production," *Keizai Kenkyu* 19 (October 1968):358–62. Appraisals by other scholars include Henry Rosovsky, "Rumbles in the Ricefields: Professor Nakamura vs. the Official Statistics," *Journal of Asian Studies* 27 (February 1968):347–60, and Colin Clark's review of Nakamura's book in the September 1967 issue of *Journal of Agricultural Economics,* vol. 18, pp. 428–30.

TABLE 7-1. Land-labor endowments and relative prices in agriculture: United States and Japan, selected years

	1880	1900	1920	1940	1960	1980
UNITED STATES						
(1) Agricultural land area (million ha.)	327	465	458	452	440	427
(2) Arable land area (million ha.)	93	157	194	189	185	191
(3) Number of male farm workers (thousand)	7,959	9,880	10,221	8,487	3,973	1,792
(4) (1)/(3) (ha./worker)	41	47	45	50	111	238
(5) (2)/(3) (ha./worker)	12	16	19	22	47	107
(6) Value of arable land ($/ha.)	109	106	341	178	696	3,393
(7) Farm wage rate ($/day)	0.90	1.00	3.30	1.60	6.60	25.31
(8) (6)/(7) (days/ha.)	188	106	103	111	105	134
JAPAN						
(9) Agricultural land area (thousand ha.)[a]	5,509	6,032	6,958	7,102	7,042	5,729
(10) Arable land area (thousand ha.)	4,749	5,200	5,998	6,122	6,071	5,461
(11) Number of male farm workers (thousand)	8,336	8,483	7,577	6,362	6,230	2,674
(12) (9)/(11) (ha./worker)	0.66	0.71	0.92	1.12	1.13	2.14
(13) (10)/(11) (ha./worker)	0.57	0.61	0.79	0.96	0.97	2.04
(14) Value of arable land (yen/ha.)	343	917	3,882	4,709	1,415,000	7,642,000
(15) Farm wage rate (yen/day)	0.22	0.31	1.39	1.90	440	5,054
(16) (14)/(15) (days/ha.)	1,559	2,958	2,793	2,478	3,216	1,512

Source: Data from Appendix Tables C-2 and C-3.

[a] Agricultural land areas in Japan for 1880–1960 are estimated by multiplying arable land areas by 1.16, the ratio of agricultural land area to arable land area in the 1960 Census of Agriculture; this conversion factor changed to 1.05 for 1980 based on the 1980 Census of Agriculture.

Resource Endowments and Prices

Japan and the United States are characterized by extreme differences in relative endowments of land and labor (Table 7-1). In 1880 total agricultural land area per male worker was more than sixty times as large in the United States as in Japan, and arable land area per worker was about twenty times as large. The differences have widened over time. By 1980 total agricultural land area per male worker was more than one hundred times as large and arable land area per male worker about fifty times as large in the United States as in Japan.

The relative prices of land and labor also differed sharply in the two countries. In 1880 in order to buy a hectare of arable land (compare rows 8 and 16 in Table 7-1) a Japanese hired farm worker would have had to work eight times as many days as a U.S. farm worker. In the United States the price of labor rose relative to the price of land, particularly between 1880 and 1920. In Japan the price of land rose sharply relative to the price of labor, particularly between 1880 and 1900. By 1960 a Japanese farm worker would have had to work thirty times as many days as a U.S. farm worker in order to buy one hectare of arable land. This gap was reduced after 1960 partly because of extremely rapid increases in wage rates in Japan during the two decades of ''miraculous'' economic growth. In the United States land prices rose sharply in the postwar period primarily because of the rising demand for land for nonagricultural use and the anticipation of continued inflation. Yet in 1980 a Japanese farm worker still would have had to work eleven times as many days as a U.S. worker to buy one hectare of land.

Production and Productivity Growth

In spite of these substantial differences in land area per worker and in the relative prices of land and labor, both the United States and Japan experienced relatively rapid rates of growth in production and productivity in agriculture (Table 7-2). Overall agricultural growth for the entire one-hundred-year period was very similar in the two countries. In both countries total agricultural output increased at an annual compound rate of 1.6 percent, total inputs (aggregate of conventional inputs) increased at a rate of 0.7 percent, and total factor productivity (total output divided by total input) increased at an annual rate of 0.9 percent. Labor productivity measured by agricultural output per male worker increased at rates of 3.1 percent per year in the United States and 2.7 percent in Japan. It is remarkable that the overall growth rates in output and productivity were so similar despite the extremely different factor proportions that characterize the two countries.

Although there is a resemblance in the overall rates of growth in production and productivity, the time sequences of the relatively fast-growing phases and the relatively stagnant phases differ between the two countries. Figure 7-1 indicates that in the United States agricultural output grew rapidly up to 1900;

TABLE 7-2. Annual compound rates of growth in output, input, productivity, and factor proportions in U.S. and Japanese agriculture, 1880–1980, selected periods (percentage)

| | Subperiods | | | | | Entire period |
	1880 to 1900	1900 to 1920	1920 to 1940	1940 to 1960	1960 to 1980	1880 to 1980
United States						
Output (net of seeds and feed)	2.2	0.8	1.3	1.9	1.9	1.6
Total inputs	1.6	1.4	0.2	0.1	0.3	0.7
Total productivity (output/total inputs)	0.6	-0.7	1.1	1.9	1.6	0.9
Number of male workers	1.1	0.2	-0.9	-3.7	-3.8	-1.5
Output per male worker	1.1	0.6	2.2	5.9	6.1	3.1
Agricultural land area	1.8	-0.1	-0.4	0.2	-0.2	0.3
Arable land area	2.7	1.1	-0.1	-0.1	0.1	0.7
Output per ha. of agricultural land	0.4	0.8	1.7	1.7	2.1	1.3
Output per ha. of arable land	-0.4	-0.3	1.4	2.0	1.8	0.9
Agricultural land area per male worker	0.7	-0.3	0.5	4.1	3.9	1.8
Arable land area per male worker	1.5	0.9	0.8	3.8	4.2	2.2
Japan						
Output (net of seeds and feed)	1.6	2.0	0.7	1.8	1.9	1.6
Total input	0.4	0.5	0.3	1.6	1.0	0.7
Total productivity	1.2	1.5	0.4	0.2	0.9	0.9
Number of male workers	0.1	-0.6	-0.9	-0.1	-4.2	-1.1
Output per male worker	1.5	2.6	1.6	1.9	6.3	2.7
Arable land area (= agric. land area)	0.4	0.7	0.1	-0.04	-0.5	0.1
Output per ha. of arable land	1.2	1.3	0.6	1.8	2.4	1.5
Arable land area per male worker	0.4	1.3	1.0	0.1	3.8	1.2

Source: Data from Appendix Tables C-2 and C-3.

167

FIGURE 7-1. Changes in total output, total input, and total productivity (1880 = 100), the United States and Japan, 1880–1980, semilog scale. (Data from Appendix Tables C-2 and C-3.)

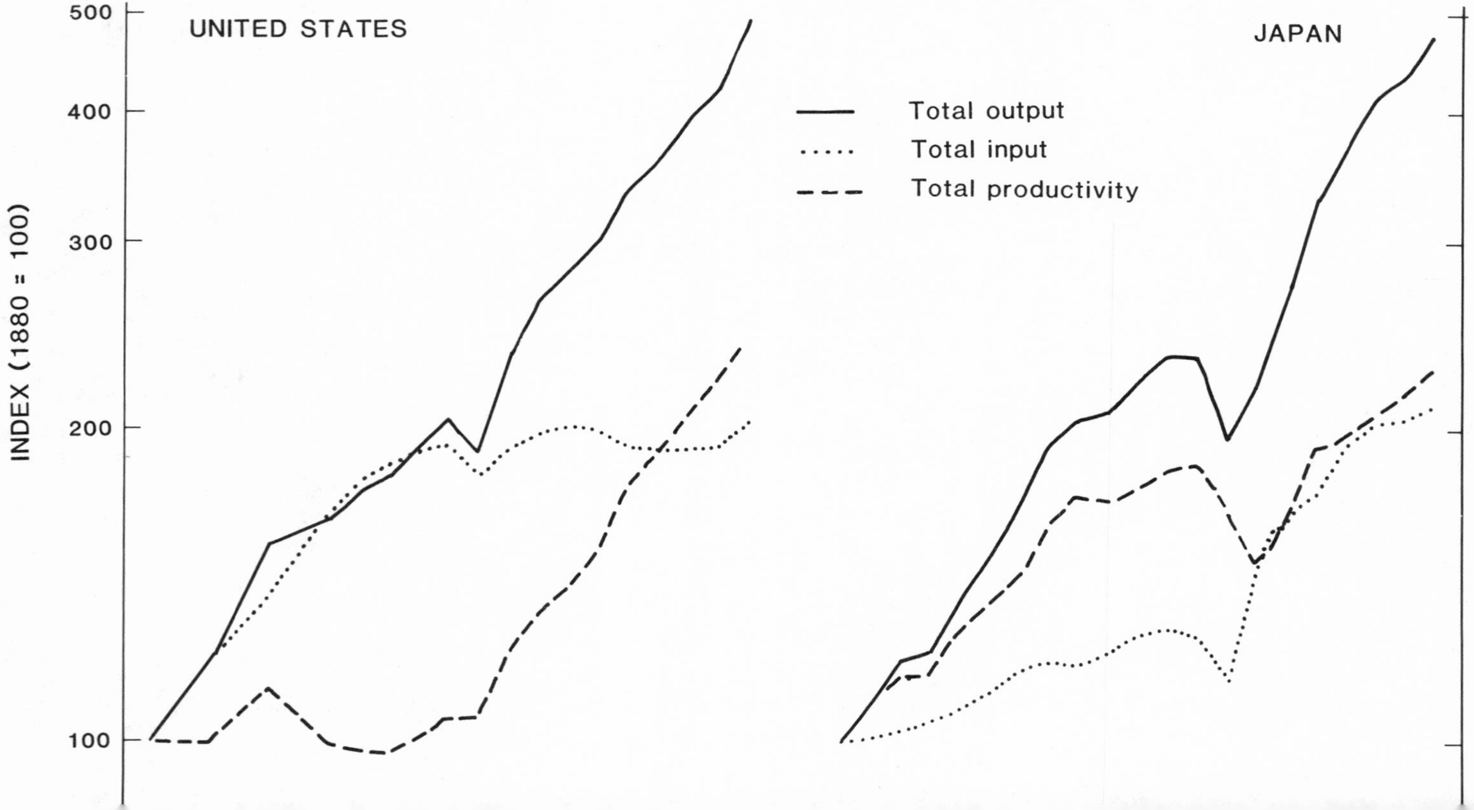

JAPAN

UNITED STATES

Total output
Total input
Total productivity

INDEX (1880 = 100)

500
400
300
200
100

168

then the growth rate decelerated. From the 1900s to the 1930s there was little gain in total productivity. This stagnation phase was succeeded by a dramatic rise in production and productivity in the 1940s and 1950s. Japan experienced rapid increases in agricultural production and productivity from 1880 up to the 1910s, then entered into a stagnation phase that lasted until the mid-1930s. Another rapid expansion phase commenced during the period of recovery from the devastation of World War II. The United States experienced a stagnation phase roughly two decades earlier than Japan and also shifted to the second development phase two decades earlier.

Components of Labor Productivity Growth

In the course of agricultural development, there have been substantial differences in the growth of labor productivity in the United States and Japan. According to the identity used in Chapter 5, the growth in output per worker (Y/L) can be partitioned between two components—land area per worker (A/L) and land productivity (Y/A). Given the differences in the prices of land and labor in the United States and Japan we would expect that growth in output per worker (Y/L) in the United States would be closely associated with changes in land area per worker (A/L) and in Japan with changes in land productivity (Y/A).

These expectations are confirmed by the data on land area per male worker and output per hectare plotted in Figure 7-2. In the United States land area per worker (A/L) rose much more rapidly than in Japan. In Japan land productivity (Y/A) rose much more rapidly than in the United States. As shown in Table 7-2, for the period 1880–1980 increase in land area per worker explains about 70 percent of the labor productivity growth in the United States, whereas it explains less than 40 percent in Japan.

Both the United States and Japan experienced successive stages of rapid growth and relative stagnation followed by rapid growth in labor productivity. In the United States the stagnation phase was associated with a reduction in the rate of growth in land area per worker (A/L). In Japanese agriculture it is clearly the movements in land productivity (Y/A) which are most closely associated with the sequence of the development and stagnation phases before World War II. Rapid increases in labor productivity (Y/L) in the United States and Japan after World War II were associated with increases in both land area per worker (A/L) and land productivity (Y/A). This similarity suggests that U.S. and Japanese agricultural growth patterns began to converge in the postwar period as the scarcity of labor relative to land increased in Japan and the scarcity of land relative to labor increased in the United States.

PROGRESS IN MECHANICAL AND BIOLOGICAL TECHNOLOGY

In agriculture it appears consistent with the technical conditions of production to consider growth in land area per worker (A/L) and output per hectare

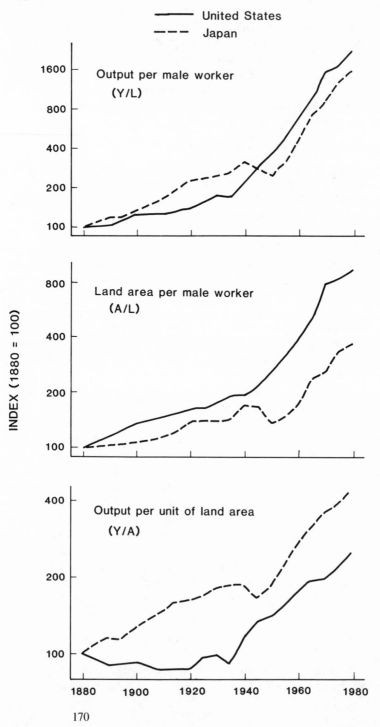

(*Y/A*) as "somewhat independent, at least over a certain range."[3] As discussed in previous chapters, the major source of increases in land area per worker has been progress in mechanical technology that facilitated the substitution of other sources of power for human labor. Similarly, the major source of increase in land productivity has been progress in biological technology that facilitated the conversion of a higher percentage of the solar energy falling on an area into higher levels of plant and animal production through improvements in the supply and utilization of plant nutrients.

The associations between mechanical and biological innovations and the contrasting growth patterns in land area per worker (*A/L*) and in land productivity (*Y/A*) in the United States and Japan are shown in Figures 7-3 and 7-4. In Figure 7-3 the three indicators of the land-labor ratio (*A/L*) are compared with the number of work animals (horses, mules, and work cattle) and tractor horsepower per worker.[4] There are considerable differences in the three indicators of land area per worker (*A/L*). Especially noteworthy in the case of the United States is the divergence between the series of agricultural land and arable land; arable land area increased much faster between 1900 and 1930 as grazing land was converted into arable land in response to population growth in frontier areas. Equally remarkable is the divergence in the land-labor ratio in Japan between the series using male workers and work-hours. The latter increased much more slowly or even declined slightly between 1880 and 1910 because the number of work-hours per worker per year increased considerably during this period.

When comparing long-term trends between the United States and Japan, however, such differences become relatively minor and the general pattern is not altered by the choice of indicator. In the United States the number of work animals increased up to the 1920s and then began to decline. The increase in tractor horsepower more than compensated for the decline in work stock. The increase in nonhuman power per worker seems to have been closely associated with the increase in land area per worker (*A/L*). The increases in power per worker represent a convenient index of the adoption of mechanical innovations. For example, the substitution of the self-raking reaper for the hand-rake reaper and the substitution of the binder for the self-raking reaper required more horses per worker. Those innovations involved the substitution of power for labor, thereby causing an increase in the land area used per worker in agriculture.

In Japan, corresponding to the slow rate of growth in land area per worker (*A/L*), the number of work animals increased slowly, especially before the 1920s. The tractor was not adopted extensively until after World War II.

3. Zvi Griliches, "Agriculture: Productivity and Technology," *International Encyclopedia of the Social Sciences*, vol. 1 (New York: Macmillan and Free Press, 1968), pp. 241–45.
4. When it is difficult to choose a single data series to represent a single variable adequately, it is reasonable to try several alternatives and to accept the results as conclusive only if the several results are consistent with one another.

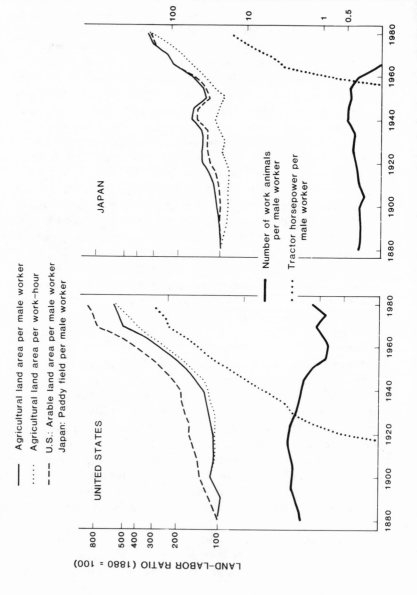

FIGURE 7-3. Land-labor ratio and power-labor ratio, the United States and Japan, 1880–1980, semilog scale. (Data from Appendix Tables C-2 and C-3.)

—— Agricultural land area per male worker

······ Agricultural land area per work–hour

– – – U.S.: Arable land area per male worker
Japan: Paddy field per male worker

NUMBER OF WORK ANIMALS OR TRACTOR HORSEPOWER PER MALE WORKER

—— Number of work animals per male worker

······ Tractor horsepower per male worker

JAPAN

UNITED STATES

LAND–LABOR RATIO (1880 = 100)

172

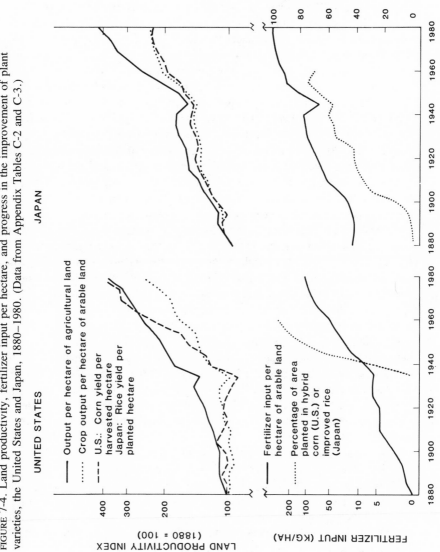

FIGURE 7-4. Land productivity, fertilizer input per hectare, and progress in the improvement of plant varieties, the United States and Japan, 1880–1980. (Data from Appendix Tables C-2 and C-3.)

173

Figure 7-4 illustrates the contrasting relationship between land productivity (*Y/A*) and the progress of biological technology in the United States and Japan. Here, again, two indicators of land productivity (*Y/A*) are shown in order to check whether different conclusions are implied by the different choices of data. The percentages of total corn area planted to hybrid corn and of total rice area planted to improved varieties are treated as proxy variables representing an index of advances in biological technology in the United States and Japan.

The evidence from these two crops is certainly not conclusive (the percentages are poor proxies even for corn and rice improvements). But it seems fairly safe to say, based on a comparison of the corn and rice adoption ratios with the trends in fertilizer inputs, that in Japan the significant yield-increasing innovations date from the 1880s, while in the United States they began only in the 1930s. The yield-increasing varieties are almost invariably associated with high levels of plant nutrient utilization. Biological innovations of the yield-increasing type involve the development of crop varieties that can respond to higher levels of fertilization. The parallel increases in fertilizer input per hectare and in percentage of area planted in improved rice varieties in Japan indicate that significant biological innovations were already under way in Japan as early as the 1880s. In the United States the introduction of hybrid corn (and other high-yielding crop varieties) is closely associated with the growth in fertilizer use. A major factor in the development, introduction, and adoption of hybrid corn, and other new crop varieties, was greater responsiveness to the higher-analysis commercial fertilizers that were becoming available at continuously lower real prices.

In connection with the complementarity between fertilizer input and the development of yield-increasing varieties, it is suggestive that Japan's level of fertilizer input per hectare in the 1880s was almost the same as the level in the United States in the 1930s. Furthermore, these dates represent the beginning of periods in which advances in biological technology, accompanied by rapid growth in fertilizer consumption, began to exert a significant impact on crop production in both countries.

This parallelism does not appear to hold for the period before the 1930s. Initially, increases in fertilizer input were not accompanied by increases in yield per hectare in the United States. This contradiction was apparently due to the use of commercial fertilizers primarily for the purpose of offsetting declining yields resulting from depletion of soil fertility. Prior to 1930, use of commercial fertilizer was concentrated in the South for the production of cotton and tobacco, crops which were classified as soil depleting.[5] Depletion of the soil fertility from virgin land would have been significant, especially in the newly opened Great Plains (see Chapter 8). The increase in commercial

5. Rosser H. Taylor, "The Sale and Application of Commercial Fertilizer in the South Atlantic States to 1900," *Agricultural History* 21 (January 1947):46–52.

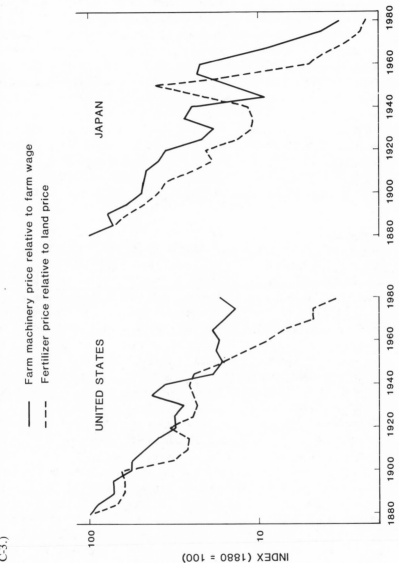

FIGURE 7-5. Farm machinery price relative to farm wage, and fertilizer price relative to arable land price (1880 = 100), the United States and Japan, 1880–1980, semilog scale. (Data from Appendix Tables C-2 and C-3.)

——— Farm machinery price relative to farm wage

– – – Fertilizer price relative to land price

175

fertilizer input per hectare and the stagnant or even declining land productivity (Y/A) between 1880 and 1935 are consistent with the inference that the supply of plant nutrients from all sources (including both natural and commercial sources) was stagnant or even declining during this period.

Increases in power per worker and in fertilizer input per hectare were accompanied by dramatic declines in the price of machinery (a proxy for the price of power and machinery) relative to the wage rate and the price of fertilizer relative to the price of land (Figure 7-5). These trends in factor price ratios, along with the trends in the price of land relative to labor (Table 7-1), are consistent with the hypothesis that the differential progress in mechanical and biological technologies in the United States and Japan represented a process of dynamic factor substitution in response to the changes in relative factor prices.

THE INDUCED TECHNICAL INNOVATION PROCESS

In the previous sections we have observed sharp contrasts in the patterns of agricultural growth in the United States and Japan. In the United States it was primarily the progress of mechanization which facilitated the expansion of agricultural production and productivity by increasing the area operated per worker. In Japan it was primarily the progress of biological technology, represented by seed improvements that increased the yield response to higher levels of fertilizer application, which permitted the rapid growth in agricultural output in spite of severe constraints on the supply of land. U.S. agriculture has experienced significant biological innovations since the 1930s, and farm mechanization has been progressing at an accelerating pace since the 1950s. In Japan, the advance of biological technology exerted a major impact on the growth of production and productivity before World War II. Japanese agriculture has experienced dramatic progress in mechanization in the postwar period in response to sharp increases in farm wage rates because of the rapid transfer of labor to the industrial and service sectors.

The manner in which differences in factor price movements in Japan and the United States have influenced the process of technical change and the choice of inputs in the two countries is consistent with the induced technical innovation hypothesis developed in Chapter 4. The contrasting patterns of productivity growth and factor use in U.S. and Japanese agriculture can best be understood as a process of dynamic adjustment to changing relative factor prices along a metaproduction function—dynamic in the sense that production isoquants change in response to the changes in relative factor prices.

In the United States the long-term decline in the prices of land and machinery relative to wages (Table 7-1 and Figure 7-5) before 1960 could be expected to encourage the substitution of land and power for labor. This substitution generally involved progress in the application of mechanical technology to agricultural production. With fixed technology represented by a certain type of machinery, there is little possibility of factor substitution. For example, an optimal factor combination with the reaper (such as the McCormick or Hussey), assuming two weeks for harvesting and two shifts of horses, was approximately five workers, four horses (two horses for original models), and 140 acres of wheat. Only when a new technology, in the form of the binder, was introduced was it possible for the farmer to change this proportion to two workers, one reaper (binder), four horses, and 140 acres.[6] Although we do not deny the possibility of substitution within a limited range (e.g., through a change from two shifts to three shifts of horses), such enormous changes in factor proportions as observed in Figures 7-3 and 7-4 could hardly occur as a result of substitution among available alternatives in the absence of new technical possibilities.

Dramatic increases in land area and power per worker of the magnitude that occurred in the United States indicate a response to mechanical innovations which raised the marginal rate of substitution in favor of both land and power for labor.[7] This has been a continual process. The introduction of the tractor, which can be considered the single most important mechanical innovation in agriculture, greatly raised the marginal rate of substitution of power for labor by making it much easier to command more power per worker. Substitution of higher-powered tractors for low-powered tractors has a similar effect.

In Japan the supply of land was inelastic and the price of land rose relative to wages. It was not profitable, therefore, to substitute land and power for labor. Instead, the new opportunities arising from continuous declines in the price of fertilizer relative to the price of land were exploited through advances in biological technology. Seed improvements were directed to the selection of more fertilizer-responsive varieties. The traditional varieties had equal or higher yields than the improved varieties at the lower level of fertilization, but they did not respond to higher applications of fertilizer (as illustrated in Table 4-2, Chapter 4). With fixed biological technology represented by a certain variety of seed, the elasticity of substitution of fertilizer for land was low. The enormous changes in fertilizer input per hectare, as observed in Japan since 1880 and in the United States since the 1930s, reflect not only the effect of a decline in the price of fertilizer but the development of fertilizer-responsive

6. Leo Rogin, *The Introduction of Farm Machinery in Its Relation to the Productivity of Labor in the Agriculture of the United States during the Nineteenth Century* (Berkeley: University of California Press, 1931).

7. This is consistent with the emphasis on the importance of the effect of mechanical innovations on the substitution between new and old machinery in terms of the relative price changes as analyzed by David: Paul A. David, "The Mechanization of Reaping in the Ante-Bellum Midwest," *Industrialization in Two Systems,* ed. Henry Rosovsky (New York: Wiley, 1966), pp. 3–39. In fact, the decline in the price of new machines (relative to old machines) in efficiency terms represents a measure of the contribution of the farm machinery industry to technical changes in agriculture.

crop varieties in order to take advantage of the decline in the real price of fertilizer.

In Japan, because of the secularly rising trend of wages and drastically falling fertilizer prices relative to land prices, there was a strong inducement for farmers and experiment station workers to develop biological innovations such as the high-yielding, fertilizer-responsive crop varieties. It is significant that in the United States the biological innovations represented by hybrid corn began about ten years after the rate of increase in arable land area per worker decelerated (around 1920) and that biological innovations and fertilizer application were accelerated after acreage restrictions were imposed by the government. It seems that the changes in land supply conditions, coupled with a dramatic decline in fertilizer prices, induced a more rapid rate of biological innovation in the United States after the 1930s. It may be that when the increase in fertilizer input per hectare resulting from this relative price decline exceeded the amount of natural fertility depleted from the soil, the demand for biological innovations became a pressing need, which, coupled with the change in the supply condition of arable land, induced the dramatic advantages in biological technology in the United States since the 1930s.

According to our hypothesis postulated in Chapter 5 such adjustments in factor proportions in response to changes in relative factor prices represent movements along the iso-product surface of a metaproduction function—the envelope of less elastic production surfaces corresponding to specific types of machinery or varieties as illustrated in Figure 5-6.

The movements along the metaproduction function may be inferred from Figures 7-6 and 7-7, in which U.S. and Japanese data on the relationship between farm draft power (from both tractors and draft animals) per male worker and the machinery-labor price ratio, and between fertilizer input per hectare of arable land and the fertilizer-land price ratio, are plotted. Despite the enormous differences in climate and other environmental conditions, the relation between these variables is almost identical in both countries. This suggests that U.S. and Japanese agricultural growth has involved a movement along a common metaproduction function.

FACTOR SUBSTITUTION ALONG THE METAPRODUCTION FUNCTION[8]

The hypothesis developed in the previous section can be summarized as follows: Agricultural growth in the United States and Japan during the period 1880–1980 can best be understood when viewed as a dynamic factor-substitution process. Factors have been substituted for each other along a metaproduction function in response to long-run trends in relative factor prices. Each point on the metaproduction surface is characterized by a technology that can

8. Readers who are not interested in the technical detail may wish to skip this section.

FIGURE 7-6. Relation between farm draft power per male worker and power-labor price ratio (= hectares of work days which can be purchased by one horsepower of tractor or draft animal), the United States and Japan, quinquennial observations for 1880–1980.

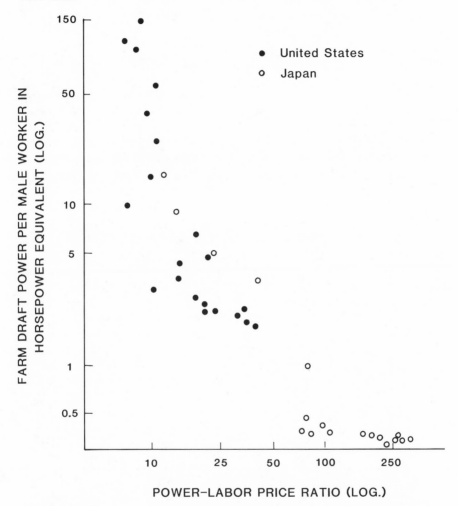

POWER–LABOR PRICE RATIO (LOG.)

Source: Data from Appendix C: Number of male workers = U3 and J4, power = U7 + U8 and J7 + J8, land price = U19 and J19, power price = average retail price of tractor per horsepower extrapolated by U21 from the 1976–80 average of 216 dollars for the United States, and extrapolated by J21 from the 1976–80 average of 65,170 yen for Japan.

FIGURE 7-7. Relation between fertilizer input per hectare of arable land and fertilizer-arable land price ratio (= hectares of arable land which can be purchased by one ton of N + P_2O_5 + K_2O contained in commercial fertilizers), the United States and Japan: quinquennial observations for 1880–1980.

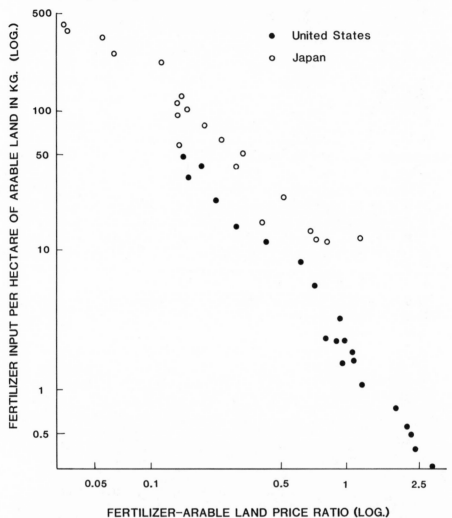

Source: Data from Appendix C: Land area = U6 and J6, fertilizer input = U9 and J9, land price = U19 and J19, fertilizer price = U23 and J22.

be described in terms of specific sources of power, types of machinery, crop varieties, and animal breeds. Movements along this metaproduction surface involve technical changes. These technical changes have been induced to a significant extent by the long-term trends in relative factor prices.

As a test of this hypothesis, we have tried to determine the extent to which the variations in factor proportions, as measured by the land-labor, power-labor, and fertilizer-land ratios, can be explained by changes in factor price ratios. In a situation characterized by a fixed technology it seems reasonable to presume that the elasticities of substitution among factors are small. This permits us to infer that innovations were induced if the variations in these factor proportions are explained consistently by the changes in price ratios. The historically observed changes in those factor proportions in the United States and Japan are so large that it is hardly conceivable that these changes represent substitution along a given production surface describing a constant technology.[9]

To specify the regression form adequately, we have to be able to infer the shape of the underlying metaproduction function and the functional form of the relationship between changes in the production function and in factor price ratios. Because of a lack of adequate a priori information, we have simply specified the regression in log-linear form without much claim for theoretical justification. If we can assume that the production function is linear and homogeneous, the factor proportions can be expressed as factor price ratios alone and are independent of product prices.

Considering the crudeness of the data and the purpose of this analysis, we used quinquennial observations (stock variables measured at five-year intervals and flow variables averaged for five years) instead of annual observations for the regression analysis.[10] A crude form of adjustment is built into our model, since our data are quinquennial observations and prices are generally measured as the averages of the five years preceding the year when the quantities are measured (for example, the number of workers in 1910 is associated with the 1906–10 average wage).

The results of regression analyses are summarized in Tables 7-3 and 7-4. Table 7-3 presents the regressions for land-labor and power-land proportions.

9. Griliches has shown, using a distributed lag model, that increases in fertilizer input by United States farmers can be explained solely in terms of the decline in fertilizer prices. See Zvi Griliches, "The Demand for Fertilizer: An Economic Interpretation of a Technical Change," *Journal of Farm Economics* 40 (August 1958):591–606. The relation he estimated can be identified as the movement along the metaproduction function. A very high elasticity of substitution between labor and capital in the order of 1.7 was estimated for U.S. agriculture by Yoav Kislev and Willis Peterson, "Prices, Technology, and Farm Size," *Journal of Political Economy* 90 (June 1982):578–95. We consider their estimates to represent the elasticity of substitution along the metaproduction function rather than the elasticity along a given technology production function.

10. For earlier periods annual observations were either unavailable or, if available, very crude and often inconsistent in definition and measurement (e.g., measured on the crop-year basis for some years and on the calendar-year basis for others).

TABLE 7-3a. Regressions of land-labor ratios and power-labor ratios on relative factor prices: United States, 1880–1980, quinquennial observations

Regression number	Dependent variables	Coefficients of price of			Coeff. of det. (R̄²)	S.E.	Durbin-Watson statistics
		Land relative to farm wage	Machinery relative to farm wage	Time dummy			
	Land-labor ratios:						
(W1)	Agricultural land per male worker	-.248 (.191)	-.313 (.107)	.984 (.118)	.922	.155	1.82
(W2)	Arable land per male worker	-.042 (.182)	-.592 (.102)	.902 (.112)	.945	.148	1.92
(W3)	Agricultural land per work-hour	-.182 (.206)	-.267 (.115)	.971 (.127)	.898	.167	1.55
(W4)	Arable land per work-hour	.024 (.195)	-.545 (.109)	.889 (.120)	.929	.158	1.67
	Power-labor ratios:						
(W5)	Horsepower per male worker	-1.040 (.466)	-1.060 (.261)	1.839 (.287)	.928	.378	1.73
(W6)	Horsepower per work-hour	-.974 (.480)	-1.013 (.269)	1.826 (.295)	.919	.389	1.65

Source: Data from Appendix C: Number of workers = U3, number of work-hours = U4, agricultural land area = U5, arable land area = U6, power in horsepower equivalents = U7 + U8, farm wage = U8, land price = U18, machinery price = U20, machinery price = U21.

Note: Equations are linear in logarithm. Standard errors of the estimated coefficients are in parentheses. The time dummy variable is zero for 1880–1960 and one for 1965–80.

182

TABLE 7-3b. Regressions of land-labor ratios and power-labor ratios on relative factor prices: Japan, 1880–1980, quinquennial observations

| Regression number | Dependent variables | Coefficients of price of | | Coeff. of det. ($\bar{R}^2$) | S.E. | Durbin-Watson statistics |
		Land relative to farm wage	Machinery relative to farm wage			
	Land-labor ratios:					
(W7)	Arable land per male worker	−.147 (−.068)	−.408 (.034)	.893	.123	1.00
(W8)	Arable land per work-hour	.069 (.067)	−.354 (.060)	.680	.215	.48
	Power-labor ratios:					
(W9)	Horsepower per male worker	.221 (.375)	−1.146 (.188)	.695	.675	.37
(W10)	Horsepower per work-hour	.143 (.430)	−1.091 (.216)	.615	.773	1.74

Source: Data from Appendix C: Number of workers = J3, number of work-hours = J4, arable land area = J6, power in horsepower equivalents = J7 + J8, farm wage = J18, land price = J20, machinery price = J21.

Note: Equations are linear in logarithm. Standard errors of the estimated coefficients are in parentheses.

183

TABLE 7-4a. Regressions of fertilizer input per hectare of arable land on relative factor prices: United States, 1880–1980, quinquennial observations

Regression number	Coefficients of price of			Coeff. of det. ($\bar{R}^2$)	S.E.	Durbin-Watson statistics
	Fertilizer relative to land	Labor relative to land	Machinery relative to land			
(W11)	-1.512 (.119)	.850 (.212)	-.025 (.233)	.983	.177	2.02
(W12)	-1.521 (.053)	.843 (.216)	–	.984	.189	2.02
(W13)	-1.641 (.063)	–	–	.972	.250	.88
(W14)	-1.295 (.092)	1.118 (.129)	-.066 (.176)	.991	.129	2.01
(W15)	-1.328 (.038)	1.076 (.114)	–	.992	.134	2.04
(W16)	-1.524 (.075)	–	–	.954	.318	1.04

Source: Data from Appendix C: Fertilizer input = U9, arable land area = U6. In case of (W11), (W12), and (W13), farm wage = U17, land price = U19, machinery price = U21, fertilizer price = U23. In case of (W14), (W15), and (W16), farm wage = U20, land price = U18, land price = U18, machinery price = U21, fertilizer = U24.
Note: Equations are linear in logarithm. Standard errors of the estimated coefficients are in parentheses.

185

TABLE 7-4b. Regressions of fertilizer input per hectare of arable land on relative factor prices: Japan, 1880–1980, quinquennial observations

Regression number	Coefficients of price of			Coeff. of det. ($\bar{R}^2$)	S.E.	Durbin-Watson statistics
	Fertilizer relative to land	Labor relative to land	Machinery relative to land			
(W17)	-1.033 (.347)	.432 (.209)	.019 (.487)	.884	.388	1.67
(W18)	-1.020 (.082)	.427 (.173)	–	.891	.388	1.67
(W19)	-1.037 (.093)	–	–	.862	.449	1.29
(W20)	-1.626 (.311)	.496 (.180)	.906 (.437)	.909	.345	.63
(W21)	-1.001 (.082)	.587 (.190)	–	.892	.386	1.06
(W22)	-1.028 (.098)	–	–	.844	.477	1.07

Source: Data from Appendix C: Fertilizer input = J9, arable land area = J6. In case of (W17), (W18), and (W19), farm wage = J17, land price = J19, machinery price = J21, fertilizer price = J22. In case of (W20), (W21), and (W22), farm wage = J18, land price = J20, machinery price = J21, fertilizer price = J23.
Note: Equations are linear in logarithm. Standard errors of the estimated coefficients are in parentheses.

In those regressions we originally included other variables, such as the fertilizer-labor price ratio and the exponential time trend. But, probably because of high intercorrelations, the coefficients for those variables either were nonsignificant or they resulted in implausible results for the other coefficients. Those variables were dropped in the subsequent analysis.

Table 7-3a shows the results for the United States. A major anomaly in our initial U.S. regressions on land-labor and power-land ratios (not shown) was that very poor results were obtained for signs and significance levels of estimated coefficients, coefficients of determination, and the Durbin-Watson statistics when the regressions were estimated for 1880–1980, yet good results were obtained for 1880–1960 (see Table 6-3a in the 1971 edition of this book). This anomaly seems to be explained by the deficiency of data on land prices. We measured land price by the average unit of land in farms. This is a measure of the price of land as a stock but not the price of the service of land for agricultural production. As is well known, agricultural land prices in the United States diverged rapidly from agricultural land rents during 1960–80 because of the rising demand for land for nonagricultural uses and the anticipation of continued inflation.[11] As a result, the stock price of land rose relative to the farm wage rate after 1960. But land rents seem to have declined relative to the farm wage rate although national aggregate time-series data on agricultural land rents are not yet available.

To adjust for the divergence between the stock and the service prices of agricultural land, the regressions in Table 7-3a include a time dummy variable, which is specified as zero for 1880–1960 and one after 1960. About 90 percent of the variation in the land-labor ratio and in the power-labor ratio is explained by the changes in their price ratios together with the dummy variables. The coefficients are all negative, except the land-price coefficient in regression (W4). Such results indicate that the marked increases in land and power per worker in U.S. agriculture over the past one hundred years have been closely associated with declines in the price of land and of power and machinery relative to the farm wage rate. The hypothesis that land and power should be treated as complementary factors is confirmed by the negative coefficients. This seems to indicate that, in addition to the complementarity along a fixed production surface, mechanical innovations that raise the marginal rate of substitution of power for labor tend also to raise the marginal rate of substitution of land for labor.

The results from using the same regressions for Japan (Table 7-3b) are greatly inferior in statistical criteria, probably because the ranges of observed variation in the land-labor and power-labor ratios are too small in Japan to detect meaningful relationships between the factor proportions and price

11. For the divergence between agricultural land prices and land rents in the United States since 1960, see John P. Doll and Richard Widdows, *A Comparison of Cash Rent and Land Values for Selected U.S. Farming Regions* (Staff Report, U.S. Department of Agriculture, Economic Research Service, National Economics Division, Washington, D.C., 1982).

ratios. It may also reflect the fact that the mechanical innovations in Japan were developed and adopted primarily to increase yield, rather than as a substitute for labor, for the period before World War II.

The results for the United States of the regression analyses of the determinants of fertilizer input per hectare of arable land are presented in Table 7-4a. The results indicate that variations in the fertilizer-land price ratio alone explain more than 90 percent of the variation in fertilizer use. They also show that the wage-land price ratio is a significant variable, indicating a substitution relationship between fertilizer and labor. Over a certain range, fertilizer input can be substituted for human care for plants (for example, weeding). A more important factor in Japanese history would be the effects of substitution of commercial fertilizer for the labor allocated to the production of self-supplied fertilizers such as animal and green manure.[12]

A comparison of Table 7-4a with Table 7-4b indicates a striking similarity in the structure of demand for fertilizer in the United States and Japan. The results in these two tables seem to suggest that, despite enormous differences in climate, initial factor endowments, and social and economic institutions and organization in the United States and Japan, the agricultural production function, the inducement mechanism of innovations, and the response of farmers to economic opportunities have been essentially the same.

Overall, the results of the statistical analysis are consistent with the hypothesis stated at the beginning of this section: in both Japan and the United States factors have been substituted for each other along a metaproduction function, primarily in response to long-run trends in factor prices.

A TEST OF THE INDUCED TECHNICAL CHANGE HYPOTHESIS[13]

According to our hypothesis, factor substitution along the metaproduction function involves changes in the fixed-technology production surface in a direction of saving the factors that become relatively more expensive than the other factors. The discussion of the induced technical change hypothesis presented in the previous section has established rather clearly the plausibility of the induced technical change hypothesis. But to test more rigorously the

12. Biological innovations represented by improvements in crop varieties, characterized by greater response to fertilizer, tend to be land-saving and labor-using. The yield potential of the improved varieties is typically achieved only when high levels of fertilization are combined with high levels of crop husbandry and water management. On this score, the introduction of high-yielding varieties enhances the substitution of fertilizer and labor for land. On the other hand, commercial fertilizers have significant labor-saving effects as they substitute for self-supplied fertilizers. In Japan, the production of such self-supplied fertilizers as manure, green manure, compost, and night soil has traditionally occupied a significant portion of a farmer's work hours. With the increased supply of commercial fertilizers, farmers can divert their labor to the improvements in cultural practices in such forms as better seed bed preparation and weed control.

13. Readers who are not interested in the technical detail may wish to skip the mathematical presentation in this section and turn to Figures 7-8 to 7-10.

induced innovation hypothesis it is necessary to decompose changes in factor proportions into (a) the effect of factor substitution along a fixed-technology isoquant in response to changes in relative factor prices and (b) the effect of biased technical change. In addition, it is necessary to see whether the biased technical change effect is in the same direction as the price-induced factor substitution effect.

In this section we attempt to conduct such a test using the 1880–1980 quinquennial data for U.S. and Japanese agriculture. A method of measuring biases of technical change with many factors of production was originally developed by Hans Binswanger using the transcendental logarithmic (translog) function. His method has found a number of applications in the analysis of agricultural production.[14] In this study we employ the two-level constant elasticity of substitution (CES) production function, which is more robust in estimation and more clear-cut in interpretation than the translog function.[15]

In order to measure the effect of biased technical change it is convenient to specify that technical change is of the factor-augmenting type. Output is assumed to be produced by n inputs $(X_1, \ldots, X_n)$ with corresponding factor-augmenting coefficients $(E_1, \ldots, E_n)$ where E_i represents the efficiency of X_i:

(1) $$Q = f(E_1 X_1, \ldots, E_n X_n)$$

where the production function (f) is assumed to be linear homogeneous and well-behaved.

When a competitive market equilibrium is assumed, the following relation

14. Hans P. Binswanger, "The Measurement of Technical Change Biases with Many Factors of Production," *American Economic Review* 64 (December 1974):964–76; and "Measured Biases of Technical Change: The United States," *Induced Innovation,* ed. Binswanger and Ruttan, pp. 215–42. The Binswanger method was applied to Japanese agriculture by Toshiyuki Kako, "Decomposition Analysis of Derived Demand for Factor Inputs: The Case of Rice Production in Japan," *American Journal of Agricultural Economics* 60 (November 1978):628–35; and Le Thanh Nghiep, "The Structure and Changes of Technology in Prewar Japanese Agriculture," *American Journal of Agricultural Economics* 61 (November 1979):687–93.

15. The two-level CES production function was originally developed by Kazuo Sato, "A Two-Level Constant-Elasticity-of-Substitution Production Function," *Review of Economic Studies* 34 (April 1967):201–18. This production function was first applied to the analysis of Japanese agriculture by Masahiko Shintani and Yujiro Hayami, "Nogyo ni okeru Yosoketsugo to Henkoteki Gijutsushimpo" (Factor combination and biased technical change in agriculture), in *Kindai Nihon no Keizai Hatten* (Economic development of modern Japan) (Tokyo: Toyokeizaishimposha, 1975), pp. 228–48. More recently, the two-level CES production function was advocated for its relevance to the analysis of agricultural production in general by Hiromitsu Kaneda, "Specification of Production Functions for Analyzing Technical Change and Factor Inputs in Agricultural Development," *Journal of Development Economics* 11 (August 1982):97–108. According to Kaneda, the two-level CES function has advantages over the translog function in parsimony in parameters, ease of interpretation and computation, and interpolative and extrapolative robustness. For an earlier attempt to adopt the CES production function to estimate elasticities of substitution among more than two factors see Terry Roe and Patrick Yeung, "A CES Test of Induced Technical Change: Japan," *Induced Innovation,* ed. Binswanger and Ruttan, pp. 243–60.

can be derived (see Supplement A for derivations) for accounting for changes in factor proportions:

$$(2) \quad \sum_{j \neq i} s_j \left(\frac{\dot{X}_i}{X_i} - \frac{\dot{X}_j}{X_j} \right) = \sum_{j \neq i} s_j \sigma_{ij} \left(\frac{\dot{P}_j}{P_j} - \frac{\dot{P}_i}{P_i} \right) + \sum_{j \neq i} s_j (1 - \sigma_{ij}) \left(\frac{\dot{E}_j}{E_j} - \frac{\dot{E}_i}{E_i} \right)$$

where the dot denotes the time derivative (hence, for example, $\dot{X}_i/X_i$ represents the growth rate of X_i); P_i is the real factor price of input i; s_i is the factor share of input i; σ_{ij} is the Allen partial elasticity of substitution representing the curvature of the fixed-technology isoquant between input i and input j, assuming optimal adjustments in other factor inputs.

The left-hand side of equation (2) is the weighted average of the rates of change in the proportion of factor i relative to all other factors using factor shares as weights. This term may be called a "generalized change in the factor proportion" of the ith input ($GCFP_i$). Since $GCFP_i$ can also be expressed as

$$\frac{\dot{X}_i}{X_i} - \sum_j s_j \frac{\dot{X}_i}{X_j},$$

it can be interpreted as an excess of the growth rate of X_i over the average growth rate of all factor inputs.

The first term on the right-hand side of equation (2) measures the contribution of changes in relative factor prices to $GCFP_i$ as it represents the effect of factor substitution along a fixed isoquant. The second term measures the contribution of biased technical change as it represents the effect of differential rates of factor augmentation among inputs. In short, the right-hand side of equation (2) decomposes $GCFP_i$ into the price-induced factor substitution and the biased technical change effects.

Following the Hicksian definition, factor-using bias in technical change may be defined for the many factor cases as ith factor-using, neutral, and ith factor-saving depending on whether the second term on the right-hand side of equation (2) is positive, zero, or negative, respectively.

Factor-using bias can also be evaluated using changes in factor shares. The rate of change in the ith factor share can be expressed as

$$(3) \quad \frac{\dot{s}_i}{s_i} = \sum_{j \neq i} s_j (\sigma_{ij} - 1) \left(\frac{\dot{P}_j}{P_j} - \frac{\dot{P}_i}{P_i} \right) + \sum_{j \neq i} s_j (1 - \sigma_{ij}) \left(\frac{\dot{E}_j}{E_j} - \frac{\dot{E}_i}{E_i} \right).$$

In the above equation, the rate of change in the ith factor share is decomposed into (a) the price-induced factor substitution effect (the first term on the right-hand side) and (b) the biased technical change effect (the second term). The factor-using bias can be defined by the signs of the second term of equation (3) in the exactly same manner as for equation (2).

For the measurement of technical change biases we use equation (3). The technical change biases were measured by the changes in factor shares that would have occurred in the absence of factor price changes. First, the rate of change in the factor share for inputs that would have occurred during year t in the absence of factor price changes (b_{it}) is estimated by subtracting the first term on the right-hand side of equation (3) from the left-hand side. The cumulative change in a factor share owing to biased technical change that would have occurred for input i from the base year (1880) up to year t (B_{it}) can be calculated as

$$B_{it} = S_{i,1880} \cdot \prod_t (1 + b_{it}) - S_{i,1880}$$

where $S_{i,1880}$ is the actual factor share in the base year (1880). The estimates of B_{it}'s are shown in Table 7-5.

The first term on the right-hand side of the above equation may be called the "constant-price factor share" ($S'_{i,t}$), which is a hypothetical factor share that would have existed in year t if the factor prices had remained the same as for 1880. Note that the factor shares used for the calculation of b_{it}'s were the constant-price factor shares instead of the actual shares. The index of factor-using bias for input i in year t may be calculated by

$$\frac{S'_{it}}{S_{i,1880}} \times 100$$

where $S_{i,1880}$ is the actual factor share in 1880.

For the estimation of B_{it} it is necessary to estimate the partial elasticities of substitution (σ_{ij}) and factor shares (s_i). The partial elasticities of substitution were estimated with the use of the two-level CES production function (see Supplement B). The data of factor shares were estimated as explained in Supplement C.

The induced innovation hypothesis will be accepted if the factor-using bias for input i is associated with a decline in the price of input i relative to other input prices. Therefore, for testing the induced innovation hypothesis, it is necessary to have the indexes of input prices relative to the aggregate input price index. The aggregate input price index was constructed by aggregating the indexes of labor, land, power, and fertilizer prices using factor shares as weights (see Supplement C). The relative factor price indexes were obtained by deflating the indexes of individual factor prices by the aggregate input price indexes as shown in Table 7-5.

The time-series data for factor inputs and prices used for the analysis in this section are the same as for the analysis in the previous sections, except that the work-hour data were used exclusively for the labor variable (L). For the production function analysis, assuming market equilibrium conditions, flow measures of inputs, such as the number of work-hours, are more appropriate to use than stock measures, such as the number of workers. The stock measures were still used for land (A), for agricultural land area, and power (M),

TABLE 7-5. Cumulative changes in factor shares owing to biased technical change in agriculture (B_{it}) and the indexes of factor prices relative to the aggregate input price index, the United States and Japan, 1880–1980

| | United States | | | | | | | | Japan | | | | | | | |
| | Factor-using bias (B_{it}) (Percent) | | | | Relative factor price 1880 = 100 | | | | Factor-using bias (B_{it}) (Percent) | | | | Relative factor price 1880 = 100 | | | |
Year	Labor (L)	Land (A)	Power (M)	Fertilizer (F)	Labor (L)	Land (A)	Power (M)	Fertilizer (F)	Labor (L)	Land (A)	Power (M)	Fertilizer (F)	Labor (L)	Land (A)	Power (M)	Fertilizer (F)
1880	0.	0.	0.	0.	100	100	100	100	0.	0.	0.	0.	100	100	100	100
1885	-0.4	-0.5	0.8	0.2	102	111	88	76	6.2	-6.8	0.2	0.4	83	134	96	95
1890	-1.0	-1.7	2.3	0.3	108	109	78	67	4.5	-7.3	0.9	1.9	81	146	86	87
1895	-3.3	-0.4	3.1	0.6	107	111	79	69	10.4	-13.9	1.8	1.6	74	177	72	84
1900	-2.9	0.9	1.2	0.8	116	107	66	69	6.4	-12.4	3.2	2.8	80	170	61	67
1905	-2.6	0.1	1.3	1.3	106	141	59	45	6.9	-14.4	3.3	4.1	77	180	64	64
1910	-2.6	-0.8	1.8	1.6	110	143	52	38	5.9	-16.8	4.6	6.1	80	191	53	48
1915	-3.6	-1.0	2.7	1.8	112	147	45	38	7.5	-21.8	5.8	8.4	77	220	48	41
1920	-6.4	-0.1	4.2	2.2	125	126	39	43	-16.4	-0.6	7.7	9.2	96	159	37	33
1925	-8.6	2.3	4.5	1.8	123	134	40	33	-12.1	-5.9	8.3	9.6	101	179	28	24
1930	-11.2	2.4	6.6	2.1	135	114	38	26	-6.0	-13.1	8.8	10.3	89	220	27	24
1935	-12.0	-0.9	10.2	2.8	118	119	51	29	-13.9	-7.5	9.2	12.0	91	203	32	22
1940	-13.0	-2.8	12.6	3.1	127	109	46	28	-28.1	4.4	10.4	13.2	110	158	27	18
1945	-21.4	1.1	17.0	3.4	159	82	31	20								
1950	-28.5	3.8	20.5	4.2	166	84	28	14								
1955	-38.4	5.4	28.0	5.2	161	91	29	11	-26.3	0.1	10.9	15.2	115	133	32	18
1960	-46.5	12.6	29.1	4.8	164	97	28	9	-18.8	-8.9	11.5	16.1	99	217	28	11
1965	-54.4	12.8	35.5	6.1	158	100	29	7	-31.1	-1.9	13.1	19.7	133	181	20	7
1970	-58.7	15.3	36.9	6.3	176	112	26	5	-40.2	5.0	14.6	20.6	169	166	14	5
1975	-61.8	16.1	37.4	8.2	181	119	24	6	-49.6	10.2	16.0	23.4	205	160	10	4
1980	-63.3	12.5	43.8	7.1	156	134	24	5	-47.3	7.9	16.0	23.4	195	183	8	4

for horsepower, because flow data were not available. The 1945–50 observations for Japan, the period following the devastation of World War II, were discarded from the analysis because government price controls and rationing preclude the possibility that the assumption of competitive market equilibrium from which our model was deduced would hold during that period.

To test the induced innovation hypothesis, the indexes of factor-using biases, as measured by $(S_{it}/S_{i,1880})$, are compared with the index of relative factor prices for each individual input for the United States in Figure 7-8 and for Japan in Figure 7-9. In both the United States and Japan, movements in the indexes of factor-using bias are negatively associated with those of relative factor prices with only a few exceptions. The results render support to the induced innovation hypothesis, indicating that technical change in both countries was directed toward using (or saving) the factors that became less (or more) costly relative to other factors.

A major difference in the historical sequences of technical change biases was observed between the United States and Japan. Technical change in U.S. agriculture was biased in the labor-saving direction for the entire period in response to the continuous rise in the labor wage rate relative to other input prices. Technical change in the United States was almost neutral with respect to the use of land between 1880 and 1900, a period of relative stability in land prices. It then became land-saving until 1940, apparently induced by the rise in land prices from 1900 to 1915.

In contrast, the direction of technical change in Japan was largely labor-using and land-saving until about 1915 in response to the relative decline in the wage rate and the relative rise in the price of land. After 1915, the directions of labor and land biases were reversed in response to reversals in the movements in their relative prices. Such contrasts suggest that in the early stage of economic development, labor was relatively scarce and land relatively abundant in the United States and that labor was relatively abundant and land relatively scarce in Japan. Thus technology in both countries was directed to saving the relatively scarce factors, which were different in the two countries.

The direction of factor-using biases in the United States and Japan tended to converge during the period after World War II. A major inconsistency was found in the case of land in the United States in that period, when a land-using bias was positively associated with sharp increases in the price of land. This anomaly may have been more apparent than real because of the deficiency in land price data as a measure of the price of the factor service of land (see note 12). It seems reasonable to expect that the recent inconsistency between the trends in land bias and land prices might be solved, or at least considerably reduced, when national land rent data become available.

Another possible explanation for the recent inconsistency is the difficulty of distinguishing between the cause and effect of factor-using bias from ex post empirical data, especially for the input with inelastic supply. Given the

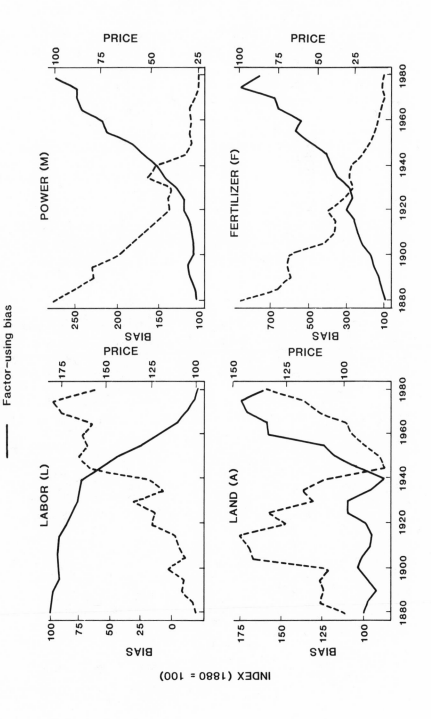

FIGURE 7-8. Individual comparisons between the indexes of factor-using biases in technical change ($S'_{it}/S_{i,1880}$) and the indexes of factor prices relative to the aggregate input price index, the United States, 1880–1980. (Data from Table 7-5.)

193

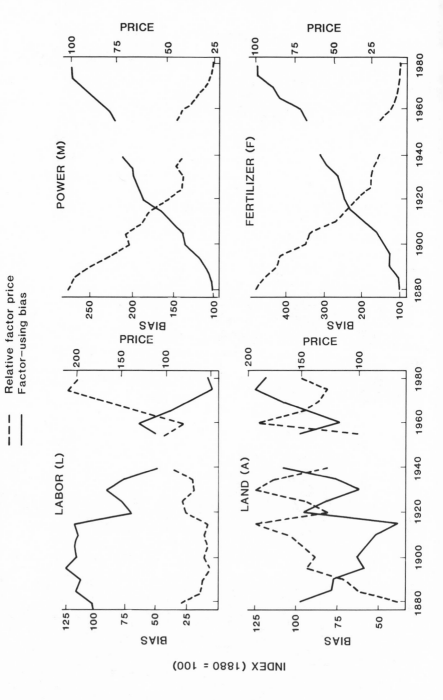

FIGURE 7-9. Individual comparisons between the indexes of factor-using biases in technical change ($S'_{it}/S_{i,1880}$) and the indexes of factor prices relative to the aggregate input price index, Japan, 1880–1940 and 1955–80. (Data from Table 7-5.)

Relative factor price
Factor-using bias

inelastic supply of land, if technical change were very responsive to a decrease in land prices in the land-using direction, the land price would then fall less than it would in the absence of technical change. In an extreme case it might not fall at all.[16] When we consider this possibility, together with the problem of the land price data, the apparent inconsistency between the land bias and the land price trend in the United States for recent years can hardly be taken as a significant qualification of the induced innovation hypothesis.

Our estimates of factor-saving biases in U.S. agriculture are largely consistent with Binswanger's. With respect to the induced innovation hypothesis, however, he found a major inconsistency between machinery-using bias and an increase in the relative price of machinery and concluded that an innate bias in technical change existed, in a machine-using direction. His conclusion was strongly criticized by Yoav Kislev and Willis Peterson on the ground that the USDA machinery price index used by Binswanger overestimates the price increase since it is not adjusted for quality change in machinery.[17] In our case, the machinery prices were adjusted for quality change (Appendix C-2), which may explain why the inconsistency did not appear.

Our results for Japan were different from those of Le Thanh Nghiep,[18] especially regarding his findings of labor-saving bias in technical change during the prewar period. The labor-saving bias in his case was based on labor measured by the number of workers. The number of workers increased much less than the number of work-hours used in our analysis. In addition, his analysis covered only the period after 1903 and did not cover the earlier period for which the labor-using bias was observed in this study.

The index of factor-using bias $(S'_{it}/S_{i,1880})$ used for the analysis in Figures 7-8 and 7-9 shows the rates of change in factor shares owing to biased technical change. This index is an appropriate measure of the extent to which a factor input increased relative to other inputs because of biased technical change. But it is not an appropriate measure of the absolute effect on the agricultural production cost structure of increasing the input of that factor relative to other factors as a result of technical change. For example, even if the rate of increase in factor-using bias for an input as measured by $(S'_{it}/S_{i,1880})$ is high, the absolute effect of that bias on factor shares will be small if the factor share in the base period $(S_{i,1880})$ is very small. On the other hand, a modest increase in $(S'_{it}/S_{i,1880})$ may result in a large change in the corresponding constant price factor share if the factor share in the base period is large. To compare the absolute effects of biased technical change on the production cost structure, it is more appropriate to use the absolute change

16. This problem was pointed out by Binswanger, "Measured Biases of Technical Change," p. 216.

17. Yoav Kislev and Willis Peterson, "Induced Innovations and Farm Mechanization," *American Journal of Agricultural Economics* 63 (August 1981):562–65.

18. Nghiep, "Structure and Changes of Technology in Prewar Japanese Agriculture."

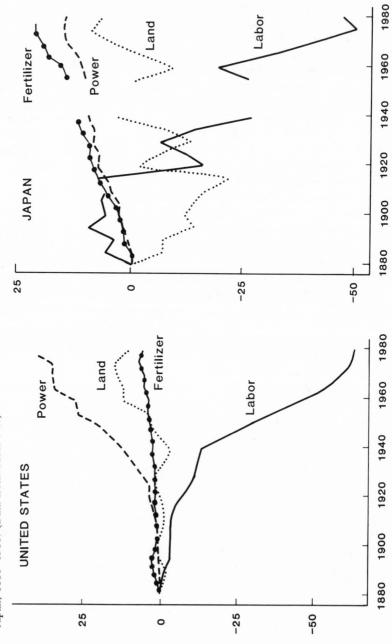

FIGURE 7-10. Cumulative changes in factor shares owing to biased technical change in agriculture (B_{it}), the United States and Japan, 1880–1980. (Data from Table 7-5.)

between the constant-price factor share and the actual factor share in the base period ($B_{it} = S'_{it} - S_{i,1880}$) rather than the relative change ($S'_{it}/S_{i,1880}$).

The cumulative changes in factor shares resulting from biased technical change are compared in Figure 7-10 for both the United States and Japan. The absolute effects of biased technical change on the agricultural production cost structure as measured by the cumulative changes are quite different between the United States and Japan. In the United States, biased technical change resulted in a major increase in the share of power in total production cost and an associated decrease in the share of labor. Although the rate of increase in fertilizer-using bias was high, as measured by ($S'_{it}/S_{i,1880}$), its absolute effect on the factor-share structure was relatively small because the initial factor share for fertilizer was very small. It seems clear that the dominant effects of biased technical change in U.S. agriculture on the production structure were labor-saving and power (cum machinery)-using throughout the entire period of analysis.

In contrast, in Japan the absolute effect of factor-using bias on factor shares was largest for fertilizer and second largest for power, and the factor-saving effect was largest for labor for the entire period. The dominant effects of biased technical change during the early phase of economic development until about 1915 were land-saving and labor-using. It seems clear that, during the early period in which labor was relatively abundant and land represented the major constraint on agricultural production, the major efforts of technological development in Japan were geared for facilitating substitution of labor for land. Later, as labor wage rates rose primarily because of increased demand for labor from the nonagricultural sectors, technological development seems to have been redirected toward the labor-saving direction by facilitating substitution of power and fertilizer for labor.

GUIDING TECHNOLOGICAL CHANGE
ALONG ALTERNATIVE PATHS

Despite extremely different resource endowments, both the United States and Japan were successful in sustaining growth in agricultural output and productivity over the 1880–1980 period. A common thread of the success in both countries identified from the analysis in this chapter was the capacity to develop agricultural technology to facilitate the substitution of relatively abundant factors for scarce factors in accordance with market price signals.

Rapid growth in agriculture in both countries could not have occurred without such dynamic factor substitution. If factor substitution had been limited to substitution along a fixed production surface, agricultural growth would have been severely limited by the inelastic supply of the more limiting factors. Development of the continuous stream of new technology, which altered the production surface to conform to long-term trends in resource endowments and factor prices, was the key to success in agricultural growth in the United States and Japan.

For both the United States and Japan, vigorous growth in the industries that supplied machinery and fertilizers at continuously declining relative prices has been an indispensable requirement for agricultural growth. Equally important were the efforts in research and extension to exploit fully the opportunities created by industrial development. Without the creation of fertilizer-responsive crop varieties, the benefits from the lower fertilizer prices would have been limited. The success in agricultural growth in both the United States and Japan seems to lie in the capacity of their farmers, research institutions, and farm supply industries to exploit new opportunities in response to the information transmitted through relative price changes.

Agriculture in the United States and Japan, starting from entirely different initial factor endowments and factor supply conditions, experienced comparable rates of growth in production and productivity over the 1880–1980 period. There is little reason to believe that presently developing countries cannot attain the same success if they exploit the opportunities available to them. Their patterns of growth would be expected to be different from those of either the United States or Japan, since factor supply conditions reflect the unique endowments of each country. In addition, product demand in most developing countries is rising at a rate that exceeds the historical rates experienced in either Japan or the United States. Efforts must be directed to creating a unique pattern of growth for each developing country. An important element in this effort appears to be an institutional environment which is capable of reflecting accurately the economic implications of factor endowments to producers, public institutions, and private industry.

The results of our tests of the induced technical change hypothesis for the United States and Japan are consistent with a number of more limited studies of the effects of distortions in relative factor prices on technical change. Studies in Brazil, in Pakistan, and in Senegal suggest that exchange rate distortions and subsidies have led to premature mechanization.[19] Such factor price distortions have both short-run and long-run effects. In the short run they encourage, within the constraints imposed by existing factor-substitution possibilities, an inefficient choice among available technologies. Over the longer run they induce biases in the invention of new technology and in the direction of productivity growth. Because of the lags between research, development, and adoption, current policies that distort relative factor prices affect the technology choices that become available to farmers a decade or more in the future.

19. John H. Sanders and Vernon W. Ruttan, "Biased Choice of Technology in Brazilian Agriculture," *Induced Innovation,* ed. Binswanger and Ruttan, pp. 276–96; John P. McInerney and Graham F. Donaldson, *The Consequences of Farm Tractors in Pakistan* (Washington, D.C.: World Bank, Staff Working Paper 210, February 1975): Dryek Byerlee et al., "Employment-Output Conflicts, Factor-Price Distortions, and Choice of Technique: Empirical Results from Sierra Leone," *Economic Development and Cultural Change* 31 (January 1983):315–36.

SUPPLEMENT A. MATHEMATICAL DERIVATION OF EQUATIONS FOR MEASURING THE EFFECT OF BIASED TECHNICAL CHANGE

Assuming the production function as specified in equation (1) and also assuming the competitive market equilibrium, the cost function that relates production cost (C) to output and real input prices $(P_1, \ldots, P_n)$ can be derived as

$$(4) \qquad C = Q \cdot g \, (P_1/E_1, \ldots, P_n/E_n)$$

where g is the unit cost function. The input prices $(P_i$'s) are divided by the factor-augmenting coefficients $(E_i$'s) because a proportional increase in E_i has the same effect as a proportional decrease in P_i. From Shephard's lemma, we obtain

$$(5) \qquad \frac{\delta C}{\delta P_i} = X_i = \frac{Q}{E_i} \left(\frac{\delta g}{\delta P_i} \right), \qquad i = 1, \ldots . n.$$

The unit cost function is related to the Allen partial elasticity of substitution (σ_{ij}) in the following way:[20]

$$(6) \qquad \sigma_{ij} = \frac{\dfrac{\delta^2 g}{\delta P_i \delta P_j} g}{\dfrac{\delta g}{\delta P_i} \dfrac{\delta g}{\delta P_j}}$$

The differentiation of equation (5) with respect to time (t) using equation (6) results in

$$(7) \qquad \frac{\dot{X}_i}{X_i} = \frac{\dot{Q}}{Q} - \frac{\dot{E}_i}{E_i} + \sum_j s_j \sigma_{ij} \left(\frac{\dot{P}_j}{P_j} - \frac{\dot{E}_j}{E_j} \right)$$

where the dot denotes the time derivative and s_j is the factor share of the jth input. Equation (7) is the factor demand function in the growth equation form. Since $s_j \sigma_{ij}$ is the demand elasticity of input i with respect to the price of input j, and the factor demand is homogeneous of degree zero with respect to input prices, the following relation holds:[21]

$$(8) \qquad \sum_j s_j \sigma_{ij} = 0$$

Equation (2) in the text can be obtained by incorporating the above equation into equation (7) and using the relations, $\sum_j s_j = 1$ and $\dot{Q}/Q = \sum_j s_j (\dot{X}_j/X_j + \dot{E}_j/E_j)$.

20. This relation is based on Hirofumi Uzawa, "Production Functions with Constant Elasticities of Substitution," *Review of Economic Studies* 29 (October 1962):291–99.
21. See. R. G. D. Allen, *Mathematical Analysis for Economists* (London: Macmillan, 1938), p. 504.

Equation (3) in the text can be derived as follows: The rate of change in the ith factor share is expressed as

$$(9) \qquad \frac{\dot{s}_i}{s_i} = \frac{\dot{P}_i}{P_i} + \frac{\dot{X}_i}{X_i} - \frac{\dot{Q}}{Q}.$$

Since total output is fully distributed to inputs so that $Q = \sum_j P_j X_j$, the following relation holds:

$$(10) \qquad \frac{\dot{Q}}{Q} = \sum_j s_j \left(\frac{\dot{P}_j}{P_j} + \frac{\dot{X}_j}{X_j} \right).$$

Substitution of equation (10) into equation (9) results in

$$(11) \qquad \frac{\dot{s}_i}{s_i} = \sum_{j \neq i} s_j \left(\frac{\dot{P}_i}{P_i} - \frac{\dot{P}_j}{P_j} \right) + \sum_{j \neq i} s_j \left(\frac{\dot{X}_i}{X_i} - \frac{\dot{X}_j}{X_j} \right).$$

Equation (3) is obtained by inserting equation (7) into equation (11).

SUPPLEMENT B. ESTIMATION OF THE TWO-LEVEL CES PRODUCTION FUNCTION

The two-level CES production function is specified for agriculture including labor (L), land (A), machinery (M), and fertilizer (F) as four factors of production to produce output (Q) gross of intermediate products. Since it is reasonable to assume that machinery is a factor substituting mainly for labor, and fertilizer is a factor substituting for land, it seems appropriate to specify the first-level equation of the two-level CES function as

$$(12) \qquad Z_1 = [\alpha(e^{\delta_L' L})^{-\rho_1} + (1 - \alpha) (e^{\delta_M' M})^{-\rho_1}]^{-1/\rho_1}$$

$$(13) \qquad Z_2 = [\beta(e^{\delta_A' A})^{-\rho_2} + (1 - \beta) (e^{\delta_F' F})^{-\rho_2}]^{-1/\rho_2}$$

where ρ's are substitution parameters; α and β are distribution parameters; and δ_i's $(i = L, M, A, F)$ are the rates of factor augmentation for respective inputs, which are assumed to be constant for the relevant periods. It is also assumed that both functions are linear homogeneous.[22]

To use the terms of Amartya K. Sen[23], Z_1 is considered an aggregate of "laboresque" inputs and Z_2 is an aggregate of "landesque" inputs. Since it is

---

22. In equations (12) and (13), input variables are normalized to be one and time is set to be zero at the base period. In estimates of the CES function based on equations (18), (19), and (23), 1960 was used as the base period.

23. Amartya K. Sen, "The Choice of Agricultural Techniques in Underdeveloped Countries," *Economic Development and Cultural Change* 7 (April 1959):279–85.

reasonable to expect that the laboresque and the landesque inputs are largely separable, the relation between output (Q) and the two categories of inputs may be expressed by the second-level CES function as follows:

$$(14) \qquad Q = [\gamma \, (Z_1)^{-\rho} + (1 - \gamma) \, (Z_2)^{-\rho}]^{-1/\rho}$$

where ρ and γ are the parameters of substitution and distribution, respectively.

While the direct elasticities of substitution are expressed as $\sigma_1 = 1/(\rho_1 + 1)$, $\sigma_2 = 1(\rho_2 + 1)$ and $\sigma = 1/(\rho + 1)$, the Allen partial elasticities of substitution are expressed by

$$(15) \qquad \sigma_{LA} = \sigma_{LF} = \sigma_{AM} = \sigma_{MF} = \sigma$$

$$(16) \qquad \sigma_{LM} = \sigma + \frac{1}{s_1} (\sigma_1 - \sigma)$$

$$(17) \qquad \sigma_{AF} = \sigma + \frac{1}{s_2} (\sigma_2 - \sigma)$$

where s_1 and s_2 are the factor shares of the first and the second categories of inputs, respectively.

The CES production parameters are estimated using the competitive market equilibrium conditions as follows:

$$(18) \qquad \ln \left(\frac{M}{L} \right) = - \frac{1}{\rho_1 + 1} \ln \left(\frac{\alpha}{1 - \alpha} \right) + \frac{1}{\rho_1 + 1} \ln \left(\frac{P_L}{P_M} \right)$$
$$+ \frac{\rho_1}{\rho_1 + 1} (\delta_L - \delta_M) t$$

$$(19) \qquad \ln \left(\frac{F}{A} \right) = - \frac{1}{\rho_2 + 1} \ln \left(\frac{\beta}{1 - \beta} \right) + \frac{1}{\rho_2 + 1} \ln \left(\frac{P_A}{P_F} \right)$$
$$+ \frac{\rho_2}{\rho_2 + 1} (\delta_A - \delta_F) t$$

$$(20) \qquad \ln \left(\frac{Z_2}{Z_1} \right) = - \frac{1}{\rho + 1} \ln \left(\frac{\gamma}{1 - \gamma} \right) + \frac{1}{\rho + 1} \ln \left(\frac{P_1}{P_2} \right)$$

where P_L, P_A, P_M, and P_F are the prices of labor, land, machinery, and fertilizer, respectively, and P_1 and P_2 are the prices of Z_1 and Z_2, which are calculated by

$$(21) \qquad P_1 = (P_L L + P_M M)/Z_1$$

$$(22) \qquad P_2 = (P_A A + P_F F)/Z_2$$

From the regression estimation of equations (18) and (19) we can obtain estimates of ρ_1, ρ_2, α, β, $(\delta_L - \delta_M)$, and $(\delta_A - \delta_F)$ but cannot obtain δ_L, δ_M,

TABLE 7-6. Regressions for estimating the parameters of the two-level CES production function: the United States and Japan, 1880–1980, quinquennial observations (1945–50 observations are discarded for Japan)

Regression number	Dependent variables	Coefficients of			dummy variables for		Coeff. of det. ($\bar{R}^2$)	S.E. of estimates	Durbin-Watson statistics
		Intercept	Relative price	Time trend	Intercept	Time trend			
United States									
First level									
(R1)	Machinery-labor ratio (M/L)	−2.121 (.114)	.191 (.110)	.037 (.017)	2.027 (.120)	.334 (.013)	—	.083	.98
(R2)	Fertilizer-land ratio (F/A)	−.174 (.135)	.349 (.112)	.183 (.021)	.176 (.139)	.073 (.017)	—	.102	1.39
Second level									
(R3)		−.514 (.364)	.191 (.276)	.198 (.050)	.611 (.367)	−.093 (.042)	.997	.099	1.18
Japan									
First level									
(R4)	Machinery-labor ratio (M/L)	−1.160 (.134)	.111 (.153)	−.019 (.023)	1.237 (.125)	.704 (.052)	—	.116	1.72
(R5)	Fertilizer-land ratio (F/A)	.183 (.132)	.182 (.210)	.187 (.042)	−.099 (.182)	−.110 (.047)	—	.157	.71
Second level									
(R6)		.055 (.093)	.239 (.109)	.219 (.018)	−.109 (.116)	−.582 (.047)	.996	.080	1.20

Source: Data from Appendix C. U.S. data: Labor (L)=U4, land (A)=U5, power (M)=U7+U8, fertilizer (F)=U9, wage rate (P_L)=U18, land price (P_A)=U20, power price (P_M)=U21, fertilizer price (P_F)=U24; dummy variable=0 for 1880–1925; =1 for 1930–1980. Japanese data: Labor (L)=J4, land (A)=J5, power (M)=J7+J8, fertilizer (F)=J9, wage rate (P_L)=J17, land price (P_A)=J20, power price (P_M)=J21, fertilizer price (P_F)=J23; dummy variable=0 for 1880–1940; =1 for 1955–1980.

Note: The first-level equations are estimated by generalized least squares. The second-level equations are estimated by ordinary least squares. Standard errors of the estimated coefficients are in parentheses.

δ_A, and δ_F separately. Therefore, Z_1 and Z_2 cannot be measured directly and, hence, equation (20) cannot be estimated. Therefore, in order to proceed to the second-level estimation, we define as

$$\hat{Z}_1 = e^{-\delta_{M}t}Z_1; \quad \hat{Z}_2 = e^{-\delta_{F}t}Z_2;$$

$$\hat{P}_1 = e^{\delta_{M}t}P_1; \quad \hat{P}_2 = e^{\delta_{F}t}P_2,$$

which can be obtained from equations (18), (19), (21), and (22). Substitution of those relations into equation (20) produces the following estimable equation:

$$(23) \quad \ln\frac{\hat{Z}_2}{\hat{Z}_1} = -\frac{1}{\rho + 1}\ln\left(\frac{\gamma}{1 - \gamma}\right) + \frac{1}{\rho + 1}\ln\frac{\hat{P}_1}{\hat{P}_2} + \frac{\rho}{\rho + 1}(\delta_M - \delta_F)t.$$

From the regression estimates of $(\delta_L - \delta_M)$, $(\delta_A - \delta_F)$, and $(\delta_F - \delta_M)$ based on equations (18), (19), and (23), the differential rates of factor augmentation for any pairs of inputs can be obtained.

In the regression analysis a time dummy variable was included to adjust for possible structural change among different phases of economic development. The dummy takes the value of zero for 1880–1925 and one for 1930–80 in the United States, and zero for 1880–1940 and one for 1955–80 in Japan. The time demarcation for Japan in the pre–World War II and the postwar periods should be natural considering the obvious structural change in agriculture as well as in the entire economy. It is not so clear, however, what time demarcation may be used for the United States. Therefore, we tried a number of alternative demarcations and chose the one that gave the best results in terms of goodness of fit and statistical significance of estimated parameters. Through this procedure, the entire period was divided into two subperiods— before 1930 and since 1930.

For the estimation of the first-level equations (18) and (19), the generalized least squares (GLS) method is used. For the second-level equation, OLS is applied. Slope dummies for the relative prices were deleted from the regressions because their coefficients were either insignificant or irrelevant in sign. The results of estimation using data in Appendix C are summarized in Table 7-6. The Allen partial elasticities of substitution derived from the results in Table 7-6 are shown in Table 7-7.

TABLE 7-7. Estimates of the Allen partial elasticities of substitution

Allen partial elasticity of substitution	United States		Japan	
	1880–1925	1930–1980	1880–1940	1955–1980
σ_{LM}	.191	.191	.029	.013
σ_{AF}	.777	.741	.093	.108
Other	.191	.191	.239	.239

TABLE 7-8. Factor shares and the aggregate input price indexes in the United States and Japan, 1880–1980

	United States					Japan				
	Factor shares (%)				Aggregate input price index (1880 = 100)	Factor shares (%)				Aggregate input price index (1880 = 100)
Year	Labor	Land	Power	Fertilizer		Labor	Land	Power	Fertilizer	
1880	52.9	21.2	24.8	1.1	100	52.8	28.8	10.9	7.6	100
1885	53.4	22.6	22.9	1.1	108	52.8	28.8	10.9	7.6	88
1890	55.1	21.1	22.6	1.2	104	50.2	30.7	10.6	8.5	95
1895	52.3	22.7	23.4	1.5	102	51.5	31.0	9.7	7.8	117
1900	56.3	23.2	18.8	1.7	98	52.1	31.0	9.5	7.5	176
1905	51.4	29.6	17.1	2.0	122	50.9	30.7	9.9	8.6	183
1910	53.2	28.8	15.8	2.2	145	50.6	30.2	9.8	9.3	234
1915	53.1	29.3	15.1	2.4	152	49.0	29.7	10.3	11.0	273
1920	57.9	24.7	14.4	2.9	237	49.1	29.6	10.2	11.1	656
1925	54.8	28.1	14.7	2.4	232	52.9	26.2	10.0	10.9	746
1930	56.3	24.8	16.3	2.6	229	54.6	23.4	10.5	11.6	574
1935	52.3	22.5	21.9	3.3	153	48.0	27.6	11.1	13.3	457
1940	54.6	18.5	23.3	3.6	168	47.1	27.2	11.6	14.1	789
1945	61.4	13.2	21.8	3.6	275					
1950	55.3	15.8	24.5	4.4	430					
1955	44.0	18.5	32.3	5.3	530	48.9	22.9	12.1	16.1	141,000
1960	35.7	26.2	33.2	4.9	601	42.2	28.7	12.5	16.5	201,000
1965	26.8	27.2	39.8	6.2	729	43.4	23.1	13.5	19.9	292,000
1970	23.3	29.9	40.3	6.4	896	42.1	22.5	14.8	20.7	434,000
1975	20.0	31.3	40.4	8.3	1274	38.0	22.6	16.0	23.4	806,000
1980	13.3	32.4	47.2	7.2	2230	38.0	22.6	16.0	23.4	1,177,000

204

SUPPLEMENT C. FACTOR SHARES AND AGGREGATE INPUT PRICE INDEXES IN THE UNITED STATES AND JAPAN

Factor shares for labor, land, machinery, and fertilizer in the United States were estimated by Binswanger for 1912–68.[24] We extrapolated Binswanger's estimates of factor shares by the input value indexes, which were the products of input quantity indexes and price indexes calculated from the data in Appendix C. The shares of labor, land, power (machinery), and fertilizer were adjusted to add up to 100. For Japan, the estimates by Sakuro Yamada were used.[25] It was assumed that the factor shares of capital and current inputs correspond to the shares of power and fertilizer, respectively. This assumption may be justified as a first approximation, considering the dominant weights of draft animals and machinery in the value of capital and of fertilizer in the value of current inputs in Japanese agriculture. It was also assumed that the factor shares for 1880 and 1980 were the same as for 1885 and 1975.

The aggregate input price index was constructed by aggregating indexes of labor and of power and fertilizer prices by using factor shares as weights. The factor share weights are changed for every five-year interval, and the indexes constructed with the different weights are chain-linked into a single aggregate input price index. The input price data used for the U.S. index were (U18) for labor, (U20) for land, (U21) for power, and (U24) for fertilizer. The input price data used for the Japanese index were (J17) for labor, (J20) for land, (J21) for power, and (J23) for fertilizer.

The results of the estimation of factor shares and the aggregate input price indexes are shown in Table 7-8.

24. Binswanger, "Measured Biases of Technical Change," pp. 222–23.
25. Saburo Yamada, "The Secular Trends in Input-Output Relations of Agricultural Production in Japan, 1878–1978," *Agricultural Development in China, Japan and Korea,* ed. Chi-ming Hou and Tzong-shian Yu (Taipei: Academia Sinica, 1982), p. 53.

8

Science and Progress in Agriculture

Advances in agricultural science and technology clearly represent a necessary condition for releasing the constraints on agricultural production imposed by inelastic factor supplies. Yet, for a country in the early stages of economic development, technical innovations are among the more difficult products to produce. Institutionalization of the process by which a continuous stream of new agricultural technology is made available to a nation's farmers is particularly difficult to achieve.

In both Japan and the United States the "socialization" of agricultural research has been deliberately employed as an instrument of modernization in agriculture. In both countries the modernization process involved the development of experiment station and industrial capacity capable of producing the biological and mechanical innovations adapted to factor supply conditions. In this chapter, we review the process by which the scientific and technological capacity to produce technical change in agriculture was effectively institutionalized in the two countries. We then discuss the implications of technical change on commodity market relationships and on the structure of agriculture.

THE SOCIAL CLIMATE FOR SCIENTIFIC RESEARCH

Public support for education and research as an instrument of economic progress represents a major institutional innovation in modern society. In Germany this innovation was initiated with the deliberate intention of utilizing education and research as an engine of economic growth.[1] At the middle of the nineteenth century Germany was a generation behind Britain in industrial and agricultural development. Public support for advances in science, technology, and education was undertaken for the deliberate purpose of overcom-

1. David S. Landes, "Technological Change and Development in Western Europe, 1750–1914," *The Cambridge Economic History of Europe VI: The Industrial Revolution and After,* Part I, ed. H. J. Habakkuk and M. Postan (Cambridge: Cambridge University Press, 1966), pp. 274–601; Vernon W. Ruttan, *Agricultural Research Policy* (Minneapolis: University of Minnesota Press, 1982), pp. 71–75.

ing the gap in industrial technology and economic power between Germany and Great Britain.

Britain, which led the world in the Industrial Revolution, left technical training and scientific research to private enterprise because of its strong laissez-faire tradition, while "the German states generously financed a whole gamut of institutions, erecting buildings, installing laboratories, and above all maintaining competent and, at the highest level, distinguished faculties." In the latter half of the nineteenth century Britain fell behind Germany in human capital formation, including (a) the ability to read, write, and calculate; (b) the engineer's combination of scientific principle and applied training; and (c) a high level of scientific knowledge, theoretical and applied, with the possible exception of the working skills of the craftsman and mechanic.[2] As a result, there was a rapid closing of the gap in industrial productivity between Britain and Germany in the 1860s and 1870s, and Germany emerged as an industrial leader in fields such as chemicals and electrical machinery.

Although Britain, at the beginning of the nineteenth century, was regarded by Continental reformers as the "school for agriculture," it was not a coincidence that the first publicly supported agricultural research institution was set up in Germany rather than Britain. It had been a British tradition since Jethro Tull and Charles Townshend (admired by such great pioneers in German agricultural science as Albrecht Thaer) that agricultural improvements were carried out by country gentlemen. The famous Rothamsted Experimental Station was established (1843) and financed personally by Sir John Bennet Lawes throughout the nineteenth century. The Edinburgh Laboratory (founded in 1842), from which early advocates of the state agricultural experiment stations in the United States (such as John P. Norton and Samuel Johnson) received great inspiration, was supported by the Agricultural Chemistry Association of Scotland, a voluntary agricultural society. The laboratory was dissolved in 1848 as a result of the association members' impatient demands for practical results.

In contrast, a publicly supported agricultural experiment station was successfully established in Germany (at Möckern, Saxony) in 1852 as an answer to the "search, stirring in the German provinces since the publication of Justus von Liebig's treatise in 1840, for methods of applying science to agriculture."[3] The Saxon farmers drafted a charter for the station, which the Saxon government legalized by statute, and secured an annual appropriation from the government to finance the experiment station operations. Although the German system of agricultural research evolved later than the British, it provided a more effective environment for the "enlargement" of new scientific and technical knowledge. As a specialized institution, operating under its

2. Landes, "Technological Change," pp. 571, 566–67.
3. H. C. Knoblauch et al., *State Agricultural Experiment Stations: A History of Research Policy and Procedure* (Washington, D.C.: U.S. Department of Agriculture, Miscellaneous Publication 904, May 1962), p. 16.

own charter and supported by the state, it was not as subject to the pressures for immediate practical results as the privately supported research of the English landowners or even the cooperatively organized Edinburgh Laboratory. The development of publicly supported agricultural research institutions was based on the establishment, in Germany, of a social and political climate which regarded science and technology as instruments of economic growth and viewed their advance as a major responsibility of the state.[4]

The German concept of socialized agricultural research was transplanted to the United States and Japan and has evolved beyond the German model in response to the enormous differences in resource endowments and social and economic traditions of the two countries. Japan and the United States, as relative latecomers in industrial development, were responsive to the role of education and research as a means for economic growth. This was fertile soil into which the concept of socialized agricultural research could be transplanted and grown. Agriculture in these two countries was characterized by predominantly peasant- or family-operated farms, in contrast to the large-scale system of farming in England and Prussia. Individual farmers in the United States and Japan had but limited capacity to conduct research and little possibility of realizing a significant share of any gains from the results of research. The gains from technical progress tended to be rapidly externalized with consumers rather than farm producers realizing the major share of the returns. Under such conditions, there were strong social incentives to socialize scientific research in agriculture.

THE UNITED STATES EXPERIENCE

A belief that the application of science to the solution of practical problems represented a sure foundation for human progress has been a persistent theme in the intellectual and economic history of the United States. The nation "was born of the first effort in history to marry scientific and political ideas."[5] However, the institutionalization of public responsibility for advances in science and technology, as an instrument of national economic growth, developed slowly.[6]

4. W. O. Atwater, *Agricultural-Experiment Stations in Europe* (Washington, D.C.: U.S. Department of Agriculture, Report of the Commissioner of Agriculture for the year 1875, 1876), pp. 517–24.
5. Don K. Price, *The Scientific Estate* (Cambridge, Mass.: Harvard University Press, 1965), p. 5. According to Price, "The United States was founded at a time when philosophers were beginning to believe in the perfectibility of mankind. Ever since Benjamin Franklin and Thomas Jefferson, Americans have been inclined to put their faith in a combination of democracy and science as a sure formula for human progress" (p. 1).
6. Even as late as 1860 "the United States still hesitated to embrace the theory that the government should have a permanent scientific establishment. . . . Sciences that only the government could easily coordinate, such as meteorology and aid to agriculture, failed to find adequate organizational expression. The attempts of the government to use science in regulation and aid of technology had been timid and intermittent." A. Hunter Dupree, *Science in the*

Progress in Mechanical Technology in the Nineteenth Century

In the nineteenth century progress in agricultural science and technology was, as in England, primarily the product of innovative farmers, inventors, and the emerging industrial sector. Progress in mechanical technology was impressive throughout the last half of the nineteenth century, and advances in tillage and harvesting machinery, induced by the westward march of the land frontier and the associated shortage of labor relative to land, resulted in rapid growth of labor productivity.[7] Mechanization was the most important single source of labor productivity growth.[8] In the case of the small grains (wheat and oats) most of the increase in labor productivity was accounted for by mechanization of seeding and of harvest and postharvest operations. In the case of corn, nearly all of the decline in labor inputs per acre occurred from improvements in preharvest operations.

The advances in mechanical technology were not accompanied by parallel advances in biological technology.[9] Nor were the advances in labor productivity accompanied by comparable advances in land productivity. In most areas fertility and the yields of staple crops declined within a decade or two

---

Federal Government: A History of Policies and Activities to 1940 (Cambridge: Harvard University Press, 1957), p. 114. See also I. Bernard Cohen, *Science and American Society in the First Century of the Republic* (Columbus: Ohio State University, 1961). Margaret W. Rossiter, *The Emergence of Agricultural Science: Justus Liebig and the Americans, 1840–1880* (New Haven: Yale University Press, 1975); Charles E. Rosenberg, *No Other Gods: On Science and American Thought* (Baltimore: Johns Hopkins University Press, 1976); Lawrence Bush and William B. Lacy, *Science, Agriculture and the Politics of Research* (Boulder, Colo.: Westview Press, 1983).

7. Leo Rogin, *The Introduction of Farm Machinery in Its Relation to the Productivity of Labor in the Agriculture of the United States during the Nineteenth Century* (Berkeley: University of California Press, 1931); Clarence H. Danhof, *Change in Agriculture: The Northern United States, 1820–1870* (Cambridge, Mass.: Harvard University Press, 1969); Irwin Feller, "Inventive Activity in Agriculture, 1837–1890," *Journal of Economic History* 22 (December 1962):560–77. Feller indicates that "while considerable inventive activity was devoted towards agriculture in the early nineteenth century, these efforts did not have an appreciable effect on output until the middle of the century" (p. 561).

8. William N. Parker and Judith L. V. Klein, "Productivity Growth in Grain Production in the United States, 1840–60 and 1900–10," *Output, Employment and Productivity in the United States after 1800*, NBER Studies in Income and Wealth, vol. 30 (New York: Columbia University Press, 1966), pp. 523–82. In the case of wheat, approximately 60 percent of the growth in labor productivity was due to mechanization, 20 percent to the westward shift in the location of production, and 20 percent to changes in land yields and interaction effects. There is some evidence that Parker and Klein underestimate the contribution of the westward movement to expansion of agricultural production. See Franklin M. Fisher and Peter Temin, "Regional Specialization and the Supply of Wheat in the United States, 1867–1914," *Review of Economics and Statistics* 52 (May 1970):134–49.

9. This is not to imply that significant advances in biological technology were not achieved; for example, "all of the farmers of the Lower South accepted as their standard strain a new upland cotton developed by Southwestern plant breeders during the early decades of the 1800's. This new variety, the famous Mexican hybrid, improved the yield and quality of American cotton to such an extent that it deserves to rank alongside Eli Whitney's gin in the Old South's hall of fame" (p. 95). John Hebron Moore, "Cotton Breeding in the Old South," *Agricultural History* 30 (July 1956):95–104. See also, Rosser H. Taylor, "The Sale and Application of Commercial Fertilizer in the South Atlantic States to 1900," ibid. 21 (January 1947):46–52.

after settlement. By 1800 declines in fertility and yields were characteristic of even the more fertile areas of the East. By the 1840s declines in productivity were beginning to be serious in Ohio and by the 1860s as far west as Iowa. In the meantime efforts were being made in the eastern states to introduce the English "new husbandry." Improved breeds of livestock were introduced from England. Use of natural organic (animal manure, green manure, and guano) and mineral (gypsum, lime, and lime phosphate) fertilizers was being initiated on a modest scale. "The English succeeded in inducing American farmers to adopt their livestock, but they were less successful in persuading Americans to use English field culture and agricultural machinery." The aggregate impact of the new crop production technology was barely sufficient to offset the effects of soil depletion on yields.[10]

Explanations for the differential advances in mechanical and biological technology in U.S. agriculture in the nineteenth century can be sought both in the state of scientific development on which advances in mechanical and biological technology draw and in the economic environment in which American farmers operated prior to 1860.[11] It has been pointed out, for example, that "invention in biology and chemistry was, by modern standards, far less advanced in the nineteenth century than invention of mechanical equipment."[12]

A more fundamental response must be sought in the economic environment in which American farmers operated during the nineteenth century. During the first half of the century, labor was too expensive relative to land, even in the older areas of the country, to employ labor-intensive systems of conservation farming economically.[13] Instead, mechanical technology was sought in order to increase the land area that each worker could cultivate. The Civil War added further impetus, in the form of labor shortages and inflation of product prices, for farmers to adopt mechanical technology.

10. Rodney C. Loehr, "The Influence of English Agriculture on American Agriculture, 1775–1825," ibid. 11 (January 1937):12; Danhof, *Change in Agriculture*, pp. 251–77.

11. For a general discussion of historical evidence on whether technical change is knowledge-induced or demand-induced see Jacob Schmookler, *Invention and Economic Growth* (Cambridge, Mass.: Harvard University Press, 1966). Based on an extensive review of 235 important inventions in agriculture, 284 in petroleum refining, 185 in paper making, and 230 in railroading between 1800 and 1955, Schmookler concludes that technical change has been primarily demand-induced, pp. 66, 67, 176.

12. Parker and Klein, "Productivity Growth," p. 525.

13. Danhof, *Change in Agriculture*. According to Danhof, "The approach to soil utilization pursued by the majority of farmers was a product of the circumstances in which early settlers had found themselves. The known fertility-maintaining practices . . . were impractical because . . . the available labor was fully occupied to more immediate advantage . . . including the clearing of new land" (p. 251). "The maximum returns desired were obtained by cultivating with a minimum of labor the largest possible acreage planted in the most immediately valuable crops. . . . Most farms were established with acreages that required many years to bring into cultivation, and as long as virgin land remained available, the breaking of new land was the reaction to declining fertility" (p. 252). "Among those who did attempt to apply fertility conservation and renovating techniques, many found returns inadequate, so that they too joined the search for new lands" (p. 253).

In an economic environment characterized by a strong demand for labor-saving mechanical technology, the industrial sector responded by introducing a continuous stream of new mechanical equipment. Advances in the design and diffusion of tillage, seeding, and harvesting equipment resulted in a system of agriculture based on "horse mechanization," even though mechanization of motive power was not developed until introduction of the tractor (see Figure 4-1). The introduction of wire fencing sharply reduced the cost of enclosing the western lands and the conversion from a grazing to a crop agriculture.[14]

During the nineteenth century the process by which new mechanical and other industrial inputs were generated by the private industrial sector appeared to be relatively consistent with the demand for progress in mechanical technology by the agricultural sector. The typical process by which new mechanical technology was introduced involved initial invention and production by innovating farmers, inventors, mechanics, or small machinery firms. After demonstration of the technical feasibility and market potential, the production rights were typically acquired by larger firms, which proceeded to make further engineering improvements and adapt the design to the requirements of mass production and distribution.[15]

The patent system provided sufficient protection to induce inventors and manufacturers to undertake the research and development costs necessary to introduce a continuous stream of new industrial inputs designed to bring more land into cultivation and to reduce labor requirements per unit area.[16]

By the beginning of the twentieth century the earlier consistency between the pattern of technical change generated in the industrial sector and the growth requirements of American agriculture was breaking down. The rate of

14. Earl W. Hayter, "Barbed Wire Fencing—A Prairie Invention; Its Rise and Influence in the Western States," *Agricultural History* 13 (October 1939):189–207.

15. See Walter Prescott Webb, *The Great Plains* (Boston: Ginn and Co., 1931), pp. 295–318, for a history of the farmer invention of the barbed wire fence, the litigation over patent rights, and the final monopolization of barbed wire production by a subsidiary of U.S. Steel. For a more recent example see James H. Street, "Mechanizing the Cotton Harvest," *Agricultural History* 31 (January 1957): 12–22.

16. "The patent system raises the returns to invention and innovation by increasing the costs and difficulties of imitation. It makes private property out of what otherwise would, in the absence of secrecy, be in the public domain." Richard R. Nelson, Merton J. Peck, and Edward D. Kalachek, *Technology, Economic Growth, and Public Policy* (Washington, D.C.: Brookings Institution, 1967), p. 160. Nelson et al. also point out that "broadening of the incentive to invent is one of the most important social benefits of the patent system. These benefits do not come without cost . . . the patent system involves a transfer of income from the general public or a subgroup of the public to successful innovators. . . . Rather than tapping public tax revenues, the patent system effects the income transfer by granting the inventor a monopoly right. . . . It is in the social interest that existing knowledge be free for use wherever it may be of positive social value. In contrast, it is in the interest of a particular producer to limit the use of knowledge so as to give it a scarcity value" (pp. 161, 162). See also D. D. Evenson, J. D. Putnam, and R. E. Evenson, "Legal Systems and Agricultural Invention: International Comparisons," mimeograph, paper presented at the Workshop on Asian Agricultural Growth, Yale University, June 20–21, 1983.

growth in labor productivity was beginning to decline, growth of total productivity was turning negative, and the rate of growth of agricultural output fell below the rate of growth in demand. Prices of agricultural products were beginning to rise relative to the general price level. In spite of a continued flow of new mechanical technology, U.S. agriculture appeared to be entering a period of diminishing returns consistent with the classical model of economic development. These changes set the stage for a dramatic increase in investment in public sector agricultural research and for advances in biological technology.

Setting the Stage for Advances in Biological Technology, 1860–1920

The institutionalization of public sector responsibility for research in the agricultural sciences and technology in the United States can be dated from the 1860s. The Act of May 15, 1862, "establishing the United States Department of Agriculture" and the Act of July 2, 1862, "donating public lands to the several states and territories which may provide colleges for the benefit of American agriculture and the mechanic arts" became the first federal legal authority under which a nationwide agricultural research system was to develop.

The institutional pattern that emerged for the organization of agricultural research drew heavily on the German experience.[17] As noted earlier, a tradition of public support for research laboratories and agricultural experiment stations had been established in Germany in the 1850s. A number of the leaders in the movement to establish state experiment stations had studied in Germany, and there was a substantial traffic of young Americans to European, particularly German, centers of study for graduate education in the fields of agricultural science. The results of foreign training were, however, not unlike those observed in many underdeveloped countries today. "European professors were puzzled by American students who, after beginning well abroad, lapsed into mediocrity upon returning home. And one recalls cases in which Americans, inspired by European science, actually began to make basic contributions; but never went on to a fulfillment of the potentialities so revealed."[18]

In institutionalizing agricultural research the United States created a dual federal-state system. The federal system developed more rapidly than the state system. Yet it was not until the later years of the nineteenth century that the U.S. Department of Agriculture achieved any significant capacity to provide the scientific knowledge needed to deal with urgent problems of agricultural

17. Rossiter, *Emergence of Agricultural Science;* Knoblauch, *State Agricultural Experiment Stations.*

18. Richard Harrison Shryock, "American Indifference to Basic Science during the Nineteenth Century," *The Sociology of Science,* ed. Bernard Barber and Walter Hirsch (New York: Free Press of Glencoe, 1962), pp. 104–5. Shryock attributes this lack of accomplishment in basic science to orientation toward applied science which "seems to promise most for utility in the near future" (p. 110).

development. The emergence of a viable pattern of organization, toward the end of the century, involved breaking away from a discipline-oriented pattern of organization and the organization of scientific bureaus focusing on a particular set of problems or commodities. A. Hunter Dupree cites the Bureau of Animal Industry, established in 1884, as an example: "The Bureau of Animal Industry thus had most of the attributes of the new scientific agency at its birth—an organic act, a set of problems, outside groups pressing for its interests, and extensive regulatory powers."[19]

The capacity of the land-grant colleges to produce new scientific and technical knowledge for agricultural development was even more limited than that of the Department of Agriculture. The first state experiment station, the Connecticut State Agricultural Experiment Station, was not established until 1877. Prior to passage of the Hatch Act in 1887, which provided federal funding for the support of land-grant college experiment stations, only a few states were providing any significant financial support for agricultural research at the state level.[20]

It was well after the turn of the century before the new state experiment stations could be regarded as productive sources of new knowledge or significant contributors to productivity growth in U.S. agriculture.[21] And it was not until 1914, with the passage of the Smith-Lever Act, that a firm institutional basis, in the form of a cooperative federal-state extension service, was established for the educational functions of the Department of Agriculture and the land-grant colleges.[22] By the early 1920s a national agricultural research and extension system had been effectively institutionalized at both the federal and state levels.

In reviewing the history of agricultural research between 1880 and 1930, the most interesting question is not, what did the system contribute to the growth of agricultural production and productivity, but rather, why did it contribute so little? There are several answers. In total, federal and state expenditures on agricultural research were less than $2 million in 1900 and

19. "The department gradually evolved an adequate social and political mechanism, the government bureau. . . . The ideal new scientific bureau had clearly defined characteristics. In the first place, the center of interest was a problem, not a scientific discipline. . . . Thus the ideal bureau chief sought continuity by means of a grant of power in the organic act of Congress. . . . In the second place, the ideal bureau aimed at a stable corps of scientific personnel which was not only competent but also loyal to the bureau and confident that its work was important to the country. . . . In the third place, the ideal bureau established as harmonious relations as possible with many groups outside itself," Dupree, *Science in the Federal Government,* pp. 158–59, quotation on p. 165.
20. Knoblauch, *State Agricultural Experiment Stations,* pp. 29–52. Prior to the passage of the Hatch Act in 1887 only four of the land-grant colleges had established experiment stations— California in 1880, Tennessee in 1882, Wisconsin in 1883, and Kentucky in 1885.
21. Ibid., pp. 191–206.
22. Prior to 1914, "the state experiment stations and colleges, along with the agricultural journals, had borne the brunt of extension work for many years in a disorganized way. . . . In 1914 the Smith-Lever Act put the Extension Service on a separate and permanent basis. One feature of the law was the '50–50' plan by which each federal dollar was matched by one from the states." Dupree, *Science in the Federal Government,* pp. 181, 182.

TABLE 8-1.   Expenditures on agricultural research and extension in the United States (in millions of current dollars), 1880–1980

	State experiment station research				Other federally funded agriculturally related research[a]	Research by private industrial firms[b]
Year	Federal funds	Nonfederal funds	Total	USDA research		
1880	–	0.1	0.1	0.5		
1890	0.7	0.2	0.9	0.8		
1900	0.7	0.3	1.0	0.8		
1910	1.3	1.3	2.6	4		
1920	1.4	6	7.4	7		
1930	4	12	16.0	15		
1940	7	13	20.0	22		
1950	13	47	60.0	47		
1960	31	111	142.0	92		325
1965	47	180	227.0	167	365	460
1970	90	192	282.0	177		
1980	262	543	805.0	469	521	2,000

Sources: 1880–1965: Robert E. Evenson, "The Contribution of Agricultural Research and Extension to Agricultural Production" (Ph.D. dissertation, University of Chicago, 1968), p. 3, 1970–80: State and federal expenditures are from U.S. Department of Agriculture, Current Research Information System Printout. Research by other federal agencies is based on USDA Science and Education Administration, *Inventory of Research, Extension and Higher Education Related to Food and Agriculture Conducted by Federal Agencies Other Than USDA, FY1981,* (Washington, D.C., March 1982). For research by private industrial firms see Vernon W. Ruttan, *Agricultural Research Policy* (Minneapolis: University of Minnesota Press, 1982), pp. 183–86. About half of the private sector expenditures in 1980 were in support of agricultural production and half in the area of postharvest technology and marketing.

[a]Research indirectly related to agriculture, including research by private foundations and non-land-grant universities.

[b]The estimated expenditures for research by private firms for 1960 and 1965 are the only estimates available for this effort. The 1960 estimate includes some agriculturally related research.

less than $15 million in 1920 (Table 8-1). But why, in spite of more than half a century of effort, did the evolution of public sector investment in agricultural research proceed so slowly? The answer must be sought in the same conditions that induced the rapid development of mechanical technology in American agriculture before 1900. Neither movements in relative factor prices nor factor-product price ratios were such as to induce yield-increasing innovations or the adoption of available yield-increasing technology until the closing years of the nineteenth century.

Progress in Biological Science and Technology—The Case of Corn Improvement

The institutional innovations in the organization of public sector agricultural research, development, and extension between 1860 and 1920 proved capable, during the 1920–65 period, of absorbing new resources at a relatively rapid rate and of generating rapid growth in new scientific and technical knowledge. By and large, the private sector had contributed little to advances in biological technology. Similarly, public sector agricultural research institutions were much more effective in generating advances in biological (or biological and chemical) technology than in generating advances in mechanical technology. In this section we devote special attention to the institutional aspects of technical advance in corn production.

Corn (maize) has occupied a unique role in U.S. agricultural development from colonial times to the present. It was indigenous to the Americas at the time of their discovery. Maize culture represented the agricultural basis for the pre-Columbian civilization. In the United States it has, in the past, occupied an important role as both a food grain for human consumption and a feed grain for work animals. It is valued today, however, primarily as a feed grain for meat animals. In 1980 approximately 80 percent of domestic use of corn was for animal feed. A small but increasing amount of corn has been used in the production of corn sweeteners and starches and as a feedstock for liquid fuel (ethanol). Exports account for about one-third of annual production.

Corn production increased rapidly between 1880 and 1900, remained relatively stable between 1900 and 1920, declined from 1920 to 1937, and has risen rapidly since 1937 (see Figure 8-1a). Between 1880 and the mid-1920s corn yields per acre remained essentially unchanged at approximately twenty-seven bushels per acre. From the early 1920s until the end of the drought years of the 1930s national average corn yields declined. Yields have risen dramatically since the late 1930s. Between 1880 and 1920 the growth in corn production was attributable to expansion of area cultivated. Between the late 1930s and the late 1960s rapid growth in yields was accompanied by a reduction of more than 25 percent in the area planted to corn. During the 1970s expansion of both area and yields made important contributions to growth in production.[23]

The first third of the twentieth century was a period of relative stagnation in corn production. The growth of demand pressed against supply. Corn prices, which had started to rise relative to the general price level in the 1880s, rose dramatically between 1900 and 1920 (Figure 8.1b). James O. Bray and Patricia Watkins have argued that the trend toward declining yields, despite the movement toward better land, "suggests that increases in the total production of corn between 1870 and 1937 were, to a large degree, brought about by fertility-depleting operations. Capital in soil fertility was transformed into animals and machines which, in turn, enabled the process to be accelerated. . . . After the beginning of the 20th century, the effectiveness of further improvements in extractive techniques began to be restricted by the fertility

23. W. Burt Sundquist, Kenneth M. Menz, and Catherine F. Neumeyer, *A Technology Assessment of Commercial Corn Production in the United States* (St. Paul: University of Minnesota Agricultural Experiment Station Bulletin 546, 1982).

FIGURE 8-1a. U.S. grain corn yield, acreage, and production, 1879–1982.

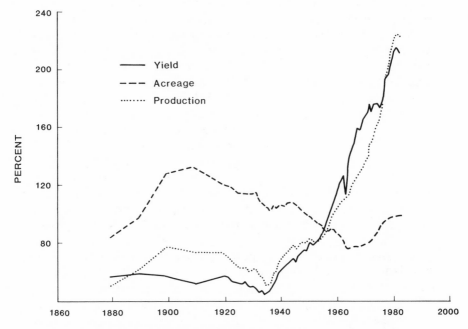

Source: Agricultural Statistics 1981 (Washington, D.C.: Government Printing Office, 1981, and earlier years).

Note: Data from 1879 to 1909 are Census of Agriculture estimates; from 1919 to 1981 annual survey data collected by the Statistical Reporting Service; for 1982 a preliminary estimate from *Crop Production,* SRS, USDA, November 10, 1982. Series are plotted as five-year moving averages from 1919 to 1982.

barrier.''[24] The evidence from corn yields during the first third of the twentieth century clearly supported the view of the English classical economists concerning diminishing returns to additional "doses" of land and labor.

By the mid-1920s, however, three developments were beginning to call into question the implications of projections based on the classical model. These included (a) mechanization of motive power, (b) the invention of hybrid corn, and (c) sharply declining real costs in the production of commercial fertilizer.

The critical significance of the mechanization of motive power—the substitution of tractors for horses—was that it sharply reduced the demand for corn and other feed grains as an energy source for draft power. Feed ac-

24. James O. Bray and Patricia Watkins, "Technical Change in Corn Production in the United States, 1870–1960," *Journal of Farm Economics* 46 (November 1964):751–65.

FIGURE 8-1b. Real prices of wheat and corn, 1866–1981.

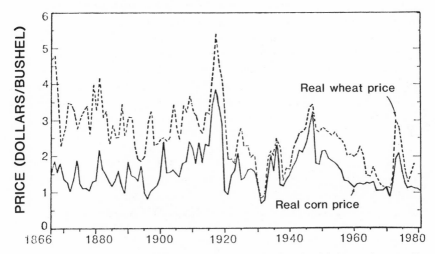

Source: Michael V. Martin and Ray F. Brokken, "The Scarcity Syndrome: Comment," *American Journal of Agricultural Economics* 65 (February 1983):159.

counted for approximately three-fourths of the cost of maintaining horses.[25] As "tractorization" continued it also released the constraints on labor productivity imposed by farm production of power and fuel in the form of horses and feed grains and on the size of equipment imposed by the capacity of horse-powered machines.

Increasingly intensive efforts to improve corn yields through the selection and the diffusion of the best varieties produced by farmers and commercial "seedmen" and the efforts to develop more effective cultivation practices were made by the land-grant college experiment stations and extension services and the U.S. Bureau of Plant Industry after 1900.[26] These efforts had little impact on yield at the farm level until the introduction of hybrid varieties in the 1920s and 1930s.

25. The effects of the substitution of tractors for horses on productivity have been described by Sherman E. Johnson, *Changes in American Farming* (Washington, D.C.: U.S. Department of Agriculture Miscellaneous Publication 707, 1949); see also Allan G. Bogue, "Changes in Mechanical and Plant Technology: The Corn Belt, 1910–1940," *Journal of Economic History* 43 (March 1983):1–25; Naum Jasny, "Tractor versus Horse as a Source of Farm Power: Their Competition in Various Countries of the World," *Agricultural Economic Review* 25 (December 1935):708–23. According to Jasny, substitution of tractors for horses was affected by the relative prices of feed and fuel, the relative prices of horses and tractors, the price of labor, and the number of horses or tractor days of work per horse or per tractor per year.

26. The efforts made in Illinois and Iowa have been carefully documented in Martin L. Mosher, *Early Iowa Corn Yield Tests and Related Later Programs* (Ames: Iowa State University Press, 1962).

The development of hybrid corn has been characterized as the most signifi-
cant contribution in applied biology in the first half of the twentieth century.[27]
It involved not one but several inventions. These included the crossing tech-
niques for producing hybrid corn plants developed by William Beal at the
Michigan Agricultural Experiment Station and the studies of inheritance by
George H. Schull at the Carnegie Institution, which led to the understanding
of the theoretical basis for hybrid vigor. The development of inbred lines by
Edward M. East and the double-cross method of mass seed production by
Donald Jones, both of the Connecticut Agricultural Experiment Station, set
the stage for commercial hybrid seed production.

The work by Beal was completed before the turn of the century; Schull
presented his results in papers published in 1908 and 1909; East's work in
Connecticut began in 1905; and Jones's work was conducted between 1915
and 1917. According to Paul C. Mangelsdorf, "Hybrid corn was transformed
from Schull's magnificent design to the practical reality it now is when Jones'
method of seed production made it feasible and his theory of hybrid vigor
made it plausible."[28] By the early 1920s hybrid corn breeding programs were
initiated in many states; by the 1930s hybrid corn was in commercial production on a substantial scale; and by 1950 more than three-fourths of the total
corn acreage in the United States was planted to hybrid corn.

The production of commercial varieties of hybrid corn involves three complex steps: (a) isolation of inbred lines, (b) testing of inbred lines in various
crossing combinations to determine their hybrid performance, and (c) combining the selected inbred lines to produce commercial hybrid seed.[29] Because second-generation progeny of a hybrid decline markedly in yield, the
farmer cannot save his own seed but must buy new hybrid seed each season.
Furthermore, hybrid corn varieties must be individually "tailored" to a particular environment. The primary factors limiting geographic adaptability are
varietal sensitivity to temperature and to photoperiod (flowering is triggered
by day length). These factors limit adaptability in a north-south direction but
not necessarily in an east-west direction. Other ecological factors, such as
rainfall and pathogens, combine to make most hybrid corn varieties relatively
location-specific.

The development of hybrid corn, therefore, represents an "invention of a
method of inventing" varieties adapted to each growing region, rather than
the invention of varieties that can then be diffused from the original location

---

27. Paul C. Mangelsdorf, "Hybrid Corn," *Scientific American* 185 (August 1951):39–47.
The basic reference on the biological aspects of corn improvement is George F. Sprague, ed.,
Corn and Corn Improvement (New York: Academic Press, 1955; 2d ed. 1977). For more
personal accounts see Herbert Kendall Hayes, *A Professor's Study of Hybrid Corn* (Minneapolis:
Burgess Publishing Co., 1963), and A. Richard Crabb, *The Hybrid Corn Makers: Prophets of
Plenty* (New Brunswick, N.J.: Rutgers University Press, 1947).
28. Mangelsdorf, "Hybrid Corn," p. 42.
29. Ibid., p. 43; H. D. Hughes, "Introduction" to Crabb, *Hybrid Corn Makers*, pp. xv–xxv.

through normal marketing and extension education processes.[30] As a result, the successful development and diffusion of commercial hybrid corn varieties was characterized by the evolution of an increasingly complex research, development, distribution, and educational system involving close cooperation among public sector research and extension agencies, a series of public, semipublic, and cooperative foundation seed-producing organizations, and private sector research and marketing agencies.

Entry of the private sector into the development and marketing of new hybrid corn varieties was encouraged by the complex technology of seed production. The existence of superior proprietary inbred lines provided a protection to the innovating firm, similar to the protection afforded to mechanical inventions by the patent system.[31] As a result, the private sector has come to play a more significant role in the development of new hybrid corn varieties than in most other areas of crop improvement. By the mid-1950s the private sector had become the dominant source of new hybrid corn research, although inbred lines released by the experiment stations continued to be of great importance to the hybrid seed industry. The expanded role of the private sector in varietal improvement and in the production and distribution of seed resulted in the allocation of much larger resources to the achievement of corn yield increases than if the effort had been confined primarily to the public sector.

By introducing a significant shift up and to the right in the yield-response curve (as represented by the shift from u_0 to u_1 in Figure 5-6, Chapter 5), a movement along the metaproduction function occurs. The use of both higher levels of fertilizer and higher levels of management then becomes profitable. Almost since the introduction of hybrid corn, there has been a continuing argument regarding the relative contribution of the new varieties, as compared to the contribution of higher levels of fertilization and advances in crop management. According to D. Gale Johnson and Robert L. Gustafson, the corn yield increase between 1920–29 and 1946–54 resulted, in approximately equal proportions, from seed improvement, higher levels of fertilization, and increase in mechanization.[32] Between the mid-1950s and 1980, varietal improvement appears to have accounted for slightly less than half of the increase in corn yield. Increased use of material inputs, primarily fertilizer and

30. Zvi Griliches, " 'Hybrid Corn': An Exploration in the Economics of Technological Change," *Econometrica* 25 (October 1957):501–22. For a reanalysis see Robert Dixon, "Hybrid Corn Revisited," *Econometrica* 48 (September 1980):1451–61.

31. An effort has been made to provide incentives for private investment in the development of open-pollinated crop varieties through "breeders' rights" legislation designed to establish patent or patentlike property rights in new crop varieties. For a review of the issues involved see Vernon W. Ruttan, "Changing Role of Public and Private Sectors in Agricultural Research," *Science* 216 (April 2, 1982):23–29.

32. D. Gale Johnson and Robert L. Gustafson, *Grain Yields and the American Food Supply: An Analysis of Yield Changes and Possibilities* (Chicago: University of Chicago Press, 1962), p. 92. See also Bray and Watkins, "Technical Change in Corn Production," p. 761.

FIGURE 8-2. Nitrogen fertilizer's contribution to U.S. corn yields during the periods 1954–60, 1961–70, and 1971–80.

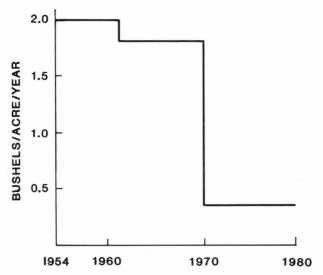

Source: W. Burt Sundquist, Kenneth M. Menz and Catherine F. Neumeyer, *A Technology Assessment of Commercial Corn Production in the United States* (St. Paul: University of Minnesota Agricultural Experiment Station Bulletin 546, 1982), p. IV–4.

pesticides, and improvements in management practices have accounted for slightly more than half of the yield increase (Figure 8-2).[33] Attempts to sort out the separate factors that have contributed to yield increases must be undertaken with caution because of the strong interactions among the several technology components. Higher levels of fertilizer use have been associated with higher plant populations, but neither would have been profitable in the absence of varietal improvement. And the higher yield ceilings associated with the improved hybrids have made it profitable to develop and adopt more effective materials and practices to protect plants.

The long-term decline in the price of fertilizer relative to the price of corn and of land (Chapter 7) was a consequence of technical change in fertilizer production and marketing.[34] This price decline, particularly for nitrogen fer-

33. Sundquist, Menz, and Neumeyer, *Technology Assessment of Commercial Corn Production,* p. IV-4.

34. The contribution of technical change in fertilizer production and distribution to the decline in the price of fertilizer relative to other input and product prices has been documented by G. S. Sahota, "The Sources of Measured Productivity Growth: United States Fertilizer Mineral Industries, 1936–1960," *Review of Economics and Statistics* 48 (May 1966):193–204; Gian S. Sahota, *Fertilizer in Economic Development: An Econometric Analysis* (New York: Praeger, 1968). Between 1936 and 1960 the price of fertilizer declined by 52 percent relative to the GNP implicit price deflator. Of this total decline (a) 26 percent was accounted for by productivity increases in the fertilizer sector, (b) 12 percent by increased competition, and (c) 10 percent by decline in the price of inputs used by the fertilizer industry.

tilizer, together with the shift in the fertilizer response curve resulting from the new hybrids, led to the corn yield explosion that began in the late 1930s (Figure 8-1a). Higher yields enhanced the potential gains from more effective crop protection and induced the development of a new series of highly effective chemical pesticides that also contributed to the yield increases. The advances in fertilizer and pest control technology were induced, at least in part, by the same economic forces that led to the introduction and rapid diffusion of hybrid corn. Both were a response to the declining price of fertilizer relative to the prices of both land and product (corn and agricultural commodities generally) in the latter nineteenth and early twentieth centuries.

Public sector research played an important role in the evolution of fertilizer technology and in the diffusion of fertilizer use. The National Fertilizer Development Center operated by the Tennessee Valley Authority has been an important source of new knowledge about the physical and chemical properties of fertilizer materials, soil-fertilizer-plant relationships, and new technology in the field of process engineering.[35] There is also evidence that public sector fertilizer research has contributed to the decline in the real price of fertilizers to farmers through efforts to maintain and strengthen competition in the fertilizer industry.[36]

By the mid-1970s there was a growing concern about what appeared to many to be an excessive energy dependency in U.S. agriculture.[37] Mechanization had reduced the labor required to produce one hundred bushels of corn from more than fifty hours in 1940 to only four hours in 1980. The environmental costs imposed by the new "second-generation" chemical pesticides were recognized, but the emergence of a new "third generation" of environmentally compatible chemical and biological pest-control agents proceeded less rapidly than anticipated. Fertilizer prices more than doubled during the energy crisis of the mid-1970s.

In retrospect it appears that these concerns about energy dependence, although not without foundation, were overdrawn. It now seems clear, for example, that the rapid escalation of fertilizer prices in 1973, 1974, and 1975 was the result of short-run production capacity constraints rather than energy supply constraints or high energy prices.[38] By the late 1970s fertilizer prices

35. Tennessee Valley Authority, *The TVA Fertilizer Program* (Knoxville: Tennessee Valley Authority, 1965); Office of the General Manager, "The Federal Government's Role in Fertilizer Research and Development," mimeograph (Knoxville: Tennessee Valley Authority, June 1978).

36. Jesse W. Markham, *The Fertilizer Industry* (Nashville: Vanderbilt University Press, 1958); Vernon W. Ruttan, "Positive Policy in the Fertilizer Industry," *Journal of Political Economy* 68 (February 1960):634.

37. David Pimentel, L. E. Hurd, A. C. Bellotti, M. J. Forster, I. N. Oka, O. D. Sholes, and R. J. Whitman, "Food Production and the Energy Crisis," *Science* 182 (November 2, 1973):443–49; John S. Steinhart and Carol E. Steinhart, "Energy Use in the U.S. Food System," *Science* 184 (April 19, 1974):307–16; also Vernon W. Ruttan, "Food Production and the Energy Crisis: A Comment," *Science* 187 (February 14, 1975):560–61.

38. For a definitive discussion of the relationship between energy prices and fertilizer prices see Mohinder S. Mudahar and Travis P. Hignett, *Energy and Fertilizer: Policy Implications and Options for Developing Countries* (Muscle Shoals, Ala.: International Fertilizer Development

were no higher, relative to the price of corn, than in the late 1960s and early 1970s, and they were substantially lower, relative to the price of land, than they had been a decade earlier.[39]

Even though the worst fears about the impact of the energy shortage on fertilizer availability and prices failed to materialize, it is doubtful that growth in fertilizer use can continue to be a dynamic source of productivity growth in U.S. corn production, or in U.S. agriculture generally. By 1980 U.S. farmers were applying an average of 120 pounds of nitrogen plus an additional 60 pounds of phosphorus (P_2O_5) and 70 pounds of potash (K_2O) per acre of corn. In 1954–60 increases in nitrogen use were adding approximately two bushels per acre to annual corn yield increases; during 1971–80 increases in nitrogen application were adding less than half a bushel per acre to the annual increases in corn yield (Figure 8-2).[40]

How will increases in U.S. corn yields be generated in the future? A combination of scientific advance and enhanced concern about sources of productivity growth has induced intensified efforts to explore new approaches to the development of less energy-intensive and more environmentally compatible biotechnologies for corn production. These include biorational and biological approaches to pest control, photosynthetic enhancement, plant growth regulations, cell and tissue culture, biological nitrogen fixation, and cellular-level gene transfer. These new biotechnologies, even if successful, are not expected to exert a measurable impact on U.S. corn yields until the late 1980s (Table 8-2), but if pursued vigorously they could become the dominant source of increase during the 1990s.[41]

Agricultural Adjustment and Structural Change

During the last half-century American agriculture has been transformed from a resource-based to a technology-based industry. Until 1900 almost all

---

Center, 1982), pp. 61–75. See also Gian S. Sahota. *The Role of Fertilizer in the New International Economic Order* (London: Trade Policy Research Centre, 1977), pp. 18, 24; Per Pinstrup-Andersen, *Agricultural Research and Technology in Economic Development* (London: Longman, 1982), pp. 166–68.

39. Sundquist, Menz, and Neumeyer, *Technology Assessment of Commercial Corn Production,* pp. IV-17, 18.

40. During the 1950s there was a substantial disequilibrium in fertilizer productivity and use. Production function studies frequently indicated marginal returns of above $2 for each $1 of fertilizer applied. See Earl O. Heady and John I. Dillon, *Agricultural Production Functions* (Ames: Iowa State University Press, 1961), p. 556. By the late 1970s the disequilibrium had largely been eliminated. Between 1954–60 and 1971–80 the marginal physical product of nitrogen fertilizer in corn production declined from .80 bushels to .15 bushels of corn per pound of nitrogen applied. For a review of the evidence on the decline in both the marginal physical product and the marginal returns from fertilizer use see Sundquist, Menz, and Neumeyer, *Technology Assessment of Commercial Corn Production,* p. IV-4.

41. For an assessment of the potential sources of productivity growth for the U.S. agricultural sector for the period 1980–2000 see Yao-chi Lu, Philip Cline, and Leroy Quance, *Prospects for Productivity Growth in U.S. Agriculture* (Washington, D.C.: U.S. Department of Agriculture, Economics, Statistics and Cooperatives Service, Agricultural Economics Report 435, 1979); Yao-chi Lu, ed., *Emerging Technologies in Agricultural Production* (Washington, D.C.: USDA Cooperative State Research Service, 1983).

TABLE 8-2.   Potential impact of various technologies on maize yields, 1980–2000

| | Marginal annual yield increases (bushels/acre/year) | | | | |
Year	Technology trend[a]	Additional nitrogen	Production management	Emerging biotechnologies[b]	Total
1980	1.0	.4	.2	–	1.5
1985	1.0	.2	.3	–	1.5
1990	1.0	.1	.3	.2	1.6
1995	1.0	–	.2	1.2	2.4
2000	1.0	–	.2	1.7	2.9

Source: W. Burt Sundquist, Kenneth M. Menz, and Catherine F. Neumeyer, *A Technology Assessment of Commercial Corn Production in the United States* (St. Paul: University of Minnesota Agricultural Experiment Station Bulletin 546, 1982), p. XII–10; K. M. Menz and C. F. Neumeyer, "Evaluation of Five Emerging Biotechnologies for Maize," *BioScience* 32 (September 1982):675–76.
[a]Mainly as a result of conventional plant breeding and related technologies.
[b]Includes biological nitrogen fixation, photosynthetic enhancement, plant growth regulations, cell or tissue culture, and genetic engineering.

increases in agricultural output in the United States were based on expansion in area cultivated. Since World War II almost all increases have been based on growth in output per unit area cultivated. This transformation was made possible by a series of institutional innovations, including the emergence of public and private sector suppliers of new technology, public sector agricultural extension services to transfer new technical knowledge to farmers, the emergence of corporate and cooperative research, input supply and marketing organizations, and the development of more efficient labor, credit, and commodity markets.

The technical changes and productivity growth generated by these institutional innovations have in turn induced the development of new programs to modify market behavior in relating growth of agricultural production to growth in the demand for agricultural commodities. And the new technology and new market institutions have contributed to dramatic changes in the structure of American agriculture. In this section we briefly review some of the institutional changes that have been induced by productivity growth in U.S. agriculture.

Commodity policies.[42]   One effect of the technical changes that began to exert a measurable impact on productivity growth in the mid-1920s (Chapter

42. The best historical review of the development of commodity policy is Willard W. Cochrane, *The Development of American Agriculture: A Historical Analysis* (Minneapolis: University of Minnesota Press, 1979); see also Willard W. Cochrane and Mary E. Ryan, *American Farm Policy, 1948–1973* (Minneapolis: University of Minnesota Press, 1976); and Wayne D. Rasmussen and Gladys L. Baker, *Price-Support and Adjustment Programs from 1933 through 1978: A Short History* (Washington, D.C.: U.S. Department of Agriculture, ESCS, Information Bulletin 424, 1979).

7) was to generate political stress over the partitioning of the new income streams generated by technical change. What portion of the income growth generated by technical change would be transmitted, through the market, to consumers in the form of lower food prices? And what share would be retained within the agricultural sector in the form of higher net incomes to farm operators, landowners, and workers? These issues began to emerge as important items on the political agenda in the 1920s. Since the passage of the Agricultural Adjustment Act of 1933 the government has continued to intervene in agricultural commodity markets with programs intended to slow the transfer of income from the agricultural to the nonagricultural sector—to retain more of the agricultural surplus within the agricultural sector.

The attempts to resolve the conflicts between efficiency in commodity production and equity in the distribution of income through commodity market interventions have been central to the debates about U.S. agricultural policy since the mid-1920s. These conflicts were partially muted during the great depression of the 1930s, when distributional objectives became paramount, and during World War II, when efficiency objectives tended to be weighted heavily.[43]

During the 1950s, the major controversy in farm policy debates was the issue of high, fixed price supports versus flexible price supports. The policies that prevailed combined relatively high fixed prices with weak production controls. The result was the accumulation of large agricultural surpluses. Throughout this period, a major program instrument used to transfer income to farmers was the nonrecourse commodity loan. The nonrecourse loan was first employed to support the price of cotton, at ten cents per pound, in 1933. Under the nonrecourse arrangement, the government loaned the farmer an amount equal to the support price (loan level) on the amount of the farmer's crop that was eligible for support. If the market price remained below the loan level, the government stood ready to accept the commodity in full satisfaction of the loan. If the market price rose above the loan level, the farmer could choose to redeem his crop by repaying the loan, plus interest and a service charge, and sell the crop at the market price. The nonrecourse feature insured the farmers against price declines below the loan level but allowed them to gain from any price rise above the loan level.

During the 1930s and again after the mid-1950s, efforts were made to limit the accumulation of surpluses by diverting land from crop production. In the 1930s, acreage allotments, based on historic land use, were established for each major crop. The farmer was required to divert a portion of his base acreage from production to be eligible for a price-support loan. Under the Soil Bank program that was initiated in 1957, payments were made to farmers (a) to reduce the land planted to specific crops, such as wheat, cotton, corn,

---

43. Even during wartime, however, equity objectives at times tended to dominate efficiency objectives. See the chapter "The Iowa Margarine Incident" in Charles M. Hardin, *Freedom in Agricultural Education* (Chicago: University of Chicago Press, 1955), pp. 119–25.

tobacco, peanuts, and rice, and to convert the land to soil-conserving uses (the acreage reserve); and (b) to designate a certain portion of their cropland to be devoted to conservation use (the conservation reserve).

During the 1950s and early 1960s the U.S. dollar became increasingly overvalued relative to the currencies of its major trading partners.[44] The costs of disposing of agricultural surpluses through export subsidies, partially disguised as food aid to developing countries, became excessive. In the early and mid-1960s a new set of programs was designed to price the major tradable agricultural commodities at levels that would permit them to move into international markets through normal commercial channels.

The new agricultural commodity programs of the 1960s and 1970s have tended to place more reliance on the use of direct payments to farmers as incentives to adjust production to demand and less reliance on price supports to transfer income to farmers. Under the Food and Agriculture Act of 1965, farmers were given the option of participating in the programs. Additional flexibility was introduced by the Agricultural Act of 1970. Receipt of price-support payments for feed grains, for example, was not tied directly to planting restrictions on feed grains. Farmers were eligible for price-support loans on feed grains if they diverted a specified percentage of their total crop land from production. The diverted acreage could come out of any crop, not just feed grains. In 1971 the only requirement for diversion payments and price-support loans was that the farmer leave idle a quantity of crop land equal to 20 percent of the base acreage. Additional payments were also made available as an inducement to divert acreage beyond the mandatory minimum.

The Agricultural and Consumer Protection Act of 1973 was passed during a period of world food shortage. World demand, spurred by devaluation of the dollar, export subsidies, and crop failures in the USSR and in parts of Africa and Asia, had liquidated the stocks that had accumulated under previous price-support programs. Commodity prices had risen dramatically so that they exceeded loan rates and target prices by substantial margins. The new legislation reflected the more optimistic perspective on the world market for U.S. agricultural commodities that prevailed at that time. The 1973 act placed increased reliance on market arrangements to facilitate the movement of agricultural commodities into world markets as follows: (a) the price-support loan rates were set at levels that were intended to be below market prices to encourage production for domestic consumption or export rather than for accumulation in government hands; and (b) payments to farmers were made only when market prices fell below target prices. Target prices were to be adjusted annually to reflect changes in productivity and prices paid by farmers

44. G. Edward Schuh, "The Exchange Rate and U.S. Agriculture," *American Journal of Agricultural Economics* 56 (February 1974):1–13; Schuh, "The New Macroeconomics of Agriculture," *American Journal of Agricultural Economics* 58 (December 1976):802–11; Robert G. Chambers, "Interrelationships between Monetary Instruments and Agricultural Commodity Trade," *American Journal of Agricultural Economics* 63 (December 1981):934–41.

for inputs. The payments, termed deficiency payments, were equal to the difference between the target price and the market price, but they could not exceed the difference between the price-support loan level and the target price.

The Food and Agricultural Act of 1977 reflected less buoyant market conditions. Prices of food and feed had receded from the 1973–75 highs. Producers and their friends in the Congress were again concerned with problems of oversupply and depressed prices. The administration was eager to avoid excessively high program costs. Both agreed, however, on the continued use of target prices and of loans at lower levels than target prices to allow crops to move freely in international trade. The policy debate focused more on target prices, loan levels, and deficiency payment levels than on general principles.

It seems apparent that the dominant trend in the development of policy governing agricultural commodities in the United States has been toward using markets to achieve greater precision and efficiency in allocating resources. This trend was influenced in part by the high fiscal and resource costs of the more restrictive programs of the 1950s and early 1960s. It also reflected a desire on the part of both farmers and the government to take advantage of expanding international trade opportunities. These concerns led to an attempt to separate the commodity market from the equity objectives of agricultural programs. Programs to achieve equity in income distribution between farmers and nonfarm families, and among farm families, came to rely more heavily on the use of direct payments such as the deficiency payments referred to above and on the extension of services and income-support programs such as Social Security, Medicare, family assistance, food stamps, and other programs that do not directly affect commodity prices.

In the early 1980s the consensus that had guided agricultural commodity and income policy since the mid-1960s broke down. Because of an ideological commitment to free market economic policies combined with a commitment to reduce both taxes and budget deficits, the Reagan administration initially failed to make effective use of the commodity program instruments available to it to adjust production to the slower growth of demand until excessive surpluses had accumulated. It responded to large commodity surpluses in 1983 with a massive program to divert land from grain production. At the same time it attempted to reverse the growth of equity-oriented entitlement programs that had evolved during the 1960s and 1970s, when agricultural commodity policies were becoming more market-oriented. As a result the future direction of agricultural commodity programs was more confused in the mid-1980s than at any time since the early 1960s.

Structural change. With the rapid growth in agricultural productivity and the slow growth in demand for agricultural products, the labor market became an increasingly important link between the farm and nonfarm sectors of the

TABLE 8-3.   Median income of farm and nonfarm families, United States, 1960–1980 (current $)

	1960	1970	1980
Nonfarm	5,620	10,006	21,151
Farm	2,875	6,773	15,755
Farm as a percent of nonfarm	51.2	67.7	74.5

Source: Data for 1960 and 1970 were obtained from Table 530 of the *Statistical Abstract of the United States, 1972,* U.S. Department of Commerce, July 1972. The 1980 figures were obtained from Table 1139 of the *Statistical Abstract of the United States, 1982–83,* U.S. Department of Commerce, December 1982.

U.S. economy. During the period 1950–70, when demand for agricultural output grew at less than 2 percent per year and labor productivity rose by more than 6 percent per year, the burden of adjustment on the labor market was extremely heavy. It was particularly difficult in the low-income agricultural regions, where local nonfarm employment did not expand fast enough to absorb both the excess agricultural labor force and the new entrants to the labor force from rural areas.

Between 1940 and 1960, the annual net emigration out of agriculture averaged close to 1 million people. During this same period, total employment on farms declined from 9.5 million to 5.5 million workers. Between 1960 and 1980, farm employment declined by another 2.1 million workers to 3.4 million. The balance between the size of the farm population and the availability of farm and nonfarm employment in rural areas is better today than in the past. In the 1950s the incomes of farm families averaged less than 60 percent of those of nonfarm families. In the 1970s, farm incomes, when adjusted for cost-of-living differences, were close to parity with nonfarm incomes (Table 8-3).

One of the more surprising developments in the agricultural labor market was the slowing of the decline in farm employment during the 1970s. The average annual employment of hired farm workers rose from 1.17 million in 1970 to approximately 1.25 million in 1980, while the employment of operator and family workers declined from 2.29 million to 2.21 million. Hired farm workers remain the most disadvantaged group of American workers.[45] They have less protection than other workers from arbitrary action by employers, and they receive fewer employment-related benefits when they are out of work.

A fundamental limitation in achieving legislation to improve the position of farm workers is that they are not organized to protect their own economic interests. Organization of farm workers is more difficult than organization of

45. See Stephen H. Sosnick, *Hired Hands: Seasonal Farm Workers in the United States* (Santa Barbara, Calif.: McNally and Loftin, West, 1978).

industrial workers because of the seasonal nature of much of farm work and the casual attachment of many farm workers to the agricultural labor force. It is also difficult because weak legal protection is given to organization efforts of farm workers. The interests of farm operators are represented through general farm organizations, commodity organizations, and cooperatives. The neglect of the problems of hired farm workers in America is in particularly striking contrast to the attention that has been given to the economic problems of farm operators and organized workers in other sectors.

In spite of improvements in the prosperity of the families that produce most of the nation's food and fiber (Table 8-3) there has been a growing unease about the future role of rural people and rural communities. Three issues have been of particular concern to American farm people and to rural communities.[46]

Who will control agricultural production?   Agricultural production has been increasingly concentrated. The number of farms has declined from a peak of nearly 7 million in the 1930s to 2.7 million in the late 1970s. These numbers are somewhat misleading. A farm is defined unrealistically in the official statistics as any place with annual sales of $1,000 or more.

In 1978, 82 percent of farm sales were accounted for by the 577,000 farms with sales of more than $40,000. The share of sales accounted for by the 50,000 largest farms rose from 23 percent in 1967 to 36 percent in 1977. It is not difficult to anticipate that by the year 2000 close to two-thirds of farm sales could be accounted for by the 50,000 largest farms and 80 percent by the 100,000 largest farms.

Who will own the 100,000 farms that will account for most of U.S. farm output in the future? Will they be family farms or will they be owned by agribusiness firms that integrate production, processing, and marketing activities? It seems clear that, unless remedial action is taken, an increasing share of the production on specialized farms engaged, for example, in cattle feeding and poultry production, fruit and vegetable production, nursery and greenhouse plant production, and sugarcane production will be corporate farms. Family farms will probably continue to dominate in the more diversified farming systems and in the production of soybeans, food and feed grains, dairy products, and pork. Even in these areas, however, many family farms may incorporate so as to facilitate the intergeneration transfer of resources.

The rapid inflation of land prices in the 1970s is another factor that has led to a concentration of landownership. Prices for agricultural land more than doubled in the decade between 1970 and 1980. Land rents, which rose much less rapidly than land prices, suggest that by the early 1980s land had become substantially overvalued for agricultural purposes.[47]

46. The USDA has produced a series of reports on structural issues. See U.S. Department of Agriculture, *Structural Issues of American Agriculture* (Washington, D.C.: USDA/ESCS Agricultural Economic Report 438, 1979).

47. John P. Doll and Richard Widdows, *A Comparison of Cash Rents and Land Values for Selected U.S. Farming Regions* (Washington, D.C.: USDA, ERS, NED Staff Report, 1982).

The combination of larger farm size and higher prices for land and other assets has made it more difficult for young people to get started in farming without substantial family backing. This problem has led to a concern that the ownership of farmland may become increasingly concentrated in the hands of the wealthy—that rural America will be owned by a class of hereditary landed proprietors and by integrated corporate enterprises. An important issue for the future will be whether changes should be made in the tax and inheritance laws that would reduce the incentives for farmland ownership by those who are not operating farmers.

Is there a role for the small farm? Since World War II, small farms have been regarded by most agricultural scientists, farm-program administrators, and farm-organization and political leaders as outside the mainstream of American agriculture. Small farms have been viewed as subsistence operations for those with no alternative employment opportunities; as retirement residences for those who are no longer active farmers or who have retired to rural areas; and as a source of part-time employment or income supplementa-

FIGURE 8-3. Farm and off-farm income per farm operator family by value of farm products sold in 1978.

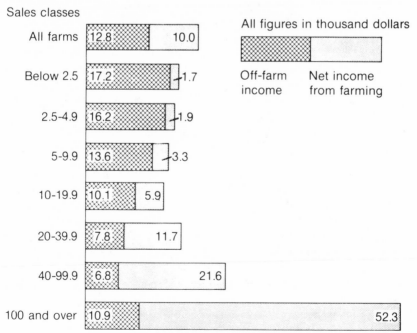

1978 data. Net income before adjustment for inventory change.

Source: 1979 Handbook of Agricultural Charts (USDA/ESCS Agriculture Handbook 561), 1979, chart 8.

tion for persons employed in nonagricultural occupations. The information presented in Figure 8-3 supports the view that, for small farmers as a group, income from farming accounts for a relatively small share of total income.

One outgrowth of the environmental movement of the 1960s and the pessimism over food and energy of the 1970s was popular concern about the future of the small farm in American agriculture. This concern induced an attempt, at the official level, to reexamine the role of the small farm in contemporary American agriculture. The Rural Development Act of 1972 and the Food and Agriculture Act of 1977 included provisions for research and extension directed to the agricultural production problems of small farmers. A number of small farm pilot programs were started by the state agricultural extension services. Others have been started with the help of private philanthropic foundations. In Mississippi and Alabama, two programs modeled on the Israeli *moshav* farm-cooperative concept were initiated. Each farm involves twelve hundred acres and forty farm families. The projects, which were initially heavily subsidized from both public and private sources, are managed by the Small Farm Development Corporation. Such programs are controversial. One newspaper that objected to the assistance provided by the USDA ran the following headline: "Government Will Establish Collective Farms under the Guise of Family Farm Development."

The most active support for the strengthening of small farms comes from what is often referred to as the "alternative-agriculture" movement.[48] The alternative-agriculture movement emphasizes both technological and social alternatives to the dominant trends in U.S. agricultural and rural development over the last fifty years. In the area of technology, it emphasizes organic approaches to maintaining and improving soil fertility, stressing alternatives to the intensive use of pesticides and chemical fertilizers. Less capital-intensive systems of crop production are employed. At the social level, smallness, self-sufficiency, decentralization, and the development of the rural community and culture are emphasized.

What is the future of the rural community?   During the 1970s, the long-term decline in population in many rural areas was reversed. The non-metropolitan areas of the southern Appalachians, the Ozark uplands, and the upper Midwest that had lost population in the 1950s and 1960s were among the regions with the most rapid population growth in the 1970s. Improved health and education services in rural communities have made them more attractive places in which to live. Decentralization of employment opportunities has made them more attractive places in which to work. And the new

48. For an introduction to the philosophy of alternative agriculture, see Wendell Berry, *The Unsettling of America: Culture and Agriculture* (New York: Avon Books, 1978). For an attempt to present an economic rationale see Robert C. Oelhaf, *Organic Agriculture* (Montclair, N.J.: Allanheld Osmun, 1978, and New York: Halsted/Wiley, 1979). For a sympathetic review of Oelhaf's book see David Vail, "The Case for Organic Farming," *Science* 205 (July 13, 1979):180–81.

preference for rural living has resulted in a more positive view of the advantages of rural life.

As the population of rural areas has expanded, the nonagricultural character of the rural economy and the rural community has become more pronounced. As a result, economic-development and community-development programs must address the needs of the entire rural and small-town population if they are to have any chance of success. The need to respond to expanding needs for improvements in the quality of education, to meet the health and housing needs of the elderly, and to provide for water, sanitation, and fire-protection services is placing increasing pressure on the capacities of voluntary community agencies and local governments.

A major challenge that will face rural communities in the future is how to respond to the opportunities and pressures for growth without losing the very qualities that have led farm people and other rural residents to prefer rural life.

THE JAPANESE EXPERIENCE

Until shortly before the beginning of the Meiji period (1868–1911), Japan had been isolated from the influence of Western technology for more than two centuries.[49] Because of the real danger of colonization by the Western powers, quick acquisition of Western technology and industrial productivity was regarded as of utmost urgency. Progress in education, science, and technology was viewed, as in Germany, as an effective instrument of national progress. Productivity growth in agriculture, the dominant sector of the economy, not only was required to contribute to social welfare by increasing the consumers' surplus but also was essential to finance industrialization and various modernization measures.

Leaders of the new Meiji government felt this need keenly. Partly because the need was so urgent and partly because they were impressed by the superiority of Western industrial technology, their first attempt to develop agriculture was the direct importation of the large-scale farm machinery and implements employed in England and the United States. It was natural for the Meiji leaders, reasoning from the analogy with industrial technology, to iden-

49. This section heavily depends on Nogyo Hattat Sushi Chosakai (Research Committee for the History of Agricultural Development), *Nihon Nogyo Hattat Sushi* (History of Japanese agricultural development), 10 vols. (Tokyo: Chuokoronsha, 1953–58): henceforth abbreviated as *NNHS*. Its abbreviated edition is Seizo Yasuda, ed., *Meiji Iko ni Okeru Nogyo Gijutsu no Hattatsu* (Progress of agricultural technology since Meiji) (Tokyo: Nogyo Gijutsu Kyokai, 1952). English readers may refer to Takekazu Ogura, ed., *Agricultural Development in Modern Japan* (Tokyo: Fuji Publishing Co., Ltd., 1963). Interest in Western science by Japanese intellectuals had, however, developed rapidly during the last century of the Tokagawa period. See Donald Keene, *The Japanese Discovery of Europe, 1720–1830* (rev., Stanford: Stanford University Press, 1969). In spite of their isolation Keene argues that "by the end of the eighteenth century the Japanese were better acquainted with European civilization than the people of any other nonwestern country" (p. 123).

tify Western agricultural technology with modern large-scale farm machines. This identification was not unique to Japanese leaders.

In 1870 Hirotumi Ito (later to be a prime minister) brought back from the U.S. 700 dollars worth of farm machinery. In order to exhibit the new machines, and the ones to be imported later, the Western Farm Machinery Exhibition Yard was opened in 1871 in Tsukiji, Tokyo. The machines were demonstrated at the Naito Shinjuku Agricultural Station (set up in 1873). In 1879 the Mita Farm Machinery Manufacturing Plant was established to produce farm machinery modeled after the imported machines.

The government also invited instructors from Britain to the newly opened Komaba Agricultural School (founded in 1877 and redesignated the University of Tokyo, College of Agriculture, in 1890), and from the United States to the Sapporo Agricultural School (in 1875), which was designed to develop the last frontier, Hokkaido.[50] The curriculum at the new agricultural colleges was based on the same view of the requirements for agricultural development that led to the importation of Anglo-American mechanical technology.

These innovations were one example of the broad effect of borrowing agricultural and industrial technology from the Western world. But, unlike the case in industry, it was unsuccessful, except in Hokkaido. The factor endowments in Japanese agriculture (average arable land area per worker of less than 0.5 hectare) were incompatible with the large-scale Anglo-American machinery. A farmer, observing the imported machinery, remarked, "These machines may be applicable in the vast area as in Hokkaido, but it would be as if a camel were to dress in the hide of an elephant to use them in the small patches of land as in our region."[51] Although the importation of modern industrial machinery, as in the Tomioka Model Silk Reeling Plant, led to modern industrial development, the importation of farm machinery failed to provide momentum for agricultural development.[52]

The teaching of the British instructors at the Komaba School was equally ineffective. Kizo Tamari, a first graduate of the Komaba School and later a professor at the University of Tokyo, recollected in his memorial lecture, "Instructions concerning agronomy were based on the extensive livestock farming in England and hardly applicable to the real problems of Japan. . . . How could one translate such words as 'plow,' 'harrow,' 'furrow,' and 'rotation'? First of all, did such things even exist in Japan?"[53]

Rationalization of indigenous techniques. The Meiji government quickly perceived the failure of the attempt to develop a mechanized agriculture based

---

50. John A. Harrison, "The Capron Mission and the Colonization of Hokkaido, 1868–1875," *Agricultural History* 25 (April 1951):135–42.

51. *NNHS,* 2:114.

52. The government also tried to transplant foreign plants and livestock. The Mita Botanical Experiment Yard (1874), the Shimofusa Sheep Farm (1875), the Kobe Olive Farm (1877), and the Harima Grape Farm (1880) represent such trials. This effort also failed because the importation was not selective and there was no adequate basis of adaptive research.

53. *NNHS,* 9:761.

on the Anglo-American model and redirected its agricultural development policy toward the search for a modern technology compatible with the factor endowments of the Japanese economy.

In 1881, as soon as the contracts of the British agricultural instructors at the Komaba School were completed, they were replaced by a German agricultural chemist (Oskar Kellner) and a German soil scientist (Max Fesca). The curriculum of agricultural education in Japan was reorganized to place primary emphasis on German agricultural chemistry and soil science of the von Liebig tradition.

The facilities for the demonstration of the Western machinery, plants, and livestock were largely discontinued during the 1880s. The newly founded Ministry of Agriculture and Commerce (1881) established an itinerant instructor system in 1885, in which the instructors traveled throughout the country holding agricultural extension meetings. The government employed as instructors not only the graduates of the Komaba School but also veteran farmers (*rōnō*), in order to combine the best practical farming experience with the new scientific knowledge of the inexperienced college graduates. In contrast with the earlier emphasis on the direct transplanting of Western technology, the itinerant instructor system was designed to diffuse the best seed varieties already in use by Japanese farmers and the most productive cultural practices used in the production of Japan's traditional staple crops, rice and barley. In order to provide better information for the itinerant lecturers, the Experiment Farm for Staple Cereals and Vegetables was set up in 1886. In 1893 the experimental farm at Nishigarhara was further strengthened and designated the National Agricultural Experiment Station, with six branches over the nation. The itinerant instructor system was subsequently absorbed into the program of the National Agricultural Experiment Station.

The initial research conducted at the Experiment Farm for Staple Crops and Vegetables and at the National Agricultural Experiment Station was primarily at the applied end of the research spectrum. The major projects were simple field experiments comparing the varieties of seeds or husbandry techniques (for example, checkrow planting of rice seedlings versus irregular planting). Facilities, personnel, and, above all, the state of knowledge did not permit conducting research beyond simple comparative experiments.

Nevertheless, such experiments provided a basis for the rapid growth of agricultural productivity during the latter years of the Meiji period because substantial indigenous technological potential could be further tested, developed, and refined at the new experiment stations. In addition, farmers with whom the research workers interacted effectively showed a strong propensity to innovate.

During the three hundred years of the Tokugawa period preceding the Meiji Restoration farmers were subject to the strong constraints of feudalism. Personal behavior and economic activity were highly structured within a hierarchical system of social organization. Farmers were bound to their land

and were, in general, not allowed to leave their village except for such pilgrimages as the Ise-Mairi (the Pilgrimage to the Ise Grand Shrine). Neither were they free to choose what crops to plant or what varieties of seeds to sow. Barriers that divided the nation into feudal estates actively discouraged communication. In many cases, feudal lords prohibited the export of improved seeds or cultural methods from their territories. Under such conditions diffusion of superior seeds and husbandry techniques from one region to another was severely limited. Although the Tokugawa period was characterized by significant growth in agricultural productivity, Japanese agriculture entered the Meiji period with a substantial backlog of unexploited indigenous technology.[54]

With the reforms of the Meiji Restoration such feudal restraints were removed. Farmers were free to choose what crops to plant, what seeds to sow, and what techniques to practice. Nationwide communication was facilitated with the introduction of modern postal service and railroads. The cost of information diffusion concerning new technology was greatly reduced. The land tax reform, which granted a fee-simple title to the farmers and transformed a feudal sharecrop tax to a fixed-rate cash tax, increased the farmers' incentive to innovate.

The farmers, especially of the *gōnō* class (landlords who personally farm part of their holdings), vigorously responded to such new opportunities. They voluntarily formed agricultural societies called *nodankai* (agricultural discussion society) and *hinshukokankai* (seed exchange society) and searched for higher-payoff techniques. Such rice production practices as use of salt water in seed selection, improved preparation and management of nursery beds, and checkrow planting were discovered by farmers and propagated by the itinerant instructors and sometimes enforced by the sabers of the police. The major improved varieties of seeds, up to the end of the 1920s, were also the result of selections by veteran farmers. For example, the *Shinriki* variety, which was more widely diffused in the western half of Japan than any other single variety that has since been propagated, was selected in 1877 by Jujiro Maruo, a farmer in the Hyogo prefecture (the variety was called *Shinriki* meaning the "Power of God" by the farmers who were surprised by its high yield). Also, the *Kameno-o* variety, which was propagated widely and contributed greatly to stabilizing the rice yield in northern Japan, was selected in 1893 by Kameji

---

54. There has been some disagreement among students of Japanese agricultural history about the effectiveness of the feudal restraints on the diffusion of technology. It has been argued, for example, that Japanese agriculture "underwent notable technological (though not mechanical) changes long before the modern period. Between 1600 and 1850 a complex of such changes greatly increased the productivity of land, altered that of labor both in specific operations and over-all, and contributed to lasting changes in agrarian institutions. . . . Few changes were the result of inventions; most resulted from the spread of known techniques from the localities in which they had been developed to areas where they were previously unknown or unused." Thomas C. Smith, *The Agrarian Origins of Modern Japan* (Stanford: Stanford University Press, 1959), p. 87.

Abe, a farmer in the Yamagata prefecture. The development and diffusion of these *rōnō* varieties were initiated within the western part of Japan, which includes the most advanced regions (Kinki and Northern Kyushu). Then this process was transmitted to the relatively backward eastern part of Japan (Figure 8-4).[55]

Experiment station research was successful in testing and refining the results of farmer innovations. The *rōnō* techniques (veteran farmers' techniques) were based on experiences in the specific localities where they originated. They tended to be location-specific and to require modification when transferred to other localities. Simple comparative tests effectively screened the *rōnō* techniques and varieties, thereby reducing greatly the cost of technical information for farmers. Slight modifications or adaptations of indigenous techniques on the basis of experimental tests often gave them universal applicability. A good example is the technique of rice seed sorting in salt water. Jikei Yokoi, who later became a foremost leader of agriculture and agricultural science in Japan, found this technique practiced by farmers when he was a young instructor at a vocational agricultural school in the Fukuoka prefecture. After he perfected the technique and it was subjected to repeated tests at the national experiment station, it was propagated throughout Japan. It is interesting that a person like Yokoi, who advocated very strongly the superiority of modern agricultural science over the *rōnō* knowledge throughout his life, contributed to the propagation of the *rōnō* technique.

The techniques developed by veteran farmers were strongly constrained by the resources available to Japanese farmers. In Japan the major motivation was, of necessity, to increase land productivity. The success of agricultural productivity growth in the Meiji period was achieved by a reorientation of agricultural development policy toward the development of a technology suited to the resource endowment situation in Japan. Effective interaction between farmers and scientists was deliberately encouraged as part of the process of screening, adapting, and diffusing the best indigenous technology.

Another important element in the effective response of technical change to Japanese resource endowments was improvement in the supply of inputs that substitute for land, i.e., fertilizer. This depended on the progress in the intersectoral division of labor accompanying industrialization and economic growth. Agricultural suppliers, particularly fertilizer supply firms, perceived the pressing demand by farmers for land substitutes and exploited the opportunity. Improved efficiency in transportation, especially the introduction of the steamship, greatly reduced the cost of herring meal from Hokkaido. Search for a cheaper source of nitrogen brought about the enormous inflow of Manchurian soybean cake in the 1900s and 1910s.

The story of Kumejiro Tagi, founder of the Tagi Fertilizer Company,

---

55. See Yujiro Hayami and Saburo Yamada, "Technological Progress in Agriculture," *Economic Growth: The Japanese Experience since the Meiji Era*, ed. Lawrence Klein and Kazushi Ohkawa (Homewood, Ill.: Irwin, 1968), pp. 135–61.

FIGURE 8-4. Changes in the percentage of area planted in improved varieties to total area planted in rice, Japan, 1875–1963.

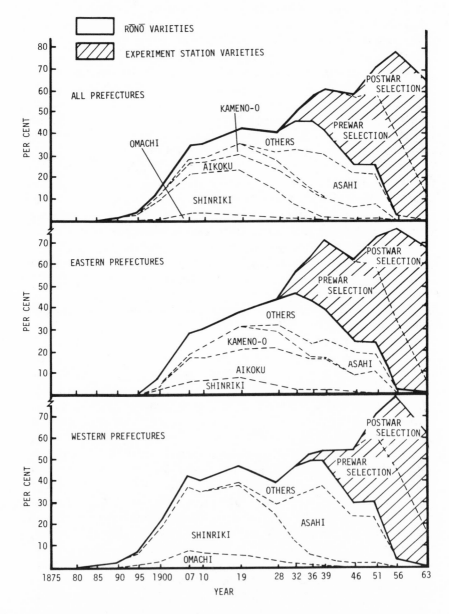

Source: Yujiro Hayami and Saburo Yamada, "Technological Progress in Agriculture," *Economic Growth: The Japanese Experience since the Meiji Era,* ed. Lawrence R. Klein and Kazushi Ohkawa (Homewood, Ill.: Irwin, 1968), pp. 135–61.

illustrates the interaction between farmers and agricultural supply firms. Tagi belonged to the *gōnō* class in the Hyogo prefecture, where he owned eleven hectares of arable land, of which he cultivated a little less than a hectare himself. He also manufactured soya sauces as a family enterprise. Perceiving the strong demand for fertilizer and the rising price of sardine meal Tagi started the manufacture of bonemeal. Overcoming several difficulties, including the revulsion against animal bones among farmers and his employees stemming from the Buddhist tradition, he further expanded his enterprise during the fertilizer shortage of the Sino-Japanese War (1894–95) and developed it to become one of the largest producers of superphosphate of lime and mixed fertilizer. His vigorous extension and sales promotion activities, more than his engineering dexterity, have been identified as the secret of his success.[56]

Increasing demand induced innovations in the fertilizer industry, which in turn reduced the cost of fertilizer and induced further innovations using fertilizer in crop varieties and production. The history of seed improvement in Japan is a history of developing varieties that were increasingly more fertilizer-responsive. Varieties selected by *rōnō* in response to the inflow of cheap Manchurian soybean cake (such as *Shinriki* and *Kameno-o*) were characterized by high fertilizer-responsiveness—varieties that did not easily lodge and were less susceptible to disease at higher levels of nitrogen application. Both economic logic and pressure from farmers motivated agricultural scientists to develop a technology geared to high levels of fertilizer application and yield, the so-called "fertilizer consuming rice culture."[57] In this respect the discipline of agricultural chemistry and soil science of the German tradition was extremely effective.

Through the dialectic interaction among farmers, scientists, and agricultural supply firms in response to relative factor prices that reflected Japan's resource endowments, Japan was able to evolve a unique and highly productive system of agricultural technology called *Meiji Noho* (Meiji agricultural technology).

Toward scientific maturity in experiment station research. The high payoff of simple applied agricultural research in the Meiji period was based on the backlog of indigenous technological potential previously dammed by feudal constraints.[58] This potential was exhausted as it was exploited. In due course it became necessary for the research institutions to recharge the declin-

---

56. Nippon Kagakushi Gakkai, ed., *Nippon Kagaku Gijutsushi Taikei* (History of Japanese science), vol. 22 (Tokyo: Daiichi Hoki Shuppan, 1967), pp. 383–85.

57. Ogura, *Agricultural Development in Modern Japan*, pp. 365–77.

58. For more detail on the historical process described in this section, see Yujiro Hayami and Saburo Yamada, "Agricultural Research Organization in Economic Development: A Review of the Japanese Experience," *Agriculture in Development Theory*, ed. Lloyd G. Reynolds (New Haven: Yale University Press, 1975), pp. 224–49. See also Hayami and Yamada, "Technical Progress."

ing potential by conducting more sophisticated and basic research. By the beginning of this century the accumulation of human capital and scientific knowledge had approached the stage at which such research could be initiated. In addition to the national system, the prefectures had gradually established their own experiment stations. This trend was encouraged by the Law of State Subsidy for Prefectural Agricultural Experiment Stations (1899), and in 1900, twelve new stations were set up, bringing the total number of prefectural stations to thirty-three. Those prefectural stations gradually accepted responsibility for conducting the more applied research tests and demonstrations. Agricultural associations organized under the Agricultural Association Law (1899) into a pyramidal structure, with the Imperial Agricultural Association on the top and village associations on the bottom, began to take on extension activities by employing agricultural technicians (the number of these extension workers grew to 5,200 in 1914, 10,000 in 1924, and 14,000 in 1933). Relieved of those activities, the National Agricultural Experiment Station could now direct its resources toward more basic research.

Thus, for the first time, in 1904, the National Agricultural Experiment Station launched an original crop-breeding project at the Kinai Branch with Koremochi Kato in charge of rice breeding. The objective of this project was to develop new seed varieties by crossbreeding. It took almost two decades before new varieties of major practical significance were developed, though the project contributed greatly to the accumulation of experience and knowledge.[59] Another project was started in 1905 at the Rikuu Branch to improve rice varieties by pure line selection. This approach brought about quicker practical results. Thereafter the main efforts of crop breeding in the Taisho era (1912–25) were directed to pure line selection.

Although scientific research gradually evolved into a major source of new biological technology, Japanese agriculture continued to rely heavily on *rōnō* techniques during the Taisho era and even into the early period of the Showa era (1926–present). Major rice varieties were still predominantly of *rōnō* selection. The *Asahi* variety, which substituted for *Shinriki* because of its high responsiveness to ammonium sulfate, was selected (1911) by Shinjiro Yamamoto, a farmer in Kyoto. The *Ginbozu* variety, which was propagated in the north central region because of its strong pest and insect resistance under the high application of nitrogen, was selected (1907) by Iwajiro Ishiguro in the Toyama prefecture. The pure line selection at the experiment stations was essentially a sophistication of *rōnō* varieties. It contributed to productivity growth through the exploitation of indigenous potential rather than creating new potential.

The exploitation and consequent exhaustion of indigenous potential became evident in the 1910s. The rate of increase in rice yield started to decele-

59. The first variety of major practical significance developed by hybridization was the *Rikuu No. 132* (1922). This variety was characterized by strong cold-weather-resistance and replaced *Kameno-o* in northern Japan.

rate. When this productivity lag coincided with the increase in demand caused by World War I, Japan faced a population-food problem. The rising price of food, which exceeded increases in wage rates, caused serious disruption in urban areas and culminated in the *Kome Sodo* (rice riot) of 1918. The riot, triggered by fishermen's wives in the Toyama prefecture, swept over all the major cities in Japan.

The first reaction of the government was to increase rice imports from the overseas colonies, Taiwan and Korea. Through the squeeze on income in Taiwan and Korea by taxes and monopoly sales, on the one hand, and the investment in irrigation and agricultural research, on the other, Japan was successful in organizing large-scale rice imports from the colonial territories. The importation of colonial rice, which coincided with the contraction of demand after World War I, was successful in bringing down the price of rice to consumers. It also had the effect of reducing income and dampening production incentives for Japanese agriculture.[60]

The government reacted by partially blocking rice imports from the colonies. At the same time the government tried to rescue domestic agriculture by investing in research and physical infrastructure. Under such circumstances, the nationwide coordinated crop-breeding program called the Assigned Experiment System (the system of experiments assigned by the Ministry of Agriculture and Forestry) was established, first for wheat (1926) and second for rice (1927).[61]

Under the Assigned Experiment System the national experiment stations were given the responsibility for conducting hybridization up to the selection of the first several filial generations. The regional stations, in each of eight regions, conducted further selections so as to achieve adaption to the regional ecological conditions. The varieties selected at the regional stations were then sent to prefectural stations to be tested for their acceptability in specific localities. The varieties developed by this system were called *Norin* (abbreviation of the Ministry of Agriculture and Forestry) varieties.[62]

This system was outstandingly successful. *Norin No. 1* was selected in 1931 at the headquarters of Hokuriku (north central region) located at the Niigata prefectural station. This variety proved to be superior in yield, fertilizer-responsiveness, early maturity (a required characteristic in northern regions), and palatability. *Norin No. 1* spread rapidly, especially after 1935,

60. Yujiro Hayami and Vernon W. Ruttan, "Korean Rice, Taiwan Rice, and Japanese Agricultural Stagnation: An Economic Consequence of Colonialism," *Quarterly Journal of Economics* 84 (November 1970):562–89.

61. This system was expanded to cover other crops and livestock. See Ogura, *Agricultural Development in Modern Japan,* p. 326.

62. It is of interest that the Mexican dwarf wheat which is revolutionizing Mexican and Indo-Pakistan agriculture was based on the *Norin* wheat varieties brought back to the United States by C. S. Salmon, a USDA scientist on loan to the occupation army as an agricultural adviser. See Dana G. Dalrymple, *Development and Spread of High-Yielding Varieties of Wheat and Rice in the Less Developed Nations,* 6th ed. (Washington, D.C.: U.S. Department of Agriculture Foreign Agricultural Economic Report No. 95, 1978).

and was planted on approximately 160,000 hectares in 1939. It saved rice farming in this region, which was on the verge of collapse because of competition from colonial rice.

It appears that with the establishment of the Assigned Experiment System, scientific research finally had become a major supplier of new technological potential and a dominant source of productivity gain in agriculture. The *Norin* numbered varieties successively replaced older varieties in the latter half of the 1930s (see Figure 8-4). If the supply of fertilizer and agricultural inputs had not been restricted by the diversion of resources for the production of munitions during World War II, Japanese agriculture would have probably experienced a second epoch of agricultural productivity growth beginning in the late 1930s. The history of the Assigned Experiment System seems to suggest that the institutional response to changes in the supply of factors and products, reflected by changes in relative prices, occurs with a significant time lag. The production of new knowledge embodied in new varieties and materials occurs only after a further lag. The first crossing of parents of *Norin No. 1* was made in the Rikuu Branch of the National Experiment Station in 1922. The fifth filial generation was sent to the Niigata regional headquarters of the Assigned Experiment System in 1927, and three years later *Norin No. 1* was selected as the eighth filial generation. Further tests at prefectural stations were involved before it was finally recommended by extension workers.

The agricultural stagnation in Japan during the interwar period seems to be explained by this time lag in the adjustment of the public research complex to changes in the demand and supply of production factors and products. The Japanese experience was, in this respect, similar to the U.S. experience discussed earlier in this chapter.

Postwar Agricultural Development

After World War II, Japan was left with a territory reduced by almost one-half and a population increased by repatriation from overseas territories. The productive capacity of manufacturing plants was devastated, and industrial production declined to one-fourth of its prewar level. It was of the utmost urgency to secure food supplies from domestic agriculture.

The critical impediment to the recovery of agricultural production was the shortage of fertilizers. In the program for the rehabilitation of industry, called *Keisha Seisan Hoshiki* (differential production scheme), which began in 1946, the fertilizer industry was given high priority together with the coal-mining and iron and steel industries. In this scheme government funds were first allocated to coal mining; the increased outputs of coal were delivered to the fertilizer, iron, and steel industries; and the increased output in food from fertilizers and in iron and steel were returned to coal mining to expand the cycle of reproduction.

Meanwhile, the policies of democratizing agrarian society and institutions were promoted under the direction of the U.S. occupation forces. Of special significance were land reform and the reorganization of the agricultural cooperative associations.

The land reform, which became effective in postwar Japan, was carried out for the 1946–50 period in accordance with the strong recommendations of the occupation authorities.[63] The government was authorized to enforce the purchase of all farmlands owned by absentee landlords as well as the landholdings of resident landlords exceeding one hectare (four hectares in Hokkaido), which were to be sold to tenants within two years after the proclamation of the law.

The land prices paid to the landlords were determined as forty times the annual rent in the case of paddy fields and forty-eight times the rent in the case of upland fields. In this formula the rents paid in kind were evaluated by the commodity prices of November 1945. Consequently, during the process of hyperinflation from 1945 to 1949, the real burden of tenant farmers in procuring land was reduced to a negligible level.

For the four years from 1947 to 1950, the government purchased 1.7 million hectares of farmland from landlords and transferred 1.9 million hectares, including state-owned land, to tenant farmers, which amounted to about 80 percent of the formerly tenanted land area. As a result, the ratio of farmland under tenancy declined from 45 percent in 1945 to 9 percent in 1955. Further, for the remaining land under tenancy, the rights of tenants were strengthened and rents were controlled at very low levels by the Agricultural Land Law (1952). This law also imposed a limit on landholding of three hectares (twelve hectares in Hokkaido) to prevent the revival of landlordism.

The land reform promoted more equal assets and income distributions among farmers, thereby contributing critically to the social stability of the rural sector, although the farm-size distribution was fixed and the small-scale farms were maintained even though they became less efficient in the process of economic development. Although land reform contributed to an increase in the level of living and consumption, its contributions to capital formation and productivity growth in agriculture have not been clearly visible or are not significant when analyzed quantitatively.

Another reform that had a major impact on the agricultural economy and rural society was the reorganization of the agricultural cooperative associations. During the war, the agricultural associations and the agricultural cooperatives were integrated into a semigovernmental organization called Nogyokai (agricultural society) that was designed to share the responsibility of controlling and mobilizing village economies for war purposes. This organization was dissolved by direction of the U.S. General Headquarters Organization (GHO). All the economic functions of the Nogyokai, including market-

63. Shigeto Kawano, "Effects of the Land Reform on Consumption and Investment of Farmers," *Agriculture and Economic Growth: Japan's Experience,* ed. Kazushi Ohkawa, Bruce F. Johnston, and Hiromitsu Kaneda (Tokyo: University of Tokyo Press, 1969, and Princeton: Princeton University Press, 1970), pp. 374–97.

ing and credit, were transferred to the agricultural cooperative associations reestablished by the Agricultural Cooperative Law in 1947.

The agricultural cooperative associations inherited some nationwide organizations from the Nogyokai. The village associations, numbering more than ten thousand, were organized into prefectural and national federations. The national federations at the top of the pyramid included the National Federation of Agricultural Cooperatives for marketing; the Central Bank of Agriculture and Forestry for credit; the National Federation of Mutual Insurance for life and casualty insurance; and the Central Union of Agricultural Cooperatives for political lobbying.

When the Nogyokai was dissolved with the formation of the new agricultural cooperative associations, the extension service activities that it had carried out were assumed by the prefectural governments, again according to the instruction of the GHO. The new system was modeled after the U.S. system of agricultural extension services. Unlike the trinity of education, research, and extension in the U.S. land-grant college system, the new extension service was established separately from the experiment stations and agricultural colleges. Yet because both the prefectural experiment station and the extension services were placed under the auspices of the same agricultural departments of the prefectural governments, they operated in close cooperation. In many cases senior extension specialists were stationed in the experiment stations as contact persons. Activities in the prefectural extension services were reinforced by subsidies from the central government amounting to about 40 percent of the total extension budget.

Agricultural production in Japan recovered rapidly from its 1945–47 low point. The growth rates of agricultural output and productivity have decelerated since the mid-1950s, when the recovery was completed, but they have been maintained at much higher levels than the prewar growth rates.

The major factor underlying rapid agricultural growth in the post–World War II period may be identified as the backlog of technological potential accumulated since the 1930s under the Assigned Experiment System—a potential that had been dammed by a critical shortage of fertilizers and other complementary inputs during the war. The new potential of agricultural technology was quickly realized with the recovery of the supply of those technical inputs. This process was also assisted by the rehabilitation and improvement of flood-control and irrigation facilities. Projects to improve the land infrastructure promoted by government investment and credit covered 1.6 million hectares of paddy fields, as much as 60 percent of the total area, for 1946–57.

The postwar agricultural growth was further enhanced by the supply of new industrial inputs, such as chemical pesticides, insecticides, and garden tractors and tillers. Such inputs were based on the progress of industrial technology and scientific knowledge accumulated during the war. Agricultural scientists developed techniques that pushed the fertilizer-consuming rice culture toward its limits. Basic to this move forward was a dynamic interaction among various scientific and engineering disciplines. Increased fertilizer application made rice plants susceptible to pests and insects, inducing research on agricultural chemicals, plant physiology, and entomology. Success in these areas reinforced the development of varieties that were even more responsive to high levels of fertilizer application.

A distinct aspect of postwar agricultural development was the progress in farm mechanization. Before World War II, mechanization in Japanese agriculture was limited to irrigation, drainage, and postharvesting operations, such as threshing. The introduction of tractors was attempted only on an experimental scale. The postwar spurt of "minitractorization," a rapid introduction of small tractors of less than ten horsepower, was paralleled by a spurt of industrial and economic development since the mid-1950s that resulted in the rapid absorption of the agricultural labor force by the nonagricultural sector.

Such rapid progress in tractorization was induced by the relative rise in farm wage rates resulting from labor outmigration from agriculture. At the same time it was supported by the capacity of the machinery industry to supply the farm machinery and implements suitable for the farming conditions of Japan. The hand tractors were first manufactured according to designs from the United States. They had two defects: heavy body weights relative to power and engines without waterproof devices, which made operation in wet fields difficult. The replacement of draft animals by tractors was made possible by the development of new designs that overcame these critical defects. The engineering capacity in Japanese industry, which had increased during the war, served as a backlog for the local adaptation and diffusion of mechanical technology in agriculture for the postwar period.

Until the late 1960s the use of tractors had largely been limited to land preparation, such as plowing and harrowing. Transplanting and harvesting were still performed manually, creating sharp seasonal peaks in labor requirements. Substantial efforts have been made in developing rice-transplanting and harvesting machines, such as the cutter, binder, and small-scale combine. Small-scale mechanization for the entire process of rice production in Japan was nearly completed by the late 1970s.

Introduction of large riding tractors for farm operations began in Hokkaido in the late 1950s. Their usage has increased rapidly nationwide since the acceleration of labor outmigration from agriculture after the 1960s.

Agricultural Adjustment Problems

When Japan recovered from the devastation of the war and set off on its "miraculous" economic growth after the mid-1950s, agriculture began to face serious adjustment problems.[64]

64. This section draws heavily on Yujiro Hayami, "Adjustment Policies for Japanese Agriculture in a Changing World," *U.S.-Japanese Agricultural Trade Relations*, ed. Emery N. Castle

The rate of growth in agricultural productivity, which was rapid by international standards, was not rapid enough to keep up with the growth in the industrial sector. The growth rate of real per-worker output in manufacturing was almost twice that of agriculture. After the Korean War, intersectoral terms of trade did not improve for agriculture during the 1950s partly because of the impact of surplus agricultural production in the United States and other exporting countries and partly because the domestic demand for major staple cereals, especially rice, approached the saturation point after the bumper crop of 1955. In consequence, the levels of income and living for farm households lagged behind those for urban households.

In such a situation, the major goal of agricultural policy shifted from an increase in the production of food staples to a reduction in the rural-urban income gap. To attain this goal, the Agricultural Basic Law, a national charter for agriculture, was enacted in 1961. The law declared that it was the government's responsibility to raise agricultural productivity and thereby close the gap in income and welfare among farm and nonfarm people. Among the measures identified as necessary for this purpose were encouragements to expand selectively the production of agricultural commodities in response to a changing demand structure and to enlarge the scale of the production unit.

In spite of such efforts the rate of agricultural productivity growth was not raised sufficiently to prevent the rural-urban income gap from widening. Farmers reacted against the deterioration in their economic position by taking group action to force government support for higher prices for farm products. They also transferred more labor to nonfarm employment to supplement the income from farming.

The demand to support prices took the form of pressuring the government to raise the price of rice, which had been kept under the direct control of the Food Agency. In 1960 strong political pressure from farm organizations resulted in a rice price-determination formula called the Production Cost and Income Compensation Formula. By this formula the price of rice is determined by the cost of production. A critical point in this formula is that wages for family labor are valued by nonfarm wage rates so as to guarantee "fair returns" for the labor of rice producers.

With this formula the price received by producers of rice rose rapidly. By the early 1980s the support price was between three and four times the price of rice in international markets. The price-support program resulted in a substantial loss in economic efficiency. High rice prices have reduced consumers' welfare by contracting the demand for rice and by obstructing the shift of

---

and Kenzo Hemmi with Sally A. Skillings (Washington, D.C.: Resources for the Future, 1982; distributed by Johns Hopkins University Press, Baltimore, Md., and Johns Hopkins Press, Ltd., London), pp. 368–92. For additional references see the other essays in the Castle-Hemmi volume. These issues have also been discussed by Takekazu Ogura, *Can Japanese Agriculture Survive? A Historical and Comparative Approach,* 2d ed. (Tokyo: Agricultural Policy Research Center, 1980).

TABLE 8-4.   Changes in food self-sufficiency rates (percentages)

	1960	1970	1975	1980
All grains	83	48	43	29
Food grains	90	79	76	60
Rice	102	106	110	87
Wheat	39	9	4	10
Feed grains	66	6	2	2
Beans	44	13	9	7
Vegetables	100	99	99	97
Fruit	100	84	84	81
Dairy products	89	89	82	86
Eggs	101	97	97	98
Meats	93	89	77	80

Source: Japan Ministry of Agriculture, Forestry and Fishery, *Food Balance Sheets* (various issues).

resources from rice to other high-demand agricultural products, such as livestock and vegetables. High rice prices have induced substantial private investment in rice production capacity and excessive public investment in land development and research.[65] Even more wasteful was the rapidly accumulating surplus rice in government storage and the increasing cost of the food subsidy program, which rose to 30 to 40 percent of the government budget for agriculture. The government has also been forced to adopt a very expensive acreage-control program with incentive payments for the retirement of paddy fields from rice production or diversion to nonrice crops.

For the past two decades changes in Japanese agriculture have been progressively linked to the international division of labor. With the shift of comparative advantage in favor of manufacturing, imports of agricultural products increased sharply. Food self-sufficiency rates have declined (Table 8-4). Especially dramatic was the decline in self-sufficiency in nonrice cereals and soybeans.

Despite such rapid expansion in agricultural imports and the steep decline in food self-sufficiency, Japan has been strongly criticized for the high rate of agricultural trade protection. The reason for this increased protection is the decisive comparative advantage that Japan has achieved in manufacturing production with a secular surplus in the trade balance. Although trade liberalization has progressed rapidly in Japan, it has not been rapid enough to satisfy the demand of agricultural exporting countries in the face of an extremely rapid expansion in manufacturing exports from Japan.

Table 8-5 compares the nominal rates of agricultural protection of Japan and nine other industrialized countries. In 1980 the nominal protection rate in

65. Keijiro Otsuka, *Role of Demand in a Public Good Market: Rice Research in Japan* (New Haven: Yale University Economic Growth Center, 1979).

TABLE 8-5.   Comparison of the nominal rates of agricultural protection among ten industrialized countries (percentages)[a]

	1955	1960	1965	1970	1975	1980
United States	2.4	0.9	8.2	10.9	4.0	−0.1
EEC[b]	30.7	32.8	40.3	47.1	27.1	35.7
France	31.2	23.4	28.2	44.1	28.0	29.6
West Germany	28.0	40.6	46.8	44.3	35.8	42.0
Italy	43.3	46.5	60.2	64.2	35.6	53.8
Netherlands	11.9	19.2	30.7	34.4	28.6	24.9
United Kingdom	34.9	33.7	18.9	24.9	5.6	32.1
Denmark	4.5	3.2	4.6	16.3	18.3	24.4
Sweden	31.3	40.3	46.3	61.3	40.9	55.9
Switzerland	53.0	55.0	64.9	84.2	86.8	113.2
Japan	17.5	41.1	67.6	72.7	74.4	83.5

Source: Yujiro Hayami and Masayoshi Honma, "Kokusai Hikaku kara mita Nihon Nogyo no Hogo Suijun" (The agricultural protection level of Japan in an international comparative perspective) (Tokyo: Forum for Policy Innovation, 1983), mimeo.

[a]The nominal rates of agricultural protection are calculated by subtracting the value of agricultural output in international prices from the value of agricultural output in domestic prices and dividing the remainder by the value of agricultural output in international prices.

[b]Weighted average of France, West Germany, Italy, and the Netherlands for 1955–70; plus United Kingdom and Denmark for 1975–80.

Japan was 83.5 percent of total domestic output valued in international prices. This figure was almost twice as high as the EEC average of 35 percent and was not much lower than that of Switzerland, which is known for its exceptionally high level of agricultural protection for the preservation of Alpine agriculture. It is noteworthy that Japan's nominal rate of agricultural protection in 1955 was only 17.6 percent, which was lower than the EEC average of 30.4 percent. It rose very rapidly, however, exceeding the EEC level in 1960 and approaching the Swiss level in 1965. The period from 1955 to 1965 was characterized by exceptionally high rates of industrial growth in Japan. If the interindustrial adjustments corresponding to a rapid shift in the comparative advantage from agriculture to industry had been left to market mechanisms, the rural-urban income disparity and labor migration would have increased to an extent that would have been socially and politically intolerable. Thus it seems reasonable to hypothesize that Japan reduced the cost of interindustrial adjustment by paying the cost of agricultural protection.

Having achieved rapid economic growth and having established clearly the comparative advantage for its industry, however, Japan is faced with strong pressures to liberalize agricultural imports. It is therefore critical to achieve structural adjustments in agriculture in order to compete internationally. The basic factor limiting Japanese agricultural productivity is the small farm size. Japan's average farm size of 1.1 hectares of agricultural land or 0.9 hectare of arable land is well below the farm sizes of other industrialized countries. With such a small scale of operation, it is difficult for Japanese agriculture to make efficient use of modern labor-saving technologies so as to be internationally competitive.

The average farm size showed virtually no increase during the period of rapid economic growth. The number of people employed in agriculture declined by approximately one-half between 1960 and 1978, yet the number of farm households declined by only 20 percent. Together with the conversion of some agricultural land to nonagricultural uses, these reductions held the average farm size to a 15 percent increase over the period (0.8 percent per annum)—a rate of increase which would require some ninety years for a mere doubling.

The reason there was so little decline in the number of farm households despite the decline in the agricultural population is, obviously, the increase in the number of part-time farm households. Whereas approximately one in three farm households was engaged in farming full time in 1960, this figure is now one in eight. During the same period, the number of Class II part-time farm households (those whose nonagricultural income exceeds their agricultural income) has jumped from 30 percent to 70 percent of the total. It has thus become common for farmers with secure nonagricultural employment to hold onto their land and to continue farming in their spare time, by drawing upon supplemental labor from available family members (generally women and old people). As a result, full-time farmers have found it difficult to expand their operational scale. As of 1977, the per-farm area under cultivation for full-time farm households was a mere 2.3 hectares.

Part-time farm households tend to concentrate on rice farming because rice is a very stable crop offering a high return on only intermittent labor. Because rice marketing is carried out exclusively by the government, rice farmers are guaranteed a high price and can easily sell their product through the agricultural cooperative, the sole agent of government rice marketing. In addition, agricultural research and extension services have traditionally been concentrated on the rice crop with the result that rice cultivation has become highly standardized, making it easier for part-time farmers to grow rice rather than other crops and livestock. That rice production in Japan has been geared to part-time farming in this way is a major factor in encouraging part-time farming and impeding any decline in the number of farm households.

The land-tenure policies pursued since the postwar land reform have rejected any separation of ownership and cultivation rights. Tenancy rights have been very strongly protected, and it has been almost impossible for landlords to evict tenants. Land rent has been controlled at an extremely low level. Therefore, part-time farmers have had no incentive to lease out their holdings, even if their operation is very inefficient.

The spread of part-time farming has in turn impeded attempts by full-time farmers to expand operational scale and improve productivity. The increase in off-farm earnings, however, has made it possible to achieve the goal of income equalization between farm and nonfarm families. In the 1960s, aver-

TABLE 8-6.   Income levels of farm and urban wage-earner households (thousand yen)

	Farm households				Urban households per capita (C)	Income ratio (B/C)
	Per household			Per capita (B)		
	Agricultural income	Nonagricultural income[a]	Total (A)			
1960	225	224	449	78	115	0.68
1965	365	470	835	157	194	0.81
1970	508	1,084	1,592	326	358	0.91
1975	1,146	2,815	3,961	867	760	1.14
1980	952	4,642	5,594	1,271	1,114	1.14

Sources: Japan Ministry of Agriculture, Forestry and Fishery, *Farm Household Economy Survey* (various issues); Japan Prime Minister's Office, Bureau of Statistics, *Urban Household Economy Survey* (various issues).

[a]Nonagricultural income for farm households includes money earned by family members as seasonal laborers.

age per capita farm household income was about 30 percent below that of urban wage earners (Table 8-6). This disparity was narrowed during the process of rapid economic growth until per capita farm household income exceeded per capita urban wage-earner income by nearly 15 percent in 1975. The main source of this rapid increase in farm household income has been off-farm earnings. Nonagricultural income rose from approximately 50 percent of all farm household income in 1960 to over 80 percent in 1980.

So far, the expansion in part-time farming has been seen as a factor inhibiting expanded operational scale for full-time farmers, but this same turn to part-time farming has also helped to equalize agricultural and non-agricultural income levels and has contributed importantly to social stability by preventing rural depopulation and urban overcrowding. The dual demands for creating internationally competitive agriculture and preserving social stability can best be met by enabling part-time farmers to stay in the rural villages and to reduce their own operations by transferring production to full-time farmers. The farmer's strong attachment to the land and the expectation that such land will become increasingly valuable make it impossible to expand the scale of agricultural operations through transferring landownership. The only way left to expand operational scale is through development of a land rental market.

Japanese agriculture should thus aim at creating the following features in the future. First, while guaranteeing highly stable employment opportunities in nonagricultural sectors, it should promote institutional innovations in order to develop a more effective land rental market. Arrangements could be developed that would permit some 90 percent of Japan's five million farm families to remain in rural villages, keeping 0.1 hectare or so for home gardens, while they work in nonagricultural occupations and consign the cultivation rights to the rest of their land to full-time farmers. If this is done, the approximately 10 percent of full-time farmers will be able to expand the scale of their operations to an average of 8 to 10 hectares. This scale is comparable to that of West Germany.

Even if Japan achieves an operational scale on a par with EC levels, it will be difficult to compete internationally in wheat or feed grains with countries in new continents such as the United States or Australia. A major reorientation of agricultural production toward livestock-centered farming will be required by making positive use of cheap imported grains and encouraging domestic production of roughages and pasture. It will be an extremely difficult task to switch Japanese farmers, accustomed to producing the traditional rice and cereal crops, to livestock-centered farming. Such a reorganization of agricultural production will require a major reorientation of agricultural research, farmer education, and extension.

In the early stage of economic development, Japan was successful in transforming traditional agriculture into a modern dynamic sector, which excelled the world in land productivity. This change was accomplished through a series of technological and institutional innovations under conditions of very unfavorable man-land ratios. Japanese agriculture now faces the challenge of improving labor productivity in agriculture in a manner consistent with the growth in labor productivity in the nonagricultural sector. Since the 1960s Japan has entered a new era in which the absolute size of the agricultural labor force has declined rapidly and wage rates have risen faster than land prices. But improvements in labor productivity have been inadequate to permit Japanese farmers to remain competitive in internationally traded commodities. The result has been political pressure for greater agricultural protectionism. As a result of Japan's development into an industrial superpower, Japanese agriculture is now faced with new demands for institutional innovation. These pressures for structural reform are comparable in many respects to the pressure that induced the dramatic advances in biological technology during the first century following the Meiji Restoration.

ARE THERE RELEVANT LESSONS?

Both the United States and Japan were successful in achieving sustained growth in agricultural productivity by generating a stream of technological innovations throughout a century of modern economic growth. Resources saved from the productivity growth in agriculture were transferred to the nonagricultural sectors in various forms, such as reduced food prices, foreign exchange earnings from agricultural commodity exports, and a supply of labor from agriculture. Thus the technological innovations in agriculture that enabled the transfer of resources to the nonagricultural sectors were the critical basis of industrialization and overall economic development, especially in the early phase. The most important lesson that can be drawn from the historical experience of U.S. and Japanese agricultural development is the process by which institutional innovations were developed to facilitate technological innovations. Another major lesson is the way in which both the United States and Japan dealt with the serious agricultural adjustment problems in the later stage of economic development as the result of their success in achieving agricultural productivity growth and overall economic development.

A major institutional innovation that underlay the success in generating technological innovations was the development of publicly supported agricultural education and research systems, which were especially important in advancing the biological sciences and technology. Both the U.S. and Japanese experiences suggest that the public sector must play an important role in the advance of biological technology if the pattern of technical progress is to approach an optimal rate or avoid excessive bias in the direction of mechanical technology and those areas of biological and chemical technology which can be embodied in proprietary products. Failure effectively to institutionalize public sector agricultural research can result in serious distortion of the pattern of technological change and resource use.

Market incentives have been much more effective in inducing innovation in mechanical than in biological technology. A bias in the productivity growth path inconsistent with relative factor endowments can be expected from failure to balance the effectiveness of the private sector's response to inducements for advances in mechanical technology (and those areas of biological technology in which advances in knowledge can be embodied in proprietary products) with appropriate public incentives for advances in biological technology.

It seems reasonable to hypothesize that failure to invest in public sector experiment station capacity is one of the factors responsible in some developing countries for the unbalanced adoption of mechanical, relative to biological, technology. Failure to develop adequate public sector research institutions has also been partially responsible in some countries for the almost exclusive concentration of research expenditures on plantation and export crops such as bananas and sugar.

The emphasis on public sector research in biological science fields does not mean that research and development leading to new technology have been unimportant in the private sector. On the contrary, the development by agricultural supply firms of improvements in farm machinery and implements and of more efficient technology for the production of fertilizer and agricultural chemicals has been a major source of agricultural productivity growth in the United States and Japan. The development of research capacity in the private sector has been supported by public sector research and training programs. The public sector has been responsible for much of the basic and generic research and for the training of scientists and technicians. The public sector has also encouraged private research and development through patents to protect property rights in mechanical and chemical inventions and patentlike protection for inventions in some areas of biological technology.

A major lesson to be learned from the United States and Japanese experiences is that public investment in education in the biological sciences related to agriculture and in experiment station research capacity is absolutely essential if a nation is to (a) successfully test and diffuse the indigenous technology employed by its own farmers, (b) transfer and adapt the agricultural technology developed in other countries, and (c) conduct the basic and applied research necessary to provide its farmers with a continuous stream of new biological and chemical technology. This implication, which will be examined in greater detail in subsequent chapters, is particularly significant for most developing countries because their factor endowments clearly suggest that their optimal path of technical progress would place a relatively heavy emphasis on biological technology.

One of the major organizational features of public sector agricultural research in the United States and Japan has been a reasonably effective balance between centralization and decentralization in research decision making. The U.S. public agricultural research system consists of the centrally managed research program of the U.S. Department of Agriculture and a decentralized system of state agricultural experiment stations managed by the state agricultural colleges and universities. The U.S. Department of Agriculture has played a coordinating role relative to the state experiment stations but has not determined research priorities or directed research resource allocations by the state stations. The role of the central government has been somewhat stronger in Japan. Yet there is considerable decentralization of decision making about research priorities and resource allocation at the prefectural level. This decentralization had helped make the Japanese system responsive both to market forces and to the needs of farmers in each prefecture. In general, concentration of decision making at the center tends to obstruct the induced innovation process. The induced innovation process is dependent on close articulation between research performers and research users. An important factor in protecting both the United States and the Japanese systems against overcentralization has been the substantial funding of research by the state and prefectural governments.

It must be recognized, however, that effective institutionalization of agricultural education and research in presently developing countries will involve new institutional innovations rather than the direct transfer of the Japanese or U.S. models. Neither the English nor the German models, on which the Japanese and the United States drew in designing their agricultural research systems, were adequate for the needs of Japan or the United States. Changes in rural institutions that were needed to achieve an effective balance between advances in mechanical and biological technology in Japan and the United States are quite different—both in timing and design.

The manner in which the United States and Japan have dealt with the serious agricultural adjustment problems in the later stage of economic development also provides a number of useful lessons for the newly industrializing countries, which are now experiencing high rates of economic growth. When a country reaches a high-income stage, the rate of growth in the domestic demand for food declines. At the same time the capacity to expand food production continues to increase because the well-developed agricultural research infrastructure generates rapid technical change. Given the low price elasticity of food demand, the lag in the shift in demand relative to the shift in supply will result in a sharp decline in agricultural prices and income. Because the intersectoral transfer of resources, especially labor, through the market is slow relative to the requirement of agricultural supply adjustments there is a strong demand by farmers for government interventions, such as agricultural trade protection and price supports.[66] The United States reached such a stage in the 1930s, Japan in the 1960s.

Political pressure to implement agricultural price-support programs and protectionist trade policies to relieve the disruptive effects of demand-supply imbalance became very large at the time the countries began to experience agricultural adjustment problems. But the government interventions, once initiated, have reinforced the vested interests of agricultural producers in trade restrictions and price supports. They have been able to maintain these programs beyond the period when they made an effective contribution to the solution of agricultural adjustment problems. Extremely large social costs have been involved in the form of both the high fiscal costs of commodity price-support programs and the consequent high food prices to consumers.

The lessons that the newly developing countries can learn from the failure of the United States and Japan to cope with their agricultural adjustment problems are as important as the lessons that can be learned from their success in achieving agricultural productivity growth in the early stage of development.

66. For a very useful analysis of the problem of agricultural adjustment under conditions of relatively fixed resources see Glenn L. Johnson and C. Leroy Quance, *The Overproduction Trap in U.S. Agriculture* (Baltimore: Johns Hopkins University Press, 1972). For an earlier analysis see Clark Edwards, "Resource Fixity and Farm Organization," *Journal of Farm Economics* 41 (November 1959):747–59.

IV

CAN GROWTH BE TRANSFERRED?

9

International Transfer of
Agricultural Technology

In attempting to explain productivity differentials among countries (Chapter 6), we found that a substantial share of the differences is accounted for by differences in the proxy variables for knowledge (general and technical education). The more detailed comparisons between the United States and Japan (Chapters 7 and 8) indicate that dialectic interaction among farmers, public institutions, and private farm supply firms resulted in a highly developed mechanical technology in U.S. agriculture and a highly developed biological technology in Japanese agriculture consistent with the resource endowments of the two countries.

It was also argued that the conventional treatment of technical change in agriculture in most development models, as a factor that shifts the production function without imposing any substantial demands on resource inputs, is inadequate. The production of technical change in agriculture imposes a substantial pressure on resource utilization, particularly the relatively limited pool of scientific and technical manpower available to the agricultural sector in most developing economies. The short-run supply of such manpower, and of the new scientific and technical knowledge required for agricultural development, appears to be relatively inelastic with respect to increases in expenditures on research personnel in both developed and less developed countries.

Enormous differences in agricultural productivity among countries seem to imply that less developed countries can acquire substantial gains in agricultural productivity by borrowing advanced technology existing in developed countries. In fact this was the premise on which the diffusion model was adopted as a major foundation for technical assistance after World War II, leading to an extension bias in development assistance programs in the 1950s (Chapter 3).

Efforts to achieve agricultural development by the direct transfer of agricultural technology from other agroclimatic regions have been largely unsuccessful. Modern agricultural technology has evolved primarily in the developed countries of the temperate zone and is adapted to their ecology and factor endowments.[1] Inadequate recognition of the location-specific character of agricultural technology was a major reason for the lack of effectiveness of much of the technical assistance effort of national and international agencies during the 1950s and 1960s. Major emphasis was placed on extension projects designed primarily to transfer materials and practices from the developed to the less developed countries and on the implementation of multipurpose, and frequently superficial, community development efforts. In reviewing the agricultural efforts of the 1950s and early 1960s, Albert H. Moseman points out that "this 'extension bias' met with only limited success because of the paucity of applicable indigenous technology and the general unsuitability of U.S. temperate zone materials and practices to tropical agricultural conditions."[2]

Yet the effective transfer of technology is critically important to the agricultural development process. Although there exist a few ready-made technologies (for example, particular machinery or seeds) for international diffusion, transfer of knowledge and the development of indigenous capacity to generate an ecologically adapted and economically viable agricultural technology are vital to the progress of less developed countries.

In this chapter we attempt to draw insights from earlier research on the diffusion of culture and technology that may contribute to a more adequate understanding of the processes involved in the international diffusion of agricultural technology. This analysis leads us to place particular emphasis on adaptive research and development as the critical elements in the international transfer of agricultural technology. Finally, we specify the implications of our analysis for the continued diffusion of the technical potential opened up by the green revolution of the late 1960s. We also attempt to place in historical perspective the changes in grain production in the tropics since the late 1960s. We draw particularly on the impact of the diffusion of Japanese rice technology in Taiwan and Korea in the 1920s and 1930s.

DIFFUSION MODELS AND INTERNATIONAL TECHNOLOGY TRANSFER

There are multiple traditions of research on diffusion processes: in anthropology, economics, geography, sociology, and other disciplines. Each tradition has evolved a somewhat different model of the diffusion process.[3]

1. The role of ecological and environmental factors has largely been neglected in the economic development literature. For a useful discussion of the special constraints on agricultural development associated with tropical environments see Andrew M. Kamarck, *The Tropics and Economic Development* (Baltimore: Johns Hopkins University Press, 1976). Kamarck suggests that the recent neglect of climate as a factor in economic development was probably a reaction against an earlier school of geographic determinists.

2. Albert H. Moseman, *Building Agricultural Research Systems in the Developing Nations* (New York: Agricultural Development Council, 1970), p. 71.

3. For a review of these several traditions see Elihu Katz, Herbert Hamilton, and Martin L. Levin, "Traditions of Research on the Diffusion of Innovation," *American Sociological Review*

Aside from differences in terminology, real differences among these models exist because they are concerned with different aspects of diffusion phenomena. The main focus of sociologists and geographers has been on the impact of communication (or interaction) and sociocultural resistance to innovation on the pattern of diffusion over time and across space. There has been particular concern with understanding how the different sociocultural characteristics of adopters create a spectrum ranging from innovators to laggards, and how these characteristics determine the means of communication that are most effective in accelerating the diffusion process.[4] The models of economists have focused on how economic variables such as the profitability of innovation and the asset position of firms influence the rate of diffusion.[5]

These models have, with a few exceptions, only limited relevance for the international transfer of technology in agriculture. They have typically been designed to describe or analyze diffusion within a particular area over time. The attributes of the technology and of potential adopters until recently have been taken as givens.[6] The assumption of ready availability and of direct transferability of the technology within the area represents a critical limitation in using these diffusion models to understand the process of international

28 (April 1963):237–52. For an attempt to develop and implement a model that incorporates the concepts and variables drawn from the sociological, spatial, and economic diffusion literature see Robert K. Lindner, "Adoption as a Decision Theoretic Process" (Ph.D. dissertation, University of Minnesota, 1981). For useful reviews of diffusion studies in agriculture see Gershon Feder, Richard Just, and David Zilberman, "Adoption of Agricultural Innovations in Developing Countries: A Survey," *Economic Development and Cultural Change* (January 1985):255–98; Stephen D. Biggs and Edward J. Clay, "Generation and Diffusion of Agricultural Technology: A Review of Theories and Experiences" (Geneva: International Labor Organization Working Paper 122, 1983).

4. Everett M. Rogers, *Diffusion of Innovations*, 3d ed. (New York: Free Press of Glencoe, 1983); Allan Pred, "Postscript," in Torsten Hägerstrand, *Innovation Diffusion as a Spatial Process* (Chicago: University of Chicago Press, 1967), pp. 299–324; Lawrence A. Brown, *Innovation Diffusion: A New Perspective* (New York: Methuen, 1981).

5. Zvi Griliches, "Hybrid Corn: An Exploration in the Economics of Technological Change," *Econometrica* 25 (October 1957):501–22; "Hybrid Corn and the Economics of Innovation," *Science* 132 (July 29, 1960):275–80. For a retest of the Griliches model see Robert Dixon, "Hybrid Corn Revisited," *Econometrica* 48 (September 1980):1451–61. For the diffusion of industrial technology see Edwin Mansfield, "Technical Change and the Rate of Imitation," *Econometrica* 29 (October 1961):741–66; "The Speed of Response of Firms to New Techniques," *Quarterly Journal of Economics* 77 (May 1963):291–311; "Size of Firm, Market Structure, and Innovation," *Journal of Political Economy* 71 (December 1963):556–76; "Intrafirm Rates of Diffusion of an Innovation," *Review of Economics and Statistics* 45 (November 1963):348–59; Bela Gold, "Technological Diffusion in Industry: Research Needs and Shortcomings," *Journal of Industrial Economics* 29 (March 1981):247–69.

6. This has been of concern to some of the leaders in the field of diffusion research. Hägerstrand, in summarizing his work, points out: "In the models attention was directed to the processes of change, to how the distribution of g_n generates the distribution of g_{n+1}. The location of the starting point of the diffusion process was stated among the assumptions. However, we observe that when agricultural indicators and agricultural elements are involved, the same small areas within the region seem repeatedly to be the starting points for new innovation. . . . The origin of such centers is a problem in itself." Hägerstrand, *Innovation Diffusion*, p. 293.

diffusion of technology in situations where variations in ecological conditions and factor endowments among countries severely restrict the direct transfer of agricultural technology.

The Role of Research in Technology Diffusion

The study by Griliches of the diffusion of hybrid corn is a rare attempt to incorporate the mechanism of local adaptation into a diffusion model.[7] The study is of relevance because the diffusion of hybrid corn among geographic areas, through the development of locally adapted varieties, is similar to our view of the process of the international technology transfer in agriculture. "Hybrid corn was the invention of a method of inventing, a method of breeding superior corn for specific localities. It was not a single invention immediately adaptable everywhere. The actual breeding of adaptable hybrids had to be done separately for each area. Hence, besides the differences in the rate of adoption of hybrids by farmers . . . we have also to explain the lag in the development of adaptable hybrids for specific areas."[8]

The procedure employed by Griliches was to summarize the diffusion path for each hybrid corn maturity area by fitting an S-shaped logistic trend function to data on the percentage of corn area planted with hybrid seed. The logistic trend function is described by three parameters—an origin, a slope, and a ceiling. Griliches used differences in the *slope,* which measures the rate of acceptance, and the *ceiling,* which measures the percentage of acceptance at which use of hybrid seed tended to stabilize, of the S-shaped logistic curve to measure changes in the demand for hybrid seed. He interpreted his results as indicating that differences among regions in the rate (slope) and level (ceiling) of acceptance are both functions of the profitability of a shift from open-pollinated to hybrid corn. Variations in these two parameters among regions are thus explained in terms of farmers' profit-seeking behavior. In this respect Griliches's model is similar to other diffusion models employed by economists.

What makes Griliches's study so relevant to the problem of international

---

7. Griliches, "Hybrid Corn: An Exploration" and "Hybrid Corn and the Economics of Innovation." The Griliches studies are also of interest because subsequent discussions helped to clarify the role of economic and sociocultural factors in the diffusion process. See Lowell Brandner and Murray A. Straus, "Congruence versus Profitability in the Diffusion of Hybrid Sorghum," *Rural Sociology* 24 (December 1959):381–83; Zvi Griliches, "Congruence versus Profitability: A False Dichotomy," ibid. 25 (September 1960):354–56; Everett M. Rogers and A. Eugene Havens, "Adoption of Hybrid Corn: A Comment," ibid. 27 (September 1962):327–30; Zvi Griliches, "Profitability versus Interaction: Another False Dichotomy," ibid. 27 (September 1962):327–30; Jarvis M. Babcock, "Adoption of Hybrid Corn: A Comment," ibid. 27 (September 1962):332–38; Gerald E. Klonglan and E. Walter Coward, Jr., "The Concept of Symbolic Adoption: A Suggested Interpretation," ibid. 35 (March 1970):77–83; Kenneth J. Arrow, "Classification Notes on the Production and Transmission of Technological Knowledge," *American Economic Review* 59 (May 1969):29–35. Arrow points out that "the economists are studying the demand for information by potential innovators and sociologists the problems in the supply of communication channels" (p. 33).

8. Griliches, "Hybrid Corn: An Exploration," p. 502.

technology transfer is that he incorporated into his model the behavior of public research institutions and private agricultural supply firms in making locally adapted hybrid seeds available to farmers. He identified the date of *origin* as the date at which an area began to plant 10 percent of its ceiling acreage to hybrid corn as an indicator of commercial availability. The 10 percent level was chosen as the origin to indicate that the development had passed through the experimental stage and that superior hybrids were available to farmers in commercial quantities. The average lag between technical availability and commercial availability was approximately two years. He attempted to explain variations in the date of origin, or of commercial availability, by the size and density of the hybrid seed market, estimated from the size and density of corn production.

From this analysis Griliches derived the conclusion that the efforts of both the agricultural experiment stations and the commercial seed companies were guided by the expected return to research, development, and marketing costs. In spite of the lack of a direct market test of the returns to research and development, in the case of the publicly (USDA and state) supported experiment stations, the "contribution of the various experiment stations is strongly related to the importance of corn in the area. In the 'good' corn areas the stations did a lot of work on hybrids and in the marginal areas, less."[9] This implies, as hypothesized in our discussion of the induced innovation model (Chapter 4), that public research institutions are motivated and in fact attempt to maximize social returns (social returns of the region) to their research expenditure.

Similar interregional variations in development and marketing activities are consistent with the private profit maximization behavior of the commercial seed companies. Larger size and higher density of market imply larger potential sales and lower marketing costs of the firms. In addition, the cost of commercial development of local hybrids would be lower in those regions characterized by the most intensive hybrid corn research.[10]

One of the great merits in the Griliches model is that it incorporates the mechanism of local adaptation in the interregional transfer of agricultural technology. This mechanism is based on the behavior of public research institutions and private agricultural supply firms. Modification of the model is needed, however, when we apply it to the study of international technology transfer.

In the United States there exist a large stock of scientific and technical manpower, a well-structured federal-state experiment station network, and vigorous entrepreneurship in private farm supply firms. The mechanism for inducing the research and development necessary for local adaptation of technology functions efficiently. When these conditions are not met, even if the

9. Ibid., p. 511.
10. A Richard Crabb, *The Hybrid-Corn Makers: The Prophets of Plenty* (New Brunswick: Rutgers University Press, 1947).

expected payoff from the transfer of a particular technology is potentially very high, the supply of adaptive research may be very inelastic. The problem of facilitating international technology transfer as an instrument of agricultural development is, therefore, how to institutionalize an elastic supply of adaptive research and development. We hypothesize that the most serious constraints on the international transfer of agricultural technology are limited experiment station capacity in the case of biological technology and limited industrial capacity in the case of mechanical technology. The inelastic supply of scientific and technical manpower represents a critical limiting factor in both cases.

Phases of International Technology Transfer

The international diffusion of agricultural technology is not new. The classical studies by Sauer and Vavilov indicate that intercountry and intercontinental diffusion of better husbandry practices and of crop varieties and livestock breeds was a major source of productivity growth even in prehistory.[11] It is well known that transfer of new crops such as potatoes, maize, and tobacco from the new continents to Europe after the discovery of America had a dramatic impact on European agriculture.[12] Before agricultural research and extension were institutionalized, this diffusion took place as a by-product of travel, discovery, and trade. Over a long gestation period (several decades or centuries) exotic plants and techniques were gradually adapted to local conditions. But by the latter half of the nineteenth century the process of international transfer of crop plants and domestic livestock had become highly institutionalized.[13]

This natural diffusion can be a significant source of agricultural productivity growth in preindustrial economies in which the required rate of growth in agricultural output is in the range of 1.0 percent per year. This does not seem consistent with the requirements of economies characterized by modern rates of growth in demand for agricultural output in the range of 3 to 6 percent per year.

It appears useful to distinguish the three phases of international technology transfer as (a) material transfer, (b) design transfer, and (c) capacity transfer. The first phase is characterized by the simple transfer or import of new

11. See Carl O. Sauer, *Agricultural Origins and Dispersals: The Domestication of Animals and Foodstuffs*, 2d ed. (Cambridge, Mass.: Massachusetts Institute of Technology Press, 1969), pp. 113–34; N. I. Vavilov, *The Origin, Variation, Immunity and Breeding of Cultivated Plants*, trans. from the Russian by K. Starr Chester, *Chronica Botanica*, vol. 13, nos. 1–6 (1949–50). See also David R. Harris, "New Light on Plant Domestication and the Origins of Agriculture: A Review," *Geographical Review* 57 (January 1967):90–107.

12. See Folke Dovring, "The Transformation of European Agriculture," *The Cambridge Economic History of Europe*, vol. 6, *The Industrial Revolution and After*, Part II, ed. H. J. Habakkuk and M. Postan (Cambridge: Cambridge University Press, 1966), pp. 604–72.

13. See Nelson Klose, *America's Crop Heritage: The History of Foreign Plant Introduction by the Federal Government* (Ames: Iowa State College Press, 1950); Lucile H. Brockway, *Science and Colonial Expansion: The Role of the British Royal Botanic Gardens* (New York: Academic Press, 1979).

materials such as seeds, plants, animals, machines, and techniques associated with these materials. Local adaptation is not conducted in an orderly and systematic fashion. The naturalization of plants and animals, the local adaptation of borrowed technology, and the development of new machines tend to occur primarily as a result of trial and error by farmers, blacksmiths, and mechanics.[14]

In the second phase, the transfer of technology is primarily through the transfer of certain designs (blueprints, formulas, books, etc.). During this period the imports of exotic plant materials and foreign equipment are made in order to obtain new plant breeding materials or to copy equipment designs, rather than for their use in direct production. New plants and animals are subject to orderly tests and are propagated through systematic multiplication. Domestic production of the machines imported in the previous phase is initiated. This phase usually corresponds to an early stage of evolution of publicly supported agricultural research in that experiment stations conduct, primarily, simple tests and demonstrations.

In the third phase, the transfer of technology is made through the transfer of scientific knowledge and capacity which enable the production of locally adaptable technology, following the "prototype" technology which exists abroad. Increasingly, plant and animal varieties are bred locally to adapt them to local ecological conditions. The imported machinery designs are modified in order to meet climatic and soil requirements and factor endowments of the economy. An important element in the process of capacity transfer is the migration of agricultural scientists. In spite of advances in communications, diffusion of the ideas and craft of agricultural science depends heavily on extended personal contact and association.[15] The transfer of scientists is often

14. See, for example, R. H. Green and S. H. Hymer, "Cocoa in the Gold Coast: A Study in the Relations between African Farmers and Agricultural Experts," *Journal of Economic History* 26 (September 1966):299–319. The crucial innovations leading to the rapid growth of Gold Coast cocoa production "were made in the 1880's by Ghanaians, and they succeeded in spite of, not because of, the colonial department's efforts" (p. 302); Arthur J. Dommen, "The Bamboo Tube Well: A Note on an Example of Indigenous Technology," *Economic Development and Cultural Change* 23 (April 1975):483–89; Edward J. Clay, "The Economics of the Bamboo Tubewell: Dispelling Some Myths about Appropriate Technology," *Ceres* 13 (May–June 1980):43–47. For a discussion of the possible strengths and limitations of informal (in contrast to institutional) research and development see Stephen D. Biggs and Edward J. Clay, "Sources of Innovation in Agricultural Technology," *World Development* 9 (April 1981):321–36.

15. For insight into the relationships between the transfer of ideas and the migration of individuals and groups see Warren C. Scoville, "Minority Migrations and the Diffusion of Technology," *Journal of Economic History* 11 (Fall 1951):347–60; Fritz E. Redlich, "Ideas— Their Migration in Space and Transmittal over Time," *Kyklos* 6 (1953):301–22; Robert Solo, "The Capacity to Assimilate an Advanced Technology," *American Economic Review* 56, Papers and Proceedings (May 1966):91–97. The embodiment of scientific and technical knowledge in individuals and institutions is one of the reasons that the multinational firm occupies such an important, and often controversial, role in the transfer of industrial technology. It is also the basis for the policies of the national governments in developing countries to encourage multinationals to establish local research and development facilities, to upgrade local production, technical, and management skills, and to purchase components from local suppliers. See Edwin Mansfield, Anthony Romeo, Mark Schwartz, David Teece, Samuel Wagner, and Peter Brach, *Technology*

of critical importance to ease the constraint of the short supply of scientific and technical manpower in the less developed countries. It is necessary to speed up the entrance of these countries into the capacity transfer phase. These phases of international technology transfer of a biological technology can be illustrated by the international transfer of sugarcane technology.[16]

Transfer of Biological Technology: The Case of Sugarcane

Robert Evenson's study of the development of sugarcane varieties is of interest because it represents a major example of the international transfer of biological technology in agriculture, and because the process has evolved from a simple transfer of plants to the phase of capacity transfer.[17]

Evenson identified four stages of development in sugarcane varieties: Stage 1—Natural Selection (Wild Canes). The cane plant reproduces asexually. Until the late 1800s relatively few wild or native varieties were commercially produced. These varieties apparently were the result of natural asexual reproduction. They were transmitted between countries, but the transmission was extremely slow. For example, the "Bourbon" cane, the major Stage I cane in the nineteenth century, was not introduced to the British West Indies until 1785, almost a hundred years after it was a commercial cane in Madagascar.

Stage II—Sexual Reproduction (Noble Canes). The discovery of the fertility of the sugarcane plant in 1887, independently in Barbados and in Java, established the basis for the breeding of new varieties. Under proper conditions the cane plant can be induced to flower and produce seedlings. Each new seedling is then a potential new variety since it can be reproduced asexually. The early man-made varieties were produced using the existing commercial

---

Transfer, Productivity and Economic Policy (New York: W. W. Norton, 1982), pp. 14–24, 64–107.

16. There is also a large literature on the international transfer of industrial technology. This literature has stressed the role of product market rather than factor market inducements for technological innovation and transfer. Much of this literature stems from the seminal paper by Raymond Vernon, "International Investment and International Trade in the Product Cycle," *Quarterly Journal of Economics* 80 (May 1966):190–207. See also the several articles in Raymond Vernon, ed., *The Technology Factor in International Trade* (New York: Columbia University Press, 1970), and Mansfield et al., *Technology Transfer, Productivity and Economic Policy.*

17. This section draws on R. E. Evenson, J. P. Houck, Jr., and V. W. Ruttan, "Technical Change and Agricultural Trade: Three Examples—Sugarcane, Bananas, and Rice," *The Technology Factor in International Trade,* ed. Raymond Vernon (New York: Columbia University Press, 1970), pp. 415–80; Robert Evenson, "International Transmission of Technology in the Production of Sugarcane," *Journal of Development Studies* 12 (January 1976):208–31; Robert E. Evenson and Yoav Kislev, *Agricultural Research and Productivity* (New Haven: Yale University Press, 1975), pp. 140–55; Robert E. Evenson, "Cycles in Research Productivity in Sugarcane, Wheat and Rice," *Resource Allocation and Productivity in National and International Agricultural Research,* ed. Thomas M. Arndt, Dana G. Dalrymple, and Vernon W. Ruttan (Minneapolis: University of Minnesota Press, 1977) pp. 209–36; Robert E. Evenson and Hans P. Binswanger, "Technology Transfer and Research Resource Allocation," *Induced Innovation: Technology, Institutions, and Development,* ed. Hans P. Binswanger and Vernon W. Ruttan (Baltimore: Johns Hopkins University Press, 1978), pp. 164–211.

80-chromosome cane species *Saccharum Officinarum* as parent varieties. Between 1900 and 1920 numerous varieties resulted from this effort. These varieties were transferred widely over the world from experiment stations in Java, India, Barbados, British Guiana, and Hawaii; and when introduced they appeared to be definitely superior to the native varieties. Only simple tests and demonstrations are required, if any, for recipient countries to propagate these varieties. In many cases, however, they were susceptible to diseases and their yield advantages were lost.

Stage III—Interspecific Hybridization (Nobilization).[18] The experiment station in Java (Proefstation Oost Java, P.O.J.) achieved a major advance in cane breeding by introducing the species *Saccharum Spontaneum* into its breeding programs after 1915. Through a series of crosses and back crosses new interspecific hybrids were developed that incorporated the hardiness and disease-resistance of this noncommercial species. Later, the station at Coimbatore, India, developed a series of tri-hybrid canes by introducing a third species, *Saccharum Barberi*. The local *S. Barberi* species resulted in new varieties adaptable to local climate, soil, and disease conditions. The Stage III varieties were disease-resistant and high-yielding, notably those from Java and India. They were transferred to every producing country in the world. While this international transmission was widespread, it did not occur easily without the aid of research and extension efforts in the recipient countries.

Stage IV—Location-Specific Breeding. The Coimbatore, India, station set the stage for modern breeding activity. More than 100 experiment stations are now in existence. In most cases they are pursuing programs that involve systematic selfing and crossing of parent varieties suitable to the specific soil, climate, disease, and economic conditions of relatively small regions. Very little international transfer of varieties is now taking place because most regions are producing cane from varieties produced by the region's experiment station.

It appears possible to interpret sugarcane variety transfers during Evenson's Stages I and IV as clearly belonging to the material transfer and the capacity transfer stages, respectively. Stage II appears to be a transition from the material transfer to the design transfer; and Stage III a transition from the design transfer to the capacity transfer.

Significant implications of this sequence are the increasingly important role which public research has played in developing and "naturalizing" of sugarcane varieties and the sequence running from initial international diffusion of superior varieties to the international diffusion of the capacity to "invent" location-specific varieties superior to the "naturalized" varieties.

18. Interspecific hybrids should be distinguished from single- or double-cross hybrids. Interspecific hybrids are produced by the crossing of two species. The backcross method may be used as in the above case to transfer a single, readily identifiable characteristic such as disease resistance from one variety to another. The backcross method cannot be expected to improve the variety more than the increment achieved by the addition of the single selected character. This is in contrast to hybrid vigor obtained by combining inbred lines (as in corn).

TECHNOLOGY TRANSFER AND THE STRENGTHENING
OF AGRICULTURAL RESEARCH CAPACITY

Technological transfer is intimately linked with institutional development. The most dramatic example of agricultural technology transfer during the last several decades has involved the development and rapid diffusion of modern high-yielding varieties (MVs) of rice, wheat, and other cereals in the tropics. The development and diffusion of the new cereals technology was made possible by a series of institutional innovations in the organization, management, and financing of agricultural research in the less developed countries of the tropics.

The process by which East Asian rice technology and Western wheat technology were transferred from the temperate to the tropical and subtropical zones has been particularly significant. It involved the international migration of scientific manpower and the development of research institutions rather than the direct transfer of materials and designs. The two key elements in the process were (a) the development of an international system of agricultural research and development institutes and (b) the strengthening of national agricultural research systems.

The International Agricultural Research System

At the end of World War II, the Food and Agriculture Organization (FAO) of the United Nations was established to perform the functions of a global ministry of food and agriculture.[19] The FAO headquarters was established in Rome. Through its technical assistance and its educational and regional communication and networking activities the FAO has made significant contributions to the development of national research capacity in agriculture. But the FAO's Governing Council and Program Committee, dominated by ministries of agriculture from developed countries, was reluctant to approve a substantial role in the sponsorship and conduct of research as part of the FAO's regular program. There was also a pervasive perception, at the time the FAO was established, that lagging agricultural development was primarily a consequence of failure to make effective use of available technology. Lack of more productive technology was not itself seen as a major barrier to agricultural development.

By the late 1950s, this view had changed. Technical assistance and community development programs, based explicitly or implicitly on the diffusion model (Chapter 3), had failed to generate either rapid modernization of traditional farms and villages or rapid growth in agricultural production (Chapter 12). The perception of declining growth in food production, particularly in

19. This section draws heavily on the chapter "The International Agricultural Research System" in Vernon W. Ruttan, *Agricultural Research Policy* (Minneapolis: University of Minnesota Press, 1982), pp. 116–46. For a history of the establishment and early development of the FAO, see Gove Hambidge, *The Story of FAO* (New York: Van Nostrand, 1955).

South Asia, during the late 1950s led to the placing of the development of agricultural research capacity in the tropics higher on the agenda of development assistance institutions and of national governments.[20] The decision to invest in strengthening research capacity in the developing countries was reinforced by the growing evidence, articulated most effectively in Theodore W. Schultz's book *Transforming Traditional Agriculture,* of the larger growth dividends from agricultural research.[21]

During the 1960s the international research and training institutes emerged; they were perceived by the assistance agencies as the most effective way to organize scientific capacity to generate technical change in agriculture in the developing countries. The international institute model draws on two historical traditions. One is the experience of the great colonial agricultural research institutes that played such an important role in increasing the production of a number of tropical export commodities, including rubber, sugar, tea, and sisal. The Rubber Research Institute of Malaya and the sugar research institutes in Barbados, Java, and India, referred to earlier in this chapter, were important examples.[22]

The international institute model drew more immediately on the experience of the Rockefeller Foundation in Mexico and the Ford and Rockefeller foundations in the Philippines.[23] The Rockefeller Foundation's agricultural sciences program was initiated in 1943 with the establishment of the Oficina de Estudies Especiales in cooperation with the Mexican Ministry of Agriculture. Field research programs were first initiated with wheat and corn. The program was later expanded to include field beans, potatoes, sorghum, vegetable crops, and animal production. A U.S. specialist was brought in as each commodity program was initiated. Each specialist assembled a staff of young Mexican university graduates, who were trained in research methods and practices through participation in the research programs. Some of the most promising were later selected for further training at the postgraduate level.

20. Max F. Millikan and David Hapgood, *No Easy Harvest: The Dilemma of Agriculture in Underdeveloped Countries* (Boston: Little, Brown, 1967).

21. Theodore W. Schultz, *Transforming Traditional Agriculture* (New Haven: Yale University Press, 1964).

22. Charles Jeffries, *A Review of Colonial Research, 1940–1960* (London: HMSO, 1964); Geoffrey B. Masefield, *A History of the Colonial Agricultural Service* (Oxford: Clarendon Press, 1972).

23. For an account of these developments see E. C. Stakman, Richard Bradfield, and Paul C. Mangelsdorf, *Campaigns against Hunger* (Cambridge, Mass.: Harvard University Press, 1967); also Sterling Wortman and Ralph W. Cummings, Jr., *To Feed This World: The Challenge and the Strategy* (Baltimore: Johns Hopkins University Press, 1978), pp. 113–85; J. G. Crawford, "Development of the International Agricultural Research System," *Resource Allocation and Productivity in National and International Agricultural Research,* ed. Thomas M. Arndt, Dana G. Dalrymple, and Vernon W. Ruttan (Minneapolis: University of Minnesota Press, 1977), pp. 281–94. For an account of these same developments written from a Marxian perspective see Edmund K. Oasa and Bruce H. Jennings, "La naturaleza de la investigación social en la agricultura internacional; La experiencia Norte Americana, el IRRI y el CIMMYT" (The nature of social inquiry in international agricultural research: A reproduction of the American experience at IRRI and CIMMYT), *El trimestre económico* 49 (October–December 1982):975–1002.

The wheat program was successful almost from the beginning. Stem rust was diagnosed as a major factor limiting wheat production. Resistant wheat varieties were being distributed to farmers by the fall of 1948. By 1956 the impact on productivity was sufficient to make Mexico independent of the need for imported wheat.

The success of the program in expanding wheat production in Mexico and the perception of an emerging crisis in food production in Asia led to conversations between the Ford Foundation and the Rockefeller Foundation about the possibility of collaborating on a program in Asia. An agreement was reached between the two foundations and the government of the Philippines to establish the International Rice Research Institute (IRRI) in the Philippines in 1959. By 1962 the IRRI facilities had been constructed, a staff was being recruited, and the program was initiated. In 1963 the Rockefeller Foundation's program staff in Mexico was reorganized, with Ford Foundation financial support, to establish the International Center for the Improvement of Maize and Wheat (CIMMYT) to facilitate a stronger international collaborative research effort for these commodities.

During the 1960s the Ford and Rockefeller foundations again collaborated in the establishment of the International Institute of Tropical Agriculture (IITA) in Nigeria and the International Center for Tropical Agriculture (CIAT) in Colombia. With the establishment of these two new centers it became apparent that the financial requirements of the system would soon exceed the capacity of the two foundations. Consultations were held between the Ford and Rockefeller foundations, the World Bank, the Food and Agriculture Organization, and the United Nations Development Program (UNDP) in 1969. Following several informal discussions, a formal meeting was held in May 1971 to organize the Consultative Group on International Agricultural Research (CGIAR). The initial membership included the World Bank, the FAO, and the UNDP as sponsors, plus nine national governments, two regional banks, and three foundations.

The leadership for the Consultative Group is now centered at the World Bank, which provides a chairperson and a secretariat. The Consultative Group established a Technical Advisory Committee (TAC) to provide technical guidance for its work. The TAC consists of a chairperson and twelve scientist members. The FAO provides the TAC secretariat. Technical matters such as new institute initiatives and program changes at existing institutes are referred to the TAC for technical review before action by the CGIAR. The TAC develops draft policy statements for the CGIAR's consideration on priorities within the system and has the authority to initiate investigations and to suggest initiative and program changes to the Consultative Group on its own initiative. Since 1976 the TAC has been charged with the responsibility of organizing comprehensive quinquennial reviews of the programs of the several international research centers and with the periodic analysis of programs that have common elements in the several centers, such as cropping systems or mechanization research.

The international research system grew rapidly under CGIAR sponsorship. Expenditures rose from $1.1 million in 1965 to almost $180 million in 1984. The number of institutions in the CGIAR system expanded to include ten research institutes and three research-related programs (Table 9-1).

By the early 1970s the new international agricultural research system was making a major contribution to the growth of agricultural production in the developing countries. The area planted to the new wheat and rice varieties, initially developed at CIMMYT and IRRI and adapted and disseminated by national agricultural research and extension systems, had expanded rapidly (Table 9-2 and Figure 9-1).

Even the most conservative estimates of the research done at IRRI suggest that by the crop year 1974–75 the supply of rice in all developing countries was approximately 12 percent higher than it would have been if the same total resources had been devoted to the production of rice using only the traditional varieties available before the mid-1970s. The impact of CIMMYT's

FIGURE 9-1. Estimated area planted to modern high-yielding varieties of wheat and rice in Asia (East and South), excluding Communist Asia and Taiwan.

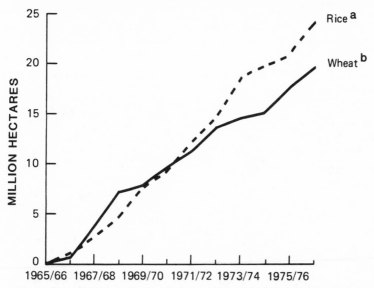

Source: Dana G. Dalrymple, *Development and Spread of High-Yielding Varieties of Wheat and Rice in the Less Developed Nations,* 6th ed. (Washington, D.C.: U.S. Department of Agriculture, Economic Research Service, Office of International Cooperation and Development, Foreign Agricultural Economic Report 95, 1978), p. 117.

Note: [a]Bangladesh, Burma, India, Indonesia, Korea (South), Malaysia (West), Nepal, Pakistan, Philippines, Sri Lanka, Thailand. [b]Bangladesh, India, Nepal, Pakistan.

TABLE 9-1.   The international agricultural research institutes

Center	Location	Research
IRRI (International Rice Research Institute)	Los Baños, Philippines	Rice under irrigation, multiple cropping systems; upland rice
CIMMYT (International Center for the Improvement of Maize and Wheat)	El Batan, Mexico	Wheat (also triticale, barley): maize (also high-altitude sorghum)
ITTA (International Institute of Tropical Agriculture)	Ibadan, Nigeria	Farming systems: cereals (rice and maize as regional relay stations for IRRI and CIMMYT); grain legume (cowpeas, soybeans, lima beans); root and tuber crops (cassava, sweet potatoes, yams)
CIAT (International Centre for Tropical Agriculture)	Palmira, Colombia	Beef; cassava; field beans; swine (minor); maize and rice (regional relay stations to CIMMYI and IRRI)
WARDA	Monrovia, Liberia	Regional cooperative effort in adaptive rice research among 13 nations with IITA and IRRI support.
CIP (International Potato Centre)	Lima, Peru	Potatoes (for both tropical and temperate regions)
ICRISAT (International Crops Research Institute for the Semi-Arid Tropics)	Hyderabad, India	Sorghum; pearl millet; pigeon peas; chickpeas; farming systems; groundnuts
IBPGR (International Board for Plant Genetic Resources)	FAO, Rome, Italy	Conservation of plant genetic material with special reference to crops of economic importance
ILRAD (International Laboratory for Research on Animal Diseases)	Nairobi, Africa	Trypanosoiasis; theileriasis
ILCA (International Livestock Center for Africa)	Addis Ababa, Ethiopia	Livestock production system
ICARDA (International Centre for Agricultural Research in Dry Areas)	Lebanon, Syria	Crop and mixed farming systems research, with focus on sheep, barley, wheat, broad beans, and lentils
IFPRI (International Food Policy Research Institute)	Washington, D.C. United States	Food policy
ISNAR (International Service for National Agricultural Research)	The Hague, Netherlands	Strengthening the capacity of national agricultural research programs

Sources: J. G. Crawford, "Development of the International Agricultural Research System," *Resource Allocation and Productivity in National and International Agricultural Research,* ed. Thomas M. Arndt, Dana G. Dalrymple, and Vernon W. Ruttan (Minneapolis: University of Minnesota Press, 1977), pp. 282–83. Budget data for 1984 were obtained from the Secretariat for the Consultative Group on International Agricultural Research, World Bank, Washington, D.C.

Coverage	Date of initiation	Core budget for 1984 ($000,000)
Worldwide, special emphasis on Asia	1960	22.5
Worldwide	1966	21.0
Worldwide in lowland tropics, special emphasis on Africa	1967	21.2
Worldwide in lowland tropics, special emphasis on Latin America	1968	23.1
West Africa	1971	2.9
Worldwide, including linkages with developed countries	1971	10.9
Worldwide, special emphasis on dry semiarid tropics, nonirrigated farming. Special relay stations in Africa under negotiation	1972	22.1
Worldwide	1974	3.7
Mainly Africa	1973	9.7
Major ecological regions in tropical zones of Africa	1974	12.7
West Asia and North Africa, emphasis on the semiarid winter precipitation zone	1976	20.4
Worldwide	1975	4.2
Worldwide	1980	3.5

TABLE 9-2.   Estimated area planted to modern high-yielding varieties of wheat and rice, 1976–1977 (hectares)

Region	Wheat	Rice	Total
Asia (South and East)	19,672,300	24,199,900	43,872,200
Near East (West Asia and North Africa)[a]	4,400,000	40,000	4,440,000
Africa (excl. N. Africa)[a]	225,000	115,000	340,000
Latin America	5,100,000[a]	920,000	6,020,000
Total	29,397,300	25,274,900	54,672,200
		Percent	
Asia (South and East)	72.4	30.4	41.1
Near East (West Asia and North Africa)[a]	17.0	3.6	16.5
Africa (excl. N. Africa)[a]	22.5	2.7	6.5
Latin America	41.0[a]	13.0	30.8
Total	44.2	27.5	34.5

Source: Dana G. Dalrymple, *Development and Spread of High-Yielding Varieties of Wheat and Rice in the Less Developed Nations*, 6th ed. (Washington, D.C.: U.S. Department of Agriculture, Economic Research Service, Office of International Cooperation and Development, Foreign Agricultural Economic Report 95, 1978), pp. x–xi. See also the report by R. W. Herdt and C. Capule, *Adoption, Spread, and Production Impact of Modern Rice Varieties in Asia* (Los Baños, Laguna, Philippines: International Rice Research Institute, 1983). The Herdt-Capule study indicates that 25.1 million hectares were planted to modern rice varieties in 1976–77 and 32.9 million hectares in 1980–81 in Asia.
[a]Particularly rough estimate of area.

research on wheat production probably exceeded the impact of IRRI on rice production.[24]

One result of the very high returns to the initial investments in research at IRRI and CIMMYT has been to create expectations about the performance of the other institutes in the CGIAR system that are unlikely to be realized. In retrospect the wheat and rice programs were able to draw on a large backlog of past research accomplishments on wheat and rice in the temperate regions. Other centers are working on commodities and farming systems specific to the tropics. For commodities such as the millets, tropical legumes, and cassava there was no comparable backlog of scientific and technical knowledge anywhere in the world to be drawn on. As a result, the flow of new technology from the newer institutes, and its impact on agricultural production, has proceeded more slowly. Accomplishments have taken the form of incremental gains rather than revolutionary breakthroughs.

24. R. E. Evenson and P. M. Flores, "Social Returns to Rice Research," *Economic Consequences of the New Rice Technology*, ed. Randolph Barker and Yujiro Hayami (Los Baños, Laguna, Philippines: International Rice Research Institute, 1978), pp. 243–65. See also the discussion of economic returns to international research in Per Pinstrup-Andersen, *Agricultural Research and Technology in International Development* (London: Longman, 1982), pp. 105–23.

But the newer institutes have made significant contributions.[25] The International Centre for Tropical Agriculture (CIAT) has developed bean varieties that are being produced in several South American and Central American countries. Cassava varieties with resistance to mosaic and bacterial wilt developed at the International Institute of Tropical Agriculture (IITA) are being grown by African farmers. The International Crops Research Institute for the Semi-Arid Tropics (ICRISAT) has incorporated resistance to downy mildew into varieties of pearl millet that are now being grown in India and in the Sahelian zone in Africa. Each of the institutes has established major germ plasm collections that are available to national programs. The International Board for Plant Genetic Resources (IBPGR) has organized collection expeditions, assisted in the development of computerized systems for the storage of germ plasm collections, and organized an international collaborative network for gathering, maintaining, and distributing genetic materials.

By the early 1980s the international agricultural research system was being faced with a series of questions about the allocation of research resources and about its effectiveness in the generation of new technology.[26] Questions have been raised about the role of the institutes as centers of genetic resource conservation and germ plasm enhancement relative to their role as centers of crop variety development. The relative importance of different approaches to cropping and farming systems and of pre- and postharvest mechanical technology has also been questioned. The institutes have been challenged to direct their research specifically to the development of "small farmer technology." And critics have questioned the environmental compatibility of the new technology that has been generated by the institute. We will return to these issues in subsequent chapters; here we focus on the process of international technology transfer.

The Development of National Agricultural Research Systems

The institutes of the international agricultural research system were developed to facilitate the transfer of agricultural technology from the temperate to the tropical zone and among countries in the tropical zone through the transfer of research capacity. They represent a highly productive institutional innovation. Yet it is clear that the international research centers alone are insufficient to exploit fully the potential gains from international agricultural technology transfer. Agricultural technology is highly location-specific. The process of its transfer involves the adaptation of crops, animals, machines, and farming systems to the environmental conditions of individual countries and to the

25. CGIAR Review Committee, *Second Review of the CGIAR* (Washington, D.C.: Consultative Group on International Agricultural Research Secretariat, World Bank, 1981), pp. 15–21. For more detailed information the reader will find the quinquennial reviews of individual institute programs, available from the CGIAR Secretariat, of value.
26. Ruttan, *Agricultural Research Policy*, pp. 132–42.

different ecological regions within countries. This task requires an intensive network of national and local experiment stations.

By the early 1970s it was generally perceived that the limited capacity of many national research systems was the most serious constraint on realization of the potential gains from new knowledge and new technology that had been generated at the international institutes. One reflection of this concern was the establishment by the Rockefeller Foundation of the International Agricultural Development Service (IADS) in 1977 and by the CGIAR of the International Service for National Agricultural Research (ISNAR) in 1979 to work with bilateral and multilateral assistance agencies and with national governments in efforts to strengthen national agricultural research systems in the developing countries. Both the bilateral and multilateral donors also expanded their direct support of national agricultural research systems in the 1970s.[27]

Investment in the development of national agricultural research systems in the developing countries has expanded rapidly during the 1960s and 1970s. We now are able to trace the trends in the numbers of research scientists and extension workers available to national agricultural research and extension systems (Table 9-3).[28] Such countries as Brazil, India, Nigeria, and the Philippines have made very substantial progress in the development of their national research systems during the last twenty years. Others, including Argentina and Colombia, have experienced a decline in research capacity during the 1970s.

A second observation that stands out in the data presented in Table 9-3 is that the developing countries tend to be relatively extensive-intensive. The lower-income countries tend to employ a larger number of extension workers than research scientists. In contrast, the developed countries tend to employ more research scientists than extension workers. Evenson's analysis supports the conclusion that the developing countries have substituted relatively low-cost extension workers for higher-cost research scientists. And our own observations suggest that commodity specialists, with relatively little research training or capacity, often occupy many of the support and leadership positions in the weaker national research systems.

The supply of extension workers and commodity specialists is more elastic than the supply of research scientists. Many developing countries are still faced with the necessity of trying to conduct agricultural research without

27. Ibid., pp. 125–29.

28. Robert E. Evenson and Yoav Kislev, "Investment in Agricultural Research and Extension: A Survey of International Data," *Economic Development and Cultural Change* 23 (April 1975):507–21; James K. Boyce and Robert E. Evenson, *National and International Agricultural Research and Extension Programs* (New York: Agricultural Development Council, 1975); M. Ann Judd, James K. Boyce, and Robert E. Evenson, "Investing in Agricultural Supply" (New Haven: Yale University Economic Growth Center, Center Discussion Paper 442, 1983). See also Peter A. Oram and Vishva Bindlish, *Resource Allocations to National Agricultural Research: Trends in the 1970's* (The Hague: International Service for National Agricultural Research, and Washington, D.C.: International Food Policy Research Institute, 1981).

TABLE 9-3. Trends in numbers of research scientists and extension workers, 1959–1980

Region/Subregion	Research scientists[a]			Extension workers			Ratio of extension workers to research scientists		
	1959	1970[b]	1980	1959	1970[b]	1980[c]	1959	1970	1980
Western Europe	6,251	12,547	19,540	15,988	24,388	27,881	2.56	1.94	1.43
Northern Europe	1,818	4,409	8,027	4,793	5,638	6,241	2.64	1.23	0.78
Central Europe	2,888	5,721	8,827	7,865	13,046	14,421	2.72	2.28	1.63
Southern Europe	1,545	2,417	2,686	3,330	5,704	7,219	2.16	2.36	2.69
Eastern Europe and USSR[d]	17,701	43,709	51,614	29,000	43,000	55,000	1.64	0.98	1.07
Eastern Europe	5,701	16,009	20,220	9,340	15,749	21,546	1.64	0.98	1.07
USSR	12,000	27,700	31,394	19,660	27,251	33,454	1.64	0.98	1.07
North America and Oceania	8,449	11,688	13,607	13,580	15,113	14,966	1.61	1.29	1.10
North America	6,690	8,575	10,305	11,500	12,550	12,235	1.72	1.46	1.19
Oceania	1,759	3,113	3,302	2,080	2,563	2,731	1.18	0.82	0.83
Latin America	1,425	4,880	8,534	3,353	10,782	22,835	2.35	2.21	2.68
Temperate South America	364	1,022	1,527	205	1,056	1,292	0.56	1.03	0.85
Tropical South America	570	2,698	4,840	2,369	7,591	16,038	4.16	2.81	3.32
Caribbean and Central America	491	1,160	2,167	779	2,135	5,505	1.59	1.84	2.54
Africa[d]	1,919	3,849	8,088	28,700	58,700	79,875	14.96	15.25	9.88
North Africa	590	1,122	2,340	7,500	14,750	22,453	12.71	13.15	9.60
West Africa	412	952	2,466	9,000	22,000	29,478	21.80	23.11	11.95
East Africa	221	684	1,632	9,000	18,750	24,211	40.72	27.41	14.84
South Africa	696	1,091	1,650	3,200	3,200	3,733	4.60	2.93	2.26
Asia[d]	11,418	31,837	46,656	86,900	142,500	148,780	8.55[e]	7.28[e]	5.06[e]
West Asia	457	1,606	2,329	7,000	18,800	16,535	15.31	11.71	7.10
South Asia	1,433	2,569	5,691	57,000	74,000	80,958	39.80	28.80	14.23
Southeast Asia	441	1,692	4,102	9,500	30,500	33,987	21.54	18.03	8.29
East Asia	7,837	13,720	17,262	13,400	19,200	17,300	1.71	1.40	1.00
China	1,250	12,250	17,272	—	—	—			
World total	47,163	108,510	148,039	177,521	294,483	349,337	3.87[e]	3.06[e]	2.67[e]

Source: M. Ann Judd, James K. Boyce, and Robert E. Evenson, "Investing in Agricultural Supply" (New Haven: Yale University Economic Growth Center, Center Discussion Paper 442, 1983).

[a] Estimates for research scientists include only workers with advanced degrees. An attempt has been made to include only research workers engaged in production-related agricultural research. Research on postharvest technology is, for example, not included in these estimates.

[b] 1970 data are an average of data for 1968 and 1971.

[c] 1974 data are used when more recent data are not available. In other cases, the 1980 data are averages for 1974–80.

[d] Data for extension workers in Eastern Europe, USSR, Africa, and Asia are estimated.

[e] Excludes China, for which data on extension workers were not reported.

agricultural scientists. A basic constraint on the ability of developing countries to build more effective agricultural research institutions is their limited domestic capacity to train research scientists. A few countries, such as India, Brazil, and the Philippines, have made substantial progress in building such capacity. But the strengthening of national capacity to train scientists and the design of research institutions capable of making productive use of scarce scientific resources remain among the most critical problems for both national governments and international assistance agencies if they are to make significant progress in exploiting the potential gains from technology transfer and development.[29]

An Induced Technology Transfer Hypothesis for the New Cereals Technology

In the previous section the new tropical grain production technology was viewed as a result of agricultural technology transfer between different ecological zones through the transfer of scientific knowledge and the development of local experiment station capacity. This process involved institutional innovations designed to promote capacity transfer. In this section, we present a model of the economic forces that have induced international and national agencies to change development policies and to design institutional innovations leading to the creation of a new potential for grain production in the tropics.

The modern high-yielding varieties of rice recently developed in tropical Asia, similar to the prototype high-yielding varieties in Japan (demonstrated in Table 4-1, Chapter 4), are distinguished by high fertilizer responsiveness. Their fertilizer-responsive capacity is fully realized only when they are accompanied by improved husbandry practices (for example, weed and insect control) and by adequate water control. Traditional varieties had long survived with little fertilization under unfavorable environmental conditions, including a precarious water supply and rampant weeds. In such conditions the traditional varieties represented an optimal technology.[30]

---

29. Assistance agencies and national governments will also need to address themselves to the question of how to provide external assistance in a manner that strengthens rather than weakens the capacity of national research systems to generate domestic, political, and economic support. In some countries donor assistance has contributed to distortion in the allocation of research resources. A number of national research systems have experienced severe erosion of research capacity following the decline of external support. See Jorge Ardila, Eduardo Trigo, and Martin Piñeiro, "Los recursas humanos en la investigación agropecuria: Tres casos en América Latina," *Desarrollo rural en las Americas* 12 (September–December 1980):233–58; and Vernon W. Ruttan, "Reforming the Global Agricultural Research Support System," *Issues in Third World Development,* ed. Kenneth C. Nobe and Rajan K. Sampath (Boulder, Colo.: Westview Press, 1983).

30. Peter R. Jennings, "Plant Type as a Rice Breeding Objective," *Crop Science* 4 (January–February 1964):13–15, presents the classic statement of the new crop-breeding strategy focusing on models of biologically efficient plant types. See also Te-Tzu Chang, "Genetics and Evolution of the Green Revolution," *Replies from Biological Research: Proceedings of the Symposium on Biology and Ethics: Problems and Positive Results of Scientific Research in*

FIGURE 9-2. Hypothetical process of the induced development of a modern high-yielding variety of rice.

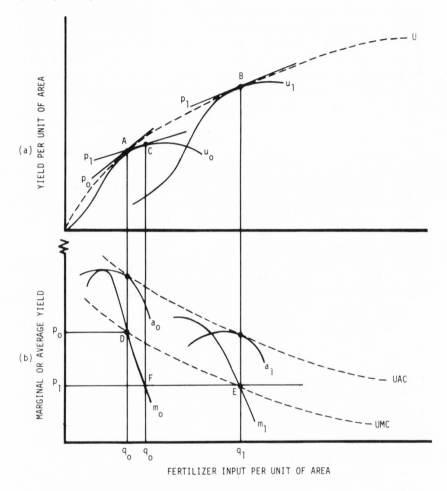

The fertilizer response curves for the traditional varieties and the MVs are typically drawn as u_0 and u_1, respectively, in Figure 9-2a (same as Figure 5-8). We assume the metaproduction function (U), which is the envelope of many such response curves, each representing a variety characterized by a different degree of fertilizer-responsiveness; a_0 and m_0, a_1, and m_1, and UAC and UMC in Figure 9-2 are the average and marginal product curves corre-

Genetics, ed. Roman de Vicente (Madrid: Consejo Superior de Investigaciones Cientificas, 1979), pp. 187–209; and M. S. Swaminathan, "Rice," *Scientific American* 250 (January 1984):80–93.

sponding, respectively, to u_0, u_1, and U; u_0 represents an optimal (profit-maximizing) variety for the fertilizer-rice price ratio, p_0; and u_1 represents an optimum for p_1. However, even if the fertilizer-rice price ratio declines from p_0 to p_1, individual farmers cannot move from A (or D) to B (or E), and will be trapped at C (or F) unless u_1 becomes available. C represents an equilibrium for a response curve (u_0) that is actually available for farmers, but a disequilibrium in terms of potential alternatives described by the metaproduction function (u_1). It is hypothesized that the development of a new variety (u_1) is undertaken when the benefit of adjustment from C (or F) to B (or E) exceeds the cost of development of u_1. This is an oversimplified picture. The location and shape of the fertilizer response curve depends on the conditions of water control and husbandry practices. If water supply and control are inadequate, the MVs would fail to show the fertilizer-responsive character. On the other hand, it is possible that in the paddy fields having good irrigation and drainage facilities the MVs produce higher yields than the traditional varieties, even at the zero level of artificial fertilization. In such fields, significant amounts of plant nutrients are supplied from the efficient decomposition of organic materials and from nutrients carried in by irrigation water. Yield response to fertilizer is also dependent on effective weed control, because short-stalked MVs are more subject to competition for sunlight from vigorous growth of weeds encouraged by the high level of fertilization. Application of herbicides and weed-preventing practices, such as checkrow planting, become of crucial importance in accurate measurement of the fertilizer-response relationships. In this formulation the fertilizer input per hectare should be regarded as an index representing the level of the package of inputs complementary with fertilizer in realizing the yield potential of the MVs.[31]

Adjustments along the metaproduction function involve time and costs. The development of fertilizer-responsive MVs requires investment in research. Better husbandry practices must be developed and learned. Complementary investment in irrigation and drainage may be required to secure adequate control of water. It takes time to reorient the efforts of public agencies in such directions in response to price changes. It is particularly costly and time-consuming to build adequate institutions and competent research staff.

These processes may be inferred with respect to Table 9-4, which compares for Japan and other selected countries in Asia the price of fertilizers relative to the price of rice and rice yield per hectare of paddy area planted. The data in the table indicate (a) that the higher rice yield per hectare in Japan

31. The choice of varieties (u_0 or u_1) depends not only on fertilizer and rice prices but also on the costs of water control and cultural practices. It is a reasonable assumption, however, that the rise in marginal productivity of fertilizer due to the development of the MVs (u_1) raises the marginal productivities of these complementary inputs. A decline in the price of fertilizer can thus play a leading role in changing the economic return on investment in developing the MVs. And the development of higher-yielding varieties can sharply increase the return on investment in irrigation and in plant protection.

TABLE 9-4.   Fertilizer-rice price ratio and rice yield per hectare in selected Asian countries, 1955–57, 1963–65, and 1975–77, and in Japan, 1883–1962

Country	Currency unit	Price of fertilizer per m. ton of nitrogen (1)	Price of rice per m.ton of milled rice[a] (2)	Fertilizer-rice price ratio (1)/(2)	Rice yield per ha, m.ton of paddy[b] (3)
Intercountry comparison					
1955–57					
India	rupee	1,675	417[c]	4.0	1.3
Philippines	peso	962	352	2.7	1.1
Thailand	U.S.$	393	79	5.0	1.4
Japan	1,000 yen	119	77	1.5	4.8
1963–65					
India	rupee	1,750	595	2.9	1.5
Philippines	peso	1,048	530	2.0	1.3
Thailand	U.S.$	229	70	3.3	1.6
Japan	1,000 yen	97	99	1.0	5.0
1975–77					
India	rupee	4,541	1,606	2.8	1.9
Philippines	peso	3,877	1,687	2.3	1.8
Thailand	U.S.$	530	180	2.9	1.8
Japan	1,000 yen	134	343	0.4	6.0
Japan's time series					
1883–87	yen	450	42	10.7	2.6
1893–97	yen	670	69	9.7	2.6
1903–07	yen	815	106	7.7	3.1
1913–17	yen	803	125	6.4	3.5
1923–27	yen	1,021	277	3.7	3.6
1933–37	yen	566	208	2.7	3.8
1953–57	1,000 yen	113	75	1.5	4.3
1963–67	1,000 yen	100	85	1.2	5.1
1973–77	1,000 yen	125	305	0.4	5.8

Sources: Intercountry data: FAO, *Production Yearbook, Fertilizer Annual Review,* and *Fertilizer Yearbook,* various issues. Japan data: Kazushi Ohkawa et al., eds., *Long-term Economic Statistics of Japan,* Vol. 9 (Tokyo: Toyokeizaishimposha, 1966), pp. 202–3; Nobufumi Kayo, ed., *Nihon Nogyo Kisotokei* (Tokyo: Norin Suisangyo Seisankojokaigi, 1958), p. 514; Toyokeizaishimposha, *Bukka Yoran* (Tokyo: 1967), p. 80; Institute of Developing Economies, *One Hundred Years of Agricultural Statistics in Japan* (Tokyo, 1969), p. 136; Japan Ministry of Agriculture, Forestry and Fisheries, *Norinsho Tokeihyo,* various issues.

[a]Wholesale price at a milled rice basis. Data for Japan are converted from a brown rice basis to a milled rice basis assuming 10 percent for processing cost.

[b]Data for Japan are converted from a brown rice basis to a paddy basis assuming 0.8 for a conversion factor.

[c]Price at Sambalpur, Orissa.

than in Southeast Asian countries was associated with a considerably lower price of fertilizer relative to the price of rice; (b) that there was an inverse association between the rice yield per hectare and the fertilizer-rice price ratio in the Japanese time-series data; (c) that the substantial decline in the fertilizer-rice price ratios from 1955–57 to 1963–65 in other Asian countries was

associated with only small gains in rice yield per hectare; (d) that the fertilizer-rice price ratios in the South and Southeast Asian countries in 1963–65,
the years immediately preceding the green revolution, were much more favorable than those that prevailed in Japan at the beginning of this century and
earlier; and (e) that significant gains in rice yield per hectare in the South and
Southeast Asian countries from 1963–65 to 1975–77 were not associated with
further decreases in the fertilizer-rice price ratios.

If we consider the yield comparisons in Table 4-1, it seems reasonable to
infer that the considerable differences in the rice yield and the price ratios
between Japan and Southeast Asian countries can best be interpreted in terms
of the different fertilizer-response curves as shown in u_0 and u_1 in Figure 9-2.
The consistent rise in the rice yield per hectare, accompanied by the consistent
decline in the fertilizer-rice price ratio in the historical experience of Japan,
indicates a process of movement along the metaproduction function. The
history of the development of Japanese agricultural technology, including the
deliberate efforts of veteran farmers to select and propagate superior varieties,
the vigorous activities in experiment stations and other research institutions,
and the remarkable shifts of rice varieties over time, is clearly inconsistent
with an assumption of movement along a fixed production response curve
(u_0).

When we examine the data for Southeast Asia, some intriguing questions
remain unanswered. Why did rice yields per hectare in the Southeast Asian
countries increase so slowly before the mid-1960s, in spite of the substantial
decline in the fertilizer-rice price ratio? And why did rice yields in these
countries remain at low levels despite fertilizer-rice price ratios that were
more favorable than in Japan at the beginning of this century? The answer
must be sought in the time lag required to move along the metaproduction
function. This time lag tends to be extremely long in situations characterized
by lack of adequate institutions and human capital to generate the flow of new
techniques. Apparently before 1960, even though the fertilizer-rice ratio declined from p_0 to p_1, the countries in Southeast Asia could not move from A
(or D) to B (or E) in Figure 9-2 because of a lag in the investment in the
experiment station capacity necessary to create a new technology (u_1). They
seem to have been trapped at C (or F). On the other hand, movements of their
positions from 1963–65 to 1975–77 seem to have been the ones represented
by the movement from C (or F) toward B (or E).

The dramatic appearance of the MVs after 1965 can be interpreted in this
light. The efforts of the International Rice Research Institute, the University
of the Philippines College of Agriculture, and the Bureau of Plant Industry in
the Philippines, of the Japanese plant breeders in Malaysia under the Colombo
Plan, of the Indian Council of Agricultural Research, and of various other
national research organizations were designed to develop fertilizer-responsive
MVs. By the mid-1960s a number of varieties satisfying these requirements,

including IR-8, C4-63 Malinja, and ADT-27, were being released to farmers. It now seems clear that these innovations were induced by a potential high payoff of investment in crop-breeding research, permitting the adjustment from C (or F) to B (or E). Indeed, even though the fertilizer price relative to the rice price did not decline further from 1963–65 to 1975–77, rice yields per hectare increased significantly as the result of MV development that enabled the movement from inside to the surface of the metaproduction function.

Because the prototype high-yielding varieties were already in existence in Japan, the United States, and other temperate zone rice-producing countries before the green revolution, it was possible to realize major advances in potential productivity from a relatively modest research investment. A critical element is that realization of the high payoff to investment in research was dependent on a social decision to invest in research rather than on decisions made by individual firms. The farms operated by Asian producers are, except in the cases of a few export commodities, too small to capture the gains necessary to pay for research investments. It is only when public agencies (or semipublic agencies such as foundations) perceive this opportunity and allocate funds for such research that technological transfer or development becomes feasible.

Declines in the price of fertilizer relative to the price of rice during the 1950s and 1960s were the result of increased productivity in the chemical fertilizer industry in the developed countries. These lower costs were initially transmitted to less developed countries through international trade and later through the growth of domestic fertilizer production.[32] In most parts of Asia characterized by high population density the increase in population and food demand has resulted in increasing pressure against land. It seems reasonable to hypothesize that the payoff of the crop-breeding research was enhanced by the capacity of the MVs to facilitate the substitution of an increasingly abundant factor (fertilizer) for an increasingly scarce factor (land). It seems valid to regard the agricultural research that produced the new fertilizer-responsive varieties as a response to a decline in the price of fertilizer relative to the price of land and to the price of rice. In the absence of a decline in the real price of fertilizer, such research might not have been attempted and, even if attempted, the results would have been incompatible with price relationships among factors and products and would have been similar to earlier attempts to introduce mechanization in tropical rice production. Success of research depends on whether it is directed to the generation of a technology compatible with the market prices that reflect product demand and factor endowments of the economy.

32. Subrata Ghatak with Derek Deadman and Christine Eadie, *Technology Transfer to Developing Countries: The Case of the Fertilizer Industry* (Greenwich, Conn.: JAI Press, 1981).

TRANSFER OF RICE PRODUCTION TECHNOLOGY
FROM JAPAN TO TAIWAN AND KOREA

In this section we attempt to test the hypothesis proposed in the previous section against the experience of transmitting Japanese rice technology to Taiwan and Korea during the 1920s and the 1930s.[33] To be more specific, the hypothesis to be tested is that (a) fertilizer-rice price ratios in Taiwan and Korea before the 1920s had already been favorable enough to make it rewarding to develop the fertilizer-responsive MVs but because of the lack of local research and development capacity in Taiwan and Korea this opportunity had not been exploited; (b) only when the colonial governments, pressed by the demand from the mother country, responded to this opportunity by investing in rice-breeding research were the MVs adaptable to the local ecologies of Taiwan and Korea actually developed; and (c) these MVs represent a technical change biased toward the fertilizer-using and land-saving direction that was compatible with changes in the factor endowments of the economy. As is the case with the recent development of MVs in tropical Asia, this represents a transfer of prototype agricultural technology existing in developed countries (Japan) to less developed countries (Taiwan and Korea), through the transfer of scientists. It is hypothesized that institutional innovations and the increased public investment in research leading to this technology transfer were induced by the high social payoff expected from adjustment from a secular disequilibrium (C in Figure 9-2) to a secular equilibrium (B in Figure 9-1), although the social payoff in this case was primarily in terms of the benefits to Japan rather than to Taiwan and Korea.[34]

Background

The recent development of new MVs in the tropics involved the application of science to the production problems of peasant agriculture, with the ultimate goal of promoting overall economic growth. This was the process of agricultural development in Japan, Taiwan, and Korea until the collapse of the Japanese Empire during World War II. The primary purpose was to finance and support industrial development in metropolitan Japan by generating agricultural surpluses through increased productivity. The technological potentials available in the late nineteenth and early twentieth centuries were first exploited in domestic agriculture in Japan, and when they were exhausted, the colonial agricultural development policy was launched.

---

33. This section draws on Yujiro Hayami, ''Elements of Induced Innovation: A Historical Perspective for the Green Revolution,'' *Explorations in Economic History* 8 (Summer 1971):445–72.

34. For further discussion of the relevance of Japan's experience with technical change for contemporary experience in Southeast Asia see Shigeru Ishakawa, *Essays on Technology, Employment and Institutions in Economic Development: Comparative Asian Experience* (Tokyo: Kinokuniya Co., 1981), pp. 151–251.

FIGURE 9-3. Indices (in logs) of total production and yield per hectare of rice, Japan, Korea, and Taiwan, five-year moving average, 1890–1935. 1917–22 = 100.

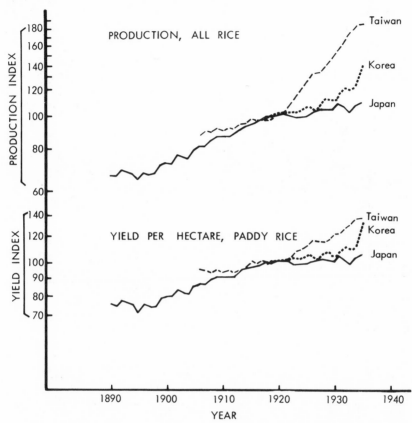

Sources: Japan—*LTES,* 9:166–67; *Norimsho Ruinen Tokeihyo* (Historical statistics of Ministry of Agriculture and Forestry), (Tokyo, 1945), p. 24. Korea—*Chosen Sotokutu Tokeihyo* (Statistical yearbook of Government General Korea), 1925 issue (p. 94), 1930 issue (p. 92). Taiwan—Chinese-American Joint Commission on Rural Construction, Taiwan Agricultural Statistics (Taipei, 1966), pp. 23–27.

This process is reflected in the movements in rice production and yield per hectare in Japan, Taiwan, and Korea (Figures 9-3 and 9-4).[35] The major source of rice output increase necessary to meet the increase in consumer demand, associated with rapid industrialization and urbanization in Japan through the first two decades of the twentieth century, was primarily yield increases in domestic agriculture in the western part of Japan until around

35. It should be remembered that double cropping of rice is commonly practiced in Taiwan while it is virtually nonexistent in Japan and Korea. Productivity of land in Taiwan is, therefore, higher, relative to Japan and Korea, than the rice yield per hectare planted indicates.

FIGURE 9-4. Rice yields per hectare planted for Japan, Taiwan, and Korea, five-year moving average, 1895–1935.

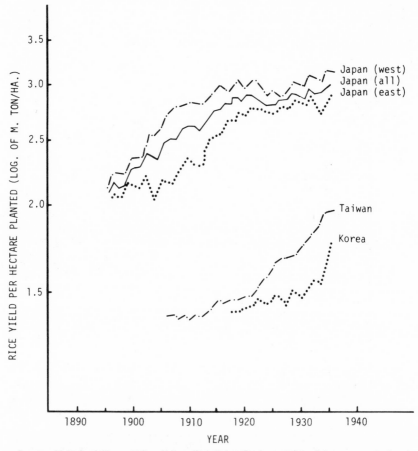

Sources: Nobufumi Kayo, *Nihon Nogyo Kiso Tokei* (Basic statistics of Japanese agriculture) (Tokyo: Norin-Suisangyo Seisansei Kojo Kaigi, 1958):607–52; Taiwan Government-General, *Taiwan Nogyo Nenpo* (Yearbook of Taiwan agriculture), (Taipei), various issues; Korea Government-General, *Nogyo Tokeihyo* (Agricultural statistics) (Seoul), various issues.

1905 and in the eastern part from 1905 to 1920. These differential rates of growth in the East and West reflect the lag in diffusion of improved varieties and techniques to the East.

As we indicated in Chapter 8, the agricultural productivity growth of Japan in the Meiji period (1868–1911) was supported by the propagation of techniques, practiced by the better farmers, which were screened and tailored by experiment station workers following the modern agricultural science traditions observed in Germany. The initial phase of rice yield increase was caused by the diffusion of superior varieties selected by veteran farmers (*rōnō*) in the western part of Japan, which included the most advanced regions (Kinki and Northern Kyushu). The superior varieties in the West provided the prototype for farmers and experiment station workers in the East in developing improved varieties for their ecologies. Regional patterns in the spread of the *rōnō* varieties (Figure 8.4, Chapter 8) are consistent with movements in rice yields (Figure 9-4).

It appears that this process of rice productivity growth in Meiji Japan—a significant decline in the fertilizer-rice price ratio, the spread of improved varieties, and increases in fertilizer input and rice yield per hectare from 1895 to 1915 (rows 1–4, Table 9-5)—indicates movement along the metaproduction function in response to a decline in the fertilizer-rice price ratio, as represented by a movement from *A* to *B* in Figure 9-2.

The development and diffusion of these high-yielding varieties were also based on the relatively well-established water-control facilities in Japanese paddy fields, which raised the potential payoff of the improved varieties. Even at the beginning of the Meiji Restoration almost 100 percent of the paddy fields in Japan were irrigated, although the water supply was not necessarily sufficient, and appropriate drainage was lacking in many cases.[36] These irrigation systems had been built during the long, peaceful feudal Tokugawa period, primarily by communal labor under the encouragement of feudal lords.

As described in Chapter 8, the exploitation of indigenous potential and the lag in scientific research in supplying new potential, when confronted with the expansion of demand during World War I, resulted in a serious rice shortage and forced the rice price upward to an unprecedented level. This caused serious disruption in the urban areas, culminating in the *Kome Sodo* (rice riot) in 1918.

Japan was then faced with a choice between high rice prices, high cost of living, and high wages, on the one hand, and a drain on foreign exchange by large-scale rice imports, on the other. Both were unfavorable to industrial development. The reaction of the government was to organize programs to import rice from the overseas territories of Korea and Taiwan. In order to release rice for export to Japan, short-run exploitation policies, which involved importing millet to Korea from Manchuria, forced Korean farmers to substitute lower-quality grain for rice in domestic consumption. A similar squeeze was also practiced in Taiwan, forcing Taiwanese farmers to substitute sweet potatoes for rice in their diet. This was enforced by a squeeze on real income through taxation and government monopoly sales of such commodities as liquor, tobacco, and salt. The longer-run program was to intro-

---

36. The fact that no statistics have ever been collected on the irrigated area is consistent with the fact that in Japan "paddy field" and "irrigated field" have been regarded as identical. Construction of drainage facilities has been the primary objective in land improvement projects in Japan.

TABLE 9-5. Fertilizer-rice price ratio, seed improvement, fertilizer input, and rice yield per hectare: Japan, Taiwan, and Korea, selected years

	1895	1905	1915	1920	1925	1930	1935
Japan							
1) Fertilizer-rice price ratio (m. tons of brown rice purchasable with a ton of $N + P_2O_5 + K_2O$	7.0	5.2	4.4	3.5	3.0	3.0	2.2
2) Ratio of area planted in improved varieties to total paddy area planted in rice	0.04	0.30	0.40	0.42	0.42	0.56	0.56
3) Fertilizer input per ha. (kg of $N + P_2O_5 + K_2O$)	13	24	49	63	79	96	104
4) Rice yield per ha. (m. tons of brown rice)	2.06	2.46	2.79	2.91	2.84	2.89	3.04
Taiwan							
5) Fertilizer-rice price ratio (m. tons of brown rice purchasable with a ton of $N + P_2O_5 + K_2O$)					4.5	4.5	4.2
6) Ratio of area planted in Ponlai varieties to total paddy area planted in rice					0.13	0.23	0.46
7) Fertilizer input per ha. (kg of $N + P_2O_5 + K_2O$)				12	20	33	55
8) Rice yield per ha. (m. tons of brown rice)			1.47	1.47	1.63	1.75	1.97
Korea							
9) Fertilizer-rice price ratio (m. tons of brown rice purchasable with a ton of $N + P_2O_5 + K_2O$)				3.3	3.0	3.5	2.5
10) Ratio of area planted in Japanese varieties to total paddy area planted in rice				0.22	0.57	0.72	0.84
11) Fertilizer input per ha. (kg. of $N + P_2O_5 + K_2O$)				1.3	3.4	12	28
12) Rice yield per ha. (m. tons of brown rice)				1.43	1.50	1.48	1.82

Notes: Data are five-year averages, centering at the years shown except for arable land area, which is measured at the years shown.
1) Unit price of plant nutrients in commercial fertilizer divided by unit price of rice. (*Source:* Kazushi Ohkawa et al., ed., *Long-term Economic Statistics of Japan since 1868* [abbreviated as *LTES*] 9 [Tokyo: Toyokeizaishimposha, 1966]: 146–47, 166–68 and 194–201.)

2) Series J10 in Appendix Table C-3.

3) Plant nutrients contained in commercial fertilizers per hectare of arable land. (*Source:* Series J6 and J9 in Appendix Table C-3.)

4) Yield per hectare planted in paddy rice. (*Source:* Series J10 in Appendix Table C-3.)

5) Unit price of plant nutrients in commercial fertilizer divided by unit price of rice. Commodity flow estimates of fertilizer consumption (production + import − export) after 1932 were spliced to the estimates for preceding years based on rural survey by multiplying by the 1929–32 average ratio. (*Source:* Michio Kanai, "Taiwan," *Koshinkoku Nogyo Hatten no Shojoken* (Conditions of agricultural development in less developed countries) in Chujiro Ozaki, ed. [Tokyo: Institute of Development Economies, 1968], pp. 82–112 and 101; Taiwan Government-General, *Taiwan Nogyo Nenpo* [Yearbook of Taiwan agriculture], various issues.)

6) *Taiwan Nogyo Nenpo*, various issues.

7) Plant nutrients contained in commercial fertilizers applied to crops other than sugarcane per hectare of arable land area minus sugarcane area. Kanai's estimates of total plant nutrient consumption were apportioned to sugarcane and other crops in proportion to the values of commercial fertilizers applied to sugarcane. The data of fertilizer applications by crops are available only until 1932. The data after 1932 were estimated by fixing the compositions to 1929–32 values. (*Source:* Kanai, "Taiwan"; *Taiwan Nogyo Nenpo*, various issues. The 1920 figure is estimated by linear extrapolation using the rate of growth from 1925 to 1930.)

8) Yield per hectare planted in paddy rice. (*Source: Taiwan Nogyo Nenpo*, various issues.)

9) Unit price of plant nutrients in commercial fertilizers divided by unit price of rice. (*Source:* Korea Government-General, *Nogyo Tokeihyo* [Agricultural statistics], various issues.)

10) *Nogyo Tokeihyo*, various issues.

11) Plant nutrients contained in commercial fertilizers per hectare of arable land. (*Source: Nogyo Tokeihyo*, various issues.) Total quantities of plant nutrients were calculated from the quantities of individual fertilizer consumed using the following conversion factors:

	Fish meal	Bone meal	Other animal matters	Soybean cake	Other oil seed cakes	Brans	Other vegetable matters	Ammonium sulphate	Sodium nitrate	Super-phosphate of lime	Potassium sulphate	Other chemical fert.	Mixed fert.
N	0.08	0.04	0.08	0.07	0.06	0.02	0.06	0.21	0.15	0	0	0.08	0.08
P_2O_5	0.07	0.23	0.07	0.01	0.03	0.04	0.02	0	0	0.17	0	0.08	0.08
K_2O	0.03	0	0.03	0.02	0.01	0.02	0.02	0	0	0	0.50	0.05	0.05

12) Yield per hectare planted in paddy rice. (*Source: Nogyo Tokeihyo*, various issues.)

duce development programs designed to increase the yield and output of rice in those colonial territories.[37] Before the rice riot, "development efforts in Taiwan were concentrated on sugar production and little was done in Korea. It was claimed that the development of rice production in those overseas territories should be suppressed since it would foster competition against Japan agriculture."[38]

Under the program titled *Sanmai Zoshoku Keikaku* (Rice Production Development Program), the government invested in irrigation and water control and in research and extension, in order to develop and diffuse high-yielding Japanese rice varieties adapted to the local ecologies of Korea and Taiwan. The expenditure for agricultural development by the Government-General of Korea before and after the start of the Rice Production Development Program (1920) clearly indicates this drastic policy reorientation. The total agricultural development expenditure jumped from a 1915–19 total of 3.5 million yen to a 1920–24 total of 18.6 million yen; expenditure for experiment stations increased from 1.1 million yen to 2.8 million yen; and the expenditure for land improvement projects, including irrigation and drainage facilities, went from only 334 thousand yen to 12 million yen.[39] Rapid increases in rice yields in Taiwan and Korea, accompanied by stagnation in Japanese rice yields, were the result of this policy reorientation.

Taiwan Case

A spectacular success was attained in Taiwan with the development of the Ponlai varieties. The Ponlai varieties are rice varieties "developed by cross-breeding of Japanese varieties or between Japanese and traditional Taiwan (Chailai) varieties to have photo-sensitivities different from the original Japanese varieties."[40] They are more fertilizer-responsive, high-yielding, with adequate water control and cultural practices, and are better suited to the Japanese taste than are the Chailai varieties (Indica).

37. This reorientation of the colonial agricultural development policy, in response to the shortage of rice in Japan, is clearly described by Tobata and Ohkawa in reference to Korea: "Since the Rice Riot Japan has faced a so-called 'population-food problem.' Rapid increase in population and even more rapid increase in nonagricultural population, as the result of industrial development, have been pressing the need for an increase in rice production. In Japan, however, rice farming had already approached a technical limit of intensification, and economically there was little possibility of increasing rice production. Therefore, the solution of the population-food problem was sought in the direction of enlarging the rice production area. In this connection Korea represented the biggest hope, where extensive and underdeveloped farming have been practiced without progress for hundreds of years. It was anticipated that if Korean agriculture were to be developed by the weapons of modern science it would be possible to increase its intensity as well as to expand the paddy field area." Seiichi Tobata and Kazushi Ohkawa, *Chosen Beikoku Keizairon* (A treatise on rice economy in Korea) (Tokyo: Nihon Gakujutsu Shinkokai, 1935), p. 7.

38. Nihon Nogyo Hattatsushi (History of Japanese agricultural development), 10 vols. (Tokyo: Chuokoronsha, 1953–58), 9:597, henceforth abbreviated as *NNHS*.

39. Kuro Kobayakawa, ed., *Chosen Nogyo Hattatsushi: Seisakuhen* (History of Korean agriculture: Policy volume) (Tokyo: Yuhokyokai, 1959), pp. 117–18.

40. Eikichi Iso, *Horaimai Danwa* (Discourse on the Ponlai rice) (Yamaguchi: Udokukai, 1964), p. 18.

It was not easy to adapt Japanese varieties to the tropical climate of Taiwan. Even before the policy reorientation after the rice riot, when the effort of the Government-General was directed to improving the Chailai varieties to satisfy Taiwan's domestic demand, research to adapt Japanese varieties to tropical ecology had been conducted, although on a small scale. A breakthrough occurred when Eikichi Iso of the Agricultural Division, Central Research Institute of the Government-General, found that the Japanese varieties could be grown successfully by reducing by one-half the time the rice seedlings remained in the nursery bed.[41]

With this breakthrough, and under the pressing demand of Japan, the Government-General shifted the emphasis from improvement of the Chailai varieties to the development and propagation of the Ponlai varieties. Areas planted with the Ponlai varieties grew from 400 hectares in 1922, the first year this statistic was recorded, to 131,000 hectares in 1930, and 296,000 hectares (almost one-half of the paddy field area planted) in 1935. This rapid diffusion was based on the high payoff of the Ponlai varieties. According to the rice production costs survey conducted by the Government-General in 1926–27, both profit (total revenue minus total cost) and farm family income (profit plus family labor wages) per *chia* (0.97 hectare) were very much higher with the Ponlai varieties than with the Chailai varieties (Table 9.6).

In the cost comparison in Table 9-6 differences in (a) fertilizer expense, (b) wages, and (c) rent are particularly significant. Larger expenditures for fertilizer for the production of Ponlai varieties clearly reflect their higher fertilizer-responsiveness.[42] Higher wage costs show that the Ponlai varieties require more labor and better husbandry, including checkrow planting, deep plowing, more intensive weeding, and insect control. Higher rent for the Ponlai varieties indicates that these varieties were grown in areas with better water control. It appears that the economic implications of the Ponlai varieties for Taiwan in the 1920s were essentially equivalent to those of the modern rice varieties in the tropics today.[43]

41. From fifty to sixty days to twenty to forty days in the first crop: from thirty to forty days to fifteen to twenty days in the second crop. Ibid., pp. 76–77.

42. The fertilizer-responsive character of the Japanese varieties from which the Ponlai varieties were developed relative to the Chailai varieties is demonstrated by the following results of experiments, which compare the average fertilizer responses of four Japanese varieties and four Chailai varieties:

	No fertilization	Level of ordinary fertilization	Double of ordinary level of fertilization
	---------------------- metric tons per hectare[a] ----------------------		
Taiwan Chailai	2.024	2.701	2.815
Japanese Ponlai	1.587	2.713	3.081

Source: NNHS, 9:221.
[a]Brown rice basis.

43. Randolph Barker and E. V. Quintana, "Returns and Costs for Local and High Yielding Rice Varieties," *Philippine Economic Journal* 7 (Second Semester, 1968):145–61. The entire

TABLE 9-6.   Comparison of the costs of Ponlai and Chailai rice production per *chia**

| | 1926 second crop | | | 1927 first crop | | |
	Ponlai (1)	Chailai (2)	(1)–(2)	Ponlai (3)	Chailai (4)	(3)–(4)
	yen					
Seed	8.12	3.97	4.15	8.31	4.17	4.14
Fertilizer[a]	51.26	25.50	25.76	63.58	26.90	36.68
Wage:	112.38	93.86	18.52	126.20	103.83	22.37
Family labor	73.30	54.57	18.73	81.51	62.75	18.76
Hired labor	39.08	39.29	−0.21	44.69	41.08	3.61
Implements and building	3.76	4.24	−0.48	4.55	4.83	−0.28
Miscellaneous	2.46	1.01	1.45	9.25	11.73	−2.48
Tax and rate	1.41	1.66	−0.25	1.81	1.57	0.24
Rent	147.20	121.70	25.50	176.40	133.42	42.98
Total cost	326.59	251.94	75.15	390.10	286.45	103.65
Total revenue[b]	382.04	285.31	96.73	466.76	285.26	181.50
Profit[c]	55.45	33.37	22.18	76.66	−1.19	77.85
Farm family income[d]	128.75	87.94	40.81	158.17	61.56	96.61

Sources: Taiwan Government-General, Bureau of Colonial Development, *Shuyonosanbutsu Keizai Chosa* (Economic survey of major agricultural products) No. 6, pp. 11, 48–49, 62–63, 82–83, 112–113, 241, 249; and No. 9, pp. 11, 13, 15, 17, 50–51, 64–65, 118–19, 152–53 (Taipei, 1928). Data are for tenant farmers.
*1 chia = 0.97 hectares.
[a]Include self-supplied fertilizers.
[b]Include the value of straw.
[c]Profit = total revenue − total cost.
[d]Farm family income = profit + wage for family labor.

A remarkable aspect of the rapid diffusion of the Ponlai varieties during the 1920s and 1930s is that it was not accompanied by an appreciable decline in fertilizer prices relative to rice prices, as was the case with the improved varieties in Japan prior to 1920 (compare row 1 and row 5 in Table 9-5). As discussed previously, the spread of improved varieties in Japan, accompanied by a decline in the fertilizer-rice price ratio, suggests movement from A to B in Figure 9-2. In contrast, the rapid propagation of the Ponlai varieties in Taiwan, without any significant decline in the fertilizer-rice price ratio, seems to indicate a movement from C to B. Since Taiwan had been included in the Japanese Empire common market, it seems reasonable to assume that the fertilizer price in Taiwan declined relative to the rice price, parallel with its decline in Japan prior to 1920 (from p_0 to p_1). In the absence of comparable levels of development of scientific knowledge in Taiwan, this opportunity could not be exploited, and rice production in Taiwan was trapped at C on the

issue contains the papers presented at a seminar-workshop on the economics of rice production held at the International Rice Research Institute, December 8–9, 1967.

response curve of the Chailai varieties (u_0). When foreign (Japanese) agricultural scientists turned their attention to this situation, in response to the demand of the mother country, the potential was exploited through the dramatic development and propagation of the Ponlai varieties (u_1).

Korean Case

The Korean experience as summarized in Table 9-5 (rows 9–12) indicates that (a) the ratio of the price of fertilizer relative to the price of rice was almost as low as in Japan; (b) propagation of Japanese varieties in the 1920s was not accompanied by a significant reduction in the relative price of fertilizer; and (c) in spite of an earlier start in propagation of Japanese varieties, fertilizer input per hectare in the 1920s was at a much lower level than in Taiwan. As a result, the rice yield did not start to increase until the late 1920s.

Korea was situated closer to Manchuria, Japan's major supplier of nitrogen in the form of the soybean cake until the 1920s. In the 1930s Japanese industrialists, attracted by abundant hydroelectric power, built large-scale modern nitrogen plants in North Korea. Korean agriculture thus had access to cheaper sources of plant nutrients than did Taiwan. Rapid diffusion of Japanese rice varieties and rapid yield increases, in spite of stagnant relative prices of fertilizer, can be explained by the movement from C to B in Figure 9-2. This was the same as in the case of Taiwan.

There is, however, an apparent contradiction in the Korean experience. In spite of an earlier start in the diffusion of Japanese varieties, the level of fertilizer input per hectare was low and the yield take-off lagged in Korea relative to Taiwan. The key to this contradiction seems to be the difference in the level of irrigation and water control. Table 9-7 compares progress in paddy field irrigation between Taiwan and Korea. Since data on the area of irrigated paddy fields are not available for Taiwan, we calculated the ratio of irrigated paddy field area to total paddy field area on the assumption that irrigation was developed only for rice and sugar production (which seems a reasonable approximation). The ratios thus calculated check well with the ratios of double-cropped paddy areas. In Taiwan, irrigation is required for double-cropping of rice.

From Table 9-7 it is apparent that irrigation construction lagged in Korea compared with Taiwan. In terms of the ratio of irrigated paddy area to total paddy area, Korea in 1925 did not reach the level of Taiwan in 1915. Judging from the movements in double-cropping ratios (which are not comparable with Taiwan in absolute level because of the different climate) it seems reasonable to assume that progress in water control in Korea was greatly accelerated during the 1925–35 period. This is compatible with the expenditure patterns for land improvement projects of the Government-General, as seen earlier. In the literature on Korean agriculture it is common to identify the lack of irrigation as the critical cause for low productivity. Seiichi Tobata and Kazushi Ohkawa wrote in 1935: ''The first technical condition of rice

TABLE 9-7. Irrigation and double-cropping ratios in paddy field: Korea and Taiwan, selected years

		Year				
		1915	1920	1925	1930	1935+
Taiwan						
1) Paddy area	1,000 ha.	343	367	374	396	479
2) Sugarcane area	1,000 ha.	83	105	127	106	118
3) Irrigated area	1,000 ha.	239	268	350	442	466
4) Double-cropping paddy area	1,000 ha.		246	266	292	313
5) Ratio of irrigated area	(3) ÷ [(1) + (2)]	0.56	0.57	0.70	0.88	0.78
6) Ratio of double-cropping area	(4) ÷ (1)		0.67	0.71	0.74	0.65
Korea						
7) Paddy area	1,000 ha.	1,168	1,531	1,551	1,605	1,668
8) Irrigated paddy area	1,000 ha.	160	240	758	953	1,152
9) Double-cropping paddy area	1,000 ha.			266	353	429
10) Ratio of irrigated area	(8) ÷ (7)	0.14	0.16	0.49	0.59	0.69
11) Ratio of double-cropping area	(9) ÷ (7)			0.17	0.22	0.26

Sources: Taiwan—Taiwan Government-General, *Taiwan Nogyo Nenpo* (Yearbook of Taiwan agriculture), various issues. Korea—Korea Government-General, *Nogyo Tokeihyo* (Agricultural statistics) and *Chosen Tochikairyo Jigyo Yoran* (Summary report of Korean land improvement projects), various issues.
Note: (1) Area of paddy field; (2) area of sugarcane harvested; (3) irrigated arable land area; (7) area of paddy field; (8) irrigated paddy field area.

production is nothing but water control. But paddy field in Korea is so called 'rain-fed paddy field,' . . . accordingly marshy paddy field with drainage difficulty, which is considered of low quality in Japan is considered good paddy field. . . . Who would dare to apply fertilizers under such conditions?''[44] It was natural to place a high investment priority on irrigation when the Rice Production Development Program was initiated in 1920.

The climate of Korea is much more like that of Japan than is Taiwan's. Rice varieties from northern Japan were directly transferable to Korea. But because of the precarious water supply, even in most of the so-called ''irrigated paddy field'' areas, the Japanese varieties introduced into Korea were not the high fertilizer-responsive varieties. Koremochi Kato, director of the Agricultural Experiment Station in Korea, remarked in 1926: ''It is natural that our experiment station since its establishment has worked to select those from many Japanese varieties, which have better results under low level of fertilization. . . . But, as water control has been developing recently farmers have been increasing fertilizer application and have become dissatisfied with the results.''[45] In response to the demand for fertilizer-responsive varieties the South Korean Branch of the Agricultural Experiment Station was set up in 1930, with the primary purpose of developing fertilizer-responsive high-yielding varieties. During the 1930s, varieties with higher fertilizer-responsiveness, such as *Ginbozu* and *Rijuu No. 132,* rapidly replaced less fertilizer-responsive Japanese varieties, such as *Tamanishiki* and *Kokurato.*[46]

In short, for almost a decade the development of high-yielding varieties in Korea, comparable to the Ponlai varieties, lagged relative to development of high-yielding varieties in Taiwan because of the constraint of water control, which worked to depress the payoff of investment in developing the high-yielding varieties. We may then ask, why was irrigation developed earlier in Taiwan? Many factors were involved: (a) annexation of Korea to Japan occurred a decade later than for Taiwan, so that investment in infrastructure in general was later in starting;[47] (b) irrigation had been developed in Taiwan during the early days of colonization to promote the production of sugarcane, and the facilities could be used for rice production; (c) production of Korean rice (Japonica) had been a direct menace to Japanese rice producers and was suppressed, while Taiwan Chailai rice (Indica) was not a direct competitor; (d) the Taiwan Government-General enjoyed revenue surpluses during the

44. Seiichi Tobata and Kazushi Ohkawa, *Chosen Beikoku Keizairon* (A treatise on rice economy in Korea) (Tokyo: Nihon Gakujutsu Shinkokai, 1935), pp. 2–3.
45. *NNHS,* 9:176–77.
46. The area planted to *Tamanishiki* and *Kokurato* was more than 30 percent of the area planted to rice and close to 50 percent of the area planted to Japanese varieties in Korea during the late 1920s. According to the experiments conducted by the Agricultural Experiment Station of the Government-General of Korea for 1927–29, both of those two varieties recorded lower yields in high fertilization plots, while such varieties as *Ginbozu* recorded higher yields in the high fertilization plots. *NNHS,* 9:177–78.
47. Taiwan was conceded to Japan by China in 1895 as a result of the Sino-Japanese War. Korea became a protectorate of Japan in 1905, and it became a territory of Japan in 1910.

TABLE 9-8.   Factor shares in the cost of rice production, Japan and Taiwan

	Japan 1925–27 average	Taiwan			
		Ponlai		Chailai	
Factor		1926 Second crop	1927 First crop	1926 Second crop	1927 First crop
Fertilizer[a]	15.9	15.7	16.3	10.0	9.4
Wage	35.8[b]	34.4	32.2	37.3	36.2
Rent	41.5	45.1	45.2	48.3	46.6
Others	6.8	4.8	6.3	4.3	7.2
Total cost	100.0	100.0	100.0	100.0	100.0

Sources: Japan: Calculated from Yukio Ishibashi, *Teikoku Nokai Kome Seisanhi Chosa Shynsei* (Compilation of rice production cost survey by the Imperial Agricultural Society) (Tokyo: National Research Institute of Agriculture, 1961), pp. 82–95. Data are for tenant farmers. Taiwan: Calculated from Table 9-3.
[a]Includes self-supplied fertilizer.
[b]Includes livestock labor.

half-decade preceding 1910 (called the "Golden Age" of the Taiwan Government-General's treasury) and could afford to invest in large-scale construction of physical infrastructure, including railways, ports, and irrigation.[48]

Transfer of Production Function: A Process of Biased Technical Change

It appears that the emergency and propagation of improved varieties in Taiwan and Korea during the 1920s and 1930s can be represented by the movement from *C* to *B* in Figure 9-2. This movement was made possible by the organized research of Japanese agricultural scientists and investment in irrigation by the colonial governments. This process of technology transfer involved the transfer of prototype Japanese rice production technology to Taiwan and Korea through coordinated adaptive research.

This process is illustrated in Table 9-8, which compares factor shares in the cost of rice production in Japan with those of the Ponlai and Chailai varieties in Taiwan. The factor shares in the case of the Ponlai varieties are very similar to those in Japan. If we assume a production function of the Cobb-Douglas type and equilibrium under competitive factor markets, the factor shares represent production elasticities of the respective inputs. In the propagation of the Ponlai varieties, Japan's rice production technology was assimilated by Taiwan.

Both in the cases of Japan and of the Ponlai varieties in Taiwan, the share accounted for by fertilizer is larger and the share accounted for by rent is smaller than in the case of the Chailai varieties. This clearly reflects the

48. Shigeto Kawano, *Taiwan Beikoku Keizairon* (A treatise of rice economy in Taiwan) (Tokyo: Yuhikaku, 1941), p. 11; Tadao Yanaihara, *Teikokushungika no Taiwan* (Taiwan under imperialism) (Tokyo: Iwanami, 1929), pp. 91–117.

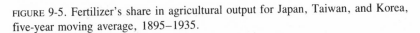

FIGURE 9-5. Fertilizer's share in agricultural output for Japan, Taiwan, and Korea, five-year moving average, 1895–1935.

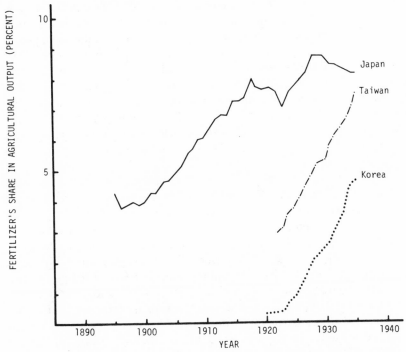

Sources: Kazushi Ohkawa et al., eds., *Long-term Economic Statistics since 1968,* 9 (Tokyo: Toyokeizaishimposha, 1966):146–47 and 194–95; Taiwan Government-General, *Taiwan Nogyo Nenpo* (Yearbook of Taiwan agriculture), various issues; Korea Government-General, *Nogyo Tokeihyo* (Agricultural statistics), various issues.

Note: Fertilizer's share is the total value of commercial fertilizer consumption divided by the gross value of agricultural production (both in current prices). In the case of Taiwan, fertilizers applied to sugarcane and sugarcane production are deducted, respectively, from fertilizer consumption and agricultural production (see estimation procedures in the note to Table 9-7).

fertilizer-using and land-saving character of the new technology embodied in fertilizer-responsive high-yielding varieties. This bias in technical change was consistent with a land-saving demand of the Taiwan economy in which the population pressure against land was raising the price of land relative to the prices of other factors.[49]

Figure 9-5 shows the changes in fertilizer's share in the total output in

49. During the period 1920–35 arable land area increased by 11 percent and agricultural population by 21 percent, resulting in a decline in the land-man ratio of 10 percent in Taiwan. In Korea, during the same period, arable land area increased by 3 percent and agricultural population by 11 percent, resulting in a decline in a land-man ratio of 8 percent. Although comparable data are unavailable for Taiwan and Korea, Japan recorded a rise in the price of arable land relative to the prices of other inputs from 1880 to 1960 (Table 7-1, Chapter 7).

Japan, Taiwan, and Korea. Because of data limitations, self-supplied fertilizers, such as manure and compost, are not included in the fertilizer totals. In Taiwan, because of its special nature, the sugarcane sector is excluded from the calculations (fertilizer input in sugarcane is deducted from total fertilizer inputs and sugarcane output is deducted from total agricultural output).[50] There is a remarkable association between the movement of fertilizer's share and of rice yield per hectare (Figure 9-4) in Japan, Taiwan, and Korea. This suggests strongly that growth in rice yields in these three regions was a process of replacement of traditional varieties by fertilizer-responsive high-yielding varieties (for example, Chailai by Ponlai). It indicates the process of assimilation of Japanese technology by Taiwan and Korea. In other words, it represents the transfer of Japan's agricultural production function to Taiwan and Korea.

Fertilizer's share of output in Japan rose rapidly until the end of the 1910s and decelerated thereafter. This corresponds to the emergence and propagation of improved varieties based on the exploitation of technological potential through a dialectic process of farmers' trials and scientific research, followed by the exhaustion of the yield potential of the *rōnō* varieties, as discussed previously. This movement in fertilizer's share may appear to be similar to what Bent Hansen has called the learning process in reference to Egyptian and U.S. agriculture: the process by which farmers learn how to use new inputs, i.e., chemical fertilizers.[51] Our interpretation of the experience of Japan, Taiwan, and Korea is somewhat different. Even though farmers are well-informed about the properties of new fertilizers, the shift to a new production function is difficult for individual farmers unless more fertilizer-responsive high-yielding varieties are made available. The growth in fertilizer's share in Japan, Taiwan, and Korea in Figure 9-4 involved not only farmers' learning but also the creation of new technology through a dialectic interaction between farmers' experience and scientific research, and its transfer through adaptive research.

PERSPECTIVES ON THE RECENT DEVELOPMENT
OF MODERN VARIETIES IN THE TROPICS

We have hypothesized that the technical basis of the green revolution has involved a movement from a production function that had been optimal for the factor and product prices that once prevailed in premodern society to another production function optimal at currently prevailing prices. This adjustment process lagged until the mid-1960s in most parts of Asia because of the lack of

50. Sugarcane was produced either by plantations owned by sugar companies or by peasant farmers by contract under the supervision and guidance of the sugar companies. Fertilizer inputs in sugarcane were high even before the 1910s.

51. Bent Hansen, "The Distributive Shares in Egyptian Agriculture, 1897–1961," *International Economic Review* 9 (June 1968):175–94.

investment in the local research and development capacity needed to make this adjustment possible. The result was a disequilibrium between actual and potential technology—between the production functions available to farmers in tropical and subtropical Asia and the metaproduction function. The transfer of scientific research capacity, induced by this disequilibria, resulted in revolutionary advances in rice production technology.

Japan's experience in the Meiji period indicates that in the creation and diffusion of more fertilizer-responsive high-yielding varieties the effective interaction among innovative veteran farmers and emerging agricultural science brought about continuous adjustments in response to declining fertilizer-rice price ratios. This Japanese experience suggests that movements along the metaproduction function can be accomplished relatively smoothly, given the existence of indigenous human capital and an adequate institutional and physical infrastructure.

Without these two factors, disequilibrium had mounted in Taiwan until about 1920, when Japan, to alleviate her own food problem, transferred to Taiwan the technical knowledge embodied in Japanese agricultural scientists. This resulted in a dramatic success in the creation of the Ponlai varieties. The experience of Taiwan has special relevance in that it involved the transfer of technology to a different climatic condition, where the direct transfer of seeds and techniques was not feasible. Korea's adjustment lagged behind that of Taiwan, mainly because of a lag in the construction of physical infrastructure, especially irrigation. Korean experience is particularly relevant for many areas in Southeast Asia where the adjustment to a new optimum through the diffusion of MVs may be severely constrained both by limitations in human capital and by inadequate physical infrastructure, especially water-control facilities. It appears possible to interpret the experience of Taiwan and Korea as representing the response of public agencies (colonial governments) to a potential high payoff (for Japan) of investment in research leading to adjustments from a secular disequilibrium toward an equilibrium for the fertilizer-rice price ratios prevailing at that time.

Viewed from the historical perspective of agricultural development in Japan, Taiwan, and Korea, the recent development of MVs in Asia represents a response by national and international agencies to changes in product and factor prices, particularly rice and fertilizer prices, resulting from changes in demand for rice and in the technology of fertilizer production during the 1950s and the early 1960s. Also it appears that the technical changes embodied in the new high-yielding cereal varieties are biased toward saving the increasingly scarce factor (land) and using the increasingly abundant factor (fertilizer) in the economy.

A large number of contemporary studies drawing on experience from South and Southeast Asia, Latin America, and Africa since the introduction of modern high-yielding varieties tend to confirm the inferences from historical experience in East Asia. Studies by Mark Pitt and Gunawan Sumodiningrat are particularly useful because they were specifically designed to test the model of Figure 9.2.[52] Both studies drew on data on the response of traditional and modern rice varieties to differences in the prices of variable and fixed inputs in Indonesia. The results obtained by Pitt indicate that the elasticity of fertilizer demand with respect to the rice-fertilizer price ratio for traditional varieties (U_0 in Figure 9-2) was .347 and for modern varieties (U_1 in Figure 9-2) was .366. But the elasticity along the metaproduction function (U in Figure 9-2), which takes into account the shift from traditional to modern varieties, was .508. Thus the shift in the response function, associated with a change in varieties, sharply increased the opportunity for Indonesian rice producers to expand rice production by substituting fertilizer for land. Sumodiningrat found that failure to take into account the effect of variety shifts also tended to underestimate the elasticity of demand for several other factor inputs. The capacity to respond to higher levels of fertilizer and other inputs was embodied in the genetic characteristics of the modern varieties. The effect was to augment the productivity of the other factors used in producing the modern rice varieties.

We have argued in this chapter that the seed-fertilizer technology of the green revolution has occurred as a delayed response to the disequilibrium brought about by changing factor endowments and growth in demand. We have argued, in effect, that the seed-fertilizer technology has been "appropriate" when evaluated against the changes in factor-factor and factor-product price ratios arising out of economic growth. This perception, however, has been widely questioned. One group of critics has questioned whether the biological and chemical technology used to generate and protect the higher yields is ecologically sound. A second group of critics has questioned the compatibility of the new technology with the institutions and cultural endowments of the peasant societies into which the new technology has been introduced. In many cases the two criticisms have been used to reinforce each other.[53]

The first group has challenged the "sustainability" of a technology that is dependent on high levels of energy-intensive fertilizers and chemical control of pests and disease. The most extreme among the ecologically oriented

52. Mark M. Pitt, "Farm-Level Fertilizer Demand in Java: A Meta-Production Function Approach," *American Journal of Agricultural Economics* 65 (August 1983):502–8; Gunawan Sumodiningrat, "Varietal Choice and Input Demand in Rice Production in Indonesia" (Ph.D. dissertation, University of Minnesota, 1982), pp. 118–25. Among other particularly useful studies are Salem Gafsi and Terry Roe, "Adoption of Unlike High-Yielding Wheat Varieties in Tunisia," *Economic Development and Cultural Change* 28 (October 1979):119–33; and Surjit S. Sidhu and Carlos A. Baanante, "Estimating Farm-Level Input Demand and Wheat Supply in the Indian Punjab Using a Translog Profit Function," *American Journal of Agricultural Economics* 63 (May 1981):237–46.

53. For a review see Kenneth A. Dahlberg, *Beyond the Green Revolution: The Ecology and Politics of Global Agricultural Development* (New York: Plenum Press, 1979), pp. 76–88. For the second argument see Keith Griffin, *The Political Economy of Agrarian Change: An Essay on the Green Revolution*, 2d ed. (London: Macmillan Co., 1979).

critics have viewed the development of modern varieties for the tropics as a plot by multinational firms and foundations to make peasant producers in poor countries dependent on chemical fertilizer and pest-control materials. The more moderate critics point to the potential loss of genetic diversity as the traditional crop varieties (landraces) are displaced by widespread use of new varieties based on a narrow range of genetic materials. There is also concern that intensive use of chemical insecticides and herbicides could lead to resistance to insect and other pest populations and that new varieties that do not incorporate the natural resistance of some of the traditional crop varieties could lead to explosive growth of pest populations.

Some of these concerns clearly are valid. Stephen Biggs has pointed out that in 1977 "the wheat crop in Sonora Valley, the home of the Mexican dwarf wheat varieties, was threatened by a large-scale outbreak of rust because of lack of genetic diversity in the available commercial varieties. . . . The Pakistan wheat crop was hit badly by rusts in 1978. The official analysis indicated that the severity of the loss was due to excessive acreage being planted with a single high-yielding variety, Sonalika, which had become susceptible." The most dramatic examples of ecological damage have come from areas where DDT and other synthetic organic insecticides have been used heavily. Excessive use of such insecticides for the control of insect pests in cotton production in Mexico and several Central American countries has led to the emergence of resistant strains of the malaria mosquito, which in some areas has led to the abandonment of cotton production and the resurgence of malaria.[54]

We do not regard the ecologically oriented criticisms as a fundamental challenge either to the long-term viability of the seed-fertilizer revolution or to the induced innovation hypothesis.[55] Rather, we see the environmental spillover impacts of the new technology inducing a focus on the part of both ecologically and agriculturally oriented agricultural scientists toward the invention of cropping, pest management, and farming systems that are both ecologically and economically viable. And we also see the spillover effects inducing a response by social scientists and political entrepreneurs to invent new institutions to regulate and manage the pest-control technologies in a manner that limits the spillover effects on national environments, agricultural practices, and human health.

The second group of critics has been more concerned with the impact of technical change on the viability of rural community institutions and on the distribution of the new income streams generated by growth in agricultural

---

54. Stephen D. Biggs, *Agricultural Research: A Review of Social Science Analysis* (Norwich: University of East Anglia School of Development Studies, Discussion Paper 115, 1982); Georganne Chapin and Robert Wasserstrom, "Agricultural Production and Malaria Resurgence in Central America and India," *Nature* 293 (September 17, 1981):181–85.

55. See Vernon W. Ruttan, "Technology and the Environment," *American Journal of Agricultural Economics* 53 (December 1971):707–17.

production. An attempt is made to assess the evidence on the distributional impact of technical change in Chapter 11, "Growth and Equity in Agricultural Development."

In our judgment, the most serious issue that continues to face the countries now experiencing advances in modern seed-fertilizer technology is whether the potential commodity surpluses resulting from the new biological technology will be used to generate viable economic growth in the total economy, or whether the surpluses will be absorbed by even higher levels of population growth or by public consumption that fails to sustain or generate economic growth. Most developing economies face the choice between the historical examples provided by Java and Japan—between involution and development.[56] This issue will be discussed in the final chapter of this book.

56. Clifford Geertz, *Agricultural Involution; The Process of Ecological Change in Indonesia* (Berkeley: University of California Press, 1966); Bruce F. Johnston and John Cownie, "The Seed-Fertilizer Revolution and Labor Force Absorption," *American Economic Review* 59 (September 1969):569–82.

10

Technology Transfer
and Land Infrastructure

Lhe transfer of Japanese rich technology to Taiwan and
Korea, analyzed in the previous chapter, clearly demonstrates a key role of
irrigation infrastructure in the diffusion process. A unique aspect of agricultural production as a biological process is that it is basically conditioned by
natural environments. In general, the interregional transfer of agricultural
technology involves (a) adapting location-specific technology to different
natural environments and (b) modifying local environments to suit the technology. Natural environments have always been hostile to domesticated
plants and animals. Only as natural environments have been modified by
cultivation and such infrastructure investments as terracing, irrigation, and
drainage has it been possible to achieve high levels of output per hectare and
per worker.[1]

The diffusion of agricultural technology and investment in land infrastructure reinforce each other. The modification of environmental conditions (e.g.,
better control of water by irrigation) is often a precondition for efficient use of
new technology (e.g., modern semidwarf varieties of rice), and the introduction of such technology induces environmental modification by raising the
expected rate of return to investments in improving the land infrastructure. In
terms of the model illustrated in the right-hand diagram of Figure 4.2, the
development of the seed-fertilizer technology, represented by a shift from i_0
to i, is associated with complementary increases in fertilizer input and investment in land infrastructure. The dynamic interactions between technological
change and investment in land infrastructure involve institutional innovations
to organize public efforts to undertake those tasks.

Like research, land infrastructure is characterized by some of the attributes
of a "public good," especially in a rural society composed of a large number
of small farmers, each of whom operates a unit that is too small to internalize
the gains from investments in large-scale land infrastructure projects such as

1. For a historical perspective see Ester Boserup, *Population and Technological Change: A
Study of Long-Term Trends* (Chicago: University of Chicago Press, 1981).

gravity-irrigation systems. The failure of the market to provide such services must be corrected by institutional innovations to enable cooperation at the local community level or to mobilize public resources at the provincial or regional level.

In a historical perspective such dynamic interactions among land infrastructure, technology, and institutions may be viewed as a process of augmenting (or saving) land in order to overcome growing population pressure on limited land resources. With the closing of the land frontier the constraints on agricultural production were removed by investment in land and water development and by the development of crop varieties and production practices suited to more intensive cultivation. The development and diffusion of an intensive seed-fertilizer technology for rice production in Japan, and its transfer to Taiwan and Korea and more recently to tropical Asia, is one example of such a process. It is the purpose of this chapter to illustrate the dynamic interaction between technology and development of land infrastructure from a comparison of the recent experience in the Philippines with the experience of Japan, Korea, and Taiwan. The Philippine experience is particularly relevant because it involves a tropical rice-producing region in contrast to Japan or Korea, which are located in the temperate region, and Taiwan, which is semitropical.

CHANGING PATTERNS OF AGRICULTURAL
GROWTH IN THE PHILIPPINES

Before comparing the Philippine experience with that of Japan, Taiwan, and Korea,[2] it is useful to review the historical changes in the pattern of agricultural growth in the Philippines that have emerged as the result of population pressure. Similar background information for Japan, Taiwan, and Korea has already been presented in previous chapters.

Until the end of the 1950s, Philippine agriculture followed the traditional vent-for-surplus pattern of agricultural development characteristic of much of Southeast Asia. Growth was brought about primarily by expansion of the cultivated area in response to an increased world demand for export crops such as sugar and copra. The area planted to food staples, such as rice and corn, was then increased in response to the growth in domestic demand resulting from the export-stimulated growth in income and population. Some efforts had been made to increase the yield of plantation crops (notably by

---

2. This section draws heavily on Yujiro Hayami, Cristina C. David, Piedad Flores, and Masao Kikuchi, "Agricultural Growth against a Land Resource Constraint: The Philippine Experience," *Australian Journal of Agricultural Economics* 20 (December 1976):144–59. See also Randolph Barker, "Recent Trends in Labor Utilization and Productivity in Philippine Agriculture with Comparisons to Other Asian Experiences," *Village-Level Modernization in Southeast Asia: The Political Economy of Rice and Water*, ed. Geoffrey B. Hainsworth (Vancouver: University of British Columbia Press, 1982), pp. 141–72.

introducing improved sugarcane varieties from Java and Hawaii), but the possibility of increasing the yields of food staples was largely ignored. Expansion of the area under cultivation at a rate rapid enough to absorb the growing labor force was possible as long as large unused land areas existed. Agricultural growth along this traditional path was bound to be limited, however, by the closing of the land frontier.

With the rapid growth of population after World War II, the supply of unexploited land became progressively exhausted. Toward the end of the 1950s the rate of expansion of cultivated land began to decline in the Philippines, but the number of workers in agriculture continued to grow at about the same rate, as shown in Figure 10-1. As a result, cultivated area per worker began to decline. Development of irrigation facilities was accelerated during this period. The expansion of the irrigation system since the 1950s made an important contribution to the rapid diffusion of modern semidwarf varieties of rice since the mid-1960s.

This transition was accompanied by a major change in the pattern of growth in agricultural output and factor use (Table 10-1). During the 1950s, the rapid growth of output, 4.1 percent per year, was accompanied by a 3.4 percent annual increase in land area under cultivation. Expansion of area cultivated accounted for more than 80 percent of output growth. Increases in yield per hectare of cultivated land area accounted for less than 20 percent. The agricultural labor force (number of farm workers) increased at an annual rate of 2.7 percent. Approximately one-half of the gain in labor productivity (1.5 percent per year) was explained by the increase in area per worker.

The pattern of agricultural growth in the 1960s is in sharp contrast to that of the previous decade. The rate of expansion of the cultivated area dropped by almost one-half, but population growth did not drop appreciably. Increases in labor productivity became totally dependent on increases in land productivity. The rate of increase in cultivated land area declined further from the 1960s to the 1970s, and the relative contributions of land productivity growth to the increases in total agricultural output and labor productivity became larger. The data in Table 10-1 clearly suggest that Philippine agriculture experienced a transition from a traditional growth pattern, based on the expansion of cultivated area, to a new pattern based on increase in land productivity.

Another remarkable aspect of the change in growth pattern is that the application of modern inputs and technology, which had previously been limited to export crops, became increasingly focused on food crops. During the 1950s the increases in yields per hectare were confined to export crops such as sugar. During the 1960s the yields per hectare of food crops such as rice for domestic consumption began to increase (Table 10-2).

Such contrasts seem to reflect a basic change in the direction of the growth of Philippine agriculture. The demand-induced technical changes, which previously had been generated by world demand for export crops, were complemented during the 1960s by rapid growth in domestic demand for food crops

FIGURE 10-1. Comparisons in the trends of cultivated and irrigated land areas and of number of farm workers in the Philippines, three-year moving averages, semilog scale.

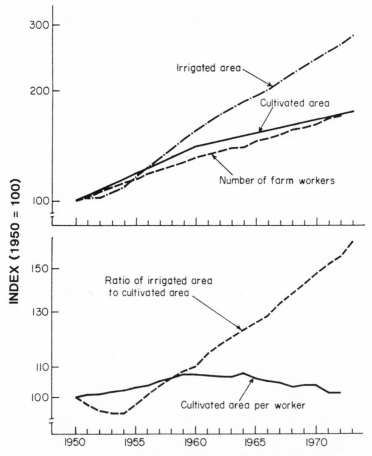

Source: Yujiro Hayami and Masao Kikuchi, "Investment Inducements to Public Infrastructure: Irrigation in the Philippines," *Review of Economics and Statistics* 60 (February 1978): 71.

generated by the population explosion. This trend was reinforced by changes in relative factor prices, which induced land-saving technical change and investment in land infrastructure.

The nature of this "epochal change" in the growth pattern of Philippine agriculture is comparable to the experience of Taiwan agriculture during the period between the two world wars. Agricultural growth in Taiwan before the mid-1920s was based primarily on expansion of area cultivated. Increases in output per worker were associated with increases in cultivated area per worker. As population growth in Taiwan rose from 1 percent per year during the

TABLE 10-1.   Contribution of area and land productivity to the growth in output and labor productivity in Philippine agriculture (percentages)

	1948–52 to 1958–62		1958–62 to 1968–72		1968–72 to 1978–82	
	Annual growth rate	Relative contribution	Annual growth rate	Relative contribution	Annual growth rate	Relative contribution
Total agricultural output	5.1	100	3.2	100	6.2	100
Cultivated land area	3.3	65	1.4	44	−0.6	−10
Output per ha of cultivated land area	1.8	35	1.8	56	6.8	110
Agricultural output per farm worker	2.7	100	0.8	100	3.8	100
Cultivated land area per farm worker	0.9	33	−1.0	−125	−3.0	−79
Output per ha of cultivated land area	1.8	67	1.8	225	6.8	179

Source: Cristina C. David, Randolph Barker, and Adelita Palacpac, "The Nature of Productivity Growth in Philippine Agriculture, 1948–1982" (Paper presented at the Symposium on Agricultural Productivity Measurement and Analysis, APO, Tokyo, Japan, October 2–8, 1984).

TABLE 10-2.   Contribution of area and yield to growth in total output of rice and sugar in the Philippines (percentages)

	Annual growth rate			Relative contribution		
	Output	Area	Yield	Output	Area	Yield
1948–52 to 1958–62						
Rice	3.5	3.5	−0.05	100	101	−1
Sugar	6.2	4.6	1.5	100	75	25
1958–62 to 1968–72						
Rice	3.2	0.1	3.1	100	3	97
Sugar	3.7	4.8	−1.1	100	130	−30
1968–72 to 1978–82						
Rice	4.3	0.7	3.6	100	17	83
Sugar	2.3	1.3	1.0	100	57	43

Source: Cristina C. David, Randolph Barker, and Adelita Palacpac, "The Nature of Productivity Growth in Philippine Agriculture, 1948–1982" (Paper presented at the Symposium on Agricultural Productivity Measurement and Analysis, APO, Tokyo, Japan, October 2–8, 1984).

1910s to 2.5 percent in the 1930s, there was no more area into which to expand, and the land-labor ratio began to decline. At the same time there was a spurt in land productivity. The growth in yield per hectare of cultivated land was brought about by increased cropping intensity and the development and diffusion of Ponlai varieties. The increase in the intensity of land use was based on investment in irrigation, which was accelerated during the 1910s. As a result, agricultural output and labor productivity in Taiwan continued to rise in spite of the decline in the land-labor ratio.

The similarity of the Philippine and Taiwan experiences is demonstrated in Figure 10-2. Both Taiwan and the Philippines moved to higher levels of labor productivity (iso-labor-productivity curves are represented by plotted contours) through changes in land productivity (Y/A) and land area per worker (A/L). It is clear that the turning point in agricultural growth from a pattern based on expansion of area to one based on increase in yields occurred in Taiwan in the mid-1920s and in the Philippines from the late 1950s to the early 1960s. The change in the agricultural growth pattern in both countries seems to have occurred in response to population pressure on land.

SEQUENCES IN TECHNOLOGICAL CHANGE AND LAND INFRASTRUCTURE DEVELOPMENT

The epochal change in the agricultural growth momentum in the Philippines between the 1950s and the 1960s is clearly reflected in the spurt in rice

FIGURE 10-2. Historical growth paths of labor productivity in relation to land productivity and land-labor ratio in the Philippines and Taiwan.

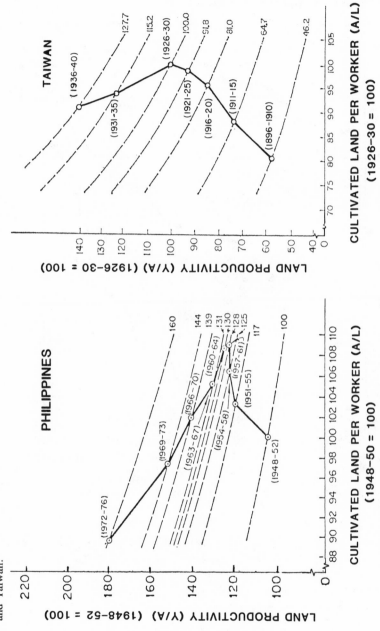

Source: Cristina C. David, Randolph Barker, and Adelita Palacpac, "The Nature of Productivity Growth in Philippine Agriculture, 1948–82" (Paper presented at the Symposium on Agricultural Productivity Measurement and Analysis, Asian Productivity Organization, Tokyo, October 2–8, 1984); and adapted from Teng-hui Lee, Intersectoral Capital Flows in the Economic Development of Taiwan, 1895–1960 (Ithaca: Cornell University Press, 1971), p. 51.

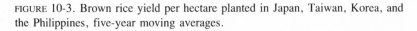

FIGURE 10-3. Brown rice yield per hectare planted in Japan, Taiwan, Korea, and the Philippines, five-year moving averages.

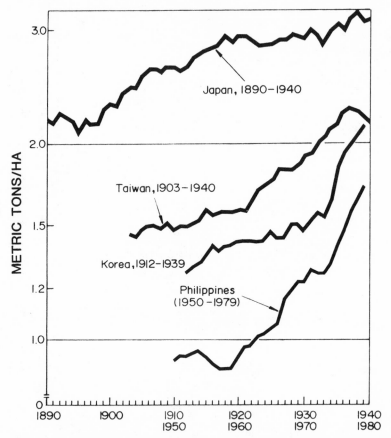

Sources: Masao Kikuchi and Yujiro Hayami, "Agricultural Growth against a Land Resource Constraint: A Comparative History of Japan, Taiwan, Korea, and the Philippines," *Journal of Economic History* 38 (December 1978): 847, © Economic History Association; Adelita C. Palacpac, *World Rice Statistics* (Los Baños, Philippines: International Rice Research Institute, 1982).

yield per hectare in the 1960s.[3] Figure 10-3 compares the trend in rice yield per hectare in the Philippines for 1950–79 with those of Japan, Taiwan, and Korea before World War II. It is apparent that the spurt in rice yield in the Philippines since the 1960s was similar to that experienced in Taiwan and Korea during the interwar period.

3. This and the next two sections draw heavily on Masao Kikuchi and Yujiro Hayami, "Agricultural Growth against a Land Resource Constraint: A Comparative History of Japan, Taiwan, Korea, and the Philippines," *Journal of Economic History* 38 (December 1978):839–64.

As emphasized in the previous chapter, the take-off in rice yield per hectare in Taiwan and Korea can best be understood as a technology transfer involving adaptive research and improvements in land infrastructure, especially development of irrigation systems. A cursory glance at Figure 10-3 suggests that the technology transfer that resulted in the boosts in rice yield in Taiwan and Korea during the interwar period finally reached the Philippines in the 1960s.

The apparent similarity in rice-yield trends in Taiwan, Korea, and the Philippines is matched by the similarity in the process that accounted for these increases. Figure 10-4 compares trends in the diffusion of new rice varieties and the development in land infrastructure in Japan, Taiwan, Korea, and the Philippines. The sequences of technology diffusion and land infrastructure development in Taiwan, Korea, and the Philippines show a striking similarity. In those three cases the development of irrigation systems preceded the diffusion of improved varieties, reflecting the necessity for an adequate water supply for the fertilizer-responsive, high-yielding varieties.[4]

The development of irrigation systems in Taiwan preceded by almost a decade the introduction of the Japanese Ponlai varieties of rice, which had been adapted to Taiwan's environment (see Figure 10-4). The improved infrastructure led to an increase in rice output by enabling the transplanting of Japanese rice varieties in the 1920s, in accordance with the policy of developing Taiwan as a granary for Japan. In effect, the infrastructure development created the conditions for increasing land productivity, thus compensating for the decline in the land-labor ratio.

The lead-lag relation between irrigation and seed-fertilizer technology for Korea is less clear. An increase in the ratio of irrigated paddy area to total paddy field area paralleled an increase in the area planted to the Japanese rice varieties, although those initially introduced in the absence of adequate irrigation facilities were not highly fertilizer-responsive (see Chapter 9). As the irrigation infrastructure was improved, in response to the Rice Production Development Program launched in 1920, those varieties were replaced by the new Japanese varieties with higher fertilizer responsiveness, such as *Ginbozu* and *Rikuu 132* (see Figure 10-4c).

The sequence of irrigation and technology diffusion in the Philippines was similar to that in Taiwan and Korea. The dramatic development and diffusion of modern semidwarf varieties since the late 1960s was preceded by a rapid increase in investment in irrigation systems over more than a decade (see Figure 10-4d).

The sequence of development of land infrastructure followed by introduc-

---

4. The critical importance of irrigation for the introduction of seed-fertilizer technology in monsoon Asia has been emphasized by Shigeru Ishikawa, *Economic Development in Asian Perspective* (Tokyo: Kinokuniya Bookstore Co., 1967). See also S. C. Hsieh and Vernon W. Ruttan, "Environmental, Technological, and Institutional Factors in the Growth of Rice Production: Philippines, Thailand, and Taiwan," *Food Research Institute Studies* 7 (1967):307–41.

FIGURE 10-4. Trends in the development in irrigation improvement and in seed-fertilizer technology: Japan, Taiwan, Korea, and the Philippines, five-year moving averages.

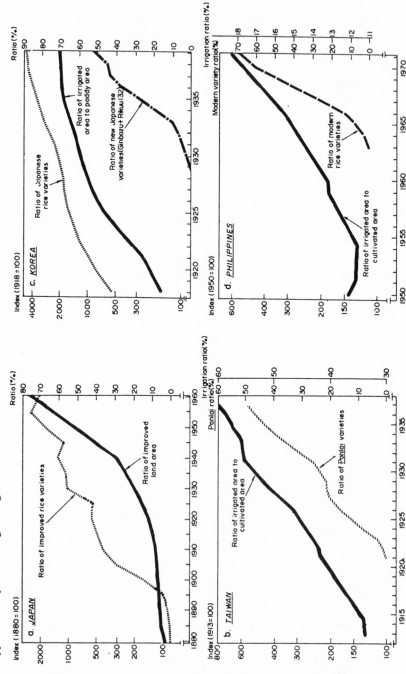

Source: Masao Kikuchi and Yujiro Hayami, "Agricultural Growth against a Land Resource Constraint: A Comparative History of Japan, Taiwan, Korea, and the Philippines," Journal of Economic History 38 (December 1978): 848, © Economic History Association.

308

tion of high-yielding rice varieties in Taiwan, Korea, and the Philippines stands in sharp contrast to the sequence in Japan. In Japan, the initial yield increases during 1890–1920 were paralleled by an increase in the ratio of area planted in improved varieties to total rice area (see Figure 10-4a). At this time the ratio of area covered by land improvement projects (irrigation, drainage, and land consolidation) to total cultivated land area did not improve appreciably. Instead, the ratio of the improved land area began to rise during the 1910s when the ratio of improved varieties began to level off.

The initial lag of investment in land infrastructure behind the development of seed-fertilizer technology in Japan was a result of unbalanced regional development resulting from Japan's traditional feudal system. By the beginning of the modern era the irrigation and drainage systems in the advanced areas of Japan, such as Kinki and North Kyushu, had been developed sufficiently to introduce the fertilizer-responsive high-yielding varieties. Those varieties were selected mostly by veteran farmers (*rōnō*) and were further tested and improved by experiment stations. As the diffusion of the technology approached the limit of the area endowed with adequate water-control facilities, however, land infrastructure became the major constraint on rice production.

When land infrastructure became a bottleneck in rice production, anxiety over domestic food supply induced public investment and institutional innovation to mitigate the constraint. As early as 1899 public concern about national security, arising from Japan's position as a net importer of rice after the Sino-Japanese War (1894–95), resulted in the enactment of the Arable Land Replotment Law (revised in 1905 and 1909). The law authorized compulsory participation by farmers and landlords in a land improvement project if consent were obtained from two-thirds of the landlords owning two-thirds of that area. The rice riots caused by high rice prices during World War I resulted in further institutional innovation—the promulgation of the Rules of Subsidization of Irrigation and Drainage Projects. The rules authorized the central government to give a 50 percent subsidy to large irrigation and drainage projects undertaken by the prefectural governments.[5]

This Japanese case illustrates the dynamic sequences whereby technical and institutional changes are prompted through imbalance or disequilibrium inherent in the process of economic development. Through this process, the ratio of improved land area in Japan experienced a sharp increase after the late 1910s (see Figure 10-4a).

---

5. For more detail about the history of land infrastructure development in Japan, see Yujiro Hayami, with Masakatsu Akino, Masahiko Shintani, and Saburo Yamada, *A Century of Agricultural Growth in Japan* (Minneapolis: University of Minnesota Press; and Tokyo: University of Tokyo Press, 1975), pp. 170–92.

THE PROCESS OF LAND AUGMENTATION: A HYPOTHESIS

We now draw on the experiences of Japan, Korea, Taiwan, and the Philippines to develop an operational hypothesis to interpret the mechanism underlying the process of land productivity increases in response to growing population pressure against land resources.

Increase in land productivity from improving land infrastructure and developing seed-fertilizer technology has the same effect on agricultural output as expansion in cultivated land area. The former may be called "internal land augmentation" as opposed to "external land augmentation" for the latter.[6] The shifts in the momentum of agricultural output growth from external to internal land augmentation, as observed in the histories of Japan, Taiwan, Korea, and the Philippines, can be conceptualized along the following lines.

As population pressure pushes the cultivation frontier into marginal areas, we expect the marginal cost of agricultural production via expansion of cultivated area to rise relative to the marginal cost of production via intensification. Eventually the economy will reach a stage at which internal land augmentation becomes a less costly means of increasing agricultural output than external land augmentation. Curve *A* in Figure 10-5 represents the marginal cost of increasing agricultural output or income by opening new land; curve *I* represents the marginal cost of raising agricultural production by constructing irrigation facilities. With abundant land resources, curve *A* would remain horizontal and below curve *I*, indicating a relative advantage of external expansion over internal augmentation. As unused land resources are exhausted and the cultivation frontier moves from superior land to inferior land, curve *A* would rise and cross curve *I*. When the economy reaches the crossover point *P*, irrigation becomes a more profitable base for agricultural growth than the opening of new land.

As the area under irrigation expands, however, irrigation development moves from the relatively easier and less costly projects to the more difficult and more costly ones. As a result, the marginal cost of adding irrigated area increases. The rise in the cost of irrigation will eventually reduce the incentive to invest in land infrastructure.

At the same time, other forces act to offset the rising trend in irrigation costs. The improvement of irrigation permits the introduction of new seed-fertilizer technology. Because of their high complementarity, use of fertilizers and improved seeds reduces the cost of irrigation required to produce a unit of additional output, as is illustrated in Figure 10.5 by the shift of the irrigation cost curve downward from *I* to *I'*. Curve *A* may also be affected to some extent by biological and chemical innovations, but their impacts on curve *I*

6. We have used the term "internal land augmentation" for what the followers of Ricardo referred to as expansion of production along the "internal margin" of cultivation; the term "external land augmentation" corresponds to the Ricardian concept of expansion along the "external margin." See note 6 in Chapter 2.

FIGURE 10-5. Hypothetical relations between the marginal cost curves of agricultural production by opening new land and by building irrigation systems.

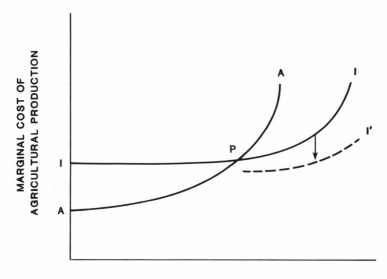

TIME

Source: Masao Kikuchi and Yujiro Hayami, ''Agricultural Growth against a Land Resource Constraint: A Comparative History of Japan, Taiwan, Korea, and the Philippines,'' *Journal of Economic History* 38 (December 1978): 853, © Economic History Association.

would be much larger because of the strong complementarity between irrigation and the seed-fertilizer technology. The increased advantage of irrigation over expansion of external area increases the incentive to invest in land infrastructure.

The relation illustrated in Figure 10-5 is not a logically deduced theoretical one, but rather a ''stylized fact'' that emerges from the historical transition of agricultural growth momentum from the expansion of external area to the increase in land productivity.[7] Theoretically, it may appear anomalous to assume that the marginal cost of agricultural production from irrigation will

7. Other stylized models would be appropriate under other ecological conditions or different land-labor resource endowments. In the more humid upland farming areas of North America, for example, the closing of the frontier was followed initially by the development of yield-increasing crop varieties and only later by supplemental irrigation and more intensive tillage practices (see Chapter 8). In arid-region agriculture, irrigation and other forms of water management might be expected to precede the development of high-yielding varieties by a much longer time than in the more humid areas of East and Southeast Asia. See, for example, Alan Richards, *Egypt's Agricultural Development, 1800–1980: Technical and Social Change* (Boulder, Colo.: Westview Press, 1982). For an attempt to test a model similar to that presented in this chapter against African experience see Prabun Rancali, Yves Biget, and Hans P. Binswanger, ''Agricultural Mechanization and the Evolution of Farming Systems of Subsaharan Africa,'' mimeograph (Washington, D.C.: World Bank, 1984).

312 Can Growth Be Transferred?

be below the marginal cost of opening up new land to cultivation because the optimal resource allocation will equate the marginal rates of return among investment alternatives. Yet this apparent disequilibrium can be explained by the time lag in adjusting to the economic opportunity represented by the crossover point.

In an economy with an open land frontier, private individuals typically settle in the new area, either as legal homesteaders or as illegal squatters. They open the new land with their own labor and capital. In contrast, the construction of irrigation systems, especially the gravity systems prevalent in monsoon Asia, is characterized by indivisibility and externality. Group action by farmers or public investment by the government is required and in turn demands both leadership and discipline. These qualities cannot be developed immediately as the need arises; such organizational capacity and habit grow in a rural society only over time, perhaps several generations. Therefore, when the economy reaches the point of a sharp rise in the marginal cost of opening new land, the marginal cost of increasing production by building irrigation systems may lie below the marginal cost of increasing production from new land for some time because of the slow development of social overhead capital.

The government, of course, may fill this gap. But the allocation of public resources is also a political process involving compromises among vested interests. It can hardly be expected that when population pressure causes the economy to pass to the right of point P in Figure 10-5, government investment in irrigation will increase so promptly as immediately to reestablish equality in the marginal rates of returns to opening new land and building irrigation systems. Of course, a government response of investment in production infrastructure depends on its ability to perceive the shift in the social rate of return in favor of land infrastructure investment as well as on its revenue. During the rise of great dynasties in Asia efficient bureaucracy and relatively abundant government revenue resulted in large-scale construction and rehabilitation of the irrigation systems. Later, as the bureaucracy gradually lost its vitality and revenues fell short of expenditures, irrigation systems deteriorated and agricultural production declined.[8]

In accordance with our hypothesis, the modern agricultural histories of Japan, Taiwan, Korea, and the Philippines may be reinterpreted as follows. Before modern economic growth began in the Meiji period, Japan was already located to the right of point P in Figure 10-5 as a result of gradual population growth in the feudal Tokugawa period. But because the shift was very gradual, there was sufficient time for village communities to develop an organizational capacity to mobilize communal labor to build and maintain local irriga-

8. This theme has been developed by Karl A. Wittfogel, *Oriental Despotism: A Comparative Study of Total Power* (New Haven: Yale University Press, 1957); also "The Hydraulic Civilizations," *Man's Role in Changing the Face of the Earth,* Vol. 1, ed. William L. Thomas, Jr. (Chicago: University of Chicago Press, 1956), pp. 152–64.

tion facilities. Feudal lords had also taken the responsibility for controlling rivers and major irrigation systems. A decentralized power structure that permitted economic and political competition among the holders of feudal fiefs contributed to the interest of the rulers in the possibilities of local economic development. As a result, Meiji Japan inherited a well-developed irrigation infrastructure. The stage had been set for a move from curve *I* to curve *I'* by developing the high-yielding seed-fertilizer technology.

It appears that Korea was also located to the right of *P* before its modern agricultural growth began. Partly because of the incapacity of the Yi dynasty in its late stage and partly because of the highly centralized despotic structure of the government, the irrigation infrastructure had not been properly developed. Initial large-scale investment in irrigation was required before the shift from curve *I* to curve *I'* could commence.

Taiwan's economy, in contrast, seems to have reached *P* in the late 1910s. The increase in government investment in irrigation during this period, supported by the budget surplus of the colonial government, played a large role. But an even more basic factor appears to have been the increase in the relative advantage of irrigation over land opening. The government irrigation investment provided the conditions for shifting from *I* to *I'* in the 1920s and 1930s.

The Philippines seems to have reached *P* only in the late 1950s. The nationalistic desire to achieve self-sufficiency in food, together with foreign exchange considerations, helped focus public attention on the need to invest in irrigation, which had become a relatively less costly means of increasing rice output. The conditions necessary to induce a shift from *I* to *I'* in the mid-1960s had thus been established.

Estimating the Cost Curves

As a test of our hypothesis we have attempted to estimate curves *A*, *I*, and *I'* in terms of the marginal cost of irrigation development and land opening to produce an additional unit of income from agricultural production. The marginal cost-benefit (*C/B*) ratios are calculated as follows:[9]

$$(C/B) = [i \cdot \frac{(1 + i)^{m+n}}{(1 + i)^n - 1} \cdot K + O]/B$$

where
B = annual benefit flow owing to the investment per hectare,
K = capital cost per hectare,
O = annual operation and maintenance costs per hectare,
i = interest rate (assumed 10 percent),

9. For data sources, see Kikuchi and Hayami, "Agricultural Growth against a Land Resource Constraint," p. 857. For more detail about calculation procedures and results, see Hayami et al., *A Century of Agricultural Growth in Japan*, pp. 179–89; and Masao Kikuchi, "Irrigation and Rice Technology in Agricultural Development: A Comparative History of Taiwan, Korea and the Philippines" (Ph.D. dissertation, Hokkaido University, 1976).

m = median year of the capital construction period,
n = period of usable life.

Simplifying assumptions adopted in the above formula are that (a) the entire capital cost is spent in the median year of the construction period, and (b) both the benefit and operation-maintenance costs begin to emerge in the year following completion of the construction and are fixed throughout the period of usable life.[10]

The cost (C) consists of the annual service flow of initial capital investment and the annual costs of operation and maintenance per hectare of new area brought into either cultivation or irrigation. The corresponding benefit flow (B) is measured by an increase in gross value added. The increase is estimated by subtracting the cost of seeds, fertilizers, and chemicals from the value of output produced from the new area.[11] Both costs and benefits are measured at constant prices (1934–36 prices for Japan, Taiwan, and Korea; 1970 prices for the Philippines). In the Japanese case, "irrigation" includes not only irrigation per se but also drainage and land consolidation projects.

In estimating the marginal C/B ratios for irrigation, we assume four levels of seed-fertilizer technology for each country in order to analyze the complementarity between irrigation and seed-fertilizer technology. In Japan, for example, the first two levels assume the use of traditional varieties with applications of 40 kg and 80 kg of nitrogen per hectare, respectively. The second two levels assume the use of improved varieties with applications of 80 kg and 120 kg of nitrogen.

In addition to the C/B ratios, the internal rates of return are calculated as r's that satisfy

$$\frac{K}{B - O} = \frac{(1 + r)^n - 1}{r(1 + r)^{m+n}}.$$

10. The operation and maintenance costs for irrigation are assumed: 3 percent of initial capital costs for Japan; 18 yen per hectare for Taiwan; 13 yen per hectare for Korea; and 60 pesos per hectare for the Philippines. The $O\text{-}M$ costs for land opening are assumed as zero for all countries except Korea, for which the same amount of $O\text{-}M$ costs as for irrigation are assumed because all land-opening projects included in our analysis had irrigation facilities. The median years of the capital construction periods are assumed to be 2, 1.5, 1.5, and 1.5 years in the case of irrigation, and 2.5, 2.5, 4.5, and 1.5 years in the case of land opening, for Japan, Taiwan, Korea, and the Philippines, respectively. The periods of usable life are assumed to be 50 years for all countries in the irrigation case, and infinite for the land-opening case, except for Korea, for which it is assumed to be 50 years.

11. Increase in labor costs for crop production owing to irrigation and land opening were not subtracted. This assumes that the increments in labor are available at zero opportunity cost. In fact, because of irrigation there is little change in labor input for the wet-season crop. Labor use in the dry season (for Taiwan and the Philippines) increases as irrigation enables planting in the dry season. It seems reasonable, however, to assume that during the dry season, farmland, which remains primarily idle if there is no irrigation, has a very low opportunity cost. Also, it seems reasonable to assume that the workers who are resettled by the government land-opening projects (for which our C/B calculations were made) are those who had difficulty in finding productive employment in their prior locations.

TABLE 10-3. Changes in the costs of irrigation construction and land opening required to produce an additional unit of agricultural income

| | Irrigation | | | | Land opening | |
| | Traditional varieties | | Improved varieties | | | |
Japan[a]	N = 40kg	N = 80kg	N = 80kg	N = 120kg	Case A	Case B
1902	0.89 (11)	0.64 (15)				
1905	0.80 (13)	0.57 (17)				
1910	1.11 (9)	0.80 (12)				
1915	1.25 (8)	0.90 (11)				
1920	1.32 (7)	0.96 (10)	0.70 (14)	0.64 (15)	1.00 (10)	
1925	1.26 (7)	0.92 (11)	0.66 (15)	0.61 (16)	0.78 (12)	
1930	1.49 (6)	1.07 (9)	0.78 (13)	0.67 (14)	1.06 (10)	
1932	1.32 (7)	0.95 (10)	0.69 (14)	0.64 (15)	1.17 (9)	
Taiwan[a]	N = 0kg	N = 50kg	N = 50kg	N = 100kg	Case A	Case B
1907	0.40 (26)	0.33 (31)				
1910	0.60 (17)	0.49 (21)			0.96 (10)	1.15 (9)
1915	0.76 (13)	0.62 (16)				
1920	0.65 (16)	0.53 (19)				
1925	0.87 (11)	0.71 (14)	0.47 (20)	0.42 (22)		
1930	1.15 (9)	0.94 (11)	0.61 (15)	0.55 (17)		
1932	1.27 (8)	1.04 (10)	0.68 (14)	0.61 (16)		
Korea[a]	N = 0kg	N = 50kg	N = 50kg	N = 100kg	Case A	Case B
1911	0.53 (28)	0.42 (36)				
1915	0.61 (19)	0.49 (26)				
1920	0.52 (24)	0.42 (30)			0.61 (17)	
1925	1.02 (10)	0.82 (13)	0.42 (27)	0.39 (29)	0.70 (15)	0.48 (22)
1930	1.04 (10)	0.84 (13)	0.43 (26)	0.39 (28)	1.20 (8)	0.82 (13)
1932	1.11 (9)	0.89 (11)	0.46 (24)	0.42 (26)	1.26 (8)	0.86 (12)
Philippines[b]	N = 0kg	N = 15kg	N = 20kg	N = 60kg	Case A	Case B
1951	0.44 (26)	0.42 (27)				
1955	0.48 (24)	0.45 (25)				
1960	0.61 (18)	0.58 (19)				
1965	0.59 (19)	0.56 (20)				
1970	0.69 (15)	0.65 (16)	0.35 (32)	0.31 (36)	1.19 (9)	0.80 (12)
1972	0.76 (14)	0.72 (15)	0.38 (28)	0.34 (32)		

Source: Masao Kikuchi and Yujiro Hayami, "Agricultural Growth against a Land Resource Constraint: A Comparative History of Japan, Taiwan, Korea, and the Philippines," Journal of Economic History 38 (December 1978): 859. © Economic History Association.
[a] 1934–1936 constant prices. Figures inside parentheses are the internal rates of return.
[b] 1970 constant prices. Figures inside parentheses are the internal rates of return.

The results of estimation of the C/B ratios and the internal rates of return are summarized in Table 10-3. As expected, the real cost of irrigation development to produce an additional unit of agricultural income tends to rise with each level of technology in every country, although it fluctuates around the trend line with a tendency for costs relative to benefits to rise more rapidly when irrigation investment expands rapidly.

The rising trends in the marginal cost-benefit ratios for irrigation were totally compensated by the successive downward shifts of curve I to I'. These results support our hypothesis that the development of seed-fertilizer technology tended to counteract the rising cost of irrigation because of the movement of irrigation construction from easier to more difficult sites. The momentum of internal land augmentation was maintained through the complementarity of technology and land infrastructure.

Only incomplete data are available for investments in opening new land. In the case of Japan, aggregate time-series data are available for the period after 1918. The estimates for Japan in Table 10-3 show that the marginal costs of opening land to produce an additional unit of income in agriculture were about the same as those for irrigation, if the traditional varieties were used. But since the improved varieties had already been introduced widely in Japan by the 1920s, the profitability of investment in irrigation would clearly have been higher than in opening land.

The time-series data for Japan are not sufficient to test the relation between the cost curves for opening land and development of irrigation hypothesized in Figure 10-5 (A, I, and I'). The data for Korea are more informative in this respect. Cases A and B for Korea in Table 10-3 correspond to the technology level of "Traditional 0N" (applying zero nitrogen for traditional varieties) and "Improved 100N" (applying 100 kg of nitrogen for improved varieties), respectively, for rice planted in newly opened paddy fields. The real cost of both opening land and irrigation for the traditional technology (Case A) rose sharply from the beginning of the 1920s (Figure 10-6). The irrigation cost curve rose sharply until the mid-1920s, reflecting increasing short-run costs caused by the sudden jump in government investment in irrigation based on the Korean Rice Production Development Program. The longer-run trend, however, seems steeper for the land-opening curve than for the irrigation curve.

Another interesting observation for Korea is the relation between the land-opening and the irrigation curves for the improved technology (Case B in Table 10-3). Although the development of seed-fertilizer technology was successful in counteracting the increase in irrigation costs to produce additional agricultural income, it did not reverse the rise in the land-opening cost curve. The divergence between the land-opening and the irrigation curves for Case B demonstrates clearly the role of complementarity between irrigation and technology in shifting the momentum of agricultural growth from external to internal land augmentation.

FIGURE 10-6. Comparison of the trends in the cost-benefit ratios for building irrigation systems and opening new land for Korea, 1934–36 constant prices.

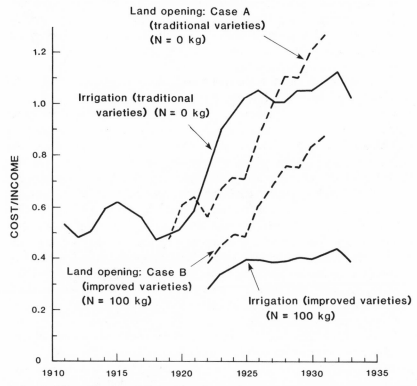

Source: Masao Kikuchi and Yujiro Hayami, "Agricultural Growth against a Land Resource Constraint: A Comparative History of Japan, Taiwan, Korea, and the Philippines," *Journal of Economic History* 38 (December 1978): 860, © Economic History Association.

Unfortunately, no aggregate time-series data on land-opening investment are available for Taiwan and the Philippines. In the case of Taiwan, the estimated costs of land opening are for the government land settlement project for 1909–17. Cases A and B assume that different crops were planted in the new land: two crops of upland rice and one crop of sugarcane, respectively. The results show much higher cost-benefit ratios for land-opening than for irrigation investments, which suggests a rationale for the Taiwan colonial government's heavy investment in irrigation since the mid-1910s for the purpose of raising agricultural output.[12]

12. In an earlier stage of development in Taiwan, several land-settlement projects were undertaken by the colonial government and the sugar companies. Those projects were unsuccessful. Taiwan Government-General, *Kanei Imin Jigyo Hokokusho* (Report on government land settlement projects) (Taipei, 1919); Tadao Yanaihara, *Teikokushhugi ka no Taiwan* (Taiwan

In the case of the Philippines, the estimates of the costs of opening land are from 1973 land-opening projects of the Bureau of Land Resettlement. Cases A and B assume that one crop of upland rice and two crops of corn are planted in the newly opened upland area, respectively. The results show that irrigation improvement was a much more profitable and less costly means of generating an additional unit of income in agriculture, especially with modern fertilizer-responsive varieties.

The four countries have in common rising irrigation cost curves. But there were differences in the levels of the marginal cost-benefit ratios for irrigation, which are clearly seen in Figure 10-7. The curves of irrigation cost-benefit ratios for Japan for different technologies are located well above those for Taiwan and Korea throughout the period under study.

As previously stated, modern Japan inherited from the feudal period relatively well-developed irrigation systems; the easier sites for building irrigation facilities had largely been exhausted by the time modernization began. In Taiwan and Korea, on the other hand, the inadequacy of irrigation infrastructure for the successful introduction of seed-fertilizer technology during their early stages of agricultural development implies that relatively large areas suitable for irrigation development were left unexploited. The possibility of achieving an increase in agricultural output at a relatively low cost by exploiting the underdeveloped irrigation potential can be identified as a basic factor that induced public investment in irrigation systems in Taiwan and Korea under the Japanese colonial rule.

The gap in the irrigation cost-benefit ratio between Japan and its colonies continued to narrow during the 1920s as a result of the rapid exhaustion of less costly sites for irrigation development concurrent with the rapid expansion of irrigation-command areas in Taiwan and Korea. Had there been no agricultural depression in Japan in the 1930s, and thus no interruption in the irrigation development programs, the irrigation cost-benefit ratio of Taiwan and Korea would have approached the level of Japan. Such a process seems to imply a movement toward an equilibrium in rice-production costs within the Japanese Empire.

The marginal cost-benefit ratio of irrigation for the Philippines in the 1950s was at the same level as for Taiwan and Korea in the initial stage of their agricultural development, which may imply that the Philippines was endowed with an equally large potential for irrigation development. The failure of the irrigation cost curve in the Philippines to rise in the 1960s as fast as in Taiwan and Korea in the 1920s may mean that the potential for irrigation development in the Philippines was exploited less rapidly than in Japan and Korea. In any

---

under imperialism) (Tokyo, 1929). Almost the only project that was successful in settling the emigrants was the project analyzed here, and it was terminated in 1917, leaving a large part of the original plan incomplete. These unsuccessful attempts were consistent with the low rates of return to land opening estimated in this study.

FIGURE 10-7. Comparison among the trends in the cost-benefit ratio for irrigation improvement in Japan, Taiwan, Korea, and the Philippines.

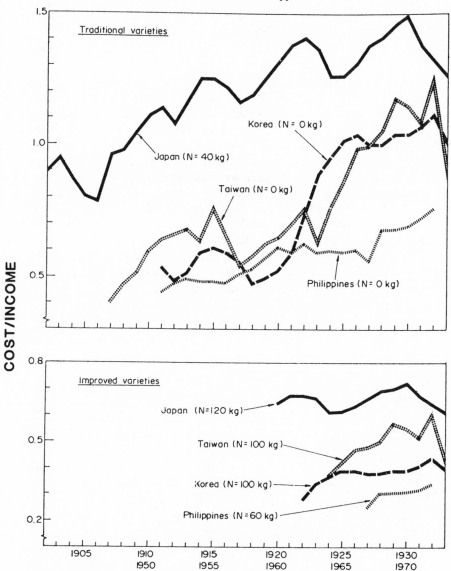

Source: Masao Kikuchi and Yujiro Hayami, "Agricultural Growth against a Land Resource Constraint: A Comparative History of Japan, Taiwan, Korea, and the Philippines," *Journal of Economic History* 38 (December 1978): 862, © Economic History Association.

case, it is clear that the Philippines still has a very large potential for profitable irrigation development.

BARRIERS TO EFFICIENT RESOURCE ALLOCATION TO LAND INFRASTRUCTURE

The comparative history of Japan, Taiwan, Korea, and the Philippines outlined in previous sections clearly shows a mechanism by which technology transfer and land-infrastructure development were induced in a mutually reinforcing manner in response to growing population pressure on limited land resources. This process is not limited to the Philippines. It seems pervasive among developing countries today. In fact, in countries of South and Southeast Asia, deteriorations in the man-land ratio as measured by increases in the number of agricultural workers per hectare of arable land have been associated with a steady increase in the percentage of arable land under irrigation (Table 10-4). This infrastructure development has enabled the new seed-fertilizer technology to diffuse rapidly in those countries.

A major difficulty in achieving efficient allocation of resources to the development of land infrastructure stems from the fact that its benefits do not

TABLE 10-4.   Changes in the man-land ratio of arable land and the ratio of area under irrigation

	1955	1965	1975
Man-land ratio (workers/ha of arable land)			
Bangladesh	1.84	1.98	2.27
India	0.82	0.88	0.96
Pakistan	0.55	0.49	0.56
Sri Lanka	1.20	1.11	1.30
Indonesia	1.46	1.55	1.59
Philippines	0.81	0.91	1.05
Thailand	0.93	0.91	0.89
Ratio of arable land area under irrigation (percent)[a]			
Bangladesh	5	7	16
India	14	16	19
Pakistan	56	61	74
Sri Lanka	19	21	22
Indonesia	23	24	24
Philippines	13	14	18
Thailand	16	14	19

Source: Yujiro Hayami and Masao Kikuchi, *Asian Village Economy at the Crossroads* (Tokyo: University of Tokyo Press, 1981; and Baltimore: Johns Hopkins University Press, 1982), pp. 40 and 43.

[a]Figures for 1965 are as of 1966.

necessarily accrue to those who pay the cost. Like agricultural research, land infrastructure is endowed, to a significant extent, with such public-goods attributes as indivisibility, externality, and jointness in supply and use. The supply of such goods at a socially optimal level depends on the efficiency of public sector decision-making and resource-allocation institutions.

The public-goods characteristics are weaker for land infrastructure than for agricultural research. Capacity constraints in the irrigation and drainage systems limit the scope of joint use. Also, it is easier to exclude from the use of the facilities those who do not share the costs. Therefore, group action of farm producers plays an important role in the provision of land infrastructure. The efficient allocation of resources to land infrastructure depends critically on the design of local institutions that facilitate the organization of group action by farm producers to construct and manage irrigation and drainage systems locally. The provision of the larger-scale irrigation system infrastructure is, however, appropriately a government responsibility.

The need for collective action in irrigation and drainage depends on socioeconomic conditions such as farm-size distribution as well as on natural conditions such as water sources and topography. Where farm size is large and groundwater that can be lifted by relatively small-sized pumps is available, resources can be allocated efficiently to irrigation if left to private producers. An example was sharp increases in private investment in irrigation pumps in Pakistan and Punjab-Haryana in India concurrent with the spread of modern varieties of wheat and rice.[13] But the diffusion of modern varieties down the Gangetic Plain into eastern India and Bangladesh has been slow. The heavy monsoon rain in this area reduces the benefit from irrigation in the wet season. More crucially, the small farm size and fragmented holdings make it uneconomical for most farmers to install pumps individually. The inability of private profit incentives to allocate resources efficiently to the development of land infrastructure is more pronounced in the case of gravity irrigation systems in communities of small peasants.

One obvious answer to the problem of capital lumpiness is to organize group action by farm producers. The organization of irrigation projects at the local community level is highly desirable not only because it solves the problem of capital lumpiness but also because it facilitates mobilization of local resources at low opportunity cost for the construction and maintenance of highly productive infrastructure. Typically, in the rural sector of low-income, labor-abundant economies, labor is idle during the dry season. The

13. Inderjit Singh, "The Landless Poor in South Asia," *Growth and Equity in Agricultural Development*, Proceedings, Eighteenth International Conference of Agricultural Economists, Jakarta, Indonesia, August 24–September 2, 1982, ed. Allen Maunder and Kazushi Ohkawa (Aldershot, Hampshire, England: Gower Publishing Co., Ltd., 1983), pp. 379–400. See also Inderjit Singh, *Small Farmers and the Landless in South Asia* (Baltimore: Johns Hopkins University Press, in press).

rates of return to communal irrigation projects that effectively mobilize off-season labor have proved to be extremely high.[14]

The organization of irrigation projects depends on the capacity of community leadership to convince a sufficient number of people that it is to their mutual advantage to participate and to convince the government that the project is worthy of support. As Randolph Barker explains:

> Both are formidable tasks, and the rules of the game—persuasion, coercion, forging signatures when necessary—are not part of economic literature. . . . A major problem is that a leader who takes on both the formidable task . . . will benefit only marginally from the project if he is a small landholder. So only a rare individual dedicated to the community good will offer to organize a community project. On the other hand, if the leader is a large landholder, he will benefit substantially, but other members of the community will see the project as a means of promoting his interests rather than contributing to the common benefit. In this case, it would be extremely difficult to persuade the community members to contribute their labor.[15]

Because enlightened and dedicated leadership is rare, only a few such projects are successful and a large potential of irrigation in developing countries remains unexploited. And even when enlightened leadership does exist, it can be rendered ineffective if local institutions are designed to facilitate control from the center rather than to facilitate mobilization of local resources.

In a broader perspective the lack of effective leadership and of willingness of community members to support it are deeply rooted in the culture. An intensive network of small-scale irrigation systems in Japan has been built and maintained mainly by communal efforts since the feudal period. This system provided a favorable environment for the development and diffusion of modern seed-fertilizer technology during the Meiji period. The organizational capacity of local communities to mobilize communal labor for irrigation developed gradually over generations in response to gradual population pressure on available land. The social system had become tightly structured so that community members were expected to conform closely to traditional social norms. One such norm was the obligation of village elites to exercise leadership and of other villagers to participate in the construction, operation, and maintenance of irrigation infrastructure vital for the survival of their community.

14. See Masao Kikuchi, Geronimo Dozina, Jr., and Yujiro Hayami, "Economics of Community Work Programs: A Communal Irrigation Project in the Philippines," *Economic Development and Cultural Change* 26 (January 1978):211–25; Geronimo Dozina, Jr., Masao Kikuchi, and Yujiro Hayami, "Mobilizing Local Resources for Irrigation Development: A Communal System in Central Luzon, Philippines," International Rice Research Institute, *Irrigation Policy and Management in Southeast Asia* (Los Baños, Philippines, 1978), pp. 135–42; Anwar Hafid and Yujiro Hayami, "Mobilizing Local Resources for Irrigation Development: The Subsidi Desa Case of Indonesia," ibid., pp. 123–33.

15. Randolph Barker, "Barriers to Efficient Capital Investment in Agriculture," *Distortions of Agricultural Incentives*, ed. Theodore W. Schultz (Bloomington: Indiana University Press, 1978), p. 149.

In contrast, most parts of Southeast Asia were characterized until recently by an abundant supply of unused land, so that the increasing population could easily be supported by opening new land for cultivation. Although the cultivation frontiers have been closing and the man-land ratio has deteriorated rapidly in recent years, the social system molded under the land-abundant conditions does not change so quickly. Compared with Japan, the social structure in Southeast Asia has remained loose, making it easier to avoid than to participate in group activities.[16]

In such a society, the task of organizing community members for construction and maintenance of irrigation infrastructure is difficult, and leadership does not readily emerge because it is not a trait traditionally expected of village elites. Thus the cultural endowments and communal institutions have resulted in a weaker base for responding to the rapidly increasing returns to development of irrigation infrastructure in Southeast Asia than in East Asia.

The ineffective organization of local communities also puts a burden on the national irrigation systems. The efficient design and implementation of government irrigation projects require an understanding between the government and the farmer users so that the users' interests are reflected in the system's design and operation. In the absence of pressure from the farmers' organizations, the design of national systems tends to be dominated by engineering criteria, and cultural institutional considerations are neglected by both the government and the international lending agencies.[17] This problem is aptly described by Barker:

> Commonly, one observes the following progression of events in the development of national systems. The government initially may construct the primary and secondary canals in the system in anticipation that the local community will complete the tertiary canals and farm ditches. Partly because village organization and leadership are lacking, as described earlier, the local community takes no action. The farmers may lack the organizational capacity or even the simple ditching and leveling equipment and technical advice needed to complete the job. In many cases, due to poor management of water in the major laterals, there may be essentially no benefits to be gained. The farmers blame the irrigation authority who, in turn, blames the farmers. Amidst complaints that the system is not working properly, the national irrigation authority responds in the only way that it can, with more capital investment to undertake land consolidation and lay out the tertiary canals and farm ditches. The construction cost per hectare doubles.

16. John Embree, an American anthropologist, first characterized Thailand as a "loosely structured" society, in contrast to Japan. See Embree, "Thailand—A Loosely Structured Social System," *American Anthropologist* 52 (April–June 1950):181–93. Several comparative studies of rice villages in Japan and Southeast Asia indicate that the villages in Southeast Asian countries are, in general, less tightly structured than those in Japan. See *A Comparative Study of Paddy-Growing Communities in Southeast Asia and Japan*, ed. Masuo Kuchiba and Leslie E. Bauzon (Tokyo: Toyota Foundation, 1979).

17. For a detailed discussion of problems of reform of water institutions see Daniel W. Bromley, Donald C. Taylor, and Donald E. Parker, "Water Reform and Economic Development: Institutional Aspects of Water Management in the Developing Countries," *Economic Development and Cultural Change* 28 (January 1980):365–87.

As with construction, the major weakness in the operation and maintenance of the system seems to be institutional or organizational rather than technical. The water delivered to each farm cannot be metered. Normally everyone is charged an equal amount per hectare, usually only enough to cover operation and maintenance costs. However, those managing the system take no steps to ration the water and insure its equitable distribution. The farms at the head of the canal waste water; the farms at the end seldom have enough. The system operates with an efficiency well below that projected in the initial feasibility studies.

The choice among system designs at the national level is influenced by the thinking of the engineers who are primarily responsible for both designing and operating the system. The more "modern" the system, the better. . . . This natural bias toward engineering efficiency and capital intensity is reinforced by personal experience. Those who run the system know that a more labor-intensive solution does not work because it is difficult to obtain active participation of the farmers. Thus, the existing organizational and institutional structure of the irrigation network, and the weak linkage between those delivering the water and the end-users, serve as the ultimate constraint to the maximization of social benefits in the design, operation, and maintenance of the system.[18]

In short, the lack of active participation and organized pressure from local communities results in a bias toward high-capacity intensity in national irrigation systems in economies with abundant labor and scarce capital. The effect is to reduce the area served by the systems for a given amount of public resources allocated.

BREAKING THE LAND-RESOURCE CONSTRAINT

According to Ricardo and other classical economists, population pressure on land will result eventually in agricultural and economic stagnation, high food prices, real wages barely sufficient for subsistence, and a land rent that is a high share of total income (Chapter 2). The Ricardian perspective remains a real threat for many villages in the developing world, where population growth has been on the order of 2.5 percent per year and the cultivation frontier has been closing rapidly. One way to escape the Ricardian trap is to increase the land productivity by developing land infrastructure and seed-fertilizer technology in a mutually reinforcing manner.

A comparison of agricultural growth in the Philippines since the 1950s with the experience of Japan, Taiwan, and Korea before World War II suggests that several mechanisms are available to relax the land-resource constraint on production. The most important finding from the comparative history of these countries is the process and sequence by which irrigation and technology were developed. In Japan, the feudal heritage of relatively well-developed irrigation systems preceded the development of modern seed-fertilizer technology. But as the technology diffused rapidly, the land infrastruc-

18. Barker, "Barriers to Efficient Capital Investment," pp. 153–54.

ture became a bottleneck that induced public investment and institutional innovation for the further development of land infrastructure. In both Taiwan and Korea, the initial irrigation infrastructure was inadequately developed to take advantage of the transfer of the seed-fertilizer technology from Japan when the transfer was attempted during the interwar period. Large-scale investments in irrigation by the colonial governments were necessary to take advantage of the higher yield potentials. Developments in irrigation and technology proceeded concurrently, thus reinforcing each other.

The rise in land productivity in the Philippines in the 1960s was induced by the stagnation in production associated with the closing of the land frontier. As this change occurred the Philippines began to follow a route of agricultural growth similar to that of Japan, Taiwan, and Korea. The take-off in government irrigation investment in the late 1950s established a favorable environment for the dramatic diffusion of modern semidwarf varieties of rice after the mid-1960s. The rising cost that accompanied the increased amount of cultivated area irrigated was partially offset by the development of new rice technology. If this technology had not been developed, the Philippines would have been caught in a Ricardian trap resulting from sharply rising costs of agricultural production under strong population pressure and land-resource constraints. Whether the Philippines is capable of using these new opportunities for growth to escape the Ricardian trap, rather than merely postpone it, is still an open question.

Population growth will continue to press hard on the economies of the developing countries for several decades. The capital requirement for developing irrigation infrastructure at a pace consistent with increasing food needs will be extremely large. As irrigation systems expand, the lowest-cost construction sites will be progressively exhausted. It will become increasingly more difficult to counteract the rising cost of irrigation by the diffusion of seed-fertilizer technology alone. It will be important to reduce the cost of irrigation by substituting local resources that have low opportunity costs (especially labor during the off season) for more capital-intensive forms of development that are dependent on the limited fiscal capacity of national governments and international lending agencies.

A major impediment to the effective mobilization of local resources is the limited organizational capacity in rural communities. Most parts of Southeast Asia have traditionally been characterized by an abundant supply of unused land resources. Primarily because of the population explosion since World War II, it was only recently that the critical need arose to increase the productivity of existing cultivated land. There has not yet been sufficient time for rural communities to adapt to the development of irrigated agriculture.

A major policy problem is how to shorten the time required for rural communities to develop their organizational capacity in response to the need for land and water development. Serious research, education, and training efforts should be made by national and international development agencies to correct the bias toward engineering efficiency criteria and to design institutions capable of mobilizing local participation in design, development, and maintenance. Efforts to organize farmers into irrigation associations and to facilitate other group development activities should accompany the construction of irrigation facilities. Communal activities for the rehabilitation and maintenance of rural infrastructure should be promoted through financial incentives and technical assistance. Delivery of institutional credit and inputs should be designed to encourage group action by irrigators.

More effective policy design should be based on intensive investigations at the village level and should draw on the organizational potential that is latent in traditional water mangement institutions. It now seems clear that land and water development programs in which there is excessive concentration of planning and decision making at the center tend to inhibit the mobilization of local knowledge and resources. There needs to be additional experimentation with management systems that can take advantage of center technical capacity and local knowledge and resources.[19]

Such efforts should not be limited to irrigable lowland areas. In developing countries today, tropical forests that play a critical role in holding water for downstream irrigation systems have been denuded rapidly for timber exports, firewood, and cultivation. The result has often been serious soil erosion and flooding, increased cost of irrigation maintenance, and reduction in the usable life of dams and canals. The development of irrigated agriculture in lowland areas must be supported by forestry management programs in hills and mountains. Public expenditure for reforestation should accompany the programs to promote rational agroforestry management so that foods and fuels for mountain people can be reproduced without destroying the ecological balance. A crucial element in such programs is the effective organization of local communities.

The dynamic interactions between technological change and land-infrastructure development may not work efficiently enough to prevent the Third World from slipping into the Ricardian trap. There is a need for institutional innovations that will reduce the cost of the collective action needed to develop the infrastructure that will make the new technologies productive.

---

19. For an indication that such approaches are now being developed in the Philippines see Frances F. Korten, "Building National Capacity to Develop Water Users' Associations: Experience from the Philippines (Washington, D.C.: World Bank Staff Working Paper No. 528, July 1982). For a critical discussion of the conditions under which local participation can be most effective see John D. Montgomery, "When Local Participation Helps," *Journal of Policy Analysis and Management* 3 (1983):90–105.

V

RETROSPECT AND PROSPECT

11

Growth and Equity in Agricultural Development

The intercountry cross-section analysis in Part II, the time-series comparison of Japan and the United States in Part III, and the analysis of international technology transfer in Part IV have all made it clear that technological progress consistent with resource endowments and ecological conditions is the key to growth in agricultural output and income. Our investigation into the nature of international technology transfer in Part IV supports the view that development and diffusion of modern varieties of rice and wheat in the tropics since the late 1960s were highly appropriate in view of the resource endowments of the countries into which these varieties were introduced. This new biological technology has facilitated the substitution of increasingly abundant factors (such as fertilizer) for increasingly scarce factors (such as land).

Introduction of the green revolution or MV technology has not been without controversy, however. Critics have argued that the gains in production have been offset by losses in equity—that the new technology has made the rich richer and the poor poorer.[1] In this chapter we attempt to clarify, at a conceptual level, the relationship between technical change and income distribution during the process of agricultural development and to test our understanding of these relationships against empirical evidence.[2]

---

1. See, for example, the series of reports prepared under the general direction of Andrew Pearse and summarized in *The Social and Economic Implications of Large-Scale Introduction of New Varieties of Foodgrain: Summary of Conclusions of a Global Research Project* (Geneva: United Nations Research Institute for Social Development [UNRISD], Report 74.1, 1974). For a more complete report see Andrew Pearse, *Seeds of Plenty, Seeds of Want: Social and Economic Implications of the Green Revolution* (Oxford: Clarendon Press, 1980); also, Keith Griffin, *The Political Economy of Agrarian Change: An Essay on The Green Revolution* (Cambridge, Mass.: Harvard University Press, 1974), pp. 51–52; and Francis Moore Lappé and Joseph Collins, with Cary Fowler, *Food First: Beyond the Myth of Scarcity*, rev. ed. (New York: Ballantine, 1979), pp. 121–68.

2. For a review of literature see William R. Cline, "Distribution and Development: A Survey of Literature," *Journal of Development Economics* 1 (February 1975):359–400.

AGRICULTURAL TECHNOLOGY AND RURAL EQUITY

The view that modern technology is both subversive of traditional institutions and regressive in its impact on rural incomes is strongly rooted in public consciousness. This belief is supported by both Marxian ideology and populist sentiment. Much discussion on this issue is badly confused. There is often a failure to distinguish between the different income-distribution effects of mechanical-engineering and biological-chemical technology. There is also a tendency to focus on single-factor explanations and to ignore the effects of such factors as the growing population pressure against land resources.

Technology and Agrarian Structure

The perspective was advanced by Karl Marx and elaborated by Karl Kautsky and Vladimir Lenin that an inevitable consequence of both modern technology and capitalism is to polarize the peasantry into commercial farmers and wage laborers.[3] In this perspective the institutions of precapitalist village society, such as communal landownership, mutual-help associations, and patron-client ties, were thought to assure the subsistence needs of the poorest members of the rural community. As those traditional institutions were replaced by modern market institutions, such as private property rights, village elites began to accumulate land for commercial production by encroaching on the commons, by evicting tenants, and by purchasing or appropriating the holdings of small peasants. The introduction of modern machine technology further enhanced the efficiency of large-scale relative to small-scale operations, enabling large capitalist farms to displace the small peasants from their land and convert them into landless laborers. Those who were not able to find employment in agriculture owing to the labor-saving effect of modern agricultural technology were forced to migrate and join the urban lumpen or the reserve army of industrial workers.

The model for this polarization process, as conceived by Marx, was the Second Enclosure Movement in England, although Marx recognized that the English model might not be replicated in its ideal form in other countries. The Marxian predictions did not materialize in the other countries of western Europe and Japan that followed England in industrialization.[4] Even in the

---

3. Karl Marx, *Capital*, Vol. 3 (New York: International Publishers, 1967); and *Theories of Surplus Value* (Moscow: Progress Publishers, 1968); Karl Kautsky, *Die Agrarfrage* (Hannover: Verlag J.H.W. Dietz nachf., 1966, facsimile reprint of the Stuttgart 1899 ed.); Vladimir I. Lenin, *The Development of Capitalism in Russia* (Moscow: Progress Publishers, 1964).

4. In western Europe, except the United Kingdom, industrialization was accompanied by the persistence, or even the increase, rather than the elimination of small-scale peasant production units, which led to a major controversy between orthodox and revisionist Marxians on the "agrarian question." See David Mitrany, *Marx against the Peasant: A Study in Social Dogmatism* (Chapel Hill: University of North Carolina Press, 1951), chaps. 1–3; Alain de Janvry, *The Agrarian Question and Reformism in Latin America* (Baltimore: Johns Hopkins University Press, 1981), pp. 94–140; Michael Lipton, *Why Poor People Stay Poor: Urban Bias in World Development* (Cambridge, Mass.: Harvard University Press, 1977), pp. 107–30. More recent

United States, where the development of labor-saving technology proceeded most rapidly, family farms continue to account for a high share of agricultural production. Unlike the industrial sector, large-scale farm firms characterized by hired labor and management did not become the dominant mode of production in the modern capital-intensive system of agriculture practiced in the United States.

Why did the Marx-Lenin prediction fail to materialize in the course of capitalist development? The primary reason seems to be that intensive polyculture systems require high levels of husbandry skill. Only a few crops, such as sugarcane and cotton, have lent themselves to production by gangs of unskilled laborers working under the direction of hired overseers. Unlike the industrial sector in which the machine process makes work highly standardized and easy to monitor, the biological process of agricultural production is subject to infinite variations in response to ecological conditions. Very different treatments for a crop or an animal are often required in response to slight differences in temperature and soil moisture. It matters a great deal whether a laborer performs his work with care and judgment. Furthermore, the quality of such work is extremely difficult to monitor. The scattering of agricultural operations over a wide space adds to the difficulty of monitoring.[5]

This difficulty multiplies as the farming system becomes more complex, involving more intensive crop and animal husbandry. As John M. Brewster put it, "In areas more suitable for multiple enterprise farms, family operators have the advantage. Increasing the number of enterprises so multiplies the number of on-the-spot supervisory-management decisions per acre that the total acreage which a unit of management can oversee quickly approaches the acreage which an ordinary family can operate."[6] Thus the development of biological technology geared to increase output per unit of land area by applying more labor, together with increased biological and chemical inputs for more intensive crop and animal husbandry, gives small family farms an advantage over large farms dependent on hired wage labor. Perhaps the strongest evidence of the relative inefficiency of the estate or plantation system, based on the use of large numbers of unskilled workers carrying out standardized tasks under hired overseers, is its tendency to disappear whenever urban demand for labor has generated upward pressure on agricultural wage rates.[7]

historical research suggests that even in the United Kingdom the impact of population increase rather than parliamentary enclosure was primarily responsible for the growth of landlessness. See the review by David Grigg, *The Dynamics of Agricultural Change: The Historical Experience* (New York: St. Martin's Press, 1982), pp. 195–214.

5. For a discussion of the unique nature of the biological production process, see Yujiro Hayami and Masao Kikuchi, *Asian Village Economy at the Crossroads: An Economic Approach to Institutional Change* (Tokyo: University of Tokyo Press, 1981, and Baltimore: Johns Hopkins University Press, 1982), pp. 12–16.

6. John M. Brewster, "The Machine Process in Agriculture and Industry," *Journal of Farm Economics* 32 (February 1950):69–81.

7. The inefficiency of agricultural production based on the use of large numbers of unskilled workers was a major reason for the decline of the manor system in western Europe during the

It is critical to recognize that modern technologies are not homogeneous in their effects on agrarian structure. Advances in mechanical technology are usually accompanied by scale economies, resulting in economy in management effort as well as in the use of labor in production. It is much easier to supervise one tractor driver than a large number of bullock teams. The development of mechanical technology has increased the relative efficiency of large farms as Marx and Lenin envisaged. Biological technology, in contrast, is generally embodied in divisible inputs such as improved seed and fertilizer and requires intensive on-the-spot supervisory management decisions. Its effect is to raise the relative efficiency of small family farms and promote a unimodal farm-size distribution.

Marx and Lenin failed to predict the course of agrarian change, primarily because they failed to understand the complexity of the biological production process and the potential contribution of advances in biological technology to productivity growth.

Our perspective is consistent with historical changes in the size distribution of operational holdings in Japan (Table 11-1). As observed in previous chapters, significant progress of biological technology before World War II was associated with the increasing concentration of farms into the middle-size (0.5 to 2 hectares) class, with a decrease in the percentage shares of both small (less than 0.5 hectares) and large (more than 2 hectares) farms. This process was not confined to the modern era after the Meiji Restoration. It was well under way during the Tokugawa period. In the early Tokugawa period the dominant mode of farming had been large holdings, ranging from a few hectares to a few dozen hectares, which were cultivated with labor supplied by the extended family, hereditary or indentured servants, or both.

As population pressure increased and irrigation systems were built, especially after the middle of the eighteenth century, more labor-intensive and land-saving technologies were developed, such as double-cropping, improved crop varieties, and fertilizers. These advances often were applied first to commercial crops such as cotton, tobacco, and indigo with sericulture. These more complex farming systems were intensive both in labor use and in their managerial requirements and therefore were more efficient than large units. As a result, the share of land cultivated by large farms was gradually reduced through the dissolution of the extended family or renting land to members of the servant class. Thus the small-scale family farm of around one hectare became the dominant mode of agricultural production toward the end of the Tokugawa period.[8]

---

sixteenth century. See Immanuel Wallerstein, *The Modern World-System I: Capitalist Agriculture and the Origins of the European World-Economy in the Sixteenth Century* (New York: Academic Press, 1974), pp. 87–116.

8. Yujiro Hayami, with Masakatsu Akino, Masahiko Shintani, and Saburo Yamada, *A Century of Agricultural Growth in Japan* (Minneapolis: University of Minnesota Press, and Tokyo: University of Tokyo Press, 1975), pp. 44–45; also see Thomas C. Smith, *The Agrarian Origins of Modern Japan* (Stanford: Stanford University Press, 1959).

TABLE 11-1. Distribution of farms by size of cultivated area (percentages)

	Farms			
Year	Less than 0.5 ha	0.5–2.0 ha	More than 2 ha	Total
1908	37.3	52.1	10.6	100.0
1910	37.5	52.4	10.1	100.0
1920	35.3	54.0	10.7	100.0
1930	34.3	56.4	9.3	100.0
1940	33.3	57.3	9.4	100.0

Source: Institute of Developing Economies, *One Hundred Years of Agricultural Statistics in Japan* (Tokyo, 1969), p. 116.

There is no denying that institutional factors in addition to technology, such as agricultural associations and credit cooperatives, contributed to the unimodal farm-size distribution in Japan. Those institutions, however, promoted the unimodal structure mainly by facilitating rather than restraining the development and diffusion of modern technology. In effect, these institutional innovations were induced by the potential gains from a unimodal structure of agricultural production. In the absence of development of scale-neutral technology, there would have been few gains from such institutional innovations and it is unlikely that they would have emerged.

Technology and Population Pressure

The relation between new technology and factor income shares is closely related to the characteristics of both the new technology and the structure of the economy into which it is introduced. The extent to which the income generated by a new technology embodied in factors such as a new seed variety or a new machine will augment the productivity and the income accruing to other factors will depend on the technical characteristics of the production function, the elasticity of supply of the several factors, and the institutional environment into which the new technology is introduced.[9]

In rural communities the major source of inequality in income distribution is the inequitable distribution of landownership, which often corresponds to the inequitable distribution of operational holdings. If the share of agricultural income accruing to labor increases, the income position of tenants and agricultural laborers improves relative to that of landlords and owner-cultivators. The reverse occurs if the income share accruing to land increases. Therefore,

9. For a technical discussion of embodiment and augmentation see Hans P. Binswanger, "A Note on Embodiment, Factor Quality, and Factor Augmentation," Appendix 5-1, in *Induced Innovation: Technology, Institutions, and Development,* ed. Hans P. Binswanger and Vernon W. Ruttan (Baltimore: Johns Hopkins University Press, 1978), pp. 159–63. The critics of the green revolution have often failed to understand the distinction between embodiment and augmentation.

land-saving and labor-using technological changes that raise the economic return to labor relative to land have the effect of equalizing the income distribution between the landless and the landowning classes. In contrast, labor-saving and land-using technological changes contribute to greater inequality.

Since biological technology saves land by applying labor and biological inputs more intensively, its diffusion might be expected to contribute to a more favorable income distribution in rural communities. Nevertheless, the new seed-fertilizer technology has often been blamed for benefiting landlords at the expense of tenants and laborers on the ground that land rents increased while wage rates stayed the same or even declined in many areas where MVs and related inputs were introduced. These arguments have often ignored a critical factor coinciding with the MV diffusion—the growing pressure of population on the land.

During the past two decades the labor force engaged in agricultural production in countries in South and Southeast Asia increased at rates of 1.0 to 2.5 percent per year.[10] Meanwhile, arable land area has increased at rates of about 1.0 percent or less. The deterioration in the man-land ratio has been even more serious than the data imply because the cultivation frontier has been expanded largely into marginal, less productive areas. Classical economists such as Ricardo predicted that as the cultivation frontier expands onto lower-quality land the marginal return to additional labor input would decline and the cost of food production would rise—real wage rates would decline and rents would rise (Chapter 2). If this process had not been partially offset by the adoption of land-saving technology, incomes would have fallen further and a larger portion of agricultural income would have accrued to landlords.

Several highly simplified models are presented in Figure 11-1 to clarify the effects of technological change and population pressure on wage rates, land rent, and factor share.[11]

For the sake of simplicity, let us assume an agricultural production function in which output is produced from labor (L) and land (A). Output may be considered as value added after current inputs are deducted, and land may be considered as land-cum-capital. The upper diagrams in Figure 11-1 represent aggregate demand and supply of labor in the market and the lower diagrams the production function (f) that relates output per hectare ($q = Q/A$) to labor input per hectare of physical land area ($l = L/A$). The shape and the location of f are determined by technology, broadly defined to include land infrastructure such as irrigation and drainage. The classical assumption of decreasing return to labor applied per unit of land is adopted.

Case I represents one polar example in which the labor demand curve (the

10. Hayami and Kikuchi, *Asian Village Economy*, pp. 39–40.
11. These models are developed more fully in Hayami and Kikuchi, *Asian Village Economy*, pp. 49–52.

FIGURE 11-1. The effects of technological change and population pressure on income distribution among laborers and asset holders.

I Technology constant and population increasing   II Technology progressing and population constant

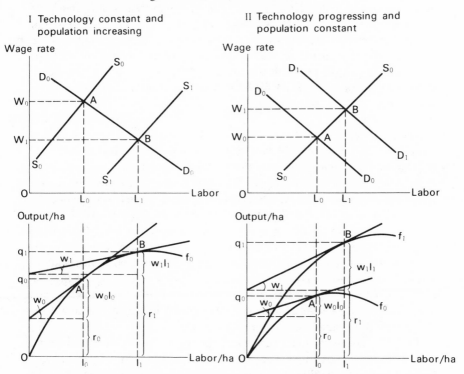

Source: Yujiro Hayami and Masao Kikuchi, *Asian Village Economy at the Crossroads: An Economic Approach to Institutional Change* (Tokyo: University of Tokyo Press, 1981, and Baltimore: Johns Hopkins University Press, 1982), p. 50.

marginal product schedule for labor) stays constant at D_0, reflecting no progress in technology (f_0), while the labor supply schedule shifts from S_0 to S_1 as a result of population growth. Corresponding to a change in the market equilibrium point from A to B, the wage rate declines from w_0 (OW_0) to w_1 (OW_1) and the land rental rate rises from r_0 to r_1. If the increased labor is applied to the fixed production function (f_0) at a zone of decreasing return to labor such that the elasticity of substitution of labor for land is less than one (i.e., less than a 1 percent increase in the labor-land ratio results from a 1 percent decrease in the wage-rent ratio), the relative income share of labor declines from ($w_0 l_0 / q_0$) to ($w_1 l_1 / q_1$). If the labor application per hectare continues to increase, a point will eventually be reached beyond which the elasticity of factor substitution becomes so small that labor's income declines absolutely in response to any further increase in labor input.

Case II represents another polar example. Let us assume that the labor supply schedule remains constant at S_0 and the labor demand schedule shifts from D_0 to D_1, reflecting the upward shift in the production function from f_0 to f_1. In response to the change in market equilibrium from A to B, the wage rate rises from w_0 to w_1 and the absolute income of labor from $(w_0 l_0)$ to $(w_1 l_1)$. Whether the relative income share of labor improves or not depends on the nature of the shift in the production function. The relative share of labor (w_1/q) increases if the production function shifts in such a way as to increase the labor-land ratio ($l = L/A$) for a constant rent-wage ratio (r/w) at competitive equilibrium—the land-saving and labor-using technological change in Hicks's definition.

In the real world both the demand for and the supply of labor shift simultaneously. The evidence presented in the previous section shows, however, that in many developing countries the shift in the supply of labor caused by rapid population growth has outpaced the shift in demand for labor caused by technological progress. The result has been a decline in the real wage rate. In such a situation, the income distribution would become more skewed because the rate of return to land (r) would rise relative to that of labor (w) and an increasing share of income would be captured by the landowning class. In most developing countries the level of living of the rural poor, the landless laborers, and tenants whose incomes consist mainly of earnings from their labor will continue to decline both absolutely and relatively unless land-saving technical change results in more rapid growth in demand for labor than the growth in the supply of labor in rural areas.

This does not imply that every change in technology is beneficial to the poor. Some technological changes reduce labor's income by displacing labor by machinery and herbicides and are labor-saving in the Hicksian sense. In the right-hand diagram of Figure 11-1, labor-saving (and land-using) technological change is represented by a shift in the production function in such a way as to reduce the labor-land ratio ($l = L/A$) for a constant rent-wage ratio (r/w) in competitive equilibrium. This is equivalent to a shift of the unit isoquant from I_0 to I_1 in the left-hand diagram of Figure 4-2. If a technological change is labor-saving, the relative income share of labor (w_1/q) declines. It is theoretically possible for the labor-saving bias to be so strong that the absolute income of labor will decline.

GREEN REVOLUTION CONTROVERSIES

The discussions in the previous section should make it clear that the development of biological technology designed to increase agricultural output per unit of land area is a critical factor in offsetting tendencies toward a worsening of income distribution in the rural sector in response to growing population pressure on land. The MV technology is in this category. Yet since its introduction, often heralded as the green revolution, MV technology has frequently been viewed as a source of inequity in income distribution and of polarization in rural communities.[12]

The critics of the green revolution have argued that (a) the new technology tends to be monopolized by large farmers and landlords who have better access to new information and better financial capacity even though MVs and related inputs are divisible and, hence, applicable to small farms; (b) small farmers are unable to use MVs efficiently because financial constraints make it difficult for them to purchase cash inputs such as fertilizers and chemicals; (c) monopoly of the new technology by large farmers enables them to use their profits to enlarge their operational holdings by consolidating small farmers' holdings; and (d) as farm size increases it becomes profitable to purchase large-scale machinery and reduce the cost of labor management.[13] The effect is to reduce employment opportunities and to lower wage rates for the growing number of landless workers.

How valid is the suggested sequence? Have large holders dominated the adoption of MV technology? Does the technology make large-scale operations relatively more efficient and profitable? Does MV technology induce mechanization and reduce employment and earnings? These are the issues that must be tested against empirical data.

Was MV Technology Monopolized by Large Farmers?

The available evidence indicates that neither farm size nor tenure has been a serious constraint to MV adoption. The data on adoption of modern wheat varieties in Pakistan, presented in Table 11-2, are fairly typical of those available for other areas where MVs are technically well adapted. Similar

12. This section draws heavily on Yujiro Hayami, "Induced Innovation, Green Revolution, and Income Distribution: Comment," *Economic Development and Cultural Change* 30 (October 1981):169–76; Hayami and Kikuchi, *Asian Village Economy*, pp. 52–59; and Vernon W. Ruttan, "The Green Revolution: Seven Generalizations," *International Development Review* 19 (August 1977):16–23.

13. These concerns were expressed in Clifton R. Wharton, "The Green Revolution: Cornucopia or Pandora's Box?" *Foreign Affairs* 47 (April 1969):464–76; Bruce F. Johnston and John Cownie, "The Seed-Fertilizer Revolution and Labor Force Absorption," *American Economic Review* 59 (September 1969):569–82; Walter P. Falcon, "The Green Revolution: Generations of Problems," *American Journal of Agricultural Economics* 52 (December 1970):698–710; Ingrid Palmer, *The New Rice in Asia: Conclusions from Four Country Studies* (Geneva: United Nations Research Institute for Social Development, 1976). Even more extreme views have been expressed in Francine R. Frankel, *India's Green Revolution: Economic Gains and Political Costs* (Princeton: Princeton University Press, 1971); Harry M. Cleaver, Jr., "The Contradictions of the Green Revolution," *American Economic Review* 62 (May 1972):177–86; Ali M. S. Fatemi, "The Green Revolution: An Appraisal," *Monthly Review* 24 (June 1972):112–20; and Keith Griffin, *The Political Economy of Agrarian Change: An Essay on the Green Revolution* (Cambridge, Mass.: Harvard University Press, 1974). For a useful comment on the sources of bias in the early assessment studies of the green revolution see John Harriss, "Bias in Perception of Agrarian Change in India," in *Green Revolution: Technology and Change in Rice-growing Areas of Tamil Nadu and Sri Lanka,* ed. B. H. Farmer (London: Macmillan, 1977), pp. 30–36, and Robert Chambers, "Beyond the Green Revolution: A Selective Essay," *Understanding Green Revolutions: Agrarian Change and Development Planning in South Asia,* ed. Tim Bayliss-Smith and Sudhin Wanmali (Cambridge: Cambridge University Press, 1984), pp. 362–79.

TABLE 11-2.   Mexican-type wheat acreage as percentage of all wheat acreage, by size and tenure of holdings: 1969–70 post-monsoon season in Lyallpur, Sahiwal, and Sheikhupura districts, Pakistan

Number of acres in holding	Owner holdings	Owner-cum-tenants	Tenant holdings	All holdings
Less than 12.5	71.0	80.4	66.7	72.5
12.5 to 25	63.3	71.7	69.2	68.0
25 to 50	71.9	92.7	81.9	82.0
50	73.2	87.3	57.3	78.6
All sizes	69.4	80.5	70.0	73.4

Source: K. M. Azam, "The Future of the Green Revolution in West Pakistan: A Choice of Strategy," *International Journal of Agrarian Affairs* 5 (March 1973):408. Original source: Government of the Punjab, Planning and Development Department, Statistical Survey Unit, *Fertilizer and Mexican Wheat Survey Report* (Lahore, 1970), p. 38.

results have been reported for wheat in India, rice in India, Indonesia, Malaysia, and the Philippines, and maize in Kenya.[14]

There are, of course, cases in which small farmers lagged significantly behind large farmers in MV adoption. One example was found in a rice village in Andra Pradesh, India, covered by an international project and coordinated by the International Rice Research Institute to study the changes in rice farming in selected areas of Asia.[15] This village was characterized by extremely skewed farm-size distribution. Its experience supports the hypothesis that the introduction of MV technology into a community in which resources are very inequitably distributed tends to reinforce the existing inequality.

14. See Bandhudas Sen, *The Green Revolution in India: A Perspective* (New Delhi: Wiley Eastern, 1974), pp. 32–54; Mahar Mangahas, Virginia A. Miralao, and Romana P. de los Reyes, with Normando de Leon, *Tenants, Lessees, Owners: Welfare Implications of Tenure Change* (Quezon City: Ateneo de Manila University Press, 1976), pp. 23–49; Mahar Mangahas, "Economic Aspects of Agrarian Reform under the New Society," *Philippine Review of Business and Economics* 11 (December 1974):175–87; Irlan Soejono, "Growth and Distributional Changes of Paddy Farm Income in Central Java, 1968–1974" (Ph.D dissertation, Iowa State University, 1976); Soejono, "Growth and Distributional Changes in Paddy Farm Income in Central Java," *Prisma (Indonesian Journal of Social and Economic Affairs)*, no. 3 (May 1976), pp. 26–32; John Gerhart, *The Diffusion of Hybrid Maize in Western Kenya* (Mexico, D.F.: Centro Internacional de Mejoramiento de Maiz y Trigo, 1975); Richard H. Goldman and Lyn Squire, "Technical Change, Labor Use, and Income Distribution in the Muda Irrigation Project," *Economic Development and Cultural Change* 30 (July 1982):753–75; C. J. Bliss and N. H. Stern, *Palanpur: The Economy of an Indian Village* (Oxford: Clarendon Press, New York: Oxford University Press, 1982), pp. 124–210. For a more complete review of literature on the income distribution effects of the MV technology in Asia see Inderjit Singh, *Small Farmers and the Landless in South Asia* (Baltimore: Johns Hopkins University Press, in press); and Randolph Barker and Robert Herdt with Beth Rose, *The Asian Rice Economy* (Baltimore: Johns Hopkins University Press, 1985), chap. 13.

15. G. Parthasarathy, "West Godavari, Andhra Pradesh," *Changes in Rice Farming in Selected Areas of Asia* (Los Baños, Philippines: International Rice Research Institute, 1975), pp. 43–70.

FIGURE 11-2. Cumulative percentage of farms in three size classes adopting modern varieties and tractors in thirty villages in Asia.

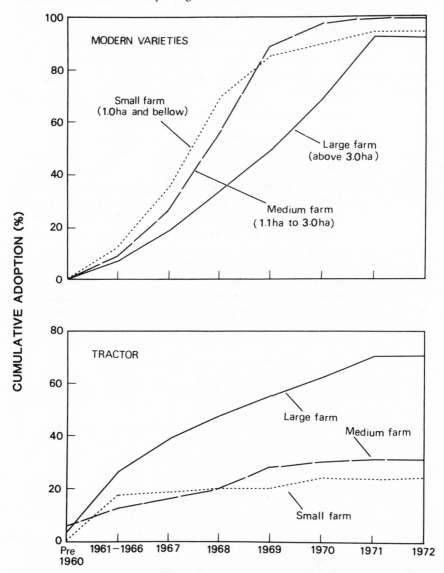

Source: International Rice Research Institute, *Interpretive Analysis of Selected Papers from Changes in Rice Farming in Selected Areas of Asia* (Los Baños, Philippines, 1978), p. 91.

This village is an exception rather than a norm, however. Of the thirty-six villages studied by the project, it was the only one where a significant differential in the MV adoption among farm-size classes was observed. On the average, small farmers adopted the MV technology even more rapidly than large farmers (see the upper diagram of Figure 11-2). The pattern of MV diffusion contrasts sharply with the pattern for the diffusion of tractors in which large farmers achieved a distinctly faster and higher rate of adoption (lower diagram in Figure 11-2).

Did the MV Technology Make Large Farms Relatively More Efficient?

There is now a large body of evidence that suggests that small farmers make more efficient use of available land than large farmers.[16] They apply higher levels of labor input, particularly family labor, and they usually have more livestock per unit of land than large farms. Surjit Sidhu's carefully conducted study of the adoption of modern wheat varieties in the Indian Punjab showed that MV wheat represented a neutral technological change with respect to farm scale—both small and large farms achieved approximately equal gains in efficiency.[17]

A study by K. M. Azam in Pakistan interpreted the data from the Pakistan Punjab to indicate that, although "the smaller farmers do face relatively more severe constraints of irrigation water and credit, the difference in the severity of these constraints is not serious enough to have caused any significant differences in the yields obtained by the small farmers as compared with large farmers."[18] Similar results have been reported for rice from the Philippines by Mahar Mangahas and from Indonesia by Irlan Soejono.[19]

Again, in some cases differential productivities were recorded, although they seem to be exceptional. For example, among the thirty-two villages

16. The literature on the relationship between farm size and productivity has been reviewed by R. Albert Berry and William R. Cline, *Agrarian Structure and Productivity in Developing Countries* (Baltimore: Johns Hopkins University Press, 1979).

17. Surjit S. Sidhu, "Relative Efficiency in Wheat Production in the Indian Punjab," *American Economic Review* 64 (September 1974):742–51. Sidhu concludes "(1) that small and large wheat producing farms have equal relative economic efficiency and equal relative price efficiency and (2) that tractor-operated and non-tractor operated wheat producing farms have equal relative *economic efficiency* and equal relative *price efficiency.* . . . This implies that these farms also have equal *technical efficiency,*" p. 746.

18. K. M. Azam, "The Future of the Green Revolution in West Pakistan: A Choice of Strategy," *International Journal of Agrarian Affairs* 5 (March 1973):418. The impact of the green revolution on income distribution in Pakistan has been vigorously debated. See M. H. Khan, *The Economics of the Green Revolution in Pakistan* (New York: Praeger Publishers, 1975); M. Ghaffar Chaudhry, "Green Revolution and the Redistribution of Rural Incomes: Pakistan's Experience," *Pakistan Development Review* 21 (Autumn 1982):173–205; M. H. Khan, "Green Revolution and Redistribution of Rural Incomes: Pakistan's Experience—A Comment," *Pakistan Development Review* 22 (Spring 1983):47–56; M. Ghaffar Chaudhry, "Green Revolution and Redistribution of Rural Incomes: Pakistan's Experience—A Reply," *Pakistan Development Review* 22 (Summer 1983):117–24.

19. Mangahas et al., *Tenants, Lessees, Owners;* and Soejono, "Growth and Distributional Changes."

throughout Asia covered by the IRRI-coordinated project, significant differences in rice yields per hectare between large and small farmers were recorded in only eight villages.[20]

A major puzzle is why, in view of the evidence, planners and officials in developing countries and officials in national and international development assistance agencies remain skeptical about the efficiency of small farms. One reason may be that as a country develops and the opportunity cost of labor rises, the special efficiency advantage of small farms tends to disappear. It thus becomes natural to associate large farms with a highly developed national economy. But this inference is irrelevant in most developing economies in which the absolute size of the agricultural labor force is continuing to increase.

Did the MV Technology Promote Mechanization?

The popular perception that MV technology stimulates the introduction of labor-displacing machinery has not been borne out by careful analysis. The data in Figure 11-2 indicate that large farmers began to adopt tractors before the introduction of MVs. Nor was there any indication that adoption of tractors was accelerated by the dramatic diffusion of MVs from the late 1960s to the early 1970s.

Much of the growth in the use of tractors in South and Southeast Asia can be attributed to distortions in the price of capital by such means as overvalued exchange rates and concessional credits from national governments and international lending agencies. Also, the ease of supervising the operation of one tractor with an operator relative to that of supervising a large number of laborers and bullock teams seems to have worked as a strong inducement to tractorization on large farms.[21] This factor should have been especially serious where regulation of land rent and tenure arrangements depressed the incentive of large landowners to rent out their holdings in small operational units.

Did the MV Technology Reduce Labor Employment and Earnings?

An extensive review of the literature by William Bartsch indicates that the introduction of MVs into traditional wheat and rice production systems has

20. International Rice Research Institute, *Interpretive Analysis of Selected Papers from Changes in Rice Farming in Selected Areas of Asia* (Los Baños, Philippines: International Rice Research Institute, 1978), p. 96.
21. Randolph Barker, William H. Meyers, Cristina Cristostomo, and Bart Duff, "Employment and Technological Change in Philippine Agriculture," *International Labour Review* 106 (August–September 1972):111–39; John P. McInerney and Graham F. Donaldson, "The Consequences of Farm Tractors in Pakistan" (Washington, D.C.: World Bank Staff Working Paper 210, 1975); Bart Duff, "Mechanization and Use of Modern Rice Varieties," *Economic Consequences of the New Rice Technology,* ed. Randolph Barker and Yujiro Hayami (Los Baños, Philippines: International Rice Research Institute, 1978), pp. 145–64; Hans P. Binswanger, *The Economics of Tractors in South Asia* (New York: Agricultural Development Council; and Hyderabad, India: International Crops Research Institute for the Semi-Arid Tropics, 1978).

TABLE 11-3. Percentages of farms adopting MVs and tractors and use of labor man-days per hectare for rice production in Laguna, Philippines, 1966–75, wet seasons

	1966	1970	1975
MV adopters (percent of farms)[a]	0	76	94
Tractor adopters (percent of farms)[a]	26	71	90
Average paddy yield (metric tons/ha)	2.5	3.4	3.5
Labor input (man-days/ha)			
Land preparation	18.7	11.1	9.0
Transplanting	10.2	10.2	10.9
Weeding	13.8	17.8	31.3
Other preharvest operations	9.4	14.8	20.2
Harvesting and threshing	31.6	33.6	31.6
Postharvest operations	4.4	5.4	3.4
Total	88.1	92.9	106.4

Source: Randolph Barker and Violeta G. Cordova, "Labor Utilization in Rice Production," *Economic Consequences of the New Rice Technology in Asia,* ed. Randolph Barker and Yujiro Hayami (Los Baños, Philippines: International Rice Research Institute, 1978), pp. 120 and 127.
[a]Averages for wet and dry seasons.

typically resulted in substantial increases in annual labor use per unit of cropped area and, in some cases, in higher cropping intensity. Similarly, data assembled by Randolph Barker and Violeta Cordova from various areas in Asia show that labor input per hectare of area in rice was higher for MVs than for traditional varieties by 10 to 50 percent.[22]

Sidhu's econometric investigation indicates a very substantial shift to the right of the labor demand function on wheat farms in Indian Punjab as a result of the introduction of MVs. Similar results were obtained by both C. H. Hanumantha Rao and William Staub.[23]

Increases in labor use associated with MVs were often realized despite the concurrent progress in mechanization. The data on labor use in rice production from the Laguna province in the Philippines, as presented in Table 11-3,

22. William H. Bartsch, *Employment and Technology Choice in Asian Agriculture* (New York: Praeger Publishers, 1977), indicates that in wheat production, under a wide variety of technologies ranging from primary dependence on human labor to fully mechanized production, the shift from traditional varieties to high-yielding MVs leads to increased labor inputs per hectare. When this shift to MV technology was accompanied by a simultaneous shift to a fully mechanized technology, labor input per hectare declined. In all cases output per unit of labor input rose. Randolph Barker and Violeta G. Cordova, "Labor Utilization in Rice Production," *Economic Consequences of the New Rice Technology,* ed. Randolph Barker and Yujiro Hayami (Los Baños, Philippines: International Rice Research Institute, 1978), pp. 113–36.

23. Surjit S. Sidhu, "Economics of Technical Change in Wheat Production in the Indian Punjab," *American Journal of Agricultural Economics* 56 (May 1974):217–26; C. H. Hanumantha Rao, *Technological Change and Distribution of Gains in Indian Agriculture* (Delhi: Macmillan Company of India, 1975), p. 227; and William J. Staub, *Agricultural Development and Farm Employment in India* (Washington, D.C.: U.S. Department of Agriculture, Economic Research Service, Foreign Agricultural Economic Report 84, 1973).

are typical. This province experienced rapid diffusion of both modern rice varieties and tractors. Tractorization reduced the amount of labor needed for land preparation, but the reduction was more than compensated for by increases in labor use for weeding and in other areas of crop husbandry.

The econometric test by Sidhu on Punjab wheat production shows that the new technology was neutral with respect to factor use, implying that labor's income rises proportionally with the incomes accruing to land and capital. A similar study by Chandra G. Ranade and Robert W. Herdt on rice in the Philippines suggests that the MV technology is biased in the land-saving direction.[24]

Several other studies, however, show that the labor share of income declined and the land share increased over the period of MV diffusion. Dayanatha Jha's data indicate that the factor share to land rose in India between 1960–61 and 1970–71. Data assembled by John Mellor and Uma Lele indicate that a disproportionately small percentage of the increased output attributable to MV adoption was allocated to labor.[25] The data on relative shifts in factor shares cannot be interpreted without further analysis to indicate that landowners have gained relative to tenants and laborers from the adoption of MVs. Considerable confusion has resulted from neglect of the fact that while the income share of land increased, as Jha's data clearly show, not only did technology change but labor supply increased. As the model in Figure 11-1 illustrates, if the labor supply increases faster than demand for labor, it is possible for the factor share of land to rise even if the technological change is biased in the land-saving and labor-using direction.

Much of the data that indicated a rise in the factor share to land, such as that presented by Mellor and Lele, was obtained during the initial stages of MV adoption. At that time MVs accounted for only a small percentage of area cultivated and of output. There was, therefore, only a modest shift in aggregate wheat or rice production or in aggregate factor demand. Early adopters were able to capture large excess profits from the use of more efficient technology without forcing down product prices or bidding up factor prices appreciably. As the technology is diffused more widely, innovators' excess profit tends to be lost as product and factor prices move toward a new equilibrium. In the long run, the relative share of labor will return to the same level as before the introduction of MVs if MVs represent a neutral technological change. It will become larger if the technology is biased in the land-saving and labor-using direction. This sequence is supported by a number of studies; for example, Pranab Bardhan found that in North India at the begin-

24. Sidhu, "Relative Efficiency in Wheat Production"; Chandra G. Ranade and Robert W. Herdt, "Shares of Farm Earnings from Rice Production," *Economic Consequences of the New Rice Technology*, ed. Barker and Hayami, pp. 87–104.

25. Dayanatha Jha, "Agricultural Growth, Technology and Equity," *Indian Journal of Agricultural Economics* 29 (July–September 1974):207–16; John W. Mellor and Uma J. Lele, "Growth Linkages with the New Foodgrain Technologies," *Indian Journal of Agricultural Economics* 28 (January–March 1973):35–55.

ning of MV diffusion the green revolution had no significant effect on the demand for rural labor. An analysis by Deepak Lal in the same region for a later period, however, shows clearly that as MV use diffused more widely the net effect of the resulting increase in demand for labor was a significant rise in the real wage rates in Punjab and other parts of North India at a time when real wage rates were constant or declining in other parts of India where MV diffusion was limited.[26]

How do we interpret the critical assessments of the effects of the green revolution on income distribution in view of the findings reported in this section? First, it is apparent that many of the assessments that were made during the initial years of the green revolution were based on limited data and, in some cases, an excessively casual approach to analysis of the data that were available. Second, there was a general failure to understand that the impact of a technical change on income distribution is a function both of the character of the technology and of the economic and institutional environment into which it is introduced. There is as yet no evidence that the MV technology is heavily biased against labor. There is substantial evidence that in most areas where it has been adopted it has increased the demand for labor.[27] And there is a growing body of evidence that the impact on production and on demand for labor has had a positive effect on the quality of life in rural villages. In his study of a Punjab village, for example, Murray J. Leaf notes that farmers now "grow more per hectare . . . and more per capita overall. As measured by food, medical care, educational facilities, and housing, there have been substantial improvements in general welfare. . . . The gains have gone at least as much to the poorer villagers as to the wealthier. . . . The poorer families are remaining in the village and finding work and improved living conditions. . . . They are able to send increasing numbers of their children to school. . . . The wealthier families, who have already invested more in education . . . are sending members out . . . to white-collar and other types of service employment."[28] In addition, the MV technology and the increased agricultural income resulting from its adoption have had the important effect

26. Pranab K. Bardhan, " 'Green Revolution' and Agricultural Labourers," *Economic and Political Weekly* 5, nos. 29–31 (Special Number, July 1970):1239–46; Deepak Lal, "Agricultural Growth, Real Wages, and the Rural Poor in India," *Economic and Political Weekly* 11, no. 26 (June 1976):A47–61.

27. A limitation of most of the studies that are presently available is that they tend to employ a microeconomic partial equilibrium analysis. A series of sector-level general equilibrium econometric studies are now under way which should provide more definitive results than are now available. For a preliminary report see Robert E. Evenson, "Economics of Agricultural Growth: The Case of Northern India," *Issues in Third World Development*, ed. Kenneth C. Nobe and Rajan K. Sampath (Boulder, Colo.: Westview Press, 1983), pp. 145–91, and "Population Growth and Agricultural Development in North India" (Paper presented at Conference on Recent Population Trends in Southwest Asia, New Delhi, February 2–8, 1983).

28. Murray J. Leaf, "The Green Revolution and Cultural Change in a Punjab Village, 1965–1978," *Economic Development and Cultural Change* 31 (January 1983):268. See also George Blyn, "The Green Revolution Revisited," *Economic Development and Cultural Change* 31 (July 1983):705–25.

of creating employment opportunities in the nonagricultural sector through increased demand for nonagricultural goods and services by the agricultural sector.[29]

A VIEW FROM TWO VILLAGES IN JAVA

The empirical evidence fails to confirm that the MV technology (in combination with irrigation and fertilizer) has contributed to more inequitable income distribution. In general, both small and large farmers have adopted MVs at more or less equal rates and have achieved efficiency gains of the same order. It is likely that the MV technology was neutral or biased, if anything, in the land-saving and labor-using direction. It has generally resulted in increases in demand for labor, even in areas where it has been accompanied by concurrent progress in mechanization.

We do, however, see a real danger of growing inequality in rural areas, not because of new technology but because of insufficient progress in the development and diffusion of new technology. If technological progress is not sufficiently rapid, the increase in demand for labor will fail to keep up with the increase in the supply of labor arising from rapid population growth. As the model in Figure 11-1 indicates, the wage rate is bound to decline, the return to land to rise, and the income position of laborers and tenants to deteriorate relative to that of landowners when the rate of growth of the rural labor force exceeds the rate of growth in demand for labor.

A comparative analysis by Yujiro Hayami and Masao Kikuchi of two villages located in the same geographic district in Java—one characterized by technological stagnation and the other by significant technological progress—demonstrates this point with remarkable clarity.[30] A comparison of the two cases shows the separate effects of technological change and population growth.

The two villages chosen for the comparative analysis are located in the Regency (*kabupaten*) of Subang in West Java, adjacent to the north of the Bandung Regency and about 120 km east of Jakarta. One village is located at the foot of the mountains in the southern part of the Subang Regency and is identified as the South Village. Much of the land belonging to the South Village consists of terraced rice fields. The other village, identified as the North Village, is located about 20 km south of the South Village and is on a completely flat coastal plain along the Java Sea. These two villages were

---

29. Mellor and Lele, "Growth Linkages with the New Foodgrain Technologies"; Raj Krishna, "Measurement of the Direct and Indirect Employment Effects of Agricultural Growth with Technological Change," *Externalities in the Transformation of Agriculture,* ed. Earl O. Heady and Larry R. Whiting (Ames: Iowa State University Press, 1975), pp. 305–27; Uma Lele and John W. Mellor, "Technological Change, Distributive Bias and Labor Transfer in a Two Sector Economy," *Oxford Economic Papers* 33 (November 1981):426–41.
30. This section draws on Hayami and Kikuchi, *Asian Village Economy,* chaps. 8 and 9.

among those covered by the Rice Intensification Survey (Intensifikasi Padi Sawah), which was conducted by the Agro-Economic Survey of Indonesia during 1968–72. The data collected from this survey provide the initial benchmark information. New surveys were conducted during January 1979 in the South Village and during November–December 1979 in the North Village.

Population Pressure and Technological Change

Java is known for its extremely high population density. The two villages under study are also characterized by very unfavorable man-land ratios. In the South Village, as many as 419 persons obtained their primary subsistence from only about 25 hectares of wet rice (Sawah). The situation was somewhat better in the North Village. Its population of 774 persons had 64 hectares of rice land.[31]

Although the population density was higher in the South Village, the rate of population growth seems to have been much faster in the North Village. Data on the number of children per mother (Table 11-4) suggest that over the past forty years the natural rate of population growth in the South Village declined from about 3 percent per year to 1 percent. There was no indication of a significant inflow of migrants. Although data for the higher age brackets are not available, a comparison of the average numbers of children per mother suggests that the natural rate of population growth was much faster in the North Village than in the South Village. Moreover, there were a large number of migrants into the North Village. Older villagers recalled that in 1940 there were about 40 households. At the time of our survey the number had in-creased to 191. Assuming no change in average family size, the rate of population growth for the past four decades was about 4 percent per year.

These demographic differences can be explained by the different histories of settlement and technological change in the two villages. The South Village is old; no one could recall when it was first settled. The North Village was settled after 1920. The settlement was late because it was more difficult to build a gravity irrigation system with only local resources in the flat coastal plain than in the small mountain valley where the South Village was located.

The economy of the South Village experienced little change in recent times. The local irrigation systems had been well developed for as long as people could remember and permitted rice production on about 90 percent of the paddy field area even in dry seasons. There had been no significant improvements in the system and no expansion in cultivated area since World War II. Growing population pressure resulted in increased fragmentation of landholdings through inheritance. The number of landless and near-landless families increased.

31. In addition to wet rice fields, the South Village had 3 hectares and the North Village had 8 hectares of land used for home gardens and fish ponds.

TABLE 11-4. Average numbers of surviving children per mother by mother's age and the estimates of the natural rates of population growth in the South and North Villages in the Regency of Subang, West Java, Indonesia

	South Village		North Village	
Mother's age	Children per mother (n) No.	Population growth rate[a] (r) %/year	Children per mother (n) No.	Population growth rate[a] (r) %/year
80 years and above	4.80	3.0	n.a.	–
60–79	3.93	2.3	n.a.	–
50–69	3.49	1.9	n.a.	–
40–49	2.71	1.0	3.25	1.6
(36–45)	(2.48)	(0.7)	(3.16)	(1.5)
30–39	1.95	–	2.57	–
20–29	0.84	–	1.80	–

Source: Yujiro Hayami and Masao Kikuchi, *Asian Village Economy at the Crossroads: An Economic Approach to Institutional Change* (Tokyo: University of Tokyo Press, 1981, and Baltimore: Johns Hopkins University Press, 1982), pp. 176 and 198.
[a]Calculated by the formula: $n = 2(1 + r)^{30}$, assuming 30 years for the period of mothers' reproductive capacity.

MVs were introduced in the late 1960s under the Bimas Program, a nationwide effort to intensify rice production based on a package of modern inputs, credit, and extension. But because the first MVs introduced were highly susceptible to the brown planthopper and tungro, a virus disease, many farmers who tried them shifted back to traditional varieties. From 1968–71 to 1978 the MV adoption rate increased slowly from 11 to 14 percent, although as many as 83 percent of the farmers had tried MVs at least once. As a result, the average rice yield per hectare increased only slightly, from 2.6 to 2.9 tons per hectare.

The population pressure on limited land resources under a stable technology apparently reached a saturation point by the 1950s. The data in Table 11-4 indicate that the villagers responded by reducing their birth rate even before 1975, when a government birth control program was introduced. Villagers indicated that many wives had practiced abortion by indigenous methods that were often harmful to their health. The South Village appears to be an example of the impact of the Malthusian check on population growth.

In contrast to the stagnation in the South Village, the economy of the North Village was highly dynamic. The initial settlers opened the land and practiced an extensive system of rainfed rice production. Because rice yields under the rainfed system were very low, a relatively large farm was required to meet the subsistence needs of a family. The population density was low by Java standards until the Jatiluhur Irrigation System, the largest irrigation system in Indonesia, was extended to the village.

The Jatiluhur System had a dramatic impact on the economy of the North Village. Major laterals were built by 1968, but it was not until 1972 that secondary and tertiary laterals were completed and the entire area of the village became suitable for rice double-cropping. In 1968–71, double-cropping was practiced in about half of the rice land. By 1979 the entire area was double-cropped.

The introduction of double-cropping rice production was facilitated by the diffusion of early-maturing and nonphotosensitive MVs. According to the Rice Intensification Survey, 7 percent of farmers planted MVs in 1968–71. The ratio rose to 100 percent in 1978–79. There was no difference in the MV adoption rate among farm-size and tenure classes. The MVs commonly used in 1979 were IRRI varieties (IR26, IR36, IR38) and the Asahan variety developed by the Central Agricultural Experiment Station at Sukamana' located near the North Village.

With the diffusion of MVs and the increased application of fertilizer, the average yield per hectare of rice crop area increased from 2.4 tons in 1968–71 to 3.5 tons in 1978–79. The cropping index rose from 1.5 to 2.0. Thus the average rice output per hectare of rice land per year rose by more than 80 percent between 1968 and 1978.

Employment, Wages, and Factor Shares

The different patterns of technological progress (defined here broadly as a shift in the production function resulting from both irrigation improvement and MV diffusion) between the two villages were reflected in sharp differences in the use of rice production inputs and in input prices (Tables 11-5 and 11-6).

In the South Village, where technology was stagnant, the input of fertilizer per hectare of crop area increased at a rate lower than the rate of decline in the real price of fertilizer. In the North Village, where the fertilizer-responsive MVs were widely adopted, the per-hectare input of fertilizer increased at a rate six times as fast as the rate of decline in the price of fertilizer.

Changes in the use of labor and animal power in relation to their price changes also produced dramatic contrasts. In the South Village, an increase in labor input was associated with a decline in the real wage rate. Meanwhile, a rise in the real rental rate of draft animals (carabao and cattle) resulted in a sharp decline in the use of animal power. As a result, because of the decline in the labor wage rate relative to animal rental costs, hand hoeing was substituted for animal plowing and harrowing. It is clear that the population pressure on land under a stagnant technology resulted in a decline in the value of human labor relative to the values of both capital and food.

In contrast, in the North Village higher labor inputs were associated with a significant increase in the real wage rate. The average labor input per hectare of rice increased only modestly. But the labor input per hectare of rice area per year increased more than 40 percent over the decade as a result of the

TABLE 11-5. Changes in inputs per hectare of rice crop area and input prices for rice production in the South Village, 1968–71 to 1978

	1968–71[a]	1978[b]	Percent change from 1968–71 to 1978
Inputs			
Fertilizer (kg/ha)	191	229	20
Labor (hours/ha):			
Land preparation	420	494	18
Total (preharvest)	736	928	26
Carabao and cattle for land preparation (days/ha)	16.4	9.2	−44
Real input prices (in paddy)[c]			
Fertilizer (kg/kg)	1.5	1.1	−27
Labor wage (kg/day)[d]	9.5	8.5	−11
Carabao rental (kg/day)	6.2	9.5	53

Source: Yujiro Hayami and Masao Kikuchi, *Asian Village Economy at the Crossroads: An Economic Approach to Institutional Change* (Tokyo: University of Tokyo Press, 1981, and Baltimore: Johns Hopkins University Press, 1982), pp. 180 and 181.

[a]Averages for wet and dry seasons.
[b]Dry season.
[c]Nominal price divided by paddy price.
[d]Wage for land preparation, assuming eight hours per day; includes meals.

TABLE 11-6. Changes in inputs per hectare of rice crop area and input prices for rice production in the North Village, 1968–71 to 1978–79

	1968–71[a]	1978–79[b]	Percent change from 1968–71 to 1978–79
Inputs			
Fertilizer (kg/ha)[c]	75	209	179
Labor (hours/ha):			
Land preparation	219	233	6 (42)[g]
Total (preharvest)	638	701	10 (46)[g]
Carabao and cattle for land preparation (days/ha)[d]	9.6	13.2	38 (83)[g]
Real input prices (in paddy)[e]			
Fertilizer (kg/kg)	1.5	1.0	−33
Labor wage (kg/day)[f]	7.9	11.5	46
Carabao rental (kg/day)[d]	8.8	14.1	60

Source: Yujiro Hayami and Masao Kikuchi, *Asian Village Economy at the Crossroads: An Economic Approach to Institutional Change* (Tokyo: University of Tokyo Press, and Baltimore: Johns Hopkins University Press, 1982), pp. 201 and 203.

[a]Averages for wet and dry seasons.
[b]Averages for 1978–79 wet season and 1979 dry season.
[c]Urea and TPS.
[d]Data for wet season only.
[e]Nominal price divided by paddy price.
[f]Wage for land preparation, assuming eight hours per day; includes meals.
[g]Outside of parentheses are the rates of increase in labor input per ha of cropped area. Inside of parentheses are the rates of increase per ha of paddy field area per year.

increase in the multiple-cropping index (figures in parentheses in the last column of Table 11-6). At the same time, the use of animal power increased even more rapidly than the use of human labor despite a rapid rise in the real cost of animal rental. It is clear that the increase in demand for labor owing to technological progress outpaced the increase in labor supply owing to population growth. As a result, the real wage rate rose in spite of the effort to substitute capital (animal power) for human labor.

How were the major differences in technological change reflected in different patterns of income distribution between the South and North villages? Estimates of changes in the average factor shares of rice output per hectare of crop area in the two villages are shown in Tables 11-7 and 11-8. The factor payments are expressed in terms of paddy (rough rice) by multiplying factor inputs by factor-product price ratios.

In the South Village, the average rice yield per hectare increased by about 10 percent from 1968–71 to 1978. Both the payment to hired labor and the imputed cost of family labor increased by less than 5 percent. For owner farmers, operators' surplus (residual) rose sharply. For tenant farmers, operators' surplus was almost zero and land rent paid to landlords was equivalent to the owner farmers' surplus. These results indicate that for the owner farm-

TABLE 11-7. Changes in factor payments and factor shares in rice production per hectare of crop area in the South Village, 1968–71 to 1978

	Factor payment (kg/ha)			Factor share (percent)		
	1968–71[a]	1978[b]		1968–71	1978	
	Owner	Owner[c]	Tenant[d]	Owner	Owner	Tenant
Rice output	2,600	2,942	3,080	100.0	100.0	100.0
Factor payment[e]						
Current input[f]	345	293	321	13.3	10.0	10.4
Capital[g]	136	125	76	5.2	4.2	2.5
Labor	1,257	1,301	1,341	48.3	44.2	43.5
(Family)	(427)[h]	(438)	(476)	(16.4)	(14.9)	(15.4)
(Hired)	(830)[h]	(863)	(865)	(31.9)	(29.3)	(28.1)
Land	0	0	1,262	0	0	41.0
Operators' surplus	862	1,223	80	33.2	41.6	2.6

Source: Yujiro Hayami and Masao Kikuchi, *Asian Village Economy at the Crossroads: An Economic Approach to Institutional Change* (Tokyo: University of Tokyo Press, 1981, and Baltimore: Johns Hopkins University Press, 1982), p. 191.
[a] Averages for wet and dry seasons.
[b] 1978 dry season.
[c] Averages of 74 owner farmers cultivating 20.4 ha.
[d] Averages of 9 tenant operators cultivating 1.8 ha.
[e] Factor payments converted to paddy equivalents by the factor-output price ratios.
[f] Seeds, fertilizers, and chemicals.
[g] Animal rental and irrigation fee.
[h] Assume the same composition of family and hired labor as for 1978.

TABLE 11-8.   Changes in factor payments and factor shares in rice production per hectare of crop area in the North Village, 1968–71 to 1978–79

	Factor payment (kg/ha)			Factor share (percent)		
	1968–71[a]	1978–79[b]		1968–71[a]	1978–79[b]	
	Owner	Owner	Tenant[c]	Owner	Owner	Tenant[c]
Rice output	2,342	3,203	3,272	100.0	100.0	100.0
Factor payment[d]						
Current input[e]	152	300	280	6.5	9.4	8.5
Capital[f]	47	154	154	2.0	4.8	4.7
Labor	947	1,322	1,295	40.4	41.0	39.6
(Family)	(117)	(252)	(357)	(5.0)	(7.9)	(10.9)
(Hired)	(830)	(1,070)	(938)	(35.4)	(33.4)	(28.7)
Land	0	0	1,495	0	0	45.7
Operators' surplus	1,196	1,427	48	51.1	44.5	1.5

Source: Yujiro Hayami and Masao Kikuchi, *Asian Village Economy at the Crossroads: An Economic Approach to Institutional Change* (Tokyo: University of Tokyo Press, 1981, and Baltimore: Johns Hopkins University Press, 1982), p. 206.

[a] Averages for wet and dry seaons.
[b] Averages of 1978–79 wet season and 1979 dry season.
[c] Data for share tenants.
[d] Factor payments converted to paddy equivalents by the factor-product price ratios.
[e] Seeds, fertilizers, and chemicals.
[f] Animal and machine rental and irrigation fee.

ers the operators' surplus consisted mainly of the return to their land. This implies an increase in the economic rent to land. The decline in the relative share of labor and the rise in the relative share to land imply that the income position of landlords and large owner farmers rose relative to that of marginal farmers, tenants, and agricultural laborers.

It seems likely that the size distribution of income became even more skewed than the data in Table 11-7 indicate. From 1968–71 to 1978, the number of landless and near-landless households in the South Village increased faster than the number of farmers. Therefore, the share of income per landless household probably declined by a greater extent than the share of labor income per hectare. It is highly likely that per household or per capita income from rice production for landless and near-landless households declined in absolute terms even though the rice income per hectare increased slightly.

The situation was very different in the North Village. There the average yield per hectare per year, over both the wet and dry seasons, increased by more than 80 percent. In spite of the rapid increase in output, the relative share of labor stayed almost constant. Meanwhile, the current inputs and capital shares increased. Owner farmers' operators' surplus declined.

The operators' surplus for tenant farmers was almost zero, and the land rent paid to landlords was equivalent to the owner farmers' surplus. This implies that the operators' surplus for owner farmers consisted mainly of the return to their land. Thus the results in Table 11-8 are consistent with the hypothesis that technological progress in this village was biased in a land-saving and capital-using direction and was more or less neutral with respect to the use of labor. These results for the North Village are in sharp contrast to those for the South Village, where the share of land increased sharply at the expense of that of labor.

The comparison of these two villages shows clearly that growing poverty and inequality are almost certain to result if the efforts to generate technological progress are insufficient to overcome the decreasing return to labor resulting from the growing population pressure on land.

PRODUCT MARKET EFFECTS OF NEW TECHNOLOGY

So far we have discussed the equity implications of new technology mainly from a factor market perspective. In this section we discuss the more elusive product market effects of technological change on income distribution.[32]

The "Agricultural Treadmill"

Technological progress in commodity production results in a downward shift in the cost function and hence a shift to the right in the supply function. The total economic welfare or economic surplus, defined as the sum of Marshallian consumers' and producers' surpluses, invariably increases. The distribution of the total welfare gain between consumers and producers depends on the price elasticities of demand and supply. If the demand curve is downward sloping as normally assumed, consumers' welfare increases through the consumption of a larger quantity at a lower price. Producers also gain if they are able to increase output and/or lower costs sufficiently to more than compensate for the price decline. If the price elasticity of demand is very low, however, the price may fall so sharply that the total revenue from the sale of output decreases more than the cost reduction, resulting in a net loss to the producers.

Such an adverse effect of technological progress on farm producers through the product market is most severe in the case of commodities that are not internationally traded (home goods) characterized by low demand elasticities in high-income, fully commercialized economies, such as the United States or the European Economic Community, where farmers market almost all their production and the domestic demand for farm commodities is very inelastic. Ironically, it is in such economies that the capacity to develop and diffuse new technology is the strongest. When product prices decline under

32. This section draws heavily on Yujiro Hayami and Robert W. Herdt, "Market Price Effects of Technological Change on Income Distribution in Semisubsistence Agriculture," *American Journal of Agricultural Economics* 59 (May 1977):245–56.

the pressure of increased supply resulting from technological progress, farmers try to reduce production costs by introducing new technology. The early adopters of innovations enjoy entrepreneurial profits. But as the innovation is diffused the aggregate supply curve shifts to the right, resulting in a fall in prices and the elimination of excess profits. The late adopters are forced to adopt the new innovations so as to avoid incurring losses. This process by which agricultural incomes are squeezed out to benefit urban consumers has been termed the product market "treadmill" by Willard Cochrane. In this process the farmers who are unable to keep up with the treadmill are "ground out" of agriculture and into the nonfarm labor market. Thus in market economies, technological progress in agriculture works to transfer both food and labor from the agricultural to the nonagricultural sector. Wyn Owen has termed this the "double developmental squeeze" on agriculture.[33]

A Model of Semisubsistence Agriculture

The theory of the agricultural treadmill implies that technological progress benefits urban consumers at the expense of agricultural producers in the fully commercialized economies. The situation is quite different in semisubsistence economies, where a large fraction of the commodity is consumed in the households of producers or in the villages in which it is produced. In such economies a large fraction of consumers' surplus resulting from technological progress accrues to the producers. Even if producers' surplus decreases according to the treadmill effect, the loss may be more than compensated for by the increase in consumers' surplus accruing to producers, particularly small producers and landless laborers.

This process is illustrated in Figure 11-3, in which we analyze the market demand and supply relationships for a subsistence crop. The vertical line $D_H H$ is the demand curve of producers for home consumption. It is assumed that producers' households consume a given quantity and sell the rest in the market irrespective of price.[34] $D_M D$ represents the market demand for the product, and the horizontal difference between $D_M D$ and $D_H D$ measures the quantity purchased by nonfarm households. The total demand for the crop is represented by $D_H D_M D$.

$S_0 O$ and $S_1 O$ are the supply curves before and after a technical change. Corresponding to the shift in the supply, the market equilibrium point moves from A to B. Consumers enjoy the increased consumption (OQ_0 to OQ_1) at the reduced price (OP_0 to OP_1). Consumers' surplus increases by $AP_0 P_1 B$, of which $ACGB$ accrues to nonproducer consumers and $CP_0 P_1 G$ accrues to producers themselves. Meanwhile, producers' surplus changes from $AP_0 O$ to

33. Willard W. Cochrane, *Farm Prices, Myth and Reality* (Minneapolis: University Of Minnesota Press, 1958). Wyn F. Owen, "The Double Developmental Squeeze on Agriculture," *American Economic Review* 56 (March 1966):43–70.
34. This conclusion does not change for the first-order approximation even if home consumption is somewhat responsive to price changes instead of being inelastic.

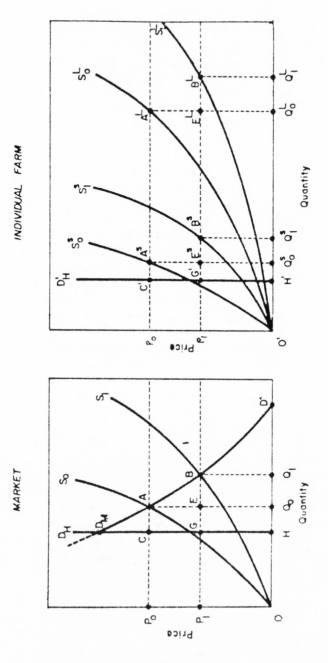

FIGURE 11-3. The impact of technological change on a subsistence crop.

TABLE 11-9. Distribution among producers and consumers of economic welfare gains resulting from technological progress in a subsistence crop, as percent of initial production value ($Y = p_o q_o$)[a]

	Fully commercialized (market surplus ratio: $r = 1.0$)		Semisubsistence (market surplus ratio: $r = 0.4$)	
Consumers' surplus				
To nonproducers				
(ΔCSC)	14.3	(200)	5.7	(80)
To producers				
(ΔCSP)	0		8.6	
Producers' surplus				
(ΔPS)	-7.2		-7.2	
Producers' net gain				
($\Delta NGP = \Delta CSP + \Delta PS$)	-7.2	(-100)	1.4	(20)
Total economic surplus				
($\Delta CSC + \Delta NGP$)	7.1	(100)	7.1	(100)

[a]Calculated from equations (3)–(7), assuming that elasticity of supply (β) = 0.4, elasticity of demand ($-\eta$) = -0.3, and supply shift (k) = 10 percent.

BP_1O. It should be clear that the more vertical or more price inelastic the aggregate demand is, the more likely it is that the producers' surplus decreases. If the quantity of home consumption (OH) is large relative to that sold in the market (HQ_0), however, the more likely is the increase in consumers' surplus accruing to producers (CP_0P_1G) to outweigh the possible decrease in producers' surplus (AP_0O - BP_1O). (For a more formal mathematical treatment of those relationships see the supplement at the end of this chapter.)

A Numerical Illustration

The distributional implications of technological progress in subsistence crops can be illustrated by a specific numerical illustration using empirically relevant parameters. Let the price elasticity of supply (β) be 0.4; the price elasticity of demand ($-\eta$) be -0.3; and the marketed surplus ratio (r) be 0.4. These values are based on empirical estimates from the Philippines. They are reasonably representative of the parameters for major food grains in developing countries in general.[35] We will examine the effect of a 10 percent shift in the supply function (k).

The distributional implications of technological change in a staple food crop in a semisubsistence ecomomy ($r = 0.4$), in contrast to the case of a fully commercialized economy ($r = 1.0$), are shown clearly in Table 11-9. In both cases a 10 percent shift to the right in the supply function owing to tech-

35. The conclusion from this analysis is not sensitive to moderate differences in parameter values. For a sensitivity test, see Hayami and Herdt, "Market Price Effects of Technological Change," p. 251.

TABLE 11-10. Differential impacts of technological progress in a subsistence crop on small and large farms, as percent of initial production value $(p_{oi}q_{oi})$

	Specified parameters			Percentage changes		
	Market surplus ratio (r_i)	Supply elasticity (β_i)	Technical change (k_i)	Consumers' surplus to producers (ΔCSP)	Producers' surplus (ΔPS)	Producers' net gain $(\Delta NGP = \Delta CSP + \Delta PS)$
Case I						
Small farms[a]	0.2	0.4	.10	11.4	−7.1	4.3
Large farms[a]	0.8	0.4	.10	2.9	−7.1	−4.2
Case II						
Small farms[b]	0.2	0.3	.07	11.4	−9.8	1.6
Large farms[b]	0.8	0.5	.14	2.3	−4.4	−2.1

[a]The same rate of technical change ($k = 0.1$), supply elasticity ($\beta = 0.4$), and demand elasticity ($-\eta = -0.3$) is assumed for small and large farms.
[b]Different parameters are assumed for small and large farms. For small farms, technical change is 0.07, supply elasticity β_S is 0.3, and demand elasticity ($-\eta$) is -0.3. For large farms technical change is 0.14, supply elasticity is 0.5, and demand elasticity ($-\eta$) is -0.3.

nological progress results in an increase in total economic surplus of about 7 percent of the value of total output in the base period. The effects on income distribution are quite different for the different marketable surplus ratios. In the fully commercialized economy, nonproducer consumers gain twice the value of total welfare gain at the expense of producers who incur a net loss as large as the total welfare gain. In contrast, in the semisubsistence economy, producers are able to capture 20 percent of the total gain because the reduction in producers' surplus is more than compensated for by a gain in consumers' surplus accruing to producers.

The differential effects of technological progress on small and large farmers in the semisubsistence economy are illustrated in Table 11-10. Two cases are considered: Case I assumes the same rate of technological progress for the small and large farmers ($k = k_S = k_L = 10\%$) and the same magnitudes for their price elasticities of demand ($\beta = \beta_S = \beta_L = 0.4$). Case II assumes a rate of technological progress by the large farmers twice that of the small farmers ($k_S = 7\%$, $k_L = 14\%$). A higher price elasticity for large farmers than that for the small farmers ($\beta_S = 0.3$, $\beta_L = 0.5$) is also assumed to take account of differences in their capacity to finance the resource adjustments needed to adopt the new technology. In both cases, it is assumed that larger farmers sell to the market a much higher proportion of their produce than small farmers ($r_S = 0.2$, $r_L = 0.8$).

In Case I, which may be fairly representative of the green revolution experience in many parts of Asia, the 10 percent shift in the supply function increases the economic welfare of the small farmers and reduces that of the large farmers by more than 4 percent. Even when technological progress occurs twice as rapidly for large as for small farmers (Case II), the small farmers are better off and the large farmers are worse off. It is clear that improved biological technology in a subsistence crop tends to equalize incomes among producers.

Implications for Export Crops

The analysis in this section has so far assumed a closed economy. Although this assumption is not entirely realistic for an individual country, it is not unrealistic for a larger region, such as the rice economy of monsoon Asia, for which the aggregate demand is likely to be inelastic. The implications of our model for the case of export cash crops, for which international trade has a critical role, need to be considered.

In terms of the model developed in Figure 11-3, the export cash crops differ from the subsistence crops in that home consumption is small and the aggregate demand curve is horizontal, at least in the case of a small country. Thus the entire benefit from technological progress accrues to producers in the form of increased producers' surplus.[36] Since technical progress does not

36. The gains may also accrue almost entirely to producers when a country is pursuing a self-sufficiency or import-substitution policy. See Goldman and Squire, "Technical Change, Labor Use, and Income Distribution."

result in a fall in the product price, the gains from technical change are realized entirely in the form of producers' surplus. Technological progress in export cash crops does not have the income-equalizing effects among producers nor are the gains passed on to domestic consumers, as in the case of subsistence crops. This seems to explain why, during the colonial period, the large plantation owners organized themselves into associations and pressed the government to establish research institutions for export crops such as rubber in Malaysia and sugar in Java.

To the extent that producers face an elastic international demand, they are free from the effects of "product market treadmill." This applies, however, to individual countries. The aggregated demand facing the producers of the export cash crops will be more inelastic. The agricultural treadmill effect would operate for the export cash crops on a global scale in a way similar to the calculations for the fully commercialized case in Table 11-10. In this case it is possible, as emphasized by the structuralist and dependency schools, that the benefit from technological progress accrues to consumers in developed countries at the expense of producers in developing countries (Chapter 2). On the other hand, failure to achieve rapid technical change in export crops may lead to the substitution of industrial products, such as synthetic for natural fibers, for the raw materials produced in the developing countries.

TOWARD GROWTH WITH EQUITY

Our examination of the relationship between technological change and income distribution in this chapter suggests that the commonly assumed trade-off between growth and equity appears to be more relevant as an issue for ideological debate than as a description of contemporary development experience. The development and diffusion of new technology that is consistent with factor endowments is a necessary condition for agricultural output and productivity growth. The new technologies that meet the test of efficiency and productivity are also those most likely to advance equity objectives.[37]

In the agriculture of developing countries, in which land is becoming increasingly scarce and expensive relative to labor as population pressure increases against land resources, the development of biological and chemical technologies is the most efficient way to promote agricultural growth. Technological progress of this type tends to make small-scale operations relatively more efficient. It thereby induces an agrarian structure characterized by a unimodal distribution of small family farms rather than a bimodal distribution consisting of large commercial farmers and large numbers of landless or near-landless laborers. Moreover, because such technological progress tends to be

37. This section draws heavily on Yujiro Hayami, "Growth and Equity: Is There a Trade-Off?" in *Growth and Equity in Agricultural Development*, Proceedings, International Conference of Agricultural Economists, Jakarta, Indonesia, Aug. 24–Sept. 2, 1982, ed. Allen Maunder and Kazushi Ohkawa (Aldershot, Hampshire, England: Gower Publishing Co., 1983), pp. 109–16.

generally biased, or at least neutral, toward labor use, it helps counteract the effect of population pressure on land rent and wages.

Technological progress, by definition, results in a downward shift in the cost curve and a shift to the right in the product supply curve. In developed market economies where producers sell a large share of their output in the market, the shift to the right in supply, when confronted with the inelastic demand, causes a disproportionately large fall in product prices. The effect is to transfer the gains from technical change from producers to consumers. When technological progress occurs in a semisubsistence economy, where producers consume a large fraction of their produce, a significant portion of consumers' surplus remains with the producers. The consumers' surplus gain may more than compensate for the loss in producers' surplus. The producers' gain, in the form of consumers' surplus, is proportionately larger for small farmers, who consume a larger share of their production, than for large farmers. Thus, although large commercial farmers may lose from the decline in product prices, small subsistence farmers are more likely to share the benefit from technological progress.

The development of more productive biological and chemical technologies capable of offsetting the effect of growing population pressure appears to be a necessary condition for the simultaneous achievement of both growth and equity in developing countries today. If developing countries fail to achieve sufficiently rapid technological progress, greater poverty and greater inequity in rural areas will be the inevitable result. As the growth of population presses against limited land resources under existing technology, the cultivation frontier is forced onto more marginal land. Greater amounts of labor must be applied per unit of cultivated land with the result that the cost of food production increases and food prices rise. The long-run effect will be, as in the South Village case of the Indonesian village study, the reduction of wages to a subsistence level with the available surpluses captured by landlords in the form of land rent.

It is clear that a necessary condition for escape from the Ricardian trap is land-saving and labor-using technical change. But even if such technology is developed, its contribution to growth and equity will be small if it does not achieve rapid diffusion. If it is confined to a few regions or if adoption is limited to a few large farmers in each village, the aggregate product supply and the aggregate labor demand will not shift appreciably. There will be only a limited impact on product prices and wage rates. The adopters will continue to enjoy innovators' excess profits, but the landless population will not be able to share in the benefits of technological progress in the form of higher wages and lower food prices.

The MV technology, enthusiastically heralded as the green revolution, has often been regarded as a source of inequity in rural incomes. This view is generally inconsistent with the green revolution experience. The MV technology diffused rapidly among farmers irrespective of farm size and land tenure in the areas where it was superior to traditional technology. For numerous cases, however, small or poor farmers lagged significantly behind the large or wealthy farmers in the adoption of MVs and related inputs. Such cases are largely a reflection of institutional rather than technical bias. Institutional reforms are necessary to partition equitably the new income streams generated by an appropriate technology.

Richard Grabowski has listed the necessary reforms:

> Research activities must be directed at developing new seeds for the majority of farmers who lack irrigation. Research activities need to be oriented toward improving cultivation practices and irrigation techniques in order to increase cropping intensity. Credit must be made available to allow farmers with small farms to irrigate their land and thus increase their cropping intensities. . . . Larger farmers' privileged access to machinery must be eliminated. . . . All of these require an increase in the power and influence of farmers with small farms, relative to those with large farms, on government decisions concerning rural research and credit priorities. This could possibly be accomplished through land reforms or, a less radical solution, the organization of small farmers into groups which could put pressure on government agencies to recognize and respond to the interest of small farmers.[38]

These reforms are clearly desirable. But under what conditions would they be economically and politically viable? It is a common observation that, in a society characterized by extreme bias in economic and political resources, it is difficult to bring about institutional reforms that are biased against those who possess substantial economic and political resources. A disproportional share of institutional credit and subsidized inputs will, in such situations, be directed into the hands of the larger farmers. Land reform programs are likely to lead to eviction of tenants and conversion of land use from labor-intensive crops such as rice to more extensive crops such as sugar. It is exceedingly difficult to implement institutional changes that are neutral or biased toward the poor in a society characterized by extreme inequality in economic resources and political power.

A relevant question, given the extreme inequality in wealth and power in many developing countries, is whether the development of the green revolution technology should have been withheld because of its possible adverse effect on income distribution. Even the most severe critics of the green revolution technology have seldom been willing to advocate such a policy. MV technology has been diffusing in Asia with sufficient speed to shift the product demand and the labor supply schedules significantly. There have been substantial gains to both producers and consumers. In the absence of the new technology many developing countries would have moved several steps closer to the Ricardian trap of economic stagnation and even greater stress over the

---

38. Richard Grabowski, "Induced Innovation, Green Revolution, and Income Distribution: Reply," *Economic Development and Cultural Change* 30 (October 1981):180–81.

distribution of income. The conclusion that should be drawn from this experience is not that growth has been "immizerizing" but that stagnation has.[39]

A further reason for encouraging the development and diffusion of new biological and chemical technologies, even in societies characterized by inequitable distribution of economic and political resources, is that the new income streams generated by technical change represent a powerful source of demand for institutional change. It seems clear that in many countries the potential gains from the new technology have generated effective demand for institutional reform. The gains from the new technology can be fully realized only if land tenure, water management, and credit institutions perform effectively. Markets for the inputs that embody the new technology—seeds, fertilizer, and pesticides—must perform efficiently. Product markets in which prices are distorted against either producers or consumers fail to generate the potential gains from new technology. In a society in which technology is static and marketable surpluses are not increasing, there are few gains, either to producers or consumers, from the reform of market institutions. But when rapid growth of production and of productivity becomes possible, the gains become larger and the incentives that act to induce institutional reforms become more powerful. Similarly, unless the potential gains from land tenure and other institutional reforms are enhanced by technical change, it will be difficult to generate the effort needed to bring about these reforms.

We do not argue, of course, that the dialectical interaction between technical and institutional innovation always functions to enhance both growth and equity. Simon Kuznets and others have documented the tendency for income distribution to worsen during the initial stages of development.[40] The potential gains from technical change set in motion both private and bureaucratic efforts to capture the gains from technical change in the form of institutional rents rather than allowing the market to partition the gains among factor owners and consumers. The possibilities for bias in institutional innovations are greatest in societies with highly unequal distribution of economic and political resources.

These institutional biases may in turn induce further bias in the direction of technical change. In a bimodal rural society with a few large estate owners and

39. Inderjit Singh, "The Landless Poor in South Asia," *Growth and Equity in Agricultural Development*, Proceedings, Eighteenth International Conference of Agricultural Economists, Jakarta, Indonesia, August 24–September 2, 1982, ed. Allen Maunder and Kazushi Ohkawa (Aldershot, Hampshire, England: Gower Publishing Co., Ltd., 1983), pp. 379–400.

40. Simon Kuznets, "Economic Growth and Income Inequality," *American Economic Review* 45 (March 1955):1–28; Edmar L. Bacha, "The Kuznets Curve and Beyond: Growth and Changes in Inequalities," *Economic Growth and Resources*, Vol. 1, *The Major Issues*, Proceedings of the Fifth World Congress of the International Economic Association, Tokyo, Japan, 1977, ed. Edmond Malinvaud (New York: St. Martin's Press, 1979), pp. 52–71. Kuznets has also emphasized that a successful developed country has had to acquire the capacity both to encourage technological innovation and to design institutions that can accommodate the uneven distributional impact of technology on different social groups. Simon Kuznets, "Driving Forces of Economic Growth: What Can We Learn from History?" *Weltwirtschaftliches Archiv* 116 (1980):409–31.

a large number of landless or near-landless laborers, for example, the factor prices that are taken into consideration in the decision making of the estate owners may be very different from social opportunity costs. For the estate owners, unit labor costs may be substantially higher than market wage rates because a significant cost is involved in supervising a large number of hired laborers. They may also have access to capital at a price cheaper than its social opportunity cost through such means as subsidized credits and overvalued exchange rates. In such situations the research system may respond to the demand of the larger farmers by producing technologies biased in a labor-saving and capital-using direction even if a socially optimal direction of technological change may be labor-using and land- and capital-saving. Those technologies, in turn, may strengthen the existing social system by making large-scale farms relatively more efficient.[41]

We should emphasize that even the most appropriate technical changes have a limited impact on the growth and distribution of income in rural areas when unaccompanied by effective development efforts in other sectors. Growth in rural incomes and in returns to labor is critically dependent on rapid growth in nonagricultural employment opportunities and on effective intersector labor markets. (This issue has been discussed in Chapter 5 and will be discussed again in Chapter 13). We do not argue, therefore, that rapid and appropriate growth in agricultural productivity is a solution to either the income level or income distribution problem in rural areas. We do insist that it is a necessary condition.

SUPPLEMENT: THE MATHEMATICS OF PRODUCERS' AND CONSUMERS' SURPLUS

The relations of Figure 11-3 may be more clearly visible if the changes in producers' and consumers' surpluses are expressed mathematically. Denote p and q for the price and the quantity, respectively, concerned; $(-\eta)$ and β for the price elasticities of demand and supply, which are assumed constant; r for the ratio of marketable surplus to total output in the initial period ($r = HQ_0/OQ_0$); k for the rate of technological progress defined as the rate of shift in the supply function; ΔCS for the change in total consumers' surplus of which ΔCSC accrues to nonproducer consumers and ΔCSP accrues to producers ($\Delta CS = \Delta CSC + \Delta CSP$); ΔPS for the change in producers' surplus; ΔNGP for a net welfare gain of producers ($\Delta NGP = \Delta PS + \Delta CSP$); Y for the total output value in the initial period ($p_0 q_0$).

Changes in the price and quantity because of a k-percent shift in the supply

---

41. See the Argentine example discussed in Chapter 4. The Argentine case draws from the work of Alain de Janvry, "A Socioeconomic Model of Induced Innovations for Argentine Agricultural Development," *Quarterly Journal of Economics* 87 (August 1973):410–35.

function can be approximated by the Taylor expansion up to the first-order terms:

$$(1) \qquad \frac{\Delta p}{p_0} \cong - \frac{k}{\beta + \eta}$$

$$(2) \qquad \frac{\Delta q}{q_0} \cong \frac{k\eta}{\beta + \eta}$$

Correspondingly, the first-order approximations of changes in consumers' surpluses relative to the total output value are

$$(3) \qquad \frac{\Delta CS}{Y} \cong \frac{k}{\beta + \eta}$$

$$(4) \qquad \frac{\Delta CSC}{Y} \cong \frac{kr}{\beta + \eta}$$

$$(5) \qquad \frac{\Delta CSP}{Y} \cong \frac{k(1 - r)}{\beta + \eta}$$

which shows that consumers' surplus is divided between nonproducer consumers and producers in proportion to the ratios of marketable surplus and home consumption. (Those first-order approximations are invariable for whatever magnitude is assumed for the price elasticity of home consumption.)

Meanwhile, producers' surplus changes by

$$(6) \qquad \frac{\Delta PS}{Y} \cong \frac{\eta - 1}{(1 + \beta)(\beta + \eta)}$$

which is likely to be negative for subsistence crops such as rice and wheat, for which η is less than one even in very poor countries.

As a result, the net gain in producers' economic welfare can be approximated by

$$(7) \qquad \frac{\Delta NGP}{Y} \cong k \frac{\eta - r + \beta(1 - r)}{(1 + \beta)(\beta + \eta)}$$

which indicates that the gains of producers will increase if r decreases. In other words, technological progress in subsistence crop production in a less commercialized economy not only would benefit nonproducer consumers but also producers.

The fact that the marketable surplus ratio (r) is a critical parameter to determine whether the technological progress benefits producers has an important implication on the income distribution among individual producers. The individual farm diagram of Figure 11-3 illustrates the changes in equilibrium points in individual farm producers corresponding to changes in market equilibrium points in the market diagram. $O'S_0^S$ and $O'S_0^L$ represent the supply curves for small and large farms, respectively, before technological advance, which correspond to OS_0 in the market diagram. $O'S_1^S$ and $O'S_1^L$ represent the supply schedules of the small and large producers after the technology change, which correspond to OS_1. Home consumption is assumed to be the same for both the small and the large farmers. The assumption seems reasonable considering the nature of subsistence crops. (The relaxation of this assumption for a relevant range does not affect the conclusion.)

Corresponding to the changes in technology and market prices, the equilibrium of the small producers moves from A^S to B^S, accompanied by a change in producers' surplus from $A^S P_0 O$ to $B^S P_1 O$. Likewise, the large farmers' equilibrium moves from A^L to B^L with a change in producers' surplus from $A^L P_0 O$ to $B^L P_1 O$. Meanwhile, consumers' surplus accruing to the producers increases by the same magnitude ($C'P_0 P_1 G'$) for both large and small farmers. The net effect on producers' economic welfare depends on the relative changes in revenue and cost, but it is likely that the small farmers gain more or lose less than the large farmers because their loss as producers is smaller relative to their gain as consumers.

Aggregate price elasticity of supply (β), which determines market prices, is the weighted average of the price elasticities of supply of individual producers, $\beta = \Sigma_i w_i \beta_i$, where β_i is the price elasticity of supply of the ith producer ($i = L$ for large producer and $i = S$ for small producer), and w_i is the share of the ith producer in total output. Likewise, the rate of shift in the aggregate supply is an average of the rates of supply shift of individual producers, $k = \Sigma_i w_i k_i$.

The first-order approximations of the impacts of k-percent shift in the aggregate supply function on the ith producers' share in consumers' surplus (ΔCSP_i), producers' surplus (ΔPS_i), and producers' net welfare gain (ΔNGP_i) are

$$(8) \qquad \frac{\Delta CSP_i}{Y_i} = \frac{k(1 - r_i)}{\beta + \eta}$$

$$(9) \qquad \frac{\Delta PS_i}{Y_i} = k_i - \frac{k_i \beta_i}{1 + \beta_i} - \frac{k}{\beta + \eta}$$

$$(10) \qquad \frac{\Delta NGP_i}{Y_i} = k_i - \frac{k_i \beta_i}{1 + \beta_i} - \frac{kr_i}{\beta + \eta}$$

where r_i represents the market surplus ratio of the ith producer.

Whether technical progress in the subsistence crop has a positive effect on the welfare of the ith producer (a positive value for equation 10) depends to a large extent on the magnitudes of k_i and β_i relative to k and β. It is clear, however, that as r_i becomes smaller, the increase in income becomes larger (or the decline is smaller). In other words, the income position of farmers who sell a small portion of their produce in the market will improve relative to that of farmers who sell a large fraction, given a technical change.

This model also applies to technical change in the relative incomes of landlords and tenants. If rent is paid in kind as a fixed part of output, say 50 percent, the supply curve of a tenant is obtained by shifting the supply curve of an owner-operator to the left by 50 percent. If costs are shared in the same proportion by the landlord, the tenant's supply curve is the same as an owner-operator's. In this case, the changes in revenue, cost, and income of both landlords and tenants as a result of the technological change are all 50 percent of the changes in the case of the owner-operator and can be expressed by multiplying equations 8, 9, and 10 by 0.5. The major difference between the landlords and the tenants would be expressed by the values of *r;* the marketable surplus ratio of the small share tenant will be small, whereas the ratio of the large landlords will be nearly 1.

In the case of leasehold tenure, with rent paid in kind in fixed quantity, the tenant's marketable surplus is reduced by the quantity of the rent (shown by a rightward shift of $D'_H H'$ in Figure 11-3). Assuming that landlords sell the rice they collect as rent, the aggregate market supply would be the same as for an owner-operator. The change in income of the tenant owing to the technical change can be expressed by equation 10 with a smaller value of *r*. The income of the landlords receiving a fixed quantity of rent in kind would be reduced by the rate of decline in the product market price, as expressed by equation 1.

Thus technical progress in subsistence crop production narrows the income gap between large farms (or landlords) and smaller farms (or tenants) and contributes to more equal income distribution in the rural sector.

Moreover, the decline in the price of staple food grains corresponding to technological progress tends to benefit poor consumers proportionately more than rich consumers in the urban sector, too, because the impact of a decline in the price of staple foods on the real income of individual urban households depends on the importance of the staple in the total consumption expenditure. The poor classes normally spend a higher proportion of their income for such products than the wealthy, hence they benefit more.

Assume that total income (*y*) is spent either for the staple food (*s*) or for other commodities (*x*) as $y = p_s q_s + p_x q_x$, where p_s, p_x, q_s, and q_x represent, respectively, the prices and the quantities of the staple and the other commodities. Then the rate of increase in real income caused by a decline in the staple price can be approximated by

(11)
$$\frac{\Delta y}{y} - e \frac{\Delta p_s}{p_s}$$

where $e = p_s q_s / y$ is the ratio of expenditure for the staple to total household income.

According to equation 1, the percentage change in market price of the subsistence food crop corresponding to a *k*-percent shift in the supply curve is $k/(\beta + \eta)$. Therefore, the rate of increase in real income is approximated by

(12)
$$\frac{\Delta y}{y} \cong \frac{ek}{\beta + \eta}$$

which is larger for poorer consumers since e is inversely correlated with per capita income. Moreover, if the income elasticity of demand is negative so that the absolute quantity of consumption of the staple is also inversely related to per capita income, the real income gain owing to the price decrease is larger in absolute terms for the poor than for the rich.

12

Disequilibrium in World Agriculture

$\mathbf{I}$n the international economic system that emerged by the end of the nineteenth century, agricultural commodities and raw materials were exported from the most recently settled countries of the temperate region and from the tropical-colonial areas to the developed countries. Industrial products were exported by the developed countries to the less developed world. It was believed to be to the economic advantage of both the developed and the less developed countries for each nation to pursue its comparative "natural advantage."

This system gradually broke down after World War I. The period between the two world wars was characterized by great instability and slow economic growth.[1] Protectionism contributed to and was reinforced by the Great Depression of the 1930s. The period since World War II has been characterized by unprecedented rates of growth in production and trade. Yet the policies pursued by both the DCs and the LDCs have intensified the disequilibrium in world agriculture. Serious imbalances in the growth of agricultural products have been reflected in the underproduction of food, resulting in chronic malnutrition in the LDCs, and in the overproduction of food, resulting in depressed prices of farm products and the accumulation of surpluses in the DCs. Differences in agricultural productivity between the DCs and the LDCs have widened (Chapter 5), and the LDCs have become, on balance, net importers rather than net exporters of food. It is the purpose of this chapter to identify some of the policy biases that underlay the widening disequilibrium in world agriculture.

---

1. W. Arthur Lewis, *Aspects of Tropical Trade, 1883–1965* (Stockholm: Almquist and Wiksell, 1969); W. Arthur Lewis, *Growth and Fluctuations, 1870–1913* (London: George Allen & Unwin, 1978), pp. 225–45; W. Arthur Lewis, "The Slowing Down of the Engine of Growth," *American Economic Review* 70 (September 1980):555–64.

CONSEQUENCES OF POLICY DISTORTIONS

The period of rapid economic growth since World War II was accompanied by a widening disequilibrium in agricultural production and trade relationships. In the developed countries human capital and technical inputs, as demonstrated by the intercountry production function analysis (Chapter 6), became the dominant sources of growth in agricultural production. The basis for comparative advantage in agricultural production shifted from natural resource endowments to scientific and industrial capacity. Agriculture in the developed countries evolved from a resource-based to a science-based industry.

During the 1960s and 1970s a number of developing countries also began to make the transition to higher levels of productivity. There was rapid diffusion of research capacity and wide adoption of biological and mechanical technology (Chapter 9). But a significant unanswered question is why so many developing countries failed to realize the relatively inexpensive sources of growth in agricultural output and productivity that have been available to them.

In retrospect, it seems clear that the domestic economic policies adopted by both developed and less developed countries have contributed to a widening, rather than a narrowing, of the disequilibrium in world agriculture.[2] Typically, the developed countries have adopted policies that protect domestic agriculture by supporting agricultural prices and restricting agricultural imports. In contrast, the less developed countries have often adopted policies that have forced the agricultural sector to bear the costs of protecting domestic industry.

In this section we examine some of the protectionist policies of the developed countries that have contributed to disequilibrium in world agriculture. We then turn to some of the industrial and trade policies of developing countries that have constrained the growth of agricultural production and have dampened growth in the income of agricultural producers. Finally, we attempt to use the induced innovation perspective to interpret the implications of these distortions for agricultural development.

Agricultural Protectionism in the Developed Countries

During the thirty years between 1950 and 1980 the developed countries significantly reduced the barriers to international trade in industrial products. Although these reductions were sometimes offset by nontariff protection against imports from developing countries, the overall trend has been toward

2. This theme has been developed most forcefully by D. Gale Johnson, *World Agriculture in Disarray* (London: Macmillan and Fontana, and New York: St. Martin's Press, 1973); Michael Lipton, *Why Poor People Stay Poor: Urban Bias in World Development* (Cambridge, Mass.: Harvard University Press, 1977); Theodore W. Schultz, "On Economics and Politics of Agriculture," *Distortions of Agricultural Incentives,* ed. Theodore W. Schultz (Bloomington: Indiana University Press, 1978), pp. 3–23.

greater trade liberalization.[3] The LDCs have responded by increasing their share of world exports of manufactured products.

The decline in industrial protectionism has been accompanied by an increase in agricultural protectionism, which has resulted, to a very substantial degree, from nontariff barriers imposed to assure the effectiveness of domestic agricultural programs. Since 1950 the share of primary commodity exports, mainly foodstuffs and raw materials, accounted for by the LDCs has declined continuously.[4]

The increasing agricultural protectionism of the developed countries since World War II has been fundamentally different in its rationale, though perhaps not in its impact on trade, from the earlier protectionism which followed the Industrial Revolution. Historically, the demand for agricultural protectionism rested (a) on the wide differential in productivity and income between workers in the agricultural and industrial sectors and (b) on a loss of comparative advantage relative to foreign agricultural producers, as nations have shifted an increasing share of their resources from agriculture to industry during the process of modernization. The demand for protection by the agricultural producers in the developed countries since World War II, especially in the exporters of agricultural commodities such as the United States and some of the EEC countries, has rested on a different basis. As agriculture in the developed countries has shifted from a resource-based to a science-based industry, productivity growth in agriculture has often exceeded productivity growth in the industrial sector. Confronted with a relatively inelastic demand for agricultural products in domestic markets, agricultural producers in the industrial countries have demanded protection against declining domestic prices.

The governments of the developed countries have responded to the demands of agricultural producers by erecting an increasingly complex system of national policies for the protection of domestic agriculture. These systems have typically involved some combination of (a) devices that directly discourage imports (import duties, quantitative restrictions, state trading, and multiple exchange rates); (b) devices that directly encourage exports (export subsidies and multiple exchange rates); and (c) devices that directly encourage

3. Helen Hughes and Jean Waelbroeck, "Can Developing-Country Exports Keep Growing in the 1980s?" *World Economy* 4 (June 1981):127–47; Judith L. Goldstein, "The State, Industrial Interests and Foreign Economic Policy: American Commercial Policy in the Postwar Period" (Paper presented at National Science Foundation Conference on the Politics and Economics of Trade Policy, Spring Hill Conference Center, Minnesota, October 29–31, 1981).

4. Rachel Dardis and Elmer W. Learn, *Measures of the Degree and Cost of Economic Protection of Agriculture in Selected Countries* (Washington, D.C.: U.S. Department of Agriculture, Economic Research Service, Technical Bulletin 1384, 1967); Jimmye S. Hillman, *Nontariff Agricultural Trade Barriers* (Lincoln: University of Nebraska Press, 1978); Alexander J. Yeats, *Trade Barriers Facing Developing Countries* (New York: St. Martin's Press, 1979), pp. 36–63; Alberto Valdés and Joachim Zietz, *Agricultural Protection in OECD Countries: Its Cost to Less-Developed Countries* (Washington, D.C.: International Food Policy Research Institute, Research Report 21, 1980).

domestic production (price supports and deficiency payments). The net effect has been an increase in the degree of protectionism.

The response of national economic policy to protectionist pressure has varied widely among nations. In nineteenth-century Great Britain, where the comparative advantage clearly rested in the industrial sector and foreign markets for industrial products were highly elastic, agricultural protectionism was forced to give way to free trade. The Corn Laws were repealed in 1846, well over half a century after the Industrial Revolution had resulted in a clear shift of comparative advantage from agriculture (particularly in grain production) to manufacturing. It seems likely that the conditions that led to the repeal of the Corn Laws were unique, even in Great Britain. In his classic history of the English Corn Laws, Donald Grove Barnes points out that "only for a brief period in Great Britain were the interests of the manufacturers and consumers identical. Both wanted cheap food, although for different reasons, and hence they united against their common enemy, the agriculturists, and brought in free trade. But in no other country has this union of the trading and manufacturing interests with the consumers taken place, because their interests have never been identical."[5]

It seems apparent that the failure of the other developed countries to follow the example of Great Britain in the latter half of the nineteenth century reflected a situation in which the comparative advantage of the industrial sector was less clear and foreign markets for industrial products were viewed as less elastic. The response of France and Germany to the large-scale inflow of grains from the new continents, which coincided with the world depression during the 1870s and 1880s, was protectionist. The tariff on grain imports introduced in Germany by Bismarck in 1879 was the result of a united campaign by Junkers and iron-steel industrialists to protect both agricultural and industrial products. Later, in the 1890s, the tariff rate was reduced as policy was reoriented toward trade expansion (Caprivi's Der Neue Kurs), but the protection was never completely abandoned. In France tariffs on agricultural produce were revived by Méline in 1892, strengthened in 1895, raised again after World War I, and supplemented again during the Great Depression of the 1930s. Support for protectionist policies was based both on the weak competitive position of French industry and on the threat of lower-priced grain imports from Russia, Australia, and America. A succession of aristocratic, republican, and socialist governments discovered that the economic demands of the peasantry were stronger than economic theory.[6]

5. Donald Grove Barnes, *A History of the English Corn Laws from 1660–1846* (1930; rpr. New York: Augustus M. Kelley, 1961), p. 239.

6. For a comparison of the responses of Great Britain, Germany, France, Italy, and Denmark to the world decline in the price of wheat after 1870, see C. P. Kindleberger, "Group Behavior and International Trade," *Journal of Political Economy* 59 (February 1951):30–46. See also Alexander Gerschenkron, *Bread and Democracy in Germany* (Berkeley and Los Angeles: University of California Press, 1943); Alfred Whitney Griswold, *Farming and Democracy* (New York: Harcourt Brace, 1948); Gordon Wright, *Rural Revolution in France: The Peasantry in the Twentieth Century* (Stanford: Stanford University Press, 1964), pp. 6–18.

The Great Depression in the 1930s was a major blow to trade liberalism. Countries throughout the world raised tariff walls. This was the period when agricultural price supports emerged as a permanent feature of United States agricultural policy. The tariffs, price supports, and production quotas were originally designed as emergency measures to relieve agricultural prices and income from collapse due to rapidly contracting demand against the inelastic supply of agricultural products during the depression.[7] The persistence and further strengthening of protectionist policies in the industrial countries during the postwar period has been due, to a substantial degree, to rapid growth in agricultural output in the developed countries because of the rapid shift from a resource-based agriculture to a science-based agriculture and a secular decline in the income elasticity of demand for food by consumers. The result was a shift in the internal terms of trade against agriculture.

The impact of rapid growth in labor productivity pressing against an inelastic demand for farm products created particularly difficult resource adjustment problems. In the United States, for example, labor productivity rose by more than 3 percent per year between 1925 and 1950 and by more than 6 percent per year between 1950 and 1980. The growth in demand was approximately 2 percent per year. The slow expansion in demand for farm products and the rapid growth in labor productivity in agriculture placed the major burden of adjustments to the shift in the domestic terms of trade against agriculture on the intersector labor markets. Labor market adjustments of this magnitude, involving a transfer of farm labor to the nonfarm sector in the range of 4 percent per year, have been extremely difficult to achieve even in a rapidly growing urban-industrial economy. The burden of adjustment was particularly difficult in those regions where local nonfarm employment has expanded slowly and for the older farm workers, the less well-educated, and the ethnic and racial minorities.[8] In this environment, to ease the burden of adjustment, agricultural producers pressed for increased agricultural protectionism as well as for more effective domestic price supports and land-use controls.[9]

The economic rationale for protectionist policies has been strengthened by a number of social and political factors. In France, Japan, and the United States there has been a broad base of public support by farmers for protection from the full impact of market forces. Agricultural "fundamentalism"—the view that an agrarian system in which the basic unit of production was the family farm, owned and operated by the cultivator, represented the only sound foundation of social equality and political stability—has persisted. In

---

7. D. Gale Johnson, "The Nature of the Supply Function for Agricultural Products," *American Economic Review* 40 (September 1950):539–64.

8. Dale E. Hathaway, "Migration from Agriculture: The Historical Record and Its Meaning," *American Economic Review* 50 (May 1960):379–91; Vernon W. Ruttan, "Agricultural Policy in an Affluent Society," *Journal of Farm Economics* 48 (December 1968):1100–1120.

9. "Nationalism in developed countries justifies protection as a means of preserving old industries at the expense of both the consumer and the foreigner, particularly the poor foreigner, who could supply the product cheaper," Harry G. Johnson, *Economic Policies toward Less Developed Countries* (Washington, D.C.: Brookings Institution, 1967), p. 79.

western Europe and Japan the economic position of the peasantry has been reinforced by political alliances between the peasant parties and the moderate and conservative parties against the left.

Perhaps of equal importance in explaining the continued use of protectionist devices, price supports, and land-use controls to manage agricultural prices and output has been a dramatic rise in the capacity of the government administration and control that started in World War I and has greatly accelerated since World War II—by what Sir John Hicks has termed the "administrative revolution in government."[10] Before this revolution, the tariff was the only practical technique available to governments to manipulate prices, manage production, and redirect income flows in favor of or against agriculture. Today the governments of the developed countries have the capacity to administer a much more complex and precise set of policy measures and direct controls. Furthermore, the economic growth of the total economy and the relative decline of the agricultural sector have made both the government and the general public in the developed countries much less sensitive to the distortions in resource use and the social costs incurred as a result of the policies adopted to protect agriculture from market forces.

The failure of developed countries to manage price and trade policies in the mutual interest of both the developed and developing countries can be illustrated in an extreme form in the case of sugar.

Protectionist policies toward sugar. Protectionist policies have limited access to developed country markets for LDC sugar exporters and have contributed to extreme price variation in world sugar markets (Figure 12-1).

During the 1950s and 1960s, U.S. sugar policy was highly protectionist.[11] It was effective in maintaining a considerable margin between domestic and world prices (Figure 12-1). The principal instrument of the policy was the imposition of quotas intended to achieve a level of domestic production and imports consistent with domestic consumption requirements. From 1960 to 1971 the domestic price of sugar was never less than 97 percent of the target

10. "It is impossible to have a strong administration . . . unless it can be paid for. . . . But the 'amount' of control that can be 'purchased' for a given expenditure may be large or may be small; there can be no doubt that in the Modern Phase it has been very sharply increased. The change that has ensued is so important, and so potent, that we cannot get on without naming it; . . . the *Administrative Revolution*. It is partly a matter of organization . . . but it is partly . . . a matter of application of capital equipment. Modern governments, one would guess, over-use the aeroplane; but where would they be without the telephone—and the typewriter? The contribution of the computer . . . is only beginning to be seen. It is already the case that it would be easier (technically) to govern New Zealand from London than it was to govern Scotland from London in the eighteenth century," John Hicks, *A Theory of Economic History* (London: Oxford University Press, 1969), pp. 99, 162.

11. For an overview of U.S. sugar policy see Roy A. Ballinger, *A History of Sugar Marketing through 1974* (Washington, D.C.: U.S. Department of Agriculture, Economics, Statistics and Cooperatives Service, Agricultural Economics Report 382, 1978); Robert D. Barry, Laurence E. Ackland, and T. Vernon Greer, "A Review of U.S. Sugar Programs and Legislative Authorities," *Sugar and Sweetener Outlook and Situation* (U.S. Department of Agriculture, Economics and Statistics Service, SSRV6N2, 1981), pp. 61–66.

FIGURE 12-1. Spot prices of raw cane sugar.

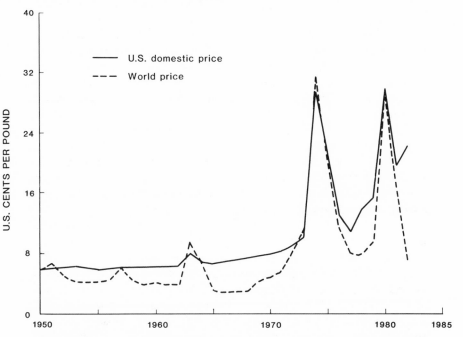

Sources: USDA, "Sugar Market Situation" and "Sugar and Sweetener Outlook and Situation," various issues.

Note: World sugar refers to bagged sugar f.a.s. Cuba, Contract #4 for 1950–60. For 1961–70, prices are for #8 contract bagged f.o.b. at Caribbean ports. Beginning in 1971, price is for #11, contract (bulk) f.o.b. at Caribbean ports. The 1982 prices are the spot prices for August 1982.

price defined by the sugar act of 1948. The quota required to achieve this level of protection has been estimated as equivalent, in its effect on the volume of imports, to a tariff on raw sugar of 106 percent.[12]

Between 1971 and 1981, however, the effect of U.S. protection was negligible as world prices moved considerably higher than the targets of the sugar act. The sugar act of 1948 was allowed to expire at the end of 1974, thus moving the United States into a brief era of free trade in sugar. Prompted by the decline in world sugar prices after 1975, the United States adopted a new support payment scheme, which was effective from 1977 to 1980. As is evident from Figure 12-1, the wedge between U.S. domestic and world sugar prices reemerged in the 1980s.

12. Tesfaye W. Tsadik, "The International Sugar Market: Self-Sufficiency or Free Trade?" *Journal of World Trade Law* 16 (March–April 1982):133–51; Hans de Kruijk, "The Effect of Tariff and Non-Tariff Barriers on U.S. Sugar Imports," *Weltwirtschaftliches Archiv* 115 (1979):315–23.

European Economic Community sugar policy has taken on increased importance in world trade in sugar. The EEC uses both price supports and a market quota system for sugar. The aggregate quota exceeds EEC domestic consumption. After the price peak of 1973–74, continued high price supports prompted an expansion of internal production in the community, which brought about a shift from a net import position of 1.7 million metric tons in 1974–75 to an export level of over 5 million metric tons in the early 1980s. EEC exports as a share of the world market rose to over 25 percent. The budgetary cost of subsidies to export this surplus averaged $700 million per year between 1977 and 1979. The growth of EEC-subsidized exports has gradually eroded the value of the commitment made by the EEC under the Lome Convention to import 1.3 million metric tons of sugar annually from African, Caribbean, and Pacific (ACP) countries. And the rise in the volume of EEC exports has clearly been an important factor in sugar prices in the depressed world during the early 1980s.[13]

The protectionist policies of DCs have also influenced the location and payoff to sugarcane research.[14] Before the increase in protectionism associated with the Great Depression, it was possible for an LDC to achieve a high return to investment in sugarcane research. The rapid growth of sugar production and exports in Java between the late 1800s and the early 1930s was based on the clear technical advantage resulting from the development of the world's major sugar research station in Java (Proefstation Oost Java). By the late 1920s cane yields in Java were the highest in the world, and Java ranked second only to Cuba as a sugar exporter. The first international sugar agreement, in 1933, and other trade-restraint policies adopted as a result of the Great Depression, were disastrous to the Java sugar industry. Since World War II, sugarcane research investment has shifted primarily to importing countries and countries with protected markets in importing countries.

The losses to both the DCs and the LDCs from agricultural protectionism are clearly very large. Alberto Valdés and Joachim Zietz have estimated that a 50 percent reduction in trade barriers and tariffs by the Organization for Economic Cooperation and Development (OECD) countries would result in an increase of approximately $8.5 billion per year (1977 prices) in the value of agricultural commodity trade.[15] LDC exporters would be expected to cap-

13. For a discussion of the development of sugar policy see Ian Smith, "Europe's Sugar Dilemma," *Journal of Agricultural Economics* 31 (May 1980):215–23. For an excellent analysis of the trade and welfare effects see Ulrich Koester and Peter Michael Schmitz, "The EC Sugar Market Policy and Developing Countries," *European Review of Agricultural Economics* 9 (1982):183–204. According to Koester and Schmitz, the preferred ACP countries realized a positive net income transfer in 1979, when EEC sugar exports amounted to 3.1 million metric tons of sugar. Developing sugar-exporting countries outside the ACP preference system were adversely affected in 1979. And as EEC sugar exports have continued to rise, the value of the preference to the ACP countries has declined.

14. Robert E. Evenson and Yoav Kislev, *Agricultural Research and Productivity* (New Haven: Yale University Press, 1975), pp. 140–55.

15. Valdés and Zietz, *Agricultural Protection*, pp. 29–38.

ture about $3.1 billion of this increase, which is equivalent to about 11 percent of total LDC agricultural exports. The gains to the LDC exporters would be substantially increased if trade liberalization were extended to cover processed agricultural products. Trade liberalization would also result in a substantial shift in processing—the roasting of coffee, refining of sugar, and extraction of vegetable oils—from DC to LDC exporters.

A continuing puzzle for economists has been why, in view of the gains from trade, protectionism by DCs has been so pervasive. During the last decade considerable progress was made in an attempt to understand the economic and political factors leading to protectionism.[16] The factors are deeply embedded in the structure of DC economic development. A rapid rise in import penetration associated with a rapid decline in employment opportunities in an industry or commodity sector almost always induces greater protectionism.

We are not, therefore, optimistic about the prospects of trade liberalization for either agricultural commodities or processed agricultural products. It is doubtful that the political resources necessary to bring about such liberalization can be mobilized as long as price-support programs are the primary device used to support farm incomes in the OECD countries. A shift to deficiency payments or other direct income-support approaches could, however, create a more favorable climate for the reform of agricultural trade relations.

The New International Economic Order (NIEO). The LDCs have been acutely sensitive to the DC protectionist policies. At the first session of the United Nations Conference on Trade and Development (UNCTAD) in 1964, Raúl Prebisch presented a report calling for a new international economic order that would give the developing countries preferred access to the DC markets.[17] This theme was taken up again in the United Nations General Assembly and at subsequent meetings of the United Nations Conference on Trade and Development. At a special session in 1974, the United Nations General Assembly adopted a Declaration and Program of Action in the Establishment of a New International Economic Order (NIEO).

The Program of Action proposed measures that would improve access to DC markets, stabilize primary raw material and commodity prices, promote the transfer of technology on more favorable terms, expand the flow of financial resources for development, and reform the international financial system. The two major concerns of the NIEO with respect to agriculture were

16. Robert E. Baldwin, "The Political Economy of Protectionism," *Import Competition and Response,* ed. Jagdish N. Bhagwati (Chicago: University of Chicago Press, 1982), pp. 263–90; Kym Anderson and Robert E. Baldwin, *The Political Market for Protection in Industrial Countries: Empirical Evidence* (Washington, D.C.: World Bank Staff Working Paper 0492, 1981).

17. *Towards a New Trade Policy for Development,* Report by the Secretary-General of the United Nations Conference on Trade and Development (New York: United Nations, 1964); Giuseppe Scida, "Toward a New International Economic Order: A Chronological Account," *Politica Internazionale* 2 (Winter 1981–Spring 1982, English edition):177–99.

(a) the reduction of tariff and nontariff barriers restricting access of the LDCs to DC markets and (b) an "integrated program for commodities" designed to maintain prices of primary commodities through a system of commodity agreements, buffer stocks, and price-support mechanisms.[18]

The proposals to establish a New International Economic Order generated much rhetoric but few reforms in economic relationships.[19] The New Economic Order dialogue also stimulated a serious reexamination of the issue of whether LDC export performance has been more constrained by restraints on external demand or internal supply. This reexamination suggests that throughout most of the postwar period, constraints on trading opportunities have been a less serious cause of the slow growth of LDC exports than failure by the DCs to take advantage of the export opportunities available to them. The obstacles to LDC export growth have been largely internal.[20]

In the next section we examine the constraints on agricultural development resulting from both the industrial policies and the agricultural commodity policies employed by the developing countries.

Industrial Development Policy Distortions in the Less Developed Countries

A second source of the widening disequilibrium in world agriculture has been the malallocation of resources resulting from industrial development policies adopted by the developing countries. These policies have often been adopted with almost complete disregard for factor endowments and have often reflected a combination of ideological bias on the part of the political elite and analytical failure on the part of development planners.

These policies were adopted in an effort to remove the constraints imposed by the political and economic dominance of the metropolitan economies. The mercantile policies of the metropolitan countries, supported by the productivity of the industrial sector of the developed countries, had resulted in a decline

18. Yeats, *Trade Barriers Facing Developing Countries,* pp. 4–8; Harry G. Johnson, "Commodities: Less Developed Countries' Demands and Developed Countries' Response," *The New International Economic Order: The North-South Debate,* ed. Jagdish N. Bhagwati (Cambridge, Mass.: MIT Press, 1977), pp. 240–51; W. M. Cordon, *The NIEO Proposals: A Cool Look* (London: Trade Policy Research Center, Thames Essay No. 21, 1979).

19. Jagdish N. Bhagwati, "Introduction," *New International Economic Order,* pp. 1–24; Goran Ohlin, "Negotiating International Economic Order," *The Theory and Experience of Economic Development: Essays in Honor of Sir Arthur Lewis,* ed. Mark Gersovitz, Carlos F. Diaz-Alejandro, Gustav Ranis, and Mark Rosenzweig (London: George Allen & Unwin, 1982), pp. 215–28.

20. Irving B. Kravis, "Trade as a Handmaiden of Growth: Similarities between the Nineteenth and Twentieth Centuries," *Economic Journal* 80 (December 1970):850–72; John R. Hanson II, "More on Trade as a Handmaiden of Growth," *Economic Journal* 87 (September 1977):554–57. See also the major OECD study by Ian Little, Tibor Scitovsky, and Maurice Scott, *Industry and Trade in Some Developing Countries: A Comparative Study* (London: Oxford University Press, 1970). The National Bureau of Economic Research (NBER) studies are summarized by Jagdish N. Bhagwati, *Foreign Trade Regimes and Economic Development: Anatomy and Consequences of Exchange Control Regimes* (Cambridge, Mass.: Ballinger for NBER, 1978), and Anne O. Krueger, *Foreign Trade Regimes and Economic Development: Liberalization Attempts and Consequences* (Cambridge, Mass.: Ballinger for NBER, 1978).

in the production of local handcraft and manufacturing and an increase in raw material specialization and commodity production.[21] The commodity- and raw-material-producing sectors were frequently dominated by foreign capital and managed by foreign personnel.

A major objective of the political leadership in most LDCs, whether impelled by a nationalist or a socialist ideology, has been to attempt to substitute new forms of economic organization for the "capitalist" form inherited from a period of colonial dominance or economic dependence and to replace the traditional "exploitive" raw-material- and commodity-producing sectors with an industrial structure that would reduce "dependence" on the metropolitan economies.[22]

Even when the motivation has been primarily nationalistic, there has generally been a preference for public enterprise over private enterprise and a distrust of the market mechanism in the allocation of resources and the direction of income flows. The implementation of nationalistic development policies has typically involved public ownership of the industries controlled by foreign capital and managed by foreign personnel, particularly those industries, such as public utilities, which tended to occupy a monopolistic position in the domestic market. In other sectors the thrust of nationalistic economic policy has frequently emphasized the development of indigenous entrepreneurship and the direction of industrial development along lines selected for their symbolic value in terms of concepts of national identity and modernization. This typically has involved the use of tax, tariff, foreign exchange, and price policies, as well as specific controls to direct the flow of resources. Where socialist ideology has reinforced the nationalistic drive, public ownership tends to be more pervasive and may even extend to small-scale industry, distribution, and agriculture.

Regardless of the motivation, these policies have contributed to the widening of disequilibrium in world agriculture. Discrimination against agriculture in both factor and product markets has depressed production incentives. The new industries developed to foster nationalistic economic objectives have often not achieved the capacity to produce the new biological, chemical, and mechanical inputs essential for agricultural development. Price policies have been directed toward extracting an economic surplus from both the peasant and plantation sectors rather than toward the effective coordination of produc-

21. See the discussion of dependency theory in Chapter 2. For a historical review of the impact of colonial development policies on the economic structure of countries in Southeast Asia see Stephen A. Resnick, "The Decline in Rural Industry under Export Expansion: A Comparison among Burma, Philippines and Thailand, 1870–1938," *Journal of Economic History* 30 (March 1970):51–73.

22. Harry G. Johnson, "A Theoretical Model of Economic Nationalism in New and Developing States," *Political Science Quarterly* 80 (June 1965):169–85; Albert Breton, "The Economics of Nationalism," *Journal of Political Economy* 72 (August 1964):376–86; M. Bronfenbrenner, "The Appeal of Confiscation in Economic Development," *Economic Development and Cultural Change* 3 (April 1955):201–18.

tion decisions at the farm level and of intersector resource-allocation decisions.

The characterization of the economic policies followed by the LDCs has been necessarily general. It is useful, therefore, to examine the working out of these policies in a particular economy. The Philippines is a useful example because of the initial success of its national development policies as well as the limitations on development resulting from these policies. During the period since independence, the objective of Philippine national economic development has been to achieve "relatively and absolutely increasing per capita real income accruing to Filipinos, with an increasing relative share of aggregate income generated by manufacturing and a diminishing relative share of aggregate income generated by specialization and external trade in primary products and, equally important, both an absolute and relative increase in the share of Filipinos in the ownership and management of the productive assets of the economy."[23]

The policies that were adopted to implement these objectives were based on the assumption that the export prospects for the traditional primary products produced by the Philippines (sugar, copra, abaca) were poor. It was concluded that the prospects for growth depended on the effective development of import-substituting industries. The legal and administrative devices employed to achieve industrial growth included (a) licensing of foreign exchange transactions, (b) administration by the government of large credit resources, and (c) use of the regulatory powers of the government to direct investment. The protective use of controls, the availability of foreign exchange at bargain prices, and the regulatory powers of the government were employed to direct resources into the manufacturing sector and into the hands of a new class of Filipino entrepreneurs. Industrial output expanded rapidly. "Between 1949 and 1960 income originating in manufacturing grew at the rate of 29% a year."[24]

In spite of impressive industrial growth the Philippine economy was beginning to experience serious difficulties by the late 1950s. There was a sharp deterioration in the balance of payments position. The foreign exchange rate (P2/$1) was under severe pressure. Between 1960 and 1962 a series of "decontrol" measures and exchange reforms was undertaken. According to Benito Legarda, the "grand design of the whole reform" was "simultaneously to lift quantitative restrictions on trade and payments under what amounted to

---

23. Frank H. Golay, *The Philippines: Public Policy and National Economic Development* (Ithaca: Cornell University Press, 1961), p. 10. See also the review of the Golay book by Amado A. Castro, "Economic Policy Revisited," *Philippine Economic Journal* 1 (First Semester 1962):66–91.

24. Benito Legarda y Fernandez, "Foreign Exchange Decontrol and the Redirection of Income Flows," ibid. 1 (First Semester 1962):22. See also Benito Legarda, Jr., "Philippine Economic Paradoxes," *Philippine Statistician* 13 (June 1964):89–112; Benito Legarda, Jr., "Back to the 'Sugar Republic,'" *Far Eastern Economic Review* 46 (October 1969):171, 172, 217.

an open general license, while at the same time . . . to prevent runaway movements of the exchange rate by credit restraints and by securing financial backing, and also to provide new forms of protection . . . by raising tariff rates on certain items.''[25] The effect of the decontrol was a substantial devaluation of the peso (to approximately P4/$1), a shift in the internal terms of trade against the emerging industrial sector, and a redirection of income flows toward the traditional commodity- and raw-material-producing sectors.

Throughout the 1960s there was a substantial professional debate concerning the effect of the economic policies of the 1950s and the reversal of economic policy in the 1960s. One major conclusion that emerged out of this debate is that the control policies of the 1950s had resulted in a severe distortion of incentives and had led to a composition of industrial output inconsistent with the nation's factor endowments. The new entrepreneurs, "encouraged by low prices on imported capital goods attributable to a policy of peso overvaluation, by incredibly low interest rates to favored industries . . . , and by high wages fostered by . . . minimum wage policy, . . . substituted capital for labor wherever their production functions allowed such possibilities.''[26] The commitment to an import-substitution pattern of industrialization, dependent on the growth of domestic consumer goods demand, set a relatively low ceiling on industrial growth. Furthermore, the effect of capital deepening at the firm level imposed severe constraints on the ability of the industrial sector to achieve gains in total factor productivity.

It is possible to provide a more positive view of the Philippine economic policies of the 1950s. An expanded industrial base was established and a new entrepreneurial class was developed. The financial system expanded and developed a capacity to service the new industrial sector. Nevertheless, the policies of the 1950s had severely underestimated the elasticity of substitution between capital and labor in the industrial sector and the response to agricultural production to changes in the prices of factors and products.[27] The decontrol resulted in a rapid rise in the price of the commercial export crops

25. Legarda, "Foreign Exchange Decontrol," p. 21.
26. Jeffrey G. Williamson, "Dimensions of Postwar Philippine Economic Progress," *Quarterly Journal of Economics* 83 (February 1969):107. See also John H. Power, "Import Substitution as an Industrialization Strategy," *Philippine Economic Journal* 5 (Second Semester 1966):167–204; Robert J. Lampman, "The Sources of Post-War Economic Growth in the Philippines," *Philippine Economic Journal* 6 (Second Semester 1967):170–88; John H. Power, with Cristina Crisostomo and Eloisa Litonjua, "The Structure of Protection in the Philippines," *The Structure of Protection in Developing Countries*, ed. Bela A. Balassa et al. (Baltimore: Johns Hopkins Press, 1971), pp. 261–88.
27. Gerardo P. Sicat, "Production Functions in Philippine Manufacturing," *Philippine Economic Journal* 2 (Second Semester 1963):107–31; Gerardo P. Sicat, "Analytical Aspects of Two Current Economic Policies," *Philippine Economic Journal* 4 (First Semester 1965):107–19; Mahar Mangahas, Aida E. Recto, and Vernon W. Ruttan, "Price and Market Relationships for Rice and Corn in the Philippines," *Journal of Farm Economics* 48 (August 1966):685–703; see also "Market Relationships for Rice and Corn in the Philippines," *Philippine Economic Journal* 5 (First Semester 1966):1–27; Randolph Barker, "The Response of Production to a Change in Rice Policy," *Philippine Economic Journal* 5 (Second Semester 1966):260–76.

relative to the domestically consumed food crops. The shift in the terms of trade between the domestic food and commercial export crop sectors was associated with a shift of resources into export production and a rapid rise in the volume of export crop production and in export earnings.

In spite of the continued growth of the export sector and the expansion of exports, the decontrol was not an unqualified success. One effect was an excess of domestic demand, which "was concentrated particularly on food, the production of which failed to grow more rapidly in the post-decontrol era because of the greater price incentives to expand export crops."[28] The result was pressure on food prices, inflation in the cost of living index, and rising imports of food commodities, particularly rice, during the mid-1960s. The inflation tended to erode the gains from decontrol by pushing labor costs upward in the export industries and by preempting the gains in foreign exchange earnings for food imports.

The inability to expand food production in the face of rising demand during the 1960s was a reflection of the failure, during both the colonial period and the 1950s, to make the investments in land and water resource development, in experiment station capacity, and in the production of the industrial inputs needed to sustain growth in agricultural productivity. Throughout this period there was little change in agricultural productivity. Output expansion was largely accounted for by expansion of traditional inputs. Output per worker rose only slightly. Output per unit of land area declined. Total productivity remained approximately unchanged. Capital investment in the industrial sector purchased too few new jobs. Failure to make the investments in agricultural research, land and water development, and the industrial inputs necessary to achieve productivity growth in agriculture imposed severe limitations on the ability of the agricultural sector to respond to growth in demand.[29]

The initial response to the decontrol and devaluation measures suggests that if the reforms had been fully implemented the momentum generated by the favorable industrial performance during the import-substitution period might have continued. But a successful transformation from import substitution to export-led growth was aborted.[30] During the import-substitution peri-

---

28. Malcolm Treadgold and Richard W. Hooley, "Decontrol and the Redirection of Income Flows: A Second Look," *Philippine Economic Journal* 6 (Second Semester 1967):125.

29. Richard Hooley and Vernon W. Ruttan, "The Philippines," *Agricultural Development in Asia*, ed. R. T. Shand (Canberra: Australian National University Press, 1969), pp. 215–50.

30. The following discussion of Philippine development in the postdecontrol period draws primarily on Robert E. Baldwin, *Foreign Trade Regimes and Economic Development: The Philippines* (New York: Columbia University Press for the National Bureau of Economic Research, 1975); Romeo M. Bautista, John H. Power et al., *Industrial Promotion Policies in the Philippines* (Manila: Philippine Institute for Development Studies, 1979); Richard Hooley, "An Assessment of the Macroeconomic Policy Framework for Employment Generation in the Philippines," mimeograph (A report submitted to USAID/Philippines, April 1981); Cristina C. David, "Economic Policies and Philippine Agriculture," mimeograph (Paper presented at the workshop on the Impact of Economic Policies on Agricultural Development sponsored jointly by the Philippine Institute for Development Studies (PIDS) and the Philippine Council for Agriculture

od Philippine entrepreneurs had become highly politicized. This political base was employed after decontrol and devaluation first to defend and then to increase tariff protection for domestic industry. During the 1970s the tariffs were supplemented by a set of implicit taxes including exchange rate over-valuation and commodity market interventions that had the effect of transfer-ring substantial resources from the agricultural to the nonagricultural sector. Cristina David has estimated that these taxes were equivalent to about 30 percent of the value added by the agricultural sector.[31]

The failure to implement the policies needed to make a transition from an import-substitution to an export-oriented strategy reduced labor absorption in the industrial sector. Factor price distortions resulting from protectionist pol-icies induced the adoption of excessively capital-intensive technology. The share of total employment in manufacturing, which had plateaued at between 11 and 12 percent in the early 1960s, remained below 12 percent throughout the late 1960s and 1970s. In the late 1970s manufacturing was absorbing less than 10 percent of the growth in employment. Most of the growth in the labor force had to be absorbed within the agricultural and service sectors. Real wage rates declined by at least 20 percent in the industrial sector and by more than one-third in the agricultural sector between the early 1960s and the early 1980s.[32]

The most impressive achievement of Philippine economic development policy during the 1970s was the rapid growth of agricultural output. The response of export crop production to decontrol during the early 1960s has already been noted. During the early 1970s production of commercial crops continued to expand in response to high prices in international commodity markets. Both the acreage and yield of food crops, particularly rice, expanded rapidly throughout the 1970s. Growth of investment in land infrastructure, particularly rapid growth in irrigation investment, permitted two crops of rice per year to be grown in many areas where it had formerly been possible to grow only one crop per year (Chapter 10). The development of a series of modern rice varieties by the University of the Philippines College of Agri-culture and the International Rice Research Institute made it possible to achieve higher yields in both the irrigated and rainfed areas.

During this same period government intervention in commodity markets increased. The sugar trade was nationalized. The National Sugar Trading Corporation became the sole wholesale buyer and seller of Philippine sugar in both domestic and international markets. A Coconut Consumer Stabilization

and Resources Research and Development (PCARRD), March 25–26, 1983, Tagaytay City, Philippines). For a more populist account of the events of this same period see Walden F. Bello, David Kinley, and Elaine Elinson, *Development Debacle: The World Bank in the Philippines* (San Francisco: Institute for Food and Development Policy, 1982).

31. David, "Economic Policies," p. 29.

32. Azizur Rahman Khan, "Growth and Inequality in the Rural Philippines," *Poverty and Landlessness in Rural Asia*, A World Employment Programme Study (Geneva: International Labour Office, 1977), pp. 233–49.

Fund and a Coconut Investment Fund were established to stabilize prices and promote new investment. The spread between farm gate and world market prices for sugar and copra widened throughout the 1970s. By the early 1980s the Stabilization Fund had become a source of price instability and the Investment Fund was being accused of diverting resources from producers to the fund managers.

By the late 1970s the rate of growth in agricultural output began to slow down. The domestic terms of trade began to shift against agriculture in the mid-1970s. This trend was reinforced by the sharp decline in commodity prices in international markets. During this same period the marketing of export crops became increasingly politicized. Export taxes, imposed in 1973 and 1975 as stabilization measures, were continued as a convenient means of taxing agricultural producers. These taxes severely dampened production incentives as world prices for agricultural commodities weakened in the late 1970s and early 1980s.

By the late 1970s the Philippine economy was facing a serious crisis reminiscent of that of the late 1950s and early 1960s. Inadequate employment growth in the industrial sector was forcing the agricultural sector to absorb an increasing number of new entrants to the labor force at lower and lower wage rates.[33] The shifts in both domestic and international terms of trade against agriculture were dampening incentives to produce.

As the dimensions of the crisis became clearer, the Philippine government, reinforced by pressure from the World Bank and the International Monetary Fund, began to initiate a new series of comprehensive tariff reforms which were to be implemented gradually over the 1981–85 period. The average effective rate of protection was scheduled to decline sharply for consumer goods and rise modestly for intermediate goods. Plans were proposed to restructure industry in favor of more labor-intensive and less capital-intensive sectors and subsectors and to encourage the exportation of nontraditional manufactured exports.

The Philippine experience is not unlike that of a number of other developing countries. Turkey, for example, has gone through three cycles involving growth, stagnation, crisis, and reform since the early 1950s.[34] Although external events have played an important role in generating such crises, it is hard to escape the conclusion that inappropriate domestic policies have been

---

33. This trend was already becoming important in the early 1970s. See Mahar Mangahas, William Meyers, and Randolph Barker, *Labour Absorption in Philippine Agriculture* (Paris: Development Centre of the Organization for Economic Coöperation and Development, 1972). For case studies of the implications of labor force expansion at the village level see Yujiro Hayami and Masao Kikuchi, *Asian Village Economy at the Crossroads: An Economic Approach to Institutional Change* (Tokyo: University of Tokyo Press, 1981, and Baltimore: Johns Hopkins University Press, 1982), pp. 67–142.

34. William Hale, *The Political and Economic Development of Modern Turkey* (New York: St. Martin's Press, 1981); Anne O. Krueger, *Foreign Trade Regimes and Economic Development: Turkey* (New York: National Bureau of Economic Research, distributed by Columbia University Press, 1974).

major contributors. This inference is reinforced by a comparison of the performance of countries such as the Philippines and Turkey with countries such as Korea and Taiwan. Philippine policy and planning officials, like those in many other countries, have found it necessary continuously to relearn the elementary lesson that the interventions designed to protect one industry or sector impose an implicit tax on some other sector or factor of production. In the Philippine case the agricultural and other raw-material-producing sectors were discriminated against. But the primary burden was on the Philippine worker, in both the agricultural and nonagricultural labor force, in the form of lower wages and earnings.

In many developing countries the effects of distortions induced by inappropriate development policies have been reinforced by distortions resulting from commodity policies designed to extract surpluses from agricultural producers. The politicization of the sugar and copra markets in the Philippines is an example. In the next section we examine the effects of commodity policy in greater detail.

Commodity Market Interventions in Less Developed Countries

Intervention by government in agricultural commodity markets, such as procurement at below market prices, has been a consistent feature of agricultural policy in the LDCs. Government intervention in commodity markets and the suppression or replacement of private market activity have often been considered necessary to achieve efficiency in market performance or to eliminate exploitation of agricultural producers by middlemen. The evidence suggests, however, that government intervention in agricultural markets has itself become, in many countries, a major source of inefficiency and exploitation.[35] We have noted, in the previous section, the emergence of such policies in the Philippines. In this section we examine the implications for agricultural development of LDC government commodity market intervention in more detail.

The political pressure to extract surpluses from producers of agricultural commodities has been generated primarily by government demand for revenue, by demand for forced savings to support industrial development, and by inefficiency and corruption in monopsonist commodity organizations. In many countries, there is also a demand generated by urban workers and employers for low-cost food. During periods of rapid inflation, pressures are particularly strong to disguise the effects of inflation by attempting to stabilize the prices of basic foods—the "wage goods." The policies adopted for export crops and domestically produced foods thus become a by-product of

---

35. Robert H. Bates, *Markets and States in Tropical Africa: The Political Basis of Agricultural Policies* (Berkeley and Los Angeles: University of California Press, 1981); Gilbert T. Brown, "Agricultural Pricing Policies in Developing Countries," *Distortions of Agricultural Incentives*, ed. Theodore W. Schultz (Bloomington: University of Indiana Press, 1978), pp. 84–113.

FIGURE 12-2. Structure of direct government intervention for major grains and staples.

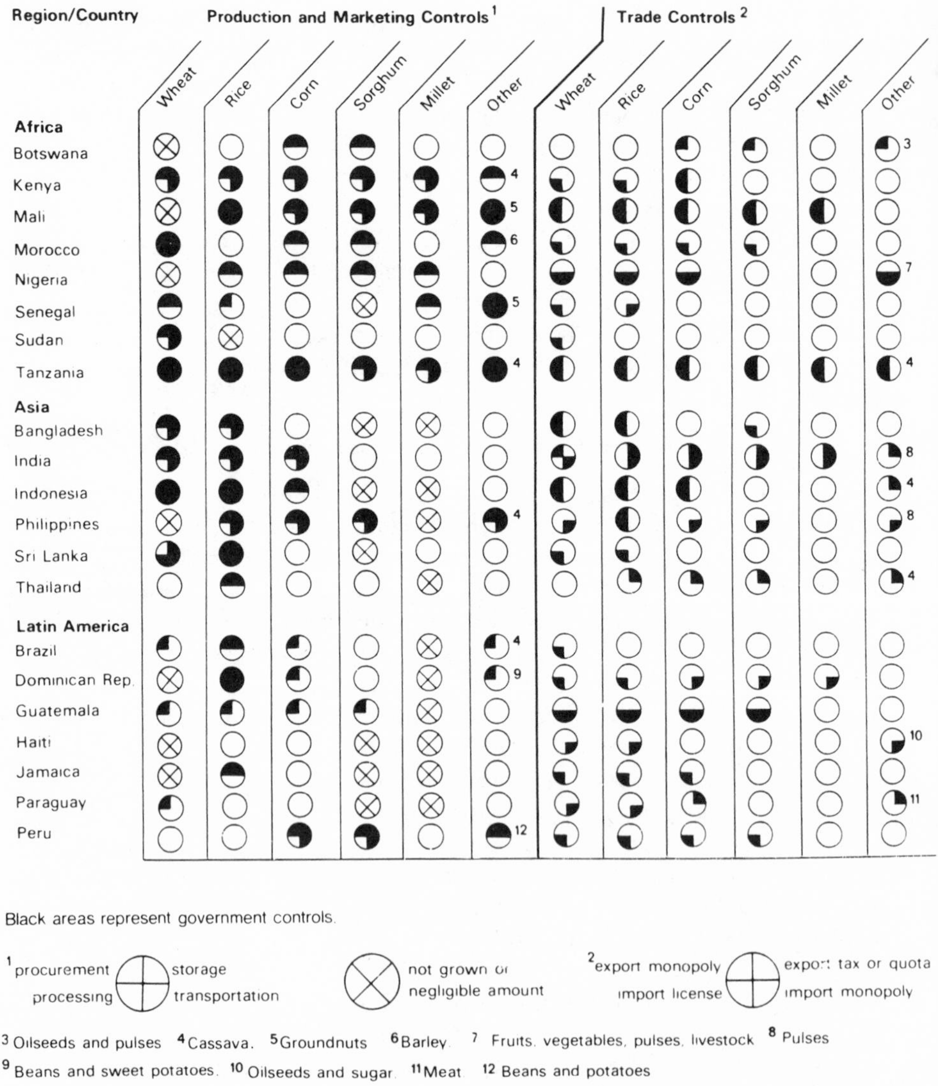

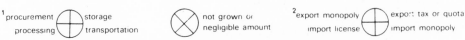

Region/Country
Production and Marketing Controls[1]
Trade Controls[2]
Wheat
Rice
Corn
Sorghum
Millet
Other
Africa
Botswana
Kenya
Mali
Morocco
Nigeria
Senegal
Sudan
Tanzania
Asia
Bangladesh
India
Indonesia
Philippines
Sri Lanka
Thailand
Latin America
Brazil
Dominican Rep.
Guatemala
Haiti
Jamaica
Paraguay
Peru
Black areas represent government controls.
1 procurement
storage
processing
transportation
not grown or negligible amount
2 export monopoly
export tax or quota
import license
import monopoly
3 Oilseeds and pulses
4 Cassava.
5 Groundnuts
6 Barley.
7 Fruits, vegetables, pulses, livestock
8 Pulses
9 Beans and sweet potatoes.
10 Oilseeds and sugar.
11 Meat.
12 Beans and potatoes

Source: Food Policies in Developing Countries (Washington, D.C.: U.S. Department of Agriculture, Economic Research Service, Foreign Agricultural Economic Report 194, 1983), p. 13.

TABLE 12-1. Nominal protection coefficients calculated for grains production in developing countries

Country	Grain	Nominal protection coefficient estimate[a]
Africa		
Egypt	maize	0.67
Ivory Coast	rice	0.97
Kenya	maize	0.91
Senegal	rice	0.70
Sudan	sorghum	0.50
Tanzania	maize	0.13
Tunisia	wheat	0.99
Zambia	maize	0.62
Asia		
India	rice	0.65
Pakistan	wheat	0.76
Philippines	rice	0.73
Thailand	rice	0.58
Europe		
Turkey	wheat	0.94
Yugoslavia	wheat	0.38
Latin America		
Argentina	wheat	0.64
Brazil	rice	0.57
Colombia	rice	0.92
Mexico	wheat	0.89
Uruguay	wheat	1.25

Source: Malcolm D. Bale and Ronald C. Duncan, "Food Prospects in the Developing Countries: A Qualified Optimistic View," *American Economic Review* 73 (May 1983): 247.

[a]The nominal protection coefficient measures the difference between the price of a product in domestic and world markets resulting from tariff and other protectionist measures. A value greater than 1.0 indicates a subsidy on production, and a value less than 1.0 indicates a tax. These estimates have been made at different points of time and now may well be out of date; moreover, the estimates vary widely from year to year within a country.

political relations between governments and their several constituencies.[36] The wide range of interventions in agricultural markets in developing countries is illustrated in Figure 12-2. The implications, in nominal protection coefficients, are illustrated for a number of countries in Table 12-1. As a

36. Bates, *Markets and States in Tropical Africa*, p. 4; Alain de Janvry, "Why Do Governments Do What They Do? The Case of Food Price Policy," *The Role of Markets in the World Economy*, ed. D. Gale Johnson and G. Edward Schuh (Boulder, Colo.: Westview Press, 1983), pp. 185–212. De Janvry notes that governments of developing countries must continually struggle with the contradiction between legitimacy and accumulation. The former calls for cheap food policies and public subsidies. The latter requires the stimulation of investment and technical change (p. 19). The political incentive for introducing price distortions may be enhanced by the possibility, as in the case of the zone price system in India, that there may be short-run gains to agricultural producers. See Yujiro Hayami, K. Subbarao, and Keijiro Otsuka, "Efficiency and Equity in the Producer Levy of India," *American Journal of Agricultural Economics* 64 (November 1982):655–63.

result, the nominal protection coefficients, calculated as the ratio of domestic prices to international prices, are less than 1.0 in most LDCs.

The policies pursued by Tanzania during the 1960s and 1970s provide a useful illustration. The government of Tanzania simultaneously attempted to pursue an import-substitution industrialization policy and a policy of self-sufficiency in food grain production. It has taxed its traditional export commodities heavily to support its industrialization policy.[37]

The state is deeply involved in nearly every aspect of food production and marketing. More than one hundred parastatal processing and retailing firms and crop authorities are involved in the marketing of agricultural commodities. An attempt has been made to maintain a single price for the entire country throughout the year, regardless of transportation costs, for agricultural inputs and products by adjusting stocks and imports.

Domestic prices of the major export crops have been held substantially below world market prices. Even at the official exchange rate, which clearly overvalued the Tanzania shilling, the implicit export tax was above 30 percent during the 1970s. The prices of maize and rice were held below the international price by 24 percent and 36 percent respectively. But the price of wheat to producers was held at about 15 percent above the import price.

How were these prices determined? Christopher Gerrard and Terry Roe have designed and estimated an econometric model to test the hypothesis that price interventions were designed to maintain the announced policy of achieving self-sufficiency in the production of maize, wheat, and rice. The results of the test indicated that the pricing policies for the three food grains were rational in terms of the announced policy goal of food grain self-sufficiency.

But Tanzania's pursuit of a rational policy to meet its objective of food grain self-sufficiency is not evidence that the self-sufficiency objective was itself rational. If domestic prices had been at world market prices during the 1970s, Tanzania would have been a net exporter of maize and rice. Imports of wheat would have been larger. The interventions have clearly had the effect of transferring incomes from producers to consumers. Tanzania's comparative advantage in rice and maize has been eroded, and the costs of autarky have risen. In the early 1980s Tanzania appeared to be initiating a number of policy

37. The Tanzania case study presented here draws primarily on Christopher D. Gerrard, "Economic Development, Government-Controlled Markets, and External Trade in Food Grains: The Case of Four Countries in East Africa" (Ph.D. dissertation, University of Minnesota, 1981); Christopher D. Gerrard and Terry Roe, "Government Intervention in Food Grain Markets: An Econometric Study of Tanzania," *Journal of Development Economics* 12 (1983):109–32. The work by Gerrard and Roe has been summarized by Shirley A. Pryor in *Food Policies in Developing Countries* (Washington, D.C.: U.S. Department of Agriculture, Economic Research Service, Foreign Agricultural Economic Report 194, 1983), pp. 46–49. The authors have also benefited from an opportunity to review the *Tanzania Agricultural Sector Report* (Washington, D.C.: World Bank, Eastern Africa Projects Department, Southern Agriculture Division, Report 4052-TA, 1982). Several other useful examples might have been selected. See, for example, the case studies of agricultural price policy in Korea, Bangladesh, Thailand, and Venezuela in George S. Tolley, Vinod Thomas, and Chung Ming Wong, *Agricultural Price Policies and the Developing Countries* (Baltimore: Johns Hopkins University Press, 1982).

changes with respect to internal pricing and marketing, for example, that could lead to greater efficiency.

The social costs of policies such as those pursued by Tanzania and many other developing countries have been consistently underestimated. In the early development literature a backward-bending supply curve for agricultural commodities in developing countries was commonly assumed. This argument was gradually put to rest by the accumulation of empirical evidence. As studies accumulated, a consensus gradually emerged to the effect that in both developing and developed economies the output of individual commodities was highly responsive to changes in the relative prices of individual commodities. The studies also tended to reinforce the perspective that aggregate supply response to changes in the domestic terms of trade (to shifts in commodity prices relative to factor costs or the costs of other consumption items) was low—in the neighborhood of .20 or less.[38]

Recent research suggests that aggregate supply is much more responsive to changes in factor price ratios than previously assumed. Willis L. Peterson has estimated long-run supply elasticities in the neighborhood of 1.3 and secular elasticities in the neighborhood of 1.6.[39] Furthermore, a separate analysis for the DCs and LDCs suggests that aggregate supply elasticities are at least as high in the LDCs as in the DCs. If Peterson's estimates are valid, modest increases in agricultural prices in the LDCs would, if sustained over several decades, be sufficient to reduce substantially the net flow of grain from the DCs to the LDCs.[40]

38. For a review see Raj Krishna, "Agricultural Price Policy and Economic Development," *Agricultural Development and Economic Growth*, ed. Herman M. Southworth and Bruce F. Johnston (Ithaca: Cornell University Press, 1967), pp. 497–540; Hossein Askari and John T. Cummings, *Agricultural Supply Response: A Survey of the Econometric Evidence* (New York: Praeger, 1976); Marc Nerlove, "The Dynamics of Supply: Retrospect and Prospect," *American Journal of Agricultural Economics* 61 (December 1979):874–88. As efforts have been made to explore the dynamics of agricultural supply response within a rational expectations framework it appears that the earlier estimates based on the Nerlove adaptive expectations model tended to underestimate farmers' response to expected changes in future prices. See Zvi Eckstein, "A Rational Expectations Model of Agricultural Supply," *Journal of Political Economy* 92 (February 1984):1–19. For an earlier attempt to model agricultural commodity policy as endogenous see Ralph G. Lattimore and G. Edward Schuh, "Endogenous Policy Determination: The Case of the Brazilian Beef Sector," *Canadian Journal of Agricultural Economics* 27 (July 1979):1–16.

39. Willis L. Peterson, "International Farm Prices and the Social Cost of Cheap Food Policies," *American Journal of Agricultural Economics* 61 (February 1979):12–21. Peterson's results were derived from estimates using a log-linear supply function fitted to cross-section data. He argues that earlier estimates based on time-series data resulted in substantial underestimates of supply elasticity because they measure the effects of short-term, year-to-year fluctuations in prices rather than long-term responses. The large and persistent differences in prices among countries provide an opportunity to measure the long-run and secular elasticities.

40. Other studies have also demonstrated the high social costs of low commodity prices. Malcolm D. Bale and Ernst Lutz have developed quantitative estimates of the effect of price distortions on agricultural output, income distribution, and employment in four developed countries (Japan, West Germany, France, and Great Britain), four less-developed market economies (Thailand, Egypt, Argentina, and Pakistan), and one less-developed socialist country (Yugoslavia). The estimates by Bale and Lutz confirm that the positive levels of protection in the four developed countries result in levels of agricultural production that are substantially higher

The efficiency losses resulting from a short-run misallocation of the resources devoted to agricultural production have been large. But even more serious have been the dynamic efficiency losses caused by lost opportunities to realize the potential gains from the technical and institutional changes that would have occurred under more appropriate market, trade, and investment policies.

An overwhelming lesson from the development experience of the last several decades is that the efficiency with which resources are allocated is a major determinant of the rate of economic growth. This lesson is contrary to the earlier expectations of many economists and planners, who believed that static allocative efficiency losses were very small.

The discussion developed in this section implies considerable slack in the use of agricultural production capacity in a large number of developing countries. In these countries substantial gains in production could be achieved by market policies that would eliminate the most serious price distortions. We do not, however, regard "getting prices right" as a sufficient condition for sustained growth in agricultural production.[41] Growth of agricultural output along a given supply response surface ultimately becomes excessively expensive in terms of the inputs that must be devoted to agricultural production. But it is hard to escape the conclusion that a large number of countries are depriving themselves of both short-run gains in output and long-run gains in productivity by imposing price regimes that provide biased signals to agricultural producers and to the private and public suppliers of agricultural technology.

REFORMING RURAL INSTITUTIONS

One of the basic premises of development thought during the first development decade after World War II was that institutional constraints represented a major barrier to technical change and to modernization in agriculture.[42] The

---

than they would be without intervention and that output in the four less-developed countries is significantly lower than it would be in the absence of distortions. Malcolm D. Bale and Ernst Lutz, "Price Distortions in Agriculture and Their Effects: An International Comparison," *American Journal of Agricultural Economics* 63 (February 1981):8–22.

41. For a similar perspective see Raj Krishna, "Some Aspects of Agricultural Growth, Price Policy and Equity in Developing Countries," *Food Research Institute Studies* 18 (1982):219–60.

42. John M. Brewster, "Traditional Social Structures as Barriers to Change," *Agricultural Development and Economic Growth,* ed. Herman M. Southworth and Bruce F. Johnston (Ithaca: Cornell University Press, 1967), pp. 66–98. The institutional constraint perspective has been restated by Gunnar Myrdal, *Asian Drama: An Inquiry into the Poverty of Nations,* 3 vols. (New York: Twentieth Century Fund, 1968), "The success of technological reforms, designed primarily to increase the cultivated acreage and raise agricultural yields through variations in techniques and the input of capital, hinges largely on the extent of prior, or at least simultaneous, institutional changes" (2:1260). For a comment on the Myrdal perspective see Kusum Nair, "Asian Drama—A Critique," *Economic Development and Cultural Change* 17 (July 1969):449–59.

perspective that emerges from the theory of induced technical and institutional innovation is that changes which enhance the productivity potential of the human and material resources in agriculture open up powerful incentives for institutional innovation. The demand for institutional innovation is also viewed as a response to new opportunities for the productive use of human and material resources opened up by changes in cultural and resource endowments and by technical advance rather than as a precondition for agricultural development (Chapter 4).

In this section we discuss efforts to reform land tenure relations and rural credit institutions and efforts to implement comprehensive programs of rural development.

Land Tenure Reform

Tenure reform has been viewed as essential to the mobilization of labor resources and the generation of productivity growth in both liberal and Marxist development perspectives. Economic logic and economic history combined in the early post–World War II period to produce a remarkable unity in doctrine to the effect that an agricultural sector in which an owner-cultivator system predominates achieves a more efficient allocation of resources and makes a greater contribution to national economic growth than under alternative systems.

Land reform after World War II. The analytical support for this position drew on a tradition that extended back through Marshall to the classical economists. The classical economists recognized that in a world of imperfect land, capital, and credit markets, sharecropping represented an improvement over wage labor because of its positive incentive effect. The classical economists also recognized that sharecropping provides the worker with less incentive to work than a fixed-rent tenant or an owner-cultivator would have. The classical perspective was confirmed by Marshall.[43] It was reexamined again within the framework of the Hicksian neoclassical theory of the firm in the 1940s and early 1950s.[44] The major conclusion that emerged from this reanalysis of the relationship between tenure and productivity, as stated by Louis S. Drake, was that "there is no substitute, from the standpoint of sheer

43. Alfred Marshall, *Principles of Economics*, 8th ed. (New York: Macmillan Co., 1948), pp. 642–49 (esp. n. 2, p. 644); Gerald D. Jaynes, "Production and Distribution in Agrarian Economics," *Oxford Economic Papers* 34 (July 1982):346–67.

44. Theodore W. Schultz, "Capital Rationing, Uncertainty and Farm-Tenancy Reform," *Journal of Political Economy* 48 (June 1940):309–24; Rainer Schickele, "Effect of Tenure Systems on Agricultural Efficiency," *Journal of Farm Economics* 23 (February 1941):185–207; Earl O. Heady, "Economics of Farm Leasing Systems," *Journal of Farm Economics* 29 (August 1947):659–78; Louis S. Drake, "Comparative Productivity of Share and Cash-Rent Systems of Tenure," *Journal of Farm Economics* 34 (November 1952):535–50; Earl O. Heady and Earl W. Kehrberg, *Relationship of Crop-Share and Cash Leasing Systems to Farming Efficiency* (Ames: Iowa State College, Agricultural Experiment Station Research Bulletin 386, 1952); Nicholas Georgescu-Roegen, "Economic Theory and Agrarian Economics," *Oxford Economic Papers* 12 (February 1960):1–40.

productivity, and irrespective of sociological considerations, for an owner-operated agricultural system."[45]

This perspective led to a major emphasis on land reform in the technical and economic assistance efforts of a number of national and international development assistance agencies after World War II. The post–World War II commitment by the United States to land reform as an instrument of political and economic policy was initiated with the reforms carried out in Germany and Japan. The success of the Japanese land reform was an important factor in U.S. support for land reform in other countries of East Asia in the early 1950s and in Latin America, under the Alliance for Progress, in the 1960s.[46]

The analytical deductions were regarded, during most of the post–World War II period, as consistent with historical experience.[47] The post–World War II land reform experience in Japan, Taiwan, and Korea has been widely interpreted as supporting the proposition that an agrarian structure consisting of extremely small owner-cultivator family farms could be economically viable, reasonably efficient, and capable of sustaining rapid increases in agricultural productivity. Analysis of the earlier modifications in tenure arrangements in Japan, beginning with the abolition of feudal privileges and the conversion of the land tax to a cash rather than a commodity basis during the early years of the Meiji Restoration, also supported the proposition that the resulting improvements in incentives complemented efforts to introduce new crop varieties, higher levels of fertilization, and other changes in cultural practices.[48]

Experience from the postwar land reforms in other developing countries, however, did not provide the same degree of support for the historical generalizations as the East Asia experience. In many countries land reform legislation was badly or perversely administered. Furthermore, the growing body of empirical evidence on the relationships among farm size, tenure, and produc-

45. Drake, "Comparative Productivity of Share and Cash-Rent Systems of Tenure," p. 549.

46. See Louis J. Walinsky, ed., *Agrarian Reform as Unfinished Business: The Selected Papers of Wolf Ladejinsky* (New York: Oxford University Press, 1977). For reviews of the land reform efforts and accomplishments of the 1950s and 1960s see Ernest Feder, "Land Reform under the Alliance for Progress," *Journal of Farm Economics* 47 (August 1965):652–68; Philip M. Raup, "Land Reform and Agricultural Development," *Agricultural Development and Economic Growth*, ed. Southworth and Johnston, pp. 267–314; Peter Dorner and Don Kanel, "The Economic Case for Land Reform," *Land Reform in Latin America: Issues and Cases*, ed. Peter Dorner (Madison: University of Wisconsin, Land Tenure Center, Land Economics Monograph 3, 1971), pp. 21–35.

47. United Nations, *Land Reform: Defects in Agrarian Structure as Obstacles to Economic Development* (New York: United Nations, Department of Economic Affairs, 1951); Agency for International Development, *Spring Review of Land Reform: Background and Country Papers* (Washington, D.C.: Agency for International Development, 1970).

48. R. P. Dore, *Land Reform in Japan* (London: Oxford University Press, 1959); Chen Cheng, *Land Reform in Taiwan* (Taipei, Taiwan: China Publishing, Co., 1961); M. Kaihara, "On The Effects of Postwar Land Reform in Japan," *Land Tenure, Industrialization and Social Stability,* ed. Walter Froehlich (Milwaukee: Marquette University Press, 1961), pp. 143–67; Takekazu Ogura, ed., *Agricultural Development in Modern Japan* (Tokyo: Fuji Publishing Co., 1963), pp. 119–44, 613–77.

tivity was frequently inconsistent with the ordering suggested by logical deductions.[49] In the smaller size ranges, share tenants frequently achieved higher yields than owner-operators. Even in the larger size classes, owner-operators seldom exhibited any clear-cut productivity differentials relative to other classes. It was frequently noted that the highest levels of productivity were achieved by owner-tenants—typically small landowners who cultivated rented land in addition to their own land.

The new land tenure economics.[50]   The lack of consistency between the logical deductions and the empirical observations regarding the efficiency of alternative land tenure institutions gave rise, in the late 1960s and 1970s, to a new land tenure economics that attempted to explore the economic rationale for the persistence of share tenancy.

As early as 1950, D. Gale Johnson questioned the empirical validity of Marshallian inefficiency based on his observation of U.S. agriculture.[51] He reasoned that landlords' refusal of contract renewal (or a threat to that effect) against share tenants who do not deliver share rents comparable to leasehold rents is a sufficiently strong enforcing mechanism to prevent obvious inefficiency. A formal proof was given by Steven N. S. Cheung three decades later. He developed a general equilibrium model in which the terms of contract such as share rate, farm size, and input levels are variables determined through negotiations between landlords and tenants, while the wage rate is determined in the market. He concluded that "the implied resource allocation under private property rights is the same whether the landlord cultivates the land himself, hires farm hands to do the tilling, leases his holdings on a fixed-

49. Vernon W. Ruttan, "Tenure and Productivity of Philippine Rice Producing Farms," *Philippine Economic Journal* 5 (First Semester 1966):42–63; Steven N. S. Cheung, *The Theory of Share Tenancy* (Chicago: University of Chicago Press, 1969); Folke Dovring, "Economic Results of Land Reforms," *Spring Review of Land Reform* (Washington, D.C.: U.S. Agency for International Development, Analytical Paper SR/LR/A-7, 1970); Yukon Huang, "Tenancy Patterns, Productivity, and Rentals in Malaysia," *Economic Development and Cultural Change* 23 (July 1975):703–18; C. H. Hanumantha Rao, *Technological Change and Distribution of Gains in Indian Agriculture* (Delhi: Macmillan Co. of India, 1975); Mahar Mangahas, Virginia A. Miralao, and Romana P. de los Reyes, with Normando de Leon, *Tenants, Lessees, Owners: Welfare Implications of Tenure Change* (Quezon City, Philippines: Ateneo de Manila University Press, 1976); Hayami and Kikuchi, *Asian Village Economy at the Crossroads;* Christopher J. Bliss and Nicholas H. Stern, *Palanpur: The Economy of an Indian Village* (Oxford: Clarendon Press; New York: Oxford University Press, 1982); Ronald J. Herring, *Land to the Tiller: The Political Economy of Agrarian Reform in South Asia* (New Haven: Yale University Press, 1983).

50. This section draws heavily on Hayami and Kikuchi, *Asian Village Economy at the Crossroads,* pp. 29–34. For a review of new land tenure economic literature, see Hans P. Binswanger and Mark R. Rosenzweig, "Contractual Arrangements, Employment, and Wages in Rural Labor Markets: A Critical Review," *Contractual Arrangements, Employment, and Wages in Rural Labor Markets in Asia,* ed. Hans P. Binswanger and Mark R. Rosenzweig (New Haven: Yale University Press, 1984), pp. 1–40; also Gerald David Jaynes, "Economic Theory and Land Tenure," ibid., pp. 43–62.

51. D. Gale Johnson, "Resource Allocation under Share Contracts," *Journal of Political Economy* 58 (April 1950):111–23.

FIGURE 12-3. Model of contractual choice.

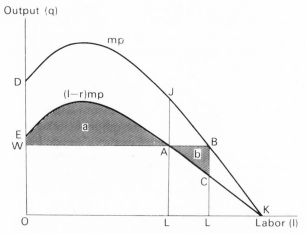

Source: Yujiro Hayami and Masao Kikuchi, *Asian Village Economy at the Crossroads: An Economic Approach to Institutional Change* (Tokyo: University of Tokyo Press, 1981, and Baltimore: Johns Hopkins University Press, 1982), p. 30.

rent basis, or shares the actual yield with his tenant,"[52] if private property rights are well-defined and the enforcement of contractual terms is costless.

Cheung's theory, as contrasted with the traditional theory of Marshallian inefficiency, is explained in Figure 12-3.[53] Curve DK represents a marginal product ($mp = \partial q/\partial l$) of labor applied to a given land area. The traditional arguments run as follows. If the market wage rate is given as OW, both the owner-farmer and the leasehold tenant will apply labor. At OL_2 the marginal product of labor (mp) and the wage rate (measured in output) are equated and the operator's residual or profit is maximized. For the share tenant, however, the marginal return to labor is lower than mp by the rate of land rent (r) that he pays to the landlord. His marginal return schedule is represented by EK. The share tenant will apply his labor only up to OL_1 where $(1 - r)mp$ equals the wage rate.

Cheung argues that, if information is perfect and transaction cost is zero, the landlord will stipulate in the contract that the share tenant should apply labor up to OL_2. Such stipulation will be accepted by the tenant through bargaining if area b is smaller than area a, because his total income as a share tenant (area $OECL_2$) is still larger than the income from his alternative employment as a wage laborer (area $OWBL_2$). Further, if the market is perfect, the landlord will be able to bid up his share rate (r) or depress the mp curve by limiting the area rented to a tenant to a level where a equals b, that is, where

52. Steven N. S. Cheung, *The Theory of Share Tenancy* (Chicago: University of Chicago Press, 1969), p. 4.

53. Hayami and Kikuchi, *Asian Village Economy at the Crossroads*, pp. 29–34.

the sharecropper's income is equal to his potential earnings as a wage laborer.[54]

Likewise, if the market is perfect, the landlord would be able to bid up the fixed rent to a level equal to his potential income as an owner-farmer. Thus in a perfect market with zero transaction cost, the resource allocation and the income distribution will be exactly the same among the three types of contract; the return to labor is invariably equivalent to area $OWBL_2$ and the return to land is equivalent to area WDB. Both the landlord and the tenant should be indifferent as to the choice of contract in a perfect market.

In the real world the choice depends on the relative magnitudes of risk and the transaction cost, especially the cost of enforcing contracts. From the side of the landlord, the risk is the lowest for the leasehold contract with fixed rent and the highest for doing one's own farming with fixed-wage labor. The transaction cost would also be highest for the use of laborers at the fixed-wage rate because of the difficulty of preventing them from shirking. The cost of enforcing a leasehold contract or of collecting fixed rent should be lower than that of enforcing a share contract because the latter involves the difficulty of ascertaining how much labor is applied and how much output is produced. Thus because of both risk and transaction cost, the landlord will prefer leasehold tenancy to share tenancy and share tenancy to fixed-wage employment.

For the tenant, the preference ordering would be exactly the opposite of that for the landlord if there were no uncertainty in the labor market. Another criterion for the tenant's contractual choice is the opportunity for the tenant to exploit his entrepreneurial ability. If this opportunity is large, the tenant will prefer leasehold tenancy to share tenancy and share tenancy to fixed-wage employment.

The actual choice of contract will depend on the relative magnitudes of risk, transaction costs, and returns to entrepreneurial ability. Cheung argued that the costs of enforcing contractual terms regarding the input levels used by share tenants could be minimized by the direct monitoring of their production activities. Even so, the transaction costs associated with the share contract would be higher than in the case of either the fixed-rent or the fixed-wage contract. He identified the advantage in risk-sharing as the major factor underlying the choice of share contracts. In contrast, C. H. Hanumantha Rao argued, drawing on Indian examples, that both the enforcement cost and the return to tenants' allocative ability can be very high for the crops charac-

---

54. Several models were also developed that consider the income-maximizing behavior of landlords but still found Marshallian inefficiency under the share tenancy. The critical assumption that led to such a conclusion is that the fixed-rent contract is not an available option for the landlord. See P. K. Bardhan and T. N. Srinivasan, "Crop-Sharing Tenancy in Agriculture: A Theoretical and Empirical Analysis," *American Economic Review* 61 (March 1971):48–64; Clive Bell and Pinhas Zusman, "A Bargaining Theoretic Approach to Cropsharing Contracts," *American Economic Review* 66 (September 1976):578–88; and Robert E. B. Lucas, "Sharing, Monitoring, and Incentives: Marshallian Misallocation Reassessed," *Journal of Political Economy* 87 (June 1979):501–21.

terized by dynamic changes in their production and demand functions. For such crops the leasehold contract would be preferred even if the risk were higher.[55] Further, David Newbery, Joseph Reid, and Joseph Stiglitz argued that risk cannot be a decisive factor in explaining the choice of share contract because the same degree of risk-sharing can be achieved by combining lease-hold and fixed-wage contracts. The indivisibility of the tenant's entrepreneurial and managerial ability, however, would make it inefficient to allocate his time between wage employment and leasehold farming on a smaller scale.[56]

Whether risk or enforcement cost is more dominant in contract choice is not a theoretical but an empirical question. It depends on the economic, social, and ecological environments.

Let us first consider a near-subsistence economy with traditional agriculture, as characterized by T. W. Schultz, in which productivity is low but resources are allocated at near the long-run equilibria and agricultural production is highly uncertain.[57] In such an economy risk aversion would dominate the tenant's preference because his income is so low that he has to worry about the probability of a subsistence crisis and, also, there is little scope for him to exploit his entrepreneurial ability.

On the other hand, risk should be a relatively minor consideration for the wealthy landlord. Because technology is stable, it is not so difficult to identify the optimal level of a tenant's input and the corresponding output level. Then it is easy to specify labor input in a sharecropping contract. It is also easy to enforce the contract because the correspondence between input and output is known, and the landlord can easily detect tenant shirking by inspecting the share rents delivered over a period long enough to average out weather variations.

Thus the reduction in transaction cost from a shift from a share to a leasehold contract would not be large. The cost increase from the conversion of sharecroppers to wage laborers, however, would likely be substantial. The cost of supervising laborers doing farm work is usually very high because most work is not standardized and requires personal judgments about production practices in response to the infinite variations in plants, animals, water, and soil. It is difficult to expect wage laborers alienated from the product of their labor to perform the tasks adequately. Thus it seems reasonable to hypothesize that the pervasive practice of sharecropping in traditional farming

55. C. H. Hanumantha Rao, "Uncertainty, Entrepreneurship, and Sharecropping in India," *Journal of Political Economy* 79 (May–June 1971):578–95.

56. Joseph E. Stiglitz, "Incentives and Risk Sharing in Sharecropping," *Review of Economic Studies* 41 (April 1974):219–55; David M. G. Newbery, "The Choice of Rental Contracts in Peasant Agriculture," *Agriculture in Development Theory*, ed. Lloyd G. Reynolds (New Haven: Yale University Press, 1975), pp. 109–37; Joseph D. Reid, Jr., "Sharecropping and Agricultural Uncertainty," *Economic Development and Cultural Change* 24 (April 1976):549–76.

57. Theodore W. Schultz, *Transforming Traditional Agriculture* (New Haven: Yale University Press, 1964).

communities is an efficient compromise between the tenant's strong risk aversion and the landlord's calculation of transaction cost. But share tenancy may become inefficient in response to changes in technology and expansion of market opportunities. The effect may be to induce a shift to leasehold tenancy.[58]

Technological change may also induce a shift from share tenancy to owner farming or the conversion of sharecroppers to wage laborers. The development of large-scale farm machinery can work as a strong inducement to this change. The large machines reduce the cost of enforcement because it is easier to supervise one tractor driver than a large number of manual laborers.[59]

It should be emphasized that close social interactions in rural communities act to assure low-cost contract enforcement. In a small community, everyone knows everyone. People watch one another closely. A tenant may be able to shirk or cheat his landlord on the amount produced for several years. But in a small community the cheating (moral hazard) will sooner or later be detected. On the other hand, the development of a reputation for dishonesty is costly for the tenant in a small community. Not only would he lose the contract with the present lessor but he would also find it difficult to rent land from other landlords. The closer the patron-client relationship between tenant and landlord, the higher the penalty because the possible detection of moral hazard in one area would endanger the full range of benefits from stable employment to emergency assistance.[60] In the course of urban-industrial development, however, such personal relations in small communities tend to be replaced by impersonal market relations. The cost of share contract enforcement is increased. This, together with the lower risk in a wider market, would induce a shift from a share to a leasehold contract.

Thus the new land tenure economics represents an antithesis to the paradigm that governed land reform programs in the post–World War II period. It demolished the traditional doctrine that share tenancy is always inefficient and thereby removed the rationale for its replacement by leasehold tenancy or owner-operatorship as a prerequisite to rapid productivity growth in agriculture. On the contrary, the new theory demonstrates that, given substantial underdevelopment or imperfection in factor and product markets, share tenure can be a more efficient method of sharing risk and minimizing transaction costs, especially in semisubsistent, semiclosed, small communities characterized by stagnant technology and intensive social interactions.

Land reform programs designed without due recognition of such socioeconomic conditions can be counterproductive, not only to farming effi-

58. Rao, "Uncertainty, Entrepreneurship, and Sharecropping in India."

59. For an interesting analysis of the effect of cotton pickers on sharecroppers in the southern United States, see Richard H. Day, "The Economics of Technological Change and the Demise of the Sharecropper," *American Economic Review* 57 (June 1967):427–49.

60. For the effect of personal interactions in small communities on labor and land contracts, see Hayami and Kikuchi, *Asian Village Economy at the Crossroads*, pp. 11–23.

ciency but also to the welfare of workers and tenants. It is common to observe that the prohibition of share tenancy, coupled with other regulations such as rent control or the prospective plan of land confiscation and redistribution, has induced landlords to cultivate their land under direct administration instead of renting it out in small parcels.[61] Because of the high cost of supervising wage laborers directly, the landlords often sought labor-saving methods of farming, either by substituting a tractor for a large number of workers and bullock teams or by shifting from labor-intensive crops such as rice to labor-extensive crops such as coconuts. The consequence was a reduction in labor use and labor earnings.[62]

The above argument does not imply that the efforts to reform land tenure relations should be abandoned or neglected. It is the role of institutions to facilitate efficient resource allocations at a certain stage of economic development. But institutions, once established, tend to persist even after changes in technology and other economic conditions have rendered them obsolete and inefficient. As product and factor markets develop, the importance of the risk-sharing role of share tenancy is reduced. Changes in agricultural technology make it more difficult for landlords to ascertain optimal levels of input and output and to specify and enforce contractual terms of share tenancy. Further, as local communities become more closely linked to wider markets, the intense social interaction, which was a basis of low-cost contract enforcement, will be weakened.

Through such processes, the disadvantages of share tenancy may come to outweigh its advantages. In that event, land tenure reform may reduce the time lag between institutional change and technological and economic change. In our induced innovation perspective, land reform should not be viewed as a precondition for productivity growth. Rather, it should be viewed as induced by opportunities created by technical change and market development. In the absence of newly created technological potential, for example, tenure reform will have little significant impact on agricultural growth. In such an environment it will be difficult to generate the political resources needed to initiate and implement land reform.

Land reform in Latin America.   The literature on the new land tenure economics has a peculiarly Asian flavor. Land reforms in Asia were carried

---

61. This tendency seems especially pervasive in India. See Kalyan Dutt, "Changes in Land Relations in West Bengal," *Economic and Political Weekly* 12 (December 31, 1977):A106–10; P. C. Joshi, "Land Reform in India and Pakistan," *Economic and Political Weekly* 5 (December 1970):A145–52; Dharm Narain and P. C. Joshi, "Magnitude of Agricultural Tenancy," *Economic and Political Weekly* 4 (September 1969):A139–42; K. N. Raj, "Trends in Rural Unemployment in India: An Analysis with Reference to Conceptual and Measurement Problems," *Economic and Political Weekly* 11 (August 1976):1281–92; and Doreen Warriner, *Land Reform in Principle and Practice* (Oxford: Clarendon Press, 1969), pp. 136–218.

62. Hans P. Binswanger, *The Economics of Tractors in South Asia* (New York: Agricultural Development Council, and Hyderabad, India: International Crops Research Institute for the Semi-Arid Tropics, 1978); and Hayami and Kikuchi, *Asian Village Economy at the Crossroads*, pp. 227–41.

out with the expectation that reforming labor and tenure relationships through elimination of intermediaries, regulation of rental arrangements, and transfer of ownership rights to the tiller would achieve both equity and productivity objectives. Most of the contributors to the new literature on land tenure economics have drawn on Asian experience.

There is a very different flavor to the literature on land tenure reform that has risen out of the Latin American experience.[63] Neither the practice nor the theory of land tenure reform in Latin America has given much weight to the achievement of productivity objectives through the transfer of landownership to the tiller.

In land reforms initiated under leftist regimes, such as Cuba in the 1960s and Chile in the late 1960s, distrust of the peasantry has often resulted in attempts to establish group farming enterprises guided or controlled by a state agency. Similar transformations have also been attempted by a number of populist or reformist governments, such as Peru in the early 1970s and El Salvador in the late 1970s. But regardless of whether the reforms have been inspired by radical, populist, or reformist ideologies, the political leadership has sought to retain control over the organization of agricultural production. The group farming enterprises resulting from such reforms have more often become a burden on development than an efficient source of food and fiber. And they have typically failed to satisfy the land hunger of the peasants.[64]

Reforms initiated by liberal or conservative regimes have often resulted in a bimodal agricultural organization. Limited land redistribution has often been undertaken in areas of most severe agrarian unrest. Simultaneous efforts have often been made to develop a modern large-scale farming sector. Improvements in the production support system, including agricultural research and extension and the development of input markets and credit institutions, were often focused on the modern sector and neglected the small-scale reform sector.[65]

The Latin American experience has been, of course, much richer than the stylized description presented here. In a large number of Latin American countries the land reforms have been successful in removing some of the most

63. See, for example, the literature reviewed in Feder, ''Land Reform under the Alliance for Progress''; Dorner, ed., *Land Reform in Latin America;* Shlomo Eckstein, Gordon Donald, Douglas Horton, and Thomas Carroll, *Land Reform in Latin America: Bolivia, Chile, Mexico, Peru, and Venezuela* (Washington, D.C.: World Bank Staff Working Paper 275, 1978); Alain de Janvry, *The Agrarian Question and Reformism in Latin America* (Baltimore: Johns Hopkins University Press, 1981).

64. See, for example, Alberto Valdés, ''The Transition to Socialism: Observations on the Chilean Agrarian Reform,'' *Employment in Developing Nations,* ed. Edgar O. Edwards (New York: Columbia University Press, 1974), pp. 405–18.

65. According to de Janvry, ''The most successful implementation of this strategy has occurred in Mexico, where political stability and democratic representation have been maintained since the reform of Cárdenas in spite of growing rural poverty and highly unequal patterns of development'' (*The Agrarian Question and Reformism,* p. 219). ''The contrasting experiences of Bolivia and Mexico—the only two Latin American countries that have undergone a long and uninterrupted process of land reform—do tend to confirm the hypothesis that potential production gains are greatest under reforms that create a transition to the farmer road'' (ibid., p. 217).

obvious sources of inefficiency and exploitation associated with the traditional hacienda system. There appear to be relatively few areas, however,
where the land reforms have been accompanied by the policies needed to
sustain productivity growth in the small-scale peasant sector. And there are
even fewer areas where the Latin American reforms have succeeded in resolving the problems of equity in the agrarian structure.

Future directions in land reform. During the 1970s great progress was
made in our capacity to understand the productivity implications of land
tenure relationships. The most important contribution of the new land tenure
economics was the demonstration that no form of land tenure is universally
efficient. The relative efficiencies of the several land tenure arrangements
depend on the environmental, technological, and institutional conditions that
influence risk, transaction costs, and entrepreneurial ability.

When we consider the implications of recent analytical advances in the
context of historical experience, we find, however, that it is hard to avoid the
conclusion that it has been a great advantage to a country to be able to enter
the period of modern agricultural growth with a unimodal, small-scale, predominantly owner-operator agrarian structure. The political costs of improving land tenure arrangements are very high even under the most favorable of
circumstances. When agriculture was organized along bimodal lines, such as
the traditional minifundia-hacienda system that characterized much of Latin
American agriculture, the political costs often permitted nothing more than
marginal adjustments toward more efficient land tenure arrangements.

It also seems clear that ideological approaches to land tenure reform have
often imposed great costs on both landowners and tenants with few gains in
agricultural production or productivity. An implication of the new land tenure
economics is that failure to take into account the complex relationships between land tenure, resource and cultural endowments, and the concurrent
level of technical and institutional development runs the risk of achieving
neither economic nor political viability. Resource and cultural endowments
and technical and institutional changes exert a powerful impact on the evolution of tenure arrangements regardless of the formal legislation that is
intended to govern land tenure.

Reforming Agricultural Credit Markets

The reform of agricultural credit markets and the provision of cheap credit
for farmers in the LDCs have dominated agricultural and rural development
support by the U.S. Agency for International Development, the World Bank,
and the several regional development banks in recent years. This emphasis on
credit is based on several perspectives.[66] First is the Schumpeterian view,

---

66. Horace Belshaw, *Agricultural Credit in Economically Underdeveloped Countries*
(Rome: Food and Agriculture Organization of the United Nations, FAO Agricultural Studies 46,
1959); C. R. Wharton, Jr., "Marketing, Merchandising, and Moneylending: A Note on Middleman Monopsony in Malaya," *Malayan Economic Review* 7 (October 1962):24–44.

which identifies innovation as the critical element in economic development and credit as the principal instrument that allows the innovator to bid resources away from other activities. A second perspective is based on a view similar to that of market reform. The farmer obtains credit and sells his output to the same middleman and is thought to be exploited in each transaction. A third perspective, closely related to the second, views public credit institutions as providing part of the supervised education and credit package designed to induce traditional farmers to adopt modern inputs. A fourth perspective views credit as an income-transfer mechanism to lessen inequities in income distribution in rural areas. A fifth perspective views subsidized credit as an incentive to farmers to expand production in spite of disincentives resulting from market interventions or exchange rate distortions that discriminate against farmers in product markets.

Before the 1970s a large share of the development assistance devoted to agricultural credit programs was directed to Latin America. Since the early 1970s external support for the development of agricultural credit institutions has been directed more heavily toward Asia and Africa. In this section we first review some of the lessons from the experience of the 1950s and 1960s and then proceed to discuss the implications of the large programs of the 1970s.

Credit programs of the 1950s and 1960s.[67]   In Latin America during the 1950s and 1960s, funds for credit activities made up a relatively large part of externally financed agricultural programs. According to Dale W. Adams, "In the ten years 1960 to 1969 the Agency for International Development (AID), the Inter-American Development Bank (IDB), and the World Bank group (IBRD) provided dollar assistance for agricultural credit worth approximately $915 million in Latin America. . . . Over half of AID's total direct assistance to agriculture in Latin America has gone into credit activities. In addition to this direct assistance, AID has helped channel to agricultural credit institutions several hundred million dollars worth of 'counterpart funds' and 'local currencies' resulting from program loans and Public Law 480 sales."[68] The World Bank stressed livestock loans. The Inter-American Development Bank tended to support colonization and farm settlement programs. AID emphasized technical assistance to credit institutions, supervised credit to family-size farms, and general expansion of loans to agriculture.

During this period organization of rural credit markets in Asia and Africa differed sharply from those in Latin America. Studies of credit markets in Asia and Africa indicate that informal credit systems (private individuals, moneylenders, and merchants) provided a large part of the total rural credit,

67. This section draws heavily on the major review of agricultural credit programs conducted by the U.S. Agency for International Development in 1972 and 1973, *Spring Review of Small Farmer Credit,* 20 vols. (Washington, D.C.: Agency for International Development, 1973). For a review of the materials prepared for the U.S. AID agricultural credit review by Gordon Donald, see *Credit for Small Farmers in Developing Countries* (Boulder, Colo.: Westview Press, 1976).

68. Dale W. Adams, "Agricultural Credit in Latin America: A Critical Review of External Funding Policy," *American Journal of Agricultural Economics* 53 (May 1971):163.

perhaps over 80 percent in many areas. The data for Latin America suggest a much smaller role for informal credit.

In spite of structural differences in credit markets there was an emerging consensus that "the high interest rate problem in informal credit markets was oversold." This perspective was best summarized by Millard Long: "Interest rates on agricultural loans in South and South-east Asia are high, possibly because of some monopoly in the credit markets, but primarily because capital is scarce, because farm loans are costly to administer, because the uncertainties of agriculture result in considerable loss through default, and because the demand for credit is seasonal."[69] The evidence from Latin America suggests that by holding interest rates down "governments have kept the private banking system and the informal credit market from providing substantial amounts of credit to agriculture."[70]

During the mid and late 1960s, however, data and analysis became available that raised serious questions concerning the assumptions on which the credit programs of the 1950s and 1960s were based.[71] It is also clear that there was a tendency to underestimate grossly the elasticity of supply of savings in rural areas. Evidence is accumulating that savings and capital formation by peasant farmers vary substantially among areas and over time, in response to profitable investment opportunities. In the Philippines, for example, capital formation was most rapid in areas of new settlement and on farms engaged in the production of commodities experiencing rapid growth in productivity.[72] In the 1950s and 1960s Taiwan was successful in mobilizing voluntary savings by raising interest rates. This experience was repeated in Korea in the late 1960s.[73]

The most obvious effects of subsidized credit are the exaggeration of credit needs and the erosion of the purchasing power of credit portfolios—effects that undermine the viability of financial markets. Credit subsidization also results in the politicization of financial markets and the concentration of credit in the hands of relatively few users.

The experience of the ACAR program in Brazil is a useful illustration of

69. Millard Long, "Interest Rates and the Structure of Agricultural Credit Markets," *Oxford Economic Papers* n.s., 20 (July 1968):287.
70. Adams, "Agricultural Credit in Latin America," p. 168.
71. Anthony Bottomley, "The Cost of Administering Private Loans in Underdeveloped Rural Areas," *Oxford Economic Papers* n.s., 15 (July 1963):154–63; Rudolph C. Blitz and Millard F. Long, "The Economics of Usury Regulation," *Journal of Political Economy* 73 (December 1965):608–19; Pantum Thisyamondol, Virach Arromdee, and Millard Long, *Agricultural Credit in Thailand* (Bangkok: Kasetsart University, 1965); Long, "Interest Rates and the Structure of Agricultural Credit Markets," p. 287; Millard F. Long, "Why Peasant Farmers Borrow," *American Journal of Agricultural Economics* 50 (November 1968):991–1008; Adams, "Agricultural Credit in Latin America," pp. 163–72.
72. L. P. de Guzman, "The Effect of Productivity and Technological Change on Savings and Capital Accumulation in Philippine Agriculture," *Philippine Economic Journal* 3 (Second Semester 1964):169–83; Levy A. Trinidad, "Private Capital Formation in Philippine Agriculture," *Philippine Economic Journal* 3 (Second Semester 1964):130–54.
73. Dale W. Adams, "Mobilizing Household Savings through Rural Financial Markets," *Economic Development and Cultural Change* 26 (April 1978):547–60.

some of these effects. The ACAR (Associacão de Crédito e Assistencia Rural) was established in 1948 under the joint sponsorship of the state of Minas Gerais and the American International Association.[74] In 1960 ACAR became a solely Brazilian agency. ACAR began as an experimental effort to test the conviction that a program of supervised credit similar to that developed by the U.S. Farm Security Administration would lead to both better living conditions in rural areas and increased agricultural production. The program as it evolved during the first few years included four activities: supervised credit, general farm and home extension education, medical care and health education, and distribution of materials. In the early years, approximately 80 percent of the total activity involved supervised credit and general extension.

A 1957 evaulation by Arthur Mosher concluded that the ACAR program had exerted a substantial impact on the levels of living and the agricultural resources of the families with which it had worked. The program had not, however, appreciably increased agricultural production in Brazil, in the state of Minas Gerais, or even in the municipalities (counties) in which the program had operated.[75] In evaluating the growth impact of ACAR, Mosher emphasized the thin technical basis on which its production recommendations rested and the prospect that the program would quickly exhaust the contribution of prior research. The difficulty of ACAR in competing for loanable funds was also identified as a potential limitation. Subsequent analysis has supported Mosher's insight.

Later evaluations by Clifton Wharton, Elisau Alves, and José P. Ribeiro and Wharton confirmed the contribution of the ACAR program to the welfare of the participating families. By 1964 ACAR had expanded its services to include approximately 30 percent of the farmers in the state of Minas Gerais. It was particularly effective in reaching small farmers, and it established an enviable record of effective administration and flexibility in response to the changing needs of the farmers it served. As an example of a combined package of supervised credit and extension, the ACAR program was clearly one of the most successful model programs in the developing world.

Nevertheless, the performance of the ACAR program as an instrument of agricultural development was disappointing. Part of the difficulty centered around the issue of concessionary credit. The nominal interest rate charged on ACAR loans ranged from 6 to 8 percent. The annual rate of inflation in Brazil fluctuated between 15 and 25 percent in the 1950s and averaged slightly more

74. From Arthur T. Mosher, *Technical Co-operation in Latin-American Agriculture* (Chicago: University of Chicago Press, 1957); Clifton R. Wharton, Jr., "The Economic Impact of Technical Assistance: A Brazilian Case Study," *Journal of Farm Economics* 42 (May 1960):252–67; José Paulo Ribeiro and Clifton R. Wharton, Jr., "The ACAR Program in Minas Gerais, Brazil," *Subsistence Agriculture and Economic Development,* ed. Clifton R. Wharton, Jr. (Chicago: Aldine Publishing Co., 1969), pp. 424–38; Elisau Roberto de Andrade Alves, "An Economic Evaluation of an Extension Program, Minas Gerais, Brazil" (Master's thesis, Purdue University, 1968).

75. Mosher, *Technical Co-operation in Latin-American Agriculture,* p. 171.

than 30 percent during the 1960s. At such rates of inflation persons securing ACAR loans were, in effect, receiving very substantial income transfer through the negative real rates of interest in the formal credit market. The interest rate subsidy helps explain the finding of Alves that non-ACAR farmers had a higher level of technical efficiency than ACAR farmers. The interest rate subsidy reinforced the incentive resulting from exchange rate distortions for ACAR farmers to overinvest in capital assets. Farmers who borrowed from ACAR were presumably following a rational strategy of maximizing net worth rather than net income or productivity. The interest rate subsidy also helps to explain Wharton's earlier finding that farmers in the largely subsistence areas (Corvelo) achieved greater gains in productivity than farmers in the more commercial farming area (Uba). The commercial farmers were in a better position to follow a strategy of maximizing net worth than the subsistence farmers.

Credit system viability. It is remarkable that the lessons learned from the more recent farm level and credit system impact studies tend to confirm the lessons learned from the studies in the 1950s and 1960s of the ACAR program.[76] Among these lessons are the following: (a) Credit is fungible. Subsidized production credit can be and is used to sustain current consumption levels, invest in consumer durables, and invest in land and relatively low-productivity capital inputs. (b) When credit is made available at below-market interest rates (sometimes at negative real rates), it must be rationed by lenders. When credit is rationed, it flows to the larger borrowers. Programs designed to subsidize credit for the poor end up making loans less available to them than if a market rate of interest were charged. (c) Subsidized credit projects often contribute to a decline in the viability of agricultural credit institutions. If agricultural credit institutions are to be viable they must solve the problems of credit mobilization and credit access. Excessive concern with the issue of credit access has made it impossible to solve the problem of mobilizing voluntary financial saving.

Why, if these lessons have been apparent for so long, did both bilateral and multilateral assistance agencies engage in such rapid expansion of support of specialized agricultural credit institutions during the 1980s? The answer must

---

76. For these lessons we draw primarily on several conferences and collections. These include John Howell, ed., *Borrowers and Lenders: Rural Financial Markets and Institutions in Developing Countries* (London: Overseas Development Institute, 1980); J. D. Von Pischke, Dale W. Adams, and Gordon Donald, eds., *Rural Financial Markets in Developing Countries: Their Use and Abuse* (Baltimore: Johns Hopkins University Press, 1983); Dale W. Adams, Douglas H. Graham, and J. D. Von Pischke, eds., *Undermining Rural Development with Cheap Credit* (Boulder, Colo.: Westview Press, 1984); Cristina C. David and Richard L. Meyer, "Measuring the Farm Level Impact of Agricultural Markets in Developing Countries," *Rural Financial Markets in Developing Countries,* ed. Von Pischke, Adams, and Donald, pp. 84–95; Campton Bourne and Douglas H. Graham, "Problems with Supply-Leading Finance in Agricultural Development," *Undermining Rural Development with Cheap Credit,* ed. Adams, Graham, and Von Pischke.

be found in the economics and politics of development assistance.[77] From the donors' perspective, it takes less effort and less skill to transfer money at below-market rates to national agricultural credit institutions than almost any other form of development assistance. Credit program loans are extensive rather than intensive in the use of technical assistance resources. There are similar advantages from the perspective of the recipient country. Because money is fungible, credit program loans provide the recipient country with foreign exchange with very few effective constraints on its use. Furthermore, lending money at below the market rate of interest requires relatively little skill on the part of LDC institutions, particularly when it can be divorced from a simultaneous savings mobilization effort. And the concentration of benefits in the hands of larger borrowers may have more political advantages than disadvantages. The benefits of the subsidy are highly concentrated, and the costs are both hidden and diffuse.

Rural Development Programs

The pervasive poverty in rural areas has been a continuing concern of national governments and development assistance agencies. One response to pervasive poverty has been to design local institutions to enable rural communities to mobilize their own resources to generate growth and improve the quality of life. Programs organized under the rubric of community development were a major focus of development assistance during the 1950s and early 1960s. During the early 1970s concern about the distributional implications of economic growth again emerged as a major theme in development thought and policy (Chapter 11). This concern gave rise to two new program approaches—integrated rural development and basic needs programs. In this section we attempt to trace the development, accomplishments, and limitations of the community development, integrated rural development, and basic needs approaches.[78]

Community development.   In the first development decade after World War II, community development became a major focus of development assistance.[79] From its inception community development included both eco-

77. Dale W. Adams and Douglas H. Graham, "A Critique of Traditional Agricultural Credit Projects and Policies," *Journal of Development Economics* 8 (June 1981):347–66; Edward J. Kane, "Political Economy of Subsidizing Agricultural Credit in Developing Countries," *Undermining Rural Development with Cheap Credit*, ed. Dale W. Adams, Douglas H. Graham, and J. D. Von Pischke (Boulder, Colo.: Westview Press, 1984).

78. This section draws on three earlier papers by Vernon W. Ruttan: "Integrated Rural Development Programs: A Skeptical Perspective," *International Development Review* 2 (1975):129–51; "Perspectives on Agrarian Reform and Rural Development," *Quarterly Journal of International Agriculture: Zeitschrift für Ausländische Landwirtschaft* 21 (July–September 1982):240–49; "Integrated Rural Development Programmes: A Historical Perspective," *World Development* 12 (1984):393–401.

79. Arthur T. Mosher, *Thinking about Rural Development* (New York: Agricultural Development Council, 1976), pp. 1–8, 170–92; Lane E. Holdcraft, *The Rise and Fall of Community Development in Developing Countries, 1950–65: A Critical Analysis and an Annotated Bibli-*

nomic and political development objectives. It held forth the promise of both building grass-roots democratic institutions and contributing to the material well-being of rural people—"without revolutionary changes in the existing political and economic order."[80]

Community development was viewed as a process which (a) involves the direct participation of people in the solution of their common problems, (b) employs the democratic process in the joint solutions of community problems, and (c) activates and/or facilitates the transfer of technology to the people of a community for more effective solutions of common problems. The process by which community goals were to be realized was itself important. The community development process was "rooted in the concept of the worth of the individual as a responsible, participating member of society. . . . It was designed to encourage self-help efforts to raise standards of living and to create stable, self-reliant communities with an assured sense of social and political responsibility."[81]

A project initiated in 1948 in the Etawah District of Uttar Pradesh, India, served as a model and inspiration for many other community development projects and programs.[82] The Etawah project employed multipurpose village-level workers to initiate self-help approaches to increasing agricultural production and strengthening rural infrastructure. In 1952 the Indian government adopted the Etawah model as the basis for a major national rural development effort. When the program was extended on a national scale, however, the government did not have the technical or bureaucratic capacity "to adopt the painstaking approach to developing a participative administrative structure able to respond to bottom-up initiates which had been the key to the Etawah project's success."[83]

The community development movement expanded rapidly during the decade of the 1950s. By 1960 more than sixty nations in Asia, Africa, and Latin America had launched national or regional community development programs. But by the mid-1960s community development was being deemphasized by both development assistance agencies and national governments. Support declined because of disillusionment on the part of political leaders in the developing countries and the officials of assistance agencies with the effectiveness of community development in meeting either their economic or political development objectives. Community development programs were

ography (East Lansing: Michigan State University Rural Development Paper 2, 1978); Jon R. Moris, *Managing Induced Rural Development* (Bloomington: International Development Institute, Indiana University, 1981).

80. Holdcraft, *Rise and Fall of Community Development*, p. 14.

81. Ibid., p. 10.

82. Albert Mayer et al., with McKim Marriott and Richard L. Park, *Pilot Project, India: The Story of Rural Development at Etawah, Uttar Pradesh* (Berkeley and Los Angeles: University of California Press, 1958); also David C. Korten, "Community Organization and Rural Development: A Learning Process Approach," *Public Administration Review* 40, no. 5 (1980):480–511.

83. Korten, "Community Organization," p. 3.

criticized for failing to improve the economic and social well-being of rural people. The criticism was also made that failure to reform the community power structure led to local elites capturing a disproportionate share of both the economic and political gains generated by the programs.[84] A related criticism, seldom stated explicitly, was that when programs were successful they set in motion political forces that were not easily controlled by the center authorities.

The global food crises, triggered by the crop failures in South Asia in the mid-1960s, shifted the attention of both national governments and development assistance agencies away from community development to a narrower focus on programs designed to enhance agricultural production. This shift was reinforced during the late 1960s as the potential of the new seed-fertilizer technology became apparent. The bilateral and multilateral assistance agencies redirected their support for institution building to attempts to strengthen agricultural research, extension, credit, and input supply systems.

Integrated rural development. After a decade of relative neglect, rural development again emerged near the top of the development policy agenda in the early 1970s. A major symposium entitled ''Agricultural Institutions for Integrated Rural Development'' was convened in Rome by the FAO in 1971. In 1973 the president of the World Bank pledged his organization to direct its resources toward improving the productivity and welfare of the rural poor in the poorest countries.[85] Integrated rural development became an increasingly important focus of efforts in bilateral and multilateral development assistance programs.

The integrated rural development approach drew on a complex of often mutually contradictory intellectual and ideological perspectives.[86] One was a perception that even rapid growth of income in rural areas did not assure either the availability or equitable access to social services and amenities. A second influence was the emergence of ''systems thinking'' about institutional design and program implementation. Recognition that rural development involves the interaction of a large number of interrelated activities was interpreted to imply that integrated program implementation could contribute to the achievement of rapid and measurable gains in agricultural production

84. Ibid.
85. Robert S. McNamara, ''Address to the Board of Governors'' (Washington, D.C.: International Bank for Reconstruction and Development, 1973); World Bank, *Rural Development: Sector Policy Paper* (Washington, D.C.: World Bank, February 1975). For a history of the evolution of poverty-oriented rural development programs at the World Bank see Robert C. Ayres, *Banking on the Poor: The World Bank and World Poverty* (Cambridge, Mass.: MIT Press, 1983), pp. 93–147.
86. Uma Lele, *The Design of Rural Development: Lessons from Africa* (Baltimore: Johns Hopkins University Press, 3d printing with new postscript, 1979), pp. 6–12, 116–26, 230–36; Mosher, *Thinking about Rural Development*, pp. 57–64; John D. Montgomery, ''The Populist Front in Rural Development: Or Shall We Eliminate the Bureaucrats and Get on with the Job?'' *Public Administration Review* 39 (January–February 1979):58–65; John M. Cohen, ''Integrated Rural Development: Clearing out the Underbrush,'' *Sociologia Rurales* 20 (1980):195–212.

and rural welfare. A third influence originated in the growing disillusionment with technocratic and bureaucratic approaches to rural development. Bureaucratic approaches were increasingly viewed as an instrument of control. This perspective led to a reemphasis on the local participation and resource mobilization themes of the earlier community development movement.

Complementarity among the several sectoral components of development was a common assumption of both the bureaucratic and populist approaches to development programs in the 1970s. This comprehensive or integrated approach distinguished the new programs from the more traditional programs designed to increase agricultural production, improve rural education, build farm-to-market roads, and supply health services or promote family planning. But widely different definitions of integration have been employed. By some definitions the integrated delivery of materials (seeds and fertilizer), credit, and extension, as in the Puebla Project in Mexico, was sufficient. A number of widely publicized integrated rural development projects served to illustrate the range of variations in the rural development programs of the 1970s (Table 12-2).

The village development program pioneered by the Bangladesh (formerly Pakistan) Academy for Rural Development at Comilla was one of the models that received particularly widespread attention.[87] The academy was established in 1959 as a training center for public officials responsible for rural development programs. The program evolved out of an effort by the academy staff to understand the rural development processes in Comilla District and to use development activities in Comilla villages as a training laboratory. The program involved three elements: (a) developing a two-tiered village and thana cooperative system; (b) inducing cooperation among public agencies in labor-intensive resource development efforts, particularly irrigation, drainage, and roads; and (c) developing the capacity of local government to coordinate and direct the efforts of departments responsible for civil administration and development (agriculture, water, health, education, and others).

---

87. Arthur F. Raper, *Rural Development in Action: The Comprehensive Experiment at Comilla, East Pakistan* (Ithaca: Cornell University Press, 1970); M. Nurul Haq, *Village Development in Bangladesh* Comilla: Bangladesh Academy for Rural Development, 1973); Akhter Hameed Khan, "The Comilla Projects—A Personal Account," *International Development Review* 16, no. 3 (1974):2–7; Robert D. Stevens, "Three Rural Development Models for Small-Farm Agricultural Areas in Low-Income Nations," *Journal of Developing Areas* 8 (April 1974):409–20. For a critical review see Azizur Rahman Khan, "The Comilla Model and the Integrated Rural Development Programme of Bangladesh: An Experiment in 'Co-operative Capitalism,'" *Agrarian Systems and Rural Development*, ed. Dharam Ghai, Azizur Rahman Khan, Eddy Lee, and Samir Radwan (New York: Holmes and Meier Publishers, 1979), pp. 113–58. The Puebla Project in Mexico has also exerted a major impact on the design of production-oriented rural development projects. For a critical review see Michael Redclift, "Production Programs for Small Farmers: Plan Puebla as Myth and Reality," *Economic Development and Cultural Change* 31 (April 1983):551–70. For a more positive perspective see Kenneth G. Swanberg, "Institutional Evolution: From Pilot Project to National Development Program— Puebla and Caqueza" (Cambridge, Mass.: Harvard Institute for International Development, Discussion Paper 132, 1982).

TABLE 12-2. Examples of integrated rural development projects

Project	Country	Dates of project	Sources of outside assistance	Project components or activities								
				Credit	Extension	Marketing	Infra-structure	Inputs supply	Health	Education	Family planning	Other
Bicol River	Philippines	1975–	AID	y		y	x	x	Proposed W/nutrition	y	Proposed	Resettlement / Tenure reform
CADU	Ethiopia	1967–	Swedish Int. Development Agency	x	x / Trained selected villagers	x	x	x	y	x		Research / Water
Comilla	Bangladesh	1959–65	Ford Foundation	x	x	x	x	x		x	x	Research
Helmand Valley	Afghanistan	1946–74 / 1975–	AID (1952)				x		x	x		Irrigation, research, and housing
Invierno	Nicaragua	1975–	AID	x	x / Trained selected villagers	x	x	x	y	y	y	Nutrition
Kigoma	Tanzania	1974–	World Bank	x	x	x	x	x	x	x		Water project
Lilongwe	Malawi	1968–78	UK / World Bank	x	x	y	x	x	x	x		Resettlement
Puebla	Mexico	1967–73	CIMMYT and Rockefeller	y	x	y		y				Research / Crop insurance
Vicos	Peru	1952–67	Cornell Univ.	x	x	x	x	x	x	x		Land tenure
Vihiga	Kenya	1970–76	AID and others	x	x		x				x	Rural industry

Source: John Cohen, "Integrating Services for Rural Development (Cambridge, Mass.: Harvard University, Lincoln Institute of Land Policy and Kennedy School of Government, 1979), pp. 12–42.

x = Project provides these components
y = Project coordinates these inputs which come from outside sources.

The Comilla program was clearly successful when evaluated for its diffusion of more productive agricultural technology, mobilization of local resources for village improvement, and the development of cooperative institutions. The cooperatives proved capable of generating modest savings and of partially replacing traditional moneylenders as a source of credit. They also became effective channels of technical information about rice production practices, health practices, and farm and cooperative management between the villagers and the technicians located at the thana center. Many of the cooperatives also proved capable of managing capital investments such as tube wells; handling the distribution of inputs such as fertilizer, insecticides, and seeds; and organizing services such as tractor plowing. Roads, irrigation, and drainage were improved. In areas where such changes occurred the value of farm output increased, the incomes of owner and tenant cultivators grew, and land values rose in response to the greater productivity and higher incomes. And the experience gained in the Comilla thana had an impact on rural administration and development in a number of other thanas in East Pakistan. After independence, the government of Bangladesh announced that the Comilla project would be used as the model for a national rural development program. But the program that was actually implemented could be described more accurately as a cooperative development program than a rural development program.

The Comilla experience and similar experiences in other countries have led some observers to question why it is so easy to identify a number of relatively successful, small-scale or pilot rural development projects but so difficult to find examples of successful rural development programs or programs in which pilot projects have made the intended transition into general practice.[88] Part of the reason is that when the programs are extended on a national scale they become mechanisms for imposing centrally mandated programs on communities rather than instruments that enable communities to mobilize their own development resources. Another reason is the dilution of technical and logistical support, which was abundantly provided at the pilot program stage. Few of the projects listed in Table 12-2 made any sustained effort to strengthen the development role of local government. Assistance agency personnel have often failed to understand the difference between decentralized administration and decentralized governance—between locating the administrative offices of center ministries at the provincial or district level and strengthening the fiscal and administrative capacity of local government.

Basic needs. In 1973 the Congress instructed the U.S. development assistance agency to direct its efforts toward meeting the basic needs of the poorest people in the developing countries. In 1974 the UN World Food

88. Naomi Caiden and Aaron Wildavsky, *Planning and Budgeting in Poor Countries* (New York: John Wiley and Sons, 1974), p. 61; Vernon W. Ruttan, "Integrated Rural Development Programs: A Skeptical Perspective," *International Development Review* 17, no. 4 (1975):9–16.

Conference adopted a declaration calling for the eradication of hunger and malnutrition by 1985. This was followed by specific program design proposals by the International Labor Organization (ILO) at the 1976 World Employment Conference.[89] These proposals and their program implications have been elaborated by staff members of the ILO, the World Bank, and the U.S. Agency for International Development.[90]

The basic needs approach represents a radical departure from conventional development strategy. As Paul Streeten and Shahid J. Burki explain, "The evolution from growth as the principal performance criterion, via employment and redistribution, to basic needs is an evolution from abstract to concrete objectives, from a preoccupation with means to a renewed awareness of ends, and from a double negative (reducing unemployment) to a positive (meeting basic needs)."[91] Meeting the basic needs of the poor is, in this view, the central focus of development policy and planning. Growth objectives are replaced by consumption targets. And the consumption targets are translated into specific program goals—"a life expectancy of 65 years or more . . . ; a literacy rate of at least 75 percent . . . ; an infant mortality rate of 50 or less per thousand births . . . ; and a birth rate of 25 or less per thousand population."[92]

The advocates of the basic needs approach did not argue that the improvement of either the material or nonmaterial needs could be achieved easily. They insisted that achievement of basic needs would require intervention by

89. United States, Congress, House of Representatives, Committee on Foreign Affairs, *Mutual Development and Cooperation Act of 1973*, Hearings, 93d Cong., 1st sess. (Washington, D.C.: U.S. Government Printing Office, 1973); United Nations, *Report of the World Food Conference, Rome, 5–16 November 1974* (New York: United Nations, 1975); International Labour Office, *Employment, Growth and Basic Needs: A One-World Problem* (Geneva: International Labour Office, 1976; New York: Praeger Publishers, 1977). The intellectual origins of the basic needs approach have been traced to the "living standards" movement of the 1930s. See Douglas Rimmer, " 'Basic Needs' and the Origins of the Development Ethos," *Journal of Developing Areas* 15 (January 1981):215–38.

90. Hollis Chenery, Montek S. Ahluwalia, C. L. G. Bell, John H. Duloy, and Richard Jolly, *Redistribution with Growth* (London: Oxford University Press, 1974); D. P. Ghai, A. R. Kahn, E. L. H. Lee, and T. Alfthan, *The Basic-Needs Approach to Development: Some Issues Regarding Concepts and Methodology* (Geneva: International Labour Office, 1977); Paul Streeten and Shahid J. Burki, "Basic Needs: Some Issues," *World Development* 6 (March 1978):411–21; Michael Crosswell, *Basic Human Needs: A Development Planning Approach* (Washington, D.C.: Agency for International Development, Discussion Paper 38, 1978); Paul Streeten, with Shahid Javed Burki, Mahbub ul Haq, Norman Hicks, and Frances Stewart, *First Things First: Meeting Basic Human Needs in the Developing Countries* (New York: Oxford University Press, 1981). Within the World Bank there were two major doctrines on poverty alleviation: (a) the "redistribution with growth" school associated with Hollis Chenery and (b) the "basic needs" school associated with Mahbub ul Haq and Paul Streeten. See Ayres, *Banking on the Poor*, pp. 76–91.

91. Streeten and Burki, "Basic Needs: Some Issues," p. 413.

92. James P. Grant, *Disparity Reduction Rates in Social Indicators: A Proposal for Measuring and Targeting Progress in Meeting Basic Needs* (Washington, D.C.: Overseas Development Council, Monograph 11, 1978), p. 9. Nonmaterial objectives are also specified in some formulations. See Paul P. Streeten, "Basic Needs: Premises and Promises," *Journal of Policy Modeling* 1 (January 1979):136–46.

national governments to redirect both production and consumption goals and a
reordering of the content and direction of effort by the development assistance
agencies. But they also insisted that a basic needs strategy could contribute to
more efficient growth than traditional assistance programs. They emphasized
the evidence that expenditures on education can be viewed as an investment
that contributes to economic growth. And they insisted that expenditures
directed to improving nutrition and health and to reducing population growth
rates should also be viewed as high-payoff investments.[93] But they also
insisted that intervention to raise both the material and nonmaterial components of consumption is a more efficient method of improving the well-being
of the poor than relying on the slow process of income enhancement.[94]

A fundamental premise of the basic needs approach is that it is possible to
realize high levels of basic needs achievement at relatively low levels of per
capita income. The Cuba, China, Kerala, and Sri Lanka experiences were
frequently cited as successful examples. In Sri Lanka life expectancy at birth
rose from 46 years in 1945–47 to 64 years in 1965–67; infant mortality
declined from 182 to 65 per thousand between 1945–49 and 1965–69; literacy increased from 68 percent in 1953 to 81 percent in 1969. And these
improvements were achieved in an economy in which per capita income was
below $200 (1974–76 U.S. dollars).[95]

An attempt by Youssef Boutras-Ghali and Lance Taylor to model the
implications of a basic needs strategy for Egypt helps to clarify some of the
implications of an attempt to move rapidly toward achieving basic needs
objectives.[96] Their analysis suggests that a basic needs strategy would be less
capital- and import-intensive than policies presently being followed. Meeting
basic needs in rural areas would be less capital- and import-intensive than in
urban areas. But a further shift of resource use toward the service and government sectors would be required. And the prices of capital goods and agricultural commodities would rise relative to the general price level. Achievement of basic needs program objectives without substantial sacrifice of
economic growth objectives would require that foreign donors' and workers'
remittances would supply over half of Egypt's foreign exchange requirements. Efforts to model the implications of basic needs strategies in the
Philippines and Korea produced the surprising conclusion that improvements
in the domestic terms of trade for agriculture were a more powerful instrument
than some of the more direct consumption interventions in shifting the distribution of income and consumption in favor of the poor.[97]

93. Bruce F. Johnston and William C. Clark, *Redesigning Rural Development: A Strategic
Perspective* (Baltimore: Johns Hopkins University Press, 1982).
94. Streeten, "Basic Needs: Premises and Promises," p. 139.
95. Grant, *Disparity Reduction Rates,* pp. 16–26.
96. Youssef Boutros-Ghali and Lance Taylor, "Basic Needs Macroeconomics: Is It Manage-
able in the Case of Egypt?" *Journal of Policy Modeling* 2 (September 1980):409–36.
97. Irma Adelman, M.J.D. Hopkins, S. Robinson, G. B. Rodgers, and R. Wéry, "A
Comparision of Two Models for Income Distribution Planning," *Journal of Policy Modeling* 1
(January 1979):37–82.

What impact did the basic needs perspective have on the organization of rural development programs? In the case of World Bank–supported projects the effect was to include more nonagricultural social service activities. Uma Lele indicates that World Bank projects started since the early 1970s in East Africa were more complex in their design and objectives than earlier projects—they involved many more activities in the productive and social service sectors than was considered feasible at earlier stages.[98] She also notes that their targets were often more ambitious than could be supported with existing technical and administrative capacity and that successful projects were difficult to replicate when governments and donors attempted to expand them into national programs.

A second problem development assistance agencies have faced in their attempts to incorporate basic needs objectives into rural development programs has been reconciling (a) a commitment to the objectives of mass participation in local decision making and the building of institutions capable of mobilizing local resources for development with (b) the achievement of measurable improvements in basic needs indicators within the relatively limited time span between program initiation and evaluation. A frequent result is that the participation and mobilization goals have been supplanted by bureaucratic approaches to program delivery.[99]

There is, of course, a danger in overemphasizing the conflict between efficiency in program design and delivery and local mobilization of economic and political resources for development. This is one of the most difficult problems for any society to resolve. Indeed, the capacity of a society to resolve this contradiction is one of the relatively sure indicators of political development.

Some conclusions and lessons.   The basic human needs orientation represented a major difference between the rural development programs of the 1970s and the community development programs of the 1950s. The community development programs of the 1950s placed major emphasis on energizing rural communities for self-help. The rural development programs of the 1970s placed more emphasis on the achievement of greater equity in the distribution of the gains from economic growth between urban and rural areas and between economic and social classes within rural areas. The result has been a

---

98. Lele, *Design of Rural Development,* p. 234.

99. For a review of the relationship between participation and success of rural development programs see Norman T. Uphoff and Milton J. Esman, *Local Organization for Rural Development: Analysis of Asian Experience* (Ithaca: Cornell University, Rural Development Committee, Center for International Studies, RLG 19, 1974); Norman T. Uphoff, John M. Cohen, and Arthur A. Goldsmith, *Feasibility and Application of Rural Development Participation: A State-of-the-Art Paper* (Ithaca: Cornell University, Rural Development Committee, Center for International Studies, Rural Development Monograph 3, 1979); also Soedjatmoko, "National Policy Implications of the Basic Needs Model," *Prisma: Indonesian Journal of Social and Economic Affairs* 9 (March 1978):3–25; Michael M. Cernea, *Measuring Project Impact: Monitoring and Evaluation in the PIDER Rural Development Project—Mexico* (Washington, D.C.: World Bank Staff Working Paper 332, 1979).

shift in program focus from the mobilization of community resources to the delivery of program inputs and services in rural development programs.

By the early 1980s the new basic needs and integrated approaches to development were coming under severe question. The decline of integrated rural development and basic needs programs did not reflect a retreat on equity goals as much as a growing recognition that the programs, particularly in Africa, were not solving one of the most fundamental rural problems— achieving a reliable food surplus.[100] Thus the reasons for the decline in emphasis on the new direction programs of the 1970s were similar to those that led to the decline of community development in the early 1960s.

But the number of families whose level of consumption falls below even the most basic of the basic needs in poor countries continues to grow. The need for the services to support agricultural production and an improvement in the quality of life in rural areas has not disappeared. It is useful, therefore, to attempt to draw the lessons that might be learned from this experience.

A clear inference from the literature on rural development is that efficient delivery of bureaucratic services to rural communities is very dependent on effective organization at the community level. Rural communities, operating through either the formal structure of local government or informal or voluntary institutions, must be able to interact effectively with the central institutions charged with responsibility for the delivery of services to local communities. They must be able to interact effectively in the establishment of priorities. They must be able to provide feedback to the agency management on program performance. And they must be able to mobilize sufficient political resources to provide incentives for effective bureaucratic performance.[101]

Many rural development pilot projects have been successful because of the relative intensity in the use of human resources devoted to organization, management, and technical assistance. When attempts were made to generalize the pilot projects as the model for a national or regional rural development program, the intensity of human resource input could not be sustained. Further, access to the higher decision-making levels of government and the administrative freedom to tailor programs precisely are frequently sacrificed to administrative convenience when the projects are generalized in the form of provincial or national programs. A highly centralized administration of national programs makes it difficult to carry out the experiments with program

---

100. Carl K. Eicher and Doyle C. Baker, *Research on Agricultural Development in Sub-Saharan Africa: A Critical Survey* (East Lansing: Michigan State University, Department of Agricultural Economics International Development Paper 1, 1982), p. 62.

101. Montgomery, "Populist Front in Rural Development"; John Friedmann, "The Active Community: Toward a Political-Territorial Framework for Rural Development in Asia," *Economic Development and Cultural Change* 29 (January 1981):235–61. For an excellent case study of the shift from a service delivery to a resource mobilization approach see Frances F. Korten, *Building National Capacity to Develop Water Users' Associations: Experience from the Philippines* (Washington, D.C.: World Bank Staff Working Paper 528, 1982). Korten notes that contribution by users to the capital costs of the project has provided communities with leverage over the performance of agency personnel (pp. 54, 55).

content and delivery methods that are essential if rural development programs are to meet the diverse needs of rural areas.

This attempt to interpret recent development experience leads to a series of five generalizations with respect to program ideology and design which are essential to the viability of any large-scale rural development effort. First, rural development program activities must be organized around activities and services that have relatively well-defined technologies or methodologies and objectives. It is important to rural communities that the technologies, methodologies, and services needed to improve rural welfare become simultaneously available but not necessarily administratively integrated. Second, rural development program activities must be organized to use the relatively low-quality (and inexperienced) human resource endowments that are available in rural areas. They must be extensive rather than intensive in their use of high-cost human capital. Third, effective implementation of rural development programs is, to a substantial degree, dependent on the development of the institutional capacity to mobilize the limited political and economic resources available in rural communities. In societies in which rural administration is organized with a strong control orientation, the political and economic conditions necessary for rural development will rarely be met. Fourth, welfare in the rural areas of most developing countries remains at least as much a problem of the level of output per person as of distribution. New sources of income growth must continue to be sought in both technical and institutional change. Fifth, given the severe constraints on the availability of high-quality technical and administrative manpower, premature transitions from a pilot project to a national program are counterproductive for the development of a viable rural development program. The human resources needed for the program can be expended only gradually through formal training and pilot program experience.

The structural characteristics of most rural communities and of the societies of which they are a part will continue to prevent them from obtaining access to many of the development opportunities which are potentially available. Rural development programs will rarely be able to mobilize the political and economic resources necessary for massive structural reform. We can expect the development of rural areas to continue to be characterized by unequal rates of income growth between rural and urban areas, among rural areas, and among classes within rural areas. A major implication is that in a society in which the distribution of political resources is strongly biased against rural people it will be difficult to mobilize the bureaucratic resources needed to make rural development programs effective. In addition, there will be strong resistance to the evolution of local institutions that have the capacity to mobilize economic and political resources to meet the basic needs of the rural poor. In such societies institutional innovation may be strongly biased toward reinforcing the existing distribution of economic and political resources.

DISEQUILIBRIUM AND DEVELOPMENT

The decade of the 1970s witnessed the opening up of unprecedented opportunities for growth in agricultural production and improvement in the well-being of rural people in the LDCs. The national and international institutions necessary to advance agricultural technology were developed and strengthened. A number of important countries, such as India, Brazil, Indonesia, and China, took advantage of this new potential for productivity growth to improve the performance of their agriculture. But a larger number of countries still lagged in developing the institutional capacity needed to invent, adopt, and diffuse more productive agricultural technologies.

There has been a major failure on the part of both the DCs and the LDCs to reform the national and international market institutions needed to enable farmers in the developing countries to take advantage of the new production opportunities that are becoming available to them. The governments of many DCs have continued to defend their domestic agriculture by erecting protectionist barriers and by imposing the burden of uneconomic production encouraged by this excessive protection on world markets. And the governments of LDCs have discouraged their farmers by exploitive pricing policies, inefficient land tenure policies, and credit policies that weaken the capacity of their credit institutions to mobilize savings for agricultural development. The result has been a widening disequilibrium between the potential productive capacity of agriculture and the growth that has actually been realized from the agricultural sector in many LDCs.

The LDCs have also been slow to encourage the development of local institutions that would enable rural people to mobilize their own economic and political resources. There is increasing evidence that the success of rural development programs in strengthening rural infrastructure or meeting the basic needs of the poor depends on the development of local representative institutions. But the strengthening of local governance is often viewed as a threat to political stability rather than as a resource for development by the national political leadership and the central bureaucracies.[102] These attitudes have sometimes been reinforced by the staffs of development assistance agencies, who often have little historical insight into the evolution of rural development institutions in the presently developed countries. The result is a widening of the disequilibrium between the potential for reducing the worst features of poverty in rural areas and the realization of that potential.

---

102. It has been argued that agricultural producers often represent relatively unattractive partners in the political coalitions that coalesce to form governments in many developing countries. Since agriculture represents a large share of total economy activity, policies that favor agriculture may be regarded as excessively costly to other coalition participants. Similarly, policies that extract resources from the agricultural sector may be viewed as attractive to a governing coalition that is able to exclude strong representation from the agricultural sector. See Robert H. Bates and William P. Rogerson, "Agriculture in Development: A Coalitional Analysis," *Public Choice* 35 (1980):513–27.

In our judgment it is now possible to contemplate a world in which all nations are able to meet the basic needs of food, clothing, shelter, health, and literacy of their poorest people. For most nations it is not unrealistic to suggest that this objective could be accomplished before the beginning of the next century. This is a judgment that we would have felt uncomfortable in making at the time we completed our earlier book.

The LDCs have several advantages as relative latecomers to the development process. The most important is the opportunity to achieve rapid productivity growth by borrowing technology from the advanced countries. But this technology can become available only if institutions are developed that are capable of facilitating the borrowing and adaptation of the technology by the latecomers.[103] By the early 1980s even the least developed countries had begun to establish the institutional capacity to borrow, adapt, and invent the agricultural technology needed to close the productivity gap between the DCs and the LDCs. The technology of human fertility control is now much superior to that available only a few decades ago. A number of poor countries have demonstrated that, with appropriate institutional support, significant reductions in the rate of population growth can be achieved in a single generation.

If the decades of the 1980s and the 1990s are as creative in institutional innovation as the 1960s and 1970s were in technical innovation, it should be possible to narrow the gap substantially between the potential level of development in rural areas and the actual levels of well-being that now prevail in the rural areas in the LDCs. But we have no illusions that the LDCs will find it easy to take advantage of the development opportunities that are available to them. Their ability to undertake the institutional reforms discussed in this chapter will be conditioned by the distribution of economic and political resources and the cultural endowments they have inherited from the past.

The authoritarian regimes that distinguish the political systems in many LDCs are caught up in accumulating and husbanding the limited political resources available to them. They are often unable or unwilling to risk the consequences of the decentralization of political power that is necessary to strengthen the institutions and mobilize the human resources needed to bring about rapid development in rural areas. In such societies it seems likely that institutional innovations will be biased toward reinforcing the existing distribution of economic and political resources.

103. This theme has been emphasized in the history of European industrialization by Alexander Gerschenkron, *Economic Backwardness in Historical Perspective, Book of Essays* (Cambridge, Mass.: Belknap Press of Harvard University Press, 1962).

13

Agricultural Transformation and Economic Growth

In the previous chapter we attempted to answer the question, Why was the record of agricultural development in the less developed countries of the world so inadequate in the years after World War II? We indicated that the basic factor underlying poor performance was neither the meager endowment of natural resources nor the lack of technological potential to increase output from the available resources at a sufficiently rapid pace to meet the growth of demand. The major constraint limiting agricultural development was identified as the policies that impeded rather than induced appropriate technical and institutional innovations. As a result, the gap widened between the potential and the actual productive capacities of LDC agriculture.

Yet it is clear that an unprecedented opportunity has opened up during the past two decades for growth of agricultural production in LDCs. Although the initial euphoria of the green revolution has waned, the national and international institutions necessary to advance agricultural technology have continued to be strengthened. Investments in land and water resource development have steadily expanded. If the technological potential thus enhanced can be accompanied by the institutional reforms needed to release agriculture's production capacity, it should be possible for the LDCs to expand output sufficiently to meet the basic food needs of the poorest segment of the population.

As LDCs reach a stage at which their capacity to expand production rapidly enough to meet basic subsistence needs of a rapidly growing population is assured, they will then be confronted by growth in demand arising out of rapid growth in per capita income. At this stage there will be a rapid shift away from consumption of the low-income elasticity of demand commodities, such as roots and cereal, and toward the consumption of commodities characterized by high-demand elasticities, such as livestock products, fruits, and vegetables. Increased consumption of livestock products in particular imposes heavy demands on agricultural production because resources must be devoted to the production of feed for animals as well as for human consumption. But the rapid growth in demand, associated with the transition from an agriculture

416

heavily based on roots and cereals to a system that places greater emphasis on livestock and other income-elastic products, creates new income opportunities for agricultural products.[1] This transformation in response to economic growth is consistent with the historical experience of the presently developed countries and is currently being experienced by a number of the newly industrializing countries as well as countries in Eastern Europe.[2]

This problem of agricultural transformation is intimately related to the role of agriculture in overall economic development as discussed in Chapter 2. In the process of modern economic development, agriculture must be able to supply food and labor to the emerging industrial and service sectors. But modern agricultural development requires an efficient supply of modern technical inputs, such as fertilizer and farm machinery, from nonagriculture. How to mobilize the dividends of agricultural growth for overall economic development is a critical issue not only for the development of modern industrial and service sectors but also for the sustained growth of agriculture itself.

In this final chapter, we explore how the advancement in agricultural technology in the LDCs, which was concentrated in food cereal production in recent years, can be strengthened further and guided to serve as a basis of successful agricultural transformation and overall economic growth.

CONDITIONS OF AGRICULTURAL GROWTH IN THE LESS DEVELOPED COUNTRIES

The performance of LDC agriculture during the 1960s and 1970s was poor primarily in relation to the growth in both aggregate demand for agricultural products and supply of labor to the agricultural sector. Growth in total agricultural output in LDCs, however, was not bad. As shown in Table 13-1, total agricultural output in the LDCs increased at an average rate of 2.9 percent per year from 1960 to 1980. This rate was substantially faster than the developed

1. The explosive growth in demand that accompanies rapid growth in per capita income in low-income countries has been emphasized by John W. Mellor in ''Accelerated Growth in Agricultural Production and the Intersectoral Transfer of Resources,'' *Economic Development and Cultural Change* 22 (October 1973):1–16; John W. Mellor and Uma J. Lele, ''Growth Linkages of the New Foodgrain Technologies,'' *Indian Journal of Agricultural Economics* 28 (January–March 1973):35–55; John W. Mellor and Bruce F. Johnston, ''The World Food Equation,'' *Journal of Economic Literature* 22 (June 1984):531–74. A number of populist writers have argued that the competition between food and feed in the rapidly growing developing countries should be dealt with by policies that attempt to discourage the emergence of ''nonsustainable'' Western patterns of food consumption. See, for example, Frances Moore Lappé and Joseph Collins, with Cary Fowler, *Food First: Beyond the Myth of Scarcity* (Boston: Houghton Mifflin, 1977), pp. 289–94; or rev. ed. (New York: Ballantine, 1978), pp. 348–56. Mellor and Johnston reject this view. They insist that a development strategy that is successful in achieving a high-level rather than a low-level food supply–demand equilibrium is more effective in expanding employment and income in rural areas.

2. Kenneth L. Bachman and Leonardo A. Paulino, *Rapid Food Production Growth in Selected Developing Countries: A Comparative Analysis of Underlying Trends, 1961–76* (Washington, D.C.: International Food Policy Research Institute, Research Report 11, 1979).

TABLE 13-1. The rates of growth in agricultural output, population, agricultural labor force (number of male workers), and agricultural land by country group, 1960–80[a] (percent per year)

	Agricultural output (Y)	Population (N)	Agricultural output per capita (Y/N)	Agricultural labor force (L)	Labor productivity (Y/L)	Agricultural land (A)	Land productivity (Y/A)	Land-man ratio Per capita (A/N)	Per worker (A/L)
Developed countries									
1960–70	2.1	1.0	1.1	−3.8	5.9	−.3	2.4	−1.3	3.5
1970–80	1.6	.6	1.0	−3.8	5.4	−.4	2.0	−1.0	3.4
1960–80	1.9	.8	1.1	−3.8	5.7	−.3	2.2	−1.1	3.5
Middle-stage countries									
1960–70	3.6	2.2	1.4	−1.1	4.7	.3	3.3	−1.9	1.4
1970–80	3.2	1.9	1.3	−2.0	5.2	.3	2.9	−1.6	2.3
1960–80	3.4	2.1	1.3	−1.5	4.9	.3	3.1	−1.8	1.8
Less developed countries									
1960–70	2.9	2.6	.3	.6	2.3	.5	2.4	−2.1	−.1
1970–80	2.9	2.4	.5	1.9	1.0	.4	2.5	−2.0	−1.5
1960–80	2.9	2.5	.4	1.2	1.7	.4	2.5	−2.1	−.8

Source: Data of output, labor, and land are from Appendix Table A-4. Data of population are from United Nations, Demographic Yearbook, various issues.
[a]For country classifications, see Table 5-2 in Chapter 5.

country average of 1.9 percent. But because the population growth rates of the LDCs was high—2.5 percent as compared to less than 1 percent for the DCs—agricultural output per capita in the LDCs increased slowly. The LDC rate of only 0.4 percent was less than half the DC rate. This slow rate of increase in agricultural output per capita was less than the growth of food demand in the LDCs given the high income elasticity of demand for food in low-income countries. Thus for the LDCs, the margin of food imports over exports increased.[3]

The agricultural growth performance of the LDCs compared with that of the DCs was even more striking relative to the growth in the agricultural labor force. As shown in Table 13-1, the labor force in the LDCs, as measured by the number of male workers in agriculture, increased absolutely. In contrast, it decreased rapidly in the DCs—at a rate of nearly 4 percent per year. As a result, the rate of increase in labor productivity in agriculture in the LDCs was less than one-third that of the DCs. It is especially noteworthy that the rate of growth in the agricultural labor force in the LDCs accelerated from 0.6 percent during the 1960s to 1.9 percent during the 1970s. Correspondingly, the growth rate of labor productivity declined from 2.3 percent to 1.0 percent. This acceleration in the rate of growth of the agricultural labor force resulted mainly from accelerated growth in the total labor force, which in turn resulted from the acceleration of total population growth during the first two decades after World War II. Another important factor underlying the rapid growth in the agricultural labor force was inadequate absorption of labor by the industrial sector because of factor price distortions resulting from the industrial and trade policies of the LDCs that were discussed in the previous chapter.

3. Most recent projections suggest that food deficits in the LDCs will increase during the rest of the twentieth century. See, for example, International Food Policy Research Institute, *Food Needs of Developing Countries: Projections of Production and Consumption to 1990* (Washington, D.C.: International Food Policy Research Institute, IFPRI Report 3, 1977); Food and Agriculture Organization of the United Nations, *Agriculture toward 2000* (Rome: FAO, 1981); Council on Environmental Quality and the Department of State, Gerald O. Barney, Study Director, *The Global 2000 Report to the President* (New York: Penguin Books, 1982); Hans Linnemann, J. De Hoogh, M. A. Keyzer, and H.D.J. Van Heemst, *MOIRA: Model of International Relations in Agriculture* (Amsterdam: North Holland, 1979). As this book was going to press a new set of more optimistic projections was being prepared by the World Bank. For a preliminary report on these projections, see Malcolm D. Bale and Ronald C. Duncan, *Prospects for Food Production and Consumption in Developing Countries* (Washington, D.C.: World Bank, World Bank Staff Working Paper 596, 1983). For a more detailed review of recent global food production trends and projections, see Glenn Fox and Vernon W. Ruttan, "A Guide to LDC Food Balance Projections," *European Review of Agricultural Economics* 10 (1983):325–46. A series of earlier global food projections was reviewed by John H. Sanders and Richard C. Hoyt, "The World Food Problem: Four Recent Empirical Studies," *American Journal of Agricultural Economics* 52 (February 1970):132–35. Increasing food trade deficits do not necessarily imply poor performance of LDC agriculture. As pointed out by D. Gale Johnson, most developing countries continue to be net exporters of nonfood agricultural products. Although food imports of the non-oil-producing developing countries increased at an annual rate of U.S. $1.4 billion between 1970 and 1977, the total agricultural export value increased at a rate of $2.9 billion. D. Gale Johnson, "The World Food Situation: Developments during the 1970s and Prospects for the 1980s," *U.S.-Japanese Agricultural Trade Relations*, ed. Emery N. Castle and Kenzo Hemmi, with Sally A. Skillings (Baltimore: Johns Hopkins University Press, 1982), pp. 15–57.

The deceleration in the labor productivity growth rate in agriculture, associated with the accelerated growth in the agricultural labor force, resulted in a deterioration in the land-man ratio in the DCs, although the agricultural land area per worker declined.

From the data in Table 13-1, it should be clear that the high rate of population growth in the LDCs, coupled with a highly elastic demand for food, meant that the growth performance of LDC agriculture was insufficient relative to growth in aggregate demand. It should also be clear that population growth, coupled with insufficient labor absorption by the nonagricultural sector, resulted in a decline in the land-labor ratio, thereby depressing labor productivity and labor income in agriculture in the LDCs. Those forces combined to widen the disequilibrium in world agriculture.

Such trends will not likely be reversed for the next couple of decades. The LDC population growth rates will continue to be high even though they began to decelerate during the 1970s. Even if the population growth rate is sharply curtailed with successful economic development, the associated increase in per capita income will reach a level at which the demand for livestock products will increase sharply and the demand for feed grains will rise explosively.

More critically, it is certain that the high rates of population growth during the past decades will be translated into high rates of growth in the labor force in LDCs over the coming decades. For the LDCs, in which the agricultural sector accounts for a high share of total employment, even very rapid growth in nonagricultural employment is insufficient to bring about either stabilization or decline in the agricultural labor force. Bruce Johnston and Peter Kilby state correctly that "in a predominantly agrarian economy, even with very rapid growth in the industrial and service sectors, the proportionate size of the agricultural labor force will fall only slowly; and for many years—in some cases many decades—the absolute size of the labor force will grow."[4] The land-labor ratio will continue to decline.

These economic and demographic conditions will characterize LDC agricultural development until the end of the twentieth century and well into the twenty-first century. As emphasized repeatedly, the situation resembles the world described by such classical economists as Ricardo, in which the in-

4. Bruce F. Johnston and Peter Kilby, *Agriculture and Structural Transformation: Economic Strategies in Late-Developing Countries* (New York: Oxford University Press, 1975), p. xvii. The annual increase in the rate of structural transformation (RST), measured by the annual increase in the nonfarm labor ratio, is a function of the initial size of the nonfarm labor ratio (L_N/L_T) and the coefficient of differential growth in the two sectors $(L'_N - L'_T)$. Thus RST $= (L_N/L_T)(L'_N - L'_T)$. If nonfarm employment is growing at an annual rate that exceeds the rate of growth of the total labor force by 1.5 percent (if, for example, $L'_N = 4.5$ and $L'_T = 3.0$), it requires approximately twenty-eight years to reduce agriculture's share in the labor force from 80 to 70 percent but only about eleven years to reduce it from 40 to 30 percent (p. 84). This relationship was developed by Folke Dovring, "The Share of Agriculture in a Growing Population," *FAO Monthly Bulletin of Agricultural Economics and Statistics* 8 (August–September 1959):1–11, reprinted in Food and Agriculture Organization of the United Nations, *FAO Studies in Agricultural Economics and Statistics; 1952–1977* (Rome: FAO, 1978), pp. 186–96.

crease in the demand for food, resulting from population growth, and the growth in the supply of labor combine to bring about a rise in both food prices and land rents and a decline in wage rates (Chapters 10 and 11). One of the necessary conditions for escape from the Ricardian trap of poverty and stagnation is the development and diffusion of land-saving and labor-using technologies.

A second necessary condition is rapid growth of employment in the nonagricultural sectors. When nonagricultural employment expands rapidly enough to pull workers into the nonagricultural labor force, it exerts an immediate impact on labor productivity and income in agriculture. This result is in contrast to a decline in the rate of population growth, which requires almost a generation to exert a significant impact on employment. A necessary condition for an increase in agricultural employment is to reverse the industrial and trade policies pursued by many LDCs since World War II that have distorted factor prices in favor of large-scale, capital-intensive, industrial enterprises.

In our view, the development and diffusion of seed-fertilizer technology in the tropics since the late 1960s, supported by massive investments in land and water resource development, represent an attempt by farmers, research scientists, and national and international development agencies to reverse the forces leading to the Ricardian trap.[5] Although strong skepticism was advanced on the effectiveness of the green revolution technology, especially during the period of the world food crisis in the mid-1970s, it is now clear that the impact of the new seed-fertilizer technology has reversed much of the former pessimism at national policy levels with respect to the potential contribution of the agricultural sector to national economic growth.

The opportunities for agricultural development that now seem apparent will not be easily secured in most developing countries. Our analysis and the experience of the 1960s and 1970s strongly support an emerging consensus that agricultural research designed to produce and continuously improve an economically viable and ecologically adaptable technology continues to be a critical link in the agricultural development process in many countries. There is a growing agreement that much agricultural research is highly location-specific. If it is to produce viable results it must be conducted in an environment in which both ecological and socioeconomic conditions approximate those where the innovation will be employed. Lack of a sufficient stock of scientific and technical manpower in the tropical and subtropical countries, which is essential to the conduct of location-specific research, imposes a

---

5. Raj Krishna has shown that under a wide range of conditions the allocation of 20–25 percent of national investment to agriculture will be necessary to meet the 3–4 percent annual rates of growth in agricultural output being experienced by many developing countries. In the past, few developing countries have allocated anywhere near this level of investment to agriculture. Raj Krishna, "Some Aspects of Agricultural Growth, Price Policy and Equity in Developing Countries," *Food Research Institute Studies* 18 (1982):219–60.

severe constraint on the exploitation of the new technical opportunities for growth.

Thus, how to manage science or to organize agricultural research so as to use most effectively the scarce limiting factor—scientific and technical man-power—is a critical factor in agricultural development.

MANAGING SCIENCE FOR TECHNICAL PROGRESS

In spite of an initial dramatic impact, the scientific and technical basis for the recent advances in grain yields in the tropics is extremely thin in most developing countries. If the momentum of the green revolution is to be main-tained, substantial investments will have to be made in agricultural experi-ment station capacity, together with investments in industrial capacity, irriga-tion, and other physical infrastructure and in the education of agricultural producers.

For that purpose it is not sufficient simply to build new agricultural re-search stations. In many developing countries existing research facilities are not employed at full capacity. They are staffed with research workers whose scientific and technical training is limited. In addition, they suffer from inade-quate financial and logistical support, isolation from the main currents of scientific and technical innovation, and an inadequate strategy for relating research activity to the potential economic value of new knowledge.

The body of knowledge relating to the organization and management of agricultural research is, if anything, even weaker than the body of research results available to agricultural producers in the LDCs.[6] There are, however, a number of principles that seem to have a substantial grounding in research that represents, as a minimum, constraints that strongly condition the produc-tivity of research investment.

The results of agricultural research tend to be relatively location-specific. Furthermore, the results tend to become more location-specific as the sophis-tication of the research and production technology advances. Although this principle applies to advances in both mechanical and biological technology, it is more obvious in the case of biological technology. The location-specific character of agricultural technology is a function of variations in the physical, biological, and socioeconomic environments in which agricultural activities are conducted. Therefore, much of agricultural research must be conducted

---

6. Among the useful references are Walter L. Fishel, ed., *Resource Allocation in Agri-cultural Research* (Minneapolis: University of Minnesota Press, 1971); Albert H. Moseman, *Building Agricultural Research Systems in the Developing Nations* (New York: Agricultural Development Council, 1970); Thomas M. Arndt, Dana G. Dalrymple, and Vernon W. Ruttan, eds., *Resource Allocation and Productivity in National and International Agricultural Research* (Minneapolis: University of Minnesota Press, 1977); Per Pinstrup-Andersen, *The Role of Agri-cultural Research and Technology in Economic Development* (London: Longman Group, Ltd., 1982); Vernon W. Ruttan, *Agricultural Research Policy* (Minneapolis: University of Minnesota Press, 1982).

and the results analyzed, tested, interpreted, and applied within a relatively decentralized system (see discussions in Chapters 3 and 8).

There are scale economies in agricultural research. Analysis by Evenson, based on state experiment stations in the United States, indicates that the marginal returns per research dollar were generally higher in stations with more scientists, more graduate students, higher staff salaries, and higher levels of staff training.[7] There was also a tendency for smaller experiment stations to produce a relatively higher proportion of final products (such as agronomic knowledge) to intermediate products (such as advances in genetics). Also, smaller stations are likely to produce fewer new material inputs in which new knowledge is embodied. Although there may be some question regarding the greater productivity of the largest stations as compared to the typical station, there can be no question that in many LDCs experiment stations are frequently too small and too poorly financed to provide the library, professional communication, and logistical support to be productive. Yet Evenson's more recent research also demonstrates that a decentralized research system, when adequately staffed and funded, makes more effective use of its resources, when evaluated by impact on technology generation, than more highly centralized systems.[8]

The production of location-specific technologies by a research system in which the individual units experience scale economies and an extensive system of regional stations is required to assure relevance in technology development imposes severe strains on the organization of agricultural research. Most national or state research administrations are faced with continuous pressure both for greater decentralization, to bring the research capacity to bear on the specific problems of regions and localities, and for strengthening of central experiment station staffs to create viable centers of professional excellence.

Effective information linkages among the units of a decentralized system are essential to achieve optimal system, in contrast to individual station, productivity. Both the Japanese and the U.S. agricultural research systems have been characterized by the capacity to mobilize research resources to respond to problems of regional and national significance, while retaining sufficient autonomy to respond to local priorities (Chapter 8).

An essential feature of both the Japanese and the U.S. research systems was the establishment of effective communication linkages among the units of the national research system and across national boundaries. The international linkages have involved intensive efforts to collect and adapt crop varieties and livestock breeds from other regions. This approach contrasts with those fol-

7. Robert E. Evenson, "Economic Aspects of the Organization of Agricultural Research," *Resource Allocation in Agricultural Research,* ed. Fishel, pp. 163–82.

8. Reported in Robert E. Evenson, Paul E. Waggoner, and Vernon W. Ruttan, "Economic Benefits from Research: An Example from Agriculture," *Science* 205 (September 14, 1979):1101–7.

lowed in some developing countries that have a nationalistic bias against "exotic" genetic materials.

The initial success of the international centers for wheat and maize research in Mexico (CIMMYT) and for rice research in the Philippines (IRRI) was facilitated by close professional and institutional linkages with related agricultural research centers in the United States, Japan, and elsewhere. These centers have, in turn, become major institutional linkages in the flow of scientific and technical information relating to wheat, maize, and rice research among the agricultural research community in the developing countries.[9]

Effective division of labor between private and public research is essential. Because public resources are severely constrained and the private sector has an inherent advantage in responding to changes in market demand and supply, the development of private research, mainly by the agricultural supply firms, is essential for the advancement of agricultural technology.[10] Private firms invest primarily in research leading to results for which excludable property rights can be established either by patents or by trade secrets that cannot be easily imitated. That is why private investments tend to concentrate on applied research mainly in the areas of mechanical and chemical engineering. In contrast, public resources have been allocated primarily to basic or generic research and to the development of biological technology. Scientific developments, such as advances in molecular biology and genetic engineering, and institutional innovations, such as the establishment of more secure property rights in new plant varieties or new life forms, are inducing greater private sector research and development in some areas of biological technology. In the early stage of economic development, when private sector research activities are weak, it is often necessary for the public sector to undertake almost complete responsibility for applied research and development even in the area of mechanical technology. But, given the constraints on the availability of public sector research resources, it is inefficient for the public sector to continue to conduct research in areas in which private incentives are adequate. The appropriate allocation of responsibility between public and private sector research requires continuous reevaluation.

An additional characteristic of a viable agricultural research system is integral involvement in education and training for research. Development of scientific and technical manpower through education and training is essential for removing the scientific manpower constraints that limit the capacity of the less developed countries to shift toward a science-based agriculture. Such

9. Ruttan, *Agricultural Research Policy,* pp. 116–46; Donald L. Plucknett and Nigel J. H. Smith, "Sustaining Agricultural Productivity: The Role of Maintenance Research," mimeograph (Washington, D.C.: Consultative Group on International Agricultural Research Integrative Report, 1984).

10. For a more detailed discussion of the role of the public and private sectors in agricultural research see Ruttan, *Agricultural Research Policy,* pp. 181–214; Carl E. Pray, "Private Agricultural Research in Asia," *Food Policy* 8 (May 1983):131–40.

education is most effective when it occurs in association with a significant research program. Moreover, the presence of students and trainees encourages a continuous interchange and flow of new ideas. Indeed, the dialectic interaction among students and teachers is a major source of scientific advance.

It may be somewhat of an overstatement to argue, as Schultz has, that "a national agricultural research center . . . that is not an integral part of a major research-oriented university is, under present conditions, an inefficient location for such research."[11] Nevertheless, even the new international commodity-research centers, which were not established as part of universities, have found it productive to establish close linkages to local educational institutions and to conduct nonacademic training programs and establish visiting scholar arrangements.

The principles of research organization outlined above do not impose any specific optimal pattern for organizing professional and institutional resources to produce new technical knowledge in agriculture. The research institute and the university are alternative methods of organizing resources to induce change. In developed societies, characterized by a highly articulated infrastructure linking the university to other public and private institutions involved in technical, social, and economic change, research within the university may be an effective link in the total system devoted to the production, application, and dissemination of new knowledge. When a single component is transplanted separately into societies lacking such institutional infrastructure, it rarely performs as an effective instrument of technical change.

In our judgment, this overemphasis on a simplified model is one of the major reasons for the substantial frustration resulting from attempts to use the land-grant university model as an instrument to generate and disseminate technical change in agriculture in many developing countries. Albert Moseman has pointed out that a major difficulty in understanding the integrated agricultural research system in the United States has been failure to recognize the active role of the USDA in regional and national research.[12] The result has been serious provincialism in attempting to guide the development of effective national systems of agricultural research in LDCs. Localized and fragmented research continues to present one of the most serious obstacles to strengthening of effective systems for agricultural science and technology in the developing nations. Many national agricultural research systems are characterized by relatively large numbers of inadequately trained and poorly paid staff and few highly trained scientists capable of exercising scientific and program leadership. In effect, such research systems are attempting

11. Theodore W. Schultz, "The Allocation of Resources to Research," *Resource Allocation in Agricultural Research,* ed. Fishel, p. 118.

12. Moseman, *Building Agricultural Research Systems;* Ruttan, *Agricultural Research Policy,* pp. 76–83.

to conduct research without scientists. A research system that undervalues science will remain unproductive.

If LDCs are to overcome the technical and institutional limitations that separate the performance of the world's high- and low-income economies, they must make efficient use of the professional competence that is their single most limiting resource in the generation of more productive inputs for agriculture. They must search for patterns of institutional organization that permit them to use the scarce scientific and technical manpower available effectively. The international research training institutes are an example of one pattern that has been exceptionally effective when the institutional infrastructure linking science to the rest of the economy is lacking. But the role of the international institutes will have to be changed as the national agricultural research system becomes stronger. It seems likely that they will occupy a smaller role as sources of new varieties and technology but will assume greater importance as genetic resource centers and as centers for the exchange of scientific and technical information.

We do not hold the international institute model, or the models followed in Japan and the United States, as idealized forms that should be transferred intact to other developing economies. Rather, they illustrate the desirability of a pragmatic rather than an ideological search for institutions consistent with the endowments of both human and nonhuman resources in the developing economies.

GUIDING TECHNOLOGY AND INSTITUTIONS FOR AGRICULTURAL TRANSFORMATION

For a new technology to be an effective instrument for agricultural development it must be consistent with changes in the conditions of factor supply and product demand in the economy. In view of strong population pressure on land, as discussed earlier, it is vitally important, in consideration of both efficiency and equity, to develop agricultural technology that is biased toward saving land and using labor or is at least neutral with respect to the use of labor. From available evidence in the LDCs as well as the historical experience of Japan, Taiwan, and Korea, it appears that the new seed-fertilizer technology is biased in the land-saving and fertilizer-using direction and is more or less neutral in scale and in the use of labor (Chapters 9 and 11).

Yet it appears that credit, extension, and related rural institutions have often been biased with respect to scale in many countries and have directed the new technology toward a labor-saving pattern of economic organization in rural areas. In the absence of adequate institutions to facilitate cooperation among small farmers, irrigation, which is vital for the introduction of new technology, has been controlled by larger-scale farmers who could install their own tube wells. The larger farmers have had better access to new knowledge and low-interest loans from cooperative or government credit agencies. These advantages have lowered the cost of capital investment and encouraged mechanization. The smaller farmers, however, have often been subject to severe capital rationing.

In contrast, traditional village communes in Japan (and the *pao-cha* system in Taiwan) were effective means of diffusing new knowledge and of mobilizing communal labor for the construction of irrigation facilities and small waterways and reservoirs and the building of other forms of social capital such as roads and schools. The village communal system provided the basis for the development of water-use and marketing cooperatives and for agricultural associations that promoted extension services through the national-prefectural-local networks (Chapter 8).

If new agricultural technology is to be guided in a land-saving and labor-using direction, new institutions have to be developed or existing institutions reformed to reverse the institutional bias in favor of larger farms and toward the substitution of capital for labor. The institutional innovations should in turn be complemented by research to generate technical changes, which raise the returns to institutional innovation at the community level.

Another major consideration is the change in demand and supply of agricultural commodities in response to technical change. If the yield-increasing technology advances and diffuses at a sufficiently rapid rate, the shift in the aggregate supply of staple cereals could exceed the shift in aggregate demand by a wide margin. The result would be a decline in the price of cereals in both international and domestic markets and a possible decline in the income of cereal producers, particularly the cereal producers located in regions where the new grain production technology is not fully adapted. This effect may be offset, however, as income growth enhances the demand for livestock products. With success in agricultural and economywide development, diversion of resources from the staple cereal sector to the production of commodities with higher income elasticities will become indispensable for maintaining incentives for the use of resources in agricultural production. New patterns of product combination and resource use, which are drastically different from traditional cereal grain monoculture, will have to be developed. The new patterns should also be consistent with the changes in factor endowments implicit in the rapid growth of population in rural areas. It is desirable that product diversification contribute to greater intensity in labor use.

The diversification will be particularly profitable for both private producers and the national economy if it is designed to use seasonally slack resources in agriculture. In some areas the new high-yielding cereal varieties are contributing to a fuller use of land and labor. Where adequate irrigation is available, their nonphotoperiod-sensitive character permits double and, in some cases, triple cropping a year. Still, the underemployment of agricultural labor between seasonal peaks is often the single most important slack in the resources in the less developed economies today, particularly in the countries that do not have adequate institutions to mobilize this slack labor for the construction of social overhead capital (see Chapter 10).

The changes in the demand and supply of products and factors expected over the next several decades will require a major agricultural transformation in the less developed economies in the tropics (the term *agricultural transformation* is defined here as a significant change in the pattern of product combination, production sequences, and resource use in agriculture). Both technological and institutional changes will be critical elements in the agricultural transformation, if they can be used to develop new patterns of agricultural production consistent with changes in factor and product markets.

It is useful to review several examples of such transformations by drawing on the historical experiences of Great Britain, Denmark, France, and Japan.

British Experience

Britain experienced a major agricultural transformation from the mid-eighteenth until the mid-nineteenth centuries.[13] We have reviewed, in Chapter 3, the transformation in eighteenth-century Britain commonly called the agricultural revolution. The technical basis for the eighteenth-century agricultural revolution was the Norfolk crop-rotation system integrating crop production with livestock production. This system intensified the recycling of nutrients among plants, livestock, and soil, thus permitting a rise in output per unit of land area, while maintaining soil fertility. The institutional basis was the enclosure—the consolidation of communal pasture and farmland into single private units—which facilitated the introduction of an integrated system of crop-livestock production.

The technology associated with the agricultural revolution was consistent with the conditions of demand and supply of factors and products. The increase in population since the second quarter of the eighteenth century expanded the demand for food and raised the price of food grains. The increase in population was followed by an increase in the labor force. Both food demand and labor supply pressed against land. It was technically feasible and economically profitable to adopt an intensive integrated crop-livestock system of agricultural production.

A second agricultural transformation in Britain occurred following the repeal of the Corn Laws and the Navigation Acts. Confronted with competition from foreign grains, British agriculture successfully transformed itself into efficient large-scale farming based on the trinity of landlords, capitalist tenants, and wage laborers. The development of "high farming" in mid-nineteenth-century England involved the substitution of industrial inputs such as farm machinery and fertilizer for labor. This process was consistent with the rapid absorption of labor by manufacturing industries in "the Workshop of the World."

13. This section draws on material previously discussed in Chapters 3, 8, and 12.

The high farming was supported technically by advances in soil conservation techniques, including underground drainage, application of guano and commercial fertilizers, and the traditional excellence of British livestock-breeding techniques, which produced numerous improved breeds. Institutionally, the establishment of an entrepreneurial tenant farming system based on the common law conventions of the compensation by landlords for tenants' investments, including soil improvements, facilitated the rational adjustment of agriculture to the changing economic environment.

In contrast to the pattern developed during the agricultural revolution, in which the primary value of livestock was the dung produced for restoring soil fertility, meat and milk became the major value of livestock production in the high farming of the mid-nineteenth century. This was, of course, a rational response to the rising animal prices relative to cereal prices in this period.

The British experience is a classical "ideal type" of agricultural transformation. Except as an illustration of effective response of technology to economic opportunities, the British experience is, however, of limited value to the developing countries today because of the extreme differences in the economic environment and technological possibilities as compared to eighteenth- and nineteenth-century Great Britain. The agricultural revolution in the eighteenth century occurred in an environment in which agriculture was a relatively self-contained system. The linkage of industry to agriculture through the supply of industrially produced inputs was not yet established. The agricultural transformation of the nineteenth century occurred at a time when the labor supply to agriculture was contracting, a situation diametrically opposite to that in developing countries today, where the absolute increase in agricultural labor force presses hard on limited land resources.

The Danish agricultural transformation experience, particularly the developments associated with the invention of the cream separator and the establishment of cooperative creameries, and the Japanese experience of development in sericulture are more relevant cases for LDCs.

Danish Experience

Agricultural development in Denmark during the last quarter of the nineteenth century and the first quarter of this century represents a case of remarkable transformation of agriculture in response to changes in product and factor market conditions.[14] Denmark was traditionally a grain exporter to the British market. When a large quantity of grains began to be imported into Britain from the new continents and grain prices fell, the traditional economic base of Danish agriculture came under severe pressure. In response to this challenge,

14. This section draws heavily on Einar Jensen, *Danish Agriculture: Its Economic Development* (Copenhagen: J. H. Schultz Forlag, 1937). See also Svend A. Hansen, *Økonomisk Vaekst i Danmark*, Bind I: 1720–1914; Bind II: 1914–1970 (Copenhagen: G.E.C. Gads Forlag, 1972 and 1974); Bruce F. Johnston, "Agricultural Development and Economic Transformation: A Comparative Study of the Japanese Experience," *Food Research Institute Studies* 3 (November 1962):223–76.

TABLE 13-2.   Farm receipts and cash expenses of a representative farm[a] in Denmark, 1881, 1901, and 1929

	1881		1901		1929	
	Kroner	Percent	Kroner	Percent	Kroner	Percent
Receipts	3,481	100	5,112	100	17,400	100
Crops	1,613	46	711	14	2,820	16
Cereals	1,509	43	645	13	2,206	13
Others[b]	104	3	66	1	614	3
Livestock	2,168	62	4,401	86	14,580	84
Butter	761	22	2,101	41	6,161	35
Pork	448	13	1,199	23	5,852	34
Others[c]	959	27	1,101	22	2,567	15
Expenses	2,310	100	3,620	100	12,042	100
Feed	228	9	511	14	4,077	34
Fertilizer	12	1	38	1	700	6
Machine repairs	100	4	200	6	500	4
Hired labor	615	27	836	23	3,425	28
Others[d]	1,355	59	2,035	56	3,340	28
Net spendable income[e] (current prices)	1,471		1,492		5,358	
Net spendable income[f] (1881 prices)	1,471		1,812		3,995	

Source: Einer Jensen, *Danish Agriculture: Its Economic Development* (Copenhagen: J. H. Schultz Forlag, 1937), pp. 258, 262, and 385.
[a]A hypothetical farm of 28 hectare located in the island of Sjaelland, Denmark, which is supposedly representative of farms in the whole east-Danish loam section.
[b]Peas, potatoes, and seed.
[c]Beef, lambs, wool, eggs, and horses.
[d]Seed, building repairs, veterinary care, insurance, light and power, real estate tax, and mortgage interest.
[e]Receipt minus expense.
[f]Income in current prices deflated by general price index (Statistical Index).

Denmark successfully transformed itself into a major exporter of butter and bacon. An important point is that this transformation was carried out while the agricultural labor force was expanding. The absolute size of the agricultural labor force in Denmark did not begin to decline until the late 1920s.

The process of transformation can be illustrated by the farm earnings and expenses of a representative farm calculated by Einer Jensen (Table 13-2). Jensen's calculation indicates that cereals were still a major item in the farm sales in Denmark in 1881, when the agricultural transformation began. In this pattern of production, labor use was highly seasonal.[15]

A dramatic change can be observed for 1901 as compared with 1881. The relative importance of livestock greatly increased, and butter replaced cereals as the most important item in farm receipts. This was clearly a rational

15. Jensen, *Danish Agriculture,* p. 261.

response to a decline in the price of wheat of more than 40 percent and a decline in the price of butter of only 15 percent during this period. Because of this transformation, the representative farmer was able to increase his real income in spite of the decline in the prices of agricultural products in Europe during this period (see the last row of Table 13-2).

In 1929 pork (for bacon) became as important an item as butter in farm receipts. The purchase of feed exceeded the sale of crops by a wide margin. The new pattern of agricultural production in Denmark was then clearly established. Through this transformation, Danish agriculture not only absorbed a growing labor force but also achieved more efficient use of labor by reducing the peaks and troughs of labor use.

A number of technological advances facilitated the transformation of Danish agriculture. These included tile drainage, increases in the application of fertilizer and lime (see Table 13-2), and improvements in seed and livestock varieties. The innovations that were most critical to the agricultural transformation were the invention and diffusion of the cream separator and the cooperative creamery system. The success of these innovations was, in turn, related to a favorable land tenure system and a high level of education among Danish farmers,[16] without which the modern agricultural production pattern in Denmark could hardly have been established.

Practically usable centrifugal cream separators were developed by the Danish inventor L. C. Nielsen in 1878 and the Swedish physicist Carl Gustav Patrik deLaval in 1879. Both were immediately used in production, and by 1881 there were eighty separators operating in Denmark.[17] Prior to this invention the production of butter was dominated by large farms or manors, which could build a "skimming hall," a large ventilated room where milk was kept fresh twenty-two to forty-six hours while the cream was rising. Small farmers who could not afford such a large capital investment were unable to participate in the profitable butter production; therefore, the expansion of dairy production was limited.

The invention of the cream separator removed this constraint. The new potential that emerged from this technical invention was exploited by an institutional innovation—the cooperative creamery. With this combination of technical and institutional innovations, Jensen reports, "the profitableness of milk production was raised on middle-sized farms and even on small-holdings, to the level of the big farms."[18]

This innovation also contributed to the integration of dairy and hog operations. Large quantities of skim milk, a by-product of butter production, pro-

---

16. "The development of the co-operative in response to a technological need . . . was the product of the prevalence of the freehold in Danish land tenure, together with the high degree of education in Danish farmers." C. P. Kindleberger, "Group Behavior and International Trade," *Journal of Political Economy* 59 (February 1951):45.

17. Jensen, *Danish Agriculture*, p. 174.

18. Ibid., p. 176.

vided cheap feed for hogs. Production of lightly cured bacon based on this integrated system was developed in Denmark, and its export to Britain came to exceed the export of bacon to Britain from the United States; "this is an outstanding example of an 'old' agricultural country entering a market fully occupied by the new over-seas competitors."[19]

The Danish experience demonstrates the critical role of technical and institutional innovations for agricultural transformation.[20] This experience is relevant to the LDCs today because the technology and institutions were so developed as to absorb a larger number of workers in agriculture and to use farm labor more fully by reducing the seasonality of agricultural production.

Retardation in French Agriculture

The contrast between the French and Danish experiences could hardly be more striking.[21] In the fifty years after 1880 the annual growth in agricultural output in France was 0.76 percent as compared to 2.07 percent in Denmark. The reasons for the slow rate of growth in France, the country with the best agricultural resources in Europe, have been a subject of considerable debate among economic historians.

According to conventional wisdom, French agriculture, during the nineteenth and well into the twentieth century, was characterized by low productivity and resistance to technical change. It was also protected from international competition. Its persistent retardation has typically been attributed to the economic and political consequences of a peasant system of agricultural organization—small owner-operated units, intensive use of family labor, unresponsiveness to the pressures of the intersector labor market, with production decisions determined by sociological rather than economic considerations.[22] Thus the structural retardation hypothesis locates the source of stagnation within the agricultural sector. It is reminiscent of much of the early literature in development economics that viewed the peasant as the primary obstacle to agricultural development.

A more careful analysis, however, locates the source of retardation in French agriculture in the poor performance of the nonagricultural sectors of the French economy and in the lack of such public sector institutional innovations as sustained rapid economic growth in Danish agriculture.

19. Ibid., p. 191.
20. Kindleberger, "Group Behavior."
21. The material in this section is presented in greater detail in Vernon W. Ruttan, "Structural Retardation and the Modernization of French Agriculture: A Skeptical View," *Journal of Economic History* 38 (September 1978):714–28. See also Rondo Cameron and Charles E. Freedeman, "French Economic Growth: A Radical Revision," *Social Science History* 7 (Winter 1983):3–30.
22. The structural retardation hypothesis in the English-language literature dates at least to the first edition of J. H. Clapham, *The Economic Development of France and Germany, 1815–1914* (Cambridge, Eng., 1921). See also George W. Grantham, "Scale and Organization in French Farming, 1840–1880," *European Peasants and Their Markets,* ed. William N. Parker and Eric L. Jones (Princeton: Princeton University Press, 1975), pp. 293–326.

In spite of what has been regarded as poor performance, the annual rate of growth in agricultural output appears to have exceeded the rate of growth in demand. Between 1880 and 1930, population growth and income growth combined to produce an annual rate of growth in demand of 0.61 percent. During this same period agricultural output grew at 0.76 percent per year. Prices received by French farmers declined. Thus between 1880 and 1930 the "inefficient" French peasant provided the urban-industrial sector with more food per capita and at lower real prices.[23]

This feat was accomplished with little assistance from the institutional infrastructure. During this period agricultural research, extension, and credit systems organized or subsidized by the public sector were developed in Denmark, Germany, Japan, and the United States but not in France. A ministry of agriculture was not established until 1881. In the thirty-three years between 1881 and 1914 there were forty-two different governments and nineteen different ministers of agriculture. Most ministers of agriculture were doctors or lawyers with little interest in or commitment to agriculture. The French agricultural research service, which was not established until after World War I, was abolished in 1935 as an economy measure. An effort in the 1920s to establish an agricultural extension service was unsuccessful.[24] It was not until after World War II that effective agricultural research and extension programs were instituted in France.

In spite of these failures in institutional development, one might ask why French agriculture did not follow the Danish example and become an exporter of livestock products to the United Kingdom market and thus release the constraints imposed by slow growth of domestic demand. Part of the response to this question is to be found in the Méline Tariff,[25] which increased the price of grain relative to that of livestock. Denmark built its livestock economy on the basis of imported feed grains and concentrates. But in France, incentives to expand the small-scale, labor-intensive livestock sector were depressed by a series of increasingly protectionist tariffs on wheat and feed grains in the 1880s and 1890s. The tariffs were erected in response to the political power of the large-scale grain producers in northern France, whose policies were directly opposed to the economic interests of the peasantry.

One might also ask why, when confronted with limited opportunities for productive employment in agriculture, French peasants did not migrate to urban centers in larger numbers in search of industrial employment. The

23. Between 1880 and 1900, agricultural prices declined in both current and real terms. Between 1900 and 1920, real prices fluctuated at near the levels of 1900. Between 1920 and 1930, real prices of agricultural products again declined. See Michael Tracy, *Agriculture in Western Europe: Challenge and Response, 1880–1980,* 2d ed. (London: Granada, 1982), p. 78; Helen C. Farnsworth, "Determinants of French Grain Production, Past and Prospective," *Food Research Institute Studies* 4 (1964):225–72.

24. Gordon Wright, *Rural Revolution in France* (Stanford: Stanford University Press, 1964), pp. 18, 34; Tracy, *Agriculture in Western Europe,* p. 81.

25. Tracy, *Agriculture in Western Europe,* pp. 76–82.

traditional response has been that the peasants withheld their labor from the market because of their ties to the land by excessive individualism, pride of ownership, and communal loyalty. A more correct answer seems to be that the demand for labor in the nonagricultural sector grew so slowly that there were limited opportunities for productive employment in the urban-industrial sector. When the demand for labor in the nonagricultural sector rose rapidly for a brief period around the turn of this century and dramatically in the 1950s and 1960s, the structuralist constraints no longer presented a serious barrier to rapid migration from rural areas.[26]

In retrospect it appears that French peasants exhibited a highly rational response to the limited economic opportunities available to them. They were constrained by a national economy that exhibited slow growth in the demand for the products the peasants produced and also for the excess labor available in rural areas. Their incentives were distorted by a tariff designed to protect the interests of the large-scale grain producers. They were denied the institutional infrastructure in research, extension, and credit that supported peasant agricultural production in Denmark.

The improvement in the performance of French agriculture since World War II was not the result of any dramatic reduction in structural constraints in the rural sector. Rather, it reflected the removal of many external constraints that had earlier limited the performance of French agriculture. New opportunities for growth in output resulted from expanded markets. New opportunities for growth in labor productivity came from the more rapid growth in the demand for labor in the nonagricultural sector. Finally, there was belated investment by the public sector in the development of the institutional infrastructure needed to serve a modern agriculture.

Development of Sericulture in Japan

A highly relevant example of agricultural transformation in the less developed countries was the development of sericulture in the early period of modern Japanese economic growth.[27] There is some question whether the development of sericulture in Japan can be correctly referred to as an agricultural transformation. It has been argued that modern agricultural development in Japan since the Meiji period was characterized by the persistence of

---

26. Jean Jacques Carré, Paul Dubois, and Edmond Malinvaud, *French Economic Growth* (Stanford: Stanford University Press, 1975), pp. 1–16, 431–37.

27. This section is based on Le Thanh Nghiep and Yujiro Hayami, "Mobilizing Slack Resources for Economic Development: The Summer–Fall Rearing Technology of Sericulture in Japan," *Explorations in Economic History* 16 (1979):163–81. See also Takekazu Ogura, ed., *Agricultural Development in Modern Japan* (Tokyo: Fuji Publishing Co., 1963), pp. 541–65; Nogyo Hattatsushi Chosakai, ed., *Nihon Nagyo Hattatsushi* (History of Japanese agricultural development), Vol. 5 (Tokyo: Chuokoronsha, 1955), pp. 134–85; Japan, Ministry of Agriculture and Forestry, Division of Statistical Research, *Yosun Ruinen Tokeihyo* (Historical statistics of sericulture) (Tokyo: Norin Tokei Kyokai, 1961).

traditional production patterns.[28] Apart from issues of terminology, however, it is clear that the development of sericulture made a critical contribution to agricultural and economic growth by raising the utilization of labor, land, and capital.

From the 1870s to the 1920s, cocoon production increased tenfold from a level of 35,000 metric tons to 350,000 metric tons, and the share of sericultural production in the total value of agricultural production rose from about 5 percent to about 15 percent. This development was vital for Japanese economic growth because silk was the major source of foreign exchange earnings, accounting for nearly 50 percent of such earnings throughout the nineteenth century and as much as 30 percent even in the 1920s.

There is an argument that attributes this development to luck. For example, Martin Bronfenbrenner attributed the development of Japanese sericulture, in addition to the existence of the world silk market, to special conditions, such as the spread of a silkworm disease in Italy and Spain and to the Taipei Rebellion in China, which coincided with the opening of Japan to the West.[29] This view is untenable because it does not explain why Japanese silk continued to increase its share of the world silk market after the elimination of the silkworm disease in Europe through the efforts of Louis Pasteur and after the Taipei Rebellion in China.

The basic element in the Japanese dominance over its competitors was the progress of technology, both in sericulture and in the silk reeling industry, supported by a number of institutional innovations. Most critical, and particularly relevant in the present context, was the development of summer-fall rearing of cocoons. Traditionally, spring—April to June—is the period of sericultural production. This period, however, coincides with the peak of the labor requirement for rice and other crop production and is hence competitive in its demand for labor.

Summer-fall culture, using the nonhibernating bivoltine varieties, had been practiced on a very small scale before the Meiji period. It was only after the discovery in 1875 by Mototada Otaka, a manager of the Tomioka Silk Reeling Mill, of a method of postponing the hatching of hibernating varieties by storing the silkworm eggs in cool caves that the summer-fall culture became practical for many farmers. Later a method of artificial hatching by chemical processing was developed. Finally, a hydrochloric acid processing method was established in 1912–13 at the Aichi Prefectural Egg Multiplication Station. In addition, the summer-fall culture was greatly facilitated by the development of F_1 hybrid varieties (originally by Kametaro Toyama in 1906). The

28. For example, see Kazushi Ohkawa and Henry Rosovsky, "The Role of Agriculture in Modern Japanese Economic Development," *Economic Development and Cultural Change* 9 (October 1960): 43–67.
29. Martin Bronfenbrenner, "The Japanese 'Howdunit,'" *Transaction* 6 (January 1969):32–36.

hybrids proved much more vigorous, and their development resulted in a dramatic improvement in the survival rate of summer-fall–reared silkworms.

There were a number of advantages to the summer-fall rearing in the use of resources. It increased the efficiency of capital use for farmers because rearing equipment and utensils could be used more than once a year. Also, reelers could economize on the use of circulating capital because they were able to divide payments for cocoons between the spring and summer-fall seasons. It reduced the risk of frost on mulberry leaves, which often damaged early spring culture. The most critical contribution, however, was the increase in the efficiency of labor use resulting from the employment of seasonally idle labor. Labor that was idle between the rice planting and harvesting periods could be mobilized for cocoon production. The result was a substantial increase in the number of work days per year per person engaged in agricultural production and an increase in labor income.

Further, the summer-fall–rearing technology was biased in favor of small peasants whose family labor endowments were large relative to land endowments, as indicated by the linear-programming (LP) analysis of a typical farm in Japan for the 1930s by Le Thanh Nghiep with Yujiro Hayami. Their calculations of the marginal product of labor in the LP solutions for different levels of family labor endowment for a given land endowment are shown in Figure 13-1.

The analysis indicates that up to a labor input of fifty man-days per month per hectare there was little difference in labor's marginal productivity between the cases with and without summer-fall rearing. As labor inputs without summer-fall rearing increased, however, marginal productivity declined sharply to zero, whereas with summer-fall rearing, marginal productivity declined more moderately and remained positive up to a labor endowment of ninety man-days. The relations observed in Figure 13-1 are consistent with the hypothesis that the contribution of the summer-fall–rearing technology to the increase in labor's marginal productivity was largest on small farms where the endowments of labor were high relative to the endowments of land.

Cocoon production from summer-fall culture rose from a negligible level at the beginning of the Meiji period (1868) to 12,000 tons in 1890, about 25 percent of total production, and to 119,000 tons in 1920, about half of total production. This innovation of summer-fall culture enabled the Japanese sericulture industry to surpass France, Italy, and China in production. It was made possible by a technical innovation that encouraged more efficient use of resources, such as labor, for which the supply was relatively elastic.

This technical innovation was supported by a number of institutional innovations, including the establishment of silk inspection stations (1895), national and prefectural silkworm egg multiplication stations (1910–11), and sericultural colleges in Tokyo (1896), Kyoto (1899), and Ueda (1920). The development of sericulture cooperatives was also important. Their activities ranged from the transmission of technical information and the cooperative

FIGURE 13-1. Marginal value productivities of labor in the linear-programming solutions for different levels of labor endowment for a typical sericultural farm in Japan during the 1930s.

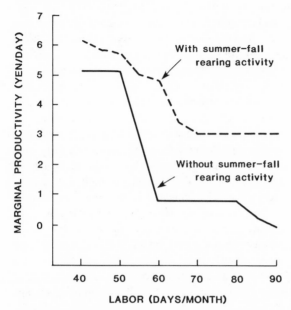

LABOR (DAYS/MONTH)

Source: Le Thanh Nghiep and Yujiro Hayami, "Mobilizing Slack Resources for Economic Development: The Summer-Fall Rearing Technology of Sericulture in Japan," *Explorations in Economic History* 16 (April 1979):163–81.

rearing of young worms to the management of cooperative silk reeling mills and even the training centers.

Implications of the Historical Experience

The development of the Danish livestock industry and the Japanese sericulture industry is of particular interest for the less developed countries as an illustration of how technological change and institutional development have been employed to achieve economic diversification in agriculture. Both the Danish and the Japanese cases illustrate the importance of "vertical" expansion in farm size under conditions of severe constraints on "horizontal" or area expansion. The livestock enterprise in Denmark and the silkworm enterprise in Japan were labor-intensive raw-material-processing activities that increased the value added in production by enabling farm families to make more effective use of available labor resources.

One of the more dramatic contemporary examples of vertical expansion is the system of milk production cooperatives developed initially by the Anand Dairy Cooperative and extended under the auspices of the National Dairy

Development Board in India.[30] The basic unit in the system is a village milk producers' cooperative composed of all milk producers in a village who wish to market their milk cooperatively. Most village cooperatives have one hundred to two hundred members. About one-third of the members are landless, and few have holdings of more than ten acres. The average herd size is less than two cows or buffalo, and the average amount of milk marketed per day is less than two liters. Individual cooperative members belong to a district cooperative union that owns and operates milk-processing and feed-compounding plants, organizes the collection of milk from village cooperatives, and distributes the milk in major urban centers. The union also provides veterinary, artificial insemination, and extension services to members.

We do not imply, of course, that there are direct transfer possibilities, either at the technological or institution levels, in the experiences of Great Britain, Denmark, or Japan. Nor are these the only experiences on which we might have drawn. The cases discussed in this section are important because the role of livestock has been relatively neglected in the literature on economic development.[31] The cases are also important because they illustrate the development of location-specific technological and institutional innovations adapted to changes in resource endowments and in product demand of a particular country or region at a particular time in economic history. These innovations occurred in response to economic possibilities rather than in response to efforts to distort the impact of economic change on domestic and world economies.

MOBILIZING AGRICULTURAL GROWTH FOR OVERALL DEVELOPMENT

A continuous sequence of technical and institutional innovations to create and evolve a pattern of agricultural production consistent with changes in product demand and factor supply conditions can sharply reduce the cost of increased income streams generated by the agricultural sector.

What are the implications of these higher income streams for economic development? It has become a generally accepted tenet of development theory

30. Ray A. Goldberg and Richard C. McGinity, *Agribusiness Management for Developing Countries: Southeast Asian Corn System and American and Japanese Trends Affecting It* (Cambridge, Mass.: Ballinger Publishing Co., 1979), pp. 466–84. The material on the Indian dairy development program was prepared by Michael Halse.

31. There has often been a negative perception of the role of livestock in development. Livestock production systems that make intensive use of feed grains have been viewed as both inefficient and competitive with the food needs of the poor. Livestock production has also been criticized for the impact of overgrazing on arid and other fragile environments. But there has been a neglect of the role of livestock in facilitating more intensive use of land and labor resources. A substantial research program on livestock and development has been conducted under the direction of Adolf Weber at the University of Kiel. See Adolf Weber and Marquard Gregersen, "The Changing Productivity Structure of the World's Cattle Industry in the Course of Economic Development," *Zeitschrift für Ausländische Landwirtshaft* 16 (1977):285–314.

that the diversion of the increments in agricultural income for the support of the emerging nonfarm sector is essential for rapid economic development (Chapter 2). In this perspective a central question of general development theory has been, "How can peasants be encouraged to produce a cumulative surplus of food and fibers over and above their own consumption, and how can this surplus largely be channeled to investment activity in the nonfarm sector without requiring in exchange an equivalent transfer of productive value to the farm sector?"[32]

Alternative approaches to the diversion of income streams generated by and the resources released from agricultural production have been employed by colonial (or plantation), socialist, and market economic systems. Our analysis supports the proposition that the market system, combined with a highly decentralized family-operated farm structure, is an effective environment for the public and private sector institutions engaged in the generation of new technical knowledge and the production of more productive inputs which are the sources of the new income streams generated by the agricultural sector.

The market system is not only effective in inducing increased streams of output. The product market is also an effective device for transferring the gains of productivity growth to other sectors of the economy. The market mechanism is, of course, not the only effective device for achieving intersectoral income transfers. Some socialist countries have been successful in designing effective intersector transfers through direct taxation or compulsory delivery. These more direct requisition or "command" systems have typically not been as successful in generating comparable rates of output and productivity growth as market systems characterized by autonomous production units.[33]

Under the colonial systems, the intersectoral income transfers were typically used to purchase growth in the metropolitan rather than the colonial economy. A large share of the growth in income streams from agriculture was transferred abroad through remittances to foreign factors—foreign capital, entrepreneurs, management, and technical personnel.[34] The efforts to substitute foreign for domestic factors through the training and education of

32. Wyn F. Owen, "The Double Developmental Squeeze on Agriculture," *American Economic Review* 56 (March 1966):43–44.

33. Hla Myint, "Market Mechanism and Planning—The Functional Aspect," *The Structure and Development in Asian Economies* (Tokyo: Japan Economic Research Center, 1968), pp. 282–313; Karl Eugen Wädekin, *Agrarian Policies in Communist Europe: A Critical Introduction* (Thottague: Martinus Nijhoff, 1982):102–18; D. Gale Johnson and Karen McConnell Brooks, *Prospects for Soviet Agriculture in the 1980's* (Bloomington: Indiana University Press, 1983), pp. 12–21.

34. Jonathan V. Levin, *The Export Economies: Their Pattern of Development in Historical Perspective* (Cambridge, Mass.: Harvard University Press, 1960); also see Robert E. Baldwin, "Patterns of Development in Newly Settled Regions," *Manchester School of Economic and Social Studies* 24 (May 1956):161–79; George L. Beckford, *Persistent Poverty: Underdevelopment in Plantation Economies of the Third World* (New York: Oxford University Press, 1972).

native people for administrative, technical, and engineering work were intentionally neglected. A significant portion of income was spent for foreign consumer goods by a class of luxury importers, who developed a taste for foreign goods, rather than spilled over into demand for domestic manufactures. Furthermore, agricultural product processing and input manufacturing were monopolized by metropolitan countries, thereby reducing the critical forward and backward linkage effects. In contrasting the economic history of Java and Japan, Clifford Geertz insists that "the real tragedy of colonial history in Java after 1830 is not that the peasantry suffered. It suffered worse elsewhere. . . . The tragedy is that it suffered for nothing."[35]

This pattern still persists in many tropical economies. Policies to promote the substitution of domestic factors for foreign factors, particularly through investments in human capital and through technical and institutional innovations, are essential for the generation of new income streams from agriculture and to direct these income streams into high-payoff investments in both the agricultural and nonagricultural sectors. Yet an abrupt break from the traditional pattern based on ideological appeal, rather than rational economic calculation, has not contributed effectively to economic growth. It is not the specialization in primary production for export or continued "dependency" on economic growth in the "center" but rather the lack of "an ability to shift resources at the dictates of the market . . . sufficient to permit shifts into new export lines or into production for the domestic market"[36] that constrains the development of the poor countries. Efforts to transform the structure and pattern of the economy, without solving this basic problem by education and by institutional and technological innovations, will continue to be unproductive.

In many developing countries, the income streams generated in the agricultural sector have been used to purchase a nonviable industrial sector or a nonproductive military and administrative bureaucracy. It has been an article of faith in development thought that it is easier for a poor country to purchase a modern steel industry than a modern agriculture. The experience of the last several decades indicates that although it may be easy for poor countries to acquire an industrial sector, particularly an industrial sector that produces manufactured products that were formerly imported, it is much more difficult to purchase an industrial sector that is capable of making a sustained contribution to income streams comparable to those generated by the agricultural sector.

If the intersector income transfers resulting from technical change in agriculture are to result in a cumulative contribution to economic growth, the new sectors purchased by these transfers must also be capable of generating inter-

35. Clifford Geertz, *Agricultural Involution: The Process of Ecological Change in Indonesia* (Berkeley and Los Angeles: University of California Press, 1966), p. 143.
36. Melville H. Watkins, "A Staple Theory of Economic Growth," *Canadian Journal of Ecnomics and Political Science* 29 (May 1963):149.

sector transfers. They must be capable of producing the industrial materials needed to sustain the process of agricultural development. They must be organized to increase the demand for labor in the industrial sector, and the impact must be transferred back to the agricultural sector or through the intersector labor market. And they must be capable of sustaining the necessary investment in education and in urban sector public infrastructure.

During the next several decades the development test will be twofold. Will the developing economies fully use the relatively inexpensive sources of growth that can be obtained by the transformation of agriculture from a traditional to a modern science-based sector? Furthermore, will the dividends from such investments be used to purchase a modern urban-industrial sector that is in turn an inexpensive source of economic growth?

INDUCED INNOVATION AND AGRICULTURAL DEVELOPMENT POLICY

The single most significant conclusion that emerges from our analysis of the agricultural development experience of Japan and the United States, and of contemporary development processes in the LDCs, is the powerful role of economic forces in inducing both technical and institutional change.

Our analysis reinforces the view that relative factor and product prices exert a pervasive impact on the direction of both the innovative and production activity of farmers and of the firms that supply the industrial inputs used in agricultural production. The analysis of induced innovation has been extended to include the behavior of public sector institutions. Although the theory of induced innovation on the part of the public sector is not complete, it is developed sufficiently to guide us in seeing that in the United States and Japan the public sector research and education institutions serving agriculture have responded effectively to economic forces in releasing the constraints on agricultural growth imposed by inelastic factor supplies. The evolution of agricultural research capacity in the LDCs, first in the export crop sectors and recently in the food crop sectors, is also consistent with the induced development hypothesis.

The pervasive role of economic forces in the resource allocation decisions of both private sector firms and public sector institutions places a major burden on the efficiency of the pricing system. Our analysis suggests that where price relationships have been distorted, either through market imperfections or government intervention in market processes, both the innovative behavior and production behavior of private firms and public institutions have been distorted. The distortion of prices in both domestic and international factor and product markets and the restrictions on resource mobility and product movements, which have been imposed in pursuit of national development policies, have clearly contributed to the widening disequilibrium in world agriculture during the interwar period and through much of the period since World War II.

In most developing economies the market systems remain relatively underdeveloped. A major challenge facing these countries in their planning is the development of a well-articulated market system capable of accurately reflecting the effects of changes in supply, demand, and production relationships. An important element in the development of a more efficient factor and product market system is the removal of the rigidities and distortions resulting from government policy itself—including the maintenance of overvalued currencies, artificially low rates of interest, and unfavorable factor and product price policies.

The dampening effect of underdeveloped and distorted domestic markets on agricultural incentives has been reinforced since the early 1970s by greater instability in international financial and commodity markets.[37] The breakdown of the post–World War II trade and financial market institutions has sharply reduced the discretion of national governments in attempting to provide agricultural producers with reasonably stable expectations regarding the behavior of factor and product markets. The short-run shocks generated by the instability in international financial and commodity markets have been primarily a result of domestic monetary and fiscal policies pursued by the major trading nations rather than a reflection of fundamental shifts in demand or trends in productivity and comparative advantage. But the effect has been to make it more difficult for the policymakers and planners in developing countries to establish the efficient market policies and infrastructure investments needed to sustain agricultural development. And it seems apparent that the excessive instability in international commodity and financial markets will continue to distort development incentives in poor countries, at least until the emergence of a new set of international trading and financial institutions.

The strategy of attempting to protect agriculture from the impact of economic forces rather than investing in institutions that would improve the capacity of the agricultural sector to respond to economic change has, in many countries, resulted in wide disparities in the economic welfare of the urban and rural populations and has severely restricted agriculture's capacity to contribute toward national economic growth. In contrast, investments in public institutions which have increased the capacity of the agricultural sector to respond to economic forces have, in the past, been critical to the success of agricultural development in countries such as Denmark, Japan, and the United States.

The capacity to move from a natural-resource-based to a science-based agriculture—to generate a continuous stream of technical innovations that are responsive to the supply of factors and product demand—depends in most developing countries on substantial investment in education and research.

37. Ian M. D. Little, *Economic Development: Theory, Policy and International Relations* (New York: Basic Books, for the Twentieth Century Fund, 1982), pp. 305–21, 334–70.

Equally important is the capacity of the country to undertake the institutional innovations and reforms necessary for agricultural producers to respond to the new technical opportunities that become available to them. Institutional innovations that permit firms and institutions to internalize the benefits of innovative activity become particularly important in creating the incentives for both innovative and productive behavior.

APPENDIXES

APPENDIX A: Intercountry Cross-Section Data

In this appendix we explain the data used for the intercountry cross-section analysis in Part II.

In general, the definitions of data and the methods of processing them follow those developed for 1960, which are explained in greater detail in Yujiro Hayami with Barbara B. Miller, William W. Wade, and Sachiko Yamashita, *An International Comparison of Agricultural Production and Productivities* (St. Paul: University of Minnesota Agricultural Experiment Station Technical Bulletin 277, 1971), although the 1960 data were revised according to new data in later publications.

Data were collected for forty-four countries for 1960, 1970, and 1980. In principle the data for flow variables, such as agricultural output and fertilizer input, were measured, respectively, as 1957–62 averages, 1967–72 averages, and 1975–80 averages; and those for stock variables, such as agricultural land area and the number of farm workers, were measured as of 1960, 1970, and 1980. The periods for averaging flow variables were determined in consideration of data availability; the 1957–62 period was adopted for 1960 because the seed and feed data are so documented in the original source; 1967–72 averages were adopted for 1970 for the sake of consistency with the 1960 series; and the 1975–80 averages were adopted for 1980 because that was the latest year for which data were available when this study was conducted.

Original data were collected mainly from the publications of United Nations organizations and other international agencies supplemented by those of individual governments and private agencies. In countries for which the original data were unavailable for specified years or obvious inconsistencies were found among data for different years, extrapolations or interpolations were extensively used for estimation and adjustments.

UN organizations discontinued publication of data for Taiwan since the early 1970s. The gap was filled mainly by Republic of China Directorate-

The authors are indebted to Toshihiko Kawagoe and Sachiko Yamashita Sidhu for assistance in revising the data series in this appendix.

General of Budget, Accounting and Statistics, *Statistical Yearbook of Republic of China* (various issues); Taiwan Provincial Government Department of Agriculture and Forestry, *Taiwan Agricultural Yearbook* (various issues); and Republic of China, Council for Economic Planning and Development, *Taiwan Statistical Data Book 1980* (1980).

When data were compiled initially for 1960 by Hayami and associates for *An International Comparison of Agricultural Production and Productivities* (and reported in the first edition of this book), the number of countries included was forty-three instead of forty-four because Bangladesh was then included in Pakistan. For this study, the Bangladesh data for 1960 were separated from those of Pakistan.

The major intercountry statistical series are presented in Table A-4 (Series K1–K36).

Agricultural Output (K1–K3)

The output variable employed in this study is specified as gross agricultural output, net of agricultural intermediate products such as seed and feed. The series of 1957–62 average agricultural outputs (K1) was estimated by the procedures described below, and the series of 1967–72 outputs (K2) and 1975–80 outputs (K3) were extrapolated from the 1957–62 data using the Food and Agricultural Organization's indices of agricultural production (FAO, *Production Yearbook*) for the respective countries.

The series of 1957–62 average outputs was estimated using the following steps: (a) deducting the seed, feed (including imported feed), eggs for hatching, and milk for calf-rearing from the quantities of individual agricultural commodities produced; (b) aggregating the quantities of the three sets of wheat relative prices derived from the farm-gate prices (or the import prices of commodities not produced domestically) for the United States, Japan, and India to produce three aggregate output series; and (c) combining these three series into a single composite series by taking their geometrical means. Denoting quantity produced of the jth commodity in the ith country by q_{ij}, the corresponding quantity to be deducted by d_{ij}, and the wheat-relative price of the United States, Japan, and India by w_{Uj}, w_{Ji}, and w_{Ij} respectively, our composite series of gross output, Y_i's, may be expressed as

$$Y_i = \sqrt[3]{Y_{Ui}Y_{Ji}Y_{Ii}},$$

where

$$Y_{Ui} = \sum_j w_{Uj}(q_{ij} - d_{ij}); \; Y_{Ji} = \sum_j w_{Jj}(q_{ij} - d_{ij});$$
$$\text{and } Y_{Ij} = \sum_j w_{Ij}(q_{ij} - d_{ij}).$$

The underlying assumptions of the above aggregation procedures are that (a) there exist three types of relative price structures characteristic of the three stages of economic development, which may be called "advanced stage," "midway stage," and "initial stage"; (b) these three stages may be represented by the United States, Japan, and India, respectively, in 1960; and (c) any bias arising from aggregating commodities by the prices of one of these representative countries will be canceled out by the determination of the geometrical means of three such series. Needless to say, it is arbitrary to assume three stages (why not four?) and to represent the three stages by the United States, Japan, and India. The availability of data rather than theory led us to the selection of the above criteria for our analysis.

Data on the quantities produced were taken from FAO's *Production Yearbook,* various issues, and data for the deduction of seed and feed from FAO's *Food Balance Sheets, 1957–59 Average and 1960–62 Average.* The availability of pertinent data in the latter publications limited the number of countries to be included for this analysis. Because of the lack of necessary information, capital formation and stock changes, especially in the form of livestock and perennial plants, are not counted in computing output. Only the products of agriculture are included in agricultural output, which excludes the products of fishery and forestry. The aggregate output of the primary sector, however, including fishery and forestry, was estimated using the price weights of Japan for the deduction of fishery and forestry workers, as explained later. In principle, quantities produced are measured in farm-gate forms, that is, sugarcane or cocoon instead of sugar or silk. Major exceptions to this rule are meat products because the availability of data in the form of meat is much greater than it is in the form of livestock.

Farm-gate prices were taken from the various sources of the three governments. Import prices into the three countries were obtained from the FAO *Trade Yearbook* (1965). If the imports do not exist in farm-gate forms (e.g., imports of cocoon to the United States), the import prices in manufactured forms (e.g., silk) were multiplied by the ratios between the prices of the manufactured goods and their source as raw materials in the exporting country (e.g., the price of cocoon relative to the price of silk in Japan).

Prices at farm gate or at port thus obtained are shown in Table A-1 as they are converted to wheat-relative prices. The results of applying the aggregation procedures, as described above, with the weighting systems in Table A-1 to determine agricultural output are presented in Table A-2.

In Table A-2 Bangladesh was included as a part of Pakistan. In order to separate the agricultural output of Bangladesh from that of Pakistan, the Bangladesh output for 1957–62 was estimated as 53 percent of the output of former Pakistan including both East and West Pakistan; this percentage was the ratio of GDP generated in the crop and livestock sectors in East Pakistan to that of former Pakistan for 1959–62 (data from East Pakistan Bureau of Statistics, *Handbook of Economic Indicators of East Pakistan* [1965], p. 169, and Pakistan Finance Division, *Pakistan Basic Fact, 1977/78* [1980], p. 16).

Number of Male Workers in Agriculture (K4–K6)

The number of male workers in agriculture was estimated from the data on the economically active male population in agricultural occupations (agriculture, forestry, hunting, and fishing), published in *Labour Force Estimates and Projections, 1950–2000,* Vols. 1–4, and *Yearbook of Labor Statistics* (various issues) by the International Labor Organization, supplemented by FAO, *Production Yearbook* (various issues). Only males were counted so as to preserve the international comparability of data.

The economically active male population in agriculture proper was estimated from that in agricultural occupations by using the following formula:

$$L_{it} = r_{it} L'_{it}$$

where L is the economically active male population in agriculture; L' is that in agricultural occupations; r is the ratio of the output in agriculture to the output of agriculture, forestry, and fishing combined, both aggregated with Japan's wheat-relative prices in 1957–62 (w_J in Table A-1); and subscripts i and t represent, respectively, country and year. The data for r_{it} are presented in Table A-3.

This method is based on the assumption that labor productivities are equal between these agricultural occupations.

Agricultural Land Area (K7–K9)

The area of agricultural land, including permanent meadows and pastures, of the year as reported in FAO, *Production Yearbook* (various issues), was used as the land variable. The 1979 data were used for 1980 because data were available only up to 1979 when this study was conducted.

The land area data for Japan, Philippines, and Taiwan, for which FAO data were not available or involve obvious statistical errors, were taken from Japan Ministry of Agriculture, Forestry and Fisheries, *Sakumotsu Tokei* (Crop statistics) (various issues); Taiwan Provincial Government Department of Agriculture and Forestry, *Taiwan Agricultural Yearbook* (various issues); and Philippine National Census and Statistics Office, *1971 Census of Agriculture,* Vol. II, *National Summary* (undated).

Livestock (K10–K12)

Data for the numbers of livestock animals existing on farms are available in FAO, *Production Yearbook* (various issues). We have aggregated the various kinds of animals in livestock units. The weights for aggregation are camels, 1.1; buffalo, horses, and mules, 1.0; cattle and asses, 0.8; pigs, 0.2; sheep and goats, 0.1; poultry, 0.01.

Fertilizer Consumption (K13–K15)

The data on fertilizer input by total physical weights of N, P_2O_5, and K_2O contained in commercial fertilizers consumed are taken from FAO, *Fertilizer Annual Review* (various issues).

Tractor Horsepower (K16–K18)

In principle, tractor horsepower data were estimated by the following formula:

$$M_{it} = h_{it}N_{rit} + 5N_{git}$$

where M is total tractor horsepower; h is average horsepower per riding tractor; N_r is the number of riding tractors; N_g is the number of garden tractors; and subscripts i and t represent, respectively, country and year. Average horsepower per garden tractor was assumed to be five for all countries.

Data for the number of tractors were taken from FAO, *Production Yearbook* (various issues). Data for average horsepower per riding tractor were estimated by using extrapolation and interpolations from the data in the Organization for Economic Cooperation and Development, *Evolution de la motorization de l'agriculture et de la consommation et des prix des carburant dans les pays membres* (June 1963); European Community statistical office, *Enquête communautaire sur la structure des exploitations agricoles 1975*, Vol. II (1978); Australia Bureau of Statistics, *Receipts, Sales and Stocks of New Tractors* (various issues); Japan Ministry of Agriculture, Forestry and Fisheries, *Sekai Noringyo Census* (World census of agriculture and forestry) (various issues); U.S. Department of Agriculture, Economic Research Service, *Economic Indicators of the Farm Sector*, Statistical Bulletin 679 (1982).

It was assumed that average horsepowers in Canada and New Zealand were the same as for the United States and Australia, respectively. Data necessary for estimating average horsepowers were unavailable for many countries, especially less developed countries. For those countries it was assumed that the average horsepowers were 30 for 1960, 35 for 1970, and 40 for 1980. For the countries for which the data for the number of garden tractors were not available, the total horsepower of garden tractors was assumed as 5 percent of that of riding tractors.

Number of Farms (K19–K21)

Data for the number of farms (agricultural holdings) were collected from FAO, *Production Yearbook* (various issues) and a large number of government and private publications mostly reporting on the results of agricultural censuses (some of those publications are listed in Hayami and associates, *An International Comparison of Agricultural Production and Productivities*).

Literacy Ratios (K22–K24)

The data for adult literacy ratios were obtained mainly from United Nations Educational, Scientific, and Cultural Organizations (UNESCO), *Statistical Yearbook* (various issues); and World Bank, *World Development Report* (various issues).

School Enrollment Ratios (K25–K27)

The school enrollment ratios relate the actual total of the number enrolled in the first and second levels of education to the population of potential enrollment. Adjustments were made to minimize the effects of differences in the school systems among countries. The data were taken mainly from UNESCO, *Statistical Yearbook* (various issues).

The school enrollment ratio represents the increase in the level of general education, primary and secondary, more adequately than the level of education itself. To convert the enrollment ratio into a measure of the stock of education, we averaged the data for three specified years at five-year intervals: averaged 1950, 1955, and 1960 to obtain the 1960 series; averaged 1960, 1965, and 1970 to obtain the 1970 series; and averaged 1970, 1975, and 1979 to obtain the 1980 series.

Number of Agricultural College Graduates per
10,000 Male Farm Workers (K28–K30)

As a proxy variable for the level of advanced technical education in agriculture, we prepared a series of the number of graduates from agricultural colleges, the third level of education, per 10,000 male workers in agriculture. Sources of the data for the number of graduates are the same as for the school enrollment ratios. For the same reason as for the school enrollment ratios as well as for reducing the effect of large annual fluctuations in the number of graduates, the data were averaged for 1957 and 1960 to obtain the 1960 series; for 1960, 1965, and 1970 to obtain the 1970 series; and for 1970, 1975, and 1980 to obtain the 1980 series. The two-year averages were used for the 1960 series because of limitation in data availability.

Farm Wage Rate (K31–K33)

The farm wage rate is here defined as the wage received by a male farm worker per day, including board. The original source of data is FAO, *Production Yearbook* (various issues). Monthly, weekly, and hourly wages are converted into daily wages by assuming, respectively (a) twenty-two work days in a month, (b) five work days in a week, (c) eight work hours in a day, and (d) an addition of 10 percent of cash wages to the data that exclude board. The wage-rate data were compiled for 1955, 1965, and 1975 instead of 1960, 1970, and 1980 for the sake of analysis in the supplement of Chapter 6.

Ratio of Nonagricultural Labor (K34–K36)

The ratio is of the economically active male population in nonagricultural occupations (other than agriculture, forestry, hunting, and fishing) to the total economically active male population. The data source is the same as for series K34–K36.

Ratio of Arable Land (K37–K39)

The ratio of arable land area to total agricultural land area is from the same data source as for series K7–K9.

TABLE A-1. Weights for aggregating agricultural products: wheat-relative prices per metric ton, 1957–62*

Commodity	U.S.A. (w_U)	Japan (w_J)	India (w_I)
Grains			
Wheat	1.00	1.00	1.00
Barley	0.61	1.00	0.69
Buckwheat	0.74	1.24	0.84
Maize	0.63	0.72	0.78
Millet	0.68	0.74	0.87
Oats	0.63	0.70	0.69
Rice (rough)	1.58	1.61	0.94
Rye	0.58	0.77	0.69
Sorghum	0.55	0.81	0.81
Mixed grain	0.61	0.74	0.69
Starchy roots			
Cassava	0.16	0.11	0.58
Potatoes	0.57	0.27	0.58
Sweet potatoes	0.81	0.22	0.58
Sugar			
Beets, not processed	0.19	0.15	0.15
Cane, not processed	0.12	0.18	0.10
Pulses and oil crops			
Copra	0.84	0.48	3.10
Cottonseed	0.75	0.83	0.78
Groundnuts	3.39	2.55	1.21
Linseed	1.30	0.66	1.50
Olives	1.66	1.31	1.13
Palm kernels	1.13	1.44	3.10
Pulses (all)	2.12	1.94	0.84
Rapeseed	0.87	1.45	1.91
Sesame seed	4.56	3.98	2.07
Soybeans	1.16	1.50	1.22
Sunflower seed	2.50	1.17	1.11
Nuts			
Unshelled	13.14	2.31	5.24
Fruits			
Bananas	0.65	1.52	0.63
Citrus	0.98	1.15	1.40
Dates	2.05	0.55	3.33
Other fresh	1.27	0.94	1.79
Unspecified	1.13	1.05	1.79
Vegetables			
All	0.83	0.42	1.31
Livestock products			
Beef and veal	12.36	9.99	5.00
Mutton and lamb	12.58	5.03	5.00
Pork	9.51	7.36	5.00
Poultry	6.47	5.15	2.98
Eggs	7.35	5.12	5.24
Milk	1.36	0.76	1.21
Fibers			
Abaca	5.77	3.88	4.12
Cotton	10.30	6.06	2.17
Flax	5.50	3.37	6.27

TABLE A-1.   (*Continued*)

Commodity	U.S.A. (w_U)	Japan (w_J)	India (w_I)
Hemp	6.94	6.29	1.70
Henequen	2.54	2.30	2.41
Jute	3.11	2.30	1.93
Silk, cocoon basis	17.32	12.86	18.88
Sisal	2.54	2.30	2.41
Wool, greasy basis	14.44	13.52	14.58
Miscellaneous			
Cocoa	8.27	6.30	6.16
Coffee	10.84	7.82	8.21
Rubber	9.33	6.74	7.14
Tea	15.70	3.44	8.88
Tobacco	19.47	8.56	4.63
Timber	—	0.15[a]	—
Marine products			
Fish	—	1.44	—
Whale	—	13.96[b]	—

*Farm-gate values of 1 metric ton of wheat in native currencies were: 67.6 dollars in the U.S.A.; 36,072 yen in Japan; and 46.4 rupees in India. See sources and estimation procedures in the main text.

[a]Per cubic meter of round wood.

[b]Per whale.

TABLE A-2. Agricultural output, 1957–62, averages of 43 countries, in 1,000 wheat units

Country	U.S.A. weights (Y_U)	Japan weights (Y_J)	India weights (Y_I)	Composite $(Y = \sqrt[3]{Y_U Y_J Y_I})$
Argentina	63,698	49,814	43,378	51,626
Australia	49,800	38,451	38,841	42,054
Austria	11,414	7,908	9,260	9,419
Belgium (and Luxemburg)	14,312	9,392	10,911	11,361
Brazil	96,753	80,409	71,317	82,162
Canada	43,960	33,340	33,554	36,633
Chile	7,605	5,658	6,705	6,607
Colombia	19,973	16,310	14,030	16,594
Denmark	18,411	12,528	12,889	14,378
Egypt	20,890	15,986	16,714	17,737
Finland	7,145	4,578	5,832	5,756
France	101,537	71,462	87,972	86,093
Germany, Fed. Rep.	70,189	48,047	54,999	57,023
Greece	13,222	8,813	11,150	10,911
India	216,477	193,272	153,821	185,986
Ireland	9,117	6,193	6,562	7,182
Israel	2,412	1,940	2,368	2,229
Italy	72,348	49,281	69,189	62,709
Japan	60,770	47,646	49,828	52,436
Libya	599	338	533	476
Mauritius	630	834	534	655
Mexico	32,811	26,572	23,483	27,354
Netherlands	21,250	13,021	16,866	16,709
New Zealand	20,724	13,149	14,702	15,882
Norway	4,118	2,496	3,174	3,195
Pakistan	56,317	40,345	40,454	45,125
Paraguay	1,215	1,066	1,183	1,153
Peru	9,046	7,100	7,252	7,751
Philippines	16,057	14,133	14,715	14,946
Portugal	9,020	6,306	8,794	7,937
South Africa	19,218	15,294	15,414	16,547
Spain	45,107	28,507	38,539	36,727
Sri Lanka	6,617	3,483	5,124	4,906
Surinam	258	206	162	205
Sweden	12,177	8,378	9,721	9,971
Switzerland	8,346	5,355	7,121	6,827
Syria	5,334	4,027	4,256	4,504
Taiwan	10,122	8,507	8,493	9,009
Turkey	37,213	25,300	34,347	31,856
U.K.	49,882	32,493	35,510	38,605
U.S.	435,480	330,953	304,332	352,619
Venezuela	5,960	5,694	4,738	5,437
Yugoslavia	20,133	14,475	17,087	17,075

TABLE A-3.   Percentage of output in agriculture to output in agriculture, forestry, and fishing combined (r)

	1960	1970	1980
Argentina	96	97	97
Australia	94	96	97
Austria	82	84	85
Bangladesh	95	94	92
Belgium (and Luxemburg)	95	96	97
Brazil	83	86	83
Canada	69	70	69
Chile	80	70	66
Colombia	84	85	83
Denmark	91	86	83
Egypt	98	99	99
Finland	40	48	55
France	91	94	95
Germany, FR	91	93	93
Greece	93	96	97
India	98	93	90
Ireland	98	98	98
Israel	99	99	99
Italy	94	96	98
Japan	71	74	76
Libya	68	86	91
Mauritius	99	98	99
Mexico	96	94	95
Netherlands	95	93	97
New Zealand	94	93	93
Norway	39	32	35
Pakistan	95	95	92
Paraguay	80	74	76
Peru	57	39	65
Philippines	90	76	79
Portugal	80	82	80
South Africa	92	83	89
Spain	90	90	93
Sri Lanka	97	85	81
Surinam	80	90	91
Sweden	55	50	54
Switzerland	91	91	92
Syria	100	100	100
Taiwan	94	95	96
Turkey	95	93	88
U.K.	94	95	96
U.S.A.	87	90	90
Venezuela	87	89	90
Yugoslavia	85	88	91

TABLE A-4. Major intercountry statistical series

Country	Agricultural Output			Number of male workers in agriculture		
	1960 (K1)	1970 (K2)	1980 (K3)	1960 (K4)	1970 (K5)	1980 (K6)
	1,000 wheat units			1,000's		
Argentina	51,626	60,407	77,872	1,478	1,373	1,221
Australia	42,054	57,760	71,489	405	341	279
Austria	9,419	11,515	12,798	309	205	141
Bangladesh	23,916	30,373	34,200	12,140	15,633	19,097
Belgium (and Luxemburg)	11,361	14,486	15,726	239	147	90
Brazil	82,162	110,026	150,425	8,852	10,622	11,380
Canada	36,633	49,262	57,692	554	432	298
Chile	6,607	7,876	8,539	581	466	432
Colombia	16,594	22,391	31,324	1,999	2,025	1,826
Denmark	14,378	15,221	16,275	310	173	124
Egypt	17,737	23,713	26,153	4,024	4,839	5,644
Finland	5,756	7,662	8,645	189	145	83
France	86,093	114,982	130,186	2,660	1,845	1,279
Germany, FR	57,023	71,631	79,113	1,535	950	696
Greece	10,911	15,644	20,242	1,200	907	786
India	185,986	228,552	286,384	86,352	86,947	92,030
Ireland	7,182	8,964	11,623	358	264	198
Israel	2,229	4,554	6,107	86	78	60
Italy	62,709	77,187	87,575	4,319	2,567	1,826
Japan	52,436	67,536	66,920	5,097	3,661	2,404
Libya	476	681	1,264	133	141	98
Mauritius	655	806	819	65	67	77
Mexico	27,354	39,914	51,072	5,316	5,886	6,825
Netherlands	16,709	21,438	28,694	388	339	263
New Zealand	15,882	21,537	24,671	113	104	105
Norway	3,195	3,342	3,760	103	46	40
Pakistan	21,209	32,662	40,721	6,768	8,674	9,805
Paraguay	1,153	1,582	2,218	235	265	341
Peru	7,751	10,186	11,273	806	609	1,112
Philippines	14,946	19,922	29,289	4,542	4,326	4,987
Portugal	7,937	9,175	8,071	1,112	769	432
South Africa	16,547	24,269	28,671	1,482	1,380	1,715
Spain	36,727	50,143	67,756	3,974	2,478	1,512
Sri Lanka	4,906	6,553	7,698	1,353	1,409	1,597
Surinam	205	371	568	15	14	12
Sweden	9,971	10,542	11,905	232	120	97
Switzerland	6,827	7,860	9,161	234	167	118
Syria	4,504	5,593	9,013	623	728	901
Taiwan	9,009	14,054	17,117	1,261	1,448	1,384
Turkey	31,856	45,181	60,367	5,245	5,166	4,746
U.K.	38,605	50,285	57,085	821	572	491
U.S.A.	352,619	414,416	497,438	3,759	2,566	1,745
Venezuela	5,437	9,244	12,197	695	660	537
Yugoslavia	17,075	22,825	28,531	2,591	2,318	1,989

TABLE A-4.   (*Continued*)

Country	Agricultural land area			Livestock		
	1960 (K7)	1970 (K8)	1980 (K9)	1960 (K10)	1970 (K11)	1980 (K12)
	1,000 hectares			1,000 livestock units		
Argentina	171,500	177,701	178,420	46,043	48,821	52,784
Australia	467,000	493,359	492,293	30,223	36,966	36,063
Austria	4,052	3,896	3,662	2,794	2,765	3,054
Bangladesh	9,546	9,695	9,730	16,645	24,127	30,168
Belgium (and Luxemburg)	1,857	1,734	1,560	3,030	3,674	3,852
Brazil	148,000	188,122	207,720	87,705	111,655	98,442
Canada	62,848	67,520	68,100	10,963	12,169	13,171
Chile	14,000	16,195	17,678	3,906	4,028	4,596
Colombia	21,047	22,138	22,800	15,194	18,348	23,434
Denmark	3,127	2,975	2,916	4,746	4,184	4,484
Egypt	2,569	2,843	2,848	5,322	5,578	4,719
Finland	2,849	2,869	2,589	2,074	1,890	1,784
France	34,586	32,495	31,853	20,949	23,071	25,185
Germany, FR	14,254	13,579	13,217	14,939	16,607	17,888
Greece	8,911	9,155	9,175	3,595	3,049	2,963
India	174,820	178,050	181,820	207,240	211,720	225,008
Ireland	4,715	4,794	4,877	4,695	5,715	6,336
Israel	1,210	1,227	1,231	267	373	634
Italy	18,430	17,680	17,608	11,762	12,268	11,402
Japan	6,071	5,797	5,474	4,558	6,584	8,380
Libya	9,809	9,567	9,264	694	412	1,159
Mauritius	98	112	114	38	74	97
Mexico	102,908	100,258	97,719	37,599	36,651	42,647
Netherlands	2,317	2,195	2,034	4,202	5,313	6,952
New Zealand	13,128	13,520	14,443	10,284	13,302	13,810
Norway	1,033	954	900	1,398	1,139	1,185
Pakistan	23,489	24,332	25,175	23,489	31,819	33,255
Paraguay	14,300	15,445	16,395	4,352	5,373	4,965
Peru	29,720	29,933	30,550	6,656	6,989	6,816
Philippines	7,076	7,795	8,442	6,305	8,052	6,971
Portugal	4,660	4,305	4,085	2,256	2,134	2,585
South Africa	102,448	97,200	95,720	15,523	14,878	14,731
Spain	32,884	32,119	31,538	9,277	8,583	8,699
Sri Lanka	2,239	2,418	2,580	2,093	2,307	2,270
Surinam	46	47	59	38	47	48
Sweden	4,282	3,743	3,720	2,797	2,176	2,312
Switzerland	2,017	2,024	2,021	1,864	2,027	2,216
Syria	14,566	13,459	13,960	1,110	1,455	2,078
Taiwan	871	907	918	1,180	1,061	1,624
Turkey	54,018	55,178	55,445	20,255	20,721	22,740
U.K.	19,894	18,879	18,452	14,971	15,804	16,875
U.S.A.	439,941	432,974	430,331	100,834	115,543	117,548
Venezuela	19,174	21,082	22,207	6,544	8,186	10,466
Yugoslavia	14,923	14,626	14,239	8,541	7,675	7,994

TABLE A-4. (*Continued*)

Country	Fertilizer consumption (N + P₂O₅ + K₂O)			Tractor horsepower		
	1960 (K13)	1970 (K14)	1980 (K15)	1960 (K16)	1970 (K17)	1980 (K18)
	1,000 metric tons			1,000 hp.		
Argentina	14	71	87	3,485	6,086	8,610
Australia	605	1,084	1,249	7,782	15,060	20,219
Austria	221	398	439	2,247	8,836	12,928
Bangladesh	17	111	281	7	48	128
Belgium (and Luxemburg)	377	512	469	1,405	2,887	5,881
Brazil	191	661	2,717	1,972	5,755	13,440
Canada	324	805	1,814	16,800	29,111	40,499
Chile	77	140	126	473	1,121	869
Colombia	38	148	261	741	1,025	1,155
Denmark	386	569	657	3,227	6,808	9,692
Egypt	204	331	526	220	645	1,029
Finland	216	431	489	2,288	5,498	8,568
France	2,183	4,172	5,200	18,996	50,460	76,126
Germany, FR	2,307	2,997	3,363	16,173	39,432	59,173
Greece	144	310	508	818	2,370	5,460
India	340	1,614	3,692	686	2,315	13,649
Ireland	174	366	525	1,243	3,029	5,727
Israel	32	51	77	214	579	1,075
Italy	816	1,236	1,764	7,536	23,769	46,527
Japan	1,577	2,154	2,105	5,234	19,263	42,544
Libya	3	11	42	71	128	546
Mauritius	18	22	25	9	10	14
Mexico	188	511	1,056	1,229	4,235	4,788
Netherlands	467	598	646	1,857	5,814	7,967
New Zealand	263	425	533	2,452	4,402	5,298
Norway	145	189	242	1,568	3,248	5,250
Pakistan	27	253	709	110	772	3,228
Paraguay	1	4	2	17	81	130
Peru	76	76	120	204	403	571
Philippines	66	165	283	128	198	672
Portugal	123	160	250	309	1,034	2,730
South Africa	213	508	838	2,250	8,085	7,560
Spain	659	1,101	1,551	1,273	9,455	20,647
Sri Lanka	57	96	117	13	281	904
Surinam	1	2	4	17	33	57
Sweden	286	463	517	4,682	6,064	7,896
Switzerland	99	141	159	652	3,095	3,717
Syria	9	31	80	123	332	1,065
Taiwan	173	191	393	37	121	450
Turkey	45	370	1,130	1,375	3,657	18,501
U.K.	984	1,797	1,958	12,989	18,108	22,981
U.S.A.	7,225	14,346	19,147	155,540	204,372	264,915
Venezuela	13	51	172	320	687	1,554
Yugoslavia	253	575	777	1,134	2,940	16,174

TABLE A-4.   (*Continued*)

Country	Number of farms		
	1960 (K19)	1970 (K20)	1980 (K21)
	1000's		
Argentina	552	538	521
Australia	252	249	222
Austria	397	381	365
Bangladesh	6,139	7,180	8,579
Belgium (and Luxemburg)	269	192	130
Brazil	4,749	4,932	5,054
Canada	481	366	317
Chile	174	287	343
Colombia	1,210	1,177	1,143
Denmark	194	143	120
Egypt	2,946	3,285	3,432
Finland	270	264	188
France	1,994	1,588	1,262
Germany, FR	1,618	1,244	928
Greece	1,156	1,047	922
India	48,882	70,493	88,918
Ireland	278	267	253
Israel	70	63	48
Italy	4,294	3,621	3,532
Japan	6,057	5,354	4,661
Libya	146	155	108
Mauritius	22	23	26
Mexico	1,365	1,511	1,752
Netherlands	301	185	143
New Zealand	77	65	72
Norway	198	155	127
Pakistan	6,016	7,710	8,715
Paraguay	161	182	234
Peru	870	657	1,200
Philippines	2,166	2,354	2,508
Portugal	835	803	770
South Africa	110	91	68
Spain	3,008	2,571	2,134
Sri Lanka	1,174	1,223	1,386
Surinam	n.a.	n.a.	n.a.
Sweden	233	155	118
Switzerland	185	149	102
Syria	418	439	460
Taiwan	808	916	891
Turkey	3,560	3,059	2,810
U.K.	396	329	281
U.S.A.	3,711	2,730	2,227
Venezuela	320	288	259
Yugoslavia	2,624	2,600	2,576

TABLE A-4. (*Continued*)

Country	Literacy ratios			School enrollment ratios		
	1960 (K22)	1970 (K23)	1980 (K24)	1960 (K25)	1970 (K26)	1980 (K27)
		percent			percent	
Argentina	91.4	92.6	93.0	70.0	77.0	86.0
Australia	98.5	100.0	100.0	81.0	83.0	85.0
Austria	99.0	99.0	99.0	74.0	81.0	82.0
Bangladesh	21.6	24.5	26.0	28.0	35.0	46.0
Belgium (and Luxemburg)	98.0	99.0	99.0	90.0	92.0	93.0
Brazil	61.0	66.2	76.0	38.0	55.0	72.0
Canada	97.5	98.0	99.0	84.0	91.0	94.0
Chile	83.6	89.0	88.0	63.0	79.0	93.0
Colombia	62.5	78.5	83.0	39.0	54.0	74.0
Denmark	98.5	99.0	99.0	85.0	88.0	90.0
Egypt	25.8	33.5	44.0	36.0	50.0	59.0
Finland	99.0	100.0	100.0	82.0	87.0	88.0
France	98.0	99.0	99.0	80.0	90.0	94.0
Germany, FR	98.5	99.0	99.0	68.0	73.0	79.0
Greece	80.4	84.4	88.0	70.0	79.0	89.0
India	27.8	33.4	36.0	28.0	47.0	51.0
Ireland	98.5	98.0	98.0	70.0	82.0	96.0
Israel	84.2	87.9	88.0	76.0	83.0	86.0
Italy	90.7	93.9	98.0	60.0	72.0	83.0
Japan	97.8	99.0	99.0	88.0	90.0	94.0
Libya	18.2	39.0	60.0	20.0	43.0	60.0
Mauritius	60.8	74.1	84.6	57.0	65.0	71.0
Mexico	65.4	74.2	81.0	43.0	59.0	78.0
Netherlands	98.5	99.0	99.0	80.0	84.0	93.0
New Zealand	98.5	99.0	99.0	88.0	91.0	93.0
Norway	98.5	99.0	99.0	83.0	87.0	93.0
Pakistan	15.4	20.7	24.0	16.0	25.0	32.0
Paraguay	74.6	80.1	84.0	58.0	63.0	67.0
Peru	61.1	72.5	80.0	50.0	67.0	82.0
Philippines	71.9	82.6	90.0	68.0	83.0	88.0
Portugal	62.0	71.0	70.0	54.0	69.0	85.0
South Africa	57.0	60.0	65.0	53.0	64.0	74.0
Spain	86.7	90.2	94.0	52.0	70.0	90.0
Sri Lanka	75.0	77.6	85.0	68.0	74.0	69.0
Surinam	72.5	65.0	65.0	73.0	75.0	75.0
Sweden	98.5	99.0	99.0	79.0	84.0	91.0
Switzerland	98.5	99.0	99.0	65.0	61.0	65.0
Syria	29.5	40.0	58.0	43.0	55.0	70.0
Taiwan	60.9	79.4	86.4	60.0	75.0	82.0
Turkey	38.1	51.3	60.0	40.0	56.0	68.0
U.K.	98.5	99.0	99.0	85.0	87.0	91.0
U.S.A.	97.8	99.0	99.0	99.0	99.0	100.0
Venezuela	63.3	76.5	82.0	50.0	69.0	74.0
Yugoslavia	76.5	83.5	85.0	62.0	80.0	84.0

TABLE A-4. (*Continued*)

Country	Number of agricultural college graduates per 10,000 male farm workers		
	1960 (K28)	1970 (K29)	1980 (K30)
	number		
Argentina	2.75	3.42	9.43
Australia	4.91	18.27	40.43
Austria	5.79	9.41	12.41
Bangladesh	0.10	0.14	0.23
Belgium (and Luxemburg)	10.75	19.73	54.11
Brazil	0.49	0.98	3.20
Canada	9.35	17.78	75.81
Chile	1.08	4.89	14.65
Colombia	0.30	1.55	4.50
Denmark	5.55	12.95	22.98
Egypt	2.14	5.33	10.79
Finland	6.40	12.83	39.40
France	2.11	3.84	4.81
Germany, FR	7.39	11.43	31.98
Greece	0.90	3.02	6.62
India	0.39	0.76	0.95
Ireland	3.91	7.31	11.06
Israel	7.56	20.13	36.33
Italy	1.42	2.54	7.10
Japan	12.63	24.91	57.52
Libya	0.23	0.78	9.49
Mauritius	4.62	5.37	4.81
Mexico	0.11	0.38	2.59
Netherlands	10.31	18.58	42.05
New Zealand	16.28	37.60	58.67
Norway	9.32	30.00	47.50
Pakistan	0.43	0.71	0.87
Paraguay	0.94	1.85	3.43
Peru	1.63	4.86	4.61
Philippines	1.26	2.51	8.92
Portugal	0.55	0.92	8.40
South Africa	0.91	1.56	1.54
Spain	0.79	1.41	5.53
Sri Lanka	0.04	0.20	0.39
Surinam	n.a.	n.a.	n.a.
Sweden	6.55	18.00	34.02
Switzerland	5.26	5.75	17.03
Syria	1.84	1.04	5.21
Taiwan	4.87	8.95	16.20
Turkey	0.69	1.33	1.60
U.K.	7.49	18.13	35.60
U.S.A.	21.21	45.52	135.14
Venezuela	0.68	2.42	10.48
Yugoslavia	3.59	6.64	9.46

TABLE A-4. (*Continued*)

	Farm wage rate per day		
Country	1955 (K31)	1965 (K32)	1975 (K33)
	U.S. dollars		
Argentina	n.a.	n.a.	2.67
Australia	n.a.	n.a.	n.a.
Austria	1.79	3.53	9.22
Bangladesh	n.a.	n.a.	n.a.
Belgium (and Luxemburg)	3.17	4.92	13.74
Brazil	n.a.	n.a.	n.a.
Canada	6.40	7.80	16.39
Chile	n.a.	n.a.	n.a.
Colombia	n.a.	n.a.	n.a.
Denmark	3.36	6.47	19.12
Egypt	n.a.	n. a.	n.a.
Finland	3.12	4.16	10.32
France	1.53	2.77	6.00
Germany, FR	2.20	5.47	15.25
Greece	n.a.	n.a.	n.a.
India	0.25	0.40	0.43
Ireland	2.38	4.00	10.05
Israel	n.a.	n.a.	7.59
Italy	n.a.	n.a.	n.a.
Japan	0.85	2.28	9.19
Libya	n.a.	n.a.	n.a.
Mauritius	0.67	1.56	1.49
Mexico	0.58	1.11	n.a.
Netherlands	n.a.	n.a.	16.46
New Zealand	5.08	5.86	10.42
Norway	3.78	6.77	20.57
Pakistan	n.a.	n.a.	0.47
Paraguay	n.a.	n.a.	n.a.
Peru	0.78	n.a.	n.a.
Philippines	1.02	0.97	0.67
Portugal	0.71	1.31	3.96
South Africa	n.a.	n.a.	n.a.
Spain	n.a.	n.a.	4.48
Sri Lanka	0.52	0.59	0.68
Surinam	n.a.	n.a.	3.45
Sweden	4.48	9.28	28.25
Switzerland	n.a.	n.a.	n.a.
Syria	n.a.	n.a.	1.23
Taiwan	n.a.	n.a.	n.a.
Turkey	0.80	n.a.	3.74
U.K.	4.29	7.26	13.16
U.S.A.	5.36	7.33	14.65
Venezuela	n.a.	n.a.	n.a.
Yugoslavia	n.a.	n.a.	5.27

TABLE A-4.   (*Continued*)

Country	Ratio of nonagricultural labor		
	1960 (K34)	1970 (K35)	1980 (K36)
	percent		
Argentina	76.0	79.7	83.5
Australia	86.1	90.3	93.4
Austria	81.3	87.3	91.8
Bangladesh	14.1	15.1	12.9
Belgium (and Luxemburg)	90.7	94.6	96.7
Brazil	43.3	48.1	55.2
Canada	83.3	89.4	93.8
Chile	63.1	70.4	76.5
Colombia	39.5	51.9	67.8
Denmark	76.4	86.3	93.9
Egypt	40.8	43.7	47.6
Finland	61.1	75.5	88.7
France	77.6	85.7	91.1
Germany, FR	89.8	94.0	96.0
Greece	50.3	62.7	67.9
India	30.4	36.2	43.6
Ireland	56.2	67.6	77.6
Israel	84.5	89.6	93.8
Italy	69.7	81.7	87.5
Japan	73.7	84.8	91.2
Libya	44.8	67.1	82.8
Mauritius	61.3	66.9	71.0
Mexico	40.9	47.6	55.7
Netherlands	87.4	89.9	93.3
New Zealand	81.9	85.5	87.5
Norway	75.6	86.4	89.7
Pakistan	40.1	42.2	47.1
Paraguay	34.4	37.2	40.2
Peru	42.4	49.1	57.1
Philippines	29.9	37.9	48.5
Portugal	50.3	63.0	78.9
South Africa	63.4	69.2	71.6
Spain	53.2	71.1	84.1
Sri Lanka	46.6	48.1	51.4
Surinam	69.7	76.7	85.7
Sweden	81.8	89.6	92.4
Switzerland	85.1	90.9	94.2
Syria	46.1	50.8	53.1
Taiwan	48.9	60.1	72.2
Turkey	32.9	43.2	54.5
U.K.	94.7	96.4	96.9
U.S.A.	91.3	94.8	96.9
Venezuela	59.0	68.5	81.7
Yugoslavia	44.0	55.0	66.7

TABLE A-4. (*Continued*)

Country	Ratio of arable land		
	1960 (K37)	1970 (K38)	1980 (K39)
		percent	
Argentina	14.6	18.7	19.7
Australia	6.4	8.8	8.9
Austria	43.3	43.1	44.3
Bangladesh	94.3	93.8	93.8
Belgium (and Luxemburg)	55.1	52.8	54.3
Brazil	18.9	18.1	19.6
Canada	66.6	64.3	65.1
Chile	28.6	32.1	33.0
Colombia	24.0	22.8	22.8
Denmark	89.0	89.9	91.0
Egypt	96.6	96.5	96.5
Finland	93.7	94.9	93.6
France	62.0	58.8	59.5
Germany, FR	60.0	59.5	60.6
Greece	41.5	42.7	42.7
India	92.2	92.7	93.3
Ireland	29.2	23.9	20.0
Israel	34.1	33.3	33.6
Italy	72.3	70.3	70.7
Japan	98.9	95.1	89.6
Libya	25.6	26.3	27.7
Mauritius	92.9	93.8	93.9
Mexico	23.1	23.4	23.8
Netherlands	44.8	39.5	42.4
New Zealand	3.8	6.2	5.9
Norway	81.7	85.3	89.6
Pakistan	81.7	79.5	80.1
Paraguay	5.6	6.1	7.3
Peru	8.8	9.4	11.2
Philippines	94.6	91.5	89.1
Portugal	88.6	87.7	87.0
South Africa	11.8	14.6	15.3
Spain	62.4	63.9	65.1
Sri Lanka	80.4	81.8	83.0
Surinam	87.0	80.9	93.1
Sweden	84.0	81.6	80.5
Switzerland	21.7	19.0	19.6
Syria	41.3	43.9	40.7
Taiwan	99.8	99.8	99.7
Turkey	47.0	49.6	50.6
U.K.	36.7	38.3	37.4
U.S.A.	42.0	44.3	48.4
Venezuela	27.1	25.1	24.1
Yugoslavia	56.0	56.1	55.5

APPENDIX B: Time-Series Data of Labor and Land Productivities of Five Selected Countries, 1880–1980

Historical time-series data of agricultural output per male farm worker and per hectare of agricultural land for selected countries (the United States, Japan, Denmark, France, and the United Kingdom) in wheat units are compiled so that they are comparable with the cross-country data; these are the data for Figure 5-5 in Chapter 5. The procedures are as follows: (a) the index of agricultural output net of inputs supplied from the agricultural sector is divided by indices of the number of male farm workers and of agricultural land area to produce the indices of output per worker and per hectare; and (b) these indices are spliced to the cross-country outputs per worker and per hectare for 1960 (Table 5-1, Chapter 5) in wheat units. These procedures are adopted to adjust for the differences between the time-series labor force and land area data that are collected for intertemporal comparability and the cross-country data that are collected for international comparability. The sources of data and the estimation procedures are summarized in Tables B-1 to B-5. Although we tried to make the time-series data in this appendix as comparable as possible with the intercountry cross-section data in Chapter 5 (and Appendix A), the available time-series data by country are not exactly the same as the intercountry data. Therefore, some of the labor and land productivity measures for 1980 in this appendix diverge slightly from those in Table 5-5.

In principle, data for a flow variable (agricultural output) are the average for the five years centering on the years shown, and those for stock variables (labor force and land area) are measured in the years shown.

The authors are indebted to Toshihiko Kawagoe and Sachiko Yamashita Sidhu for revising and updating the data in this appendix.

TABLE B-1.   Time-series data for the United States, 1880–1980

Year	Agricultural output (US 1)	Number of male workers (US 2)	Agricultural land (US 3)	Output per male worker (US 4)	Output per hectare (US 5)	Output per male worker (US 6)	Output per hectare (US 7)	Percent of male workers in nonagriculture (US 8)
	Index 1960 = 100							
	percent					WU	WU	percent
1880	29	200	46	15	64	13.0	0.5	45
1885	32	214	50	15	65	13.3	0.5	
1890	35	230	54	15	66	13.5	0.5	52
1895	40	238	64	17	64	14.9	0.5	
1900	46	248	73	18	63	16.3	0.5	57
1905	47	254	75	19	64	16.4	0.5	
1910	48	260	77	19	64	16.4	0.5	64
1915	51	259	80	20	65	17.5	0.5	
1920	53	256	83	21	64	18.3	0.5	69
1925	56	246	80	23	71	20.3	0.6	
1930	60	236	88	25	69	22.5	0.5	74
1935	56	224	94	25	60	22.0	0.5	
1940	68	214	94	32	73	25.4	0.6	78
1945	78	186	102	42	77	36.9	0.6	
1950	84	160	104	52	82	46.5	0.6	85
1955	90	130	104	69	87	61.5	0.7	
1960	100	100	100	100	100	88.8	0.8	91
1965	107	77	99	140	108	124.2	0.9	
1970	116	54	99	217	118	192.6	0.9	96
1975	126	49	98	255	129	226.3	1.0	
1980	146	45	97	324	151	287.8	1.2	97

(US 1) Index calculated from Series U1 in Table C-2, Appendix C.

(US 2) Index calculated from Series U4 in Table C-2, Appendix C.

(US 3) Index calculated from Series U5 in Table C-2, Appendix C.

(US 4) (US 1)/(US 2).

(US 5) (US 1)/(US 3).

(US 6) Index in column (US 4) spliced with intercountry cross-section series of output per worker for 1957–62 (Table 4-1, Chapter 4).

(US 7) Index in column (US 5) spliced with intercountry cross-section series of output per hectare for 1957–62 (Table 4-1, Chapter 4).

(US 8) *Sources:* Same as the source for (US 2); see Appendix C.

TABLE B-2.　Time-series data for Japan, 1880–1980

Year	Index					Output per male worker (JA 6)	Output per hectare (JA 7)	Percent of male workers in nonagriculture (JA 8)
	Agricultural output (JA 1)	Number of male workers (JA 2)	Agricultural land (JA 3)	Output per male worker (JA 4)	Output per hectare (JA 5)			
	1960 = 100					WU	WU	percent
1880	30	134	78	22	38	2.3	3.3	21
1885	33	134	79	25	42	2.6	3.6	24
1890	36	134	81	27	44	2.8	3.8	28
1895	37	135	83	27	45	2.8	3.9	31
1900	41	136	86	30	48	3.1	4.1	35
1905	46	136	87	34	53	3.5	4.6	38
1910	51	136	92	38	55	3.9	4.7	43
1915	58	132	95	44	61	4.5	5.2	47
1920	61	122	99	50	62	5.2	5.3	52
1925	62	119	97	52	64	5.4	5.5	55
1930	67	122	98	55	68	5.7	5.8	57
1935	71	121	101	59	70	6.1	6.0	61
1940	71	102	101	70	70	7.2	6.0	64
1945	59	98	95	60	62	6.2	5.3	62
1950	66	124	96	53	69	5.5	5.9	60
1955	80	118	99	68	81	7.0	7.0	66
1960	100	100	100	100	100	10.3	8.6	74
1965	113	73	99	155	114	16.0	9.8	80
1970	127	64	95	198	134	20.4	11.5	85
1975	132	48	92	275	143	28.3	12.3	89
1980	146	43	90	340	162	35.0	13.9	91

(JA 1) Index calculated from Series J 1 in Table C-3, Appendix C.

(JA 2) Index calculated from Series J 4 in Table C-3, Appendix C.

(JA 3) Index calculated from Series J 6 in Table C-3, Appendix C.

(JA 4) (JA 1)/(JA 2).

(JA 5) (JA 1)/(JA 3).

(JA 6) Index in column (JA 4) spliced with intercountry cross-section series of output per worker for 1957-62 (Table 5-1, Chapter 5).

(JA 7) Index in column (JA 5) spliced with intercountry cross-section series of output per hectare for 1957–62 (Table 5-1, Chapter 5).

(JA 8) Percentages calculated from the population census data for census years; linear interpolations for intercensus; and the percentage in 1920 (the first census year) multiplied by the ratios of the number of gainful workers in agriculture to the total number of gainful workers in Kazushi Ohkawa et al., *The Growth Rate of Japanese Economy* (Tokyo, 1957). Note that Series (JA 8) are not consistent with Series (K34)–(K36) in Table A-4, because the former are in the census definition of gainful workers and the latter are in the definition of economically active population.

TABLE B-3. Time-series data for Denmark, 1880–1980

Year	Index 1960 = 100							Percent of male workers in nonagriculture (DE 8)
	Agricultural output (DE 1)	Number of male workers (DE 2)	Agricultural land (DE 3)	Output per male worker (DE 4)	Output per hectare (DE 5)	Output per male worker (DE 6)	Output per hectare (DE 7)	
	percent					WU	WU	percent
1880	24	107	92	22	26	10.5	1.2	46
1885	25	107	93	23	26	10.9	1.2	
1890	27	108	94	26	29	11.9	1.3	49
1895	29	108	94	27	31	12.6	1.4	
1900	31	103	94	30	33	14.1	1.5	53
1905	35	111	94	31	37	14.8	1.7	
1910	41	114	93	36	44	16.9	2.0	55
1915	43	118	93	36	46	17.1	2.1	
1920	44	130	103	34	43	16.1	2.0	58
1925	48	133	104	36	46	16.9	2.1	
1930	66	131	104	51	64	23.9	2.9	62
1935	69	129	105	53	65	25.2	3.0	
1940	63	129	104	49	60	23.0	2.8	67
1945	60	122	103	49	59	23.4	2.7	
1950	76	113	102	67	75	31.9	3.4	77
1955	90	111	101	81	81	38.4	3.7	74
1960	100	100	100	100	100	47.4	4.6	77
1965	110	80	97	137	113	65.1	5.3	
1970	113	54	95	209	119	100.0	5.5	89
1975	117	44	94	268	125	127.3	5.8	91
1980	128	40	94	319	138	151.4	6.4	91

(DE 1) Index of gross agricultural output net of intermediate goods produced in agriculture. *Sources:* Kjeld Bjerke and Niels Ussing, *Studier Over Danmarks National Produkt, 1870–1950,* p. 144; for 1960–80, USDA, *Indices of Agricultural Production in Western Europe, 1950–68,* ERS-Foreign 266 (July 1969), pp. 1, 2; USDA, ERS, *Agricultural Situation in Western Europe, Review of 1972 and Outlook for 1973,* ERS-F352 (April 1973), p.1; USDA, Economics, Statistics and Cooperatives Service, *Indices of Agricultural and Food Production for Europe and the USSR,* Statistical Bulletin 620 (June 1979), p. 21; USDA, ERS, *World Indices of Agricultural and Food Production, 1972–81,* Statistical Bulletin 689 (August 1982), p. 53; 1980: 1979–81 average.

(DE 2) Index calculated from the data of the economically active males in agriculture excluding fishing, hunting, and forestry. Males in agriculture are estimated as a percentage of the total agricultural labor force given by Bjerke with data from Dovring of males in agriculture for 1900, 1930, and 1950. 1976 figure is used for 1975. *Sources:* Bjerke and Ussing, *Studier Over Danmarks National Produkt,* p.142; Folke Dovring, *Land and Labor in Europe in the Twentieth Century,* 3rd ed. (The Hague: Martines Nijhoff, 1965), p. 63; 1960, 1965, 1970: population census; 1976: Registerfolketællingen, 1976; 1980: Registerbaseret beskæftigelsesstatistik 1980.

(DE 3) Index calculated from the data of agricultural land including temporary fallow and grass plus permanent pasture. *Sources:* Einar Jensen, *Danish Agriculture* (Copenhagen: J. H. Schultz Forlag, 1937), p. 389; Danmarks Statistik, *Land Brusstatistik, 1900–1965* (Copenhagen: 1968), pp. 8–9; *Denmark's Statistik,* various issues.

(DE 4) (DE 1)/(DE 2).

(DE 5) (DE 1)/(DE 3).

(DE 6) Index in column (DE 4) spliced with intercountry cross-section series of output per worker for 1957–62 (Table 4-1, Chapter 4).

(DE 7) Index in column (DE 5) spliced with intercountry cross-section series of output per hectare for 1957–62 (Table 4-1, Chapter 4).

(DE 8) Percentage of males economically active in nonagriculture estimated from percentage of labor force in nonagriculture given by Bjerke by splicing ILO data of males in nonagriculture at 1950, 1955 average. *Source:* Bjerke and Ussing, *Studier Over Danmarks National Produkt,* p. 142; ILO, *Yearbook of Labor Statistics,* various issues.

TABLE B-4. Time-series data for France, 1880–1980

			Index 1960 = 100					Percent of
Year	Agricultural output (FR 1)	Number of male workers (FR 2)	Agricultural land (FR 3)	Output per male worker (FR 4)	Output per hectare (FR 5)	Output per male worker (FR 6)	Output per hectare (FR 7)	male workers in nonagriculture (FR 8)
			percent			WU	WU	percent
1880	43	193	100	22	43	7.4	1.1	51
1885	43	183	100	24	43	7.9	1.1	
1890	44	178	99	25	45	8.3	1.1	55
1895	46	200	100	23	46	7.6	1.1	
1900	47	195	101	24	47	8.1	1.2	56
1905	50	192	104	26	48	8.8	1.2	
1910	53	190	106	28	50	9.3	1.2	60
1915	53	183	106	29	50	9.8	1.3	
1920	54	176	104	30	52	10.2	1.3	60
1925	58	166	105	35	55	11.6	1.4	
1930	62	157	103	40	60	13.2	1.5	67
1935	62	150	101	41	61	13.8	1.5	
1940	57	150	97	38	58	12.6	1.5	
1945	52	149	93	35	56	11.6	1.4	67
1950	60	128	97	47	62	15.6	1.5	
1955	71	115	97	61	73	20.5	1.8	75
1960	100	100	100	100	100	33.3	2.5	79
1965	116	90	98	130	119	43.4	3.0	
1970	132	79	95	167	138	55.6	3.4	84
1975	144	55	93	263	154	87.5	3.8	89
1980	167	51	92	325	182	108.5	4.5	90

(FR 1) Index of gross agricultural output net of intermediate goods produced in agriculture. *Source:* J. C. Toutain, "Le produit de l'Agriculture Française de 1700 a 1958"; II: *La Croissance, Histoire Quantitative de l'Economie Française,* Vol. 2, (Paris: I.S.E.A., 1961), pp. 6, 128–29 (lumber deducted from Table 110, pp. 128–29); EEC, *Agrarstatistik* 4 (1968): 26–27. For 1960–80, USDA, *Indices of Agricultural Production in Western Europe, 1950–1968,* ERS-Foreign 266 (July 1969), pp. 1, 2; USDA, ERS, *Agricultural Situation in Western Europe, Review of 1972 and Outlook for 1973,* ERS-F352 (April 1973), p. 2; USDA, Economics, Statistics and Cooperatives Service, *Indices of Agricultural and Food Production for Europe and USSR,* Statistical Bulletin 620 (June 1979), p. 21; USDA, ERS, *World Indices of Agricultural and Food Production, 1972–81,* Statistical Bulletin 689 (August 1982), p. 53.

(FR 2) Index calculated from the data of the economically active males in agriculture excluding fishing, hunting, and forestry. 1962 figure is used for 1960. 1968 figure is used for 1970. 1965 is the arithmetic mean of 1962 and 1968 figures. 1980 is estimated from the total work force in agriculture by using the male share in 1975. *Source:* Toutain, "Le produit de l'Agriculture Française," pp. 200–201. Ministère de l'Economie, *Annuaire statistique de la France,* 1981, p. 303; Ministère de l'Agriculture, *Graph Agri 82,* p. 24.

(FR 3) Index calculated from the data of agricultural land comprised of arable land including temporary fallow and grass plus permanent pastures. *Source:* Ministère de l'Economie et des Finances, *Annuaire Statistique de la France, Résumé Retrospectif,* p. 177; *Annuaire statistique de la France,* 1967, p. 183; *Annuaire statistique de la France,* 1981, p. 304; *Graph Agri 82,* p. 6.

(FR 4) (FR 1)/(FR 2).

(FR 5) (FR 1)/(FR 3).

(FR 6) Index in column (FR 4) spliced with intercountry cross-section series of output per worker for 1957–62 (Table 4-1, Chapter 4).

(FR 7) Index in column (FR 5) spliced with intercountry cross-section series of output per hectare for 1957–62 (Table 4-1, Chapter 4).

(FR 8) Same as (FR 2).

Year	Agricultural output (UK 1)	Number of male workers (UK 2)	Agricultural land (UK 3)	Output per male worker (UK 4)	Output per hectare (UK 5)	Output per male worker (UK 6)	Output per hectare (UK 7)	Percent of male workers in nonagriculture (UK 8)
			percent			WU	WU	percent
1880	54	151	95	36	57	15.7	1.1	84
1885	55	148	96	37	57	16.4	1.1	
1890	56	145	97	39	58	17.0	1.1	86
1895	56	142	98	39	57	17.2	1.1	
1900	55	138	99	40	55	17.4	1.1	88
1905	56	140	98	40	57	17.5	1.1	
1910	56	143	98	39	57	17.3	1.1	88
1915	56	141	97	40	58	17.6	1.1	
1920	56	135	96	42	58	18.3	1.1	89
1925	57	140	100	41	57	17.8	1.1	
1930	60	134	99	45	61	19.7	1.2	90
1935	64	132	98	49	66	21.6	1.3	
1940	71	126	98	56	72	24.7	1.4	
1945	76	121	98	63	78	27.7	1.5	
1950	82	115	98	71	83	31.2	1.6	91
1955	85	109	98	78	88	34.5	1.7	92
1960	100	100	100	100	100	44.0	1.9	94
1965	119	78	99	157	120	68.9	2.3	96
1970	126	64	96	202	131	88.9	2.5	97
1975	132	60	95	226	139	99.5	2.7	97
1980	149	57	95	265	159	116.6	3.0	97

(UK 1) Index of gross agricultural output, net of intermediate goods produced in agriculture. *Sources:* Colin Clark, *The Conditions of Economic Progress* (3rd ed.; London: Macmillan & Co., 1957), p. 267. Minister of Agriculture, Fisheries and Food, *A Century of Agricultural Statistics Great Britain, 1866–1966* (London: HMSO, 1968), pp. 76–77. E. M. Ojala, *Agriculture and Economic Progress* (London: Oxford University Press, 1952), p. 210. For 1960–80, USDA, *Indices of Agricultural Production in Western Europe, 1950–1968*, ERS-Foreign 266 (July 1969), pp. 1, 2; USDA, ERS, *Agricultural Situation in Western Europe, Review of 1972 and Outlook for 1973*, ERS-F352 (April 1973), p. 1; USDA, Economics, Statistics and Cooperatives Service, *Indices of Agricultural and Food Production for Europe and the USSR*, Statistical Bulletin 620 (June 1979), p. 21; USDA, ERS, *World Indices of Agricultural and Food Production, 1972–81*, Statistical Bulletin 689 (August 1982), p. 53; 1980: 1979–81 average.

(UK 2) Index calculated from data of the economically active males in agriculture, excluding fishing, hunting, and forestry. Eighty-four percent of "farmers, partners, and directors" are assumed as male for 1970, 1975, and 1980, based on the UK government's estimate for this group in 1979. 1970 figures of "farmers, partners, and directors" are used for this group of 1965. All "salaried managers" of 1975 and 1980 are assumed as male. *Source:* Clark, *Conditions of Economic Progress*, p. 264; FAO, *Production Yearbook*, various issues; June Agricultural Census of the United Kingdom.

(UK 3) Index calculated from the data of agricultural land area including temporary fallow and grass plus permanent pasture. *Source:* Central Statistics Office, *Annual Abstract of Statistics* (London: HMSO), various issues; Central Statistical Office, *Annual Abstract of Statistics*, various issues.

(UK 4) (UK 1)/(UK 2).

(UK 5) (UK 1)/(UK 3).

(UK 6) Index in column (UK 4) spliced with intercountry cross-section series of output per worker for 1957–62 (Table 4-1, Chapter 4).

(UK 7) Index in column (UK 5) spliced with intercountry cross-section series of output per hectare for 1957–62 (Table 4-1, Chapter 4).

(UK 8) Percentage of males economically active in nonagriculture is estimated from percentage of labor force in nonagriculture given by Deane & Cole by splicing ILO data of males in nonagriculture at 1950–55 average. *Source:* Phyllis Deane and W. A. Cole, *British Economic Growth, 1688–1959* (Cambridge: Cambridge University Press, 1967), p. 142. ILO, *Annual Yearbook*, various issues.

APPENDIX C: Time-Series Data for U.S. and Japanese Agricultural Development, 1880–1980

In this section we explain the data that were primarily used for the analysis in Part III (Chapters 7–8).

The observations are quinquennial: Stock variables, such as land and labor, are measured at five-year intervals starting at 1880, and flow variables, such as fertilizer input, are five-year averages centering the year specified. Prices are measured as the average of five years ending the year specified. This is to enable consideration of the expectation and adjustment lag effects. In addition, five-year averages centering the year specified were prepared for the prices of flow variables.

Output

Data for agricultural output are in gross output net of intermediate agricultural products (seed, feed, etc.). Value added was not used in order to include such current inputs as fertilizer in our analysis. The crop output index was prepared for supplementary purposes.

Labor

Two series of labor are prepared: the number of male farm workers and the number of work-hours for all farm workers by all farm workers including females.

Land

Two series of area of land used in agriculture are compiled: arable land area and agricultural land area, which includes arable land and permanent pasture land. For the United States, arable land is identified as crop land and agricultural land is identified as the summation of crop land, and pasture and range according to the census definition. For Japan the statistics for permanent pasture land are available only after World War II. Pasture land is of

---

The authors are indebted to Toshihiko Kawagoe and Sachiko Yamashita Sidhu for revising and updating the data in this appendix.

minor importance in Japanese agriculture, however, constituting only about 10 percent of the arable land area. Since there is no reason to assume this ratio has changed significantly over time, in cases where the figure for agricultural land area is needed it was estimated on the basis of the ratio between arable land and agricultural land areas in the 1960 Census. For the consideration of the importance and the special nature of paddy fields in Japan, we used the paddy field area to obtain supplementary information. A major defect of our land statistics is that they do not incorporate quality changes due to the depletion of soil fertility or to irrigation construction and land improvement projects. Harvested area or planted area are not used because the objective of our analysis includes the process of increases in the intensity of land use (because of increases in double-cropping, etc.), which we regard as an innovational process.

Power and Machinery

Two series of nonhuman power at the farm are prepared: the number of work animals (horses, mules, and work cattle) and the tractor horsepower. Movements in these two series represent two major innovation processes: horse mechanization and tractorization. Their substitution processes are of great interest. Work animals of all ages are included. Deduction of the animals under working age was not attempted because no information was available for Japan. One underlying assumption of our analysis is that the services of machinery moved proportionally to the increase in both animal and tractor power.

Fertilizer

Our fertilizer data are the simple sums, in their physical weights, of the N, P_2O_5, and K_2O included in commercial fertilizers.

Prices

Our price data are somewhat inconsistent. Only the data of factor prices as the costs of factor services for labor and fertilizer were obtainable. Land prices in the United States as reported are (a) the average value of farm land and buildings per hectare of farmland and (b) the index of farm real estate value. In those cases where the average value of arable land was needed for comparison purposes, total value of farm land and buildings was divided by the crop land area. This, of course, overestimates per-hectare arable land value because it includes the values of pasture land and buildings. For the purpose of comparison with Japan, however, this procedure may have some merit by compensating for the overestimation of land value in Japan, where the large irrigation capital tied to paddy fields is included. The price of power and machinery presents the most serious problem, where only the conventional price index of farm machinery is available, although we attempted to adjust quality changes in machinery (see Appendix C-2). Before World War II even the conventional price index is not available for farm machinery, and it was necessary to substitute the general machinery price index.

Fertilizer prices are the unit price obtained by dividing the total value of fertilizer consumed by the total weight of plant nutrients contained therein.

Factor Shares

Our factor share data are the shares of labor, land, capital, and current input in the total cost of agricultural production.

C-1. ON THE AGGREGATION OF WORK
STOCK AND TRACTOR HORSEPOWER

In this study we constructed the series of power on the farm by aggregating work stock and tractors by the horsepower (HP) they would generate. For this aggregation we assumed one work animal is equivalent to one HP on the following reasoning: One HP is a unit of power equal to that required to raise 33,000 ft.-lbs. at the rate of one foot per minute. Two strong horses can pull a 14-inch walking plow with a 6-inch depth through soil weighing 6 lbs. per square inch at the rate of 2 miles per hour. This implies that 2 horses can pull 88,704 ft.-lbs. per minute (14 in. × 6 in. × 6 lbs. × 5,280 ft. × 2 ÷ 60 minutes). If the above assumptions hold, one horse is equivalent to 1.344 HP (88,704 ft.-lbs. ÷ 33,000 ft.-lb. ÷ 2 horses). This figure is not inconsistent with the estimates that "a 1000-lb. horse can develop 0.67 HP, a 1200-lb. horse, 0.80 to 1.00 HP, and a 1600-lb. horse, 1.07 to 1.33 HP," F. R. Jones, *Farm Gas Engines and Tractors,* 2d ed. (New York: McGraw-Hill, 1938), p. 8. Neither does it seem out of the range of the experiments conducted by James Watt as reported in Ponnell Hunt, *Farm Tractor and Machinery Management* (Ames: Iowa State University Press, 1964), p. 23.

Considering the nature of the above calculation, it is reasonable to omit the fraction and adopt one HP per horse as the factor for aggregation. We assumed mules and oxen are equivalent to horses. In any case our power series is affected little by trying fractions ranging 0.5 to 1 for mules and oxen.

One may argue against the adoption of the aggregation factor of one HP per horse, considering the nature of our data. Our work-stock data include horses, mules, and oxen of all ages on farms. The average power per head could be smaller than the power of a "representative working horse" used in the previous example. On the other hand, our tractor horsepower series does not include the power of trucks and other prime movers on the farm, which, to some extent, substituted for the work hours of horse and mules. For such considerations we estimated a factor from our aggregate data. For 1920–60 in the United States, when the substitution of tractors for horses was started and completed, we ran the following regression:

$$\log \left(\frac{A}{L}\right) = \alpha + \beta \log \left(\frac{W + kH}{L}\right),$$

where A, L, W, H, and k are respectively land area, labor force, tractor horsepower, work stock, and the factor for work stock in aggregation. The above equation expresses the relation that the area utilized or cultivated per worker is constrained by the amount of power per worker.

The equation can also be considered a production function, a relation of production of "land area cultivated" as an intermediate good for the input of power. We computed the regressions by changing k parametrically from 0.5 to 10.0 and determined the value of k giving the highest fit. The results are as summarized in Table C-1. The value of k which yields the highest fit differs depending on the data used, but in all cases it is close to one. These results, together with the previous reasoning, provide the basis for adopting one HP for the factor of aggregating work stock.

C-2. COMPUTATIONAL PROCEDURES OF QUALITY ADJUSTMENT FACTORS FOR THE FARM MACHINERY PRICE INDEX

Quality adjustment factors for the farm machinery price index (USDA index of prices paid) were calculated for 1915–60 on the basis of L. P. Fettig, "Adjusting Farm Tractor Prices for Quality Change, 1950–1962," *Journal*

TABLE C-1. The results of regression computations to determine the value of k

	Case 1		Case 2		Case 3		Case 4	
k	β	R^2	β	R^2	β	R^2	β	R^2
0.5	0.368	0.9884	0.283	0.9618	0.367	0.9908	0.282	0.9723
0.6	0.382	0.9910	0.294	0.9676	0.382	0.9926	0.293	0.9763
0.7	0.396	0.9927	0.306	0.9723	0.395	0.9934	0.304	0.9802
0.8	0.409	0.9936	0.316	0.9761	0.409	0.9936*	0.315	0.9829
0.9	0.422	0.9940	0.327	0.9792	0.421	0.9934	0.325	0.9850
1.0	0.435	0.9940*	0.337	0.9817	0.434	0.9928	0.335	0.9865
2.0	0.547	0.9807	0.428	0.9893*	0.546	0.9762	0.425	0.9879*
3.0	0.648	0.9577	0.512	0.9819	0.649	0.9523	0.509	0.9773
4.0	0.746	0.9299	0.593	0.9670	0.749	0.9248	0.592	0.9607
5.0	0.843	0.8981	0.675	0.9464	0.850	0.8941	0.675	0.9395
6.0	0.939	0.8622	0.756	0.9205	0.951	0.8600	0.759	0.9137
7.0	1.034	0.8218	0.838	0.8890	1.052	0.8217	0.845	0.8829
8.0	1.126	0.7762	0.919	0.8516	1.152	0.7785	0.931	0.8466
9.0	1.212	0.7249	0.997	0.8074	1.250	0.7297	1.016	0.8039
10.0	1.290	0.6673	1.070	0.7561	1.340	0.6744	1.097	0.8683

Source: Data from Table C-2.

    H = U 7   L = U 4 in Case 1 and Case 2   A = U 5 in Case 1 and Case 3
    W = U 8   = U 3 in Case 3 and Case 4   = U 6 in Case 2 and Case 4.
  *The highest R^2.

of Farm Economics 45 (August 1963): 599–611. The adjustment factors we calculated are originally for tractor prices, but not for the prices of farm machinery in general. The basic assumption we have to make in order to use those factors for farm machinery prices is that the quality improvement in farm machinery can be represented by or is parallel with the quality improvement in wheel tractors.

The basic approach used by Fettig to construct the quality adjusted index of farm tractors for 1950–62 is (a) to estimate the regression of tractor price on the two quality variables (average horsepower per tractor and a dummy variable for diesel engine) on cross-section data and (b) to discount the price changes due to the changes in these quality variables from the actual changes in tractor prices by the estimated regression equations.

Our quality adjustment factors for 1955–60 are based on the ratios of change in Fettig's quality adjusted index (ibid., column 4, Table 6, p. 609) to changes in the USDA index (average of columns 1–3, Table 6). The ratios calculated are 0.99 from 1950 to 1955, and 0.94 from 1950 to 1960.

For 1915–50 we calculated the adjustment factors using Fettig's linear regression equation on 1950 cross-section data (ibid., p. 606). Since the numbers of diesel-powered tractors are negligible before 1950, and also data are unavailable, the diesel dummy was dropped from the equation. The equation used is:

$$Y_t = 176.02 + 43.81 X_t,$$

where X_t is the average horsepower per tractor and Y_t is the estimate of tractor price (1950 U.S. dollars) for the corresponding horsepower in year t. Y_t divided by Y_{1915} can be interpreted as the degree of quality improvement in tractors from 1915 to year t. The inverse of (Y_t/Y_{1915}) is the quality adjustment factor (k_t).

Year	X_t	Y_t	k_t
	(HP)	(dollars)	$(1008/Y_t)$
1915	19	1,008	1.00
1920	20	1,052	0.96
1925	22	1,140	0.88
1930	24	1,227	0.82
1935	25	1,271	0.79
1940	27	1,359	0.74
1945	27	1,359	0.74
1950	27	1,359	0.74
1955			0.73
1960			0.70

k's for 1955 and 1960 are calculated by multiplying k for 1950 by the ratios of Fettig's index to the USDA index (0.99 and 0.94), as explained previously.

Data for average horsepower per tractor are calculated from U.S. Dept. of Agriculture, ERS, *Farm Cost Situation* 36 (November 1965): 14, for 1940–

60; and Austin Fox, *Demand for Farm Tractors in the United States,* Agricultural Economic Report 103 (1966), p. 33, for 1925–35. For 1915–20, the average horsepower is extrapolated from the 1925 value by a quinquennial growth rate of 7 percent (average rate for 1925 to 1940).

For 1965–80 the method used for 1950–60 was applied. The data used to estimate the regression of tractor price were supplied by David L. Debertin of the University of Kentucky. These data were earlier used by Angelos Pagoulatos, David L. Debertin, and William L. Johnson in an article titled "An Econometric Analysis of Qualitative Choice among Performance Characteristics of Agricultural Tractors," *Southern Journal of Agricultural Economics* 12 (December 1982): 83–96. Since price data used by them were retail list price, the figures were discounted by 10 percent to represent better the prices paid by farmers. Also, since these data covered only tractors equipped with diesel engines, the dummy variable for diesel engine was dropped from the estimating equation.

Linear regression equations were estimated for 1968, 1970, 1975, and 1980, and the average price of each year was calculated by using average horsepower of tractor shipped out of factory in the year, then the effect of nondiesel engine tractor on the average price was subtracted by using the coefficient of diesel engine dummy variable of Fettig's 1960 equation (Fettig, "Adjusting Farm Tractor Prices," Table 3, p. 606), and the rate of number of tractors equipped with gasoline engine to total tractors produced in the year (U.S. Bureau of the Census, *Current Industrial Reports,* Series M35S, various issues).

From regressions, price indexes (1960 = 100) were calculated using chained specification method (Fettig, "Adjusting Farm Tractor Prices," p. 608). The 1968 index was extrapolated for 1965 using the simple average of rates of change from 1965 to 1968 in farmers paid unit prices of tractors of three horsepower groups (30–39, 40–49, and 50–59) (USDA, Crop Reporting Board, *Agricultural Prices,* 1968, June 1969, p. 131). Then, price indexes were adjusted to 1954–55 = 100 by use of Fettig's index (Fettig, "Adjusting Farm Tractor Prices," column 4, Table 6, p. 609).

For the USDA index, unit prices paid by farmers for various horsepower tractor groups are used (USDA, Crop Reporting Board, *Agricultural Prices, Annual Summary,* various issues). Between 1960 and 1980, the price series of some horsepower groups were complete whereas for other groups they were only partly complete. To calculate the index values for 1965, 1970, 1975, and 1980 all the available data relevant to these years were used. The index value for 1965 (1960 = 100) was calculated as a simple average of three price indexes of 30–39, 40–49, 50–59 horsepower groups, and that for 1970 was calculated from price indexes of 30–39 and 50–59 horsepower groups. The index value for 1975 was obtained by averaging three indexes of 30–39, 50–59, and 90–99 horsepower groups. For this purpose, since 1960 and 1965 unit prices for 90–99 horsepower group were not available, first the index for

90–99 horsepower group for 1975 (1960 = 100) was estimated by multiplying the unit price ratio of 1975 and 1970 of this group with the index value for 1970 calculated above. The index value for 1980 was calculated by averaging four indexes of 30–39, 50–59, 110–29, and 170–240 horsepower groups. Prior to this calculation, the price indexes (1960 = 100) of 110–29 and 170–240 horsepower groups were estimated by use of the same method applied to the 1975 90–99 horsepower group for the same reason. Finally, each index value was adjusted to 1954–55 = 100 by use of the USDA index (average of columns 1–3, Table 6, in Fettig, "Adjusting Farm Tractor Prices").

The estimated quality adjustment factors from the above two sets of index series (1915 = 1.00) for 1965, 1970, 1975, and 1980 are 0.77, 0.90, 0.63, and 0.65, respectively.

C-3. MAJOR STATISTICAL SERIES

In principle, the data for the United States are for forty-eight coterminous states and the data for Japan are for Japan proper, including Okinawa before 1945 but not since 1945.

The following notations are adopted:
a. Values for the year shown,
b. Values for the five-year average centering the year shown,
c. Values for the five-year average ending the year shown.
Values estimated by simple linear interpolation are shown in parentheses.

The following abbreviations are used in the explanations for the individual columns:

Agricul. Statistics: U.S. Dept. of Agriculture, *Agricultural Statistics.*

Century of Agriculture: _____, *A Century of Agriculture in Charts and Tables,* Agriculture Handbook No. 318, 1966.

Production and Efficiency, 1964: _____, *Changes in Farm Production and Efficiency,* Statistical Bulletin 233, 1964.

Production and Efficiency, 1980: _____, *Economic Indicator of the Farm Sector Production and Efficiency Statistics,* 1980, Statistical Bulletin No. 679 (January 1982).

Production and Efficiency, 1981: _____, _____, 1981, ECIFS1-3 (January 1983).

JMAFF Yearbook: Japan Ministry of Agriculture, Forestry and Fisheries (JMAFF), *Norinsho Tokeihyo* (Statistical yearbook of the Ministry of Agriculture, Forestry, and Fisheries), various issues.

LTES: Kazushi Ohkawa, Miyohei Shinohara, and Mataji Umemura, eds., *Long-Term Economic Statistics of Japan since 1868.* 13 vols. (Toyokeizaishimposha).

Yamada: Saburo Yamada, "The Secular Trends in Input-Output Relations of Agricultural Production in Japan, 1878–1979," Chi-ming Hou and Tzong-shian Yu, eds., *Agricultural Development in China, Japan and Korea* (Taipei: Academia Sinica, 1982).

Yamada-Hayami: Saburo Yamada and Yujiro Hayami, "Agricultural Growth in Japan, 1880–1970," Yujiro Hayami, Vernon W. Ruttan, and Herman M. Southworth, eds., *Agricultural Growth in Japan, Taiwan, Korea and the Philippines* (Honolulu: University Press of Hawaii, 1979).

Explanations for the individual columns in Table C-2:

U1 Gross farm output net of intermediate goods supplied within agriculture.
    Sources: Production and Efficiency, 1964, p. 50; *Production and Efficiency,* 1981, p. 73.

U2 1910–80: USDA crop production index. 1880–1909: Series of production of wheat, rye, corn, oats, barley, potatoes, tobacco, cotton, and buckwheat aggregated by using 1910–14 average prices as weights and linked to USDA crop production index by multiplying by the 1910–14 average ratio.
    Source: USDA crop production index: *Production and Efficiency,* 1981, pp. 7–8; individual commodity production: *Century of Agriculture,* pp. 25–34; price weights: *Major Stat. Series,* pp. 24–34.

U3 1965–80: Economically active male population.
    1900–60: Economically active population (population census data adjusted by Kaplan and Casey). 1880–90: Number of gainful workers (population census data adjusted by Edwards).
    1980 male workers are estimated from 1980 economically active population in agriculture and 1980 male share in farm population engaged in agriculture.
    Source: A. M. Edwards, *Comparative Occupational Statistics for the United States, 1870–1940* (U.S. Department of Commerce, 1943), p. 100; D. L. Kaplan and M. C. Casey, *Occupational Trends in the United States 1900 to 1950* (U.S. Bureau of Census Working Report 5, 1958), p. 6; U.S. Bureau of Census, *U.S. Census of Population, 1960, U.S. Summary,* Final Report PC(1)-ID, 1960, p. 563; U.S. Bureau of Census, *U.S. Census of Population 1970, Industrial Characteristics,* PC(2)-7B, p. 1; U.S. Bureau of Census, *Farm Population,* Series P-27, No. 54 (August 1981), p. 4; FAO, *Production Yearbook,* 1981, p. 65.

U4 Number of person-hours used for all farm workers.
    Source: 1915–75 data from U.S. Department of Agriculture, Economics, Statistics, and Cooperatives Service, *Changes in Farm Production and Efficiency, 1978,* Statistical Bulletin 628 (January 1980). 1880–1910 data are estimated by multiplying the average work-hours per worker for 1915–20 by the number of all farm

TABLE C-2. Major time series, United States*

| Year | Agricultural production (1880 = 100) | | Labor | | Land (million ha.) | |
	All commodities b (U 1)	All crops b (U 2)	Male workers (thousand) a (U 3)	Work-hours (billion hours) b (U 4)	Agricultural land a (U 5)	Arable land a (U 6)
1880	100	100	7,959	17.6	327	93
1885	(110)	112	(8,551)	18.9	(343)	(108)
1890	119	130	9,142	20.3	358	123
1895	(137)	139	9,511	21.3	(412)	(140)
1900	155	161	9,880	22.3	465	157
1905	(160)	177	(10,120)	22.9	(460)	(167)
1910	164	182	10,359	23.6	457	177
1915	174	209	(10,290)	23.4	458	186
1920	180	217	10,221	23.3	458	194
1925	192	221	(9,818)	23.4	458	188
1930	204	228	9,414	23.2	458	194
1935	190	204	(8,950)	21.3	455	196
1940	232	247	8,487	20.5	452	189
1945	264	267	(7,419)	18.9	450	188
1950	285	288	6,352	15.6	449	193
1955	306	292	(5,163)	12.6	444	189
1960	340	329	3,973	9.8	440	185
1965	364	350	(3,042)	7.5	436	180
1970	395	384	2,128	5.9	434	191
1975	428	433	(1,960)	5.0	429	188
1980	497	519	1,792	4.1	427	191

*Values in parentheses are simple linear interpolations.

workers (male and female). 1980 data are extrapolated by the 1975–78 average growth rate.

U5 Crop land, pasture, and range in the U.S. Census of Agriculture. 1880 and 1890 are estimated from land in farm in the U.S. Census of Agriculture by multiplying by ratios of agricultural land to land in farms which are extrapolated from 1900, 1910, and 1920 ratios. 1955, 1960, 1965, 1970, 1975, and 1980 are from 1954, 1959, 1964, 1969, 1974, and 1978 censuses.

Source: Major *Stat. Series,* 2:4; H. Thomas Frey, *Major Use of Land in the United States 1974,* Agricultural Economic Report 440, USDA, Economics, Statistics, and Cooperatives Service (November 1979), p. 4; USDA, Economic Research Service, *Major Uses of Land and Water in the United States with Special Reference to Agriculture: Summary for 1964,* Agricultural Economic Report 149 (November 1967), p. 6; Hugh H. Wooten, Karl Gertel, and William C. Pendleton, *Major Uses of Land and Water in the United States: Summary for 1959,* Agricultural Economic

Power (thousand)		Fertilizer $N + P_2O_3 + K_2O$ (thousand m. tons)	Corn yield per harvested acre (bushels)	Percentage of total corn area planted with hybrid corn	Total inputs (1880 = 100)
Work stocks	Tractor horsepower				
a	a	b	b	b	b
(U 7)	(U 8)	(U 9)	(U 10)	(U 11)	(U 12)
13,775		93	25.6		100
15,858		(137)	25.4		(110)
19,171		182	27.0		119
21,595		236	25.5		(129)
21,964		356	25.9		138
22,877		518	29.0		(152)
24,851	18	730	26.9		165
26,998	475	797	25.4		177
26,112	4,920	836	26.9		184
22,754	11,968	1,047	25.9		190
19,124	21,804	1,122	24.7		193
16,683	26,410	1,064	22.6	2.5	180
14,478	42,300	1,542	30.6	30.7	191
11,950	63,600	2,591	32.9	63.5	198
7,781	91,600	3,800	39.6	79.7	202
4,309	130,400	5,330	43.6	89.4	200
3,089	153,000	6,726	57.3		193
(2,710)	176,000	10,288	71.5		191
2,331	203,000	14,600	84.6		192
1,634	222,000	17,656	85.6		193
2,271	277,000	20,799	103.4		203

Report 13, USDA, Economic Research Service (1962), p. 43; *Agricul. Statistics,* 1979, p. 419; *Agricul. Statistics,* 1981, pp. 417–18.

U6   Crop land in the U.S. Census of Agriculture. Areas of crop land used for pasture for 1880 and 1890 are estimated by multiplying the areas of "cropland used for crops and idle cropland" by 0.185 (1900 and 1910 average). 1915 cropland is estimated by dividing "cropland used for crops" by 0.92 (1910–40 average). The areas of cropland used for pasture for 1915, 1925, and 1935 are the arithmetic mean of those of 1910 and 1920, 1920 and 1930, and of 1930 and 1940, respectively. Figures are from the agricultural census year (see U 5).

Sources: Same as column U 5.

U7   Number of horses, mules, and oxen on farms on January 1. Horses include colts. 1960–80 figures are from agricultural census years (see U 5).

Source: Century of Agriculture, p. 38; W. M. Hurst and L. M.

TABLE C-2.   (*Continued*)

Year	Agricultural price (1910–14 = 100)				Farm wage	
	All farm commodities		All crops		Daily wage rate (S/day)	Index of wage rate (1910–14 = 100)
	b (U 13)	c (U 14)	b (U 15)	c (U 16)	a (U 17)	c (U 18)
1880	82	80	81	79	0.90	59
1885	76	85	75	85	0.95	65
1890	71	70	70	69	0.95	66
1895	62	68	62	68	0.85	64
1900	71	63	70	62	1.00	67
1905	81	79	81	78	1.30	76
1910	97	91	96	90	1.35	94
1915	120	99	120	98	1.40	101
1920	178	186	188	199	3.30	175
1925	145	139	150	147	2.35	169
1930	115	141	105	133	2.15	183
1935	101	84	100	81	1.35	107
1940	115	106	101	96	1.60	126
1945	222	176	216	168	4.35	257
1950	277	261	249	241	4.50	421
1955	242	267	236	251	5.30	502
1960	243	239	225	225	6.60	582
1965	248	242	236	234	7.60	680
1970	278	228	233	228	11.70	929
1975	462	397	445	370	17.23	1,358
1980	616	532	540	474	25.31	2,084

Church, *Power and Machinery in Agriculture,* USDA Miscellaneous Publication 157 (1933), p. 12; U.S. Bureau of Census, *Census of Agriculture, 1959, General Report,* 2:506; U.S. Bureau of Census, *Census of Agriculture, 1969, Livestock, Poultry, Livestock and Poultry Products,* Vol. 2, chap. 5, p. 6; U.S. Bureau of Census, *Census of Agriculture, 1978, United States,* AC78-A-51, p. 10.

U8   Horsepower on farm on January 1, 1910–20 figures are estimated by multiplying the number of farm tractors by the average horsepower per tractor which is extrapolated from 1925 average horsepower with the quinquennial growth rate of 7 percent.

Source: U.S. Department of Agriculture, *Farm Cost Situation 36,* 1965, p. 14; Austin Fox, *Demand for Farm Tractors in the United States,* U.S. Department of Agriculture, ERS, Agricultural Economic Report 103 (1966), p. 33; *Production Efficiency* (1980), p. 38.

Land price		Machinery price (1910–14 = 100)		Fertilizer price, average value of plant nutrient (S/m. ton)	
Average value of arable land (S/ha.)	Index of real estate value (1910–14 = 100)	Quality adjusted	Unadjusted		
a	c	c	c	b	c
(U 19)	(U 20)	(U 21)	(U 22)	(U 23)	(U 24)
109	46	146	146	335	358
111	55	138	138	271	292
108	52	119	119	247	251
107	52	117	117	233	251
106	48	94	94	199	194
158	79	105	105	198	195
197	95	110	110	197	195
209	103	101	101	233	208
341	138	136	142	377	368
263	143	134	152	241	271
246	120	126	154	197	216
168	84	114	144	166	159
178	84	114	154	170	169
287	103	124	168	201	195
389	167	174	235	227	216
517	222	226	309	201	215
696	268	249	356	187	188
886	337	313	407	186	188
1,079	461	341	487	164	170
1,814	697	449	712	319	259
3,393	1,379	796	1,225	476	360

U9 In terms of principal plant nutrients (N + P_2O_5 + K_2O), 1880 and 1890 figures are of the year shown.

Sources: USDA, Agricultural Research Service, Statistics on Fertilizer and Liming Materials in the United States, Statistical Bulletin 191 (April 1957), p. 105; USDA, Crop Reporting Board, Commercial Fertilizers—Consumption of Commercial Fertilizers, Primary Plant Nutrients and Micronutrients, Statistical Bulletin 472 (November 1976), p. 5; Production and Efficiency (1981), pp. 31–33.

U10 Yield per harvested acre.

Source: Century of Agriculture, p. 27; Agricul. Statistics, 1970, p. 28; Agricul. Statistics, 1980, p. 30; USDA, Crop Reporting Board, Crop Reports, CrPr 2-2 (August 1982), p. B-1.

U11 Source: Agricul. Statistics, 1963, p. 41.

U12 Sources: Production and Efficiency (1980), p. 77; Production and Efficiency (1981), pp. 60–61.

U13–16   1910–80: USDA indexes of prices received by farmers. 1880–
         1909: BLS and Warren-Pearson wholesale price indexes of farm
         commodities linked to USDA indexes by multiplying by 1911–15
         average ratio.
         Source: Historical Statistics, pp. 200–201; *Agricul. Statistics,*
         1957, p. 571; *Agricul. Statistics,* 1967, p. 563; *Agricul. Statistics,*
         1970, p. 466; *Agricul. Statistics,* 1980, p. 451; *Agricul. Statistics,*
         1981, p. 449; USDA, Crop Reporting Board, *Agricultural Prices
         Annual Summary,* 1981, Pr 1-3 (82), pp. 8–9.

U17   Farm wage per day without board. 1880, 1885, 1895, 1900, and
         1905 figures are respectively of 1879 or 1880, 1884 or 1885, 1889
         or 1890, 1899 and 1906. 1975 and 1980 are estimates from the
         annual average hourly rates by cash wage only by multiplying
         1974 ratio of farm wage per day without board to annual average
         hourly rates by cash wage only.
         Source: Historical Statistics, p. 468; *Agricul. Statistics,* 1967, p.
         530; *Agricul. Statistics,* 1976, p. 433; *Agricul. Statistics,* 1981, p.
         431.

U18   1910–1980: Simple average of seasonally adjusted quarterly index
         of farm wage rates.
         1877–1909: Simple average of indexes of farm wage ratio with
         board and room per month, with hours per month, with board and
         room per day, and without board or room per day linked to USDA
         indexes by multiplying 1911–15 average ratio.
         Source: USDA, Crop Reporting Board, *Agricultural Prices,* 1980,
         Pr 1-3 (81), p. 40; *Historical Statistics,* p. 468.

U19   Total value of farm land and buildings (from the Census of Agri-
         culture) divided by total area of arable land (from column U 6).
         1885, 1895, and 1905 figures are interpolated by use of agri-
         cultural price index (from column U 14). Figures are of Census
         Years (see U 5).
         Source: Historical Statistics, p. 457; *Agricul. Statistics,* 1967, p.
         510; *Agricul. Statistics,* 1971, p. 436; U.S. Bureau of the Census,
         *Census of Agriculture, 1969; General Report, Farms: Number
         Use of Land, Size of Farm,* Vol. 2, chap. 2, p. 14; *Census of
         Agriculture,* Alaska, Vol. 1, pt. 49, p. 2; *Census of Agriculture,*
         Hawaii, Vol. 1, pt. 50, p. vii; *Census of Agriculture, 1974, United
         States Summary and State Data,* Vol. 1, pt. 51, p. xiii; *Census of
         Agriculture, 1978, United States,* Vol. 1, pt. 51, AC 78-A-51, pp.
         266, 311.

U20   1912–80: Index of average value of farm real estate, 1912–75,
         March 1 and 1965–80, February 1.
         1880–1911: Series of average value of farm land and building per
         acre of land in farm linked to the index of average farm real estate

value by multiplying by the 1912–14 average ratio. Intercensus years are interpolated by use of the agricultural price index (from Column U 14). *Source: Historical Statistics,* p. 457; *Agricul. Statistics,* 1967, p. 517; *Agricul. Statistics,* 1973, p. 429; *Agricul. Statistics,* 1980, p. 442.

U21 Farm machinery price index adjusted for the quality changes of machinery. Column 22 multiplied by the quality adjustment factors in Appendix C-2.

U22 1965–80: USDA index of tractors and self-propelled machinery price paid by farmers.

1915–60: USDA index of farm machinery price paid by farmers. 1895–1910: BLS wholesale price index of metal and metal products linked to USDA index by multiplying by the 1911–15 average ratio.

1880–1890: Warren-Pearson wholesale price index of metal and metal products spliced to the BLS index at 1890.

Source: Historical Statistics, pp. 200–201; *Agricul. Statistics,* 1957, p. 572; *Agricul. Statistics,* 1967, p. 564; *Agricul. Statistics,* 1975, p. 454; *Agricul. Statistics,* 1981, p. 452.

U23–24 Current farm expense for fertilizer divided by quantity of principal plant nutrients consumed. Figures of 1880, 1890, and 1900 of U 23 are of the year shown. 1910 of U 23 is the average of 1909–11. 1885 of U 23 is interpolated by use of wholesale price index of chemicals and drugs. 1895 and 1905 of U 23 are interpolated by use of fertilizer price index constructed from the data of Vail by averaging the indexes of organic fertilizer and mineral fertilizer. Figures of 1880–1910 of U 24 are estimated from those of U 23 by use of wholesale price index of chemicals and drugs and fertilizer price index constructed from the data of Vail.

Source: USDA, Agricultural Research Service, *Statistics on Fertilizer and Liming Materials in the United States,* Statistical Bulletin 191 (April 1957), p. 130; *Historical Statistics,* pp. 201, 469; USDA, Economic Research Service, *Farm Income Statistics,* Statistical Bulletin 547 (July 1975), p. 49; USDA, Economic Research Service, *Economic Indicators of the Farm Sector Income and Balance Sheet Statistics,* 1981, ECIFS1-1 (August 1982), p. 62; E. E. Vail, *Retail Prices of Fertilizer Materials and Mixed Fertilizers* (Ithaca, N.Y., Agricultural Experiment Station Bulletin 545, 1932).

Explanations for the individual columns in Table C-3:

J1 Gross agricultural output net of intermediate goods supplied within agriculture. The Yamada index of total agricultural output from

TABLE C-3. Major time series, Japan

| | Agricultural output (1880 = 100) | | Labor (thousand) | | Land (thousand ha.) | | Power (thousand) | | Fertilizer N + P$_2$O$_5$ + K$_2$O (thousand m. ton) | Paddy field rice yield per unit area planted (ton/ha.) |
	All commodities b (J1)	All crops b (J2)	All workers b (J3)	Male workers a (J4)	Arable land a (J5)	Paddy field a (J6)	Workstocks a (J7)	Tractor horsepower a (J8)	b (J9)	b (J10)
1880	100	100	15,596	8,336	4,749	2,802	2,788		63	1.95
85	110	109	15,601	8,338	4,818	2,824	2,645		61	2.09
90	120	116	15,631	8,356	4,922	2,858	2,615		61	2.18
95	122	117	15,675	8,385	5,034	2,877	2,680		69	2.07
1900	138	130	15,844	8,483	5,200	2,905	2,746		86	2.30
05	152	140	15,831	8,476	5,300	2,936	2,456		128	2.46
10	170	154	15,783	8,495	5,579	3,007	2,823		224	2.62
15	193	171	15,059	8,239	5,777	3,072	2,840		286	2.78
20	205	178	13,919	7,577	5,998	3,136	2,724	0.05	378	2.92
1925	208	174	13,527	7,395	5,914	3,199	2,879	0.18	468	2.84
30	223	180	13,944	7,579	5,962	3,274	2,838	0.45	576	2.89
35	236	192	13,672	7,531	6,104	3,290	2,966	1.1	640	3.04
40	236	196	13,545	6,362	6,122	3,277	3,043	19.5	705	3.08
45	196	177	13,770	6,130	5,741	3,153	2,875	38.1	328	2.95
1950	221	198	16,000	7,720	5,858	3,231	3,296	92.1	764	3.27
55	268	229	15,410	7,350	5,982	3,302	2,880	460	1,344	3.40
60	334	271	13,390	6,230	6,071	3,381	2,089	3,957	1,579	3.93
65	379	279	11,514	4,565	6,004	3,391	1,001	14,285	1,983	4.07
70	423	284	10,252	3,973	5,796	3,415	426	19,263	2,193	4.39
1975	441	280	7,907	2,975	5,572	3,171	120	27,523	2,297	4.62
80	486	280	6,973	2,674	5,461	3,055	n.a.	42,544	2,322	4.61

486

| Year | Percentage of rice area planted with improved varieties a (J11) | Total inputs 1880 = 100 b (J12) | Agricultural price (1934–36 = 100) | | | | Farm wage | |
| | | | All farm commodities | | All crops | | Daily wage rate (yen/day) a (J17) | Index (1934–36 = 100) c (J18) |
			b (J13)	c (J14)	b (J15)	c (J16)		
1880	0.2	100	34.0	27.4	30.9	24.8	0.22	18.3
85	0.7	101	23.8	29.7	21.3	26.9	0.16	21.4
90	1.6	103	27.3	24.8	24.7	22.2	0.17	19.3
95	4.1	105	36.1	31.4	32.9	28.4	0.19	25.9
1900	13.9	108	47.8	45.4	43.8	41.6	0.31	40.3
05	29.5	112	57.0	51.4	51.9	47.1	0.31	44.9
10	35.9	118	63.6	58.4	59.6	53.4	0.41	49.5
15	39.5	120	66.9	67.2	61.7	63.3	0.46	61.9
20	42.0	119	146.3	121.3	136.3	113.7	1.39	127.3
1925	41.5	122	137.4	141.4	126.2	128.6	1.65	172.9
30	55.5	127	90.5	111.3	83.6	103.8	1.12	156.5
35	56.0	129	100.7	85.2	99.4	83.5	0.91	96.9
40	60.0	127	177.0	142.7	172.9	138.0	1.90	154.2
45	57.0	116	1,250	222.6	1,250	222.6	12.3	535.1
1950	67.4	147	25,700	13,000	25,700	13,300	248	19,250
55	75.0	166	40,050	37,800	39,300	36,800	357	36,000
60	70.0	174	42,900	39,800	42,000	39,200	440	46,600
65	n.a.	192	61,800	52,900	63,500	55,200	853	90,900
70	n.a.	204	80,700	75,200	84,200	79,100	1,611	168,000
1975	n.a.	205	140,700	110,200	149,400	119,200	3,635	356,000
80	n.a.	211	178,900	167,600	191,800	183,800	5,054	618,000

TABLE C-3. *(Continued)*

Year	Land price		Machinery price (1934–36=100) c (J21)	Fertilizer price (yen/m. ton)	
	Average value of arable land (yen/ha.) a (J19)	Arable land price index (1934–36=100) c (J20)		b (J22)	c (J23)
1880	343	10.5	65.6	402	383
85	373	12.4	55.3	260	319
90	444	14.6	54.0	354	318
95	615	21.7	55.2	399	374
1900	917	31.5	70.6	328	452
05	998	34.5	77.0	472	445
10	1,583	46.9	81.9	420	429
15	1,613	63.0	85.7	471	429
20	3,882	109.7	160.2	850	825
1925	3,711	140.3	135.0	660	672
30	3,388	132.4	103.3	432	532
35	2,783	97.1	95.7	396	381
40	4,709	131.1	137.8	620	552
45	6,154	182.5	175.5	1,429	1,136
1950	159,200	2,770	9,390	78,200	42,300
55	868,000	19,700	30,000	90,200	95,300
60	1,415,000	45,900	37,000	82,100	83,800
65	1,688,000	55,500	37,700	84,100	81,000
70	2,688,000	75,600	40,400	88,800	83,600
1975	5,235,000	135,400	54,100	165,500	123,800
80	7,642,000	225,800	73,500	223,200	194,400

1880 to 1975 is extended to 1980 by the JMAFF index of agricultural production.

Source: Yamada, series 8, Table 1, p. 26; *JMAFF Yearbook.*

J2   *Source:* Yamada, series 3, Table 1, p. 26; *JMAFF Yearbook.*

J3-4 Number of gainful workers.

Source: 1880–1960 data from Yamada-Hayami, series 1 and 3, Table J-4; 1965–80 data from the agricultural census results reported in *JMAFF Yearbook.*

J5-6 1880–1960 data from Yamada-Hayami, series 4 and 6, Table J-4; 1965–80 data from *JMAFF Yearbook.*

J7   Horses and draft cattle of all ages at the end of the year. Draft cattle before 1950 include meat cattle. Before 1950, few cattle were raised for meat alone and beef was largely a by-product of draft cattle. Since then, because animal power has been replaced by tractors, the percentage of cattle reared for meat should have increased. To deduct the number of meat cattle from the number of "draft-meat cattle" in the JMAFF statistics, it is assumed that the number of cattle reared for the draft purpose declined after 1950 parallel with that of horses; i.e., the number of draft cattle is estimated by multiplying the number of draft-meat cattle in 1950 (2,255,000) by the ratio of the number of horses in each year after 1950 to the number in 1950. The number of horses and draft cattle in 1980 is assumed to be zero corresponding to the termination of JMAFF reports on horses.

Source: LTES, 3: 166–67; *JMAFF Yearbook.*

J8   Sum of tractors multiplied by mean horsepowers in respective horsepower-size classes. It is assumed that the average horsepower of garden tractors was five and that all tractors before 1965 were garden tractors (cultivators).

Source: LTES, 3: 172; *JMAFF Yearbook.*

J9   In plant nutrients ($N + P_2O_5 + K_2O$).

Source: LTES, vol. 9, series 1, Tables 20–22, pp. 196–203; JMAFF *Pocket Hiryo Yoran* (Statistical handbook on fertilizers), various issues.

J10 On husked brown (not milled) basis.

Source: LTES, 9: 37; JMAFF, *Norinsho Ruinen Tokeihyo* (Historical statistics of the Ministry of Agriculture and Forestry), 1955, p. 24; *JMAFF Yearbook.*

J11 Estimated by interpolation from Yujiro Hayami and Saburo Yamada, "Technological Progress in Agriculture," L. R. Klein and Kazushi Ohkawa, eds., *Economic Growth: The Japanese Experience since the Meiji Era* (Homewood, Ill.: Irwin, 1968), pp. 135–61.

J12 1880–1975 data from Yamada, series 2, Table 19, p. 54. The

Yamada series is extended to 1980 by aggregating various inputs with factor share weights in 1975 (Yamada, Table 18, p. 53); the input-data are columns J3–4 for labor, columns J5–6 for land, capital extrapolated from the Yamada data (Yamada, series 7, Appendix Table 5, p. 73) in 1978 based on the average growth rate for 1975–78, and current inputs from JMAFF, *Nogyo oyobi Noka no Shakai Kanjo 1980* (Social accounts of agriculture and farm-households), 1982, p. 78.

J13–16   1876–1940 and 1950–62 data from *LTES,* vol. 8, series 4-5, Table 10, p. 165. 1941–49 data are interpolated from the LTES series by use of the wholesale price index of edible farm products (Bank of Japan, *Hundred-year Statistics of the Japanese Economy,* 1966, p. 77). 1963–80 data are extrapolated by the JMAFF indexes of rural commodity prices aggregated with the 1970 weights (*JMAFF Yearbook*).

J17   Wage of male daily contract workers. 1890 figure is of 1892.
Source: 1880–1960 data from *LTES,* vol. 8, series 24, Table 25, p. 245, and *LTES,* vol. 9, series 3, Table 34, pp. 220–21. 1965–80 data from the JMAFF surveys on rural wages (*JMAFF Yearbook*).

J18   Index of male daily contract workers' wage. Data not available from original sources are estimated by interpolation and extrapolation on the basis of the agricultural price index (Column J14).
Source: 1880–1960 data from *LTES,* vol. 9, series 3, Table 34, pp. 220–21. The index is extended to 1980 based on the data from the JMAFF surveys on rural wages (*JMAFF Yearbook*).

J19   Weighted average of the prices of the paddy field and the upland field, using the area as weights. In case of the paddy field, the 1885 price is extrapolated by the rent data and the 1880 and 1895 prices are extrapolated and interpolated by the rice price. In the case of the upland field, the 1885 price is extrapolated by the rent data, and the 1880 and 1895 prices are extrapolated and interpolated by the price index of crops except rice.
Source: 1880–1960 data are based on prices of paddy and upland field: *LTES,* vol. 9, series 9–10, Table 34, pp. 220–21; rent: *LTES,* vol. 9, series 9–10, Table 34, pp. 220–21; rice and other crop price index: *LTES,* 8: 168–71. 1965–80 data from Nihon Fudosan Kenkyujo (Japan Real Assets Research Institute), *Denbata Kakaku oyobi Kosakuryo Shirabe* (Survey on prices and rents of paddy and upland fields), various issues.

J20   Simple average of the paddy field price index and the upland field price index. 1880–1905 figures are of the years shown. 1885 figures are extrapolated by the rent data. 1880–95 figures are extrapolated and interpolated by the rice price and other crop price indexes.

Source: same as column J19.

J21   1950–80: the index of farm machinery price (price received by farmers) of the Ministry of Agriculture and Forestry. 1880–1940: the index of machinery price linked to the index of farm machinery price by multiplying by the 1951–55 average ratio.

Source: LTES, vol. 8, series 21, Table 8, pp. 160–63; *JMAFF Yearbook* and Bank of Japan, *Hundred-year Statistics,* p. 83.

J22–23   Current farm expense for fertilizer divided by the total quantity of principal nutrients consumed. 1940 figure in column J22 is of the 1938–41 average. 1880 and 1955 figures in column J23 are of the 1878–80 average and the 1952–55 average. 1945–50 data are interpolated by use of the wholesale index of chemical goods. 1965–80 data are extrapolated from 1960 by the index of fertilizer prices paid by farm producers.

Source: LTES, 9: 194–201; *JMAFF Yearbook;* Bank of Japan, *Hundred-year Statistics,* p. 78.

Index

ABOUT THE AUTHORS

Yujiro Hayami is professor of economics at Tokyo Metropolitan University and is coauthor (with Masao Kikuchi) of *Asian Village Economy at the Crossroads,* also published by Johns Hopkins.

Vernon W. Ruttan is professor in the Departments of Economics and Agricultural and Applied Economics at the University of Minnesota. His most recent book is *Agricultural Research Policy.*